The Diuguid Records 1861-1865

AND
BIOGRAPHICAL SKETCHES

Compiled by
Jerald H. Markham

HERITAGE BOOKS
2007

HERITAGE BOOKS
AN IMPRINT OF HERITAGE BOOKS, INC.

Books, CDs, and more—Worldwide

For our listing of thousands of titles see our website
at
www.HeritageBooks.com

Published 2007 by
HERITAGE BOOKS, INC.
Publishing Division
65 East Main Street
Westminster, Maryland 21157-5026

Copyright © 2007 Jerald H. Markham

All rights reserved. No part of this book may be reproduced or transmitted in any form or by any means, electronic or mechanical, including photocopying, recording or by any information storage and retrieval system without written permission from the author, except for the inclusion of brief quotations in a review.

International Standard Book Number: 978-0-7884-4292-6

Table of Contents

Acknowledgements	Pages vii-ix
Foreword	Pages xi-xiii
Part I – Narrative & Introduction	Pages 1 – 56
Part II – Old City Cemetery Listing	Pages 57-118
Part II – Other Cemetery Listings	Pages 118-122
Part III – Support Information	Pages 123-374
Part IV – Disease & Definitions	Pages 375-404
Bibliography	Pages 405-408

Sketches, Tables, Figures, Charts & Photographs:

Dedication Page - Photograph of Charles E. Hillsman

Part I:
Sketch of George A. Diuguid	-	Page 4
Map of Hospital locations	-	Page 19
Numerical Listing of Confederate Soldiers Interred in City Old Cemetery	-	Page 40
Numerical Listing of Union Soldiers Interred in Lynchburg	-	Pages 41-42
Figures 1, 2 & 3 Copies of Diuguid Log Book Pages	-	Pages 43-45
Map of the Confederate Section Old City Cemetery	-	Page 46
Photographs of City Cemetery	-	Pages 47-49
Tables I – IV Military Deaths In Lynchburg by Month & Year	-	Pages 51-55

Part III:
Photo of William G Cook

Headstone	-	Page 157
Sketch of Pvt. Robert Dilley	-	Page 168
Photo of Robert A. Eastment Headstone	-	Page 172
Sketch Gen. Samuel Garland Jr.	-	Page 182
Photo of Daniel S. Green Headstone	-	Page 181
Photo of John Harris Hayes Headstone	-	Page 196
Photo of Ariel Riddle Headstone	-	Page 266
Sketch Gen. Robert Rhodes	-	Page 269
Photo of John Kirk Seabury Headstone	-	Page 273
Photo of Natan A. Sullins Headstone	-	Page 287
Photo of Junius Fitz-James Tinsely Headstone	-	Page 294
Photo of Samuel B. Tyree Headstone	-	Page 298

The sketches of George A. Diuguid, Pvt. Robert Dilley, Generals Samuel Garland and Robert E. Rodes provided by Russell Chu. The map of hospital locations also was sketched by Russell Chu (based on Peter Houck's book <u>A Prototype of a Confederate Hospital Center in Lynchburg, Virginia)</u>.

Photographs of cemetery headstones were taken by Jerald Markham. The Junius Fitz-James Tinsely headstone was taken by the late Beau Whitaker of Lynchburg. The photograph of Chuck Hilmans on the dedication page was provided by Tony Zusman

Dedication

This book is dedicated to the late Charles (Chuck) Edward Hillsman. Born December 4, 1950 – Died December 17, 2000. Chuck will always be a true Southern gentleman, a friend, a fellow Civil War re-enactor, and my brother in Christ.

"...We can never reproduce what war was like, nor should we want to, but our endeavor is to never allow the sacrifice made by those who have gone on before us to be forgotten...."

Charles E. Hillsman
Newsweek, July 1988

Acknowledgements

As defined by Webster's dictionary acknowledgement is the act of, "To show appreciation of or admit obligation for; express thanks for." In the following few line I will attempt recognize and thank the individuals that have contributed towards making this book a reality.

Where does one begin to thank the numerous individuals that have contributed their time and efforts in assisting this writer in compiling the unique information contained herein. Without their assistance this work would not be a reality.

First and foremost I thank my creator that has provided me with the mental and physical ability to accomplish this work.

Diuguid Funeral Home in Lynchburg, Virginia for allowing me access to the burial log books (1861-1865), burial records, and the "Soldiers Book." Your kind and courteous assistance has been invaluable.

This book has several behind the scene assistants. The Book, "Behind The Old Brickwall" written by late Mrs. Lucicle Baber provided the history of the Old City Cemetery. Within her book is a listing of the initial 2,100 or so Confederate soldiers interred in the Confederate Section was the seed. Arranging these soldiers in alphabetical order, by state, by unit, by lot, row and grave was the easy part. Then came the task of going through the Diuguid records to find date of death or burial, and in which hospital they were housed. Hundreds of soldiers were handled by George A. Diuguid in preparation for burial outside of Lynchburg. Also was the task of determining the correct spelling of their last names. Find full first names not just initials. Find the cause of death (when known). Gather little known facts from their military service records or post war data. Facts such as date of birth, age, parents names, wife's name, relatives, and addresses (when possible) In order to achieve this large task I called on an army of students of the war, friends and other contacts across the South (and North) to assist with this project. These unsung heroes's are.

Jones Memorial Library, the Late Ms. Sarah Hickson and her staff, provided and abundance of assistance. In particular Mr. Wayne Rhoades, worked with me on this project almost from its concept. Wayne and I reviewed micro film together for hours. Wayne cross checked dates, names and other information. He located obituaries, old newspaper accounts, provided suggestions and on and on. Wayne's and the professional staffs assistance of Jones Memorial can not be measured.

True Southern compatriots and good friends Lawrence McFall, of Danville, Virginia, Dale Bostic and the late John Martin of Lynchburg assisted me with the research of the North Carolina troops buried in Lynchburg These gentlemen spent hours going through the rosters of North Carolina Troops 1861-1865, A Roster putting together any all pertinent information on the Tarheels interred in Lynchburg. Many thanks for the fabulous research work.

In addition to the North Carolina troops, Lawrence McFall provided assistance with the review of rosters of Georgia, Florida, South Carolina, Louisiana, and Tennessee soldiers. Lawrence found both service and post war records on several troops that helped complete the story of these men. Thank you so much for your tireless assistance.

Dennis E. Todd of Cayce, South Carolina, patiently researched the South Carolina troops at the state archives. His research of the Compiled Service Records for the South Carolina boys provided numerous details. In addition, Dennis spent time going through several of the Georgia troops. Thank you so much Dennis for your valuable work.

Unknowingly, Harold E. Howard, the genius behind the Virginia Regimental History Series, and his selected group of War Between the States historians have contributed most significantly to the information collected on the Virginia soldiers.

Thank you Bob Driver for assistance on finding information on the surgeons and assistant surgeons stationed at Lynchburg. In addition, Bob supplied addition facts on several Virginians.

Many thanks to Elizabeth Dinger-Glisan of the National Park Service, Petersburg Battlefield, Petersburg,

Virginia. Elizabeth provided burial information of Union soldiers re-interred at Poplar Grove National Cemetery at Petersburg, Virginia.

Thank you Russell Chu for the wonderful sketches and map. Russell is a good friend and a fellow Civil War re-enactor. Russell is a very accomplished artist and his contributions have added significantly to this work.

I would thank also the state archives that assisted with my research; Troup County Achieves, La Grange, Georgia, the state archives of Alabama, Texas, Mississippi, West Virginia, Vermont, Massachusetts, Pennsylvania, New Hampshire, Indiana, Rhode Island, Wisconsin, Illinois, Maine, New Jersey, and Ohio. Other archives were contacted but did not assist.

Any work such as this can never be accomplished without the help and assistance of many behind the scenes workers. I pray that I have mentioned all that were of help in putting this work together. Again thank you.

Foreword

Family bonds are not a recent phenomenon. They have existed since the beginning of time. So, it was no surprise when the young lady developed an interest in her great grandfather's life, and his death. As a result of being introduced to two dozen letters written by her ancestor during the Civil War, she read everything she could find about the conflict. Because of these letters Anna had a head start on most budding Civil War enthusiasts. She knew the name of her ancestor's military unit and the battles in which he fought. More importantly, she learned his feelings, written in his own words, about leaving his wife and five children to go away to fight for his country.

From family stories Anna had always known that her Confederate ancestor had died when General Robert E. Lee thrust his army into the center of the Union line at Gettysburg; the carnage known as Pickett's Charge. For more than 120 years her family knew of his fate but not his place of burial. That haunted Anna.

A new-found friend happened to be a Gettysburg enthusiast. He told her of a book that related the story of George Pickett's failed attack on the Union Army on that third day of fighting in Pennsylvania. Anna sought the work for more than a month and finally secured a copy through interlibrary loan. A great discovery within its pages rewarded her diligence and persistence. Overwhelming elation enveloped Anna when the book disclosed that even though her ancestor died of wounds following capture, he did receive a grave marker by his captors. Adding even more delight was the fact that in 1872, his remains, along with hundreds of others, had been removed to Richmond's Hollywood Cemetery, not far from her home. That weekend, the first of many trips to pay homage ensued.

The revelation of her ancestor's final resting place brought closure to Anna and her family. Sadly, this can not be said for missing soldiers of even more modern wars. There remain 2,200 Americans missing in Vietnam. About 8,100 American bodies were left behind after the Korean Conflict. World War II produced a staggering 78,000 servicemen left on foreign soil around the globe.

In recent years, science has made it possible to identify some of the missing when bodies are recovered. DNA tests can establish kinship and put a name to remains which are occasionally unearthed. Largely, however, the families of most Americans from these modern conflicts will never know the resting places of their loved ones. If this is true for our recent wars, how much more difficult is it to find the grave of a Civil War soldier now buried for over 140 years?

Well, Jerald Markham has made that task easier for the untold number of descendants of almost 2,500 Federal and Confederate soldiers who were laid to rest in the Old City Cemetery at Lynchburg, Virginia. These soldiers received proper preparation for burial by local undertakers of the Diuguid Funeral Home.

Established in 1820 and recognized as the second oldest institution of its kind in the United States, Diuguid generously opened its archives to Mr. Markham. This first-ever, in-depth study of the company's Civil War records enables family researchers to finally learn the grave location of their kin. A task never dreamed possible by many.

The author's transcription of facts that may have seemed mundane to the morticians, the fabrication of caskets for dead soldiers, sheds light on an obscure subject which many researchers may have deemed valueless. However, details such as these are interesting and add value to this work

A glimpse into the lives and deaths of Union prisoners of war incarcerated in the Hill City provides another interesting aside to the writer's narrative. Several quotes from authorities lend insight into the care of their captives.

Markham's decade-long effort to compile records associated with those who died in Lynchburg during the South's struggle for independence is commendable. In addition, through his untiring endeavor, perception is given into the operation of the large hospital complex there, the second largest in the South.

Day to day problems associated with the town's military compound, Camp Davis, are brought into focus with quotes from letters of the men stationed there. So too, are the good experiences such as visitation to the camp by townsfolk.

This research and its resultant publication is long overdue. Whether you seek your ancestor's place of burial or wish to learn about the war effort put forth by the authorities and citizens of Lynchburg, Markham has provided a great tool to accomplish either desire.

Lawrence McFall
Danville, Virginia
March 15, 2006

PART I

A Narrative And Introduction

Part I NARRATIVE
****

The Diuguid Records
1861 - 1865

Between May 1, 1861 and May 31, 1865 at least 2,726 soldiers (including Union) were prepared for burial in Lynchburg, by Diuguid Funeral Home. This number is based on the burial records maintained by Mr. George Alexander Diuguid (1820 - 1893), cabinetmaker and undertaker.

Using Mr. Diuguid's burial records and other sources, an effort has been made to identify each soldier, provide his burial location, date of death or burial, cause of death (if it can be determined), and any pertinent information related to that individual. Within this writing, the place of each soldier's death is referred to only as the building, site, or individual residence.

At least 144 years have passed since hospitals in Lynchburg were used to house the casualties of the Confederate and Union Armies. Tens of thousands of sick and wounded warriors, both North and South, were treated in the Lynchburg Hospital system during the war. This War, which was to become the greatest conflict ever fought on the North American Continent. This small treatise could never cover every moment of grief, pain or anguish, nor can it tell the complete story of the inglorious War of survival, which took place behind the lines. It cannot begin to identify all the soldiers, young and old, who were defending the budding Confederacy or the Union, their homes, beliefs, values and rights. Many left home in their youth, only to die on some strange and oft-times unknown or forgotten field, many miles from home.

George Alexander Diuguid

George Alexander Diuguid was the second child born to Sampson & Martha Patteson Diuguid in Lynchburg on 11/05/20, and lived with his older brother David (b. 8/25/18) and a younger sister Harriet (b. 6/07/33). Other accounts indicate there were other children born to Sampson and Martha, all of whom died at birth.

The Diuguid are descendants of French Huguenots that had fled to Scotland due to religious persecutions. The Diuguid name appears to have come from the motto "Dieu Guide" after the original forefathers left France. They lived in Scotland by one account long enough to be called "Scots". In the early 1700's four Diuguid brothers arrived in America. One of the four, George Diuguid settled in the Bent Creek area of Appomattox County (Virginia). Sampson Diuguid, the seventh child of George Diuguid, was born 10/25/1795 in Appomattox County. On 11/04/1817 he married Martha Patteson. Shortly thereafter the young couple moved to Lynchburg where he established a hand carved furniture business. The business was located at 616 Main Street.

On June 2, 1820 Sampson Diuguid was approached to fabricate a coffin for a Dr. Roberts whose son had just died. Mr. Sampson Diuguid, thus beginning the Diuguid Funeral Home, built the coffin. It was said, "A furniture maker by trade an undertaker by chance". Today Diuguid's is the second oldest funeral home in the United States of America. In that first year Diuguid listed 18 funerals in his record book. One of the funerals included a prominent Lynchburg citizen, James C. Steptoe, on October 27th.

By 1832 Sampson Diuguid's business was well established. He had bought the property at 616 Main Street. In addition he purchased a small section in the rear of the property. This area would be the location of the wood shop for the construction and storage of coffins.

On February 28, 1844 George Alexander Diuguid married Paulina Ann Davidson in Appomattox, Virginia. George and Paulina were blessed with 9 children over the next 20 years of marriage. There oldest was James Edwin born May 2, 1847. The remaining children were, Martha Elizabeth, William Davidson, Frannie, Jane Sampson, Jesse Thomas, Katherine Anna, George Alexander and Paulina Ann. The last two children George and Paulina had were twins born on 3/16/64. The third child, William Davidson (b. 9/10/51 d.2/1/23) would later taker over family business.

By the late 1840's the two sons of Sampson Diuguid, David P. and George A., were following in their fathers footsteps. By the early 1850's the two brothers were handling the family business. Following the death of Sampson Diuguid on February 15, 1856 the two brothers changed the funeral home name to D. P. & G. A. Diuguid. This partnership lasted less than 9 years. On January 1, 1865 the partnership was dissolved. George A. Diuguid made the following entry in Burial Logbook #6 on page 200 on 12/31/64, "**The firm of D P & G A Diuguid was dissolved Jan 1st 1865 and the business continues in the name of G A Diuguid**", signed G A Diuguid. The reason for the dissolving of the partnership was the death of his older brother on July 4, 1864.

The record keeping maintained by the Diuguid family was meticulous and precise. The entry in each logbook contained the date of burial, name of deceased, size of coffin (not all cases), whether cotton packing was used, use of a sheet or shroud, the type of coffin (material), cost, the name of the individual making the request and or paying for the services, and the type arrangements for paying. Cash was not always used; in some cases barter was made. Additional notes at times were made by the Diuguid as to the location the remains were to be buried, especially if the individual was not from Lynchburg. No references were noted as to which cemetery the deceased were interred in. The deceased religious conviction was not noted or any real reference to race. The only notation made to race was to indicate if the individual was black.

George A. Diuguid
1821-1893

With the secession of Virginia in April 1861 and the war, changes began to take place. During the war years the entries for deceased soldiers changed from the previous method. Initially in 1861 the recordings made in the burial logbook were essentially the same as those of the civilian community. The exception in Diuguid's entries was the state of origin (i.e. Georgia, Mississippi), regiment or unit and payment for service was made by the "Southern Confederacy". This practice or type of entry continued through 1861 and into 1862. On July 1,

Diuguid added a new type of entry in the burial logbook. This new entry was a separate page in the logbook. The heading on the page was simply, "Southern Confederacy" (Ref. Figure 1, 2 & 3 at the end of Part I for typical entries). This and the numerous pages to follow over the remaining years of the war were for the listing of the soldiers (Confederate & Union) that died in the Lynchburg Hospital System. Each line contained the individual's name, date of burial, unit/regiment/state & company and cost of burial. The 1st page covered July 1, 1862 to July 4th (not completely) and listed 22 burials at $9.00 each. Prior to that time over a 14 month period Diuguid handled 380 soldiers. In the month of July 1862 there were 192 deaths of soldiers and 123 civilians. In addition to the burial logbooks maintained, a second recording was established for the deceased soldiers. This was simply referred to as "The Soldiers Book.". The recordings began on the 19th of May 1861 and ended August 4th, 1866. The information recorded consisted of the deceased name, rank if applicable, the hospital or place of death, the row & grave number interred in the old city cemetery, next of kin and address if available, in some cases cause of death, and size of the coffin. The coffin size entry provided overall an outside length, outside width, and in some cases the depth for the coffins built. These entries for coffin size started in early 1862. Also included in this entry, at a later date, was if the deceased was later exhumed and shipped home. On occasions other information pertaining to the individual was also entered.

Formation of the Southern Army

Within days following the bombardment of Fort Sumter and subsequent capitulation, Virginia (The Old Dominion) became the eighth southern state to secede from the Union.

With the outbreak of war, steps were taken to prepare the young Confederacy to repel the "Yankee Hoards" from Southern Soil. Key areas within Virginia were designated as rendezvous areas for forming the new army. A few of the more notable Virginia cities included; Richmond, Winchester and Lynchburg where raw green recruits, and Virginia militia, were formed into infantry, cavalry and artillery units. These men were the vanguard to meet the Northern Army on the plains of Manassas.

At first, only Virginian's were learning the art of warfare in Lynchburg. Soon hundreds of new soldiers were arriving in the Hill City from all over the South on the way to the front. By mid June thousands of soldiers were in Lynchburg.

The Kanawha Canal System connected Lynchburg, which was ideally located virtually in the center of the state and on the South bank of the James River, to Richmond on the east and Buchanan on the west. Three major railroads connected Lynchburg to the major areas of the state: the Orange & Alexander Railroad to Alexandria in the north, the Southside to Richmond and Petersburg on the east; and the Virginia & Tennessee to Bristol on the west. Lynchburg was ideally located for the storage and movement of supplies and troops, which could quickly reach both the eastern and western theaters. In addition, Lynchburg became the prime location for a hospital system, second only to Richmond.

The following are letters or excerpts from letters of these new soldiers arriving in Lynchburg. These letters provide details related to the number of soldiers in Lynchburg, camp life, church and Chaplains, and their personal feelings. These young civilian soldiers, hundreds of miles from home now experiencing the military for the first time.

This letter is from a young man only identified as Holmes. He is a member of the 3rd Alabama Infantry. The 3rd Ala Inf. Was organized in April 1861 at Montgomery Ala. This unit was dispatched to Virginia shortly after organized. The letter is dated May 6, 1861.

"There is said to be 5,000 volunteers now encamped near this city, equipping thoroughly for the coming campaign. Both Alabama Volunteers are here with ten full companies each. In their ranks are to be found the very flower of the young men of the various sections of the State from which they came. I doubt very much whether two thousand finer looking, or more robust men will be found in the Confederate army during the war. Our regiment is quartered near the Fair grounds, and is being equipped as speedily as the great press upon the Quartermaster's Department will permit. The

weather is cold, rainy and of course very inclement, yet the men are cheerful, and put with the inconvenience of our present situation without murmuring.

When the weather permits, the ladies throng our encampments, and manifest their kindly feelings by generous offers of assistance in any way they can be of service to us.

The act of the convention dissolving the connection of the State with the late Union meets with universal favor. The people are alive with enthusiasm for our gallant President and the Southern Confederacy. Volunteer companies are organizing throughout the State, and "old Virginia," will give a good account of herself when Lincoln "turn loose the dogs or war," as he threatens to.

This city has already sent three thoroughly organized companies to Richmond and three more are anxiously awaiting orders to march.

Col. [Robert E.] Lee, the gallant commander of the Virginia State troops, has inspired the greatest confidence, and the people are rallying to his standard with unwonted enthusiasm. The Confederate States flag is to be seen proudly kissing the breeze from hilltop to vale all along the railroads, while the cry of determined resistance to Republican rule reverberates from the mountains to the seaboard. The "railsplitter" may devastate and ruin this fair land, he may lay its cities and towns and beautiful cottages in ashes, but he can never conquer its spirited people and make them bow their proud necks to his abject yoke – never – never!

As opportunity offers, I will comply with your request and send you an occasional letter.

      Holmes,"

This letter was written by a young private in the 6th Alabama Infantry. The 6th Ala. Inf. was organized May 1861 in

Montgomery, Ala. and arrived in Virginia in mid June 61. The letter is dated June 14, 1861.

> We arrived here yesterday at 12m., after a journey of five days. A portion of the Regiment, 600 strong, had gotten within 50 miles of Richmond where we ordered, when they were met by a dispatch from headquarters to return to this place.
>
> Our men are well with a few exceptions and eager to go forward. I was surprised to see this so large and business a place. But the best feature about it is the kind, generous and hospitable population. I have often heard and read of their proverbial hospitality and kindness, but now I have seen and had practical demonstration of the fact. Mr. Editor, say to our friends for us, that our reception in this State from the moment we entered its border, has been all that our hearts could desire. At every stopping place almost, there were congregated these kind people, who had prepared for us provisions in endless quantities and of the nicest kind. Such hams, butter, cakes, coffee, cheese, (home made) apple butter and barrels of milk just from the spring house, and numerous other things too tedious to mention were given us without stint. We are treated as though we were their brothers, husbands, and fathers from the treatment we received in portions of Tennessee, where [Andrew] Johnson, [Emerson] Ethridge, [William] Brownlow and other traitors have been doing their work; but thank God! Their day has passed and to-day a large and overwhelming majority of the people of Tennessee are with us.
>
> Seven companies of the regiment leave this evening for Manassas Gap, the balance of the Regiment to-night at 2 o'clock, for the same destination. You can judge from this what sort of chance we have of meeting the enemy soon.

We are encamped here at one of the most beautiful places I ever saw, in a oak grove, with an abundance of the coldest and purest spring water my lips ever tasted, and a fine, clear, bold running stream near by where the men can bathe, all of which we hate to leave,
and go we must, and I assure you we go not as sluggards in the great struggle, but with cheerfulness and alacrity.
PRIVATE,"

The following is portions of a letter written by Thomas D. Wright a Second Lieut. In the 3rd Battalion Georgia Volunteer Infantry. This letter is dated August 18, 1861, Camp Davis Lynchburg, Virginia.

"As I write to you, a thousand lights from our different camps illuminate the hill tops and plains, and the merry songs and ludicrous jest are heard on every side, while the pleasant breeze, blowing pure and fresh from the mountains, revives the spirit and invigorates the frames of our men. . . . Our hearts are nerved for the fray, and with a firm reliance on Providence, a determination to "conquer or die," we await our onward march. I feel more and more convinced every day that this conflict cannot last – that we are becoming more and more invincible. In truth, as the Virginians say, we will burn every bale of cotton, tumble our sugar into the Mississippi, and our tobacco into the Potomac, yet the spirit of our people is not overcome. If we are rebels, we always be rebels. . . .
. . . .The health of all in the camp, so far, is very good, though I am sorry to see much sickness in other places. Typhoid Fever is getting as formidable an antagonist as the Lincolnites. Our boys at Stanton, Monterey, and Manassas are suffering badly with this epidemic, though the measles is raging more at Manassas than anywhere else. The people

of the cities and towns are doing all they can to alleviate their sufferings. A good many will never see the dear familiar faces of the loved ones at home again, and yet it is but the fortunes of war, a great lottery, where Death secures all the prizes. Sever colds are prevalent among us here, in consequence of our change of latitude, but as the winter approaches, we hope to be free from all diseases; we have assurance from the Virginians who know this to be a fact.

. . . .There are some of the "Tigers" in the city, and inconsequence of leaving Manassas without leave, they were all ordered to be arrested. One of our Corporals went into the city, and having a red shirt and Zouave cap, was forthwith halted and commanded to go to the Bars. On inquiring the reason, the reply was, that they had orders to arrested all "Tigers" and our Corporal protested that he was no Tiger, never saw a Tiger, didn't resemble one in the least, in short, hadn't the remotest idea what a Tiger was. It was no go – a scuffle ensued, and in the scuffle our Corporal proved a real live Tiger, for he gained his liberty, and, I am happy to state, is now quite tame, and is still of the opinion that he never fought a Tiger but once, and the "lost every red." More incidents in my next.
                    Yours,   T.D.W."

The following is portions of another letter written by Thomas D. Wright. Wright was a Jr. 2nd Lieut. In the 3rd Ga. Battn. Inf. Wright was promoted to 1st Lieut. sometime in 1862. May 1863 transferred to 37th Ga. (western theater). Promoted to Captain 08/01/63.   The letter is dated September 19, 1861, Camp Davis Lynchburg, Virginia.

"The soldiers have all gone to offer up their devotions at the alters of the Most High at the various churches in the city. This manifestation of reverence for the deity, on their part, is universally commented upon by the citizens of Lynchburg – especially in reference to the Georgia troops. If I see a man, regularly as the Sabbath comes, going to church, and eagerly devouring each word of the discourse as it is uttered by the divine with prayerful attention, and the eye speaking praise to God, I cannot but think his dear parents are Christians, God loving people, and true patriot and soldier. As I now write you, our camp is almost deserted, the soldiers, in squads, under charge of an officer, have marched in good order to the houses of worship, whilst, on our right, the Mississippians are having a sermon preached them, and hither and thither they are scattered, seated on camp stools, whilst the beauties of the gospel is being unfolded to them.

Truly, I can exclaim: "Glory to God in the highest on earth; peace and goodwill towards men." What a sight for the parents of those brave men, could they but behold it! What depths of emotions would arise in the foundations of their brave hearts at such a scene. They know, by this, that the bringing up of their children "in the nurture and admonition of the Lord" is not lost upon them, even in the tented field.

. . . . A young man of noble daring, brave and chivalrous, the pride of his parents, and the favorite of the Lynchburg community, was suddenly snatched from them by this unseen power. He was at the encampment at Bull's Run on the 18th, and also at Manassas on the 21st, both of which he gallantly led on his comrades, and, though deaths was all around and about him, and men falling by the scores, yet he escaped unhurt. Immediately after, he had an attack of typhoid fever, which ended his life. He died in the bosom of his family, but no human art can give the father back his son, the mother her darling boy, the brother his dear associate, or sister her protector.

A detachment of 50 men and six lieutenants, by order of our Colonel, were detailed to pay the last, sad tribute to a stranger, but a brother soldier. We proceeded to the residence of the deceased, taking open order in front; and I never did experience such feelings as I entered the room where the deceased lay. A beautiful metallic case, all wreathed in flowers, hung entwined around it in beautiful festoons, interspersed with evergreens, first met my gaze. As we carefully raised it to bear him hence, convulsive sobs from relatives were heard, and I involuntarily, with great care, proceeded with our great task. I trod lightly the ground, for every noise was an arrow to loving hearts. They knew we had come to take their boy away, and could but bespeak our sympathies with scalding tears. We reached the cemetery – a beautiful spot near the James River; and, as the report of our fire-arms broke the stillness of the hour, I felt deeply for the parents of such a boy. Would that our country had many such sons to give in her cause.

. . . .We only live in hope. You may, therefore, look for startling and grad movements before I write you again, and your patrons my rest assured that I will give you nothing but facts – reliable facts.

T.D.W."

The young soldier that Lieut. Wright spoke of was Lieut. William Leftwich Goggins, Jr. of Co. H 11th Virginia Vol. Infantry. Goggins was buried in Presbyterian Cemetery.

Hospitals

The influx of citizen soldiers from all parts of Virginia, as well as from other Southern states in to this training/assembly camp created problems. This increase in population brought about a number of problems, including overcrowding poor sanitation, inadequate housing and personal hygiene problems. The vast majority of these new soldiers were from rural areas.

By far most of these men had earned their living as farmers. Wives and mothers had cared for these citizen soldiers now entering the military. As a result these men had the tendency as we refer today "to go native". They ignored washing themselves and or their clothes but by far the worst was they failed to follow any all regulations regarding camp sanitation. Sinks, or in today's military, latrines were dug in varying lengths by a minimum of two feet in depth. At the end of each day six inches of fill dirt was to be put over the human refuse. Initially no sinks were prepared. Even if sinks were in use many of the men refused to use this offensive foul smelling pit and went off to the wide-open spaces surrounding the camp. In general the early camps discarding of refuse and other waste was not properly done. An inspector of camps made the following statement, **"litter with refuse, food, and other rubbish, sometimes in an offensive state of decomposition; slops deposited in pits within camp limits or thrown out of broadcast; heaps of manure and offal close to the camp"**. With this filth came the infestations of flies. With these flies came disease, bacteria and viruses spreading to the men and to their rations. The end result was breeding grounds for disease. These camps were populated with young men that had never been exposed to contagious diseases. Epidemics of mumps, chicken pox, whooping cough and measles spread like a wild fire in these early military camps.

For the first time in their lives these men had to cook and prepare their own food. Both improper preparation and cooking of food introduced a whole new set of problems. With unclean hands, unclean cooking utensils, and bacteria dysentery, and diarrhea were the end result. Another illness that plagued both North and South was typhoid fever. This disease was resulted from the consumption of food or water contaminated by *salmonella* bacteria. Another illness very prevalent was pneumonia. A common cold could lead to this illness as a result of the living conditions.

At first, some of the local residents cared for the ill as best they could. By late spring of 1861 three hospitals were established for use in the city; the Warwick House (formerly a hotel on Main Street which could handle about 100 patients), Ladies' Relief Hospital (formerly the Union Hotel at the corner of 6th and Main Street with a capacity of about 100 patients), and College Hospital (previously Lynchburg College, located between Wise and 12th Street).

Two soldiers shared the first war-related deaths in the Lynchburg Hospital system. Private Thomas P. Plunkett of the 2nd Mississippi Infantry Regiment died at College Hospital on Sunday May 19, 1861. He was buried the following day. Lieutenant Joseph W. Davidson, of the 1st Tennessee, was killed that Sunday morning. He was killed at a local encampment by one of his own men as he tried to settle a dispute between two soldiers' over clothing. See Part III for details of his death as provided by the Lynchburg Daily Virginian, dated May 21, 1861.

Over the four-year period of war, a total of thirty-two sites would be used for hospitals in Lynchburg. Twenty-one of these sites remained for the duration of the war. Of the thirty-two sites, nineteen had been tobacco warehouses and factories, and fourteen of these remained open for the duration of the war as best can be determined. These names reflect the name of the owners of the facilities (see following listing).

Listing of Hospitals:
Booker's - Located @ Commerce & 7th Street (also) Court Street between 5th & 6th Street (old Jesse Hare's Factory. First recorded death, 04/25/62 and the last recorded death was 07/23/64.
Burton's - Located @ corner of 4th and Harrison Street. First recorded death, 06/25/62 and the last recorded death was 01/03/65.
Candler's - Located @ Corner of 5th & Polk Streets; on West Street. First recorded death 1/29/63 and the last recorded death was 6/20/64.
Christian's - Located @ 4th & Commerce Streets; (also) Main Street between 12th & 13th Street. First recorded death was 04/22/62 and the last was 03/21/65.
Claytor's - Located @ Salem Street & 12th Street. First recorded death was 05/21/62 and the last recorded death was 01/03/65.
Crumpton's – Located @ 12th Street between Clay & Madison Street. First recorded death was 05/17/62 and the last recorded death was 05/30/62.
Ferguson's - Located @ Main and 13th Street. First recorded death was 05/03/62 and the last recorded death was 04/10/65.
Ford's - Located @ corner of 12th & Court Streets. First recorded death was 06/07/62 and the last recorded death was 02/05/63.

*Knight's - Located @ 12th & Madison's & Harrison's Streets. First recorded death was 06/27/62 and the last recorded death was 04/13/65.
*Miller's - Located @ 12th & Madison's & Harrison's Streets. First recorded death was 07/27/62 and the last recorded death was 11/25/63.
*The Knight/Miller buildings are the only remaining today in Lynchburg.
Langhorne's - Located @ 11th & Clay Street, 8th & Clay Street - First recorded death was 05/23/62 and the last recorded death was 04/19/65.
Reid's - Located @ 5th & Church Streets. First recorded death was 05/07/62 and the last recorded death was 03/22/65.
Taliaferro's - Located @ Corner of Court & 5th Streets. First recorded death was 06/15/62 and the last recorded death was 06/28/63.
Saunder's - Located @ 4th Street between Main & Church Streets. First recorded death was 05/07/62 and the last recorded death was 03/22/65.

Five other warehouses were used as temporary hospitals;
Chamber's – Located @ Main Street between 12th & 13th Streets. First recorded death was 09/16/63 and the last recorded death was 09/16/63.
@Massie's - Located @ 13th & Monroe Streets. First recorded death was 07/05/64 and the last recorded death was 10/28/64.
@ Also used as a Prison/jail
Planter's - Located @ 515 Main Street. First & last recorded death was 06/10/63.
Sheau's - Located @ Main Street between 12th & 13th Street. Found no dates for deaths.
Wade's - Could not locate an address/location. First recorded death was 02/16/63 and the last recorded death was 08/06/63.

These tobacco warehouses (factories) were large and spacious brick buildings, generally 3 or 4 stories with gable roofs. The insides of these warehouses were far from comfortable compared to what we are accustomed to today for a hospital, they were damp, poorly lit, dingy, poorly ventilated, unsanitary and usually filled with unfamiliar smells.

In addition to the warehouses, thirteen other buildings and sites were used as hospitals, seven of which remained for the duration of the war.

Hospital Listing:
Fairgrounds - Located outside the city - per today's streets; Memorial Ave. (E.C. Glass High School) to 12th Street, from Campbell Ave. to Whitmore St., referred to as "Miller Park". This site was only used for one year only 1862. First recorded death was 06/19/62 and the last recorded death was 08/11/62.
Lynchburg College - Located @ 10th, Floyd & 11th Streets. First recorded death was 04/21/61 and the last recorded death was 01/27/65.
Pest House - Located @ 315 Wise Street (Smallpox Hospital). First recorded death was 08/21/62 and the last recorded death was 07/26/64.
Pratt's - Located @ the Old Union Station, Just off 12th & Kemper Streets. First recorded death was 06/20/64 and the last recorded death was 06/05/65.
Ladies Relief Hospital - Located @ North Corner of 6th & Main Street, formerly the Union Hotel. First recorded death was 08/26/61 and the last recorded death was 06/02/65.
Wayside Hospital - Located @ (1st) Franklin & 9th Streets; (2nd) Jefferson Street between 6th & 7th Streets. First recorded death was 10/01/63 and the last recorded death was 08/21/64.
Warwick House - No address located. First recorded death was 08/21/61 and the last recorded death was 12/31/62.

The remaining six sites were temporary hospitals;
Camp Davis - Located @ Price to Kemper Streets - 12th to 16th Streets. First recorded death was 09/02/62 and the last recorded death was 07/03/65.
Camp Nicholls - Located @ the Southeast side of city. First recorded death was 06/20/64 and the last recorded death was 07/03/65.
Dudley Hall - Located @ Church Street between 10th & 11th Street. No deaths listed.

Norvell House - Only one death recorded, it was not hospital related (See Part III, John Hight) - See map showing the location of the hospitals. That date death was 01/06/64.
Odd Fellows Hall - Located @ 12th Street between Church & Main Streets. First recorded death was 06/07/62 and the last recorded death was 09/10/63.
Washington House - No address or location found. The first and last recorded death was 09/18/61.

These individual hospitals were clustered or divided into "Hospital Divisions" and were organized into groups designated General Hospitals. As Example, **General Hospital No. 3**, contained Division 1 - (College) and Division 2 - (Ferguson's); **General Hospital No. 1** contained Division 1 - (Reid's & Booker's), Division 2 - (Langhorne's), Division 3 - (Burton's & Candler's).

By late 1863 there were three general hospitals (#1, #2, & #3) and three specialty Hospitals in Lynchburg. The first was **Wayside Hospital**, the first stop for the arriving wounded and ill. Here they were diagnosed, treated and assigned to a permanent hospital. The more critically wounded or ill were assigned to the other General Hospitals, **Ladies' Relief** and **Odd Fellows Hall**, who were better equipped for specialized care. **Odd Fellows Hall** served as what we would call an emergency room or a MASH unit, using today's vernacular.

No less than 50 private homes were used in Lynchburg to house and care for the ill and wounded during the war. In the first year of the war 28 private homes were used to care for the ill and wounded. These accounted for approximately 20%. Some of the private residences listed in Mr. Diuguid's were; J. Cundiff, Mrs. Thurman, A. Pamplin, J. W. Murrell, Mrs. Preston, Charles Scott, Jed Carter, George Lee, T. Mason, H. Bocock, Mr. McGeehe, Creed Will, Mrs. Nowlin, Mrs. Collins, A. G. Dinford, John Brown, Mr. Parrish, James Beard, H. R. Sumpters, A. Waddells, Mrs. Adams, P. Lewis, T. C. S. Ferguson, Mr. Coffee, William Langhorne, Samuel McCorkle, Samuel Garland Sr., Samuel P. Booker, and A. G. Hancock.

See the charts at the end of Part I that show the number of deaths in each hospital by month and by each of the war years. These figures are based on Mr. Diuguid's "Soldier Book".

Using Diuguid's burial logbooks and "The Soldiers Book" a total of 2,713 (recorded) soldiers were prepared and buried by George A. Diuguid during the war years. Of this number 2,174 remain in the Old City Cemetery. 201 (documented) were Union soldiers, all of which were exhumed in 1866 and re-interred at Poplar Grove National Cemetery. Another 50 Union soldiers that died in Lynchburg are not included in his records and are not included in the above total. The remaining 438 men that died in the hospitals at Lynchburg were shipped to their homes for family burial.

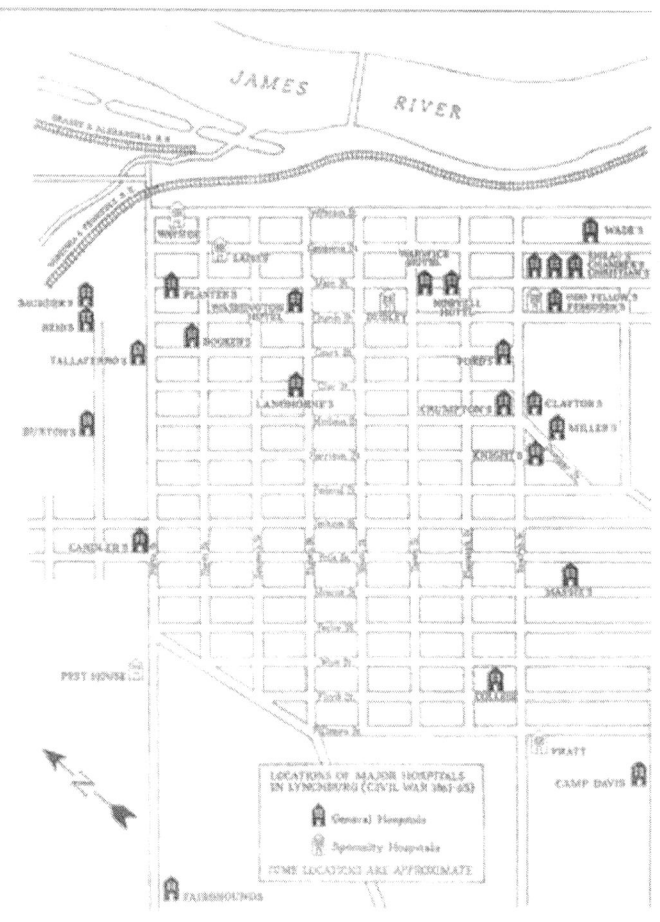

Map of Hospital Locations

The following is a listing of know surgeons, assistant surgeons, local physicians, hospital stewards, and clergy that work or served in the Lynchburg hospital system from 1861 to 1865. These few names were the more permanent medical staff known to have served at Lynchburg. During the four years of the war it is estimated that 4,000 physicians worked in the Lynchburg Hospitals.

Annan, Samuel – Surgeon, date of service was 08/16/63, age 62. Practiced medicine in Baltimore, Md. Transferred to the hospital at Buchanan, Va. Aug. 1863. Born 1800, died 1868.
Annan, T. C. – No Information
Baldwin, Robert S. – Asst. Surgeon, appointed 07/19/62, from Virginia. Resigned 12/19/63. Also served with 16th N.C. and 14th Ga.
Bartlett, T.B. – Asst. Surgeon, from Virginia.
Bass, David E. – Asst. Surgeon, appointed 08/16/62, from Virginia. Also saw service at the Culpepper, Gordonsville, and Danville hospitals.
Baylor, John C. – Asst. Surgeon from Virginia, appointed 07/01/61. Also saw service at the Beaureguard & Richmond hospitals.
Beall, F. A. – Asst. Surgeon
Blackford, Benjamin Lewis – Surgeon, date of service 01/15/63. Resident of Lynchburg, Va. age 28. Ran the Bedford (Liberty) hospitals. Enlisted 4/23/61 in Co. G 11th Virginia Inf., rank of Sgt.; promoted to Lt 5/25/61; born 1835, died 1908.
Boatwright, John G. – Asst. Surgeon, date of service 09/13/61, from Virginia. Promoted to surgeon 06/12/63. Resident of Danville after the war, died 1873, buried in Greenhill Cemetery
Bolton, James – Surgeon, date of service 07/10/63, from Virginia. Also saw service @ Richmond hospitals.
Brevard, E. A. – Asst. Surgeon, date of service 074/19/61, from Virginia. Served in 5th Va. Inf. 10/62 through 02/64.
Broun, James Conway – Asst. Surgeon, date of service 10/16/61, from Virginia. Also served in 8th Va. Inf., and at Culpepper Hospital.; resigned 10/27/62; born 1829 & died 1864.
Butler, W. M. S. – Asst. Surgeon, date of service 07/03/61, from Virginia, age 23. Also served in 3rd Va. Arty. Promoted to Surgeon 04/26/62.

Carmichael, Spotswood Welford – No military information. Resident of Fredericksburg, died there 1904. Also served as chief surgeon in Danville

Chalmers, Henry Coleman – Asst. Surgeon, date of service 05/23/61, from Virginia Age 23. Born 1837 attended UVA & Washington College. Enlisted 04/22/61 as Lt. in Co. A 11th Va. Inf.; appointed Asst. Surgeon 05/23/61. Transferred to Lynchburg (no date) – died 02/07/65.

Chandler, Samuel T. – Asst. Surgeon, date of service 08/16/62, from Virginia. Also saw service @ the Culpepper and Richmond hospitals.

Chapman, W. D. – Asst. Surgeon, date of service 11/13/61 from Virginia.

Christian, Horace B. – Asst. Surgeon, date of service 09/13/61, from Virginia.

Christian, Samuel B. – Surgeon, date of service 11/16/61, from Virginia.

Craighill, Edward D. – Asst. Surgeon, date of service 11/16/61, from Virginia. Born Charleston WVa. 11/02/1840, died in Lynchburg 01/04/1923; enlisted 06/06/61 in 2nd Va. Inf. as Pvt. @ age 21; Hospt. Stewart Winchester 06/25/61 & Manassas 09/19/61; transferred Nov./Dec. 1861 – not stated but most likely Lynchburg. Listed as Surgeon in Lynchburg 1863-65

Cunningham William D. – Asst. Surgeon, date of service 08/14/63, from Virginia; also saw service in 20th Va. Cav. & Richmond Hospitals.

Davis, John F. – Surgeon, date of service 07/03/61 from Virginia; also saw service @ Charlottesville Hospital.

Duffie, John E. – No Information

Dulaney, J. L. – Local Physician

Dulaney, William Hamilton – Surgeon, date of Service 06/01/64, from Kent County, Virginia; commissioned into F&S 13th Battn. Va. Arty. 06/05/64; promoted to surgeon 08/15/64; surgeon of station Petersburg 08/15/64; POW @ Lynchburg 04/15/65; oath of allegiance 05/20/65 (place not stated); officially paroled @ Lynchburg 06/02/65.

Early, Orville R. – Asst. Surgeon, date of service 07/19/61, from Virginia; promoted to Surgeon 10/14/62; also saw service with 12th Va. Battn. Arty.

Ellzey, Mason Graham - Asst. Surgeon, date of service 04/05/62, from Virginia; member of 8th Va. Inf.; Class of 1860

VMI; Assigned to Lynchburg (no date); shown present for duty 12/31/64; paroled @ Appomattox 04/12/65; died 03/18/1915.

Fairfax, Albert – Asst. Surgeon, date of service 04/17/62, from Virginia; also saw service in 30th Battn. Va. Shapshooter's, South Carolina units, and CSN.

Fauntleroy, Archibald McGill – Asst. Surgeon, date of service 06/27/64, from Virginia; also saw service in 6th Va. Cav.; VMI Class of 1857

Fisher, Thomas H. – Asst. Surgeon, date of service 09/02/61, from Virginia; promoted to Surgeon 02/17/62.

Fitzpatrick, Alexander B. – Asst. Surgeon, date of service 07/19/61, from Virginia; Member 51st Virginia F&S.

Galt, James Dickie – Surgeon, date of service 06/12/62, from Virginia; 07/61 Asst. Surgeon with 14th Va. Inf.; promoted to Surgeon 06/12/62 in 19th Virginia Inf.; paroled @ Lynchburg 04/13/65; M.D. from UVa 1853 & Univ. of Penn. 1854; died 09/11/1888.

Green, Daniel S. – Surgeon, date of service 07/19/61, from Virginia; also saw service in CS Navy; assigned to Lynchburg in 1862; d. 03/05/64 – See Part III for additional information.

Green, William – Surgeon; also saw service in 2nd N.C. Battn.

Hammer, Wyatt W. – Surgeon; saw service in 13th Va. Inf.

Hayes, J. A. –

Houston, M. H. (W.?) – Surgeon, date of service 07/01/61, from Virginia; also saw service @ Culpepper Hospital & Harpers Ferry

Jennings, William K. – Surgeon, date of service 07/24/61, from Virginia; also saw service in 115th Va. Militia.

Johnson, James A. – Asst. Surgeon, date of service 11/03/64, from Virginia.

Kemper, Charles R. – Surgeon, date of service 07/01/61, from Virginia; also saw service @ Culpepper Hospital

Kinner, ? – No information.

Ladd, Charles H. – Surgeon, date of Service 06/01/64, from North Carolina; also saw service in 56th N.C. Inf.

Latham, Grey Henry – Surgeon, date of service 1862, from Lynchburg, Virginia; also saw service @ Culpepper Hospital; born Lynchburg 03/04/32, died05/05/1903.

Letcher, F. Marion – Asst. Surgeon, date of service 07/14/61, from Virginia, age 33; also saw service with 13th Va. Inf. & 3rd Va. Reserves.

Lewis, Robert S. – Asst. Surgeon, date of service 07/01/61, from Virginia; appointed surgeon 10/62; also saw service with 13th Va. Inf. & 4th Va. Inf.
Luck, William Jordan – Asst. Surgeon, date of service 08/16/62, from Virginia,; promoted to surgeon, no date.
McGuire. James M. G. – Asst. Surgeon, date of service 07/101/61, from Virginia; promote to surgeon 11/62; also saw service with 1st Battn. Va. Inf. & 44th N.C. Inf.
McLaughlin, D. L. – Surgeon
Mercer, John C. – Surgeon, date of service 06/12/63, from Virginia.
Michie, Theodore A. – Asst. Surgeon, date of service 02/05/62, from Virginia; also saw service with Albermarle Arty.
Miller, John Fullenwider – Surgeon, date of service 10/30/61, from North Carolina; two records for a John F. Miller – one with 34th & one with 38th N. C. Inf. Enlisted as Asst. Surgeon in 12th N.C. 04/22/61 as a Pvt. Promoted to Asst. Surgeon 05/18/61. Transferred to F&S 38th N.C. 10/30/61. Transferred on 05/17/62 to F&S of 34th N.C. Promoted to surgeon 10/30/61 & on 05/17/62. Listed as surrendered at Appomattox 04/09/65 and paroled at Greensboro, N.C. 05/12/65
.**Minor, John W.** – Superintendent (?), date of service 05/17/61, from Virginia; also saw service with 26th Va. Inf.
Mosely, Edward Julian – Asst. Surgeon, date of service 04/17/62, from Virginia; also saw service with 18th Va. Inf. & Cutshaws Battn. Arty.
Mott, A. R. – Surgeon, date of service 07/19/62, from Virginia; resigned 05/03/64; also saw service with 2nd Va. Cav.
Murrary, James H. – Surgeon, date of service 07/19/61, from Virginia; also saw service with 49th Va. Inf.
Olden, John B. – Asst. Surgeon, date of service 09/13/61, from Virginia; also saw service with 13th Va. Cav. & 3rd Miss. Cav.
Owen, William Ottaway – Chief Surgeon Lynchburg Confederate Hospitals, date 1861, from Virginia, age 41; born in Lynchburg 10/20/20; died Lynchburg 02/20/92
Page, John Randolph – Asst. Surgeon, date of service 07/19/62, from Virginia; also saw service with 18th Va. Inf. F&S.
Palmer, William M. – Asst. Surgeon
Payne, Richard – Surgeon, date of service 07/12/61, from Virginia; also saw service with 40th Va. Inf.; resigned 12/06/61
Peters, ? – No Information

Pettison, J. R. – Local Physician
Randolph, Wilson Cary Nicholas – Surgeon, date of service 07/19/61, from Virginia; also saw service with 19th Va. Inf. F&S.
Read, Nathaniel Mason – Asst. Surgeon, date of service 07/01/61, from Virginia; resigned 10/62
Richards, Charles Taylor – Asst. Surgeon, date of service 05/13/63, from Virginia; transferred to Lynchburg 08/64; also saw service with 28th Va. Inf. Co.'s H, born 1839, attended UVa, living in Charlestown, WVa. 1898, died 1922.
Rixey, Samuel R. – Asst. Surgeon, date of service 09/02/61, from Virginia; promoted to surgeon 10/15/62; resigned 03/15/63 also saw service with 1st Va. Arty.
Rust, G. W. – Surgeon
Scott, Martin Pickett – Asst. Surgeon, date of service 07/19/62, from Virginia; also saw service with 18th Va. Inf. F&S.
Shipley, J. H. – Local Physician
Slaughter, Alfred E. – Asst. Surgeon, date of service 10/09/61, from Virginia; also saw service with 58th Va. Inf.
Smith, A. C. – Surgeon
Smith, Daniel B. – Asst. Surgeon, date of service 09/26/61, from Virginia; also served in Richmond hospitals.
Snead, Edward D. – Local Physician
Sommerville, Henry Clay – Asst. Surgeon, date of service 07/19/62, from Virginia, age 28; also saw service with 18thVa. Inf. F&S. Initial duties were as a hospital steward; test and appointed asst. surgeon 06/02/63; assigned to Danville hospital 12/30/63; reassigned to Lynchburg 03/64.
Spencer, Frank – Asst. Surgeon
Steel, David – Asst. Surgeon, date of service 12/04/62, from Virginia; also saw service with 38th Va. Battn. Arty
Taylor, R. Kidder – Asst. Surgeon, date of service 07/01/61, from Virginia; promoted to surgeon 11/13/62; also saw service with 37th Va. Inf.
Terrell, John Jay – Surgeon, date of service 08/02/62, from Virginia; also saw service with 11th Va. Inf.; born in Lynchburg 08/08/22, died Lynchburg 11/07/1922.
Thompson, Ignatius Davis – Asst. Surgeon, date of service 06/02/63, from Virginia; born Frederick Co. Md. 1836, died Baltimore, Md. 1881.
Thornhill, George William – Surgeon, date of service 05/27/61, from Virginia, age 33; enlisted in 11th Va. Inf., Co. B 04/25/61;

appointed regimental surgeon 05/27/61. Attended UVa, born 06/28/28, died in Lynchburg 01/06/93.

Tucker, Beverly St, George – Asst. Surgeon, date of service 07/15/61, from Virginia, age 23; commissioned 07/17/61 in 41st Va. Inf. F&S; Wounded in Action 06/01/62 @ Seven Pines in thigh, never returned to regiment; born 1838.

Turner, George Kempton – Asst. Surgeon, date of service 07/15/61, from Virginia; enlisted in 11th Va. Inf. 06/03/61 Co. E as a Pvt.; served in Lynchburg hospital as nurse before promotion to asst. surgeon; also served at hospital in Kinston, N.C. (no date)

Vason, Marcellus E. – Asst. Surgeon, date of service 08/19/62, from Georgia; enlisted 04/28/61 in Co. E 4th Georgia; discharged for promotion 12/04/62; 12/15/62 commissioned into F&S of 46th Va. Inf.; commissioned into F&S 32nd Va. Cav.; detailed 08/20/62 Gordonsville, Va. Hospital as Med. Director; detailed 11/15/62 place not stated; detailed 04/23/64 Bristol, Tenn. Commandant of Conscripts, last record.

Venable, Hugh A. – Surgeon

Walker, Charles W. – Asst. Surgeon, date of service 09/29/62, from Mecklenburg County, Virginia; commissioned into F&S of 32nd Va. Inf. 09/29/62; POW Amelia C.H. 04/06/65; confined 04/08/65 Newport News, Va.; took oath 07/01/65. Description 5' 8", dark complexion, blue eyes, and dark hair

Warren, William C. – Surgeon

Welburn, William J. – Asst. Surgeon

Welch, C. C. – Local Physician

Wellford, John Spotswood – Surgeon, date of service 07/19/61, from Virginia; enlisted & commissioned 07/13/61 into 41st Va. Inf.; commissioned into F&S 9th Va. Inf.; transferred out on 01/23/63 to Richmond hospitals; died 1911.

Wharton, John S. – Asst. Surgeon, date of service 11/16/61, from Virginia;

White, James, L. – Surgeon, date of service 09/11/61, from Virginia; promoted to surgeon 11/13/62; also saw service with Cutshaw's Battn. Va. Arty.

Williams, E. F. - Asst. Surgeon, date of service 02/17/62, from Virginia; also saw service with 58th Va. Militia

Williams, William J. – Asst. Surgeon, date of service 06/01/64, from Virginia; enlisted as surgeon 10th Va. Inf. No date, 3 months as surgeon with regiment; born 03/21/18

Winston, Peter – Asst. Surgeon, date of service 09/11/61, from Virginia; also saw service @ Charlottesville hospital

Delk, Jeremiah E. L. – Hospital Steward; enlisted as Pvt. 08/14/61 @ Camp Ruffin Va. In 5th Va. Cav.; transferred to Co. H 13th Va. Cav. 12/01/62; discharged by order of Sec. of War (no date); listed as a hospital steward 12/19/62; reached the rank of 1st Sgt. In 13th Va. Cav. 06/15/62; born 10/09/36, died 12/26/87, buried Urquhart Cemetery, Southampton County, Va.; post war listed as physician.

Goode, Tapely A. – Hospital Steward; enlisted in 44th Va. Inf. 04/26/61; resident of Appomattox County, Va., age 19, listed as a medical student; transferred to 20th Battn. Hvy. Arty.; detailed 03/04/62 Chimborazo Hospital, Richmond, Va. as ward master; detailed 07/06/63 to Lynchburg hospitals; detailed again to Lynchburg 06/01/64 as steward and druggist; relieved from duty 03/24/65; no further record

Lee, H. A. – Hospital Steward

Wilson, William Venable – Chaplin, Protestant, Prince William County, Va.; born Farmville, Va. 01/18/22, died Lynchburg 01/22/1908.

Miles, C. A. – Chaplin

Mitchell, Jacob Duche – Chaplin, 2nd Presbyterian, Lynchburg; born 1806, died 1877

Sears, Oscar – Chaplin, Catholic, Holy Cross, Lynchburg; born 1830, died 1867

Gache, Pere Louis-Hippolyte – Chaplin, Catholic, from Louisiana. Was Catholic Chaplin with 10th Louisiana Infantry.

Johnson, John Lipscomb – Chaplin, Baptist, Spotsylvania Co., Va.; born Forest Hill, Spotsylvania Co. 08/12/35, educated @ UVa, teacher @ Hollins Institute 1860-61, ordained Baptist minister 06/10/60; Chaplin of 17th Va. Inf.; relieved 07/09/62, assigned to Lynchburg as Chaplin 1862-65; died 03/02/1915

McGehee, William – Chaplin, Methodist, from Richmond, Va.

Duffel, John –Chaplin, from Louisiana

Daniel, C. – Chaplin, Protestant, from Covesville, Va.

The Union Soldiers – POW's & The Battle for Lynchburg

From the spring of 1862 until the later days of the war, over 10,000 Union soldiers passed through Lynchburg as

"Prisoners of War". Approximately 7,000 of these were housed in Lynchburg for some period of time before being relocated.

The first Union POWs, approximately 3,500, arrived in the city June 10, 1862 and were placed at the Fairgrounds. General T. J. Jackson's forces captured these early arrivals during the 1862 Valley Campaign. This early prisoner of war camp was established to hold prisoners temporarily either for exchange or to be shipped to other more permanent facilities. On June 17th, a short seven days after their arrival the first Union death was reported, Private Bower of the 39th New York Infantry, Company C. The last reported Union death in 1862 by Mr. G. A. Diuguid was August 11th, Corpl. Cyrenius Phipps a member of the 1st Michigan Cavalry. In a period of 2 months 74 Union POW's had died. Considering that an estimated 3,500 prisoners were housed here on a temporary basis, the mortality rate was 2.1% and would be very low as compared to some of the permanent prison sites. As a note of interest, the 42nd North Carolina Infantry commanded by Col. George C. Gibbs, was assigned as the guards of the Union soldiers held at Lynchburg. They were stationed at the "Fairgrounds" between June 14, 1862 and August 19, 1862. During this time period, 20 members of the 42nd died in the Lynchburg Hospital system from disease. The death rate of the Confederates counterparts equaled approximately 2.5%. This percentage is derived based on an estimated 800-man regiment. Based on the military records of the 42nd North Carolina, 9 of these men died of typhoid fever, 1 of scarlaina (scarlet fever) and 1 of pneumonia. The death dates were from 6/15/62 to 9/03/62. Of the 20 that died there ages ranged from 17 the youngest to 32 the oldest. The 42nd was organized in March of 1862. All of the men that died had served 5 months or less.

    The area used at the old Fairground to hold the Union prisoners was an open area with open stalls for the POW's to sleep in. The commanding officer of the 42nd North Carolina, Col. George Gibbs openly protested that the premises chosen were not adequate. In addition, Gibbs complained that the rations supplied were inadequate for both the prisoners and his regiment. This situation was resolved with the appointment of a Capt. J. V. L. Rodgers as the Asst. Q.M. to the prison camp.

Colonel Gibbs telegraphed Brig. Gen. John Henry Winder in Richmond on Wednesday June 18th about the conditions at the Fairgrounds, improper housing and rations for the prisoners. His telegraph was as follows:

"General: I wrote to you on the 15th instant.... I proceed now to make to you a detailed report of the condition of the prison and prisoners. On yesterday I received from Lt. Col. Cunningham, then commanding, 30 commissioned officers, 2230 noncommissioned officers and privates, making 2260 prisoners, exclusive of three Negroes, one of whom is said to be a slave. I inclose list of officers. The premises occupied as prison are entirely unsuited to the purpose, but the assistant quartermaster at this post reports that he can obtain no other. The sleeping quarters of the prison are vacant (open) stalls, or such tents as they can construct with blankets or oilcloths. The officers are in a different part of the grounds from their men. With a large and vigilant guard, two companies of which have been performing this duty for four and one-half months, I hope to prevent escape, but if the premises had been constructed for the express purpose they could not have been better contrived to permit the escape of prisoners. Lumber cannot be had to repair fences, gates or sheds. There is no hospital, and for the reason stated cannot be erected. There are several sick among them, but no deaths since their transfer to me. I have no prison surgeon or assistant. In consequences of some misunderstanding between captain and assistant quartermaster and assistant commissary of subsistence the prisoners were without food for twenty-four hours ending at noon today, and up to this time neither fuel nor well or water buckets have been supplied. The latter officer, Capt. Galt, signs himself as commanding the post. I have directed that no person be permitted to enter the inclosure except by my order. To prevent the possibility of unpleasant feeling (as I cannot obey orders from Capt. Galt) please cause an order to be issued on the subject. Meantime I consider myself in command of the post.

Gibbs was previously in command of the prisoner of war camp established at Salisbury, North Carolina. His command at Salisbury began on January 11, 1862 with the rank of Major. He was promoted to Col. 4/22/62, commanding "Gibbs's Prison Grd. Battalion"

As a result of Gibbs's telegraph the supply situation made a very positive change. Here are two reports dated July 17th and 31st.

July 17 (Thursday)
Capt. John M. Galt, CSA, today transferred commissary stores to Capt. J.V.L. Rodgers, the assistant quartermaster for Federal prisoners at Lynchburg, Va., imprisoned at the Fairgrounds. The supplies consisted of: 6000 pounds of bacon; 138 barrels of flour; 35 bushels of beans; 1400 pounds of rice; 1680 pounds of sugar; 16 bushels of salt; 42 ½ gallons of vinegar; and 10 gallons of whiskey. This was to feed 2248 prisoners.

July 31 (Thursday)
During the month of July, Capt. John M. Galt, Quartermaster, delivered to Capt. J.V.L. Rodgers rations for Federal prisoners at Lynchburg Fair Grounds. The 2248 prisoners were issued 33,484 rations of fresh beef, 40,651 rations of bacon, 74,135 rations of flour, 33,714 rations of beans, 40,421 rations of rice, 400 rations of coffee, 59,805 rations of sugar, 74,135 rations of salt, 10,000 rations of vinegar, 3000 rations of candles, 5500 rations of soap, and 30 gallons of whiskey.

Some of the Union POW's were used as laborers in June and July to assist with the repairs of damage to the canal following a devastating flood in the first week of June. The city's water supplied had dwindled during the repair of the canal. The city was without water for approximately six weeks.

A temporary hospital for the treatment of the Union prisoners at the Fairgrounds was established around June 18th or 19th. This hospital was situated adjacent to the Fairgrounds, "located at the top of the hill above the present Fifth Street Viaduct".

Based on the death rate experienced at the Fairgrounds, the Lynchburg military physicians began admitting Union prisoners that were ill or wounded in early 1863 to the general hospitals. They were incorporated into the Confederate population in the hospital system. Charles M. Blackford wrote, "The Yankees are all mixed up with our men and are treated exactly alike. They seem well contented." "Federal prisoners inside hospitals often wept, owning to the uniformly kind manner in which they were treated, wrote Dr. Edward Craighill. Several Union troops from the 34th Massachusetts had received medical treatment from Dr. Craighill in June 1864 following the Battle of Lynchburg and were very grateful and expressed their gratitude. These same men were a part of the larger force occupying Lynchburg in April of 1865.

For the remainder of the war Mr. Diuguid recorded an additional 126 Union burials. Of the 200 Union burials recorded by Diuguid, 2 were not listed as soldiers. A John Crawshaw listed only as a "Federal Citizen" died 10/26/64 at Crumpton's Factory. The second was Gerard Heter who died 7/08/63. Diuguid's entry was, "A German who cut his throat", "(buried...with soldiers)". (See Part III for details on these individuals).

Diuguid interred two Union Negro soldiers. The first internment was on May 17, 1864 of Union POW with the last name of Talbot who died at Knight's Factory. The second internment was Allen Bobson of the 27th US Colored Troops (Diuguid listed him as member of the 27th Ohio), Bobson died at Crumpton's Factory and was interred July 19, 1864. Both men were buried in what Diuguid referred to as "Negroes Row" in the city cemetery.

As previously stated Diuguid interred an additional 126 Union soldiers in the remaining years of the war. In 1863 there were 11 burials and 1865 there were a total of 5 more recorded. The spring and summer of 1864 saw the Union death toll increase. The total Union deaths in Lynchburg for 1864 doubled from that of 1862. Diuguid's records list 110 Union deaths; but there was at least an additional 50 not in his records.

The spring campaign of U. S. Grant against "Bobby" Lee brought about an overwhelming number of causalities both for the blue and Gray. May 5th and 6th a major battle was fought in the Wilderness. Following in quick succession was the Spotsylvania Court House Campaign (May 8th – 21st), Yellow Tavern May 11th, Drewry's Bluff May 16th, North Anna May 26th, Cold Harbor June 1st – 3rd, Trevilian Station June 11th, and Petersburg June 15th & 16th. Thousands of wounded were transported to Lynchburg. One of the surgeons in the Lynchburg Hospital system, Henry Clay Sommerville stated in May 1864 that he and the other physicians worked **"day and night with 4000 sick and wounded."** Sommerville also wrote, **"these are fearful times and fill the soul with sadness to be witness to so much suffering. Surely woe and lamentations pervade the land."** The total number of admissions to the Lynchburg hospitals exceeded 10,000 in the month of May. Of this number the total number of deaths was 127.

In connection with Grant's pressing Lee South of the Rappahannock River there was to be a second pronged attack. This attack was to be carried out by Major General David Hunter in the Shenandoah Valley. Hunter's orders from Grant were "at all hazards" to take Lynchburg. Grant regarded the capture of Lynchburg of great importance. To paraphrase Grants words "capture the town at all hazards, and hold it one day or longer if possible". Based on Hunter's record on wanton destruction of public property by fire and plunder, it is easy to imagine that his objective was to burn Lynchburg, destroy government and private property.

On June 17th & 18th 1864 the Battle for Lynchburg was fought. David Hunter retired from Lynchburg in the late hours of the 18th and early morning hours of the 19th. Confederate Surgeon John Jay Terrell was called upon to assist with the needs of the severely wounded Union soldiers left behind by Hunter's hasty exit. In Dr. Terrell's words there were eighty-five

"mortally wounded" To be cared for. Terrell also stated. **"I noted a larger and a smaller pile of limbs, the larger at least 4 feet high, indicating the surgeon had been busy in his work."**

Confederate Surgeon Edward E. Craighill went on the further describes the Union wounded. **"There were 117 of these poor crippled...maimed and famished people put in my charge. They were the...worst handled wounded men I ever saw in my whole experience (as a surgeon). They told me they were left to die...and deep and loud were there imprecations (against Hunter). We divided our scanty rations and clothing (with them) but with our best efforts, many died...their wounds...full of maggots in many instances from neglect. Probably three-fourths recovered, however."**

George Diuguid's burial records only list 26 Union deaths associated with the POW's from the Battle of Lynchburg. Twenty-three died of wounds and three as POW's based on their military records. Two of these men were listed as **"Unknown"** in Diuguid's records. A review of military records available of the Union units that participated at Lynchburg increases the Union causalities considerably. To date I have located 39 Union soldiers that were listed as **Killed in Action** on 6/17 & 18/64 and one that **Died of Wounds** two weeks later. There are no references to any of these men in Diuguid's records. The burial records for Poplar Grove National Cemetery at Petersburg, Virginia only identify two of these 39 as being reinterred there. Adding Diuguid's verified burials of 26 and the 40 military record deaths totals 66. Hunter's report of causalities for Lynchburg was 103 Killed, 564 wounded and 271 either captured or missing. By two other accounts following the battle, 80 Union dead were in one part of the field and 40 in another. Five more Union dead were accounted for on the Salem Turnpike. All of these reports, military, newspaper and personal are to some degree suspect but have some amount of factual merit. With the number of men on both sides involved, approaching 35,000, it is inconceivable to believe that were not a minimum of 1,500 casualties for both sides. Confederate records of the battle only list 40 **Killed in Action** and 160 **Wounded in Action**. To date I have been able to identify 25 to 30 Confederate soldiers that died either in the battle or from wounds.

The last recorded Union wartime deaths were in December of 1864 and January 1865. The names recorded are as follows;

Capt. John B. Hartman, 3rd New Jersey Cav., Company C, died at Crumpton's Factory and was interred on or about 12/10/64 but was removed and shipped to Philadelphia. G. Hansaker, 1st U.S. Cav., Company A, died at Crumpton's Factory and was interred on or about 12/10/64. Alfred Warwick, 3rd New Jersey Cav., Company A, died on or about 1/15/65 at Crumpton's Factory. Several other Union troops, non wartime, funerals were handled by Diuguid, the last recorded was on August 4, 1866, "Private Henry Dotting Co F 3rd Battalion 11th US Infantry".

Those Union soldiers that were interred in the city cemetery were exhumed following the war by the Federal government. The exhumation was initiated in October of 1866. Other than the remains that were claimed by their family, the bodies were reinterred at Petersburg, Virginia in a National Cemetery. George A. Diuguid made the following entry in his burial book about the removal of the Union Soldiers.

> **"The Federal Government in the removal of their dead from this place began at what I call No. 1 in 1st Line 1st Lot and numbered the coffin No. 1 proceeding numerically in the row and going back to foot of No. 1 calling it 11 and so on through the Square   Oct 14th 1866**
> **G A Diuguid**
> **So that Capt. Edmond Keys Co B 116th Ohio would be No. 43"**
>
> **GAD**

The following are two articles taken from the <u>Lynchburg Daily Virginian</u> That report the removal of the Union soldiers from the City Cemetery. The first is dated Saturday October 13th 1866.

> **The work of removing the bodies of Federal soldiers, who died here during the war, was commenced yesterday. Their remains will be taken from this place to City Point for re-interment.**

The second article was dated Wednesday October 17th 1866.

On the slopes of the hill just below the Methodist Graveyard, a group of half a dozen or more tents can be seen by passers along the dirt bridge road. Piled up along them are a great number of neat unpainted boxes. Over in the graveyard at one of the lower corners a party of men can be seen at work. This is a detachment of the Burial Corps of the United States, and the boxes are coffins to contain the remains of the Federal soldiers who are buried there. Those remains are to be taken with pious care to a national cemetery for sepulture, where monuments will be erected, flowers planted and every fitting demonstration of honor to dead be paid. This is right enough; a grateful country should honor those who died beneath its flag.

Near by are long rows of unkept and unhonored Confederate graves. Not even a wooden enclosure protects them from the tramp of the beast of the field. They are exposed to desecration, and bear no token of love. The flowers which were tenderly placed upon them in May last have withered and turned to dust. But the state of neglect, we rejoice to know, is not long to remain.

Simultaneously with the operation just mentioned, the ladies of Lynchburg were exerting themselves to procure the means to inclose and to adorn those graves. - Their hands, ever ready for good works, were busying themselves in behalf of an object so tender in all its associations. - Their Tribunitial labors are now ended. Feast, and Fair, and Tableaux, and Concert are over and the means necessary to complete the sacred work has been obtained.

The final resting place for the Union soldiers removed from the Old City Cemetery (also known, as the Methodist Cemetery) was Poplar Grove National Cemetery, Dinwiddie County, Petersburg, Virginia.

Preparation for Burial

Unfortunately, little to no information is available on what method or process George A. Diuguid used to prepare the deceased prior to burial in the city cemetery. Using existing resources, we do know that Mr. Diuguid used charcoal extensively to pack the bodies that were shipped to other localities and out of state. In addition, Mr. Diuguid's records provide us with specific cases where remains were packed in charcoal and stored, in one case, 3 years prior to burial.

Embalming, as we know it today, was in its infancy and not being practiced to any large degree in the 1860's. The chemicals/ingredients/drugs used in the embalming process were for the most part unavailable in the South during the war.

The vast majority of the soldiers interred by Mr. G. A. Diuguid in Lynchburg were placed in rough wooden coffins (varying in size) and interred. These coffins were constructed of primarily of pine and oak and based on Mr. Diuguid's notes was obtained locally within a two or three county radius. One such acquisition was recorded as follows, **"Thos A Carter is to deliver us 20,000 ft inch Pine wood & Picked timber & some what dry by the 15 Jany 1863 at 50$ per Thousand (board feet)"**. Another entry was for the purchase of walnut plank from a W. C. Jordan. The walnut was 3/4" in thickness and Mr. Diuguid offered $7.00 per one hundred board feet. Between June 20th and August 11th of 1864 Diuguid had a total of 11,579 board feet of wood supplied to him by the Confederate Government. Another undated entry read as follows, **"We offer J. W. Carpenter Rocky Point Mills $7.00 per hundred for 3/4 Walnut green & 8.00 if he can kill (sic) dry it & 4$ for 3/4 Poplar"**. Some of the suppliers listed in Diuguid's notes were Samuel A. Bailey; H. Candler (locally); J. G. Woods of Rocky Mount; Thomas W. Elliott; Mr. Moon; John Cobb, Buckingham County; Davis M. Wood, Locust Bottom, Botetourt County; William T. Barrow of Newbern, Va.; Mr. Farrer of Nelson County; J. W. Carpenter of Rocky Point Mills and Francis E. Hopkins of Lisbon, Bedford County.

For the most part each soldier was interred with only the clothing he wore when he departed this world. Very early in the war such items as socks, underwear, gloves, sheets and cotton packing were supplied at a small fee. In 1861 the standard, no-frills burial fee was $10.00. The Southern Confederacy paid G. A. Diuguid $10.00 for each soldier or individual employed in the service of the Confederacy that he buried. For a deceased member of the 3rd Georgia, R. B. Tarver, Diuguid made this entry in the burial log book for September 2, 1861, **"Cash for Draws & Socks, .90c"**. On the same day, Eldridge Robertson, a native of Lynchburg and a member of Latham's Battery was interred. The total cost for the burial was $23.00. Three dollars was the charge for a sheet & cotton packing. The Confederacy paid $10.00 of the cost; Thomas H. Robertson paid the balance. Needless to say, as the war progressed, these items became somewhat scarce and with inflation, more expensive.

In relation to the amount of wood purchased or supplied to Mr. George Diuguid a total of 1,757 entries were made with the external size of the coffin used for the burial of Confederate Soldiers. An additional 97 entries were made for Union soldiers buried. As an example, the entries made in the burial book of each coffin were recorded above each name as follows, "5'10" X 18" (5 ft. 10 in. long by 18" wide). As was previously noted, the coffins were constructed from 3/4 & 1 inch thick wooden slabs. Allowing for material thickness and room for the corpse this individual would be approximately 5'6" in height by 15" at the shoulder in width. On rare occasions Diuguid did supply the depth of the coffin, most of which were 12." The average height of the male from the 1860's would be approximately 5 ft. 9 in. and weighed about 125 to 135 pounds. George W. Lambright a member of George V. Moody's Madison Battery Light Artillery of Louisiana was the smallest prepared by Diuguid. His coffin measured 5 ft. 3 in. in length by 17 in. in width. This man probably stood no more than 5 ft. in height and weighed 100 pounds or less. In contrast, 2 Georgians share in having the largest coffins. The coffin of William B. Diamond of the 8th Georgia measured 6 ft. 10 in. in length by 26 in. in width. The coffin of Henry Clay Shropshire of the 14th Georgia measured 6 ft. 10 in. in length by 25 1/2 in. in width. Both of these men stood somewhere between 6'5" and 6'6" in height and probably weighed well over 200 pounds. These indeed were giants to the men they served with. Another entry made by Diuguid was for W. S. Holt of Company F, 9th Louisiana; no size of the coffin was given only the notation "Huge Coffin". Using the 1,854 (1,757 + 97) entries of coffin sizes that Mr. Diuguid has supplied from his records provides adequate information to help determine the average height of the Confederate and Union solider. Using the information he has supplied the average coffin length was 6 1/2 ft and the average width was 18 inches. Allowing for the material thickness, approximately 2 inches in length and width and 1 inch of space for the corpse to fit in the coffin this gives us height of 5 foot 9 1/2 inches in height by 15 inches in width. As a final note, to identify the remains, Diuguid had the individuals name placed on the lid of the coffin. It's not clear how this was done, but more than likely it was painted or stenciled.

Treating the Ill & Wounded

The treatments prescribed for cure were as numerous as the number of illnesses and diseases. Some were home remedies, while others were outlandish or potentially fatal applications. Lead, mercury and antimony and other harmful elements were used unknowingly in the treatment of several illnesses. However with time, techniques and procedures improved. Diet, proper nourishment and rest were more beneficial than some of the early war drastic treatments. The following are a few of such treatments and remarks on such cures.

For diarrhea - 4 teaspoons of Aloes, 4 teaspoons of Soda put in 12 tablespoons of warm water, a tablespoon 3 times a day for diarrhea.

Rhubarb - A medicine of made roots or rhizomes of any number of related plants. Used as a cathartic and tonic.

Diphtheria - Gargle three times a day with a mixture of vinegar, honey, black pepper, and warm water.

Dysentery – Boil together by a gentle heat, three pints of sweet milk and one ounce of mutton tallow. Then add gradually, one half tablespoonful of powdered starch, stirring constantly. Add sugar to the taste. Dosage – a wine glass several times a day.

Numerous remedies, treatments, poultices, tinctures (external and by infusion), and concoctions were used on the soldiers on this war. Some of these treatments work with great success and others failed horribly.

"Nine physicians out of ten," asserted a newspaper correspondent with Tennessee troops early in the war, **"scare their patients by long faces, looking at the tongue often, thumping the chest, shaking their heads significantly, and dosing them with quinine and ipecac. The first makes you deaf and dumb, and the other turns you inside out."**

The physicians of the 1860's as compared to today's standards were poorly trained and unprepared for medical practice. The medical schools of the time varied from one year to a matter of a few weeks. Medical schools flourished during this time period and were nothing more than diploma factories. Princeton, Yale and the University of Virginia were considered good medical schools. Of course there was another option to become a doctor; you could do an apprenticeship under and older physician. Many preferred this option of "hands on" medicine rather than classroom medicine.

Medical technology was at best very mediocre during the War Between the States. The medical staff's both North & South had no knowledge of bacteria, viruses and the use of antiseptics. However, the four years of war with all it's death and suffering did bring about refinements to medical procedures, many improvements to the medical field.

Conclusion

In the pages that follow, this author will share with you all facts and information he could gather. Each soldier listed here has been researched through current available sources. Still, there are missing bits of information, which could not be found. Some of the names are perhaps misspelled. However, every effort has been made to secure the proper spelling.

If our valiant ancestors could be heard, a multitude of stories about the war could be told by those mentioned within these pages. Think of the eyewitness accounts of that Army on the move, which could be documented concerning the life style, battle, camp life, songs, comradeship, spiritual life, close calls, humorous stories, and so many more. We will never get to hear them, not in this life.

This writing provides only the details that have been supplied to me. It is my desire that some missing link will be provided to the reader concerning their valiant ancestor. Perhaps some great-grandson or great-granddaughter might discover what happened to an ancestor who once proudly wore Confederate gray or the Union blue.

Scan the pages of this roster of the Confederate and Union heroes to learn who died here in the Lynchburg Hospital System, and/or on the field of battle.

So, now begins the story of the men that died of war wounds and disease between May 1, 1861 and May 31, 1865.

ATTACHMENT I

PART I

**A NUMERICAL LISTING OF
CONFEDERATE SOLDIERS
BY STATE OF SERVICE
INTERRED WITHIN THE CONFEDERATE SECTION
OLD CITY (METHODIST) CEMETERY**

BETWEEN MAY 1861 – MAY 1865
****

State	Confederate Section	Small Pox	*Other	Total	%
Alabama	226	9	9	244	10%
Arkansas	15	1	3	18	.007%
Florida	38	1	0	39	.0163%
Georgia	490	24	52	566	23.6%
Kentucky	4	0	0	4	.0017%
Louisiana	116	2	1	119	4.97%
Maryland	3	0	0	3	.00125%
Mississippi	111	5	5	121	5.05%
Missouri	1	0	0	1	.0004%
North Carolina	494	26	38	558	23.31%
South Carolina	181	4	15	200	8.35%
Tennessee	21	1	6	28	1.17%
Texas	29	1	0	30	1.25%
Virginia	316	21	102	439	18.34%
Unknown	14	7	3	24	1.01%
	2058	102	234	2394	

*This category indicates the number of remains prepared by Diuguid's that were either sent home for burial or interred locally other than the Confederate section of the Old City Methodist Cemetery.

North Carolina and Georgia account for 1,124 of the Confederate soldiers interred in the Old City Cemetery (a shocking 46.98%).

ATTACHMENT II
PART II
A NUMERICAL LISTING OF UNION SOLDIERS BY STATE OF SERVICE INTERRED WITHIN THE CONFEDERATE SECTION OLD CITY (METHODIST) CEMETERY

BETWEEN MAY 1861 – MAY 1865

****

State	Total Buried	Buried in National Cemetery	Shipped Home	Total
Connecticut	2	2	0	2
Delaware	2	2	0	2
Illinois	1	1	0	1
Indiana	12	12	0	12
Maine	13	13	0	13
Maryland	12	11	1	12
Mass-achutes	11	11	0	11
Michigan	15	15	0	15
New Hampshire	5	5	0	5
New Jersey	7	4	3	7
New York	45	44	1	45
North Carolina	1	0	0	1
Ohio	54	51	3	54
Pennsylvania	25	5	0	25
Rhode Island	1	1	0	1
Unknown	13	13	0	13
U.S. Regulars	5	4	1	5
USCT	2	2	0	2

Vermont	7	7	0	7
West Virginia	18	18	0	18
Wisconsin	3	3	0	3
Total	254	245	9	254

    254 Union soldiers were interred within the Old City Cemetery. A significant number of these were buried within what is now recognized as the Confederate Section.

    Of the Union soldiers interred in the cemetery 244 were exhumed and re-interred in the National Cemetery at Petersburg, Virginia following the war.

    Although all Union troops were exhumed in Oct. 1866, at least 9 were exhumed and shipped to their respective homes by Diuguid.

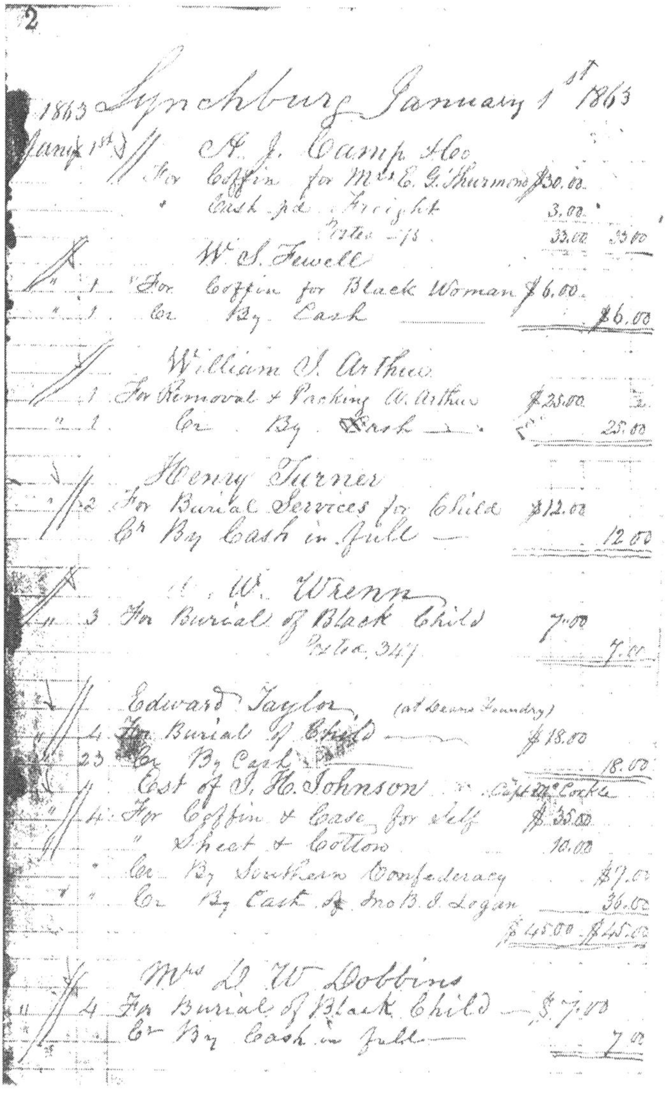
2

1863 Lynchburg January 1st 1863

Jany 1st A. J. Camp & Co
For Coffin for Mrs E. G. Thurmond $30.00
Cash pd. Freight 3.00
33.00 33.00

Wm S. Fewell
1 For Coffin for Black Woman $6.00
1 Cr By Cash $6.00

William S. Arthur
1 For Removal & Packing W. Arthur $25.00
1 Cr By Cash 25.00

Henry Turner
2 For Burial Services for Child $12.00
Cr By Cash in full 12.00

C. W. Wrenn
3 For Burial of Black Child 7.00
7.00

Edward Taylor (at Foundry)
4 For Burial of Child $18.00
23 Cr By Cash 18.00

Est of J. H. Johnson Capt McCorkle
4 For Coffin & Case for self $35.00
" Sheet & Cotton 10.00
Cr By Southern Confederacy $7.00
Cr By Cash of Jno B. J. Logan 36.00
$45.00 $45.00

Mrs L. W. Dobbins
4 For Burial of Black Child $7.00
Cr By Cash in full 7.00

Figure 1 – Typical Burial Logbook entry
Page #2 from Logbook # 6 – Dated Jan. 1, 1863

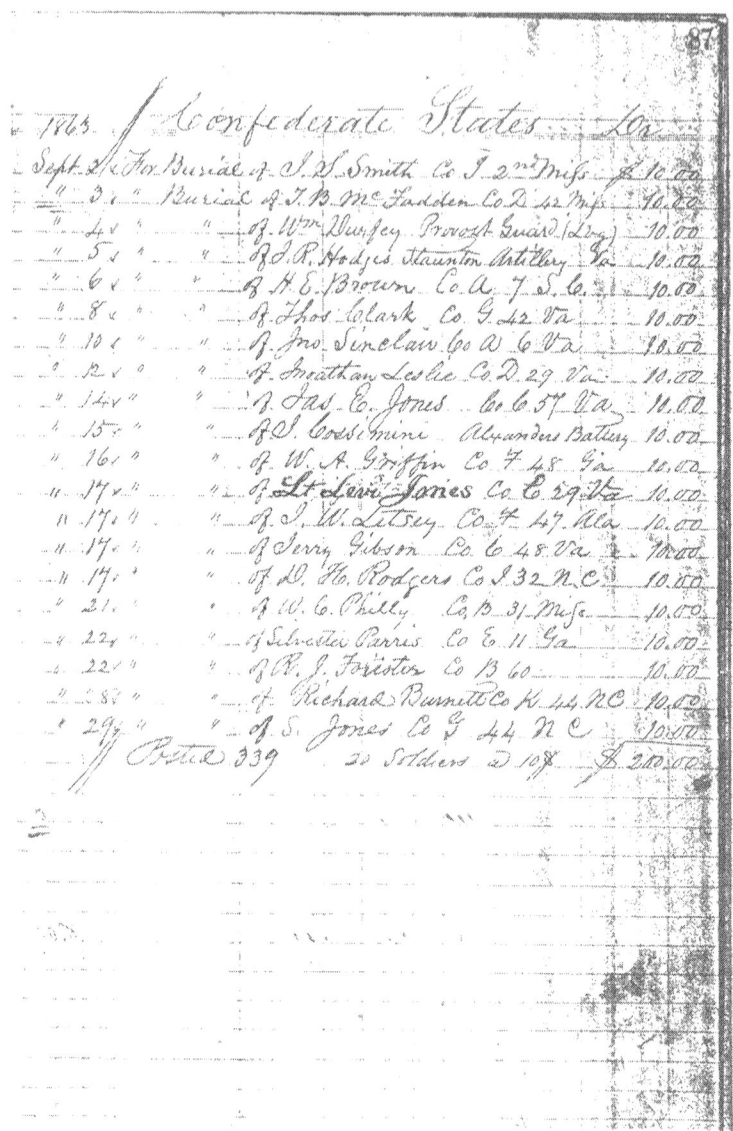

Figure 2 – "Southern Confederacy"
Typical Page taken from Logbook #6 dated Sept. 2 – 29, 1863

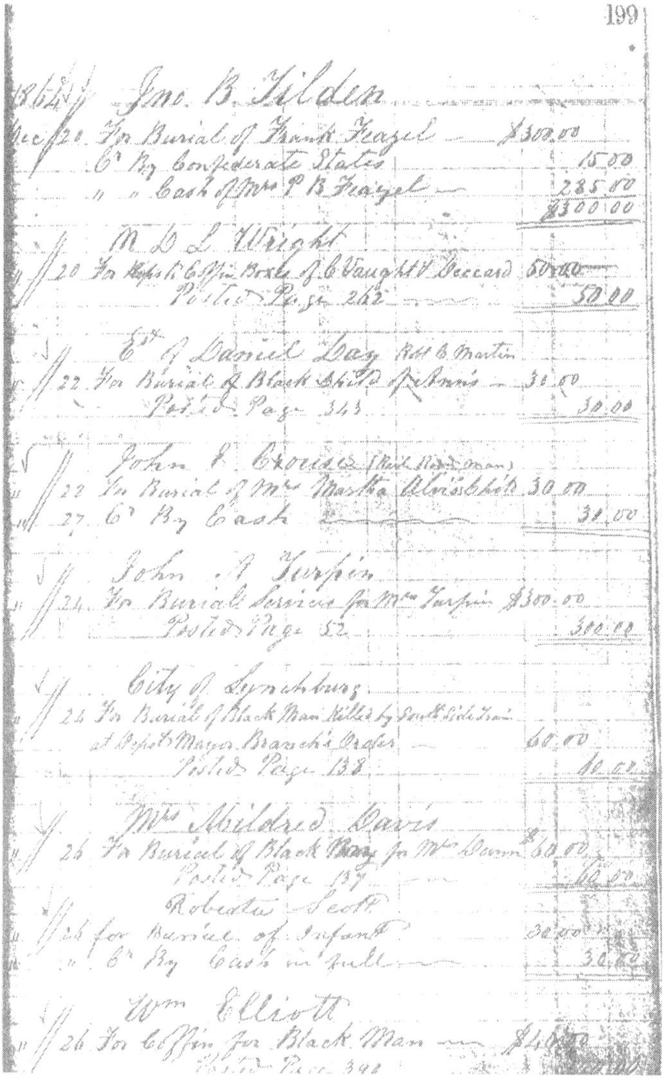

                                                                                199

1864   Jno. B. Tilden
Dec/20 For Burial of Frank Frazel — $300.00
         C° By Confederate States   15.00
          "   " Cash of Mrs P B Frazel   285.00
                                              $300.00

         M D L Wright
 /20 For Keep & Coffin Box & J C Vaught & Discard 50.00
               Posted Page 262   50.00

           E'd J Daniel Day Kill E Martin
 /22 For Burial of Black Child of his   30.00
               Posted Page 343   30.00

          John E Crouch (this man own)
 /22 For Burial of Mrs Martha Chrisbhild 30.00
  27 C° By Cash   30.00

          John A Turpin
 /24 For Burial Services for Mrs Turpin $300.00
               Posted Page 52   300.00

          City of Lynchburg
 /26 For Burial of Black Man killed by South Side Train
       at Depot Mayor Branch's Order   60.00
               Posted Page 138   60.00

          Mrs Mildred Davis
 /26 For Burial of Black Boy for Mrs Dunn 60.00
               Posted Page 139   60.00

          Roberta Scott
 /26 For Burial of Infant   30.00
       " C° By Cash in full   30.00

          Wm Elliott
 /26 For Coffin for Black Man — $40.00
               Posted Page 340

Figure 3 – Typical Burial Logbook entry
Page #199 from Logbook # 6 – Dated Sept. 1864

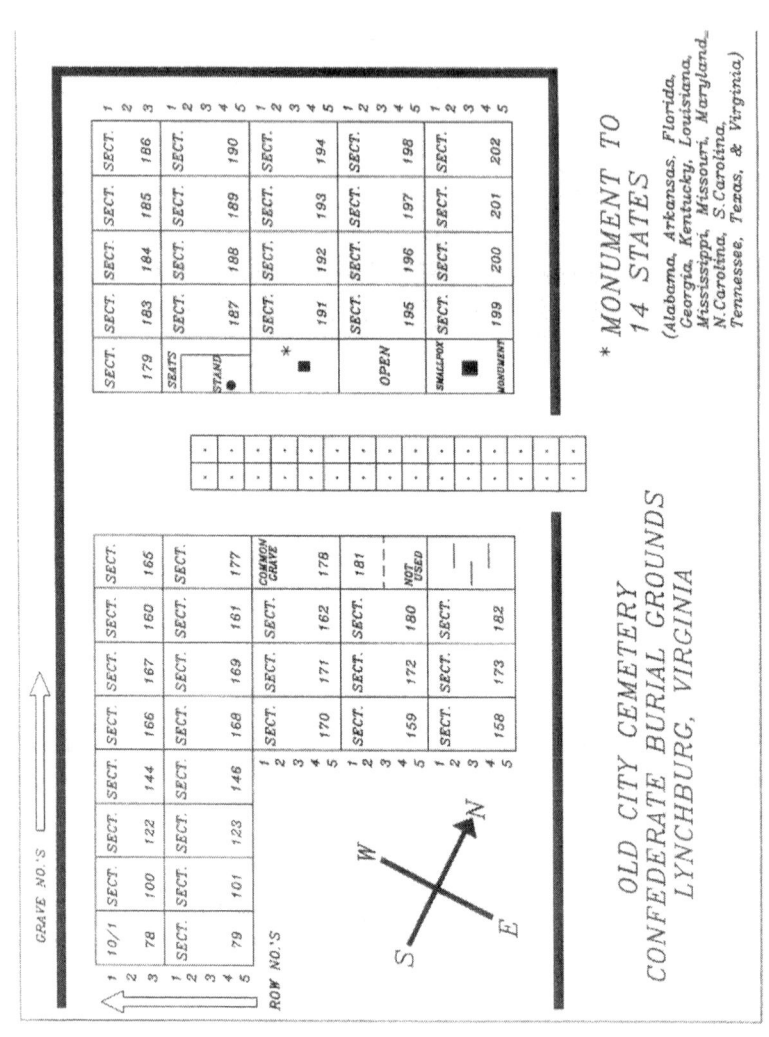

Confederate Section Map – Old City Cemetery

Photographs of the Old City Cemetery

Old City Cemetery Entrance

Old City Cemetery Entrance

Small Pox Monument

Table I - Military Deaths in Lynchburg 1861
(Based on G.A. Diuguid's Burial Records for 1861)

Hospital	May	June	July	Aug.	Sept.	Oct.	Nov.	Dec.	Total
College Hospital	5	7	1	8	4	8	3	10	46
Warwick House				3	14	4	1	3	25
Ladies Relief				2	5	6	3	4	20
Private Res.		1	6	4	8	5	3	1	28
Other	3			3	2		1	1	10
Total	8	8	7	20	33	23	11	19	129

Table II - Military Deaths in Lynchburg 1862
(Based on G.A. Diuguid's Burial Records for 1862)

Hospital	Jan.	Feb.	Mar.	April	May	June	July	Aug.	Sept.	Oct.	Nov.	Dec.	Total
Booker's				4	16	3	5	2	2	1		3	36
Burton's							7	11	8	4	4	19	53
Camp Davis													4
Candler's								4	2	2			19
Christian's				8	45	10	19	14	8	11	9	28	162
Claytor's					2	10	11	6	9	5	19	12	64
College Hospt.	2		7	8	11	5	5	16	20	9	9	4	95
Crumpton's					14	11	13	11	5	6	7	15	91
Fairground's						7	58	13			16		78
Ferguson's				1	36	17	19	11	12	9	21	30	156
Ford's						3	5	8	2	1	6	7	32
Knight's						2	7	6	2	4	6	11	38
Ladies Relief	2	3	2	8	9	6	7	13	4	2	3	3	62
Langhorne's					4	11	9	8	14	3	12	9	70
Miller's							1	7	11	11	9	5	44
Odd Fellow's						5	3	1	2		5		16
Pest House										3	1	19	23
Reid's					12	10	3	14	5	5		10	59
Saunders				2	10	5	2	5	1		2	4	31
Taliaferro's					1	3	5	5	2	1	2	6	25
Warwick House	3	1	5	12	20	5	10	13					69
Private Res.	1		1	1	7		2	4			1	1	18
Other	1	2	1	1	1	3		4	1	2			16
Total	9	7	16	45	188	116	192	176	110	79	132	191	1261

Table III - Military Deaths in Lynchburg 1863
(Based on G.A. Diuguid's Burial Records for 1863)

Hospital	Jan.	Feb.	Mar.	April	May	June	July	Aug.	Sept.	Oct.	Nov.	Dec.	Total
Booker's	1				1	1	1	1		1		3	9
Burton's	15	10	1	5	4		3	3	1	3	4	1	50
Camp Davis													
Candler's	7	7	4	7		11	4	6	3		1	1	33
Christian's	16	16	6	2		1		1	1		3		26
Claytor's	9	9	10	4	3	6	3		2	4	0	2	63
College Hospt.				3		7		3	1				42
Crumpton's	17	7	2	9	3	10	2	3	2	4	5		64
Ferguson's	26	3	4	2	1	5	2	6	1		4		54
Ford's	18	17	7	4		6	3	5			1	2	63
Knight's	8	1				1							10
Ladies Relief	7	3	8	1	1		1	1	1	2	1	1	27
Langhorne's	3	1		2	1	2	2	1		1	2		15
Miller's	12	9	7	1	8	4			3	4	2	2	53
Odd Fellow's	7	4	4	4	3	2	6	1			1		31
Pest House			1						1				2
Red's	24	19	2	5	5	4	3			1	3	2	61
Saunder's	6	1		4	4	2	1	1				2	23
Taliaferro's	6	3	2					1					13
Wade's	9	2	2	1		1		1					11
Private Res.	2	2		1	1	2						1	5
Other	1	1	1			1	1		4	2		3	7
													16
Total	194	115	61	51	35	66	32	35	20	22	27	20	678

Table IV - Military Deaths in Lynchburg 1864
(Based on G.A. Diuguid's Burial Records for 1864)

Hospital	Jan.	Feb.	Mar.	April	May	June	July	Aug.	Sept.	Oct.	Nov.	Dec.	Total
Booker's		2			8	2	2						14
Burton's	1				9	12	5	1		1		1	30
Camp Davis	1	2	3	2	9	17	22	9	2	4		1	72
Candler's	1				2	3							6
Christian's	3			1	32	23	21	6	3	4	1		94
Claytor's					2								2
College Hospt.		5	1	6	8	22	9	3	1	1	1		57
Crumpton's	3				11	16	31	15	11	5	4	5	101
Ferguson's	2	3	1	8	15	8	6	3		1	1		48
Knight's		1			18	16	15	2	3	2	1	3	61
Ladies Relief	1		1	1	11	4	3	2				1	24
Langhorne's	1	1			1	1	2	1	1			1	9
Pest House	3	7	5				1						17
Reid's	1			1	1	5	1	1	1	2	2		14
Private Res.	1		1				4	1					8
Massie's							1			3			4
Camp Nicholls						3	1						4
Wayside					3	3	1	3					10
Pratt's					4								4
Other	1			1	3	7				1	1	2	16
Total	19	21	12	21	137	142	125	47	22	24	11	14	595

Table V - Military Deaths in Lynchburg 1865
(Based on G.A. Diuguid's Burial Records for 1865)

Hospital	Jan.	Feb.	Mar.	April	May	June	Total
Burton's	1						1
Camp Davis				3	5		8
Christian's		5		1			6
College Hospt.	1						1
Crumpton's	1	4	2	2			9
Ferguson's				1			1
Knight's	3	1	1	3			8
Ladies Relief		1		1	1	1	4
Langhorne's	1			1			2
Reid's			1				1
Pratt's			1	1	4		6
Private Res.	1						1
Other	1	2			1		4
Total	9	13	5	13	11	1	52

Total Deaths Recorded by G. A. Diuguid

Total Deaths	Jan.	Feb.	Mar.	April	May	June	July	Aug.	Sept.	Oct.	Nov.	Dec.	Total
1861					8	8	7	20	33	23	11	19	129
1862	9	7	16	45	188	116	192	176	110	79	132	191	1261
1863	194	115	61	51	35	66	32	35	20	22	27	20	678
1864	19	21	12	21	137	142	125	47	22	24	11	14	595
1865	9	13	5	13	11	1							52
Total	231	156	94	130	371	325	349	258	152	125	170	225	2586

PART II

Listing of Soldiers Interred in the Confederate Section Of Old City Cemetery

Confederate Troops

Old City Cemetery (Methodist Cemetery), Lynchburg, Virginia

NAME	REGT. or UNIT	STATE	COMPANY	BRANCH of SERVICE	LOT#	Grave No.	ROW	DATE of BURIAL or DEATH	CAUSE of DEATH	HOSPITAL
Abbott, Thomas J.	5th	Florida	G	Inf.	195	6	2	02-Mar-63	Pneumonia	Burton's Factory
Ackeridge, J. B.	10th Battn.	Georgia	E	Inf.	199	4	2	10-Apr-63	---	College Hospital
* Ackerman, William Lawrence	6th	Louisiana	C	Inf.	158	7	1	18-Jun-61	---	College Hospital
Adams, Andrew Q.	15th	Alabama	F	Inf.	168	5	2	06-May-62	---	Warwick House
Adams, Charles P.	58th	Virginia	B	Inf.	198	3	4	17-Jan-64	Diphtheria	Knight's Factory
Adams, George B.	3rd	North Carolina	D	Inf.	165	8	3	30-May-63	Typhoid Perver	Christian's Factory
Adams, H. W.	8th	Louisiana	I	Inf.	Yk. Sq.	27th	1st Line	13-Feb-63	Small Pox	Pest House
Adams, Isaac	61st	Virginia	G	Inf.	79	5	2	08-Jan-63	Pneumonia	Ferguson's Factory
* Adams, James H.	11th	North Carolina	---	Inf.	Yk. Sq.	---	---	24-Jan-64	Small Pox	Pest House
Adams, Jesse	26th	Georgia	H	Inf.	123	4	3	21-Dec-62	---	Claytor's Factory
Adams, Joshua	8th	Virginia	G	Inf.	172	1	4	11-Jun-62	---	Odd Fellow's Hall
Adams, Robert W.	38th	Georgia	B	Inf.	79	8	3	05-Jan-63	---	College Hospital
Adams, William	Leesburg	Virginia	---	---	192	8	2	27-Jun-63	---	Mrs. Beckworths
Adcock, Pumphrey W.	15th	North Carolina	E	Inf.	191	5	2	06-Feb-63	Phthisis Pulmonaris	Ferguson's Factory
* Addy, Simeon L.	15th	South Carolina	C	Inf.	201	9	1	06-Jun-64	DOW 5/6/64 & Typhoid	College Hospital
Adkins, John W.	38th	Virginia	B	Inf.	166	4	3	10-May-62	Pneumonia	Ferguson's Factory
Adkins, Lewis	16th	Virginia	H	Inf.	192	3	4	06-Aug-63	---	Wade's Factory
Agerson, R.	5th	Virginia	I	Inf.	184	2	2	27-May-63	---	Ladies Relief Hospt.
Agnew, J. B.	9th	Alabama	G	Inf.	166	4	2	10-May-62	---	Ferguson's Factory
* Ahrens, Henry Wm., Sgt. Maj.	1st Orr's Rifles	South Carolina	F&S	Inf.	193	6	5	18-May-64	Dow 5/06/64	College Hospital
* Albriton, Jasper N.	8th	Florida	A	Inf.	182	1	4	15-Oct-62	Disease	Christian's Factory
* Aldridge, Francis	48th	North Carolina	K	Inf.	122	3	3	22-Nov-62	Pleuritis	Claytor's Factory
Alexander, John	55th	Virginia	A	Inf.	146	9	2	16-Dec-62	Diarrhea Chronic	Burton's Factory
Alexander, W. D.	7th	North Carolina	K	Inf.	178	6	4	08-Sep-62	Typhoid Fever	Ferguson's Factory
Allen, Abijah	8th	Louisiana	E	Inf.	168	4	4	13-May-62	---	Ferguson's Factory
Allen, John W.	2nd Battn.	Georgia	D	inf.	180	5	4	20-Oct-64	---	Claytor's Factory
* Allen, Paul 2nd Lieut.	1st Orr's Rifles	South Carolina	A	Inf.	193	8	5	17-May-64	---	Christian's Factory
Alligood, James	5th	Florida	C	Inf.	188	8	3	07-Jun-63	DOW	College Hospital
Allman, John A.	28th	Virginia	F	Inf.	168	4	1	21-Apr-62	Pneumonia	College Hospital
Allran, Jacob	11th	North Carolina	I	Inf.	197	8	1	25-May-64	Pneumonia	Ferguson's Factory
Alred, James M.	22nd	North Carolina	I	Inf.	190	9	3	27-Jun-64	Pneumonia	Christian's Factory
Almand, Graves B., Capt.	35th	Georgia	B	Inf.	201	9	2	05-Jun-64	---	College Hospital
Alphin, R. S.	3rd	Arkansas	E	Inf.	170	2	2	20-Dec-61	---	Ladies Relief Hospt.
* Altman, John Alfred	15th	South Carolina	G	Inf.	186	9	1	19-Jun-64	Gunshot Wound	Knight's Factory

* See Part III - 57

NAME	REGT. or UNIT	STATE	COMPANY	BRANCH of SERVICE	LOT#	Grave No.	ROW	DATE of BURIAL or DEATH	CAUSE of DEATH	HOSPITAL
Alverson, H. G. (T.?)	48th	Alabama	K	Inf.	197	1	3	03-Jun-64	---	Burton's Factory
Amos, James D.	26th	Georgia	M	Inf.	123	6	2	14-Mar-63	Disease	Claytor's Factory
Anderson, B	61st	Georgia	B	Inf.	187	9	2	20-Jan-63	DOW 12/13/62	Burton's Factory
Anderson, D.	26th	Georgia	I	Inf.	177	4	3	11-Sep-62	---	Claytor's Factory
Anderson, J. S.	26th	Georgia	A	Inf.	162	5	2	31-Jul-62	---	Claytor's Factory
Andley, George H.	9th	Louisiana	J	Inf.	178	1	5	30-Aug-62	---	Burton's Factory
Andrews, Daniel	47th	Alabama	I	Inf.	180	1	1	22-Sep-62	---	Odd Fellow's Hall
Andrews, R. S.	38th	Georgia	H	Inf.	146	7	3	15-Dec-62	---	Ladies Relief Hospt.
Anthony, John	9th	Virginia	Sanford's	Cav.	171	6	4	13-Jun-62	---	Odd Fellow's Hall
Appleton, J. W.	12th	Georgia	E	Inf.	173	2	2	30-Jun-62	---	Langhorne's Factory
Armistead, W. S.	2nd	Louisiana	D	Inf.	199	6	2	02-Apr-65	---	Claytor's Factory
Armstrong, Ebenezer	20th	Georgia	G	Inf.	190	4	4	04-Jul-64	DOW 5/06/64	Crumpton's Factory
Arnett, William	3rd	North Carolina	B	Inf.	183	9	2	15-Jan-63	Pneumonia	Ferguson's Factory
Arnold, Moses P.	38th	Georgia	E	Inf.	194	1	4	29-Jul-64	Disease	Camp Davis
Arss, M.	22nd	Virginia	-	Inf.	168	1	2	25-Apr-62	---	Booker's Factory
Ashwell, Pleasant T., Lieut.	28th	Virginia	G	Inf.	194	1	2	31-Jul-64	Diarrhea	Wayside Hospital
Athey, John Robert	2nd	Virginia	I	Inf.	168	6	1	22-Apr-62	Pneumonia	Christian's Factory
Athey, William A.	2nd	Virginia	I	Inf.	168	9	1	23-Apr-62	Typhoid Fever	Warwick House
Aubrey, W. F. (T.?)	Unknown	Unknown	G	Inf.	171	8	5	31-May-62	---	Booker's Factory
Aubrey, William	8th	Louisiana	G	Inf.	166	1	1	03-May-62	---	Ferguson's Factory
Autry, Daniel S.	5th	North Carolina	A	Inf.	184	7	2	23-Apr-63	Disease	College Hospital
Autry, Malcom	54th	North Carolina	C	Inf.	78	7	1	04-Dec-62	Typhoid Fever	Claytor's Factory
Ayers, R. B.	7th	Tennessee	F	Inf.	178	3	4	01-Sep-62	---	Burton's Factory
Bacon, Benjamin B.	61st	Georgia	H	Inf.	178	10	2	24-Aug-62	---	Claytor's Factory
Baggett, Elisha E.	13th	Alabama	H	Inf.	162	2	5	27-Jul-62	---	Miller's Factory
Bagwell, James	13th	South Carolina	I	Inf.	146	3	5	08-Dec-62	Diarrhea Chronic	Claytor's Factory
Bailes, George S.	13th	North Carolina	B	Inf.	161	1	2	13-Jul-62	Typhoid Fever	Crumpton's Factory
Bailey, Benjamin Franklin	52nd	Virginia	C	Inf.	186	8	3	20-Jun-64	DOW 6/18/64	Pratts Hospital
Bailey, Edward P.	53rd	Virginia	H	Inf.	Yk. Sq.	29th	3rd Line	16-Mar-63	Small Pox	Pest House
Bailey, Henry N.	60th	Georgia	H	Inf.	177	1	5	12-Aug-62	Typhoid Fever	Christian's Factory
Bailey, Jackson B.	45th	North Carolina	G	Inf.	197	2	2	04-Jun-64	---	College Hospital
Bailey, James M.	49th	Georgia	C	Inf.	184	1	1	25-Apr-63	Typhoid & Pneumonia	Camp Davis
Bailey, L.	Latham's Batty.	North Carolina	H 1st	Art.	179	9	3	12-Sep-62	Typhoid Fever	College Hospital
Bailey, William T.	33rd	North Carolina	K	Inf.	160	2	2	05-Jul-62	Diarrhea Chronic	Langhorne's Factory
Bailey, Z.	19th	Georgia	A	Inf.	179	5	1	16-Sep-62	---	Langhorne's Factory
Bain, Thomas S.	53rd	North Carolina	B	Inf.	189	4	5	07-May-64	Dysenteria Acuta	Ferguson's Factory
Baker, A. J.	1st	South Carolina	C	Inf.	201	2	2	19-Jun-64	---	Christian's Factory
Baker, John C.	20th	Mississippi	Reid's	Inf.	159	2	3	13-Sep-61	---	John Camp's
Baker, Nathan	14th	Georgia	G	Inf.	172	6	2	16-Jun-62	Chronic Diarrhea	Crumpton's Factory

* See Part III - 58

NAME	REGT. or UNIT	STATE	COMPANY	BRANCH of SERVICE	LOT#	Grave No.	ROW	DATE of BURIAL or DEATH	CAUSE of DEATH	HOSPITAL
Baker, Richard F. M.	10th	Alabama	I	Inf.	179	8	3	13-Sep-62	---	Ladies Relief Hospt.
Baker, S. J.	Stuart's Horse	Maryland	---	Art.	196	9	3	14-Aug-63	---	Ferguson's Factory
Baker, William R.	11th	Texas	F	Cav.	185	8	3	02-Mar-64	---	Ladies Relief Hospt.
Baldwin, William H.	46th	North Carolina	F	Inf.	144	5	1	18-Nov-64	Typhoid Pneumonia	Knight's Factory
Balmon, E.	14th	Louisiana	B	Inf.	198	6	1	22-Sep-64	---	Camp Davis
Barbee, H. H.	5th	North Carolina	E	Inf.	184	8	1	18-Apr-63	Diarrhea Chronic	Camp Davis
Barbee, John G.	10th	Georgia	C	Inf.	144	10	2	16-Nov-62	---	Crumpton's Factory
Barber, Henry	1st	North Carolina	H	Inf.	187	5	5	25-Jan-63	Pneumonia	Claytor's Factory
Barber, Hughey	5th	North Carolina	C	Inf.	187	2	4	05-Feb-63	Diarrhea Chronic	Knight's Factory
Barber, John H.	57th	Virginia	E	Inf.	146	3	1	08-Dec-62	---	Ferguson's Factory
Barksdale, J. H.	16th	Mississippi	F	Inf.	168	3	3	02-May-62	---	College Hospital
Barlow, William (Jos. Barley?)	1st	Tennessee	E	Inf.	123	2	3	18-Dec-62	---	Crumpton's Factory
Barnes, J.	13th	Georgia	J	Inf.	100	5	2	28-Nov-62	---	Ferguson's Factory
Barnes, James	33rd	North Carolina	A	Inf.	101	9	5	02-Jan-63	Diarrhea Chronic	Langhorne's Factory
Barnes, Thomas	38th	Georgia	H	Inf.	197	10	1	24-May-64	DOW	Knight's Factory
Barnett, Thomas	2nd	South Carolina	H	Inf.	183	4	2	21-Jan-63	Diarrhea Chronic	College Hospital
Barnett, Charles A.	48th	North Carolina	D	Inf.	162	7	5	15-Jan-64	Disease	Candler's Factory
Barnhart, Daniel E., Corpl.	2nd	Virginia	B	Inf.	168	3	1	25-Apr-62	Diarrhea Chronic	Christian's Factory
Barrett, Aaron N.	15th	North Carolina	G	Inf.	79	2	5	13-Jan-63	---	Burton's Factory
Barrett, William	19th	Georgia	H	Inf.	181	4	1	20-Oct-62	---	Christian's Factory
Barry, Howard H., Sgt.	32nd	Virginia	I	Inf.	122	7	2	22-Nov-62	---	Miller's Factory
Bartler, John A.	49th	Georgia	C	Inf.	146	6	2	14-Dec-62	---	Booker's Factory
Bartlett, William	55th	Virginia	E	Inf.	193	1	3	21-May-64	DOW 5/05/64	Crumpton's Factory
Barton, David Jr.	28th	Virginia	D	Inf.	191	1	2	07-Feb-63	Diarrhea	Christian's Factory
Bass, Blackman	59th	Georgia	E	Inf.	194	9	3	12-Jul-64	---	Knight's Factory
Bassett, J. W.	15th	Alabama	H	Inf.	173	10	5	27-Jun-62	---	Warwick House
Beach, John R.	4th	North Carolina	F	Inf.	79	6	3	11-Jan-63	---	Reid's Factory
Beachan, E. S.	17th	Virginia	H	Inf.	Yk. Sq.	25th	4th Line	05-Feb-63	Small Pox	Pest House
Bean, William M.	7th	Georgia	A	Inf.	187	10	3	20-Jan-63	Typhoid Fever	Knight's Factory
Beane, Constanine	40th	Virginia	H	Inf.	178	9	2	23-Oct-62	Typhoid Fever	Knight's Factory
Bear, William A.	5th	Virginia	H	Inf.	101	3	1	14-Mar-63	Typhoid Fever	Ferguson's Factory
Bearcroft, Thomas	40th	Virginia	F	Inf.	182	4	3	29-Oct-62	Dysentery	Reid's Factory
Beard, A. C.	2nd Battn.	Florida	E	Inf.	198	5	5	15-Oct-64	DOW	Camp Davis
Beckel, Samuel W.	33rd	North Carolina	C	Inf.	123	9	1	20-Dec-62	Diarrhea Chronic	Burton's Factory
Beckham, John	21st	Georgia	H	Inf.	171	6	3	17-Jun-62	---	Ferguson's Factory
Beckham, William J.	9th	Louisiana	F	Inf.	182	8	2	23-May-63	---	College Hospital
Bedsole, Isaiah	17th	Georgia	B	Inf.	100	4	2	24-Nov-62	---	Ford's Factory
Belcher, McHenry	45th	Virginia	A	Inf.	202	9	2	24-Mar-64	---	Crumpton's Factory
Bell, James	55th	North Carolina	A	Inf.	197	9	4	24-May-64	Dow 5/05/64	Christian's Factory
Bell, Jas.	Riley's Batty.	North Carolina	-	Art.	79	7	3	09-Jan-63	---	Christian's Factory

* See Part III - 59

NAME	REGT. or UNIT	STATE	COMPANY	BRANCH of SERVICE	LOT#	Grave No.	ROW	DATE of BURIAL or DEATH	CAUSE of DEATH	HOSPITAL
Bell, John A.	7th	Louisiana	H	Inf.	200	1	3	12-Oct-63	---	College Hospital
Beman, Stephen T.	2nd	North Carolina	I	Inf.	188	6	5	14-Jun-63	Anasarca	Reid's Factory
Bennett, James	12th	North Carolina	K	Inf.	162	10	5	27-Jul-62	Typhoid Fever	Knight's Factory
Bennett, Joseph J.	20th	North Carolina	G	Inf.	122	6	3	29-Oct-62	Pneumonia	Miller's Factory
Bennett, Julius Edward	18th	North Carolina	G	Inf.	198	10	4	05-Aug-64	Unknown	Wayside Hospital
Benson, J. B.	57th	North Carolina	K	Inf.	Yk. Sq.	28th	4th Line	07-Mar-63	Small Pox	Pest House
Benson, W. C.	2nd	Mississippi	E	Inf.	160	4	1	07-Aug-62	---	Ferguson's Factory
Berkley, J.	18th	Mississippi	F	Inf.	181	6	2	11-Nov-62	---	Langhorne's Factory
Berry, Thomas	8th	Louisiana	I	Inf.	193	10	2	14-May-64	DOW 5/05/64	Christian's Factory
Berry, William Jasper	9th	Louisiana	H	Inf.	169	6	4	28-May-62	---	Reid's Factory
Best, Thomas J.	7th	Louisiana	H	Inf.	170	3	4	13-Mar-62	---	Warwick House
Bevel, J. M.	16th	Mississippi	F	Inf.	167	4	3	14-May-62	---	Ferguson's Factory
Bevel, William D.	6th	Alabama	A	Inf.	172	8	4	16-Jun-62	---	Clayton's Factory
Bexley, Samuel	2nd	North Carolina	F	Inf.	122	6	4	12-Dec-62	Diarrhea	Candler's Factory
Bice, W.	12th	Alabama	B	Inf.	200	9	5	26-Nov-63	---	Camp Davis
Biddle, Benjamin B.	3rd	Virginia	G	Inf.	144	1	2	13-Nov-62	Pneumonia	Ford's Factory
Biggs, James P.	44th	Georgia	C	Inf.	199	6	3	02-Apr-63	---	Ferguson's Factory
Bird, A.	27th	Georgia	D	Inf.	146	3	2	10-Dec-62	---	Knight's Factory
Bird, Alfred	14th	North Carolina	K	Inf.	192	8	4	28-Jun-63	Febris Congestive	Taliaferro's Factory
Birdsong, Benjamin F.	4th	Georgia	C	Inf.	201	7	1	08-Jun-64	---	Ferguson's Factory
Birdsong, George W.	1st	North Carolina	K	Inf.	178	5	2	10-Nov-62	Dysentery	Miller's Factory
Birthaupt, J. T.	16th	Mississippi	F	Inf.	168	2	4	03-May-62	---	Ferguson's Factory
Bishop, Horton A.	52nd	North Carolina	F	Inf.	146	3	3	15-Aug-63	---	Saunder's Factory
Bishop, James M.	6th	Alabama	G	Inf.	146	2	5	09-Dec-62	DOW	Booker's Factory
Bizzell, Franklin M.	17th	Mississippi	I	Inf.	195	10	4	15-Feb-63	---	Crumpton's Factory
Black, Quincy L.	48th	Georgia	F	Inf.	179	9	2	12-Sep-62	---	College Hospital
Blackard, Granville	51st	Virginia	F	Inf.	191	6	3	17-Jul-63	Rheumatic Fever	Christian's Factory
Blackman, Hiram	4th	Alabama	C	Inf.	162	9	2	02-Aug-62	DOW (?)	Candler's Factory
Blackman, Joseph	12th	Alabama	Brown's	Inf.	159	9	1	06-Sep-61	---	Warwick House
Blackstock, James L.	14th	Virginia	H	Inf.	173	2	4	06-Jul-62	Typhoid	Taliaferro's Factory
Blair, Anthony L., 1st Sgt.	14th	Louisiana	F	Inf.	173	8	1	29-Jun-62	---	Saunder's Factory
Blake, David	14th	North Carolina	D	Inf.	192	6	5	05-Jul-63	Morbi Varii	Miller's Factory
Blake, John O.	44th	North Carolina	H	Inf.	200	1	1	15-Oct-63	Typhoid Fever	Booker's Factory
Blake, Zachariah I.	55th	Virginia	I	Inf.	161	3	4	05-Aug-62	Congestive Cerebri	Langhorne's Factory
Blalock, C. S.	15th	Alabama	G	Inf.	172	9	2	12-Jun-62	---	Langhorne's Factory
Blankenbeker, Jerome N., Sgt.	7th	Virginia	A	Inf.	160	9	1	07-Jul-62	Pneumonia	Burton's Factory
Blankenship, James T.	37th	North Carolina	E	Inf.	79	4	4	13-Jan-63	Febris Typhoides	Crumpton's Factory
Blankenship, King E.	41st	Virginia	D	Inf.	100	2	2	25-Nov-62	DOW 8/30/62	Ford's Factory
Blankenship, Thomas M.	57th	Virginia	C	Inf.	185	6	1	08-Mar-64	Pneumonia	Ferguson's Factory
Blanton, William A.	12th	North Carolina	E	Inf.	171	5	2	03-Jul-62	Typhoid Fever	Odd Fellow's Hall

* See Part III - 60

NAME	REGT. or UNIT	STATE	COMPANY	BRANCH of SERVICE	LOT#	Grave No.	ROW	DATE of BURIAL or DEATH	CAUSE of DEATH	HOSPITAL
Blaylock, W. C.	52nd	North Carolina	I	Inf.	188	7	2	03-Jun-63	Pneumonia	Clayton's Factory
Bissett, William S.	13th	Georgia	C	Inf.	162	7	1	06-Aug-62	---	Ladies Relief Hospt.
Blount, William J.	13th	Mississippi	Fletcher's	Inf.	158	7	3	05-Aug-61	---	College Hospital
Blythe, Calvin	23rd	Georgia	F	Inf.	172	3	5	29-Jun-62	Typhoid Fever	Christian's Factory
Boland, Jessey	61st	Alabama	H	Inf.	186	4	1	23-Jun-64	---	Ladies Relief Hospt.
Bondurant, William B.	58th	Virginia	B	Inf.	Yk. Sq.	24th	1st Line	27-Jan-63	Small Pox	Pest House
Bone, Joseph H.	30th	North Carolina	I	Inf.	79	4	2	10-Jan-63	Epilepsy	Candler's Factory
Booker, James	8th	Louisiana	H	Inf.	166	10	3	05-May-62	---	Warwick House
Booker, S. M.	48th	Alabama	A	Inf.	181	3	2	22-Oct-62	---	Christian's Factory
Boone, Godfrey	13th	South Carolina	H	Inf.	181	7	3	24-Oct-62	Pneumonia	Crumpton's Factory
Borders, Burrill	7th	Georgia	F	Inf.	187	9	5	20-Jan-63	---	College Hospital
Borders, Michale B.	7th	Georgia	F	Inf.	177	10	3	19-Aug-62	---	Warwick House
Borin, William (or Borens)	17th	Georgia	F	Inf.	169	1	3	19-May-62	---	Ferguson's Factory
Boston, Uriah	2nd	North Carolina	H	Inf.	190	4	1	02-Jul-64	Typhoid & Pneumonia	Ferguson's Factory
Bottoms, Aaron L.	53rd	Georgia	C	Inf.	191	3	4	14-Feb-63	Disease	College Hospital
Bowden, John	6th	North Carolina	D	Inf.	194	9	5	12-Aug-64	Disease	Ferguson's Factory
Bowen, B. F.	61st	Georgia	D	Inf.	182	5	1	30-Oct-62	---	Miller's Factory
Bowen, George A.	41st	Virginia	H	Inf.	190	4	5	04-Jul-64	Disease	Christian's Factory
Bowman, Vince P.	48th	Alabama	D	Inf.	177	1	1	19-Aug-62	---	Saunder's Factory
Bowman, William J.	7th	Georgia	C	Inf.	161	9	3	14-Jul-62	---	Warwick House
Boyd, Andrew	7th	South Carolina	D	Inf.	197	3	1	31-May-64	DOW 5/06/64	College Hospital
Bozeman, James S.	8th	South Carolina	F	Inf.	170	5	5	08-Apr-62	Pneumonia	College Hospital
Bradford, Hampton	8th	Florida	G	Inf.	101	10	4	26-Dec-62	Disease	Christian's Factory
Bradley, Edward	2nd	Tennessee	E	Inf.	170	8	3	06-Mar-62	---	@ Horse's Ford
Bradley, James O.	40th	Virginia	G	Inf.	192	3	2	13-Jul-63	Pneumonia	Booker's Factory
Bradshaw, Eaphrum	15th	Alabama	C	Inf.	Yk. Sq.	21st	3rd Line	04-Jan-63	Small Pox	Pest House
Bradshaw, James	18th	North Carolina	C	Inf.	195	9	4	18-Feb-63	Pneumonia	Burton's Factory
Bradshaw, N. Sloan	3rd	North Carolina	G	Inf.	78	2	1	03-Dec-62	Gangrene	Langhorne's Factory
Brady, Augustus	51st	Georgia	A	Inf.	194	10	5	09-Jul-64	---	Christian's Factory
Brady, Francis M.	28th	Georgia	B	Inf.	181	10	2	13-Oct-62	---	Crumpton's Factory
Bragg, John W.	15th	North Carolina	E	Inf.	123	6	4	24-Dec-62	Febris Typhoides	Saunder's Factory
Branch, Anderson	6th	North Carolina	E	Inf.	194	8	1	13-Jul-64	Disease	Camp Davis
Brandon, Solmon	48th	North Carolina	K	Inf.	190	7	2	29-Jun-64	DOW	Knight's Factory
Brannan, George W.	Phillip's Legion	Georgia	C	Inf.	78	6	2	07-Dec-62	---	Ladies Relief Hospt.
Brannan, James R.	12th	Georgia	F	Inf.	194	4	2	23-Jul-64	---	Booker's Factory
Brannan, John H. (or Branren	61st	Georgia	I	Inf.	79	8	4	07-Jan-63	---	Booker's Factory
Brannon, William C.	13th	South Carolina	F	Inf.	177	6	1	22-Aug-62	---	Ford's Factory
Brantley, Nathan	7th	North Carolina	C	Inf.	Yk. Sq.	21st	2nd Line	14-Jan-63	Small Pox	Pest House
Brantley, Robert R.	60th	Georgia	B	Inf.	161	3	3	06-Aug-62	---	Christian's Factory
Braswell, James C.	15th	Alabama	C	Inf.	169	7	4	24-May-62	Typhoid Fever	Christian's Factory

* See Part III - 61

NAME	REGT. or UNIT	STATE	COMPANY	BRANCH of SERVICE	LOT#	Grave No.	ROW	DATE of BURIAL or DEATH	CAUSE of DEATH	HOSPITAL
Breedlove, Henry	14th	Georgia	A	Inf.	200	4	2	21-Nov-63	---	College Hospital
Brewer, James W.	2nd	North Carolina	I	Cav.	101	3	5	28-Dec-62	Fever	Ferguson's Factory
Bright, John W.	26th	North Carolina	E	Inf.	188	8	2	01-Jun-63	Pneumonia	Claytor's Factory
Briley, M. E.	15th	Alabama	-	Inf.	169	7	3	28-May-62	---	Christian's Factory
Brinkley, David	33rd	North Carolina	E	Inf.	187	2	5	21-Jan-63	Febris Typhoides	Burton's Factory
* Brinsfield, Francis L.	54th	North Carolina	F	Inf.	188	4	5	05-Jul-63	Phthisis Pulmonaris	Ferguson's Factory
Britton, E.	2nd	Louisiana	D	Inf.	187	10	2	12-Feb-63	---	Claytor's Factory
Britton, W. H.	9th	Louisiana	C	Inf.	167	10	2	13-May-62	---	Saunder's Factory
Britton, William E.	1st	Tennessee	Bennett's	Inf.	158	5	1	27-May-61	---	College Hospital
* Brock, Emory M.	24th	Georgia	H	Inf.	193	10	1	11-Apr-64	Measles	Christian's Factory
Broker, Ira	33rd	North Carolina	C	Inf.	182	7	1	11-Nov-62	---	Christian's Factory
Brooks, Geroge W.	Lee's Battery	Virginia	-	Art.	170	7	1	07-Dec-61	---	Sandy Hook
Brooks, J.	61st	Alabama	F	Inf.	193	5	1	16-Dec-64	---	Camp Davis
Brooks, M. P. C., 1st Sgt.	2nd	Florida	L	Inf.	188	1	3	12-Jun-63	Fever	College Hospital
Brown, C. B. (or E. B.)	6th	North Carolina	D	Inf.	180	5	3	11-Nov-62	Unkown	Candler's Factory
Brown, H.	19th	Georgia	C	Inf.	122	6	1	19-Dec-62	---	Burton's Factory
Brown, J. A.	7th	Louisiana	B	Inf.	171	1	2	02-Jun-62	---	Ferguson's Factory
Brown, J. E.	7th	South Carolina	A	Inf.	196	5	5	06-Sep-63	Dysentery	Burton's Factory
Brown, J. H.	38th	Georgia	H	Inf.	180	2	5	25-Sep-62	---	Langhorne's Factory
Brown, Jacob J.	57th	North Carolina	G	Inf.	195	10	3	17-Feb-63	---	Langhorne's Factory
* Brown, Lewis T.	35th	North Carolina	A	Inf.	191	8	1	01-Feb-63	Typhoid Fever	Burton's Factory
Brown, Patrick	Madison Light Art.	Louisiana	-	Art.	161	10	2	10-Jul-62	---	Langhorne's Factory
* Brown, Tandy A.	9th	Louisiana	C	Inf.	169	9	2	22-May-52	---	Crumpton's Factory
Brown, William	42nd	North Carolina	D	Inf.	177	6	4	28-Aug-62	Pneumonia Typhoides	College Hospital
Brown, William N. (or Wm. L.)	7th	Georgia	D	Inf.	191	1	3	25-Feb-64	Accident	Camp Davis
Browning, Joshua	61st	Georgia	C	Inf.	160	7	3	09-Jul-62	Acute Laryngitis	Langhorne's Factory
* Browning, R. A.	23rd	South Carolina	B	Inf.	178	6	2	09-Sep-62	Typhoid Fever	Langhorne's Factory
Bruce, J. H.	2nd	South Carolina	Hale's	Inf.	159	6	1	03-Sep-61	---	Warwick House
Bruce, John W.	1st Orr's Rifles	South Carolina	L	Inf.	187	9	1	22-Jan-63	---	Saunder's Factory
* Bryan, Jas. C.	23rd	North Carolina	G	Inf.	Yk. Sq.	25th	1st Line	03-Feb-63	Small Pox	Pest House
Bryan, Joseph (Josephus?)	10th Battn.	Georgia	A	Inf.	189	2	1	06-May-64	---	Burton's Factory
Bryan, Richard	5th	North Carolina	C	Inf.	78	3	3	19-Dec-62	Diarrhea Chronic	College Hospital
* Bryant, Mills H.	41st	Virginia	H	Inf.	122	7	3	23-Nov-62	Typhoid & Pneumonia	Crumpton's Factory
Bryant, Wyatt	49th	Virginia	F	Inf.	190	7	5	30-Jun-64	DOW	Christian's Factory
Buchanan, C. B.	30th	North Carolina	H	Inf.	192	3	1	11-Aug-63	Febris	Claytor's Factory
Buchanan, Joseph	30th	North Carolina	H	Inf.	198	5	4	15-Oct-64	Diarrhea	Reid's Factory
Buckalew, W. M.	13th	Georgia	A	Inf.	197	8	3	24-May-64	DOW 5/05/64	Crumpton's Factory
* Buchanan, Robert Edward, Corpl.	17th	Virginia	H	Inf.	Yk. Sq.	-	-	23-Mar-64	Small Pox	Pest House
* Buckles, Henry	15th	South Carolina	G	Inf.	144	9	3	18-Nov-62	Pneumonia	Ford's Factory
* Buckles, John	8th	Florida	I	Inf.	198	7	2	20-Aug-64	Disease	Langhorne's Factory

* See Part III - 62

NAME	REGT. or UNIT	STATE	COMPANY	BRANCH of SERVICE	LOT#	Grave No.	ROW	DATE of BURIAL or DEATH	CAUSE of DEATH	HOSPITAL
Bugheart, E.	13th	Mississippi	B	Inf.	184	9	3	24-Apr-63	---	Camp Davis
Bulfiant, John H.	53rd	Virginia	K	Inf.	122	9	1	19-Nov-62	---	Claytor's Factory
Bumgarner, Tobias	37th	North Carolina	G	Inf.	162	1	5	03-Aug-62	Febris Typhoides	Saunder's Factory
Buncomb, P. M.	15th	Alabama	G	Inf.	166	9	3	05-May-62	---	Warwick House
Burdell, Hiram W.	14th	South Carolina	I	Inf.	194	6	3	18-Jul-64	---	Ferguson's Factory
Burkhalter, C.	20th	Mississippi	Russell's	Inf.	159	2	4	26-Sep-61	---	Ladies Relief Hospt.
Burks, Roland	5th	Texas	B	Inf.	180	7	1	02-Oct-62	Disease	Ladies Relief Hospt.
Burks, S. W.	20th	Mississippi	Graham's	Inf.	159	7	2	13-Sep-61	---	Ladies Relief Hospt.
Burks, T. T.	9th	Georgia	B	Inf.	Yk. Sq.	1st	1st Line	09-Apr-63	Small Pox	Pest House
Burningham, Benjamin	47th	Alabama	A	Inf.	Yk. Sq.	20th	4th Line	02-Jan-63	Small Pox	Pest House
Burnett, J. W.	Freeman's Batty.	Unknown	-	Art.	186	3	1	25-Jun-64	---	Knight's Factory
Burnett, Richard	44th	North Carolina	K	Inf.	196	4	1	28-Sep-63	Phthisis Pulmonaris	Candler's Factory
Burns, Henry	11th	South Carolina	H	Inf.	193	9	2	14-May-64	---	Christian's Factory
Burr, William C.	6th	South Carolina	D	Cav.	190	7	3	30-Jun-64	---	Langhorne's Factory
Burrage, C. W., Capt.	19th	Mississippi	A	Inf.	197	6	3	28-May-64	---	Reid's Factory
Burress, B. M.	8th	Tennessee	Burford's	Inf.	158	3	4	19-Aug-61	---	College Hospital
Burroughs, James G.	42nd	Virginia	C	Inf.	78	3	2	15-Jan-63	Phthisis	Christian's Factory
Burton, William John	30th	Virginia	I	Inf.	196	3	5	01-Oct-63	Murdered	Wayside Hospital
Bush, W. S.	31st	Georgia	K	Inf.	165	5	2	21-Aug-62	---	Ford's Factory
Busick, J. A.	13th	Virginia	C	Inf.	202	9	5	20-Mar-65	Dysentery	Knight's Factory
Bussey, Dempsey J.	8th	Georgia	A	Inf.	78	9	1	02-Dec-62	---	Christian's Factory
Butler, A. W. D.	45th	Georgia	C	Inf.	188	3	1	27-Jun-63	---	Langhorne's Factory
Butler, James L.	18th	North Carolina	B	Inf.	171	6	5	07-Jun-62	Typhoid Fever	Ford's Factory
Butler, James R.	30th	North Carolina	A	Inf.	Yk. Sq.	25th	2nd Line	03-Feb-63	Small Pox	Pest House
Butler, Richmond	44th	Alabama	D	Inf.	188	2	1	05-Jun-63	---	Claytor's Factory
Butler, Thomas B.	6th	Alabama	A	Inf.	179	8	1	20-Sep-62	---	Christian's Factory
Butler, William	46th	North Carolina	I	Inf.	123	2	4	18-Dec-62	Typhoid & Pneumonia	Reid's Factory
Butler, William H.	1st	Louisiana	C	Inf.	184	10	2	19-Apr-63	---	College Hospital
Buts, T. J.	61st	Alabama	D	Inf.	193	9	5	31-Jan-65	---	Langhorne's Factory
Button, J. J.	16th	Mississippi	K	Inf.	167	5	2	17-May-52	---	Reid's Factory
Buzzard, Presley	14th	South Carolina	B	Inf.	171	4	5	07-Jun-62	Febris Typhoides	Odd Fellow's Hall
Byard, E. H.	3rd	Alabama	E	Inf.	198	1	3	21-Nov-64	---	Christian's Factory
Byas, J. M.	5th	Alabama	C	Inf.	123	5	5	23-Dec-62	---	Ferguson's Factory
Byne, D. O.	Phillip's Legion	Georgia	F	Inf.	178	7	5	05-Sep-62	---	Claytor's Factory
Byrd, G. W.	32nd	North Carolina	I	Inf.	192	4	5	19-Jul-63	Bronchitis Acuta	Camp Davis
Bywaters, James Edward	6th	Virginia	B	Cav.	161	7	4	07-Aug-62	Typhoid Fever	Reid's Factory
Cabbage, W. T.	11th	Virginia	I	Inf.	160	3	2	08-Jul-62	---	Odd Fellow's Hall
Caldwell, Henry Lee	11th	Georgia	A	Inf.	188	9	5	05-Jun-63	---	Miller's Factory
Caldwell, J. B.	Graham's Batty.	North Carolina	-	Art.	Yk. Sq.	-	-	02-Mar-64	Small Pox	Pest House

* See Part III - 63

NAME	REGT. or UNIT	STATE	COMPANY	BRANCH of SERVICE	LOT#	Grave No.	ROW	DATE of BURIAL or DEATH	CAUSE of DEATH	HOSPITAL
Caidwell, John D.	1st	North Carolina	C	Art.	189	3	1	06-May-64	---	Burton's Factory
Calhoun, A.	13th	Alabama	B	Inf.	172	3	2	30-Jun-62	Phthisis	Langhorne's Factory
Calhoun, Guilford	22nd	Georgia	D	Inf.	146	6	4	14-Dec-62	---	Crumpton's Factory
Call, D. H.	31st	North Carolina	I	Inf.	194	3	3	28-Jul-64	---	Christian's Factory
Callahan, John T.	35th	Georgia	I	Inf.	178	2	5	29-Aug-62	---	Christian's Factory
Callaway, Alfred S.	28th	North Carolina	D	Inf.	199	6	4	07-Apr-63	Disease	Burton's Factory
Callis, J. W.	38th	Virginia	I	Inf.	Yk. Sq.	21st	4th Line	02-Jan-63	Small Pox	Pest House
Campbell, Atwell E.	30th	Virginia	G	Inf.	192	5	4	11-Jul-63	Dysentery Acute	Reid's Factory
Campbell, Colin J.	6th	Alabama	L	Inf.	195	5	4	06-Mar-63	---	Claytor's Factory
Campbell, E. W.	14th	Georgia	E	Inf.	201	3	4	17-Jun-64	DOW ?	Langhorne's Factory
Campbell, G. W. (James Walker)	11th	Virginia	I	Inf.	169	5	1	28-May-62	---	Langhorne's Factory
Campbell, H.	12th	South Carolina	D	Inf.	195	5	1	27-Feb-63	Pneumonia	Ferguson's Factory
Campbell, H. H.	26th	North Carolina	A	Inf.	197	2	3	05-Jun-64	Gunshot Wound	Christian's Factory
Campbell, James	3rd	South Carolina	F	Inf.	195	3	5	23-Feb-63	---	Langhorne's Factory
Campbell, James P.	23rd	North Carolina	C	Inf.	162	5	1	04-Aug-62	Diarrhea	Miller's Factory
Campbell, John	44th	Alabama	G	Cav.	199	1	5	09-Mar-63	---	Crumpton's Factory
Campbell, John M.	1st	South Carolina	A	Cav.	199	9	5	10-Apr-63	---	Camp Davis
Campbell, John W.	2nd	South Carolina	F	Inf.	195	2	3	17-Feb-63	DOW	Christian's Factory
Campbell, W. M.	13th	Georgia	D	Inf.	194	10	1	08-Jul-64	Disease	Camp Davis
Camps, A. J.	35th	Georgia	A	Inf.	188	1	2	11-Jun-63	---	College Hospital
Candleary, Peter	5th	Florida	I	Inf.	182	5	3	15-Nov-62	Pneumonia	Christian's Factory
Cannaday, John	6th	South Carolina	D	Inf.	169	6	5	25-May-62	Dow 7/21/61 & Typhoid	Crumpton's Factory
Canterbury, J. W., 2nd Lieut.	8th	Alabama	B	Inf.	101	10	3	28-Dec-62	Diarrhea Chronic	Burton's Factory
Canup, H. T.	5th	North Carolina	H	Inf.	187	1	1	26-Jan-63	---	Crumpton's Factory
Cape, William	2nd	South Carolina	C	Inf.	123	1	4	15-Dec-62	DOW 5/05/64	Ferguson's Factory
Cardwell, Parker	22nd	North Carolina	K	Inf.	194	9	2	12-Jul-64	Disease	Knight's Factory
Carlton, Alexander	7th	Georgia	A	Inf.	159	3	5	08-Oct-61	---	College Hospital
Carlton, Henry C.	38th	Georgia	H	Inf.	123	8	1	21-Dec-62	---	Langhorne's Factory
Carlton, John W.	7th	Georgia	A	Inf.	170	3	1	15-Nov-61	---	College Hospital
Carmical, Robert Y., 4th Corpl.	53rd	Georgia	D	Inf.	192	1	5	03-Jul-63	---	Christian's Factory
Carney, James	2nd	Tennessee	H	Inf.	170	6	3	27-Feb-62	Murdered 2/26/62	@ Horse's Ford
Carnley, C.	4th	Alabama	A	Inf.	Yk. Sq.	---	---	26-Jul-64	Small Pox	Pest House
Carothers, J. (James?) R.	18th	South Carolina	H	Inf.	100	6	3	03-Dec-62	---	Ferguson's Factory
Carpenter, Robert W.	28th	North Carolina	D	Inf.	193	7	1	18-May-64	Diarrhea	College Hospital
Carpenter, W. Benjamin	26th	Virginia	I	Cav.	202	8	2	12-Apr-65	---	Knight's Factory
Carr, H.	12th	Alabama	D	Inf.	200	6	4	22-Dec-63	---	Camp Davis
Carrin, M.	19th	Mississippi	C	Inf.	184	4	3	19-May-63	---	Miller's Factory
Carroll, James	1st	South Carolina	G	Inf.	187	10	4	21-Jan-63	---	Saunder's Factory
Carson, F. S., 4th Sgt.	5th	South Carolina	G	Inf.	123	5	2	21-Dec-62	Febris Typhoides	Crumpton's Factory
Carson, John H.	1st	North Carolina	K	Cav.	170	2	5	17-Mar-62	---	Warwick House

* See Part III - 64

NAME	REGT. or UNIT	STATE	COMPANY	BRANCH of SERVICE	LOT#	Grave No.	ROW	DATE of BURIAL or DEATH	CAUSE of DEATH	HOSPITAL
Carson, R. B.	9th	Louisiana	A	Inf.	168	7	5	08-May-62	---	Ferguson's Factory
Carson, William	37th	Virginia	C	Inf.	Yk. Sq.	---	---	12-Feb-64	Small Pox	Pest House
* Carter, Asbury B.	15th	South Carolina	G	Inf.	188	7	4	10-Jun-63	Febris Typhoides	College Hospital
Carter, George	42nd	Virginia	A	Inf.	182	10	5	09-Nov-62	Dysentery Acute	College Hospital
Carter, H. C.	16th	Mississippi	E	Inf.	202	5	2	14-Feb-62	---	Ladies Relief Hospt.
Carter, James L.	58th	Virginia	H	Inf.	Yk. Sq.	27th	3rd Line	15-Feb-63	Small Pox	Pest House
Carter, James Knox Polk	59th	Tennessee	B	Cav.	197	1	4	03-Jun-64	---	Blackwater Creek Camp
Carter, John	61st	Georgia	D	Inf.	172	5	2	18-Jun-62	---	Ferguson's Factory
Carter, John M.	26th	Georgia	B	Inf.	181	10	1	12-Oct-62	---	Langhorne's Factory
Carter, John O.	7th	North Carolina	C	Inf.	Yk. Sq.	14th	5th Line	15-Dec-62	Small Pox	Pest House
* Carter, Joseph M. M., 3rd Sgt.	4th	Georgia	F	Inf.	185	8	1	18-Dec-62	DOW 9/17/62	Ferguson's Factory
Carter, Reuben	61st	Georgia	D	inf.	172	6	4	14-Jun-62	---	Ferguson's Factory
* Cartwright, James G. W., Sgt.	4th	Texas	H	Inf.	197	3	3	06-Jun-64	DOW's	Christian's Factory
Caskie, John D.	1st (Hagood's)	South Carolina	D	Inf.	190	3	2	05-Jul-64	DOW 5/06/64	Christian's Factory
Cassells, C. T.	18th	Mississippi	I	Inf.	172	10	4	09-Jun-62	---	Crumpton's Factory
Cassidy, Thomas	47th	Alabama	A	Inf.	165	1	1	10-Aug-62	---	Ladies Relief Hospt.
Caston, A. H.	1st	South Carolina	I	Inf.	195	9	1	19-Feb-63	---	Ferguson's Factory
Cates, Thomas J.	33rd	North Carolina	F	Inf.	193	9	1	13-May-64	DOW 5/06/64	Burton's Factory
* Caughron, William N., 2nd Sgt.	60th	Georgia	I	Inf.	162	8	2	06-Aug-62	---	Warwick House
Causey, W. W. (Crusey)	47th	Georgia	I	Inf.	177	10	4	14-Aug-62	---	Booker's Factory
Cavanaugh, John R.	6th	Louisiana	B	Inf.	173	5	2	03-Jul-62	---	Ferguson's Factory
Cave, J.	1st	Tennessee	D	Inf.	123	3	3	20-Dec-62	---	Ladies Relief Hospt.
* Caver, James Henry (or Carver)	15th	Georgia	G	Inf.	197	4	3	31-May-64	DOW 5/10/64	Pest House
Caviness, Frederick	29th	Virginia	A	Inf.	Yk. Sq.	3rd	4th Line	29-May-63	Small Pox	Ferguson's Factory
Cay, William	5th	Florida	K	Inf.	122	8	1	21-Nov-62	---	Ferguson's Factory
* Celan, Z. H.	15th	North Carolina	C	Inf.	123	2	2	18-Dec-62	---	Christian's Factory
Chaffin, John Robert	8th	Louisiana	H	Inf.	172	4	1	23-Jun-62	Typhoid & Pneumonia	College Hospital
Chamberlain, Ewel, Sgt.	3rd	Arkansas	F	Inf.	201	2	5	17-Jun-64	DOW 5/06/64	Crumpton's Factory
Chambers, C. H.	2nd	Mississippi	K	Inf.	165	5	1	11-Sep-62	---	Langhorne's Factory
Chambers, Josephus C.	51st	Georgia	F	Inf.	122	4	2	21-Nov-62	---	Candler's Factory
Chammey, William	Unknown	Unknown	-	-	Yk. Sq.	16th	5th Line	20-Dec-62	Small Pox	Pest House
Champion, G. W.	2nd	Mississippi	C	Inf.	186	2	2	26-Jun-64	---	Knight's Factory
Chance, V. M.	1st	Texas	I	Inf.	180	10	1	25-Sep-62	---	Ferguson's Factory
Chandler, A. J.	24th	Georgia	A	Inf.	172	2	1	14-Jul-62	---	Claytor's Factory
* Chandler, Benjamin, Jr.	5th Battn.	Alabama	C	Inf.	189	2	2	05-May-64	Disease	Ferguson's Factory
* Chapman, B. F. (Benj. Franklin?)	3rd	South Carolina	H	Inf.	190	9	2	27-Jun-64	DOW 6/25/64	Christian's Factory
Chapman, William	13th	South Carolina	G	Inf.	183	6	1	14-Jan-63	Diarrhea Chronic	Langhorne's Factory
Charlton, Joseph	12th	Virginia	H	Inf.	Yk. Sq.	13th	2nd Line	30-Nov-62	Small Pox	Pest House
* Chastain, James E.	2nd	South Carolina	E	Inf.	199	2	5	29-Mar-63	Pneumonia	Saunder's Factory
* Chastain, Larkin D. V.	3rd	Arkansas	Newman's	Inf.	159	1	3	07-Sep-61	---	Mr. Creed Wills

* See Part III - 65

NAME	REGT. or UNIT	STATE	COMPANY	BRANCH of SERVICE	LOT#	Grave No.	ROW	DATE of BURIAL or DEATH	CAUSE of DEATH	HOSPITAL
Chatman, Alfred (?) S.	61st	Alabama	H	Inf.	190	1	5	06-Jul-64	---	Camp Davis
Cheney, T. B.	8th	Louisiana	H	Inf.	169	6	1	27-May-62	---	Warwick House
Childers, William	1st	Arkansas	Crawford's	Inf.	158	8	1	20-Jun-61	---	College Hospital
Childress, A. S. (or Childers)	60th	Georgia	I	Inf.	161	8	1	15-Jul-62	---	Ferguson's Factory
Childress, J. L.	17th	Mississippi	E	Inf.	144	10	3	18-Nov-62	---	Crumpton's Factory
Childress, James S.	7th	Georgia	B	Inf.	169	4	2	28-May-62	---	Booker's Factory
Childress, Thomas B.	1st	Kentucky	K	Inf.	170	10	5	27-Feb-62	---	Ladies Relief Hospt.
Chitty, Lafayette	33rd	North Carolina	C	Inf.	192	7	2	30-Jun-63	DOW 5/02/63	Miller's Factory
Chivers, E.	31st	Georgia	C	Inf.	188	9	3	03-Jun-63	---	Christian's Factory
Christian, William R.	38th	Georgia	H	Inf.	100	3	1	26-Nov-62	Diarrhea	Ladies Relief Hospt.
Church, Jackson	42nd	North Carolina	K	Inf.	178	8	4	31-Aug-62	Phthisis Pulmonaris	Ladies Relief Hospt.
Cissna, Theophilus M.	8th	Louisiana	E	Inf.	173	6	4	03-Jul-62	---	Ferguson's Factory
Clanders, W.	55th	Alabama	F	Inf.	190	10	5	27-Jun-64	---	Christian's Factory
Clark, Allen	23rd	Georgia	D	Inf.	169	9	3	27-May-62	Pneumonia	Christian's Factory
Clark, Franklin	33rd	North Carolina	E	Inf.	179	10	3	12-Dec-62	---	Claytor's Factory
Clark, James J.	1st	Texas	H	Inf.	173	3	2	18-Aug-62	Diarrhea Chronic	Claytor's Factory
Clark, John C.	9th	Louisiana	B	Inf.	161	6	1	18-Jul-62	---	Warwick House
Clark, Meredith A.	33rd	Virginia	D	Inf.	166	9	2	03-May-62	Pneumonia	Christian's Factory
Clark, Thomas	42nd	Virginia	G	Inf.	196	5	4	08-Sep-63	---	Camp Davis
Clark, W. H.	18th	North Carolina	C	Inf.	178	9	3	04-Dec-62	Diarrhea	Claytor's Factory
Clarke, Averitt Quincy	9th	Virginia	F	Inf.	123	3	1	18-Dec-62	Typhoid & Pneumonia	Crumpton's Factory
Clarke, George W.	21st	Georgia	I	Inf.	166	2	1	02-May-62	Pneumonia	Ferguson's Factory
Cleland, Robert C.	14th	Alabama	A	Inf.	162	1	2	22-Jul-62	---	College Hospital
Clemmons, John	15th	Alabama	K	Inf.	188	8	1	31-May-63	---	Knight's Factory
Clemons, J. R.	18th	Mississippi	G	Inf.	144	4	3	17-Nov-62	---	Ferguson's Factory
Cleveland, Jackson S., 1st Corpl.	44th	Alabama	F	Inf.	201	7	3	09-Jun-64	DOW	Camp Davis
Cline, A. C.	24th	Georgia	E	Inf.	162	2	4	27-Jul-62	---	Claytor's Factory
Cline, Elijah L.	37th	North Carolina	F	Inf.	122	4	1	24-Nov-62	---	Saunder's Factory
Clodfitter, J.	57th	North Carolina	B	Inf.	146	10	2	06-Dec-62	---	Christian's Factory
Clopton, W. Calvin	19th	Georgia	H	Inf.	159	8	5	08-Oct-61	---	College Hospital
Coates, William P.	13th	Georgia	A	Inf.	201	3	5	16-Jun-64	Disease	College Hospital
Coats, James	37th	Virginia	D	Inf.	197	5	1	30-May-64	DOW	Candler's Factory
Cobb, Andrew J.	13th	North Carolina	I	Inf.	190	8	3	27-Jun-64	DOW 5/21/64	Ladies Relief Hospt.
Cobb, Green B., Corpl.	2nd	Mississippi	H	Inf.	197	10	3	24-May-64	---	Christian's Factory
Cobb, Jesse	28th	North Carolina	H	Inf.	169	1	1	20-May-62	Pneumonia	Reid's Factory
Cobb, W. P.	2nd	South Carolina	I	Inf.	100	10	3	26-Nov-62	DOD	Crumpton's Factory
Cockerham, William A.	55th	North Carolina	B	Inf.	200	10	4	27-Nov-63	Febris	Reid's Factory
Cockrell, John Walter	40th	Virginia	F	Inf.	191	4	1	08-Feb-63	Fever	College Hospital
Cofield, David L.	35th	Georgia	F	Inf.	180	10	3	24-Sep-62	Small Pox (poss.)	Reid's Factory
Cofield, L. Francis	59th	Georgia	B	Inf.	189	4	2	10-May-64	DOW 5/06/64	Claytor's Factory

* See Part III - 66

NAME	REGT. or UNIT	STATE	COMPANY	BRANCH of SERVICE	LOT #	Grave No.	ROW	DATE of BURIAL or DEATH	CAUSE of DEATH	HOSPITAL
* Cogdell, Lewis D.	2nd	North Carolina	C	Inf.	101	8	1	01-Feb-63	Diarrhea	Claytor's Factory
* Cogdell, William W.	20th	North Carolina	I	Inf.	Yk. Sq.	18th	5th Line	20-Dec-62	Small Pox	Pest House
Coggin, James D.	16th	Virginia	D	Inf.	185	1	3	20-Apr-64	Necrosis	Christian's Factory
* Colburn, John W.	8th	Alabama	A	Inf.	161	7	2	16-Jul-62	---	Christian's Factory
Cole, D. F.	1st	Mississippi	F	Inf.	193	5	3	20-May-64	---	Knight's Factory
* Cole, J. J.	15th	Alabama	L	Inf.	166	7	3	16-May-62	Disease	Saunder's Factory
* Cole, S. E.	33rd	North Carolina	K	Inf.	187	4	2	26-Jan-63	DOW 12/13/62	Burton's Factory
Cole, Thomas M.	26th	North Carolina	H	Inf.	193	8	1	16-May-64	Rebeola	Camp Davis
* Coleman, Jackson J. (James Jacks	9th	Louisiana	H	Inf.	162	3	4	28-Jul-62	Typhoid	Christian's Factory
Coleman, James W., Sgt.	6th	Louisiana	D	Inf.	166	3	2	09-May-62	---	Christian's Factory
Coleman, W. F.	3rd	Alabama	E	Inf.	196	6	4	31-Aug-63	DOW	Langhorne's Factory
Coleman, William	32nd	Virginia	K	Inf.	Yk. Sq.	25th	3rd Line	04-Feb-63	Small Pox	Pest House
Collier, N. B.	3rd	Arkansas	C	Inf.	Yk. Sq.	23rd	5th Line	13-Jan-63	Small Pox	Pest House
Collins, James W.	1st	North Carolina	G	Inf.	185	7	1	24-Feb-64	DOW 11/27/63	Booker's Factory
Colwell, Glenn O.	53rd	Georgia	A	Inf.	189	3	2	04-May-64	Pneumonia	Christian's Factory
Compton, William H.	7th	Virginia	B	Inf.	168	2	2	26-Apr-62	---	Warwick House
Conkle, George Washington	44th	Georgia	D	Inf.	162	9	4	29-Jul-62	Measles	Reid's Factory
Conner, A.	Chew's Battn.	Virginia	Brother's	Art.	193	4	5	20-May-64	---	Camp Davis
Conner, J. Frank	19th	Georgia	K	Inf.	180	4	1	26-Sep-62	---	Ferguson's Factory
Conner, J. Frank	61st	Georgia	K	Inf.	180	3	1	22-Sep-62	---	Ferguson's Factory
Conner, John	7th	Louisiana	Shoat's	Inf.	170	1	2	19-Dec-61	---	College Hospital
Conroy, Thomas	Latham's Battery	Virginia	---	Art.	101	2	3	27-Dec-62	---	Caudler's Factory
* Convill, Daniel O.	44th	Alabama	H	Inf.	201	2	4	19-Jun-64	DOW	Christian's Factory
Cook, F.	32nd Battn.	Virginia	B	Cav.	188	6	4	14-Jun-63	---	Crumpton's Factory
Cook, G. W.	11th	Georgia	---	Inf.	170	5	2	05-Jan-62	---	College Hospital
Cook, James	38th	North Carolina	C	Inf.	192	5	1	06-Jul-63	Meningitis	Camp Davis
Cook, Jeremiah	4th	Georgia	B	Inf.	79	2	1	15-Jan-63	---	Ferguson's Factory
Cook, John	8th	South Carolina	L	Inf.	197	6	4	27-May-64	Gunshot Wound	Booker's Factory
Cook, William	8th	Louisiana	E	Inf.	168	1	4	03-May-62	---	Ferguson's Factory
Cooley, A. C.	1st	Virginia	C	Inf.	146	10	5	10-Dec-62	---	Ferguson's Factory
Cooper, John	48th	Georgia	H	Inf.	199	7	1	23-Mar-63	---	Claytor's Factory
Cooper, Ruben	38th	Georgia	I	Inf.	162	3	5	23-Jul-62	Chronic Diarrhoea	Ladies Relief Hospt.
Copeland, H.	21st	Georgia	D	Inf.	184	2	3	26-May-63	---	Miller's Factory
* Corbett, Jeremiah	14th	North Carolina	K	Inf.	200	2	3	27-Oct-63	Rheaul Extreme	College Hospital
* Corbett, Richard William	61st	Virginia	E	Inf.	196	4	3	05-Nov-63	Diarrhea	Crumpton's Factory
Corbin, James	48th	Alabama	D	Inf.	182	5	3	31-Oct-62	---	Christian's Factory
* Cordell, Preston J.	34th	Georgia	C	Inf.	123	9	2	22-Dec-62	---	College Hospital
* Cornett, James C., Sgt.	4th	Virginia	F	Inf.	190	10	4	26-Jun-64	---	Christian's Factory
Corprew, John J. (also Corfreau	6th	Virginia	F	Inf.	144	8	1	15-Nov-62	Pneumonia	Christian's Factory
Correy, M.	6th	Alabama	M	Inf.	184	4	1	28-Apr-63	---	College Hospital

* See Part III - 67

NAME	REGT. or UNIT	STATE	COMPANY	BRANCH of SERVICE	LOT#	Grave No.	ROW	DATE of BURIAL or DEATH	CAUSE of DEATH	HOSPITAL
Cossimini, Jasinto	Alexander's Batty.	Virginia	-	Art.	188	6	1	15-Sep-63	---	College Hospital
Cothron, S. P.	3rd	Alabama	Conscript	Inf.	146	8	2	17-Dec-62	---	Ferguson's Factory
Cotton, Authur L.	18th	Georgia	H	Inf.	173	8	5	28-Jun-62	Typhoid Fever	Ford's Factory
Cotton, Benjamin C.	61st	Virginia	B	Inf.	101	10	1	27-Dec-62	Typhoid Pneumonia	Taliaferro's Factory
County, Charles (Countz)	60th	Virginia	A	Inf.	177	9	4	14-Aug-62	---	On Car O&R Railroad
Courtney, George W., Corpl.	14th	Alabama	B	Inf.	193	5	2	19-May-64	DOW	Knight's Factory
Cowart, John W.	5th	Alabama	E	Inf.	191	6	5	03-Feb-63	---	Knight's Factory
Cox, Fountain	23rd Battn.	Virginia	H	Inf.	194	8	3	13-Jul-64	---	Camp Davis
Cox, Irby C., Sgt.	16th	Virginia	F	Inf.	185	3	2	30-Apr-64	Diphtheria	Ferguson's Factory
Cox, James M.	47th	Virginia	A	Inf.	200	7	5	18-Dec-63	---	Knight's Factory
Crabb, Asbury T.	28th	Georgia	H	Inf.	172	1	2	13-Jun-62	Erysipelas	Langhorne's Factory
Craft, Elijah	3rd	Georgia	K	Inf.	202	1	4	02-Mar-65	Small Pox	Crumpton's Factory
Craft, J. E.	Cobb's Legion	Georgia	D	Inf.	171	10	1	31-May-62	---	Crumpton's Factory
Craft, Spencer (or Croft)	61st	Georgia	F	Inf.	165	1	2	10-Aug-62	---	Saunder's Factory
Cramplin, B. F.	4th	Georgia	C	Inf.	186	7	3	20-Jun-64	---	Ferguson's Factory
Crane, John T.	48th	North Carolina	I	Inf.	100	8	3	27-Nov-62	Diarrhea Chronic	Langhorne's Factory
Craven, Robert F.	3rd	North Carolina	H	Inf.	123	10	5	22-Dec-62	Hydrothorax	Langhorne's Factory
Crawbay, G. W.	26th	Georgia	I	Inf.	180	3	2	26-Sep-62	---	Miller's Factory
Crawford, Thomas B.	28th	Virginia	B	Inf.	173	9	1	25-Jun-62	Erysipelas	Christian's Factory
Creswell, William J.	22nd	North Carolina	K	Inf.	146	5	3	12-Dec-62	---	Booker's Factory
Crider, C. W.	5th	South Carolina	C	Inf.	101	2	4	26-Dec-62	DOD	Claytor's Factory
Criger, J.	Drenwick's Batty.	Virginia	-	Art.	201	4	1	13-Jun-64	---	Christian's Factory
Crim, Jacob	21st	North Carolina	K	Inf.	194	10	2	24-Jan-65	---	Camp Davis
Crimn, E. E.	5th	Alabama	C	Inf.	182	9	5	08-Dec-62	Disease	Langhorne's Factory
Crocker, Bethel D.	15th	Virginia	F	Inf.	173	6	3	02-Jul-62	---	Claytor's Factory
Cross, R. H.	53rd	Virginia	B	Inf.	100	10	1	27-Nov-62	---	Ferguson's Factory
Crow, S.	23rd	Georgia	E	Inf.	146	7	3	15-Dec-62	---	Candler's Factory
Crowder, Allen A.	Bedford Batty.	Virginia	Jordan's	Art.	182	1	3	22-Nov-62	Disease	Ladies Relief Hospt.
Crowder, Henderson	56th	Virginia	B	Inf.	79	10	2	02-Jan-63	---	Ladies Relief Hospt.
Crowder, William A.	1st Reserves	Virginia	K	Inf.	198	1	5	05-Aug-64	---	Ferguson's Factory
Cruse, Paul	57th	North Carolina	F	Inf.	Yk. Sq.	29th	5th Line	11-Apr-63	Small Pox	Pest House
Crutchelow, Richard H.	3rd	Virginia	G	Inf.	160	8	2	10-Jul-62	Typhoid Fever	Ferguson's Factory
Culifer, William	33rd	North Carolina	F	Inf.	171	8	2	31-May-62	Typhoid Fever	Ferguson's Factory
Culverhouse, W. G.	Cutt's Battery	Georgia	B	Art.	79	9	3	05-Jan-63	---	Crumpton's Factory
Cummings, Sherman	25th	Virginia	A	Inf.	161	1	5	21-Jul-62	Typhoid Fever	Ferguson's Factory
Cunningham, M. H.	53rd	Georgia	G	Inf.	196	8	5	20-Aug-63	---	Christian's Factory
Curfee, Calvin S.	48th	North Carolina	E	Inf.	101	8	4	04-Jan-63	Pneumonia	Ferguson's Factory
Curran, Peter	9th	Louisiana	E	Inf.	198	8	1	12-Aug-64	---	Camp Davis
Currie, Daniel M.	24th	North Carolina	G	Inf.	122	2	2	19-Nov-62	Dysentery	Crumpton's Factory
Curry, Thomas	15th	Louisiana	F	Inf.	193	1	5	21-May-64	DOW 5/05/64	Christian's Factory

* See Part III - 68

NAME	REGT. or UNIT	STATE	COMPANY	BRANCH of SERVICE	LOT#	Grave No.	ROW	DATE of BURIAL or DEATH	CAUSE of DEATH	HOSPITAL
Daley, Timothy	1st Battn.	Virginia	B	Inf.	170	9	3	10-Mar-62	---	Ladies Relief Hospt.
Dameron, L. W.	10th	Virginia	K	Inf.	183	10	3	15-Jan-63	---	Ford's Factory
Danford, ---	Unknown	Unknown	-	-	Yk. Sq.	17th	5th Line	27-Dec-62	Small Pox	Pest House
Daniel, Joseph	Cutt's Battery	Georgia	---	Art.	177	8	5	23-Aug-62	---	Talliaferro's Factory
Danielly, J. M.	17th	Georgia	B	Inf.	170	3	3	01-Jan-62	Disease	College Hospital
Danielly, John M., 1st Sgt.	6th	Georgia	E	Inf.	162	1	3	08-Aug-62	---	Knight's Factory
Daugherty, Bernard (John)	33rd	Virginia	E	Inf.	167	7	2	22-May-62	---	Christian's Factory
Davenport, William H. A., Ord. Sgt.	35th	Georgia	C	Inf.	101	5	2	31-Dec-62	---	Christian's Factory
Davis, David	2nd	South Carolina	C	Inf.	182	2	3	17-Oct-62	---	Camp Davis
Davis, E. Lewis	2nd	South Carolina	K	Inf.	195	5	2	03-Mar-63	DOD	Claytor's Factory
Davis, Fountain	Phillip's Legion	Georgia	Hamilton's	Inf.	159	6	2	08-Sep-61	---	Ladies Relief Hospt.
Davis, G. A.	14th	South Carolina	G	Inf.	187	9	3	22-Jan-63	Diphtheria	Reid's Factory
Davis, George	5th	Louisiana	G	Inf.	199	3	2	31-Mar-63	---	Wade's Factory
Davis, James	27th	North Carolina	A	Inf.	189	4	4	08-May-64	---	Burton's Factory
Davis, John A.	25th	Virginia	G	Inf.	196	2	1	06-Nov-63	DOW 7/03/63	Crumpton's Factory
Davis, John B.	21st	Virginia	C	Inf.	180	4	3	30-Sep-62	Chronic Diarrhea	Knight's Factory
Davis, John W.	12th	Georgia	K	Inf.	168	10	3	07-May-62	Disease	Ferguson's Factory
Davis, Lewis E.	4th	Virginia	A	Inf.	168	4	5	03-May-62	---	Christian's Factory
Davis, Rayford	2nd	North Carolina	B	Inf.	198	1	4	29-Nov-64	Pneumonia	Crumpton's Factory
Davis, W. C.	21st	North Carolina	E	Inf.	Yk. Sq.	22nd	2nd Line	20-Jan-63	Small Pox	Pest House
Davis, W. Henry	28th	North Carolina	D	Inf.	172	10	5	09-Jun-62	Febris Typhoides	Ferguson's Factory
Davis, William	4th	Georgia	F	Inf.	180	1	4	30-Sep-62	---	Christian's Factory
Davis, William H.	21st	North Carolina	C	Inf.	194	2	5	03-Aug-64	---	Camp Davis
Davis, William H.	25th	North Carolina	D	Inf.	79	8	1	07-Jan-63	DOW 12/12/62	Ford's Factory
Day, James	18th	North Carolina	C	Inf.	79	6	5	12-Jan-63	Diphtheria	Crumpton's Factory
Day, Thomas Jefferson	6th	Alabama	D	Inf.	158	3	3	30-Jul-61	---	College Hospital
Deal, J. W.	9th	Louisiana	B	Inf.	161	5	5	25-Jul-62	---	Christian's Factory
Dean, James W.	31st	Georgia	I	Inf.	182	1	2	20-Oct-62	---	Miller's Factory
Deboard, Thomas J.	37th	North Carolina	B	Inf.	188	5	3	19-Jun-63	Pyemia	Claytor's Factory
DeFord, John W., Corpl.	61st	Virginia	A	Inf.	192	8	3	27-Jun-63	Fever Remitten	Candler's Factory
Delany, Martin	27th	North Carolina	G	Inf.	197	5	3	29-May-64	DOW 5/05/64	College Hospital
DeLoach, Andrew	15th	Alabama	E	Inf.	167	7	3	21-May-62	Disease	Warwick House
Delrack, C.	12th	South Carolina	D	Inf.	197	7	5	26-May-64	---	Booker's Factory
Denham, John T.	12th	Georgia	G	Inf.	194	8	2	13-Jul-64	DOW 05/20/64	Ladies Relief Hospt.
Denning, John J.	20th	North Carolina	H	Inf.	183	6	2	20-Jan-63	Phthisis Pulmonaris	College Hospital
Dennis, T. E.	4th	Texas	D	Inf.	173	7	1	30-Jun-62	Meningitis	Talliaferro's Factory
Denson, Charles	13th	South Carolina	A	Inf.	182	5	2	30-Oct-62	Diarrhea Chronic	Crumpton's Factory
Denton, Wesley A.	16th	North Carolina	E	Inf.	79	8	5	07-Jan-63	Febris Typhoides	Crumpton's Factory
Denton, William	4th	Virginia	H	Inf.	Yk. Sq.	-	-	02-Oct-62	Small Pox	Pest House

* See Part III - 69

NAME	REGT. or UNIT	STATE	COMPANY	BRANCH of SERVICE	LOT#	Grave No.	ROW	DATE of BURIAL or DEATH	CAUSE of DEATH	HOSPITAL
Desern, Edward	6th	North Carolina	C	Inf.	191	9	5	29-Jan-63	Typhoid Fever	Candler'd Factory
Diamond, William B.	8th	Georgia	E	Inf.	158	9	4	10-Aug-61	Disease	Jed Carter's
Dickerson, A. J.	Pate's Regt.	Unknown	Cokely's Co.	Cav.	160	1	3	04-Jul-62	...	Booker's Factory
Dickerson, S. T.	6th	Louisiana	A	Inf.	199	5	3	10-Apr-63	...	College Hospital
Dickson, E. V.	2nd	South Carolina	E or I	Inf.	79	5	4	12-Jan-63	...	Reid's Factory
Dickson, N. H. (W. H.?)	10th	South Carolina	D	Inf.	191	10	5	29-Jan-63	...	Langhorne's Factory
Didlake, G. B.	Lynch. Provost Guard	Virginia	-	Inf.	188	8	4	09-Jun-63	...	College Hospital
Dies, James	47th	Alabama	A	Inf.	193	6	4	18-May-64	...	Knight's Factory
Dilda, Joseph	7th	Georgia	E	Inf.	170	5	1	27-Nov-61	Disease	Warwick House
Dilden, Eli K. R.	13th	Alabama	K	Inf.	165	8	2	17-Aug-62	Disease	Christian's Factory
Dillard, Winberry	Holcombe's Legion	South Carolina	A	Inf.	181	2	2	07-Oct-62	Diarrhea Chronic	Miller's Factory
Dillard, W. F.	24th	Georgia	E	Inf.	183	1	1	15-Jan-63	Pneumonia	Claytor's Factory
Dillon, Michael A.	2nd	Florida	M	Inf.	178	9	1	24-Aug-62	Diptheria	Ford's Factory
Dilly, Robert W.	12th	Mississippi	B	Inf.	184	10	3	23-Apr-63	Pneumonia	Knight's Factory
Dineal, A. O.	557th	Virginia	E	Inf.	191	7	2	02-Feb-63	...	Reid's Factory
Dixon, J.	48th	Alabama	E	Inf.	161	6	3	05-Aug-62	...	Crumpton's Factory
Dodd, William (Supposed)	10th	Georgia	K	Inf.	144	5	2	18-Nov-62	...	Crumpton's Factory
Dodson, Elisha J.	41st	Virginia	G	Inf.	197	7	1	27-May-64	DOW 5/64	Claytor's Factory
Dodson, Lazarus	18th	North Carolina	H	Inf.	146	8	4	17-Dec-62	Pneumonia	Ferguson's Factory
Dodson, William	13th	Georgia	F	Inf.	181	1	3	06-Oct-62	...	Ferguson's Factory
Donahoe, M. O.	Cobb's Legion	Georgia	B	Inf.	195	5	5	08-Mar-63	...	Crumpton's Factory
Donaldson, James H.	17th	Georgia	D	Inf.	193	2	4	05-Jun-64	DOW 5/06/64	Burton's Factory
Donaldson, Peter L.	3rd	Arkansas	B	Inf.	189	1	1	08-Feb-62	...	Ladies Relief Hospt.
Donathan, Richard	2nd Battn.	North Carolina	B	Inf.	200	2	2	28-Oct-63	Pneumonia	Langhorne's Factory
Donavan, W. F.	53rd	Unknown	C	Inf.	101	2	3	28-Dec-62	...	Claytor's Factory
Dorn, William	15th	Alabama	L	Inf.	166	8	3	08-May-62	Disease	Saunder's Factory
Dougherty, James	14th	South Carolina	A	Inf.	183	6	3	19-Jan-63	Diarrhea	Langhorne's Factory
Douthit, Silas, 3rd Corpl.	60th	Georgia	F	Inf.	179	2	2	14-Sep-62	...	Claytor's Factory
Dover, E. V. (or E. B.)	60th	Georgia	H	Inf.	177	2	2	19-Aug-62	Disease	Burton's Factory
Dowdey, Benjamin	4th	Virginia	L	Inf.	159	7	1	04-Sep-61	...	Warwick House
Dowdy, Edward E.	21st	Virginia	D	Inf.	167	1	2	11-May-62	...	Ladies Relief Hospt.
Dowdy, John P.	Lynch. City Guard	Virginia		Inf.	Yk. Sq.	26th	3rd Line	12-Feb-63	Small Pox	Pest House
Downer, J. W.	20th	Mississippi	Massie's	Inf.	159	9	5	25-Sep-61	...	College Hospital
Doyel, Walter R.	2nd	South Carolina	A	Inf.	101	4	5	31-Dec-62	Pneumonia	Miller's Factory
Drewry, Samuel B.	16th	Virginia	A	Inf.	173	10	2	24-Jun-62	Rubeola	Reid's Factory
Driggers, Christopher Columbus	15th	Alabama	F	Inf.	173	5	3	04-Jul-62	Disease	Christian's Factory
Duke, Robert	46th	North Carolina	E	Inf.	198	9	4	09-Aug-64	Disease	Knight's Factory
Duke, W. C. (or W. G.)	59th	Georgia	A	Inf.	193	2	3	29-May-64	Ascites	Crumpton's Factory
Duncan, William B.	61st	Alabama	H	Inf.	197	4	2	31-May-64	Disease	Ferguson's Factory
Dunn, George Franklin	55th	Virginia	G	Inf.	181	3	1	08-Oct-62	Diarrhea Chronic	Langhorne's Factory

* See Part III - 70

NAME	REGT. or UNIT	COMPANY	STATE	BRANCH of SERVICE	LOT#	Grave No.	ROW	DATE of BURIAL or DEATH	CAUSE of DEATH	HOSPITAL
Dunn, Zacariah, S.	49th	E	Georgia	Inf.	123	2	1	17-Dec-62	Pneumonia	Christian's Factory
Durfrey, William	Lynch. Provost Guard	-	Virginia	Inf.	196	5	1	04-Sep-63	...	Temperance Hall
Durham, A. A.	3rd	C	Arkansas	Inf.	194	10	4	09-Jul-64	DOW 5/06/64	Knight's Factory
Dyess, Josiah	50th	A	Georgia	Inf.	191	6	4	03-Feb-63	Pneumonia	Knight's Factory
Eaks, Mangum Z.	23rd	I	North Carolina	Inf.	172	9	4	09-Jun-52	Measles	Langhorne's Factory
Earnhart, Clarkson	5th	B	North Carolina	Inf.	195	4	1	24-Feb-63	Febris Typhodies	Candler's Factory
Eason, William	Latham's Batty.	H 1st	North Carolina	Art.	192	10	2	21-Jun-63	Diarrhea	College Hospital
Eastman, R. A.		Walhall's	Alabama		158	8	2	17-Jul-61	...	College Hospital
Eatland, Samuel	8th	H	Louisiana	Inf.	169	5	3	31-May-62	...	Ferguson's Factory
Edge, L.	3rd	C	North Carolina	Inf.	177	4	4	30-Aug-62	Febris Typhoides	Crumpton's Factory
Edison, Mahlon	3rd	L	Alabama	Inf.	78	5	1	08-Dec-62	...	Knight's Factory
Edward, Warren M.	44th	I	North Carolina	Inf.	200	2	1	15-Oct-63	Diarrhea	Booker's Factory
Edwards, J. E.	21st	C	North Carolina	Inf.	194	4	5	24-Jul-64	Unknown	Christian's Factory
Edwards, T.	21st	D	Virginia	Inf.	202	1	3	01-Mar-65	...	Crumpton's Factory
Eldridge, L. E. W.	20th	I	Georgia	Inf.	197	3	2	03-Jun-54	Disease	Ferguson's Factory
Eller, D.	51st	B	Virginia	Inf.	202	6	4	06-May-65	...	Camp Davis
Ellington, David W.	44th	G	Georgia	Inf.	189	9	4	01-Apr-64	Chronic Diarrhoea	Ferguson's Factory
Elliott, John R., 3rd Sgt.	21st	E	Georgia	Inf.	190	5	3	02-Jul-64	Unknown	Burton's Factory
Ellis, Nathaniel	33rd	F	North Carolina	Inf.	199	7	4	03-Apr-63	...	Ferguson's Factory
Ellis, William	50th	C	Georgia	Inf.	181	2	1	11-Nov-62	Pneumonia	Candler's Factory
Ellison, M.	1st	F	Texas	Art.	199	1	3	07-Mar-63	...	Candler's Factory
Elmore, J. E.	3rd Battery	A	South Carolina	Inf.	186	9	3	20-Jun-64	...	Christian's Factory
Emmons, James	11th	D	Mississippi	Inf.	122	4	3	23-Nov-62	Disease	Home in Amherst
Epperson, Samuel	Lynch. City Guard	-	Virginia	Inf.	200	7	4	22-Dec-63	...	Christian's Factory
Epps, W.	13th	H	Mississippi	Inf.	161	3	5	15-Jul-62	...	Christian's Factory
Estes, Ruben E.	21st	F	Georgia	Inf.	169	10	4	21-May-62	Pneumonia	Ferguson's Factory
Etheridge, Lewis M.	45th	J	Georgia	Inf.	178	2	1	27-Aug-62	...	College Hospital
Ethridge, Thomas J.	5th	G	Alabama	Inf.	165	1	3	09-Aug-62	...	Christian's Factory
Eter, Isaiah	8th	I	Louisiana	Inf.	169	4	4	26-May-62	...	Knight's Factory
Eubanks, A. M. J. D.	1st Eng.	G	Virginia	Eng.	189	7	4	09-Sep-64	Pneumonia	Langhorne's Factory
Evans, Barnwell	6th	K	South Carolina	Inf.	181	6	3	11-Nov-62	Diarrhea	Claytor's Factory
Evans, J. H.	Jeff Davis Legion	B	Mississippi	Inf.	146	1	5	07-Dec-62	Diarrhea	Claytor's Factory
Evans, John	2nd	B	North Carolina	Inf.	191	1	1	06-Feb-63	Phthisis	Langhorne's Factory
Evans, William L. (or Ivens)	18th	C	Georgia	Inf.	177	8	2	17-Aug-62	...	Ladies Relief Hospt.
Evatt, W. R.	Phillip's Legion	Barclay's	Georgia	Inf.	159	7	4	05-Oct-61	...	Warwick House
Ezell, George Washington	21st	G	Georgia	Inf.	177	9	1	12-Aug-62	Diarrhea Chronic	
Fair, Lewis	18th	K	North Carolina	Inf.	Yk. Sq.	28th	5th Line	01-Apr-63	Small Pox	Pest House
Farabel, J. C.	10th	B	Virginia	Cav.	201	1	1	15-Jun-64	...	Camp Davis
Farlow, Jonas	2nd	C	Georgia	Inf.	196	7	2	23-Aug-63	...	Knight's Factory

* See Part III - 71

NAME	REGT. or UNIT	STATE	COMPANY	BRANCH of SERVICE	LOT#	Grave No.	ROW	DATE of BURIAL or DEATH	CAUSE of DEATH	HOSPITAL
Farmer, Daniel	12th	Mississippi	D	Inf.	177	7	1	20-Aug-62	---	Burton's Factory
Farmer, Elijah	1st	Tennessee	G	Inf.	190	6	4	02-Jul-64	---	Christian's Factory
Farmer, J. K.	5th	North Carolina	B	Inf.	123	7	1	23-Dec-62	Typhoid Pneumonia	Ford's Factory
Farris, Doctor	12th	South Carolina	G	Inf.	181	5	2	10-Jan-63	---	College Hospital
Farthing, Thomas J., 1st Sgt.	37th	North Carolina	E	Inf.	169	7	1	22-May-62	Typhoid Fever	Saunder's Factory
Faunt, E. H.	3rd	Alabama	H	Inf.	191	8	5	01-Feb-63	---	College Hospital
Feamster, Robert R., Lt.	11th	Mississippi	F	Inf.	158	7	4	26-Aug-61	---	Ladies Relief Hospt.
Fenley, M.	7th Battn.	Georgia	---	Inf.	161	9	4	14-Jul-62	---	Ferguson's Factory
Ferguson, Edward P.	4th	Virginia	D	Inf.	Yk. Sq.	21st	5th Line	05-Jan-63	Small Pox	Pest House
Ferguson, James	9th	Louisiana	E	Inf.	161	2	4	17-Jul-62	---	Warwick House
Ferrell, D. W.	57th	North Carolina	B	Inf.	195	3	2	26-Feb-63	---	Christian's Factory
Field, Robert	1st	Louisiana	K	Inf.	187	6	2	26-Jan-63	---	Reid's Factory
Fielder, S. T.	9th	Alabama	D	Inf.	170	2	4	09-Mar-62	---	College Hospital
Fields, John	6th	Alabama	C	Inf.	172	7	1	15-Jun-62	---	Langhorne's Factory
Fields, Mark H.	21st	North Carolina	L	Inf.	166	5	1	09-May-62	Enteritis	Ferguson's Factory
Fields, Robert	3rd	North Carolina	H	Inf.	79	1	5	09-Jan-63	Pneumonia	Christian's Factory
Fields, Samuel G.	58th	Virginia	G	Inf.	167	1	1	11-May-62	Diphtheria	College Hospital
Fincher, Moses	22nd	Georgia	C	Inf.	182	7	4	11-Nov-62	---	Miller's Factory
Fink, Daniel M.	33rd	North Carolina	A	Inf.	197	1	5	02-Jun-64	DOW 5/6/64	Burton's Factory
Finley, G. O.	26th	Georgia	D	Inf.	178	4	3	04-Sep-62	---	Ferguson's Factory
Finley, James	14th	Louisiana	H	Inf.	190	2	1	10-Jul-64	---	College Hospital
Fishel, L.	6th	North Carolina	B	Inf.	198	3	3	03-Jan-65	Typhoid Pneumonia	Burton's Factoty
Fitzpatrick, John	1st	South Carolina	C or K	Inf.	101	5	4	01-Jan-63	Diarrhea Chronic	Crumpton's Factory
Flanniken, John W., Lt.	5th	Texas	I	Inf.	187	3	2	27-Jan-63	Diarrhea Chronic	College Hospital
Flannagan, W. A.	9th	Tennessee	E	Inf.	Yk. Sq.	3rd	2nd Line	20-Apr-63	Small Pox	Pest House
Flemming, J. T.	47th	Alabama	K	Inf.	Yk. Sq.	22nd	3rd Line	05-Jan-63	Small Pox	Pest House
Fletcher, Lewis R.	60th	Georgia	C	Inf.	165	4	3	20-Aug-62	Fever	Reid's Factory
Flippin, Marian Twyman	44th	Virginia	A	Inf.	170	1	5	15-Jan-62	Frozee to Death	Found 3 mi. from City
Flohr, Charles C.	6th	Louisiana	H	Inf.	185	10	2	18-Jan-64	---	Reid's Factory
Flowers, J. C.	15th	Alabama	A	Inf.	Yk. Sq.	28th	2nd Line	19-Feb-63	Small Pox	Pest House
Floyd, R. J.	1st	Texas	D	Inf.	173	8	2	29-Jun-62	Typhoid Fever	Warwick House
Floyd, Richard	Boyce's Batty.	South Carolina	---	Art.	123	1	2	17-Dec-62	---	Burton's Factory
Folkes, W. E.	56th	Virginia	I	Inf.	195	1	4	15-Feb-63	---	Ferguson's Factory
Forbis, H. Smiley	27th	North Carolina	B	Inf.	185	7	2	13-Mar-64	Diarrhoea Chronica	Camp Davis
Porcun, Thomas M.	33rd	North Carolina	A	Inf.	169	1	5	19-May-62	Typhoid Fever	Crumpton's Factory
Ford, Ephraim Wellington	37th	North Carolina	E	Inf.	171	2	4	31-May-62	Diarrhea Chronic	Reid's Factory
Ford, J. C.	61st	Alabama	I	Inf.	189	4	3	08-May-64	---	Booker's Factory
Ford, Norman M.	21st	Georgia	C	Inf.	169	10	5	19-May-62	Measles	Christian's Factory
Ford, Thomas P.	16th	Mississippi	C	Inf.	78	6	3	07-Dec-62	---	Burton's Factory
Ford, William S.	12th	Alabama	H	Inf.	Yk. Sq.	12th	1st line	12-Oct-62	Small Pox	Pest House

* See Part III - 72

NAME	REGT. or UNIT	STATE	COMPANY	BRANCH of SERVICE	LOT#	Grave No.	ROW	DATE of BURIAL or DEATH	CAUSE of DEATH	HOSPITAL
Forehand, E. W.	10th Battn.	Georgia	A	Inf.	183	2	1	16-Jan-63	...	Claytor's Factory
Forehand, Theophilus	2nd	North Carolina	C	Inf.	199	9	1	18-Mar-63	Diarrhea Chronic	Ferguson's Factory
Forester, Richard J.	60th	Unknown	B	Inf.	196	2	3	22-Sep-63	...	College Hospital
Forrest, William	13th	Georgia	G	Inf.	202	6	3	09-May-65	...	Ladies Relief Hospt.
Forrester, Thomas	4th	Texas	K	Inf.	161	10	1	09-Jul-62	Typhoid Fever	Knight's Factory
Fort, Elias N.	8th	Florida	H	Inf.	101	4	5	29-Dec-62	Diarrhea	Reid's Factory
Foster, Baylis B.	4th	Alabama	H	Inf.	177	6	5	29-Aug-62	...	College Hospital
Foster, Francis A.	27th	North Carolina	F	Inf.	189	7	5	24-May-64	...	Burton's Factory
Fouche, Lewis	Curt's Battery	Georgia	...	Art.	196	10	2	11-Aug-63	...	Ferguson's Factory
Fountain, A. J. (or J. A.)	1st Orr's Rifles	South Carolina	G	Inf.	196	9	1	11-Aug-63	...	Ferguson's Factory
Fouts, B.	28th	Virginia	A	Inf.	202	7	4	27-Apr-65	...	Camp Davis
Fowler, A. (J.?)	1st	South Carolina	H	Inf.	187	5	1	26-Jan-63	...	Crumpton's Factory
Fowler, M. S.	16th	Georgia	B	Inf.	187	4	3	27-Jun-63	...	Claytor's Factory
Fowler, Matthew	1st (McCreary's)	South Carolina	F	Inf.	146	5	5	12-Dec-62	Pneumonia	Ferguson's Factory
Fowler, W. F.	13th	Georgia	D	Inf.	162	2	1	21-Jul-62	...	Langhorne's Factory
Fox, Alexander	7th	North Carolina	A	Inf.	200	5	1	11-Dec-63	Typhoid Fever	Langhorne's Factory
Fox, James	6th	Louisiana	B	Inf.	123	10	1	17-Dec-62	DOW 6/09/62	Christian's Factory
Fox, Samuel M.	46th	North Carolina	G	Inf.	190	7	4	30-Jun-64	Gun Shot Wound	Knight's Factory
Fox, William	7th	North Carolina	A	Inf.	100	6	2	26-Nov-62	DOW 8/29/62	Burton's Factory
Fox, William M., Jr.	37th	North Carolina	G	Inf.	146	5	1	11-Dec-62	Pneumonnia	Ford's Factory
Fraim, James W.	33rd	North Carolina	K	Inf.	146	3	4	07-Dec-62	Diarrhea	Christian's Factory
Franklin, Cicero D.	5th	Florida	H	Inf.	180	9	4	29-Sep-62	Disease	Knight's Factory
Frazier, Brice M., Lieut.	24th	Virginia	I	Inf.	79	5	1	06-Apr-63	...	Crumpton's Factory
Frazier, James M.	1st	North Carolina	G	Inf.	190	4	2	03-Jul-64	Diarrhea Chronic	Christian's Factory
Frazier, John Adams	9th	Georgia	B	Inf.	168	3	4	05-May-62	...	Warwick House
Frazier, T. J.	19th	Mississippi	A	Inf.	166	3	3	19-May-62	...	Ferguson's Factory
Fredrick, Bedford B.	13th	North Carolina	E	Inf.	180	8	4	30-Sep-62	Mobru Varai	Christian's Factory
Freeman, George Washington	44th	Georgia	B	Inf.	193	10	4	15-May-64	DOW 5/05/64	Booker's Factory
Freeman, Henry	44th	North Carolina	H	Inf.	188	2	2	11-Jun-63	Febris Typhoides	Camp Davis
Freestone, Benjamin F.	4th	Texas	A	Inf.	162	7	2	04-Aug-62	Consumption (T.B.)	Langhorne's Factory
Preller, James	29th	Virginia	B	Inf.	184	3	3	24-May-63	...	Langhorne's Factory
French, J. G.	47th	Alabama	G	Inf.	146	9	3	16-Dec-62	...	Ferguson's Factory
Fry, John	33rd	North Carolina	G	Inf.	191	5	3	07-Feb-63	Pneumonia	Ferguson's Factory
Pryar, Charles M.	18th	North Carolina	I	Inf.	169	3	2	28-May-62	Pneumonia	Booker's Factory
Fulgham, Murren	44th	Georgia	F	Inf.	186	7	2	18-Jun-64	...	Christian's Factory
Fulk, Edward	4th	North Carolina	K	Inf.	167	8	1	18-May-62	...	College Hospital
Fulks, T. P.	18th	North Carolina	I	Inf.	195	4	3	03-Mar-63	Pneumonia	Ferguson's Factory
Puller, F. M.	Wise's Legion	Virginia	Pate's	Inf.	170	1	3	06-Jan-63	...	Ladies Relief Hospt.
Fuller, J. T.	23rd	Georgia	I	Inf.	171	3	3	06-Jun-62	Gastritis	Claytor's Factory
Fuller, Joseph L.	4th	Texas	I	Inf.	186	5	1	20-Jun-64	DOW 5/06/64	Christian's Factory

* See Part III - 73

NAME	REGT. or UNIT	STATE	COMPANY	BRANCH of SERVICE	LOT#	Grave No.	ROW	DATE of BURIAL or DEATH	CAUSE of DEATH	HOSPITAL
Fuller, W. G.	7th	Georgia	H	Inf.	169	7	5	21-May-62	---	Langhorne's Factory
Fulmore, Watson	14th	South Carolina	H	Inf.	189	5	4	10-May-64	Pneumonia	Christian's Factory
Furgusson, Andrew	37th	North Carolina	H	Inf.	187	3	4	04-Feb-63	Diarrhea	Burton's Factory
* Furtick, Charles	1st (Hagood's)	South Carolina	B	Inf.	183	4	1	17-Jan-63	DOD	Crumpton's Factory
Gailory, A.	6th	Louisiana	C	Inf.	167	8	3	17-May-62	---	Ferguson's Factory
Gailespie, William	13th	Mississippi	Randall's	Inf.	158	1	4	03-Aug-61	---	Charles Scott's
* Gambill, Hugh L.	33rd	North Carolina	D	Inf.	Yk. Sq.	28th	2nd Line	23-Feb-63	Small Pox	Pest House
Gamble, William H.	47th	Alabama	H	Inf.	123	3	5	22-Dec-62	---	Ferguson's Factory
Gardner, Hezekia T.	37th	North Carolina	C	Inf.	169	6	3	28-May-62	Fever	Warwick House
Gardner, J.	8th	Louisiana	I	Inf.	Yk. Sq.	13th	1st line	11-Dec-62	Small Pox	Pest House
Gardner, S. D.	15th	Alabama	I	Inf.	173	6	5	03-Jul-62	---	Ferguson's Factory
* Garland, Samuel W.	21st	Georgia	I	Inf.	168	6	3	09-May-62	---	Christian's Factory
Garrett, E. G.	60th	Georgia	K	Inf.	191	2	1	08-Feb-63	---	Ferguson's Factory
* Garrett, J. A.	14th	South Carolina	E	Inf.	146	5	2	11-Dec-62	---	Ferguson's Factory
Garrison, J.	57th	North Carolina	I	Inf.	Yk. Sq.	---	3	18-Feb-64	Pneumonia	Pest House
Garrett, Jesse Newton	47th	Alabama	B	Inf.	79	3	3	15-Jan-63	Small Pox	Taliaferro's Factory
Gaskins, Murdock	16th	Virginia	D	Inf.	171	5	5	07-Jun-62	Disease	Ferguson's Factory
* Gates, Richard A., Lieut.	23rd	Virginia	C	Inf.	186	6	1	20-Jun-64	Rubeola	Pratts Hospital
Gatlin, J. E.	7th	Louisiana	K	Inf.	202	4	5	02-Jun-65	DOW 6/18/64	Ladies Relief Hospt.
Gaunt, Andrew	12th	Virginia	G	Cav.	201	7	2	08-Jun-64	Gunshot Wound	Reid's Factory
Gay, G. M.	15th	Alabama	L	Inf.	162	5	3	31-Jul-62	Disease	Crumpton's Factory
* Gay, Henry	30th	North Carolina	F	Inf.	183	8	1	18-Jan-63	Typhoid Fever	Claytor's Factory
* Gayhart, John	7th	Louisiana	B	Inf.	172	1	3	13-Jun-62	---	Christian's Factory
Gentry, Allen	9th	Virginia	C	Inf.	169	9	1	23-May-62	---	Ferguson's Factory
Gibbons, Eugene	13th	Virginia	C	Inf.	168	9	2	27-Apr-62	Typhoid Fever	Warwick House
* Gibson, Jeremiah (Jerry)	48th	Virginia	H	Inf.	196	4	5	17-Sep-63	Tuberculosis	Miller's Factory
Gibson, John	21st	Georgia	H	Inf.	177	5	3	30-Aug-62	---	Ford's Factory
Gibson, V. A.	33rd	North Carolina	K	Inf.	122	9	3	20-Nov-62	Phthisis Pulmonaris	Christian's Factory
Gilbert, Willis	30th	North Carolina	A	Inf.	181	9	2	12-Oct-62	Febris Typhoides	Crumpton's Factory
Gilder, M. L.	3rd	Alabama	A	Inf.	101	6	2	05-Jan-63	---	Crumpton's Factory
Gill, J. H.	3rd	Kentucky	---	Cav.	202	6	2	09-Apr-65	---	Camp Davis
Gill, Robert	13th	Virginia	K	Inf.	188	2	4	13-Jun-63	Fever	Camp Davis
Gill, W.	5th	South Carolina	A	Inf.	182	10	3	07-Dec-62	Diarrhea Chronic	Langhorne's Factory
Gillcrease, J. J.	9th	Louisiana	B	Inf.	172	1	5	10-Jun-62	---	Claytor's Factory
Gilliam, John	21st	Georgia	H	Inf.	171	1	1	03-Jun-62	Disease	Ferguson's Factory
Gilligan, John	---	Alabama	Covington's	---	158	5	2	30-Jun-61	---	College Hospital
* Gillis, Angus, 3rd Corpl.	15th	Alabama	I	Inf.	168	5	3	12-May-62	---	Ferguson's Factory
* Gills, T. O.	25th	Georgia	G	Inf.	183	1	2	17-Jan-63	---	Christian's Factory
Gilmer, R. F.	11th	Mississippi	K	Inf.	172	4	4	20-Jun-62	---	Christian's Factory

* See Part III - 74

NAME	REGT. or UNIT	STATE	COMPANY	BRANCH of SERVICE	LOT #	Grave No.	ROW	DATE of BURIAL or DEATH	CAUSE of DEATH	HOSPITAL
Gilmore, A. H.	18th	Alabama	L	Inf.	168	3	5	02-May-62	---	Christian's Factory
Gilmore, William H., 4th Corpl.	44th	Georgia	B	Inf.	202	1	1	26-Jan-65	Phthisis	College Hospital
Gipson, J.	21st	Georgia	B	Inf.	202	1	1	27-Jan-65	Phthisis	College Hospital
Givens, J. J.	5th	Alabama	B	Inf.	101	3	4	30-Dec-62	Disease	Ferguson's Factory
Gizer, John E.	8th	Louisiana	B	Inf.	168	2	5	05-May-62	---	Flynn's Shop, Ward #1
Gladden, Henry A.	60th	Georgia	K	Inf.	180	8	5	27-Sep-62	DOW 9/17/62	Camp Davis
Glasco, V. L.	2nd	Arkansas	---	Inf.	173	4	1	06-Jul-62	---	Ferguson's Factory
Glenn, John D.	1st (Hagood's)	South Carolina	D	Inf.	191	3	5	10-Feb-63	Febris Typhoides	Candler's Factory
Glenn, W. C.	5th	North Carolina	D	Inf.	170	7	5	12-Apr-62	---	Warwick House
Glover, William H.	24th	Georgia	F	Inf.	123	8	2	24-Dec-62	---	Reid's Factory
Godfrey, William	3rd	Virginia	J	Inf.	165	4	1	20-Aug-62	---	College Hospital
Godwin, James	5th	Florida	B	Inf.	78	10	2	02-Dec-62	DOW	Christian's Factory
Goens, S.	58th	North Carolina	E	Inf.	201	5	1	13-Oct-62	---	Camp Davis
Goff, William G.	21st	North Carolina	G	Inf.	180	5	2	14-Jun-64	Febris Typhoides	College Hospital
Goins, T. J.	15th	Alabama	A	Inf.	172	7	4	23-Jun-62	DOW	Ferguson's Factory
Goldsby, H. K.	6th	Louisiana	H	Inf.	173	1	1	13-Feb-64	---	Ladies Relief Hospt.
Golsby, A.	Lynch. City Guard	Virginia	---	Inf.	185	9	3	09-Sep-62	---	Knight's Factory
Goode, J. L.	14th	Alabama	A	Inf.	178	7	3	13-Jun-64	DOW	Crumpton's Factory
Goodman, H.	5th	Alabama	K	Inf.	201	4	4	21-Jul-64	---	Knight's Factory
Goodrum, C. H.	11th	North Carolina	A	Inf.	194	5	5	10-May-64	Unknown	Knight's Factory
Goodrun, J. Z.	1st Engineers	South Carolina	F	Inf.	189	7	5	21-Nov-62	---	Ferguson's Factory
Goodson, Bailey (Basley?)	2nd	Georgia	B	Inf.	122	9	2	18-Jul-62	Pneumonia	Christian's Factory
Goolsby, William M.	44th	Mississippi	E	Inf.	162	1	1	18-Nov-62	---	Ferguson's Factory
Gordin, Alexander	38th	South Carolina	G	Inf.	144	7	3	18-Aug-62	Febris Typhoides	Crumpton's Factory
Gordon, Abram	14th	Virginia	C	Inf.	161	5	4	06-Dec-62	Tuberculosis	Reid's Factory
Gordon, Benjamin F.	12th	North Carolina	I	Inf.	146	2	4	08-Jul-62	Diphtheria	Knight's Factory
Gordon, James	13th	North Carolina	D	Inf.	160	8	1	06-Dec-62	---	Crumpton's Factory
Gordon, W. D.	37th	Mississippi	B	Inf.	146	1	4	30-Jul-62	---	Ford's Factory
Govins, Joshua	18th	Georgia	F	Inf.	162	4	5	10-Jan-63	---	Reid's Factory
Gower, I. (or J.)	16th	Louisiana	I	Inf.	180	2	2	21-May-64	---	Taliaferro's Factory
Goynes, Wiley W., Sgt.	1st	Georgia	B	Inf.	193	4	2	03-Jan-63	DOW 12/13/62	College Hospital
Grace, Thomas (or Green) Co-pl.	61st	Georgia	B	Inf.	79	10	5	30-Oct-62	Pneumonia	Ferguson's Factory
Grace, William R.	49th	Georgia	F	Inf.	182	5	4	13-Aug-62	---	Ferguson's Factory
Graham, Chesley C.	23rd	Alabama	B	Inf.	177	9	3	26-Apr-62	---	Ford's Factory
Graham, Enoch	5th	Mississippi	B	Inf.	168	8	1	23-Nov-61	---	Warwick House
Graham, J. A.	19th	Louisiana	K	Inf.	170	4	1	07-Jun-64	DOW 5/12/64	Ladies Relief Hospt.
Graham, James	6th	North Carolina	B	Inf.	201	14th	3	14-Dec-62	Small Pox	College Hospital
Graham, James C.	4th	Florida	H	Inf.	Yk. Sq.	10	3rd Line	10-Nov-62	Typhoid Fever	Pest House
Graham, John R. B., 5th Sgt.	5th	Virginia	C	Inf.	182	2	1	24-Nov-62	Diarrhea	Christian's Factory
Graley, James B.	57th				100					Claytor's Factory

* See Part III

NAME	REGT. or UNIT	STATE	COMPANY	BRANCH of SERVICE	LOT#	Grave No.	ROW	DATE of BURIAL or DEATH	CAUSE of DEATH	HOSPITAL
Granger, J. M.	6th	Georgia	D	Inf.	144	7	1	17-Nov-62	---	Candler's Factory
Granger, James (also Grainger)	2nd	South Carolina	K	Inf.	180	7	4	04-Oct-62	---	College Hospital
Grant, Robert A.	14th	South Carolina	I	Inf.	182	2	2	17-Oct-62	Gunshot Wound	Ford's Factory
Grant, Thomas	8th	Louisiana	E	Inf.	171	10	3	30-May-62	---	Christian's Factory
Grant, William P.	44th	Alabama	B	Inf.	195	1	3	13-Feb-63	---	Christian's Factory
Graves, Zebedee	46th	North Carolina	F	Inf.	199	1	2	08-Mar-63	Pneumonia	Christian's Factory
Gray, Henry W.	57th	Virginia	I	Inf.	79	3	5	14-Jan-63	Pneumonia (Smallpox)	Langhorne's Factory
Gray, Lorenzo D.	44th	Alabama	C	Inf.	194	7	4	15-Jul-64	Chronic Diarrhae	Booker's Factory
Gray, Phillip F., Sgt.	12th	Alabama	F	Inf.	159	4	3	13-Sep-61	---	Warwick House
Greatheouse, Jonas, Sgt.	31st	Virginia	C	Inf.	Yk. Sq.	6th	5th Line	21-Aug-62	Small Pox	Pest House
Greathouse, Silas	31st	Virginia	C	Inf.	101	5	1	29-Dec-62	---	Candler's Factory
Green, Boswell	9th	Kentucky	E	Cav.	192	10	1	18-Jun-63	Measles	Pest House
Green, Cullen T.	14th	Georgia	B	Inf.	177	2	4	19-Aug-62	KIA ?	Reid's Factory
Green, J. J.	11th	Georgia	C	Inf.	196	7	4	26-Aug-63	---	Ferguson's Factory
Green, J. M.	10th Battn.	Georgia	B	Inf.	79	1	3	14-Jan-63	---	Claytor's Factory
Green, J. W.	9th	Louisiana	I	Inf.	179	7	5	17-Sep-62	---	Miller's Factory
Greenlee, L. B.	1st (US ?)	Tennessee	H	Cav.	202	7	2	22-May-65	---	Pratts Hospital
Gregory, Robert P.	18th	South Carolina	F	Inf.	179	6	2	15-Sep-62	Febris Typhoides	Miller's Factory
Gregory, William	54th (Deserter)	North Carolina	G	Inf.	193	3	3	23-May-64	Shot to Death	Wayside Hospital
Griffin, Benjamin	13th	North Carolina	G	Inf.	123	8	5	24-Dec-62	Pneumonia	Candler's Factory
Griffin, David H.	3rd	Georgia	D	Inf.	199	2	3	26-Mar-63	---	Candler's Factory
Griffin, Frederick	49th	Georgia	C	Inf.	180	7	2	03-Oct-62	Typhoid Fever	Christian's Factory
Griffin, John Y.	1st	North Carolina	I	Inf.	199	2	1	24-Mar-63	Pneumonia	Knight's Factory
Griffin, Nathan	13th	Georgia	G	Inf.	201	8	5	07-Jun-64	DOW 05/12/64	Christian's Factory
Griffin, Thomas A.	13th	Georgia	H	Inf.	196	3	3	01-Nov-63	---	College Hospital
Griffin, William A.	48th	Georgia	H	Inf.	196	1	5	16-Sep-63	DOW 7/21/63	Chamber's Hospital
Griffin, William H.	21st	Georgia	E	Inf.	168	3	2	26-Apr-62	Chronic Diarrhoea	College Hospital
Griffith, David H.	3rd	Georgia	L	Cav.	192	1	1	09-Jul-63	Disease	Burton's Factory
Grigg, Thomas R.	13th	Virginia	A	Inf.	194	6	2	18-Jul-64	Dysentery	Claytor's Factory
Grounds, John	8th	Louisiana	G	Inf.	161	7	1	16-Jul-62	---	Tallaferro's Factory
Gudger, Charles C.	14th	North Carolina	F	Inf.	173	4	2	09-Jul-62	Typhoid Fever	College Hospital
Guffey, Noah.	18th	North Carolina	F	Inf.	194	4	1	22-Jul-64	DOW 5/06/64	Booker's Factory
Gunn, John H.	31st	Virginia	F	Inf.	161	4	4	06-Aug-62	Typhoid Fever	Ladies Relief Hospt.
Gunter, Joseph	16th	Mississippi	D	Inf.	167	3	1	12-May-62	---	College Hospital
Hackney, John F.	21st	Georgia	D	Inf.	168	7	3	07-May-62	---	College Hospital
Haffy, Patrick	15th	Virginia	F	Inf.	169	3	4	24-May-62	---	Christian's Factory
Haggard, William R.	5th Battn.	Virginia	A	Inf.	161	2	5	11-Jul-62	---	Miller's Factory
Hagins, M. (or Hagin)	9th	Georgia	H	Inf.	192	6	2	01-Jul-63	---	Booker's Factory
Hagler, A. A.	7th	North Carolina	A	Inf.	200	8	3	09-Dec-63	Pneumonia	Booker's Factory

* See Part III - 76

NAME	REGT. or UNIT	STATE	COMPANY	BRANCH of SERVICE	LOT#	Grave No.	ROW	DATE of BURIAL or DEATH	CAUSE of DEATH	HOSPITAL
Haisten, W. P.	2nd Battn.	Georgia	D	Inf.	123	2	5	20-Dec-62	---	Ford's Factory
Haizlip, Franklin C.	57th	Virginia	D	Inf.	78	9	2	01-Dec-62	Typhoid Fever	Crumpton's Factory
Haley, John	8th	Virginia	B	Inf.	160	6	2	20-Jul-62	---	Crumpton's Factory
Hall, Edwin M.	Palmetto Sh.Shooters	South Carolina	L	Inf.	122	10	2	06-Dec-62	---	Saunder's Factory
Hall, James	21st	North Carolina	L	Inf.	159	1	2	30-Aug-61	---	Warwick House
* Hall, L. J. (James A.?)	14th	South Carolina	I	Inf.	180	6	1	06-Oct-62	Hepatitis	Knight's Factory
* Hall, Richard H.	42nd	Virginia	D	Inf.	185	5	1	12-Mar-64	Typhoid Fever	Lynch Adams House
* Hall, Richard J.	4th	North Carolina	B	Inf.	169	8	3	26-May-62	Fever	Crumpton's Factory
Hall, W. A.	60th	Georgia	C	Inf.	190	5	2	02-Jul-64	---	Camp Davis
Hall, William	3rd	Georgia	D	Inf.	123	4	4	21-Dec-62	---	Christian's Factory
Hallaway, F. W.	22nd	North Carolina	F	Inf.	184	4	2	07-May-63	---	Langhorne's Factory
Hallman, G. R.	Palmetto Sh.Shooters	South Carolina	F	Inf.	189	9	3	01-May-64	Typhoid Fever	Camp Davis
Ham, Counsel	27th	North Carolina	K	Inf.	101	9	1	02-Jan-63	Diarrhea	Taliaferro's Factory
Hamady, William	27th	North Carolina	I	Inf.	189	8	5	08-May-64	Unknown	Camp Davis
Hambrick, J.	12th	Georgia	C	Inf.	202	10	5	08-Mar-65	---	Christian's Factory
Hamby, Thomas N.	47th	Alabama	B	Inf.	193	9	4	06-Sep-64	---	Langhorne's Factory
* Hamilton, F. F.	1st	North Carolina	G	Inf.	189	7	1	07-May-64	Pneumonia	Burton's Factory
* Hamilton, H.	4th	Texas	B	Inf.	160	5	1	04-Jul-62	Typhoid Fever	Christian's Factory
Hamner, Sanford V.	11th	North Carolina	E	Inf.	159	7	3	23-Sep-61	---	Warwick House
* Hammond, Benjamin P.	1st Orr's Rifles	South Carolina	D	Inf.	197	10	4	23-May-64	DOW's 5/05/64	Knight's Factory
Hampton, E. J.	17th	Tennessee	D	Inf.	202	10	2	30-May-65	---	Crumpton's Factory
Hancock, D.	21st	Mississippi	H	Inf.	100	9	1	27-Nov-62	---	Ferguson's Factory
Hancock, J.	Phillip's Legion	Georgia	C	Inf.	183	8	2	18-Jan-63	---	Ferguson's Factory
Handy, John W.	37th Battn.	Virginia	A	Cav.	190	5	1	01-Jul-64	DOW 6/18/64	Camp Davis
Hanes, S. C.	1st Battn. S. S.	North Carolina	B	Inf.	200	5	2	10-Dec-63	Unknown	Langhorne's Factory
Haney, George W.	22nd	North Carolina	K	Inf.	146	7	4	14-Dec-62	Pneumonia	Christian's Factory
Haniford,George	20th	Mississippi	McGehee's	Inf.	158	8	4	27-Aug-61	---	T. Mason's
Hanna, Andrew Kerns	14th	Virginia	A	Cav.	198	9	2	13-Aug-64	DOW 6/17/64	Ladies Relief Hospt.
* Hardee, Isaac	1st (McCreary's)	South Carolina	C	Inf.	123	9	1	17-Dec-62	DOW 9/17/62	Burton's Factory
* Hardee, Isaac B., Corpl.	1st (McCreary's)	South Carolina	F	Inf.	173	4	5	05-Jul-62	Pneumonia	Burton's Factory
Hardee, J. A.	26th	Alabama	C	Inf.	173	5	4	03-Jul-62	---	Christian's Factory
Hardegree, Hiram	44th	Georgia	A	Inf.	79	5	5	11-Jan-63	Typhoid Pneumonia	Christian's Factory
Hardin, Elijah	28th	North Carolina	H	Inf.	177	2	3	22-Aug-62	Febris Typhoides	Miller's Factory
Hardin, Crayton Elijah	28th	North Carolina	H	Inf.	192	5	3	08-Jul-63	Febris Typhoides	College Hospital
Hardin, Samuel	2nd Rifles	South Carolina	C	Inf.	200	3	3	25-Jan-64	Disease	Crumpton's Factory
* Hardman, B.	47th	Alabama	G	Inf.	146	1	1	11-Dec-62	---	Knight's Factory
Hardman, William R.	38th	Georgia	B	Inf.	162	10	2	05-Aug-62	---	Warwick House
Hardwick, S. M.	7th	South Carolina	D	Inf.	194	6	1	16-Jul-64	Pneumonia	Christian's Factory
Hardy, Anderson	51st	Georgia	D	Inf.	181	6	1	27-Oct-62	---	Claytor's Factory
Hardy, James	49th	Georgia	C	Inf.	191	2	2	11-Feb-63	Pneumonia	Christian's Factory

* See Part III - 77

NAME	REGT. or UNIT	COMPANY	STATE	BRANCH of SERVICE	LOT#	Grave No.	ROW	DATE of BURIAL or DEATH	CAUSE of DEATH	HOSPITAL
Hardy, John W.	10th Battn.	D	Georgia	Inf.	195	3	4	23-Feb-63	---	Crumpton's Factory
Harford, Harvey	22nd	F	Virginia	Inf.	194	5	1	19-Jul-64	---	Camp Davis
Hargett, William	42nd	F	Mississippi	Inf.	196	8	4	20-Aug-63	---	Booker's Factory
Hargrove, Jesse H. (Hargraves)	60th	1	Georgia	Inf.	182	9	3	13-Nov-62	Erysipelas	Langhorne's Factory
Harmon, J. M.	48th	K	North Carolina	Inf.	187	8	5	22-Jan-63	Phthisis Pulmonaris	Christian's Factory
Harp, G. W.	7th	C	Georgia	Inf.	159	5	5	14-Oct-61	---	Warwick House
Harper, Benjamin Harrison	6th	A	Alabama	Inf.	179	6	1	16-Sep-62	---	Booker's Factory
Harper, Ellis Dallas	16th	A	Georgia	Inf.	188	1	5	28-Feb-64	---	College Hospital
Harper, Seaborn J., 2nd Corpl.	31st	H	Georgia	Inf.	177	7	4	24-Aug-62	---	Burton's Factory
Harrell, Benjamin C.	48th	E	Georgia	Inf.	192	9	2	22-Jun-63	Pneumonia	Ferguson's Factory
Harris, A. J.	47th	D	Alabama	Inf.	201	5	2	12-Jun-64	---	College Hospital
Harris, Alexander H., 3rd Lt.	47th	C	North Carolina	Inf.	201	6	5	09-Jun-64	DOW 5/8/64	Booker's Factory
Harris, Charles G.	34th	K	North Carolina	Inf.	177	8	4	22-Aug-62	Febris Typhoides	Warwick House
Harris, George W.	33rd	B	North Carolina	Inf.	123	10	2	09-Feb-63	Pneumonia	Langhorne's Factory
Harris, J. G.	19th	K	Mississippi	Inf.	161	6	2	19-Jul-62	---	Warwick House
Harris, John	25th	G	North Carolina	Inf.	Yk. Sq.	17th	4th Line	26-Dec-62	Small Pox	Pest House
Harris, John C.	11th	K	Alabama	Inf.	162	4	3	26-Jul-62	---	Ladies Relief Hospt.
Harris, Philip Andrew Jackson	10th	A	Alabama	Inf.	201	6	1	10-Jun-64	---	Camp Davis
Harris, W. J.	8th	B	Alabama	Inf.	179	5	2	14-Sep-62	---	College Hospital
Harrison, A. R.	27th	C	Georgia	Inf.	173	10	3	24-Jun-52	---	Saunder's Factory
Harrison, Franklin B.	21st	B	Georgia	Inf.	168	8	4	04-May-62	Disease	Ferguson's Factory
Harrison, Issac S.	13th	H	Virginia	Inf.	200	5	3	04-Jan-64	Tuberculosis	Crumpton's Factory
Harrison, J. H.	45th	E	North Carolina	Inf.	202	8	5	08-Apr-65	---	Knight's Factory
Harrison, James T.	16th	B	Virginia	Inf.	187	7	4	23-Jan-63	Pneumonia	Talliaferro's Factory
Harrison, John W.	17th	G	Georgia	Inf.	170	6	1	06-Dec-61	---	R. A. Lee's
Harrison, Thomas	11th	I	Georgia	Inf.	187	7	3	24-Jan-63	Disease	Reid's Factory
Harris, B.	15th	C	North Carolina	Inf.	178	6	5	17-Sep-62	Rubeola	Claytor's Factory
Harris, C. J.	15th	E	Alabama	Inf.	171	2	1	05-Jun-62	---	Claytor's Factory
Harroldson, William	49th	I	Georgia	Inf.	79	6	2	09-Jan-63	---	Miller's Factory
Harroll, D.	5th (6th?)	D	South Carolina	Inf.	171	4	1	06-Jun-62	DOD	Ferguson's Factory
Hart, Edwin	5th	F	Texas	Inf.	100	8	2	28-Nov-62	Diarrhea Chronic	Talliaferro's Factory
Hart, James H.	10th	H	Alabama	Inf.	122	2	1	15-May-63	---	Burton's Factory
Hartis, John H.	30th	K	North Carolina	Inf.	Yk. Sq.	20th	1st Line	13-Jan-63	Small Pox	Burton's Factory
Hartley, Herod C.	53rd	C	Georgia	Inf.	194	5	2	18-Jul-64	---	Christian's Factory
Hartman, Thomas H.	5th	F	North Carolina	Inf.	195	4	2	19-Mar-63	Typhoid Fever	Ferguson's Factory
Harvey, Albert G.	21st	E	Virginia	Inf.	172	6	5	19-Jun-62	---	Ladies Relief Hospt.
Hass, Henry James	1st	D	Texas	Inf.	186	1	3	26-Jun-64	DOW 5/06/64	Knight's Factory
Hass, James F., Sgt.	33rd	A	Virginia	Inf.	188	6	3	10-Jun-63	Typhoid Fever	Crumpton's Factory
Hatch, J. R.	44th	E	North Carolina	Inf.	196	3	2	06-Oct-63	Febris Typhoides	Langhorne's Factory
Hatton, William, 2nd Lt.	49th	B	Georgia	Inf.	123	6	4	23-Dec-62	Pneumonia	Ferguson's Factory

* See Part III - 78

NAME	REGT. or UNIT	STATE	COMPANY	BRANCH of SERVICE	LOT#	Grave No.	ROW	DATE of BURIAL or DEATH	CAUSE of DEATH	HOSPITAL
Havner, Willey	16th	North Carolina	M	Inf.	167	9	3	13-May-62	Phthisis Pulmonaris	Christian's Factory
Hawkins, Charles A.	33rd	North Carolina	D	Inf.	192	4	3	14-Jul-63	Febris Typhoides	Crumpton's Factory
Hawkins, E. S., 3rd Corpl.	23rd	Georgia	G	Inf.	122	1	1	23-Nov-62	:::	Candler's Factory
Hawkins, Frederick	33rd	North Carolina	E	Inf.	101	10	5	01-Jan-63	Febris Typhoides	Burton's Factory
Hawkins, Thomas	2nd Rifles	South Carolina	E	Inf.	182	4	4	30-Oct-62	Pneumonia	Claytor's Factory
Hayes, B. J.	13th	Mississippi	A	Inf.	170	8	4	07-Apr-62	:::	College Hospital
Hayes, Jesse	6th	North Carolina	K	Inf.	190	8	5	27-Jun-64	Typhoid Fever	Camp Davis
Hayes, John H.	6th	Alabama		Inf.	158	3	2	25-Jun-61	:::	College Hospital
Haynes, E.	Davis's Battery	Alabama	Lynch's	Art.	188	5	4	18-Jun-63	:::	Ladies Relief Hospt.
Haynes, W. H.	57th	North Carolina	G	Inf.	187	2	5	06-Feb-63	:::	Burton's Factory
Haynes, William S., 3rd Corpl.	19th	Georgia	H	Inf.	159	5	4	11-Nov-61	:::	College Hospital
Hayre, James J. (poss. Hayner)	16th	Virginia	B	Inf.	200	4	4	17-Nov-63	Meningitis	Knight's Factory
Hays, LeRoy (or Hayes), Corpl.	38th	Georgia	C	Inf.	162	2	3	07-Sep-62	:::	College Hospital
Hayslip, William H.	48th	Georgia	E	Inf.	190	4	3	04-Jul-64	:::	Camp Davis
Heard, W. G., 3rd Sgt.	45th	Georgia	I	Inf.	197	8	5	25-May-64	DOW 5/23/64	Crumpton's Factory
Hebberman, John	Letcher's Batty.	Virginia	-	Art.	177	1	4	01-Sep-62	:::	College Hospital
Hedrick, Peter	32nd	North Carolina	E	Inf.	200	8	4	03-Dec-63	Diarrhea	Burton's Factory
Hembree, Francis M. (or Hembry)	11th	Georgia	C	Inf.	161	10	5	09-Jul-62	Pneumonia	Christian's Factory
Hembree, Robert (Hembrey?)	13th	South Carolina	I	Inf.	180	8	1	30-Sep-62	:::	Reid's Factory
Henderson, Edmond S.	26th	Georgia	H	Inf.	180	4	2	26-Sep-62	:::	Crumpton's Factory
Henderson, J.	9th	Georgia	E	Inf.	186	2	1	25-Jun-64	:::	Crumpton's Factory
Henderson, Riley	3rd	North Carolina	B	Inf.	146	5	4	12-Dec-62	Diarrhea Chronic	Saunder's Factory
Henderson, William H.	44th	Alabama	H	Inf.	182	6	1	04-Nov-62	Fever	Miller's Factory
Hendricks, D.	30th	Virginia	C	Inf.	190	1	3	05-Jul-64	:::	Camp Nichols
Henley, John D.	14th	Tennessee	C	Inf.	179	2	3	14-Sep-62	:::	Talliaferro's Factory
Henry, R.	12th	Alabama	I	Inf.	189	5	5	09-May-64	:::	Ferguson's Factory
Hepler, William	27th	Virginia	C	Inf.	178	6	3	11-Sep-62	Typhoid Fever	Miller's Factory
Heppenstall, Samuel C.	22nd	Virginia	D	Inf.	198	7	4	14-Sep-64	Febris Typhoid	Knight's Factory
Herbert, A.	10th	Louisiana	I	Inf.	197	7	2	27-May-64	:::	Crumpton's Factory
Herendon, G. W.	49th	Georgia	E	Inf.	192	7	4	03-Jul-63	:::	Ferguson's Factory
Herrin, J. T.	15th	Alabama	H	Inf.	78	9	3	14-Dec-62	:::	College Hospital
Herrington, M. A.	17th	Mississippi	I	Inf.	170	8	5	18-Apr-62	:::	Knight's Factory
Hickman, Wiley W.	45th	Georgia	D	Inf.	198	3	5	19-Jan-65	DOW 5/06/64	Knight's Factory
Hicks, James L.	14th	Tennessee	B	Inf.	194	6	5	18-Jul-64	:::	Langhorne's Factory
Hicks, James L., Corpl.	6th	Alabama	I	Inf.	198	2	3	19-Dec-64	:::	Reid's Factory
Hicks, John M.	9th	Louisiana	D	Inf.	169	2	1	23-May-62	:::	Crumpton's Factory
Hidle, W. J. (or Hydle)	8th	Georgia	H	Inf.	160	4	3	06-Jul-62	:::	Norvell House
Hight, John C.	8th (Deserter)	Virginia	B	Cav.	200	7	1	06-Jan-64	Shot to Death	Pest House
Hill, Aaron O., (or Aaron B.)	60th	Georgia	B	Inf.	Yk. Sq.	-	-	10-Mar-64	Small Pox	Crumpton's Factory
Hill, Alexander	43rd	North Carolina	D	Inf.	188	4	3	21-Jun-63	Febris Typhoides	

* See Part III - 79

NAME	REGT. or UNIT	STATE	COMPANY	BRANCH of SERVICE	LOT#	Grave No.	ROW	DATE of BURIAL or DEATH	CAUSE of DEATH	HOSPITAL
Hill, P. M.	9th	Louisiana	H	Inf.	173	9	5	29-Jun-62	---	Ladies Relief Hospt.
Hill, G. G., 2nd Corpl.	15th	Alabama	D	Inf.	170	7	2	02-Jan-62	Disease	College Hospital
Hill, H. G.	7th	North Carolina	F	Inf.	180	4	5	02-Oct-62	Typhoid Fever	Burton's Factory
Hill, John B.	6th	Alabama	F	Inf.	202	7	3	06-Apr-65	---	Camp Davis
Hill, John D.	15th	North Carolina	K	Inf.	183	8	3	17-Jan-63	Unknown	Burton's Factory
Hill, W. C.	7th	South Carolina	D	Inf.	162	2	2	22-Jul-62	---	Ford's Factory
Hill, Wilson S.	6th	Alabama	G	Inf.	161	5	1	21-Jul-62	---	Knight's Factory
Hillhouse, Samuel Porter, Sgt.	2nd	South Carolina	L	Inf.	144	9	1	13-Nov-62	Pneumonia	Ferguson's Factory
Hilton, L. W.	53rd	Georgia	H	Inf.	144	2	2	15-Nov-62	Pneumonia	College Hospital
Hines, Stephen H.	3rd	Georgia	A	Inf.	177	5	2	22-Aug-62	---	Langhorne's Factory
Hobby, J. N.	15th	Alabama	B	Inf.	199	1	4	08-Mar-63	---	Wade's Factory
Hodge, Joseph P.	Staunton Batty.	Virginia	-	Art.	196	6	5	05-Sep-63	---	Camp Davis
Hodges, J.	1st	Alabama	B	Inf.	181	4	2	27-Oct-62	Typhoid Fever	Claytor's Factory
Hodges, Jesse	21st	North Carolina	C	Inf.	168	1	1	20-Apr-62	Febris Congestive	Warwick House
Hodges, John C.	15th	South Carolina	E	Inf.	184	5	2	07-May-63	---	Langhorne's Factory
Hodges, Josiah	41st	Virginia	F	Inf.	146	8	1	14-Dec-62	---	College Hospital
Hodoe, James R.	47th	Alabama	C	Inf.	123	1	5	19-Dec-62	---	Talliaferro's Factory
Hoffman, J. E. (of Huffman)	22nd	Georgia	D	Inf.	161	9	5	09-Jul-62	Disease	Christian's Factory
Hogg, Samuel B.	47th	North Carolina	D	Inf.	188	5	5	15-Jun-63	Rheumatism Chronic	Camp Davis
Holbert, Jacob P.	1st	Arkansas	Boswell's	Inf.	158	2	1	22-May-61	---	Piedmont House
Holbrooks, Joshua	23rd	North Carolina	B	Inf.	183	3	2	16-Jan-63	Pneumonia	Miller's Factory
Holland, B. F.	1st	Texas	A	Art.	198	9	1	07-Aug-64	DOW 5/06/64	Camp Davis
Holland, D.	Mcintosh's Battn.	Unknown	-	Inf.	194	8	5	13-Jul-64	---	Christian's Factory
Holland, James	1st	Virginia	E	Inf.	144	3	1	16-Nov-62	---	Miller's Factory
Holliday, A. J.	7th	Louisiana	H	Inf.	195	10	5	10-Feb-63	---	C. Thompson's
Hollingsworth, I.	50th	Georgia	H	Inf.	178	4	4	04-Sep-52	---	College Hospital
Hollingsworth, James M.	22nd	North Carolina	H	Inf.	192	2	1	11-Aug-63	---	Camp Davis
Hollingsworth, William A.	18th	Georgia	B	Inf.	201	9	5	07-Jun-64	DOW 5/06/64	Candler's Factory
Holloway, John	5th	Alabama	K	Inf.	177	4	5	26-Aug-62	---	College Hospital
Holloway, S. H.	7th	North Carolina	G	Inf.	146	4	5	10-Dec-62	Diarrhea	Claytor's Factory
Holly, Jesse J.	5th	Alabama	H	Inf.	178	3	5	03-Sep-62	---	Crumpton's Factory
Hollyfield, W.	5th	Alabama	D	Inf.	193	3	4	20-May-64	---	Candler's Factory
Holmes, Jas. H.	Champman's Batty	Virginia	-	Art.	198	1	1	11-Nov-64	Drowned	James River
Holmes, William H.	15th	Alabama	F	Inf.	168	5	5	06-May-62	---	Warwick House
Holt, Charles W.	42nd	Virginia	B	Inf.	168	9	5	27-Apr-62	---	Christian's Factory
Holt, Henry Alex (Alexander?)	42nd	North Carolina	C	Inf.	179	5	3	02-Aug-62	Febris Typhoides	Ladies Relief Hospt.
Holt, Jonathan	3rd	Arkansas	B	Inf.	158	7	2	17-Jul-61	---	Mrs. Preston's
Holt, W. S.	9th	Louisiana	F	Inf.	162	8	5	29-Jul-62	---	Miller's Factory
Holtzezaw, William H. B.	31st	Georgia	E	Inf.	Yk. Sq.	3rd	5th Line	27-Jul-63	Small Pox	Pest House
Holyfield, Enoch	21st	North Carolina	H	Inf.	186	8	1	18-Jun-64	Killed in Action	Battle of Lynchburg

* See Part III - 80

NAME	REGT. or UNIT	STATE	COMPANY	BRANCH of SERVICE	LOT#	Grave No.	ROW	DATE of BURIAL or DEATH	CAUSE of DEATH	HOSPITAL
Honeycut, W.	4th	North Carolina	A	Inf.	179	1	3	12-Sep-62	Gun Shot Wound	Langhorne's Factory
Hood, Daniel	9th	Alabama	E	Inf.	172	3	4	24-Jun-62	---	Ferguson's Factory
Hood, J. J.	44th	Alabama	B	Inf.	122	3	1	21-Nov-62	---	Christian's Factory
Hood, John J.	23rd	South Carolina	G	Inf.	178	10	3	25-Aug-62	Febris Typhoides	Ferguson's Factory
Hopkins, Charles	32nd	Virginia	F	Inf.	122	1	1	17-Nov-62	---	Christian's Factory
Hopkins, James F.	28th	North Carolina	D	Inf.	173	5	5	04-Jul-62	Gastro Enteritis	Langhorne's Factory
Hopkins, John J.	16th	Mississippi	F	Inf.	171	10	2	31-May-62	---	William Lane's
Hopper, W.	13th	Mississippi	B	Inf.	Yk. Sq.	27th	2nd Line	14-Feb-63	Small Pox	Pest House
Hopper, William	42nd	Virginia	A	Inf.	188	2	3	10-Jun-63	Typhoid Fever	Camp Davis
Horton, H. W.	26th	Alabama	C	Inf.	160	1	2	04-Jul-62	---	Warwick House
Hottle, Joseph	5th	Virginia	K	Inf.	168	9	3	27-Apr-62	---	Warwick House
Houchen, Charles H.	31st	Virginia	G	Inf.	Yk. Sq.	-	-	08-Dec-63	Small Pox	Pest House
Howard, Allen M., Sgt.	48th	North Carolina	G	Inf.	78	8	2	01-Dec-62	Debilitus	Christian's Factory
Howard, Wiley	54th	North Carolina	G	Inf.	79	10	3	23-May-63	---	College Hospital
Howell, G. D.	31st	Georgia	F	Inf.	162	9	5	28-Jul-62	---	Odd Fellow's Hall
Howell, William	48th	Alabama	A	Inf.	191	7	3	04-Feb-63	---	College Hospital
Howell, William W.	48th	Georgia	A	Inf.	195	3	3	23-Feb-63	---	Ferguson's Factory
Howton, William S.	41st	Alabama	H	Inf.	194	4	3	24-Jul-64	---	Camp Davis
Hoyles, Joseph P.	16th	North Carolina	A	Inf.	172	3	3	27-Jun-62	Disease	Odd Fellow's Hall
Hubbard, F. M.	48th	Alabama	D	Inf.	161	3	1	06-Aug-62	---	Reid's Factory
Huckabee, Thomas M.	14th	Louisiana	I	Inf.	177	3	3	26-Aug-62	DOWs	Reid's Factory
Hudgins, Andrew J.	52nd	North Carolina	K	Inf.	189	6	1	11-May-64	Rubeola	Camp Davis
Hudson, Everett H.	19th	Georgia	F	Inf.	159	7	4	05-Oct-61	Disease	College Hospital
Hudson, James W.	2nd Battn.	North Carolina	B	Inf.	192	9	1	22-Jun-63	---	Christian's Factory
Huffman, John W. (James?)	61st	Alabama	H	Inf.	201	1	5	15-Jun-64	---	College Hospital
Hufford, Daniel H.	8th	Georgia	H	Inf.	201	1	3	13-Jun-64	---	Ferguson's Factory
Huggins, John Joseph	18th	North Carolina	G	Inf.	178	1	2	10-Sep-62	Febris Typhoides	Odd Fellow's Hall
Hughes, N.	Lewis' Battery	Virginia	-	Art.	195	8	2	18-Mar-63	---	College Hospital
Hughes, Patrick	Lynch. Provost Guard	Virginia	H	Inf.	188	6	2	10-Jun-63	---	Planter's Warehouse
Hughes, R. F.	14th	Alabama	H	Inf.	162	6	5	30-Jul-62	---	Booker's Factory
Hughey, William M., 2nd Sgt.	5th	South Carolina	C	Inf.	159	8	4	15-Dec-61	---	College Hospital
Humbre, James F. (Hambre)	18th	South Carolina	E	Inf.	198	7	1	21-Aug-64	---	Ferguson's Factory
Humphreys, J. S.	6th	South Carolina	H	Inf.	182	7	3	10-Nov-62	---	Christian's Factory
Hunney, T. J.	2nd	Mississippi	A	Inf.	165	6	3	11-Sep-62	---	Langhorne's Factory
Hunt, Obediah	14th	North Carolina	I	Inf.	173	6	1	28-Jun-62	Diphtheria	Christian's Factory
Huntley, D. T.	26th	North Carolina	K	Inf.	193	7	3	17-May-64	---	Christian's Factory
Hurst, William E.	50th	Georgia	E	Inf.	101	2	2	30-Dec-62	Pneumonia	College Hospital
Hutchinson, Thomas A.	50th	Georgia	E	Inf.	198	1	2	11-Nov-64	DOW's 10/19/64	College Hospital
Hyatt, -----	35th	Georgia	B	Inf.	171	3	5	05-Jun-62	---	College Hospital
Hyatt, Phillip E.	21st	Georgia	G	Inf.	182	1	1	20-Oct-62	Disease	Miller's Factory

* See Part III - 81

NAME	REGT. or UNIT	STATE	COMPANY	BRANCH of SERVICE	LOT#	Grave No.	ROW	DATE of BURIAL or DEATH	CAUSE of DEATH	HOSPITAL
Hydrick, Powell	5th	Alabama	F	Inf.	162	9	1	02-Aug-62	---	Warwick House
Ingram, Andrew	28th	North Carolina	K	Inf.	197	3	5	01-Jun-64	Abscessus Chronic	College Hospital
Ingram, Benjamin F.	59th	Georgia	C	Inf.	201	2	3	18-Jun-64	DOW 5/06/64	Reid's Factory
Ingram, William	55th	Virginia	K	Inf.	165	9	3	12-Aug-62	Diarrhea Chronic	Ladies Relief Hospt.
Inmon, George	6th	South Carolina	D	Inf.	79	8	4	08-Jan-63	Typhoid Fever	Crumpton's Factory
Irwin, William A.	17th	South Carolina	C	Inf.	178	3	1	30-Aug-62	---	Ferguson's Factory
Jackson, --	Unknown	Unknown	-	-	Yk. Sq.	16th	4th Line	20-Dec-62	Small Pox	Pest House
Jackson, Allen	33rd	North Carolina	K	Inf.	191	9	3	31-Jan-63	---	Saunder's Factory
Jackson, Issac V.	19th	Mississippi	K	Inf.	160	1	1	04-Jul-62	Typhoid Fever	Claytor's Factory
Jackson, J.	53rd	Virginia	G	Inf.	78	2	3	04-Dec-62	---	Ferguson's Factory
Jackson, J. W.	54th	Georgia	C	Inf.	187	2	1	27-Jan-63	---	Claytor's Factory
Jackson, Jerry	18th	Georgia	F	Inf.	165	5	3	20-Aug-62	Typhoid Fever	Ferguson's Factory
Jackson, Joshua	55th	Virginia	D	Inf.	182	6	2	03-Nov-62	---	Ferguson's Factory
Jackson, Printice	9th	Louisiana	C	Inf.	170	7	5	01-Mar-62	---	R. Lee's
Jackson, William	48th	North Carolina	K	Inf.	123	7	5	13-Jan-63	Diarrhea Chronic	Reid's Factory
Jackson, William R.	38th	North Carolina	K	Inf.	186	10	3	19-Jun-64	DOW 5/05/64	Knight's Factory
James, A. J. (Andrew Jackson?)	15th	North Carolina	K	Inf.	183	1	3	16-Jan-63	---	Ford's Factory
James, Addison	37th	Virginia	A	Inf.	168	7	2	01-May-62	Typhoid & Pneumonia	Christian's Factory
James, David	48th	North Carolina	H	Inf.	186	5	2	22-Jun-64	Disease	Reid's Factory
James, John H.	9th	Virginia	B	Inf.	144	3	3	30-Oct-62	---	Crumpton's Factory
James, William	16th	Mississippi	F	Inf.	173	2	1	29-Jun-62	---	Reid's Factory
Jameson, W. T.	1st	South Carolina	A	Inf.	172	1	1	19-Jun-62	---	Odd Fellow's Hall
Jarnard, Alex	8th	Louisiana	C	Inf.	169	1	2	20-May-62	---	Reid's Factory
Jarratt, J. O.	Cobb's Legion	Georgia	D	Cav.	197	9	5	24-May-64	---	Christian's Factory
Jenkins, Jeremiah J., Corpl.	20th	Georgia	C	Inf.	159	3	2	30-Dec-61	---	College Hospital
Jenkins, John F.	14th	North Carolina	A	Inf.	187	7	2	27-Jul-63	Phthisis	Saunder's Factory
Jenkins, Joseph M.	25th	North Carolina	C	Inf.	183	5	1	17-Jan-63	Diarrhea	Knight's Factory
Jennergan, W. C.	8th	South Carolina	E	Inf.	161	3	2	02-Aug-62	Febris Typhoides	Knight's Factory
Jennings, Jesse, 3rd Corpl.	14th	South Carolina	B	Inf.	172	7	5	14-Jun-62	Typhoid Fever	Saunder's Factory
Jennings, John	45th	Virginia	C	Inf.	202	10	1	20-Mar-65	---	Crumpton's Factory
Jennings, R. T.	60th	Georgia	I	Inf.	161	4	3	08-Aug-62	Typhoid Fever	Burton's Factory
Jennings, S. K., Sgt.	8th	Alabama	A	Inf.	161	8	4	16-Jul-62	---	Crumpton's Factory
Jerrell, Henry Lump	21st	Georgia	D	Inf.	171	9	5	28-May-62	Typhoid Fever	Ferguson's Factory
Jester, J. A.	41st	Virginia	D	Inf.	122	8	3	23-Nov-62	---	Crumpton's Factory
Jeter, Marion J.	15th	Alabama	I	Inf.	172	8	1	12-Jun-62	Disease	Reid's Factory
Johns, James L., 4th Corpl.	44th	Alabama	I	Inf.	190	3	3	06-Jul-64	DOW	Christian's Factory
Johns, John B.	Orr's Rifles	South Carolina	F	Inf.	189	6	4	11-May-64	Typhoid Fever	Ferguson's Factory
Johnson, Andrew	15th	North Carolina	A	Inf.	179	1	1	12-Sep-62	Dysentery Acute	Miller's Factory

* See Part III - 82

NAME	REGT. or UNIT	STATE	COMPANY	BRANCH of SERVICE	LOT#	Grave No.	ROW	DATE of BURIAL or DEATH	CAUSE of DEATH	HOSPITAL
Johnson, Aris	7th	North Carolina	G	Inf.	165	10	1	12-Aug-62	Typhoid Fever	Crumpton's Factory
Johnson, George	47th	Alabama	K	Inf.	201	4	3	13-Jun-64	DOW	Camp Davis
Johnson, George	2nd	Florida	K	Inf.	179	2	1	16-Sep-62	---	College Hospital
Johnson, George	57th	North Carolina	F	Inf.	198	2	2	06-Dec-64	Pneumonia	Knight's Factory
Johnson, H.	57th	North Carolina	G	Inf.	199	2	5	27-Apr-63	---	College Hospital
Johnson, H. S. (poss. W. S.)	3rd	South Carolina	F	Inf.	144	1	1	12-Nov-62	Disease	Talliaferro's Factory
Johnson, J. F.	1st (Hagood's)	South Carolina	E	Inf.	190	2	5	29-Jul-64	DOW 5/06/64	Christian's Factory
Johnson, J. W.	54th	North Carolina	K	Inf.	198	10	1	02-Jul-64	---	Camp Davis
Johnson, James	16th	Georgia	F	Inf.	180	7	3	01-Oct-62	---	Ferguson's Factory
Johnson, Jason	26th	Georgia	C	Inf.	183	3	3	18-Jan-63	---	College Hospital
Johnson, Josiah L.	15th	Alabama	K	Inf.	166	8	1	07-May-62	---	Ladies Relief Hospt.
Johnson, R. P.	16th	Mississippi	K	Inf.	169	9	5	20-May-62	---	Christian's Factory
Johnson, Robert C. C., Corpl.	4th Battn.	Alabama	A	Inf.	193	10	5	15-May-64	---	Ferguson's Factory
Johnson, Thomas	38th Battn. (?)	Virginia	A	Inf.	198	9	5	11-Aug-64	---	Christian's Factory
Johnson, W. A.	4th	North Carolina	I	Inf.	198	2	5	25-Jan-65	Pneumonia	Knight's Factory
Johnson, Whitfield	11th	Virginia	D	Inf.	169	2	5	19-May-62	Disease	Christian's Factory
Johnson, William	20th	Mississippi	Patterson's	Inf.	158	4	4	20-Aug-61	---	George Lee's
Johnson, William S.	1st	North Carolina	-	Cav.	Yk. Sq.	20th	2nd Line	13-Jan-63	Small Pox	Pest House
Joiner, Guilford D. J.	9th	Georgia	K	Inf.	122	6	1	23-Nov-62	---	Ferguson's Factory
Jolly, Benjamin A.	28th	North Carolina	H	Inf.	169	7	2	26-May-62	Camp Fever	Saunder's Factory
Jolly, Joseph W.	60th	Georgia	H	Inf.	200	6	5	11-Dec-63	---	Ferguson's Factory
Jones, A. J., (or A. I.) Sgt.	60th	Georgia	H	Inf.	162	8	3	04-Aug-62	---	Reid's Factory
Jones, Benjamin E.	54th	North Carolina	K	Inf.	187	1	2	26-Jan-63	Febris Typhodies	Crumpton's Factory
Jones, Daniel P.	20th	Mississippi	Pettis'	Inf.	170	2	1	09-Nov-61	---	College Hospital
Jones, E.	17th	Mississippi	F	Inf.	165	6	2	11-Sep-62	---	Langhorne's Factory
Jones, Gabriel	33rd	North Carolina	K	Inf.	160	7	1	10-Jul-62	Pneumonia	Ferguson's Factory
Jones, H.	16th	Mississippi	E	Inf.	170	1	4	06-Mar-62	---	Ladies Relief Hospt.
Jones, H. B.	16th	Alabama	B	Inf.	193	9	3	15-May-64	---	Christian's Factory
Jones, Isaac	14th	Georgia	G	Inf.	182	6	5	09-Nov-62	DOW 8/09/62	Burton's Factory
Jones, J. M.	11th	South Carolina	G	Inf.	191	10	3	29-Jan-63	---	Ladies Relief Hospt.
Jones, J. T., Corpl.	18th	Mississippi	A	Inf.	190	3	5	07-Jul-64	---	Knight's Factory
Jones, J. W.	Preston's Batty.	Virginia	-	Art.	202	8	1	10-Apr-65	---	Ferguson's Factory
Jones, James, E.	57th	Virginia	C	Inf.	196	5	2	13-Sep-63	Diarrhea	Christian's Factory
Jones, John H.	15th	Alabama	E	Inf.	172	6	1	17-Jun-62	Disease	Ferguson's Factory
Jones, John W.	1st	Texas	M	Inf.	201	10	2	06-Jun-64	DOW 5/06/64	Camp Davis
Jones, Joseph M.	9th	Louisiana	D	Inf.	167	5	3	17-May-62	---	Saunder's Factory
Jones, Levi, Lieut.	29th	Virginia	E	Inf.	196	1	3	17-Sep-63	Typhoid Fever	Christian's Factory
Jones, Lewis	27th	North Carolina	I	Inf.	195	4	5	06-Mar-63	Phthisis Pulmonaris	Knight's Factory
Jones, Mosias H.	56th	Virginia	H	Inf.	179	7	2	17-Sep-62	Chronic Diarrhea	Miller's Factory
Jones, Nathan J.	3rd	North Carolina	B	Inf.	191	9	1	30-Jan-63	Plueritis	College Hospital

* See Part III - 83

NAME	REGT. or UNIT	STATE	COMPANY	BRANCH of SERVICE	LOT#	Grave No.	ROW	DATE of BURIAL or DEATH	CAUSE of DEATH	HOSPITAL
Jones, Paul (Charlotte Co.)	21st	Virginia	A	Inf.	Yk. Sq.	15th	3rd Line	17-Dec-62	Small Pox	Pest House
Jones, Robert	45th	North Carolina	K	Inf.	186	1	1	24-Jun-64	Diarrhea Chronic	Christian's Factory
Jones, Sidney	44th	North Carolina	G	Inf.	196	2	2	28-Sep-63	Diarrhea Chronic	Langhorne's Factory
Jones, Sugar	5th	North Carolina	A	Inf.	180	2	1	22-Sep-62	---	Langhorne's Factory
Jordan, B. E.	14th	South Carolina	L	Inf.	201	10	3	06-Jun-64	---	Burton's Factory
Jordan, Hudson	2nd	Virginia	I	Inf.	182	3	5	19-Oct-62	Typhoid Fever	Miller's Factory
Jordan, J. Gurney	4th	North Carolina	G	Inf.	195	6	3	03-Mar-63	Unknown	Knight's Factory
Jordan, James N.	9th	Louisiana	H	Inf.	177	7	5	23-Aug-62	---	Saunder's Factory
Jordan, W. N. (H.?)	15th	South Carolina	D	Inf.	191	5	5	06-Feb-63	---	Ferguson's Factory
Joy, William	61st (16th ?)	Alabama	H	Inf.	189	7	2	11-May-64	---	Christian's Factory
Joyce, Robert	56th	Virginia	E	Inf.	192	10	3	22-Jun-63	---	Booker's Factory
Judice, J. C.	Donaldson's Batty.	Louisiana	-	Art.	200	10	2	04-Dec-63	---	Not Stated
Juno, R.	8th	Louisiana	A	Inf.	172	5	1	22-Jun-62	---	Crumpton's Factory
Kagle, Henry	24th	Georgia	I	Inf.	162	8	4	02-Aug-62	---	Knight's Factory
Keels, C. A.	10th	Georgia	E	Inf.	201	9	4	07-Jun-64	---	Burton's Factory
Keene, Richard N. (Keen)	61st	Georgia	C	Inf.	178	8	3	04-Sep-62	---	Talliaferro's Factory
Keener, A. L.	24th	Georgia	E	Inf.	173	10	1	23-Jun-62	---	Christian's Factory
Keist, H. C.	5th	South Carolina	D	Inf.	187	8	4	23-Jan-63	DOD	Ferguson's Factory
Keller, Thomas W.	24th	Alabama	B	Inf.	199	8	5	30-Mar-63	---	Langhorne's Factory
Kelly, C. H.	Hunger's Batty.	Virginia	-	Art.	161	1	3	17-Jul-62	---	Langhorne's Factory
Kelly, J. F.	2nd Battn.	Mississippi	-	Inf.	193	6	1	19-May-64	---	Christian's Factory
Kelly, John	15th	Louisiana	D	Inf.	Yk. Sq.	-	-	17-Jun-63	Small Pox	Pest House
Kelly, M.	Graham's Batty.	North Carolina	C 1st	Art.	193	8	4	17-May-64	---	Christian's Factory
Kelly, Samuel S.	5th	South Carolina	H	Inf.	196	10	4	11-Aug-63	Typhoid Fever	Crumpton's Factory
Kelly, Wiley	7th	Georgia	H	Inf.	191	6	2	05-Feb-63	Febris Typhoides	Ferguson's Factory
Kemp, William T.	54th	North Carolina	H	Inf.	159	7	5	30-Oct-61	---	College Hospital
Kennedy, Columbus H., Sgt.	18th	Mississippi	E	Inf.	188	3	2	25-Jul-63	Febris Typhodies	Burton's Factory
Kennedy, T. P.	7th Battn.	Mississippi	G	Inf.	201	7	5	07-Jun-64	---	Crumpton's Factory
Key, Stephen William	20th	Georgia	I	Inf.	160	5	2	07-Jul-62	Chronic Diarrhea	College Hospital
Kimbrough, J. H.	21st	Mississippi	Jasper Rifle's	Inf.	101	8	3	05-Jan-63	Disease	Ford's Factory
King, David	21st	Georgia	E	Inf.	159	3	3	14-Sep-61	---	Carter's
King, George W.	2nd	South Carolina	F	Inf.	170	3	5	30-Mar-62	Disease	Warwick House
King, George Washington	5th Battn.	Alabama	C	Inf.	123	8	4	23-Dec-62	---	Crumpton's Factory
King, H. B.	49th	Georgia	D	Inf.	189	5	1	12-May-64	Disease	Ladies Relief Hospt.
King, Joseph R.	12th	Georgia	F	Inf.	180	10	2	25-Sep-62	Small Pox (poss.)	Reid's Factory
King, William	2nd	North Carolina	F	Inf.	190	1	2	05-Jul-64	DOW's	Langhorne's Factory
Kinkman, O. J.	54th	North Carolina	I	Inf.	122	5	1	24-Nov-62	---	Christian's Factory
Kinlow, James R.		North Carolina			185	10	3	26-Jul-64	DOW 7/01/64	Camp Davis
Kinney, A.	Hunger's Batty.	Virginia	-	Art.	189	8	2	03-May-64	---	Christian's Factory

* See Part III - 84

NAME	REGT. or UNIT	STATE	COMPANY	BRANCH of SERVICE	LOT#	Grave No.	ROW	DATE of BURIAL or DEATH	CAUSE of DEATH	HOSPITAL
Kirby, A. J.	8th	Tennessee	Burford's	Inf.	159	9	2	14-Sep-61	---	College Hospital
Kirby, E. L. (poss C. L.)	9th	Louisiana	G	Inf.	168	6	2	06-May-62	---	Warwick House
Kirby, G. G.	9th	Louisiana	G	Inf.	168	9	4	01-May-62	---	Warwick House
Kirch, Jacob	Franklin Co.	Virginia	---	---	146	8	5	18-Dec-62	---	John Merrill's Home
Kirksey, J. M.	8th	Georgia	F	Inf.	192	1	2	10-Aug-63	---	Burton's Factory
Kiser, Michael	21st	North Carolina	G	Inf.	190	5	5	03-Jul-65	Unknown	Camp Davis
Kitterell, Daniel (also Kintrell)	12th	South Carolina	G	Inf.	79	1	2	11-Jan-63	---	College Hospital
Knowles, John H. J.	26th	Georgia	H	Inf.	173	3	3	02-Jul-62	Parotitis	Crumpton's Factory
Knox, F.	26th	Georgia	D	Inf.	178	1	1	27-Aug-62	---	Ferguson's Factory
Kristyan, J. M.	Vol.'s	Georgia	---	---	170	8	2	31-Dec-62	---	Warwick House
Lacey, Lawrence	1st Regulars	Georgia	K	Inf.	78	8	1	02-Dec-62	---	Reid's Factory
Lackey, James H. C.	57th	Virginia	B	Inf.	181	9	1	12-Sep-62	Diphtheria	Talliaferro's Factory
Lackford, William	2nd	Virginia	E	Inf.	199	5	5	14-Apr-63	---	Ladies Relief Hospt.
Lambeth, James Madison	21st	North Carolina	M	Inf.	159	1	1	28-Aug-61	---	Warwick House
Lambright, George W.	Moody's Batty.	Louisiana	---	Art.	188	8	5	03-Mar-64	---	Camp Davis
Lancaster, William C.	Taylor's Batty.	Virginia	---	Art.	194	3	4	28-Jul-64	Chronic Diarrhea	Burton's Factory
Land, William	2nd	Georgia	C	Inf.	180	5	5	11-Oct-62	---	Burton's Factory
Lane, Richard Q.	35th	Georgia	C	Inf.	179	3	3	17-Sep-62	DOW 5/31/62 (?)	Miller's Factory
Lane, William A.	12th	Georgia	B	Inf.	197	7	3	27-May-64	DOW 5/06/64 & Pyemia	Crumpton's Factory
Laney, G.	6th	Georgia	H	Inf.	180	4	4	01-Oct-62	---	Christian's Factory
Lanford, J. M.	44th	Alabama	A	Inf.	101	10	2	29-Dec-62	---	Saunder's Factory
Langdon, Jabez M.	48th	Georgia	E	Inf.	144	9	2	15-Nov-62	Pneumonia	Candler's Factory
Langford, Francis M., 3rd Corpl.	5th	Florida	B	Inf.	184	9	1	14-Apr-63	Disease	Miller's Factory
Langley, J. T.	6th	Alabama	G	Inf.	146	7	1	16-Dec-62	---	Christian's Factory
Langston, Jesse	15th	Alabama	K	Inf.	170	3	2	01-Feb-62	---	College Hospital
Lanier, George G.	22nd	Georgia	E	Inf.	193	4	3	20-May-64	---	Booker's Factory
Lanier, William L.	38th	Georgia	D	Inf.	187	4	4	26-Jan-63	Typhoid Fever	Claytor's Factory
Lansford, Benjamin F., 2nd Sgt.	47th	Alabama	H	Inf.	180	3	3	26-Sep-62	Disease	Langhorne's Factory
Lassiter, Charles	2nd	North Carolina	D	Inf.	199	10	1	18-Mar-63	Pneumonia	Ferguson's Factory
Lassiter, Issac	12th	Georgia	A	Inf.	167	2	3	12-May-62	Typhoid & Pneumonia	Booker's Factory
Latham, John	26th	North Carolina	A	Inf.	189	7	5	07-May-64	Febris Typhoides	Wayside Hospital
Lawing, Jethro	48th	Alabama	C	Inf.	189	9	5	08-Apr-64	---	Ladies Relief Hospt.
Lawson, H. A.	26th	Georgia	H	Inf.	177	3	1	21-Aug-62	---	College Hospital
Layfield, John W.	35th	Georgia	K	Inf.	195	10	1	12-Feb-63	Typhoid Fever	Ferguson's Factory
Leatherwood, Jefferson J.	16th	North Carolina	L	Inf.	178	2	3	30-Aug-62	Pneumonia	Warwick House
Ledbetter, Anon N.	28th	North Carolina	H	Inf.	187	7	1	24-Jan-63	Unknown	Christian's Factory
Ledford, John	55th	North Carolina	F	Inf.	201	6	3	10-Jun-64	DOW 5/05/64	Knight's Factory
Ledford, John W.	48th	North Carolina	I	Inf.	193	7	1	17-May-64	Febris Typhoid	Christian's Factory
Lee, Francis Marion	50th	Georgia	H	Inf.	201	10	4	01-Jun-64	---	Knight's Factory

* See Part III - 85

NAME	REGT. or UNIT	STATE	COMPANY	BRANCH of SERVICE	LOT#	Grave No.	ROW	DATE of BURIAL or DEATH	CAUSE of DEATH	HOSPITAL
Lee, Isum S.	9th	Louisiana	F	Inf.	173	2	5	01-Jul-62	Disease	Booker's Factory
Lee, James W.	42nd	Virginia	E	Inf.	162	4	1	21-Jun-62	---	Warwick House
Leffler, William M.	5th	North Carolina	B	Inf.	146	2	3	08-Dec-62	Typhoid Pneumonia	Talliaferro's Factory
Leftwitch, G. B.	11th	Mississippi	B	Inf.	189	10	5	05-Feb-64	---	Camp Davis
Leigh, William H.	49th	Virginia	G	Inf.	173	1	4	27-Jun-62	---	Claytor's Factory
Lemmons, John Anderson	22nd	Virginia	F	Inf.	201	3	1	18-Jun-64	Killed in Action	Battle of Lynchburg
Lenear, Drewry G. H.	21st	North Carolina	A	Inf.	190	6	1	01-Jul-64	Unknown	?
Lenhman, Jean Baptist	Lynch. City Guard	Virginia	---	---	170	5	3	20-Jan-62	---	Warwick House
Leslie, Jonathan, Sgt	29th	Virginia	D	Inf.	196	5	3	11-Sep-63	---	Camp Davis
Lester, A. L.	---	Alabama	Covington's	---	158	6	4	25-Aug-61	---	College Hospital
Lester, James	31st	Georgia	F	Inf.	123	3	4	20-Dec-62	---	Claytor's Factory
Levering, Henry	3rd	Arkansas	Newman's	Inf.	158	1	3	15-Jul-61	---	Private Residence
Leving's Jacob	9th	Louisiana	D	Inf.	167	10	1	14-May-62	---	Saunder's Factory
Lewallen, John	52nd	North Carolina	B	Inf.	200	5	5	18-Nov-63	Diarrhea Chronic	Candler's Factory
Lewellen, S.	17th	Mississippi	H	Inf.	79	4	3	13-Jan-63	---	Crumpton's Factory
Lewis, James M.	46th	North Carolina	I	Inf.	201	3	2	18-Jun-64	---	Camp Nichols
Lewis, John W.	44th	Georgia	I	Inf.	162	7	4	07-Aug-62	Pneumonia	Warwick House
Lewis, N. C.	44th	Alabama	G	Inf.	190	9	1	27-Jun-64	---	Christian's Factory
Lewis, W.	1st	North Carolina	E	Inf.	181	7	7	25-Oct-62	---	College Hospital
Lightner, William H.	12th	Mississippi	Miller's	Inf.	158	8	3	07-Aug-61	---	College Hospital
Liles, Emerson H., Sgt.	37th	North Carolina	D	Inf.	171	2	2	02-Jun-62	Febris Remittens	Warwick House
Lindsay, Joseph P.	15th	Alabama	F	Inf.	160	10	2	07-Jul-62	---	Crumpton's Factory
Lindsey, F. F.	14th	Alabama	E	Inf.	180	8	3	01-Oct-62	---	College Hospital
Lindsey, John L.	51st	Georgia	E	Inf.	79	7	3	07-Jan-63	---	Crumpton's Factory
Lindsey, W. H.	9th	Alabama	K	Inf.	172	10	2	09-Jun-62	---	Saunder's Factory
Lindsey, William	51st	Georgia	I	Inf.	79	1	1	10-Jan-63	---	College Hospital
Linker, E.	57th	North Carolina	H	Inf.	199	4	1	03-Apr-63	---	Crumpton's Factory
Linsey, W. B., Sgt.	23rd	South Carolina	H	Inf.	146	1	2	05-Dec-62	DOW 8/30/52	Burton's Factory
Linton, William	Palmetto Sh. Shooter	South Carolina	M	Inf.	Yk. Sq.	23rd	3rd Line	08-Jan-63	Small Pox	Pest House
Lipes, Allen Leffel	22nd	Virginia	C	Inf.	201	2	1	18-Jun-64	Killed in Action	Battle of Lynchburg
Lipford, George	8th	Virginia	F	Inf.	190	2	4	31-Jul-64	Diarrhea Chronic	Christian's Factory
Lipscomb, Thomas H.	13th	South Carolina	I	Inf.	172	5	4	21-Sep-62	Febris Typhoides	College Hospital
Litsey, John W.	47th	Alabama	F	Inf.	196	2	5	16-Sep-63	Disease	Knight's Factory
Little, James S.	21st	Georgia	K	Inf.	168	5	4	12-May-62	DOW 5/03/63	Ferguson's Factory
Litton, William H.	48th	North Carolina	C	Inf.	189	6	3	13-May-64	Gunshot Wound	Ladies Relief Hospt.
Lock, D.	8th	Alabama	D	Inf.	197	10	5	23-May-64	---	Knight's Factory
Lockett, Thomas L.	22nd	Georgia	H	Inf.	184	10	1	13-Apr-63	---	Burton's Factory
Lockport, W. C.	22nd	Georgia	H	Inf.	Yk. Sq.	20th	3rd Line	02-Jan-63	Small Pox	Pest House
Loftis, Edward	Washington's Art.	Louisiana	3rd	Art.	191	2	3	13-Feb-63	Pneumonia	Ladies Relief Hospt.
London, Samuel	Phillip's Legion	Georgia	Hamilton's	Inf.	159	2	5	06-Oct-61	---	Ladies Relief Hospt.

* See Part III - 86

NAME	REGT. or UNIT	STATE	COMPANY	BRANCH of SERVICE	LOT#	Grave No.	ROW	DATE of BURIAL or DEATH	CAUSE of DEATH	HOSPITAL
Long, Benjamin	33rd	North Carolina	H	Inf.	187	3	3	29-Jan-63	Pneumonia	Candler's Factory
Long, D. H.	45th	North Carolina	B	Inf.	198	9	3	08-Aug-64	---	Camp Davis
* Long, Harry	33rd	North Carolina	B	Inf.	122	1	3	18-Nov-62	Diarrhea	Christian's Factory
Long, Joseph L.	54th	North Carolina	K	Inf.	194	3	2	27-Jul-64	---	Ferguson's Factory
Long, Pleasant G.	37th	North Carolina	H	Inf.	178	4	5	30-Sep-62	Diarrhea Chronic	Miller's Factory
Longbottom, Alexander	23rd	North Carolina	H	Inf.	183	5	2	25-Mar-63	Typhoid Fever	Miller's Factory
Looney, I. W.	11th	Georgia	C	Inf.	195	1	5	15-Feb-63	---	Langhorne's Factory
Loper, O. H. P.	13th	Mississippi	Carlton's	Inf.	158	5	3	03-Aug-61	---	College Hospital
* Lovell, William C.	57th	Virginia	F	Inf.	100	5	3	27-Nov-62	Diarrhea	Ladies Relief Hospt.
* Lovins, Author J.	24th	Virginia		Inf.	192	2	3	07-Aug-63	---	Crumpton's Factory
Lowder, Lee	28th	North Carolina	K	Inf.	200	9	1	09-Dec-63	Pneumonia	Reid's Factory
Lucas, Edward H.	22nd	Virginia	C	Inf.	186	5	3	22-Jun-64	Cholera Morbus	Wayside Hospital
Luggs, Holliday, Corpl.	26th	Georgia	D	Inf.	Yk. Sq.	24th	5th Line	29-Jan-63	Small Pox	Pest House
Lunceford, Noah	37th	North Carolina	E	Inf.	171	10	5	30-May-62	Pneumonia	Warwick House
Lusby, John B.	3rd	Arkansas	D	Inf.	195	6	4	02-Mar-63	Brain Fever	Miller's Factory
Lyerly, Jacob C.	28th	North Carolina	D	Inf.	192	2	2	10-Aug-63	Febris Typhoides	Burton's Factory
Lyle, W. C.	16th	Georgia	D	Inf.	Yk. Sq.	-	-	04-Feb-64	Small Pox	Pest House
Lyons, James E.	2nd Battn.	Georgia	D	Inf.	78	7	3	04-Dec-62	---	Knight's Factory
Mabe, Robert F.	4th	Virginia	C	Inf.	169	10	2	21-May-62	Diarrhea Chronic	Claytor's Factory
Mabry, S. B. (L.)	12th	North Carolina	C	Inf.	172	9	5	10-Jun-62	Disease	Langhorne's Factory
Mabry, Thomas F.	14th	North Carolina	H	Inf.	185	3	3	30-Apr-64	Dysenteria Acute	Ferguson's Factory
Maddin, Patrick	1st	Missouri	A	Inf.	196	3	1	25-Sep-63	---	College Hospital
Maddox, Edmond P.	19th	Virginia	I	Inf.	199	4	5	01-Apr-63	Consumption	Christian's Factory
Maddox, Richard	21st	Georgia	D	Inf.	161	1	1	18-Jul-62	Disease	Christian's Factory
Maddox, T. A.	26th	Alabama	I	Inf.	182	3	2	21-Oct-62	---	Ladies Relief Hospt.
Madison, Albert	4th	North Carolina	H	Inf.	201	8	3	06-Jun-64	DOW 5/19/64	Camp Davis
Mahoney, C.	8th	Louisiana	D	Inf.	200	9	2	05-Dec-63	---	Not Stated
Mangold, Micajah C.	24th	Georgia	E	Inf.	79	8	2	05-Jan-63	---	Miller's Factory
Manis, Arron W.	48th	North Carolina	A	Inf.	122	5	3	24-Nov-62	Typhoid Pneumonia	Knight's Factory
* Manning, R. L.	12th	South Carolina	B	Inf.	161	6	4	07-Aug-62	Fever	Christian's Factory
Marchbanks, I. Burrill	8th	Louisiana	K	Inf.	146	1	3	05-Dec-62	Disease	Knight's Factory
Markham, Charles H.	34th	Virginia	E	Inf.	198	8	4	21-Aug-64	---	Wayside Hospital
Marley, John F.	52nd	North Carolina	F	Inf.	197	5	2	27-May-64	Diarrhea	Ferguson's Factory
Marlow, J. S.	18th	Mississippi	A	Inf.	188	4	4	27-Jun-63	---	Langhorne's Factory
* Marshall, E. M.	5th	Texas	E	Inf.	Yk. Sq.	22nd	4th Line	05-Jan-63	Small Pox	Pest House
Marshall, George W.	33rd	North Carolina	A	Inf.	180	1	2	22-Sep-62	Erysipelas	College Hospital
Marshall, George W.	42nd	North Carolina	E	Inf.	172	5	5	15-Jun-62	Unknown	Ladies Relief Hospt.
Marshall, Henry L.	4th	North Carolina	C	Inf.	191	7	1	05-Feb-63	Pneumonia	Ford's Factory
Marshall, W. D.	2nd	South Carolina	G	Inf.	78	2	2	04-Dec-62	Disease	Langhorne's Factory

* See Part III - 87

NAME	REGT. or UNIT	STATE	COMPANY	BRANCH of SERVICE	LOT#	Grave No.	ROW	DATE of BURIAL or DEATH	CAUSE of DEATH	HOSPITAL
Marshall, William G. (or J.)	48th	Georgia	E	Inf.	79	6	1	07-Jan-63	Typhoid Pneumonia	Ferguson's Factory
Martin, Andrew Jackson	19th	Virginia	K	Inf.	171	4	4	06-Jun-62	Pneumonia	Crumpton's Factory
Martin, C. S. (or C. T.)	53rd	Georgia	K	Inf.	101	8	2	02-Jan-63	---	Crumpton's Factory
Martin, George	37th	North Carolina	E	Inf.	192	10	5	25-Jun-63	Febris Typhoides	Langhorne's Factory
Martin, J. M.	38th	North Carolina	C	Inf.	190	10	2	26-Jun-64	Diarrhea	Burton's Factory
Martin, John	Nurse	Virginia	-	Hospt.	178	4	2	05-Sep-62	---	Ferguson's Factory
Martin, John B.	1st	North Carolina	B	Inf.	189	3	4	07-May-64	Pneumonia	Knight's Factory
Martin, John L.	34th	North Carolina	K	Inf.	178	8	5	31-Aug-62	Hepatitus Acuta	Ladies Relief Hospt.
Martin, John M.	13th	North Carolina	K	Inf.	183	10	1	20-Jan-63	Unknown	College Hospital
Martin, John S.	22nd	North Carolina	B	Inf.	184	1	2	08-May-63	---	Burton's Factory
Martin, John W.	14th	Alabama	G	Inf.	171	7	4	01-Jun-62	---	Crumpton's Factory
Martin, W. H., Sgt.	8th	Georgia	H	Inf.	193	3	2	21-May-64	---	Burton's Factory
Martin, Waitman G., Sgt.	55th	North Carolina	G	Inf.	197	8	4	25-May-64	DOW 5/05/64	Knight's Factory
Mask, James Franklin	28th	North Carolina	E	Inf.	171	7	3	06-Jun-62	Typhoid Fever	Reid's Factory
Mask, W. A.	Cutt's Battery	Georgia	-	Art.	Yk. Sq.	23rd	2nd Line	25-Jan-63	Small Pox	Pest House
Mason, Anderson F.	22nd	South Carolina	K	Inf.	179	3	3	18-Sep-62	Febris Typhoides	Miller's Factory
Mason, George W.	Kirkpatrick's Batty.	Virginia	-	Art.	202	0	0	11-Apr-65	---	Pratts Hospital
Mason, Jeremiah J.	110th Militia	Virginia	-	Inf.	170	6	4	02-Apr-62	---	Ladies Relief Hospt.
Massie, W. W.	177th	Georgia	K	Inf.	169	6	2	31-May-62	---	Crumpton's Factory
Matherly, Thomas J.	37th	North Carolina	A	Inf.	195	7	2	03-Apr-63	Disease	Christian's Factory
Mathis, James Jasper	49th	Georgia	F	Inf.	162	5	4	31-Jul-62	Typhoid Fever	Christian's Factory
Mathis, John D.	3rd	North Carolina	G	Inf.	200	4	3	21-Nov-63	Pneumonia	Burton's Factory
Matlock, S. S.	3rd	Tennessee	C	Inf.	159	3	1	30-Aug-61	---	Ladies Relief Hospt.
Matthews, Aaron J., Sr.	6th	Georgia	E	Inf.	173	9	3	27-Jun-62	---	Knight's Factory
Matthews, Clifton	9th	Louisiana	F	Inf.	167	4	1	13-May-62	---	Christian's Factory
Matthews, George D.	6th	South Carolina	B	Inf.	Yk. Sq.	27th	4th Line	16-Feb-63	Small Pox	Pest House
Matthews, W. W.	20th	Georgia	H	Inf.	166	-	-	01-Jan-64	Small Pox	Pest House
Matthews, William G.	9th	Louisiana	C	Inf.	166	10	2	03-May-62	---	Christian's Factory
Mattox, William A.	17th	Georgia	F	Inf.	191	8	2	01-Feb-63	---	Langhorne's Factory
Maund, Calhoun H.	22nd	Georgia	A	Inf.	161	2	3	17-Jul-62	Fever	Claytor's Factory
Maxwell, H. C.	17th	Mississippi	A	Inf.	79	9	1	03-Jan-95	---	Claytor's Factory
May, B.	2nd	Mississippi	F	Inf.	173	5	2	17-Jul-62	---	Ladies Relief Hospt.
May, Martin Boon	21st	North Carolina	M	Inf.	159	4	2	07-Sep-61	Typhoid Fever	Warwick House
May, Silas M.	37th	North Carolina	A	Inf.	123	9	4	20-Dec-62	DOW 12/13/62	Burton's Factory
Maybin, Thomas M.	15th	Alabama	G	Inf.	167	2	2	11-May-62	Disease	Ladies Relief Hospt.
Mayfield, James	14th	North Carolina	D	Inf.	161	8	3	16-Jul-62	Ictus Solis	Claytor's Factory
Mayo, Edward C.	44th	Virginia	I	Inf.	168	5	1	27-Apr-62	Pneumonia	Christian's Factory
Mayo, Stephen J.	31st	Georgia	G	Inf.	165	2	3	08-Aug-62	Typhoid Fever	Christian's Factory
Mays, Dennett	4th	South Carolina	K	Inf.	170	6	5	10-Apr-62	Phthisis Pulmonaris	Warwick House
McAulay, Hugh E.	37th	North Carolina	C	Inf.	169	7	2	23-May-62	Febris Typhoides	Warwick House

* See Part III - 88

NAME	REGT. or UNIT	STATE	COMPANY	BRANCH of SERVICE	LOT#	Grave No.	ROW	DATE of BURIAL or DEATH	CAUSE of DEATH	HOSPITAL
McBee, G.	Conscript	Virginia	-	Inf.	202	5	4	05-Jun-65	---	Pratts Hospital
McBride, James M., 5th Sgt.	44th	Georgia	G	Inf.	146	4	2	12-May-63	---	Read's Factory
McCaskin, C. J.	29th	Georgia	H	Inf.	101	2	1	27-Dec-62	---	Burton's Factory
McCaskil, A.	8th	Alabama	G	Inf.	189	8	4	13-May-64	---	Christian's Factory
McClendon, Burwell	10th	Alabama	A	Inf.	172	9	3	11-Jun-62	---	Booker's Factory
McClendon, H.	31st	Georgia	K	Inf.	194	1	3	01-Aug-64	---	Christian's Factory
McClendon, William A.	17th	Georgia	K	Inf.	197	8	2	25-May-64	---	College Hospital
McCloud, Elisha, Sr.	31st	Virginia	E	Inf.	201	5	3	12-Jan-63	Typhoid Fever	College Hospital
McClure, D. A.	57th	North Carolina	H	Inf.	191	4	5	09-Feb-63	---	Christian's Factory
McClure, W. H.	19th	Mississippi	G	Inf.	190	2	2	27-Jul-64	---	Knight's Factory
McClure, William M.	18th	Virginia	E	Cav.	186	9	2	18-Jun-64	Killed In Action	Battle of Lynchburg
McCollon, J.	38th Battn.	Virginia	B	Art.	202	7	1	19-Apr-65	---	Langhorne's Factory
McConnell, M.	7th	North Carolina	D	Inf.	122	3	2	20-Nov-62	Typhoid Fever	Langhorne's Factory
McCool, William	2nd Rifles	South Carolina	A	Inf.	193	8	2	17-May-64	Diarrhea Chronic	Langhorne's Factory
McCord, George H.	5th	Virginia	H	Inf.	179	10	1	15-Sep-62	Haemoptysis	Langhorne's Factory
McCord, James A.	52nd	Virginia	B	Inf.	168	1	5	25-Apr-62	Typhoid Fever	College Hospital
McCord, John Thomas	2nd Battn.	Georgia	D	Inf.	Yk. Sq.	3rd	5th Line	26-Jun-63	Small Pox	Pest House
McCoy, G. (also J. J. G. W.)	48th	Georgia	A	Inf.	184	5	1	25-Apr-63	---	Christian's Factory
McCoy, W. W.	3rd	Alabama	B	Inf.	177	2	5	13-Aug-62	Febris	Christian's Factory
McCoy, William P.	13th	North Carolina	H	Inf.	171	1	3	01-Jun-62	Fever	College Hospital
McCraw, Mordecia H.	29th	Virginia	E	Inf.	188	10	4	04-Jun-63	---	College Hospital
McCukle, J.	14th	Georgia	E	Inf.	190	8	4	28-Jun-64	---	Crumpton's Factory
McCulley, James C.	22nd	Georgia	K	Inf.	196	8	1	17-Aug-63	Fever	Ferguson's Factory
McCulloch, Samuel	9th	Louisiana	G	Inf.	168	7	1	29-Apr-62	Pneumonia	Christian's Factory
McCullough, James C.	23rd	North Carolina	H	Inf.	161	8	5	11-Jul-62	Typhoid Fever	Christian's Factory
McCullough, Nathaniel (Samuel)	60th	Georgia	I	Inf.	162	7	3	06-Aug-62	---	Burton's Factory
McCurley, R. J.	9th	Louisiana	K	Inf.	161	2	1	18-Jul-62	---	Ferguson's Factory
McDade, Benjamin Franklin	21st	Georgia	C	Inf.	168	4	2	29-Apr-62	Conjestion	Saunder's Factory
McDaniel, Charles E.	14th	Tennessee	A	Inf.	177	2	1	09-Aug-62	---	Ladies Relief Hospt.
McDaniel, Ephraim H.	1st Orr's Rifles	South Carolina	C	Inf.	161	8	2	15-Jul-62	Disease	Ferguson's Factory
McDermott, Addison	22nd	Virginia	G	Inf.	190	3	1	06-Jul-64	Disease	Christian's Factory
McDill, N. L.	6th	Alabama	L	Cav.	199	9	4	31-Mar-63	---	Miller's Factory
McDonald, Charles	12th	Virginia	I	Inf.	196	3	4	03-Oct-63	Ferbis Cont. Comm.	Christian's Factory
McDonald, Harvey	12th	Virginia	I	Cav.	198	3	2	06-Nov-64	Bronchitis Chronic	Knight's Factory
McDonald, James E.	3rd	South Carolina	K	Inf.	201	7	4	05-Jun-64	DOW	College Hospital
McElvany, Augustus	20th	Mississippi	Read's	Inf.	159	8	3	24-Sep-61	---	Crumpton's Factory
McFadden, Thomas B.	42nd	Mississippi	D	Inf.	196	7	3	03-Sep-64	---	Christian's Factory
McFail, Isaac	16th	Mississippi	F	Inf.	169	2	2	22-May-62	---	Ferguson's Factory
McGaugh, M.	1st	South Carolina	C	Inf.	146	4	1	11-Dec-62	---	Ferguson's Factory
McGee, W. A.	15th	Alabama	K	Inf.	169	1	4	19-May-62	---	Ferguson's Factory

* See Part III - 89

NAME	REGT. or UNIT	STATE	COMPANY	BRANCH of SERVICE	LOT#	Grave No.	ROW	DATE of BURIAL or DEATH	CAUSE of DEATH	HOSPITAL
McGill, James M.	14th	Alabama	E	Inf.	192	5	2	08-Jul-63	---	Reid's Factory
McGinnity, John	17th	Virginia	G	Inf.	202	1	2	19-Feb-65	---	Ladies Relief Hospt.
McIntire, James	9th	Louisiana	Hodge's	Inf.	158	2	3	20-Jul-61	Measles	College Hospital
McKibbin, James E.	35th	Georgia	E	Inf.	201	5	5	11-Jun-64	Chronic Diarrhea	Knight's Factory
McKinzie, C. C.	20th	North Carolina	F	Inf.	195	8	5	20-Feb-63	Pneumonia	Christian's Factory
McLean, Allen C.	48th	North Carolina	D	Inf.	144	2	1	14-Nov-62	Pneumonia	Ferguson's Factory
McLemore, J. R.	6th	Louisiana	A	Cav.	160	2	1	05-Jul-62	Icterus	Ferguson's Factory
McMillan, Warren J.	6th	Virginia	G	Inf.	166	7	2	14-May-62	DOW 5/05/64	Warwick House
McMillian, James E., Sgt.	11th	North Carolina	H	Inf.	186	3	2	25-Jun-64	Remitten Fever	Ladies Relief Hospt.
McMinn, E.	1st	Texas	M	Inf.	178	4	1	01-Sep-62	Chronic Diarrhea	Christian's Factory
McNair, E. C.	33rd	North Carolina	K	Inf.	191	4	4	08-Feb-63	---	Christian's Factory
McNeil, George	51st	Georgia	F	Inf.	178	5	5	06-Sep-62	Disease	Ferguson's Factory
McNinch, J. L. (or I.?)	6th	South Carolina	F	Inf.	170	6	2	27-Dec-61	---	College Hospital
McPhatter, John	20th	North Carolina	I	Inf.	159	4	5	09-Oct-61	Hydrothorax	Warwick House
McPhaul, Daniel A.	38th	North Carolina	K	Inf.	78	4	2	28-Dec-62	Rubeola	Christian's Factory
McPherson, D. K.	30th	North Carolina	H	Inf.	100	1	2	25-Nov-62	Fever Intermitten	Knight's Factory
McPherson, Jesse A.	61st	Virginia	B	Inf.	198	8	5	30-Jun-64	Disease	Crumpton's Factory
McSwain, John	15th	Alabama	E	Inf.	171	1	4	29-Aug-62	Disease	Not Stated
McVay, Weberford	Unknown	Unknown	---	---	161	5	1	---	Disease	College Hospital
McVey, John B.	8th	Louisiana	E	Inf.	168	2	3	03-May-62	---	Ladies Relief Hospt.
McWhorter, D. B.	Stovall's Battn.	Georgia	A	Inf.	159	1	4	25-Sep-61	Typhoid Fever	Saunder's Factory
McWilliams, William	21st	Georgia	C	Inf.	168	8	2	30-Apr-62	DOW	College Hospital
Meadows, T. S.	3rd	South Carolina	K	Inf.	170	8	1	09-Dec-61	Phthisis Pulmonaris	College Hospital
Mears, Elihu	18th	North Carolina	H	Inf.	180	8	2	01-Oct-62	Febris Typhoides	Reid's Factory
Meeks, Nathanial	3rd	North Carolina	D	Inf.	179	1	2	12-Sep-62	Disease	Ferguson's Factory
Meeks, Thomas J.	15th	Alabama	E	Inf.	180	6	3	11-Oct-62	---	Langhorne's Factory
Melton, H. B.	8th	Louisiana	G	Inf.	171	1	5	29-May-62	Pneumonia	Burton's Factory
Melton, W. H. A.	11th	North Carolina	D	Inf.	189	4	1	08-May-64	Fever Contious	Reid's Factory
Mercer, Jacob	61st	Virginia	B	Inf.	198	5	2	12-Oct-64	Febris Cont. Comm.	College Hospital
Merritt, Samuel R.	18th	North Carolina	H	Inf.	188	3	4	17-Jun-63	Disease	Knight's Factory
Messer, D. W.	6th	North Carolina	F	Inf.	194	9	4	12-Jul-64	---	Claytor's Factory
Middleton, N. G.	2nd	Mississippi	F	Inf.	181	2	3	07-Oct-62	Disease	Ferguson's Factory
Miles, John	47th	Alabama	H	Inf.	177	8	3	22-Aug-62	---	Talliaferro's Factory
Milford, G. T. (V.?)	12th	South Carolina	P	Inf.	100	4	3	16-Jan-63	---	Crumpton's Factory
Milford, J. E.	17th	Mississippi	E	Inf.	101	1	5	26-Dec-62	---	College Hospital
Miller, Alexander	6th	Louisiana	G	Inf.	189	1	3	03-May-64	---	Crumpton's Factory
Miller, Atwell	33rd	Virginia	F	Inf.	165	7	2	20-Aug-62	Typhoid Pneumonia	Langhorne's Factory
Miller, Enoch	5th	North Carolina	H	Inf.	188	10	1	28-May-63	---	Knight's Factory
Miller, J. W.	57th	North Carolina	A	Inf.	195	7	5	05-Mar-63	---	Christian's Factory
Miller, John L. C. (Joseph?)	42nd	Virginia	E	Inf.	166	2	2	13-May-62	---	

* See Part III - 90

NAME	REGT. or UNIT	STATE	COMPANY	BRANCH of SERVICE	LOT#	Grave No.	ROW	DATE of BURIAL or DEATH	CAUSE of DEATH	HOSPITAL
Miller, Samuel E.	28th	North Carolina	C	Inf.	101	6	3	06-Jan-63	Chronic Diarrhoea	Miller's Factory
Mills, H. H.	18th	Mississippi	F	Inf.	173	6	2	03-Jul-62	---	College Hospital
Mills, William	1st (McCreary's)	South Carolina	A	Inf.	197	4	4	30-May-64	DOW 5/05/64	Knight's Factory
Mimms, John E.	3rd	Alabama	D	Inf.	182	6	4	07-Nov-62	---	Saunder's Factory
Minix, William H.	49th	Georgia	B	Inf.	191	4	2	06-Feb-63	---	Miller's Factory
Minns, John F.	Blodgetts Batty.	Georgia	---	Art.	171	3	4	01-Jun-62	---	Booker's Factory
Misenhimer, John A.	28th	North Carolina	K	Inf.	173	1	2	23-Jun-62	Typhoid Fever	Crumpton's Factory
Mitchell, B. B.	1st Orr's Rifles	South Carolina	A	Inf.	197	10	2	26-May-64	DOW 5/05/64	Christian's Factory
Mitchell, Pryon M.	12th	Alabama	B	Inf.	170	4	5	07-Mar-62	From a Fall	Ladies Relief Hospt.
Mitchell, W. P.	17th	Virginia	C	Inf.	192	3	3	17-Jul-63	---	Miller's Factory
Mitchell, William B.	1st (McCreary's)	South Carolina	A	Inf.	182	2	4	16-Oct-62	Fever	Miller's Factory
Mizell, Timothy	5th	North Carolina	F	Inf.	177	5	1	27-Aug-62	Phthisis Pulmonaris	Ferguson's Factory
Molen, James E.	27th	Georgia	C	Inf.	168	6	5	07-May-62	---	Reid's Factory
Mongomery, R. B.	9th	Alabama	A	Inf.	180	7	5	04-Oct-62	---	Reid's Factory
Montgomery, Samuel R.	Capt. Anderson's	Virginia	Anderson's	Art.	173	1	5	28-Jun-62	Not Specified	Ladies Relief Hospt.
Moody, Joel	1st Orr's Rifles	South Carolina	E	Inf.	182	5	5	01-Nov-62	---	College Hospital
Moon, A.	33rd	Virginia	---	Inf.	169	4	1	29-Jul-62	---	Ferguson's Factory
Moon, John S., 5th Sgt.	38th	Georgia	H	Inf.	198	6	3	01-Oct-64	---	Christian's Factory
Moon, W. B.	15th	Alabama	E	Inf.	169	7	5	24-May-62	---	Christian's Factory
Moore, Ezekiel Z.	23rd	North Carolina	C	Inf.	182	4	1	28-Oct-62	Phthisis Pulmonaris	Crumpton's Factory
Moore, George W.	46th	North Carolina	E	Inf.	200	8	2	14-Dec-63	Diarrhea Chronic	Booker's Factory
Moore, Green W.	9th	Virginia	H	Inf.	162	8	1	04-Aug-62	Typhoid Fever	Taliaferro's Factory
Moore, J. F.	15th	Alabama	L	Inf.	167	5	1	17-May-62	Disease	Ladies Relief Hospt.
Moore, J. V.	6th	Georgia	G	Inf.	187	4	1	29-Jan-63	---	College Hospital
Moore, James A.	2nd	South Carolina	C	Inf.	79	10	1	03-Jan-63	Pneumonia/Fever	College Hospital
Moore, James M.	52nd	North Carolina	G	Inf.	194	7	5	16-Jul-64	---	Knight's Factory
Moore, Job	55th	Virginia	H	Inf.	79	3	2	12-Jan-63	Typhoid Fever	Ferguson's Factory
Moore, John	26th	Georgia	H	Inf.	201	1	2	15-Jun-64	Pneumonia	Wayside Hospital
Moore, John Charles	6th	Louisiana	K	Inf.	199	10	4	26-Mar-63	---	Jail
Moore, Joseph D.	53rd	North Carolina	I	Inf.	192	3	5	04-Aug-63	Pneumonia	Reid's Factory
Moore, Thomas J.	13th	Virginia	D	Inf.	167	9	2	14-May-62	Measels	Christian's Factory
Moore, Thomas W.	40th	Virginia	I	Inf.	177	6	2	21-Aug-62	Fever	Miller's Factory
Moore, W. D.	5th	Virginia	D	Cav.	196	10	1	11-Aug-63	---	Camp Davis
Moore, William R.	13th	Mississippi	K	Inf.	Yk. Sq.	19th	4th Line	31-Dec-62	Small Pox	Pest House
Moorman, George Washington	15th	Alabama	D	Inf.	168	8	3	29-Apr-62	---	Ladies Relief Hospt.
Moose, William A.	4th	North Carolina	Musician	Inf.	186	2	3	26-Jun-64	Gun Shot Wound	Knight's Factory
Moreland, W. E. (or W. C.)	60th	Georgia	F	Inf.	179	4	3	13-Sep-62	---	Booker's Factory
Morgan, John L.	9th	Louisiana	C	Inf.	161	4	1	20-Jul-62	---	College Hospital
Morgan, Larkin M.	19th	Georgia	D	Inf.	146	6	1	13-Dec-62	Pneumonia	Burton's Factory
Morgan, N. W.	14th	North Carolina	K	Inf.	146	10	4	08-Dec-62	Lung Congestion	Ford's Factory

* See Part III - 91

NAME	REGT. or UNIT	STATE	COMPANY	BRANCH of SERVICE	LOT#	Grave No.	ROW	DATE of BURIAL or DEATH	CAUSE of DEATH	HOSPITAL
Morgan, Solomon	33rd	North Carolina	C	Inf.	146	1	1	19-Dec-62	Febris Typhoides	Christian's Factory
Morgan, W.	8th	North Carolina	B	Inf.	184	8	2	25-Apr-63	...	College Hospital
Morgan, William H.	12th	South Carolina	G	Inf.	193	3	5	21-May-64	DOW 5/06/64	Booker's Factory
Morris, J. F.	28th	North Carolina	D	Inf.	161	4	5	25-Jul-62	Phthisis Pulmonaris	Crumpton's Factory
Morris, James G.	21st	Georgia	I	Inf.	Yk. Sq.	18th	4th Line	27-Dec-62	Small Pox	Pest House
Morris, John R.	2nd	South Carolina	G	Inf.	100	2	3	25-Nov-62	Fever	Langhorne's Factory
Morris, O.	2nd	Mississippi	...	Inf.	167	2	3	11-May-62	...	Ladies Relief Hospt.
Morris, P. J. (poss. Norris)	26th	Georgia	C	Inf.	162	4	4	31-Jul-62	...	Langhorne's Factory
Morris, W. W.	51st	Georgia	I	Inf.	144	1	3	18-Nov-62	...	Crumpton's Factory
Morrison, Daniel L.	33rd	North Carolina	D	Inf.	146	2	2	07-Dec-62	Phthisis Pulmonaris	Christian's Factory
Morrison, J. T. B.	2nd Battn.	Mississippi	F	Inf.	177	4	2	10-Sep-62	...	Crumpton's Factory
Morton, Powhatan	24th	Virginia	F	Inf.	162	6	5	06-Aug-62	...	Ferguson's Factory
Moseley, Emsley P.	7th	Georgia	C	Inf.	196	10	5	17-Aug-63	Typhoid Fever	Camp Davis
Moseley, Thomas N.	24th	Georgia	E	Inf.	192	9	4	24-Jun-63	...	Christian's Factory
Moser, George W.	48th	North Carolina	A	Inf.	182	8	3	13-Nov-62	Typhoid Fever	Candler's Factory
Mosteller, William P.	23rd	North Carolina	B	Inf.	165	7	1	19-Aug-62	Disease	Crumpton's Factory
Mote, Elezer, 4th Sgt.	51st	Georgia	B	Inf.	185	8	2	07-Mar-64	...	College Hospital
Motes, S. T.	3rd	South Carolina	G	Inf.	101	1	2	25-Dec-62	Typhoide & Pneumonia	Reid's Factory
Motes, Tyler, Sgt.	8th	Georgia	E	Inf.	146	9	5	15-Dec-62	Disease	Ladies Relief Hospt.
Mounce, John H. E.	21st	North Carolina	F	Inf.	171	7	2	06-Jun-62	Typhoid Fever	Reid's Factory
Mourning, N.	26th	North Carolina	G	Inf.	193	1	2	22-May-64	...	Christian's Factory
Moxley, Peter H.	21st	North Carolina	L	Inf.	179	8	2	20-Sep-62	Typhoid & Pneumonia	Ferguson's Factory
Moynehan, Cornelius	7th	Louisiana	D	Inf.	172	4	5	26-Jun-62	DOW 6/09/62	Reid's Factory
Mudd, Robert J.	Lynch. Provost Guard	Virginia	-	Inf.	187	1	3	27-Jan-63	...	Ladies Relief Hospt.
Mullen, Pierce	50th	Virginia	D	Inf.	193	2	1	23-May-64	...	Ladies Relief Hospt.
Mulner, J. D.	48th	Alabama	K	Inf.	180	9	1	25-Sep-62	...	Christian's Factory
Munn, Daniel A.	14th	North Carolina	A	Inf.	183	10	2	17-Jan-63	Pneumonia	Talliaferro's Factory
Munnerlyn, Robert N.	23rd	North Carolina	A	Inf.	100	3	2	25-Nov-62	Enteritis	Ford's Factory
Murphy, Thomas J.	13th	North Carolina	I	Inf.	187	5	2	26-Jan-63	Pneumonia	Knight's Factory
Murray, James Hilliard	7th	North Carolina	E	Inf.	Yk. Sq.	-	-	08-Feb-64	Small Pox	Pest House
Myers, Henry L.	21st	Georgia	C	Inf.	171	9	4	30-May-62	...	Ferguson's Factory
Mygatt, A. H.	15th	Louisiana	G	Inf.	192	1	3	15-Jul-63	...	Camp Davis
Myres, John	28th	North Carolina	I	Inf.	123	1	3	18-Dec-62	Pneumonia	Ferguson's Factory
Nalls, Enoch B.	8th	Virginia	F	Inf.	100	7	1	03-Dec-62	Pneumonia	Miller's Factory
Nantz, Clement R.	37th	North Carolina	C	Inf.	162	3	2	25-Jul-62	Typhoides Fever	Booker's Factory
Napier, S. A.	50th	Virginia	A	Inf.	188	5	2	14-Jun-63	...	Ferguson's Factory
Neal, James	28th	North Carolina	H	Inf.	169	7	4	23-May-62	Rubeola	Booker's Factory
Neal, Moses	48th	Georgia	G	Inf.	195	8	4	21-Feb-63	...	Claytor's Factory
NeSmith, Robert P.	5th	Alabama	K	Inf.	169	2	3	25-May-62	...	Ferguson's Factory

* See Part III - 92

NAME	REGT. or UNIT	COMPANY	STATE	BRANCH of SERVICE	LOT#	Grave No.	ROW	DATE of BURIAL or DEATH	CAUSE of DEATH	HOSPITAL
Nethery, James W.	21st	C	Virginia	Inf.	168	8	5	04-May-62	---	Booker's Factory
Newborn, William H.	5th	D	Florida	Inf.	184	6	3	06-May-63	Disease	Langhorne's Factory
* Newman, William G.	58th	A	Virginia	Inf.	179	6	3	13-Sep-62	DOW 8/09/62	Burton's Factory
Newsome, William C. P.	22nd	H	Georgia	Inf.	Yk. Sq.	20th	3rd Line	02-Jan-63	Small Pox	Pest House
Newson, John R.	1st	G	Texas	Inf.	160	9	2	07-Jul-62	Typhoid Fever	Christian's Factory
Newton, Henderson	38th	I	Virginia	Inf.	167	10	3	13-May-62	Erysipelas	Christian's Factory
Newton, Isaac T.	61st	C	Georgia	Inf.	172	5	3	19-Jun-62	Disease	Ferguson's Factory
Nichols, Madison C.	14th	G	Georgia	Inf.	201	8	2	08-Jun-64	DOW 5/06/64	Christian's Factory
Nicholson, Sylvester	6th	B	North Carolina	Inf.	191	10	2	29-Jan-63	Diarrhea Chronic	Claytor's Factory
Ninniger, Giles A.	8th	H	Florida	Inf.	101	2	5	27-Dec-62	Fever	Claytor's Factory
Nipper, J. D.	38th	Casey's	Virginia	Inf.	165	3	2	17-Aug-62	---	Burton's Factory
* Nipper, John W.	50th	G	Georgia	Inf.	123	5	4	20-Dec-62	---	Talliaferro's Factory
Norrid, William S.	7th	G	Tennessee	Inf.	172	7	3	15-Jun-62	---	Christian's Factory
Norris, J. R.	9th	C	Louisiana	Inf.	101	7	4	15-Feb-63	---	Christian's Factory
* Norwood, J. C.	14th	A	South Carolina	Inf.	101	6	5	02-Jan-63	Pneumonia	Talliaferro's Factory
* Nugent, Edmund	48th	I	Alabama	Inf.	182	2	1	15-Oct-62	---	Knight's Factory
Oakley, A. N.	8th	H	Louisiana	Inf.	172	8	5	13-Jun-62	---	Reid's Factory
Oats, Abram	11th	Boyd's	North Carolina	Inf.	159	8	1	05-Sep-61	---	Warwick House
* Obarr, J. Hezekiah (or O'Barr)	5th	H	Florida	Inf.	122	7	1	22-Nov-62	Pneumonia	Burton's Factory
Obercash, M.	15th	H	Georgia	Inf.	192	6	1	03-Jul-63	Chronic Diarrhoea	Miller's Factory
O'Berry, Wesley C.	57th	C	North Carolina	Inf.	199	8	3	26-Mar-63	---	Candler's Hospital
O'Conner, D., Sgt.	8th	G	Florida	Inf.	178	9	4	24-Aug-62	Bronchitis	College Hospital
Oden, D. E.	1st Battn.	B	Virginia	Inf.	198	3	1	05-Nov-64	---	Ferguson's Factory
Odem, Allen	46th	A	Virginia	Inf.	202	1	5	05-Mar-65	---	Crumpton's Factory
Odom, Benjamin	61st	K	Georgia	Inf.	161	5	2	07-Aug-62	---	Knight's Factory
Odom, James B.	32nd	D	North Carolina	Inf.	200	6	1	20-Jan-64	Bronchitis Chronic	Christian's Factory
O'Donnell, Peter, Sgt.	50th	K	Virginia	Inf.	101	3	2	27-Dec-62	---	Ferguson's Factory
Oliver, David	24th Battn.	B	Georgia	Cav.	161	4	1	22-Jul-62	DOW 7/21/62	Ladies Relief Hospt.
O'Neal, W. R.	1st	G	North Carolina	Inf.	162	4	2	23-Jul-62	Disease	Knight's Factory
* Osborne, Thomas J.	14th	F	Alabama	Inf.	Yk. Sq.	---	---	12-Jan-64	Small Pox	Pest House
* Otis, James	1st Orr's Rifles	D	South Carolina	Inf.	193	5	4	19-May-64	DOW 5/05/64	Ferguson's Factory
* Overtrout, Preston	23rd	F	South Carolina	Inf.	182	9	4	13-Nov-62	DOW 8/29/62	Ferguson's Factory
Owen, Elias P.	Rockingham Co.	J (?)	Virginia	---	178	5	2	10-Sep-62	---	Christian's Factory
Owen, G. W.	28th	H	North Carolina	Inf.	162	10	4	29-Jul-62	Typhoid Fever	Talliaferro's Factory
* Owens, Adolphus, Sgt.	17th	G	Mississippi	Inf.	183	2	2	17-Jan-63	---	Christian's Factory
* Owens, Ezra S., 4th Sgt.	9th	D	Alabama	Inf.	189	7	3	16-May-64	---	Knight's Factory
* Oxford, J. S.	26th	M	Georgia	Inf.	178	10	1	23-Aug-62	Disease	Miller's Factory
	49th	D	Georgia	Inf.	123	7	2	16-May-63	Disease	Crumpton's Factory

* See Part III - 93

NAME	REGT. or UNIT	COMPANY	STATE	BRANCH of SERVICE	LOT#	Grave No.	ROW	DATE of BURIAL or DEATH	CAUSE of DEATH	HOSPITAL
Pace, William A., 1st Sgt.	53rd	I	Georgia	Inf.	187	2	3	05-Feb-63	---	Langhorne's Factory
Pace, William H.	Gardner's Batty.	-	South Carolina	Art.	146	6	3	12-Dec-62	Pneumonia	Langhorne's Factory
Paden, William J.	7th	H	Georgia	Inf.	162	1	4	01-Aug-62	---	Ferguson's Factory
Padgett, Alfred	8th	E	Florida	Inf.	192	1	4	18-Jul-63	Disease/Inflamation	Christian's Factory
Padgett, Arenton R.	19th	A	South Carolina	Inf.	Yk. Sq.	1st	2nd Line	21-May-63	Small Pox	Pest House
Page, John O.	15th	F	Georgia	Inf.	173	9	4	27-Jun-62	---	College Hospital
Page, Robert	16th	A	Mississippi	Inf.	169	4	5	23-May-62	---	Christian's Factory
Palmer, F. M.	1st	H	Georgia	Inf.	170	7	4	05-Apr-62	---	Ladies Relief Hospt.
Parker, B. J.	10th	E	Georgia	Inf.	162	9	3	02-Aug-62	---	Crumpton's Factory
Parker, J. C.	30th	C	North Carolina	Inf.	185	6	2	10-Apr-64	Unknown	Camp Davis
Parker, Jaby	6th	K	South Carolina	Inf.	194	4	4	25-Jul-64	DOW 10/04/63	Camp Davis
Parker, M. Turner	14th	B	South Carolina	Inf.	195	2	5	17-Feb-63	Ascities	Christian's Factory
Parker, Monroe	1st	A	Tennessee	Inf.	188	10	2	30-May-63	---	College Hospital
Parker, Samuel S.	13th	B	North Carolina	Inf.	187	3	1	27-Jan-63	Febris Remittens	College Hospital
Parks, Miles J. S.	Riley's Batty.	D	North Carolina	Art.	Yk. Sq.	14th	4th Line	14-Dec-62	Small Pox	Pest House
Parrish, Sylvester	11th	E	Georgia	Inf.	196	1	2	15-Sep-62	---	Miller's Factory
Parrish, Wesley W.	21st	A	North Carolina	Inf.	159	4	1	01-Sep-61	Disease	Warwick House
Parson, George	17th	H	Virginia	Cav.	186	10	2	19-Jun-64	DOW 6/18/64	Ladies Relief Hospt.
Parsons, Craig S.	37th	K	North Carolina	Inf.	185	6	3	28-Apr-64	Pneumonia	College Hospital
Paschall, E.	6th	E	North Carolina	inf.	190	7	1	29-Jun-64	---	Camp Davis
Pass, George	35th	H	Georgia	Inf.	200	3	3	12-Nov-63	---	College Hospital
Paterson, Martin V.	14th	D	North Carolina	Inf.	101	8	5	03-Jan-63	Pneumonia	Ferguson's Factory
Patrick, John J.	16th	F	Georgia	Inf.	78	3	1	17-Dec-62	Desease	Langhorne's Factory
Payne, A. M.	24th	C	Georgia	Inf.	79	3	4	15-Jan-63	Typhoid Fever	Christian's Factory
Payne, Crispin	38th	K	Virginia	Inf.	167	8	2	17-May-62	Typhoid Pneumonia	Crumpton's Factory
Payne, Enoch C.	24th	C (Musician)	Georgia	Inf.	184	6	1	27-Apr-63	Disease	Camp Davis
Payne, Garland A. S.	58th	D	Virginia	Inf.	160	6	3	10-Jul-62	Typhoid Fever	Christian's Factory
Payne, J. R.	60th	I	Georgia	Inf.	162	6	2	02-Aug-62	Fever	Reid's Factory
Payne, Joseph M.	47th	H	Virginia	Inf.	173	2	3	01-Jul-62	Typhoid Fever	Knight's Factory
Payne, Robert B.	37th	G	North Carolina	Inf.	123	4	5	22-Dec-62	DOW 8/27/62	Burton's Factory
Peace, George Washington	22nd	I	South Carolina	Inf.	183	7	2	18-Jan-63	---	Langhorne's Factory
Peacock, J. T.	3rd	K	Alabama	Inf.	191	7	5	03-Feb-63	---	Miller's Factory
Pearcy, Francis M.	60th	G	Georgia	Inf.	185	4	2	26-Apr-64	---	Ferguson's Factory
Pearcy, John A., 1st Sgt.	48th	I	Virginia	Inf.	179	7	1	20-Sep-62	Typhoid Fever	Langhorne's Factory
Pearsey, Joshua J.	12th	C 2nd	North Carolina	Inf.	194	3	1	26-Jul-64	Disease	Ferguson's Factory
Pearson, W. H.	14th	D	Alabama	Inf.	167	4	2	15-May-62	---	Warwick House
Peddy, John C.	3rd Battn.	F	Georgia	Inf.	159	6	5	16-Oct-62	---	Ladies Relief Hospt.
Peek, William C.	9th	K	Georgia	Inf.	159	5	1	15-Sep-61	---	Warwick House
Peel, James L.	22nd	A	Georgia	Inf.	161	7	3	21-Jul-62	Typhoid Fever	Claytor's Factory
Peel, Jesse	33rd	A	North Carolina	Inf.	101	5	5	01-Jan-63	Pneumonia	Crumpton's Factory

* See Part III - 94

NAME	REGT. or UNIT	STATE	COMPANY	BRANCH of SERVICE	LOT#	Grave No.	ROW	DATE of BURIAL or DEATH	CAUSE of DEATH	HOSPITAL
Pegram, George W.	30th	North Carolina	B	Inf.	178	3	2	30-Jul-62	---	Miller's Factory
* Pell, Joseph J.	2nd	North Carolina	A 2nd	Inf.	78	6	1	03-Dec-62	Pneumonia	Ford's Factory
* Pendergrass, Phillip H.	48th	Alabama	E	Inf.	177	10	1	12-Aug-62	---	Knight's Factory
Pendleton, Wilson	12th	Virginia	A	Inf.	197	6	1	28-May-64	DOW 5/01/64	Booker's Factory
Pendley, S. S.	60th	Georgia	C	Inf.	177	10	5	12-Aug-62	---	Warwick House
Pennington, A. G.	9th	Louisiana	G	Inf.	168	1	3	03-May-62	Disease	College Hospital
Pennington, John	7th	North Carolina	F	Inf.	Yk. Sq.	23rd	1st Line	23-Jan-63	Small Pox	Pest House
Pennybaker, John W.	5th	Virginia	K	Inf.	169	9	4	21-May-62	Diarrhea Chronic	Christian's Factory
Perdue, Andrew J.	59th	Georgia	H	Inf.	185	7	3	25-Apr-64	Disease	On Rail Car
Perkins, William A.	14th	Virginia	H	Inf.	195	9	5	19-Feb-63	---	Langhorne's Factory
Perry, James Calvin	44th	Alabama	B	Inf.	182	6	3	05-Nov-62	Pneumonia	Odd Fellow's Hall
Perry, Thomas H.	28th	Virginia	K	Inf.	170	4	3	10-Jan-62	---	Ladies Relief Hospt.
Peters, Asa C. (H.?)	6th	Alabama	F	Inf.	189	5	2	11-May-64	---	Christian's Factory
* Peters, James C.	15th	Alabama	E	Inf.	169	2	4	21-May-62	Disease	Reid's Factory
* Peters, John R.	15th	Alabama	E	Inf.	172	8	3	12-Jun-62	Disease	Ferguson's Factory
Pettie, B.	38th	North Carolina	K	Inf.	101	7	2	07-Jan-63	---	Langhorne's Factory
Petty, T. A.	18th	Virginia	E	Art./Hvy.	167	3	2	13-May-62	---	Reid's Factory
Peyton, Thomas C.	61st	Georgia	I	Inf.	161	10	3	12-Jul-62	---	Warwick House
Phelps, Joesph M.	Latham's Battery	Virginia	---	Art.	187	6	3	23-Jan-63	Typhoid Fever	Chesterfield Station
Phelps, John	Davidson's Batty.	Georgia	---	Art.	198	2	1	30-Nov-64	Dysentery Chronic	From Richmond
Phillips, Barnard J.(or Barney)	14th	Georgia	E	Inf.	189	1	4	04-May-64	Disease	Ferguson's Factory
Phillips, Isaac M.	14th	Georgia	E	Inf.	201	4	2	17-Jun-64	---	Christian's Factory
Phillips, Joesph	33rd	North Carolina	H	Inf.	123	4	2	22-Dec-62	Phthisis Pulmonaris	Christian's Factory
* Phillips, John	1st	Arkansas	McGregor's	Inf.	158	2	2	23-Jun-61	---	College Hospital
* Phillips, Robert	15th	Alabama	B	Inf.	167	1	3	10-May-62	Disease	Saunder's Factory
Phillips, Wyatt	44th	Alabama	D	Inf.	188	3	3	24-Jun-63	---	Camp Davis
Phily, W. C.	31st	Mississippi	B	Inf.	196	2	4	21-Sep-63	---	Langhorne's Factory
* Pickett, P. Willey	2nd	North Carolina	H	Inf.	194	7	1	14-Jul-64	Pneumonia	Knight's Factory
Pierce, --	Unknown	Unknown	---	---	Yk. Sq.	16th	3rd Line	20-Dec-62	Small Pox	Pest House
Pilgrim, Thomas F.	Hampton's Legion	South Carolina	K	Inf.	195	3	1	20-Jan-63	Pneumonia	Langhorne's Factory
Pinkhard, John B.	3rd	Georgia	K	Inf.	184	6	2	01-May-63	Disease	Langhorne's Factory
Pinner, William J.	9th	Virginia	F	Inf.	78	4	3	18-Dec-62	---	Crumpton's Factory
Pinson, John	2nd	South Carolina	E	Inf.	122	5	2	24-Nov-62	Typhoid Fever	Crumpton's Factory
Pitman, P. M. (F. M.)	1st	Virginia	---	Inf.	78	10	3	01-Dec-62	---	Knight's Factory
Pitt, William C.	33rd	North Carolina	B	Inf.	171	7	1	02-Jun-62	Typhoid Fever	Crumpton's Factory
Pittman, John B.	9th	Georgia	D	Inf.	173	9	2	24-Jun-62	---	Ferguson's Factory
Pitts, J. T.	Phillip's Legion	Georgia	M	Inf.	101	9	3	02-Jan-63	---	Knight's Factory
Pitts, James M.	3rd	South Carolina	B	Inf.	187	7	5	24-Jan-63	DOW	Claytor's Factory
Pitts, Thomas	Courtney's Batty.	Virginia	---	Art.	195	9	4	17-Aug-63	---	College Hospital
Platte, W. W.	1st	South Carolina	I	Cav.	199	8	1	22-Mar-63	Pneumonia	Langhorne's Factory

* See Part III - 95

NAME	REGT. or UNIT	STATE	COMPANY	BRANCH of SERVICE	LOT#	Grave No.	ROW	DATE of BURIAL or DEATH	CAUSE of DEATH	HOSPITAL
Player, Samuel P.	3rd	Georgia	F	Inf.	181	8	2	23-Oct-62	DOW 8/30/62	Burton's Factory
* Pleasant, William T.	15th	North Carolina	G	Inf.	193	6	2	19-May-64	---	Ladies Relief Hospt.
Plunkett, Thomas P.	2nd	Mississippi	---	Inf.	158	1	1	21-May-61	---	College Hospital
Poe, C. F.	13th	Mississippi	D	Inf.	123	3	2	20-Dec-62	---	Crumpton's Factory
Poe, F. H.	27th	North Carolina	F	Inf.	186	10	1	18-Jun-64	Febris Typhoides	Ferguson's Factory
Poole, E. M.	17th	Georgia	Pickett's	Inf.	170	9	5	19-Apr-62	---	College Hospital
Poovey, William F.	28th	North Carolina	C	Inf.	100	5	1	06-Dec-62	Febris Typhoides	Burton's Factory
* Pope, Elijah T.	45th	North Carolina	K	Inf.	194	2	3	02-Aug-64	---	Camp Davis
Poppell, John, 4th Corpl.	26th	Georgia	M	Inf.	177	5	5	28-Aug-62	Typhoid Fever	Christian's Factory
Porter, C. C.	12th	South Carolina	H	Inf.	197	9	3	25-May-64	Diarrhea	Christian's Factory
Porter, James	21st	Georgia	F	Inf.	158	5	4	25-May-62	---	Christian's Factory
Porter, W. C.	16th	Mississippi	G	Inf.	161	10	4	12-Jul-62	---	Talliaferro's Factory
Potts, James H.	9th	Virginia	H	Inf.	173	4	4	05-Jul-62	Fever	Burton's Factory
* Potts, John L. M.	2nd	Virginia	H	Inf.	184	5	3	09-May-63	---	Langhorne's Factory
Powe, J. W.	13th	Alabama (Miss.)	C	Inf.	165	8	1	17-Aug-62	---	Christian's Factory
Powell, James G.	50th	Georgia	F	Inf.	178	3	3	01-Sep-62	---	Camp Davis
Powell, John B.	3rd	Arkansas	Whittington	Inf.	158	6	2	15-Jul-61	---	J. W. Murrell's
* Powell, Wiley	38th	Georgia	A	Inf.	200	7	3	24-Jan-64	Tuberculosis	Ferguson's Factory
Powers, Charles W.	6th	Alabama	A	Inf.	172	10	1	08-Jun-64	---	Claytor's Factory
* Prater, Thomas L.	16th	North Carolina	F	Inf.	200	9	3	28-Nov-63	Meningitis	Ladies Relief Hospt.
Presnell, John	54th	North Carolina	K	Inf.	79	9	4	07-Jan-63	Febris Typhoides	Burton's Factory
* Prevatt, Thomas K.	8th	Florida	B	Inf.	184	7	3	03-May-63	Diarrhea	Burton's Factory
Price, A. W.	22nd	North Carolina	B	Inf.	144	4	4	16-Dec-62	Diarrhea	Miler's Factory
Price, Ashley	2nd	North Carolina	I	Inf.	196	4	4	01-Nov-63	Dysentery Chronic	Langhorne's Factory
Price, J. M.	13th	Mississippi	E	Inf.	195	1	1	14-Feb-63	---	Ferguson's Factory
Price, James T., Sgt.	33rd	North Carolina	B	Inf.	123	9	5	22-Dec-62	Pneumonia	Christian's Factory
Price, O. H.	32nd	North Carolina	K	Inf.	202	9	3	22-Mar-65	---	Reid's Factory
Price, William	11th	Alabama	K	Inf.	184	8	3	03-May-63	---	Reid's Factory
* Price, William B.	4th	Texas	K	Inf.	191	7	4	02-Feb-63	Pleuritis	College Hospital
* Price, William C.	15th	South Carolina	K	Inf.	192	8	5	30-Jun-63	Febris Typhoides	Camp Davis
Price, Wilson C.	48th	North Carolina	F	Inf.	182	7	5	11-Nov-62	Typhoid Pneumonia	Christian's Factory
Pridemore, B.	48th	Alabama	C	Inf.	182	9	1	09-Nov-62	---	Langhorne's Factory
Pringle, William A.	31st	Georgia	D	Inf.	162	3	1	24-Jul-62	DOW 6/27/62	Burton's Factory
Pritchard, Joseph	15th	Alabama	L	Inf.	166	6	3	13-May-62	---	Warwick House
Pritchett, Joseph J.	45th	Georgia	D	Inf.	181	1	2	13-Oct-62	---	Ferguson's Factory
Proctor, J. B.	22nd	Georgia	A	Inf.	173	7	5	29-Nov-62	---	Candler's Factory
Proctor, John G.	30th	Virginia	I	Inf.	101	4	2	29-Dec-62	---	Reid's Factory
Propst, Alfred	28th	North Carolina	C	Inf.	187	6	5	29-Jan-63	Typhoid & Pneumonia	Langhorne's Factory
Propst, Thomas	57th	North Carolina	C	Inf.	195	9	3	18-Feb-63	---	Burton's Factory
* Pruden, Kinch T.	44th	Alabama	F	Inf.	Yk. Sq.	15th	4th Line	17-Dec-62	Small Pox	Pest House

* See Part III - 96

NAME	REGT. or UNIT	STATE	COMPANY	BRANCH of SERVICE	LOT#	Grave No.	ROW	DATE of BURIAL or DEATH	CAUSE of DEATH	HOSPITAL
Puckett, J. Y.	2nd	Virginia	I	Inf.	197	5	4	28-May-64	---	Burton's Factory
Pugh, John	21st	Virginia	C	Cav.	Yk. Sq.	---	---	05-Apr-64	Small Pox	Pest House
Pullam, John M.	42nd	Virginia	A	Inf.	162	10	3	12-Aug-62	Diarrhea Chronic	Claytor's Factory
Purvis, Robert L.	46th	North Carolina	D	Inf.	Yk. Sq.	---	---	08-Feb-64	Small Pox	Pest House
* Putnam, L. W.	15th	North Carolina	C	Inf.	189	8	3	12-May-64	Phthisis Pulmonaris	Camp Davis
Quattlebaum, Harmond D.	14th	South Carolina	K	Inf.	200	2	4	15-Oct-63	Dysentery Acute	Christian's Factory
Quick, Richmond	5th	South Carolina	A	Inf.	78	5	3	09-Dec-62	Typhoid & Pneumonia	Reid's Factory
* Quiett, James H.	2nd	Florida	L	Inf.	192	4	4	17-Jul-63	DOW/Disease	Knight's Factory
Quinn, Peter	5th	Louisiana	G	Inf.	185	1	1	10-Apr-64	Disease	College Hospital
Radcliff, G. B.	5th	Virginia	H	Cav.	198	4	2	16-Oct-64	---	Christian's Factory
Radford, Ivey	61st	Alabama	A	Inf.	189	3	5	08-May-64	---	Christian's Factory
Ragin, Jasper	37th	Virginia	H	Inf.	Yk. Sq.	18th	3rd Line	27-Dec-62	Small Pox	Pest House
Rainbolt, William M.	1st	Tennessee	K	Inf.	189	3	3	08-May-64	---	Christian's Factory
Ralston, C. C.	Davidson's Battn.	Virginia	Rockingham	Inf.	194	8	1	12-Jul-64	---	Reid's Factory
Ramsey, Hugh	Alexander's Batty.	South Carolina	---	Art.	190	1	1	05-Jul-64	---	Ferguson's Factory
Randall, C. W.	19th	Georgia	C	Inf.	159	6	3	20-Sep-61	Typhoid Fever	College Hospital
Randolph, Charles H.	Vol's	Maryland	Shaffer's	Inf.	170	1	1	02-Nov-61	---	A. Waddell's
Rasberry, W. J.	2nd	Mississippi	C	Inf.	165	2	1	11-Aug-62	---	Ford's Factory
Rawls, Joseph	50th	Georgia	F	Inf.	189	10	2	30-Apr-64	---	Camp Davis
Ray, A. F.	Cobb's Legion	Georgia	F	Inf.	195	7	3	27-Feb-63	---	Langhorne's Factory
Ray, M. (possibly John)	37th	Virginia	G	Inf.	192	4	2	09-Jul-63	---	Ferguson's Factory
Reaves, Henry Joseph	13th	Georgia	A	Inf.	201	3	3	18-Jun-64	Fever	Burton's Factory
Reep, Laban M.	34th	North Carolina	E	Inf.	201	10	5	06-Jun-64	Gunshot Wound	Knight's Factory
Reeves, Benjamin Hatcher	13th	Georgia	I	Inf.	161	9	2	11-Jul-62	Disease	Burton's Factory
Reid, B. P., Sgt.	22nd	North Carolina	B	Inf.	201	5	4	11-Jun-64	Pneumonia	Camp Davis
* Reid, Robert Raymond	22nd	Georgia	F	Inf.	122	8	2	21-Nov-62	Pneumonia	Ferguson's Factory
* Reid, William H., Sgt.	3rd	Georgia	I	Inf.	Yk. Sq.	26th	5th Line	12-Feb-63	Small Pox	Pest House
Reid, William L.	Unknown	Unknown	---	---	177	7	3	26-Aug-62	---	Ladies Relief Hospt.
Renfrow, A.	8th	Louisiana	E	Inf.	166	10	1	04-May-62	---	Ferguson's Factory
Reynolds, J. M.	Philip's Legion	Georgia	A	Inf.	186	7	1	21-Jun-64	---	Burton's Factory
Reynolds, James T.	1st	Florida	G	Cav.	184	1	3	25-May-63	Disease	Christian's Factory
* Reynolds, Samuel	24th	Georgia	B	Inf.	190	8	2	24-Jun-64	DOW	Ferguson's Factory
Rhodes, Rash	Harrisonburg	Virginia	Militia	---	166	6	1	12-May-62	---	Reid's Factory
Rice, B.	7th	North Carolina	B	Inf.	79	3	1	14-Jan-63	Typhoid Fever	Ferguson's Factory
Rich, Hiram H.	48th	Virginia	D	Inf.	181	3	3	21-Oct-62	Diarrhea Chronic	Christian's Factory
Richards, James R.	8th	Florida	G	Inf.	182	4	2	29-Oct-62	Disease	Ferguson's Factory
* Richards, Jordan F.	26th	North Carolina	G	Inf.	185	5	3	03-May-64	---	Christian's Factory
* Richardson, C. W.	2nd	Georgia	K	Inf.	171	10	5	29-May-62	---	Ferguson's Factory

* See Part III - 97

NAME	REGT. or UNIT	STATE	COMPANY	BRANCH of SERVICE	LOT#	Grave No.	ROW	DATE of BURIAL or DEATH	CAUSE of DEATH	HOSPITAL
Richardson, John R.	37th	North Carolina	K	Inf.	165	4	2	19-Aug-62	Febris Typhoides	Warwick House
Richardson, Joseph	11th	Georgia	B	Inf.	182	4	5	29-Oct-62	Tuberculosis	College Hospital
Richardson, Robert B.	44th	Georgia	A	Inf.	187	5	4	26-Jan-63	Pneumonia	Crumpton's Factory
Richardson, W. W.	53rd	Virginia	B	Inf.	79	9	5	07-Jan-63	---	Crumpton's Factory
Ricketts, James A.	6th	Alabama	Lynch's	Inf.	158	4	2	26-Jun-61	---	College Hospital
Riddle, Ariel	2nd	Mississippi	Bramley's	Inf.	158	4	1	24-May-61	---	College Hospital
Rightsell, Milton	26th	North Carolina	G	Inf.	185	2	3	26-Apr-64	Diarrhea	College Hospital
Riley, George	15th	Alabama	G	Inf.	188	4	2	16-Jun-63	Disease	Camp Davis
Riley, John	14th	Virginia	D	Cav.	190	6	5	02-Jul-64	DOW 6/18/64	Ladies Relief Hospt.
Rilley, R. M.	16th	Mississippi	K	Inf.	167	9	1	15-May-62	---	College Hospital
Riner, William, Jr.	48th	Georgia	F	Inf.	200	9	4	29-Nov-63	Typhoid Pneumonia	Ferguson's Factory
Rippy, Richard	9th	Louisiana	H	Inf.	181	1	1	04-Oct-62	---	Miller's Factory
Risher, John S. (Jack?)	1st	South Carolina	I	Cav.	200	1	5	07-Sep-63	Diarrhea Chronic	Christian's Factory
Ritchie, Thomas J. (or I.)	12th	Georgia	B	Inf.	188	10	5	05-Jun-63	Fever	Reid's Factory
Rivere, S. F.	Lain's Battery	Georgia	---	Art.	195	4	4	15-Mar-63	---	Claytor's Factory
Rizson, J. F. (Rilson)	37th	North Carolina	H	Inf.	79	4	1	12-Jan-63	---	Crumpton's Factory
Roach, Michael	21st	Mississippi	L	Inf.	197	9	2	25-May-64	---	Christian's Factory
Roark, Harvey J.	52nd	North Carolina	H	Inf.	188	7	3	09-Jun-63	Febris Typhoides	Ladies Relief Hospt.
Robbins, S. A.	11th	South Carolina	C	Inf.	178	2	4	31-Aug-62	---	Ferguson's Factory
Robenson, G. B.	15th	North Carolina	C	Inf.	193	1	1	23-May-64	Ascites	Christian's Factory
Roberts, B. C.	6th	Louisiana	C	Inf.	201	8	1	07-Jun-64	---	College Hospital
Roberts, D. M.	17th	Mississippi	E	Inf.	168	10	1	24-Apr-62	---	Warwick House
Roberts, John R.	6th	North Carolina	B	Inf.	177	6	3	29-Aug-62	Peritonitis	College Hospital
Roberts, Marion	8th	Louisiana	G	Inf.	171	9	2	31-May-62	---	Booker's Factory
Roberts, Ryal W.	55th	North Carolina	G	Inf.	196	1	1	07-Nov-63	Compressio Cerebre	Burton's Factory
Roberts, T. Griffin	9th	Georgia	C	Inf.	190	3	4	06-Jul-64	DOW 5/06/64	Ladies Relief Hospt.
Roberts, T. J.	18th	Mississippi	I	Inf.	202	5	1	15-Jun-62	---	Crumpton's Factory
Roberts, W. M., Corpl.	9th	Alabama	H	Inf.	123	5	1	24-Dec-62	---	Knight's Factory
Roberts, Zachariah	61st	Georgia	I	Inf.	101	6	1	31-Dec-62	---	Christian's Factory
Robertson, A. M. (Robinson, A. W.?)	12th	South Carolina	C	Inf.	195	5	3	20-Apr-63	---	Miller's Factory
Robertson, Robert	30th	North Carolina	I	Inf.	200	10	5	27-Nov-63	Febris Typhoides	Candler's Factory
Robertson, Sydney A.	8th	Louisiana	A	Inf.	166	1	2	02-May-62	---	Warwick House
Robinson, Adam P.	12th	North Carolina	A	Inf.	178	10	4	24-Aug-62	Diarrhea	Reid's Factory
Robinson, J. S.	19th	Georgia	Harrold's	Inf.	159	9	5	09-Oct-61	---	College Hospital
Robinson, James A.	11th	Mississippi	Chickasaw	Inf.	158	3	1	23-May-61	---	College Hospital
Rodgers, D. W.	19th	Mississippi	K	Inf.	189	6	2	13-May-64	---	Knight's Factory
Rodgers, William	Jones' Batty.	Virginia	D	Art.	100	10	2	27-Nov-62	---	Claytor's Factory
Roebuck, Samuel H.	1st	North Carolina	H	Inf.	146	4	3	09-Dec-62	Pneumonia	Christian's Factory
Rogers, Curtis	Latham's Batty.	North Carolina	H 1st	Art.	123	10	4	19-Dec-62	Erysipelas	Miller's Factory
Rogers, David H.	32nd	North Carolina	I	Inf.	196	1	4	17-Sep-63	---	Langhorne's Factory

* See Part III - 98

NAME	REGT. or UNIT	STATE	COMPANY	BRANCH of SERVICE	LOT#	Grave No.	ROW	DATE of BURIAL or DEATH	CAUSE of DEATH	HOSPITAL
Rogers, H.	2nd	Virginia	A	Inf.	177	3	4	07-Sep-62	---	Burton's Factory
Rogers, John R.	37th	North Carolina	C	Inf.	199	1	1	08-Mar-63	Pneumonia	Ferguson's Factory
Rogers, William R.	1st	Texas	H	Inf.	192	7	5	03-Jul-63	Asthma	Miller's Factory
Roland, M. R.	Cobb's Legion	Georgia	E	Inf.	172	2	2	04-Jul-62	---	Ferguson's Factory
Roland, S. David	12th	Georgia	A	Inf.	198	7	3	04-Sep-64	---	Camp Davis
Rooks, Noah	1st	Texas	L	Inf.	173	4	3	09-Jul-62	Disease	Ladies Relief Hospt.
Roper, Barney	6th	North Carolina	A	Inf.	191	9	4	31-Jan-63	Typhoid Fever	College Hospital
Roquemore, John M.	35th	Georgia	G	Inf.	200	10	3	03-Dec-63	Typhoid Fever	Ferguson's Factory
Ross, W.	48th	Mississippi	L	Inf.	199	5	2	10-Apr-63	---	Ferguson's Factory
Rottenburg, William A.	46th	North Carolina	E	Inf.	123	8	3	22-Dec-62	Diarrhea Chronic	Laughorne's Factory
Roundtree, E.	11th	Georgia	I	Inf.	177	1	2	25-Aug-62	Measles	College Hospital
Roundtree, W. R.	Cobb's Legion	Georgia	F	Inf.	196	7	5	29-Aug-63	---	Claytor's Factory
Rowland, Waddy T.	1st	Tennessee	Bennett's	Inf.	158	6	1	30-May-61	---	College Hospital
Runnels, Richard	10th	Virginia	C	Inf.	197	4	5	30-May-64	---	Camp Davis
Russel, J. Larkin	22nd	North Carolina	A	Inf.	171	2	3	01-Jun-62	Pebris Remittens	College Hospital
Russel, Joseph C.	28th	North Carolina	E	Inf.	199	5	4	09-Apr-63	Diarrhea Chronic	Miller's Factory
Russell, Benjamin A.	5th	Florida	K	Inf.	144	1	3	14-Nov-62	Pneumonia	Ferguson's Factory
Russell, James	16th	Mississippi	Hardies'	Inf.	158	2	4	10-Aug-61	---	College Hospital
Russell, Pleasant	38th	North Carolina	C	Inf.	194	2	2	01-Aug-64	Unknown	College Hospital
Rutledge, Marion	63rd	Tennessee	G	Inf.	189	10	3	30-Apr-64	---	College Hospital
Ryan, R.	5th	North Carolina	G	Inf.	190	9	5	26-Jun-64	---	Crumpton's Factory
Ryan, William	6th	Louisiana	H	Inf.	200	7	2	05-Jan-64	---	Camp Davis
Sale, Alfred A., 1st Sgt.	54th	North Carolina	G	Inf.	191	1	5	04-Feb-63	Pebris Typhodies	Candler's Factory
Sallins, Jesse	17th	Georgia	E	Inf.	196	8	2	26-Aug-63	---	College Hospital
Salter, J. E.	Latham's Batty.	North Carolina	H 1st	Art.	101	6	4	06-Jan-63	Typhoid Fever	Ferguson's Factory
Samples, James A.	21st	Georgia	F	Inf.	194	1	5	31-Aug-64	---	Camp Davis
Sanders, B. M. (poss. Landers)	22nd	Georgia	D	Inf.	183	4	3	19-Jan-63	---	Laughorne's Factory
Sanford, J. B.	28th	Georgia	K	Inf.	169	3	5	23-May-62	---	Christian's Factory
Sanford, William John	9th	Louisiana	B	Inf.	166	3	1	04-May-62	---	Saunder's Factory
Sarrett, Peter	4th	Virginia	F	Inf.	166	2	3	06-May-62	---	Christian's Factory
Saunders, D.	61st	Georgia	B	Inf.	191	2	5	14-Feb-63	---	Burton's Factory
Saunders, James M.	34th	North Carolina	K	Inf.	165	10	3	12-Aug-62	Typhoid Fever	Ladies Relief Hospt.
Saunders, Peter M.	38th	Georgia	H	Inf.	200	3	2	08-Nov-63	Typhoid Fever	College Hospital
Saunders, W. F.	2nd	South Carolina	A	Cav.	Yk. Sq.			21-Mar-64	Small Pox	Pest House
Sawyer, Daniel	33rd	North Carolina	F	Inf.	171	8	4	31-May-62	Pneumonia	Crumpton's Factory
Saxon, Lewis A.	14th	South Carolina	C	Inf.	191	3	2	13-Feb-63	Pneumonia	Christian's Factory
Scarborough, Asa	16th	Georgia	D	Inf.	100	9	3	26-Nov-62	---	Crumpton's Factory
Scoggins, Henry M.	4th	North Carolina	K	Cav.	198	6	4	07-Oct-64	---	Christian's Factory
Scot, George P.	20th	Georgia	B	Inf.	170	9	2	26-Dec-61	---	Warwick House

* See Part III - 99

NAME	REGT. or UNIT	STATE	COMPANY	BRANCH of SERVICE	LOT #	Grave No.	ROW	DATE of BURIAL or DEATH	CAUSE of DEATH	HOSPITAL
Scott, William C., Corpl.	7th	North Carolina	G	Inf.	173	8	4	29-Jun-62	Dysentery Chronic	Reid's Factory
* Scroggins, John	6th	Alabama	F	Inf.	191	9	2	31-Jan-63	---	College Hospital
Secrist, Conrad	2nd	North Carolina	C	Inf.	180	9	3	28-Sep-62	Diarrhea Chronic	Langhorne's Factory
* Segreest, Charles T.	61st	Alabama	H	Inf.	201	4	5	13-Jun-64	DOW	Crumpton's Factory
Self, M. M.	4th	Texas	F	Inf.	171	5	3	20-Jun-62	Pneumonia	Claytor's Factory
Sellers, Daniel	19th	Georgia	McGreggor's	Inf.	159	2	1	29-Aug-61	---	At Camp
* Sellers, E. D.	15th	Alabama	L	Inf.	169	5	2	27-May-62	Disease	Ferguson's Factory
Senn, John D.	13th	South Carolina	D	Inf.	199	9	3	23-Mar-63	Disease	College Hospital
Sergeant, E. J.	24th	Georgia	J	Inf.	146	10	1	06-Dec-62	---	Christian's Factory
Sessinger, John	38th	Georgia	H	Inf.	177	7	2	20-Aug-62	---	Burton's Factory
Severs, W.	4th Battn.	Florida	H	Inf.	198	10	2	03-Aug-64	---	Camp Davis
Sexton, Simon	27th	North Carolina	F	Inf.	194	6	4	18-Jul-64	Unknown	Knight's Factory
* Shadrock, John D.	6th	Alabama	A	Inf.	169	5	5	26-May-62	---	Langhorne's Factory
Share, J. H.	57th	North Carolina	B	Inf.	190	5	4	03-Jul-64	---	Camp Davis
Sharpe, Nathan	61st	Georgia	H	Inf.	165	2	2	09-Aug-62	Brain Fever	Saunder's Factory
Shaver, Jacob Y.	42nd	Virginia	B	Inf.	180	6	5	08-Oct-62	Diphtheria	College Hospital
Shaver, James E.	42nd	Virginia	E	Inf.	144	2	3	15-Nov-62	Typhoid Fever	College Hospital
Shaw, J. Comer	2nd Battn.	Georgia	C	Inf.	Yk. Sq.	22nd	5th Line	06-Jan-63	Small Pox	Pest House
Shaw, John P.	13th	South Carolina	B	Inf.	178	7	1	06-Sep-62	Diarrhea Chronic/Fever	Langhorne's Factory
* Sheehe, Christopher	27th	Virginia	E	Inf.	158	4	3	02-Aug-61	DOW 7/21/61	College Hospital
Sheffler, B. S. (or D. P.)	21st	Georgia	G	Inf.	168	10	4	30-Apr-62	Measles	Warwick House
Shell, R. L.	17th	Mississippi	A	Inf.	186	4	2	24-Jun-64	---	Christian's Factory
Shell, Reuben	59th	Georgia	I	Inf.	144	6	2	19-Nov-62	---	Langhorne's Factory
Shelor, George T.	Stuart's	Virginia	-	Art.	173	3	2	23-Jul-62	---	Saunder's Factory
Shelton Patrick	2nd	Mississippi	H	Inf.	170	9	4	07-Nov-61	---	Ladies Relief Hospt.
Shelton, M.	3rd Reserves	Virginia	H	Inf.	202	10	4	10-Mar-65	---	Christian's Factory
* Shelton, Martin V., Corpl.	28th	Virginia	F	Inf.	178	8	1	29-Aug-62	DOW 6/27/62	Ford's Factory
Shelton, William M.	44th	North Carolina	B	Inf.	200	3	4	21-Oct-63	Diarrhea	Langhorne's Factory
Shepherd, Peter	56th	Virginia	C	Inf.	171	4	3	07-Jun-62	Erysipelas	Warwick House
Sheppard, Noah R.	52nd	North Carolina	E	Inf.	196	8	3	19-Aug-63	---	Camp Davis
Sheppard, William	5th	Alabama	A	Inf.	196	9	2	12-Aug-63	---	Claytor's Factory
Sherwood, David J.	48th	Virginia	D	Inf.	182	7	2	11-Nov-62	Typhoid Fever	Christian's Factory
Shew, William D.	33rd	North Carolina	D	Inf.	171	2	5	01-Jun-62	Febris Typhoides	Claytor's Factory
* Shierling, John Anderson, Sr.	59th	Georgia	H	Inf.	201	1	4	15-Jun-64	DOW/Typhoid Fever	College Hospital
Short, R. L.	2nd	Mississippi	B	Inf.	173	3	1	04-Jul-62	---	Langhorne's Factory
* Shropshire, Henry Clay	14th	Georgia	C	Inf.	159	2	2	01-Sep-61	---	H. Bocock's
* Shuford, Phillip S.	23rd	North Carolina	F	Inf.	197	4	1	30-May-64	DOW 5/05/64	Knight's Factory
Sightler, W. S.	1st (Hagood's)	South Carolina	K	Inf.	189	8	1	04-May-64	Pneumonia	Ladies Relief Hospt.
Sikes, J. J.	61st	Virginia	K	Inf.	194	5	3	19-Jul-64	---	Christian's Factory
Simes, W. F.	8th	Louisiana	E	Inf.	166	7	1	13-May-62	---	Christian's Factory

* See Part III - 100

NAME	REGT. or UNIT	COMPANY	STATE	BRANCH of SERVICE	LOT#	Grave No.	ROW	DATE of BURIAL or DEATH	CAUSE of DEATH	HOSPITAL
Simmons, D. (Simons?)	1st	D	South Carolina	Cav.	188	9	4	05-Jun-63	---	Claytor's Factory
Simmons, J. D.	13th	F	Mississippi	Inf.	194	9	1	09-Jul-64	---	Christian's Factory
Simmons, P. C.	6th	F	Alabama	Inf.	184	7	1	30-Apr-63	---	College Hospital
Simmons, William	5th	G	Alabama	Inf.	187	10	5	21-Jan-63	---	Crumpton's Factory
Simpkins, Benjamin	44th	I	North Carolina	Inf.	200	8	5	03-Dec-63	Diarrhea Chronic	Langhorne's Factory
Simpson, J. H.	53rd	I	Virginia	Inf.	182	1	5	01-Nov-62	---	College Hospital
Simpson, James S.	21st	M	North Carolina	Inf.	159	8	2	13-Sep-61	---	Warwick House
Simpson, Sampson B.	48th	E	Alabama	Inf.	178	5	1	03-Sep-62	---	Christian's Factory
Sims, Patrick Henry	23rd	A	Virginia	Inf.	171	6	1	06-Jun-62	Diphtheria	Booker's Factory
Sinclair, John	6th	A	Virginia	Inf.	196	6	3	10-Sep-63	---	Odd Fellow's Hall
Singletary, B.	6th	H	Alabama	Inf.	191	8	4	01-Feb-63	---	Christian's Factory
Singleton, J. P.	14th	F	South Carolina	Inf.	195	2	2	21-Feb-63	---	Candler's Factory
Sipps, William H.	9th	D	Alabama	Inf.	100	8	1	30-Nov-62	---	College Hospital
Sirbaugh, G. H.	31st	G	Virginia	Inf.	187	9	4	25-Feb-63	Disease	Christian's Factory
Skates, William	Palmetto Sh.Shooters		South Carolina	Inf.	79	7	5	11-Jan-63	---	Crumpton's Factory
Slate, Albert E.	11th	E	Georgia	Inf.	Yk. Sq.	21st	1st Line	14-Jan-63	Small Pox	Pest House
Sligh, David J.	12th	C	Georgia	Inf.	197	6	5	27-May-64	DOW 5/05/64	Burton's Factory
Sloane, R. A.	1st	C	North Carolina	Art.	185	10	1	03-Feb-64	Diarrhea	Langhorne's Factory
Snail, Thomas	45th	A	North Carolina	Inf.	189	1	5	05-May-64	Diarrhea Acute	College Hospital
Smith, --	Unknown	-	Unknown	-	Yk. Sq.	23rd	4th Line	08-Jan-63	Small Pox	Pest House
Smith, Albert	22nd	E	Georgia	Inf.	172	4	2	22-Jun-62	Typhoid Fever	Langhorne's Factory
Smith, Allen	3rd	D	Alabama	Inf.	Yk. Sq.	25th	4th Line	09-Feb-63	Small Pox	Pest House
Smith, B. T.	2nd	D	South Carolina	Inf.	196	7	1	24-Aug-63	---	Crumpton's Factory
Smith, Bennett	37th	E	North Carolina	Inf.	192	9	5	30-Jun-63	Dropsy	Burton's Factory
Smith, Cader	15th	F	North Carolina	Inf.	144	3	2	15-Nov-62	Disease	Odd Fellow's Hall
Smith, Charles W.	35th Battn.	B	Virginia	Cav.	198	4	1	16-Oct-64	---	Camp Davis
Smith, Conrad	6th	H	Louisiana	Inf.	179	10	2	17-Sep-62	Disease	Ferguson's Factory
Smith, Dillard	34th	I	North Carolina	Inf.	123	5	3	03-Jun-63	---	Burton's Factory
Smith, G. S.	51st	K	Georgia	Inf.	197	2	5	03-Jun-64	---	Ferguson's Factory
Smith, H.	34th	K	North Carolina	Inf.	202	6	5	05-May-65	---	Camp Davis
Smith, Hardy, 1st Corpl.	8th	D	Florida	Inf.	199	5	1	03-Apr-63	Diarrhea	Ferguson's Factory
Smith, Hensley L.	45th	E	North Carolina	Inf.	190	9	4	27-Jun-64	Diarrhea Chronic	Christian's Factory
Smith, Isaac	44th	F	North Carolina	Inf.	200	2	5	17-Oct-63	Unknown	Burton's Factory
Smith, J. H.	51st	B	Georgia	Inf.	178	6	2	04-Sep-62	---	College Hospital
Smith, J. M.	10th Battn.	B	Georgia	Inf.	195	2	4	21-Feb-63	---	Miller's Factory
Smith, J. S.	2nd	I	Mississippi	Inf.	196	6	2	02-Sep-63	---	Claytor's Factory
Smith, Jackson W.	1st	D	Florida	Cav.	79	6	4	06-Apr-63	DOW	Burton's Factory
Smith, James D.	61st	H	Georgia	Inf.	180	10	5	26-Sep-62	---	College Hospital
Smith, Jesse	1st (McCreary's)	A	South Carolina	Inf.	197	6	2	29-May-64	Pneumonia/wounds	Ferguson's Factory
Smith, Jesse J., Corpl.	1st (Hagood's)	G	South Carolina	Inf.	187	6	1	25-Jan-63	DOD	Ferguson's Factory

* See Part III - 101

NAME	REGT. or UNIT	STATE	COMPANY	BRANCH of SERVICE	LOT#	Grave No.	ROW	DATE of BURIAL or DEATH	CAUSE of DEATH	HOSPITAL
Smith, John	7th	Louisiana	I	Inf.	166	1	3	02-May-62	---	Warwick House
Smith, John	2nd	Mississippi	L	Inf.	Yk. Sq.	-	-	01-Oct-62	Small Pox	Pest House
Smith, John	28th	North Carolina	I	Inf.	185	9	1	05-Feb-64	Overdose Morphine	Booker's Factory
Smith, Joseph	7th	Louisiana	E	Inf.	193	8	3	17-May-64	DOW 5/05/64	Ladies Relief Hospt.
Smith, Joseph W.	16th	Georgia	A	Inf.	165	3	1	16-Aug-62	Typhoid Fever	Ferguson's Factory
Smith, R.	18th	Mississippi	I	Inf.	101	3	3	29-Dec-62	---	Ferguson's Factory
Smith, Robert	2nd	South Carolina	K	Inf.	101	4	3	30-Dec-62	---	Crumpton's Factory
Smith, Taylor	1st	North Carolina	E	Inf.	192	6	3	02-Jul-63	---	Ladies Relief Hospt.
Smith, Thomas	12th	North Carolina	I (Snow's)	Inf.	171	3	1	04-Jun-62	Typhoid Fever	Reid's Factory
Smith, W. T.	14th	South Carolina	G	Inf.	195	7	1	22-Feb-63	Diarrhea Chronic	Ferguson's Factory
Smith, William	16th	North Carolina	M	Inf.	101	7	5	14-Jan-63	DOW 8/30/62	Ford's Factory
Smith, William A., 2nd Corpl.	38th	Georgia	K	Inf.	184	3	2	04-May-63	---	Reid's Factory
Smith, William A.	8th	Florida	C	Inf.	193	2	2	23-May-64	DOW	Booker's Factory
Smith, William W.	21st	Georgia	I	Inf.	168	7	4	06-May-62	Measles	Christian's Factory
Smithey, John	2nd Battn.	Georgia	C	Inf.	Yk. Sq.	22nd	1st Line	15-Jan-63	Small Pox	Pest House
Snider, G. M.	15th	Alabama	L	Inf.	172	2	5	11-Jun-62	Disease	Saunder's Factory
Snipes, Asa	2nd	South Carolina	H	Inf.	146	9	4	17-Dec-62	Disease	Knight's Factory
Snoddy, Jesse A.	2nd	North Carolina	A	Inf.	195	2	1	17-Feb-63	Febris Typhoides	Candler's Factory
Snow, Shadrick	28th	North Carolina	A	Inf.	160	3	1	08-Jul-62	Febris	Ferguson's Factory
Sodley, David	42nd	South Carolina	C	Inf.	178	7	2	05-Sep-62	Febris Typhodies	College Hospital
Sons, A. Soloman	15th	South Carolina	C	Inf.	144	6	1	11-May-63	Phthisis Pulmonaris	Langborne's Factory
Sorrell, Joseph C.	7th	Virginia	C	Inf.	172	3	1	29-Jun-62	Diphtheria	Christian's Factory
Sparks, James S.	28th	Georgia	G	Inf.	170	2	3	10-Jan-62	---	College Hospital
Sparks, Thomas T.	48th	North Carolina	I	Inf.	100	1	3	25-Nov-62	Anasasca	Langborne's Factory
Sparks, William	47th	Alabama	K	Inf.	181	8	1	23-Oct-62	---	Knight's Factory
Sparks, William M.	12th	South Carolina	H	Inf.	171	6	2	06-Mar-63	Pneumonia	Langborne's Factory
Spears, James M.	60th	Georgia	F	Inf.	180	10	4	01-Feb-63	---	Burton's Factory
Spears, Jeremiah S.	22nd	Georgia	D	Inf.	191	10	1	28-Jan-63	Phthisis	Knight's Factory
Speer, J. A.	17th	Georgia	H	Inf.	171	5	1	06-Jun-62	---	Crumpton's Factory
Spell, Owen H., Corpl.	46th	North Carolina	I	Inf.	194	10	3	09-Jul-64	Disease	Knight's Factory
Spence, Alexander	12th	Virginia	K	Inf.	190	6	3	01-Jul-64	Disease	Christian's Factory
Spencer, W. H.	3rd	Georgia	G	Inf.	Yk. Sq.	29th	4th Line	10-Apr-63	Small Pox	Pest House
Spikes, William	3rd	North Carolina	I	Inf.	101	4	4	31-Dec-62	Pneumonia	Crumpton's Factory
Spiller, Hubbard M. (Herbert?)	1st	South Carolina	H	Inf.	189	10	4	03-Apr-64	Diarrhea Chronic	Ferguson's Factory
Spivey, Henry D.	49th	Georgia	G	Inf.	177	10	2	21-Aug-63	---	Langborne's Factory
Spratt, John H.	2nd	Florida	M	Inf.	100	7	3	30-Nov-62	Pneumonia	Claytor's Factory
Spring, Joseph L.	14th	Georgia	G	Inf.	192	5	5	11-Jul-63	DOW 12/13/62 & Erysipelas	Miller's Factory
Spurlock, Green W.	15th	Alabama	H	Inf.	169	3	3	28-May-62	Disease	Crumpton's Factory
Stafford, William M.	1st	Florida	F	Cav.	199	3	4	07-Apr-63	Pneumonia	Christian's Factory
Stagg, John H.	21st	Georgia	G	Inf.	167	6	2	21-May-62	Chronic Diarrhea	Warwick House

* See Part III - 102

NAME	REGT. or UNIT	STATE	COMPANY	BRANCH of SERVICE	LOT#	Grave No.	ROW	DATE of BURIAL or DEATH	CAUSE of DEATH	HOSPITAL
* Staggs, John	16th	North Carolina	I	Inf.	178	10	5	25-Aug-62	DOW 6/26/62	Claytor's Factory
Stallings, Andrew J.	3rd	Virginia	I	Inf.	180	2	4	24-Sep-61	Dysentery Chronic	College Hospital
Stallings, George T.	41st	Virginia	I	Inf.	101	7	3	06-Jan-63	Heart Disease	Christian's Factory
Stallings, Henry	33rd	North Carolina	K	Inf.	187	1	5	28-Jan-63	Typhoid Pneumonia	Crumpton's Factory
Stanfield, Allen J., 5th Sgt.	50th	Georgia	B	Inf.	182	8	4	11-Nov-62	---	Ferguson's Factory
Stanfield, Thomas G.	48th	Virginia	B	Inf.	181	9	3	13-Oct-62	Carditis	Christian's Factory
Stanley, E. A.	Pegram's Batty.	Virginia	-	Art.	201	6	4	10-Jun-64	---	Burton's Factory
Stanley, George W.	57th	Virginia	B	Inf.	100	6	2	30-Nov-62	Phthisis Pulmonaris	Christian's Factory
Stansil, John	Phillip's Legion	Georgia	M	Inf.	199	2	4	07-Apr-63	---	Camp Davis
Stapleton, Anderson	50th	Virginia	H	Inf.	196	9	5	17-Aug-63	---	College Hospital
Starkey, John, Jr.	58th	North Carolina	E	Inf.	173	7	4	01-Jul-62	---	Knight's Factory
* Starnes, James M.	48th	Georgia	F	Inf.	79	2	2	15-Jan-63	Typhoid Fever	Burton's Factory
Starr, Thomas	17th	Georgia	K	Inf.	160	7	2	09-Jul-62	---	Claytor's Factory
Staten, Melvin J.	9th	Louisiana	D	Inf.	171	7	5	30-May-62	---	Christian's Factory
Sterling, Isaac	Cobb's Legion	Georgia	B	Inf.	182	3	1	17-Oct-62	---	Reid's Factory
Steuart, John C.	31st	Virginia	E	Inf.	166	5	2	12-May-62	Erysipelias	Booker's Factory
* Steudham, Thomas L.	14th	South Carolina	K	Inf.	165	9	1	11-May-62	Febris Typhoides	Christian's Factory
Stewart, R. M. (Stuart?)	Boyce's Batty.	South Carolina	-	Art.	182	9	2	09-Nov-62	---	Ferguson's Factory
* Stewart, William	6th	South Carolina	C	Inf.	146	6	5	14-Dec-62	Pneumonia	Miller's Factory
Stewart, William G., Corpl.	48th	Alabama	A	Inf.	186	4	3	24-Jun-64	---	Christian's Factory
* Still, C. E.	16th	Mississippi	D	Inf.	123	7	3	26-Dec-62	---	Talliaferro's Factory
Stinson, Samuel	Phillip's Legion	Georgia	B	Inf.	79	9	2	05-Jan-63	Pneumonia	Ford's Factory
* Stogdale, Elias P.	52nd	Virginia	G	Inf.	201	8	4	07-Jun-64	DOW 5/19/64	College Hospital
* Stokes, T. A.	18th	North Carolina	C	Inf.	146	2	1	20-Dec-62	DOW 12/13/62	Claytor's Factory
* Stone, H. A.	8th	Georgia	H	Inf.	199	8	4	01-Apr-63	---	Claytor's Factory
Stone, Horbord	21st	North Carolina	H	Inf.	194	7	2	15-Jul-64	Disease	Burton's Factory
* Storie, Jesse P.	37th	North Carolina	B	Inf.	192	2	5	01-Aug-63	DOW 7/01/63	Candler's Factory
Strange, Benjamin F.	8th	Florida	B	Inf.	123	10	3	18-Dec-62	Disease	Burton's Factory
Strickland, I. L.	7th	North Carolina	E	Inf.	169	3	1	29-May-62	Typhoid Fever	Booker's Factory
Strickland, James H.	8th	Florida	B	Inf.	123	4	1	21-Dec-62	Typhoid Fever	Christian's Factory
* Strickland, Leburn	15th	Alabama	I	Inf.	161	5	3	16-Aug-62	---	Warwick House
Stubba, Marcellus	47th	Alabama	A	Inf.	78	1	1	30-Nov-62	---	Langhorne's Factory
* Sturdervant, J. D.	47th	Alabama	F	Inf.	178	1	3	01-Sep-62	---	Ferguson's Factory
Sturdivant, William R.	41st	Alabama	A	Inf.	189	2	3	06-May-64	---	Knight's Factory
Styers, N. R.	21st	North Carolina	D	Inf.	186	8	2	18-Jun-64	Killed in Action	Battle of Lynchburg
Suber, Enoch	1st (McCreary's)	South Carolina	B	Inf.	195	6	1	28-Feb-63	Pneumonia	Candler's Factory
Sublett, Smith C. (Possibly)	42nd	Virginia	C	Inf.	Yk. Sq.	2nd	2nd Line	02-May-63	Small Pox	Pest House
Sugg, Ephraim	33rd	North Carolina	K	Inf.	187	3	1	05-Feb-63	Pneumonia	Crumpton's Factory
Suggs, Jesse H.	18th	Georgia	K	Inf.	173	7	5	01-Jul-62	Heart Attack	Langhorne's Factory
* Sullins, Nathan Ashbury	61st	Alabama	H	Inf.	202	8	4	01-Apr-65	---	Ladies Relief Hospl.

* See Part III - 103

NAME	REGT. or UNIT	STATE	COMPANY	BRANCH of SERVICE	LOT#	Grave No.	ROW	DATE of BURIAL or DEATH	CAUSE of DEATH	HOSPITAL
Sullivan, Patrick	5th	Virginia	G	Inf.	196	10	3	28-Aug-63	Typhoid Fever	Crumpton's Factory
Summerlin, David	61st	Georgia	D	Inf.	165	10	2	10-Aug-62	---	Reid's Factory
Suthard, John P.	13th	Virginia	E	Inf.	79	2	4	13-Jan-63	Pneumonia	Langhorne's Factory
Suthard, William T.	13th	Virginia	E	Inf.	169	4	3	27-May-62	Enteritis	Ferguson's Factory
Sutherland, D. K.	18th	North Carolina	H	Inf.	199	6	5	27-Mar-63	Disease	Candler's Factory
Suttle, Phillip V.	34th	North Carolina	I	Inf.	188	5	1	03-Jun-63	Febris Typhoides	Claytor's Factory
Swadley, John S.	31st	Virginia	E	Inf.	180	1	3	22-Sep-62	Erypselias	Claytor's Factory
Swift, William A.	9th	Louisiana	A	Inf.	199	10	5	27-Mar-63	---	Saunder's Factory
* Swink, James William	5th	Virginia	F	Inf.	Yk. Sq.	15th	5th Line	19-Dec-62	Small Pox	Pest House
* Swinson, B. Frank	20th	North Carolina	E	Inf.	178	5	3	07-Sep-62	Fever/DOW 6/27/62	Miller's Factory
* Tackett, George C.	21st	Alabama	A	Inf.	171	8	1	31-May-62	---	Christian's Factory
* Talbert, Calvin R.	34th	North Carolina	K	Inf.	182	2	5	24-Sep-62	Febris Typhoides	College Hospital
Tankersley, J. M.	38th	Georgia	A	Inf.	161	2	2	18-Jul-62	---	Ford's Factory
Tarpley, S. S. Sr.	11th	Mississippi	Univ. Grays	Inf.	158	6	3	04-Aug-61	---	Not Stated
* Tart, Vernon H.	6th	Alabama	C	Inf.	166	5	3	13-May-62	---	College Hospital
Tate, John D.	24th	Georgia	C	Inf.	198	8	2	09-Aug-64	Disease	Christian's Factory
Taylor, Alfred	9th	Louisiana	H	Inf.	180	6	2	06-Oct-62	---	Ferguson's Factory
Taylor, F. Cicero	Rhett's Batty.	South Carolina	-	Art.	195	6	5	16-Mar-63	Pneumonia	Candler's Factory
Taylor, George W.	19th	Georgia	K	Inf.	79	4	5	14-Jan-63	---	Ferguson's Factory
Taylor, George W.	3rd	North Carolina	I	Inf.	123	10	5	13-May-63	Disease	Booker's Factory
Taylor, H. S.	7th	Georgia	H	Inf.	161	9	1	10-Jul-62	Typhoid Fever	Knight's Factory
Taylor, Henry	26th	Georgia	A	Inf.	171	4	2	08-Aug-62	---	Odd Fellow's Hall
* Taylor, Joab	24th	Virginia	C	Inf.	123	9	3	20-Dec-62	Pneumonia	Ferguson's Factory
Taylor, John M.	8th	Florida	B	Inf.	78	1	2	27-Nov-62	Pneumonia	Candler's Factory
Taylor, Jordan A.	33rd	North Carolina	B	Inf.	169	5	4	27-May-62	Typhoid Fever	Crumpton's Factory
Taylor, Lawson	16th	North Carolina	E	Inf.	194	2	1	29-Jul-64	---	Knight's Factory
Taylor, R.	49th	Virginia	E	Inf.	177	3	2	10-Sep-62	---	Miller's Factory
Teague, John	7th	North Carolina	K	Inf.	178	8	2	30-Aug-62	Typhoid Fever	Crumpton's Factory
Tempelton, George W. (M.?)	14th	South Carolina	F	Inf.	79	7	1	08-Jan-63	Phthisis Pulmonaris	Saunder's Factory
Thacker, Daniel M.	20th	Georgia	D	Inf.	123	6	3	23-Dec-62	Typhoid Fever	Christian's Factory
Thedford, Charles L.	20th	Georgia	B	Inf.	159	1	5	05-Oct-61	---	Warwick House
Thomas, A. T.	9th	Louisiana	I	Inf.	167	3	3	13-May-62	---	Christian's Factory
Thomas, Benjamin	48th	North Carolina	E	Inf.	144	4	2	16-Nov-62	Typhoid Fever	Odd Fellow's Hall
Thomas, Benjamin F., Corpl.	11th	Georgia	I	Inf.	197	4	1	02-Jun-64	KIA 5/06/64	Ferguson's Factory
Thomas, Charles R.	12th	Georgia	F	Inf.	160	5	3	21-Jul-62	---	Warwick House
Thomas, James R.	50th	Georgia	A	Inf.	188	9	2	30-May-63	DOW	Reid's Factory
* Thomas, John E.	8th	Alabama	D	Inf.	144	8	2	18-Nov-62	---	Crumpton's Factory
Thomas, Kinnon (or Kineon)	35th	Georgia	A	Inf.	179	3	2	15-Sep-62	DOW 8/09/62	Ford's Factory
Thomas, W. L. S.	9th	Louisiana	H	Inf.	168	4	3	06-May-62	---	Ladies Relief Hospt.

* See Part III - 104

NAME	REGT. or UNIT	STATE	COMPANY	BRANCH of SERVICE	LOT#	Grave No.	ROW	DATE of BURIAL or DEATH	CAUSE of DEATH	HOSPITAL
Thomas, William	8th	Alabama	G	Inf.	188	2	5	16-Jun-63	---	Claytor's Factory
Thomas, William B.	22nd	Virginia	D	Inf.	188	7	5	10-Jun-63	---	Ferguson's Factory
Thomas, William C.	48th	North Carolina	G	Inf.	Yk. Sq.	---	---	11-Jan-64	Small Pox	Pest House
* Thomas, William H.	14th	Alabama	G	Inf.	182	10	1	04-Nov-62	---	Ferguson's Factory
Thomason, Arnold D.	Holcombe's Legion	South Carolina	G	Cav.	178	1	4	31-Aug-62	---	College Hospital
Thomerson, C. H.	26th	Mississippi	F	Cav.	199	6	1	20-Apr-63	---	Langhorne's Factory
* Thompson, Allen	2nd	Georgia	L	Inf.	162	6	4	06-Aug-62	---	Miller's Factory
* Thompson, Blount James	38th	North Carolina	F	Cav.	Yk. Sq.	---	---	18-Feb-64	Small Pox	Pest House
Thompson, G. F. M.	4th	Georgia	A	Inf.	162	10	1	01-Aug-62	Typhoid Fever	Warwick House
Thompson, J. D.	1st	Mississippi	D	Inf.	188	3	5	26-Jul-63	---	Burton's Factory
* Thompson, J. N.	16th	North Carolina	C	Cav.	170	4	4	15-Mar-62	Pneumonia	Warwick House
Thompson, Jerrimiah T.	61st	Georgia	D	Inf.	182	8	5	13-Nov-62	---	Candler's Factory
Thompson, John	12th	Alabama	G	Inf.	193	7	5	17-May-64	---	Knight's Factory
Thompson, John B.	37th	North Carolina	K	Inf.	160	10	1	07-Jul-62	Febris Cont. Con.	Ferguson's Factory
Thompson, John D.	15th	North Carolina	H	Inf.	162	6	1	07-Aug-62	Typhoid Fever	Miller's Factory
Thompson, John G.	47th	Virginia	B	Inf.	187	8	3	22-Jan-63	Apoplexia	Burton's Factory
Thompson, Joseph E., Sgt.	44th	Alabama	K	Inf.	79	1	4	10-Jan-63	Chronic Diarreha	Crumpton's Factory
* Thompson, P. N.	1st	South Carolina	D	Cav.	188	7	1	03-Jun-63	---	Langhorne's Factory
Thompson, Samuel R., Sgt.	44th	Georgia	C	Inf.	179	7	2	13-Aug-63	Typhoid Fever	Crumpton's Factory
Thompson, Thompson J.	Cynthiana	Kentucky	---	---	183	7	1	17-Jan-63	Pneumonia	Knight's Factory
Thomson, L. M., Lt. (age 27)	48th	Alabama	A	Inf.	196	4	2	20-Sep-63	---	Coyner's Spring
Thornberg, Andrew M.	6th	Alabama	G	Inf.	180	1	5	02-Oct-62	---	Miller's Factory
Threadgill, John H.	24th	Georgia	D	Inf.	189	9	2	30-Apr-64	---	Ferguson's Factory
Thrower, L. B.	Thomas Legion	North Carolina	A	Inf.	122	2	3	20-Nov-62	---	Ford's Factory
Thurman, J. M.	15th	South Carolina	H	Inf.	190	1	4	05-Jul-64	---	Camp Davis
Tilton, William J.	21st	Georgia	I	Inf.	187	5	3	25-Jan-63	Splenitis	Christian's Factory
Tinker, Jacob	48th	Georgia	D	Inf.	177	3	5	22-Aug-62	Disease	Reid's Factory
Tinsley, William Vincent	12th	Georgia	C	Inf.	180	9	2	24-Sep-62	Disease	Reid's Factory
* Todd, Hudson (or Houston)	1st Orr's Rifles	South Carolina	E	Inf.	166	4	1	08-May-62	Measles	Ferguson's Factory
Todd, James Erskine	14th	Alabama	H	Inf.	177	5	4	27-Aug-62	Typhoid Fever	Crumpton's Factory
Todd, Levia A.	Palmetto Sh.Shooters	South Carolina	I	Inf.	173	3	4	03-Jul-62	---	Crumpton's Factory
* Todd, S. D.	14th	Georgia	G	Inf.	200	6	2	28-Jan-64	Disease	Ladies Relief Hospt.
* Todd, Thomas	23rd	Georgia	K	Inf.	182	3	4	17-Oct-62	Febris Typhoides	Miller's Factory
Tolbert, E. N.	35th	North Carolina	G	Inf.	162	6	2	03-Aug-62	---	Booker's Factory
* Toler, Alsey K.	53rd	Virginia	G	Inf.	193	10	3	15-May-64	Meningitis	Christian's Factory
Tomlinson, W. M.	42nd	Louisiana	K	Inf.	190	2	3	27-Jul-64	---	Knight's Factory
Tompkins, Edmund T., Sgt.	10th	Virginia	D	Inf.	165	9	2	11-Aug-62	Dysentery Acute	Reid's Factory
* Torrney, John	25th	Virginia	G	Inf.	198	6	2	28-Sep-64	---	College Hospital
Townsend, J. C.	5th	Texas	E	Inf.	Yk. Sq.	26th	2nd Line	11-Feb-63	Small Pox	Pest House
Trainer, J. A.					172	7	2	15-Jun-62	Pneumonia	Taliaferro's Factory

* See Part III - 105

NAME	REGT. or UNIT	STATE	COMPANY	BRANCH of SERVICE	LOT#	Grave No.	ROW	DATE of BURIAL or DEATH	CAUSE of DEATH	HOSPITAL
Trammel, James W.	9th	Georgia	G	Inf.	Yk. Sq.	24th	3rd Line	15-Jan-63	Small Pox	Pest House
Trammel, Thomas O.(D.?)	2nd Rifles	South Carolina	H	Inf.	189	10	3	19-Feb-64	Pneumonia	College Hospital
Trenton, Bennett	8th	Alabama	K	Inf.	185	4	3	03-May-64	---	Christian's Factory
Tribble, R. W.	7th	South Carolina	B	Inf.	170	5	4	27-Mar-62	Typhoid Fever	Warwick House
* Trivett, John E.	37th	North Carolina	E	Inf.	183	9	3	15-Jan-63	Phley Erysipelas	Ford's Factory
Trotter, William	2nd	South Carolina	K	Inf.	190	6	2	01-Jul-64	---	Christian's Factory
Trout, James M.	18th	North Carolina	E	Inf.	101	1	1	18-May-63	Disease	Burton's Factory
Troutman, Joseph	5th	North Carolina	F	Inf.	195	1	2	14-Feb-63	Diarrhea Chronic	Langhorne's Factory
Truslow, G.	50th	Virginia	I	Inf.	198	4	5	04-Nov-64	---	Crumpton's Factory
* Tucker, Charles B., Corpl.	5th	Florida	I	Inf.	184	9	2	19-Apr-96	Pneumonia	College Hospital
Tucker, Elijah D.	8th	Florida	G	Inf.	146	7	5	15-Dec-62	Disease	Candler's Factory
Tucker, J. L.	17th	Mississippi	B	Inf.	146	8	3	16-Dec-62	---	Crumpton's Factory
* Tucker, Levi T.	33rd	North Carolina	A	Inf.	197	10	1	01-Jun-64	DOW 05/06/64	Camp Davis
Tucker, W. S.	17th	Mississippi	K	Inf.	78	9	5	02-Dec-62	---	Ferguson's Factory
Turberville, J. H.	28th	North Carolina	C	Inf.	180	1	4	30-Sep-62	Pneumonia	Claytor's Factory
Turner, George L.	28th	North Carolina	H 1st	Inf.	188	1	4	14-Jun-63	Meningitis	Camp Davis
Turner, Henry	12th	North Carolina	B	Inf.	161	7	5	17-Jul-62	Tuberculosis	Warwick House
Turner, John W.	28th	Georgia	B	Inf.	161	7	5	15-Jul-62	---	Ford's Factory
Turner, M.	6th	Georgia	B	Inf.	180	2	3	24-Sep-62	---	Crumpton's Factory
Underwood, W. H.	Sumter Artillery	Georgia	B	Art.	78	8	3	03-Dec-62	---	Ferguson's Factory
Unknown	3rd	North Carolina	C or K	Inf.	160	10	3	06-Jul-62	---	Ford's Factory
* Unknown	---	North Carolina	---	---	190	10	1	26-Jun-64	DOA @ Hospital	Wayside Hospital
Unknown	Unknown	Unknown	---	---	168	2	1	23-Apr-62	---	Ladies Relief Hospt.
* Unknown	Unknown	Unknown	---	---	168	10	2	27-Apr-62	---	Warwick House
* Unknown	Unknown	Unknown	---	---	170	4	2	27-Jan-62	---	Rail Car O&A R.R.
Unknown	Unknown	Unknown	---	---	180	5	1	12-Oct-62	---	Rail Car Southside R.R.
* Vail, J. W.	5th	Alabama	E	Inf.	172	10	3	09-Jun-62	---	Langhorne's Factory
Van Winkle, J. A.	18th	Mississippi	H	Inf.	187	8	1	23-Jan-63	---	Langhorne's Factory
Vann, William A., Chaplin	13th	North Carolina	Staff	Inf.	189	9	1	29-Apr-64	Febris Typhoides	College Hospital
Vaughan, M. C.	Phillip's Legion	Georgia	M	Inf.	177	1	3	01-Sep-62	---	College Hospital
Vaughn, George Washington	31st	Georgia	H	Inf.	180	6	4	08-Oct-62	---	Christian's Factory
Venters, Washington Harmon	7th	South Carolina	E	Inf.	186	6	2	21-Jun-64	DOW	Booker's Factory
* Vernon, John Radford	22nd	North Carolina	H	Inf.	177	8	1	17-Aug-62	Febris Typhoides	Warwick House
Vernon, George M.	61st	Alabama	F	Inf.	189	6	5	10-May-64	---	Ferguson's Factory
Vernon, William H.	38th	Virginia	A	Inf.	173	1	3	10-Jun-62	Rheumatism	Reid's Factory
Vertegan, W. F. (Vertegans)	16th	Virginia	G	Cav.	202	8	3	13-Apr-65	---	Knight's Factory
Vick, Benjamin P.	41st	Virginia	H	Inf.	193	2	5	11-Jul-64	Typhoid Fever	Ferguson's Factory
Vickers, William H.	44th	Georgia	D	Inf.	Yk. Sq.	3rd	3rd Line	06-May-63	Small Pox	Pest House

* See Part III - 106

NAME	REGT. or UNIT	STATE	COMPANY	BRANCH of SERVICE	LOT#	Grave No.	ROW	DATE of BURIAL or DEATH	CAUSE of DEATH	HOSPITAL
Vickery, Richard	50th	Georgia	B	Inf.	197	3	4	03-Jun-64	---	Burton's Factory
Vinson, John	26th	North Carolina	G	Inf.	198	10	3	05-Aug-64	DOW 5/05/64	Ladies Relief Hospt.
Wade, Castleton W.	57th	Virginia	G	Inf.	Yk. Sq.	26th	4th Line	12-Feb-63	Small Pox	Pest House
Wadsworth, John C.	48th	North Carolina	E	Inf.	79	2	3	15-Jan-63	DOW 12/13/62? - Phthisis	Burton's Factory
Waesner, George W.	28th	North Carolina	E	Inf.	192	9	3	22-Jun-63	Pneumonia	Christian's Factory
Wainwright, W. T.	31st	Georgia	K	Inf.	191	6	1	06-Feb-63	Brain Fever/Cerebritis	Ferguson's Factory
Wakefield, B. F.	26th	Alabama	C	Inf.	161	6	5	17-Jul-62	---	Candler's Factory
Walden, Francis M.	44th	Georgia	D	Inf.	191	3	5	17-Feb-63	Typhoid Fever	On Rail Car
Waldrop, D.	15th	Louisiana	G	Inf.	188	10	3	17-Jan-63	---	Camp Davis
Walker, H. H.	20th	Mississippi	McGehee's	Inf.	159	4	4	30-Sep-61	---	Warwick House
Walker, J.	50th	Georgia	D	Inf.	144	8	3	18-Nov-62	---	Claytor's Factory
Walker, T. L.	2nd	Mississippi	F	Inf.	162	3	3	25-Jul-62	---	Ferguson's Factory
Wall, Richard	1st Orr's Rifles	South Carolina	B	Inf.	193	7	4	17-May-64	DOW 5/06/64	Knight's Factory
Wall, T.	21st	North Carolina	I	Inf.	100	3	3	26-Nov-62	---	Knight's Factory
Wall, Thomas J.	2nd	Virginia	B	Cav.	173	8	3	29-Jun-62	Rubeola	Schoolfield's Office
Wallace, D. W.	18th	Mississippi	H	Inf.	199	3	1	24-Mar-63	---	Claytor's Factory
Wallace, James	19th	Mississippi	K	Inf.	144	7	2	18-Nov-62	---	Crumpton's Factory
Wallace, N. (Noah?)	18th (37th?)	North Carolina	G	Inf.	165	3	3	17-Aug-62	---	Talliaferro's Factory
Walsaw, J. M.	Unknown	Unknown	---	---	Yk. Sq.	Near	Yk. Sq.	14-Dec-62	Small Pox	Pest House
Walter, J. W.	60th	Virginia	I	Inf.	202	10	3	14-Mar-65	---	Christian's Factory
Walter, Thomas B.	60th	Virginia	G	Inf.	194	2	4	02-Aug-64	---	Ferguson's Factory
Ward, B. L.	2nd	North Carolina	D	Inf.	200	10	1	06-Dec-63	---	Reid's Factory
Ward, E. W.	14th	North Carolina	E	Inf.	200	5	4	20-Nov-63	Diarrhea	Candler's Factory
Ward, Ira C.	44th	Georgia	E	Inf.	200	6	3	03-Feb-64	---	College Hospital
Ward, Peter D.	48th	North Carolina	B	Inf.	79	7	2	01-Jan-63	DOW 12/13/62	Burton's Factory
Ward, W. L.	13th	Alabama	F	Inf.	183	5	3	19-Jan-63	---	Christian's Factory
Wardlaw, Alfred W., 2nd Corpl.	24th	Georgia	F	Inf.	Yk. Sq.	28th	3rd Line	19-Feb-63	Small Pox	Pest House
Ware, John C.	20th	Georgia	E	Inf.	198	7	5	17-Sep-64	DOW 5/06/64	Christian's Factory
Warlick, Daniel	Poague's Batty.	Virginia	---	Art.	160	8	3	14-Aug-63	---	Camp Davis
Warren, Micajah	13th	North Carolina	I	Inf.	192	6	4	04-Jul-63	Febris Remittens	Camp Davis
Waterfield, Saunders	61st	Virginia	C	Inf.	101	5	3	31-Dec-62	Typhoid Fever	Crumpton's Factory
Watkins, B.	Latham's Batty.	Alabama	H 1st	Art.	191	2	4	14-Feb-63	Pneumonia	Christian's Factory
Watson, J. M.	14th	Alabama	F	Inf.	182	8	1	09-Nov-62	---	Langhorne's Factory
Watson, John William, Sgt.	47th	Virginia	I	Inf.	189	1	2	04-May-64	Pneumonia	Knight's Factory
Watson, James R.	12th	Virginia	F	Inf.	101	7	1	05-Jan-63	Abcess of Brain	Talliaferro's Factory
Watson, John A.	59th	Georgia	C	Inf.	192	2	4	07-Aug-63	Disease	Crumpton's Factory
Watson, John G.	12th	North Carolina	D 2nd	Inf.	183	2	3	15-Jan-63	Disease	Christian's Factory
Watson, John T.	15th	Alabama	G	Inf.	170	9	1	16-Dec-61	---	College Hospital
Watson, R.	1st Battn.	Virginia	A	Art.	202	5	5	07-May-65	---	Camp Davis

* See Part III - 107

NAME	REGT. or UNIT	STATE	COMPANY	BRANCH of SERVICE	LOT#	Grave No.	ROW	DATE of BURIAL or DEATH	CAUSE of DEATH	HOSPITAL
Watson, S.	6th	Alabama	B	Inf.	195	8	3	24-Feb-63	---	College Hospital
* Watts, Benjamin F.	1st	Texas	G	Inf.	172	9	1	02-Jun-62	Rubeola	Langhorne's Factory
Watts, Joseph T.	9th	Louisiana	G	Inf.	160	2	3	04-Jul-62	Disease	Talliaferro's Factory
* Watts, N. V.	48th	Alabama	F	Inf.	186	6	3	22-Jun-64	---	Christian's Factory
Watts, William Archibald	3rd	Georgia	C	Inf.	199	7	3	25-Nov-63	Disease	Miller's Factory
Wayne, Calvin C.	44th	North Carolina	I	Inf.	189	2	4	04-May-64	Febris Typhoides	Camp Davis
Weatherman, George P.	1st Battn. S. S.	North Carolina	B	Inf.	Yk. Sq.	---	---	28-Dec-63	Small Pox	Pest House
Weatherly, Samuel S.	5th	Texas	I	Inf.	187	1	4	27-Jan-63	Typhoid Fever	Burton's Factory
Weaver, Adam	18th	North Carolina	A	Inf.	78	4	1	11-Dec-62	Pneumonia	Ford's Factory
Weaver, John	60th	Georgia	I	Inf.	200	4	5	13-Nov-63	Inflamation of Liver	College Hospital
Weaver, Robert F.	55th	Virginia	A	Inf.	183	3	1	16-Jan-63	Disease	Talliaferro's Factory
Webb, Benjamin	1st (McCreary's)	South Carolina	I	Inf.	197	1	2	02-Jun-64	DOW 5/05/64	Reid's Factory
Webb, John S.	9th	Louisiana	C	Inf.	167	7	1	19-May-62	---	Ladies Relief Hospt.
* Webb, Peter D.	45th	Virginia	I	Inf.	202	9	1	26-Mar-65	---	Crumpton's Factory
Webb, Samuel, Corpl.	53rd	North Carolina	I	Inf.	194	5	4	20-Jul-64	---	Camp Davis
Webb, Thomas	11th	Virginia	B	Cav.	192	7	3	01-Jul-63	Fever Continua	Reid's Factory
Webb, W. T.	2nd	Georgia	A	Inf.	122	10	1	20-Nov-62	---	Ferguson's Factory
Webster, J. F.	1st	Maryland	I	Inf.	167	6	1	21-May-62	---	Christian's Factory
* Weddington, William A. G.	20th	North Carolina	B	Inf.	123	6	5	23-Dec-62	Diarrhea	Reid's Factory
Weeks, Cornelius	22nd (deserter)	Virginia	K	Inf.	193	4	1	21-May-64	Shot to Death	Wayside Hospital
* Weems, J. H.	1st	South Carolina	K	Inf.	199	3	3	28-Mar-63	DOWs	Claytor's Factory
Weiman, Henry	Volunteers	Virginia	Pierces'	Inf.	165	6	1	21-Aug-62	---	Christian's Factory
Welch, C. W.	10th Militia	Virginia	---	Inf.	173	7	2	01-Jul-62	Diarrhea	Saunder's Factory
Welch, J. W.	13th	North Carolina	C	Inf.	186	1	2	24-Jun-64	---	Christian's Factory
Wellington, R.	26th	Georgia	H	Inf.	Yk. Sq.	17th	3rd Line	23-Dec-62	Small Pox	Pest House
Wells, Jesse L.	2nd	North Carolina	B	Inf.	Yk. Sq.	24th	2nd Line	29-Jan-63	Small Pox	Pest House
Wells, T.	Irish Battn.	Virginia	-	Inf.	171	8	3	31-May-62	---	Crumpton's Factory
Wells, William	18th	North Carolina	C	Inf.	200	1	4	12-Oct-63	Pneumonia	Reid's Factory
Wells, William J.	42nd	Virginia	G	Inf.	166	2	2	06-May-62	---	Christian's Factory
West, Thomas Upton	46th	North Carolina	B	Inf.	191	1	4	08-Feb-63	---	Claytor's Factory
West, W. J.	28th	Georgia	B	Inf.	169	10	3	25-May-62	---	Christian's Factory
Whatley, Cicero Columbus	21st	Georgia	F	Inf.	160	9	3	26-Jun-62	---	Crumpton's Factory
* Wheatley, O.	15th	Georgia	A	Inf.	186	3	3	25-Jun-62	---	Burton's Factory
Wheeler, Marcus D.	35th	Georgia	I	Inf.	192	8	1	27-Jun-62	Erysipelas	Ferguson's Factory
Whicker, William T.	61st	Virginia	B	Inf.	195	8	1	20-Feb-63	---	Candler's Factory
Whidden, Bennett	8th	Florida	K	Inf.	165	7	3	10-Sep-62	Pneumonia	Ferguson's Factory
* Whitacker, Hugh H.	48th	Alabama	F	Inf.	183	7	3	18-Jan-63	---	Langhorne's Factory
Whitaker, W. Joshua	31st	Georgia	I	Inf.	122	10	3	20-Nov-64	---	Ferguson's Factory
White, B., Lieut.	60th	Virginia	I	Inf.	178	9	5	25-Aug-62	---	Claytor's Factory
White, Dameron S.	33rd	North Carolina	F	Inf.	195	10	2	11-Feb-63	Pneumonia	Christian's Factory

* See Part III - 108

NAME	REGT. or UNIT	COMPANY	STATE	BRANCH of SERVICE	LOT#	Grave No.	ROW	DATE of BURIAL or DEATH	CAUSE of DEATH	HOSPITAL
White, Harmon	46th	I	North Carolina	Inf.	197	2	4	03-Jun-64	DOW 5/5/64	Burton's Factory
White, Hewel L.	28th	A	North Carolina	Inf.	191	5	4	25-Nov-63	Diarrhea Chronic	Langhorne's Factory
White, James P.	28th	A	North Carolina	Inf.	177	9	2	12-Aug-62	Febris Typhoides	Claytor's Factory
Whitehead, Madison	18th	C	Georgia	Inf.	198	10	5	07-Aug-64	DOW 5/06/64	Burton's Factory
Whitehurst, Demsey	16th	G	Virginia	Inf.	200	1	2	14-Oct-63	Diarrhea	Christian's Factory
Whiteside, James H.	1st	H	South Carolina	Cav.	199	10	2	21-Feb-63	Pneumonia	Claytor's Factory
Whitfield, P. W.	2nd	A	Mississippi	Inf.	Yk. Sq.	20th	5th Line	02-Jan-63	Small Pox	Pest House
Whitley, Joshua P.	9th	C	Louisiana	Inf.	169	10	1	25-May-62	...	Reid's Factory
* Whitlock, A. Thomas	4th	G	Georgia	Inf.	193	5	5	18-May-64	Dropsy	Ferguson's Factory
Whitlock, C. D.	10th	I	Georgia	Inf.	196	6	1	21-Aug-63	Disease	Burton's Factory
* Whitlock, R. H.	18th	I	North Carolina	Inf.	191	3	3	16-Feb-63	Febris Typhoides	Wade's Factory
Whitter, G. R.	14th	C	Alabama	Inf.	171	3	2	05-Jun-62	...	Ferguson's Factory
Whittle, Isaih (also Isalm)	14th	D	South Carolina	Inf.	200	8	1	10-Dec-63	Fever	Christian's Factory
Whorley, H. C.	1st Reserves	H	Virginia	Inf.	198	8	3	14-Aug-64	...	Ladies Relief Hospt.
Wiggins, J. E.	13th	K	Alabama	Inf.	193	1	4	05-Jun-64	...	Knight's Factory
* Wiggins, William E.	59th	B	Georgia	Inf.	192	7	1	30-Jun-63	Typhoid Pneumonia	Ferguson's Factory
Wilder, J. B.	6th	H	South Carolina	Inf.	181	5	1	11-Nov-62	...	Christian's Factory
Wiles, B. F.	31st	D	Georgia	Inf.	180	3	5	30-Sep-62	DOW 9/17/62	Burton's Factory
Wiley, J. R.	17th	D	South Carolina	Inf.	181	8	3	22-Oct-62	Phthisis Pulmonaris	Christian's Factory
Wiie, Richard	Phillip's Legion	L	Georgia	Inf.	185	9	2	16-Feb-64	...	College Hospital
Wilkerson, James D.	6th	B	Louisiana	Inf.	198	4	3	23-Oct-64	...	Christian's Factory
Wilkes, F. M.	38th	C	Georgia	Inf.	198	5	3	17-Nov-64	...	Reid's Factory
* Wilkes, James H.	4th	I	Georgia	Inf.	146	4	4	09-Dec-62	Pneumonia	Talliaferro's Factory
Wilkins, T. J.	18th	B	Georgia	Inf.	191	8	3	01-Feb-63	Pneumonia	Langhorne's Factory
William, Williams M.	50th	C	Georgia	Inf.	78	1	3	28-Nov-62	Typhoid Fever	Knight's Factory
Williams, C.	22nd	C	North Carolina	Inf.	194	3	5	29-Jul-64	...	Christian's Factory
* Williams, D. R.	5th	H	Texas	Inf.	178	7	4	05-Sep-62	Tuberculosis	Claytor's Factory
Williams, F. M.	20th	I	Georgia	Inf.	159	5	2	07-Sep-61	...	Warwick House
Williams, G. B.	2nd	A	Mississippi	Inf.	172	2	3	04-Jul-62	...	Ferguson's Factory
* Williams, Hartwell Spain, Sgt.	34th	E	North Carolina	Inf.	177	4	1	23-Aug-62	Febris Typhoides	Christian's Factory
Williams, Henry	33rd	I	North Carolina	Inf.	172	6	3	18-Jun-62	Pneumonia	Claytor's Factory
Williams, J. C.	2nd Battn.	C	Mississippi	Inf.	199	10	3	31-Mar-63	...	Christian's Factory
* Williams, J. E.	Phillip's Legion	A	Georgia	Inf.	100	7	2	04-Dec-62	...	Knight's Factory
Williams, J. W.	5th	G	Alabama	Inf.	179	9	1	16-Sep-62	...	Langhorne's Factory
* Williams, James	1st	E	North Carolina	Art.	Yk. Sq.	-	-	07-Mar-64	Small Pox	Pest House
Williams, James	38th	G	North Carolina	Inf.	144	10	1	15-Nov-62	Pneumonia	Crumpton's Factory
Williams, James H.	59th	F	Georgia	Inf.	201	6	2	09-Jun-64	DOW 5/06/64	Camp Davis
* Williams, James W.	1st	E	North Carolina	Art.	123	7	4	26-Dec-62	...	Christian's Factory
Williams, Jas. J.	30th	K	Mississippi	Inf.	199	4	3	10-Apr-63	...	Ladies Relief Hospt.
Williams, Kendrick	Palmetto Batty.	-	South Carolina	Art.	201	10	1	06-Jun-64	DOW 5/06/64	Camp Davis

* See Part III - 109

NAME	REGT. or UNIT	STATE	COMPANY	BRANCH of SERVICE	LOT#	Grave No.	ROW	DATE of BURIAL or DEATH	CAUSE of DEATH	HOSPITAL
Williams, L. B.	20th	Mississippi	Pettis'	Inf.	159	9	4	06-Oct-61	---	College Hospital
Williams, P. G.	19th	Georgia	F	Inf.	187	6	5	24-Jan-63	---	Burton's Factory
Williams, S. W.	9th	Louisiana	H	Inf.	144	6	3	20-Nov-62	Pneumonia	Odd Pellow's Hall
Williams, Samuel M.	21st	North Carolina	L	Inf.	146	10	3	05-Dec-62	DOW	Ferguson's Factory
Williams, Stephen	50th	Georgia	I	Inf.	193	3	1	22-May-64	---	Ladies Relief Hospt.
Williamson, George Washington	38th	Georgia	C	Inf.	177	9	5	12-Aug-62	Small Pox	Burton's Factory
Williamson, Henry	26th	Georgia	D	Inf.	Yk. Sq.	27th	5th Line	26-Feb-63	Typhoid Pneumonia	Pest House
Williamson, Willis	4th	North Carolina	D	Inf.	101	9	2	02-Jan-63	DOW 5/02/63	Reid's Factory
Willingham, Jefferson M.	44th	Georgia	C	Inf.	188	4	1	27-Jun-63	---	Camp Davis
Willingham, John H.	47th	Alabama	D	Inf.	178	2	2	02-Oct-62	---	Langhorne's Factory
Willis, John O.	16th	Georgia	E	Inf.	185	1	2	18-Apr-64	Pneumonia	Ferguson's Factory
Wilson, Benjamin	23rd	North Carolina	I	Inf.	78	7	2	02-Dec-62	Diarrhea	Miller's Factory
Wilson, Benjamin P.	28th	North Carolina	C	Inf.	171	9	3	30-May-62	---	Christian's Factory
Wilson, E. S.	9th	Louisiana	F	Inf.	166	8	2	07-May-62	DOW 8/22/62	Ladies Relief Hospt.
Wilson, J. B.	5th	Texas	K	Inf.	181	7	2	25-Oct-62	Pleuritis	Booker's Factory
Wilson, John W.	48th	Alabama	D	Inf.	181	10	3	13-Oct-62	---	Knight's Factory
Wilson, Joseph C.	18th	North Carolina	B	Inf.	183	9	1	16-Jan-63	Disease	College Hospital
Wilson, Marion	2nd	Arkansas	Manning's	Inf.	158	1	2	21-Jun-61	---	Ladies Relief Hospt.
Wilson, Paschal	Phillip's Legion	Georgia	Cook's	Inf.	159	3	4	06-Oct-61	Typhoid Fever	Christian's Factory
Wilson, W. Davis	44th	North Carolina	A	Inf.	188	9	1	30-May-63	Small Pox	Saunder's Factory
Wilson, William (Miles?)	1st (McCreary's)	South Carolina	C	Inf.	179	4	1	19-Sep-62	Pneumonia	Ferguson's Factory
Wimberty, George E.	6th	Georgia	I	Inf.	101	1	4	27-Dec-62	Febris Typhoides	Christian's Factory
Winner, William	25th	Virginia	D	Inf.	168	10	5	27-Apr-62	Diarrhea Chronic	Pest House
Windham, Elias Charles 4th Corpl.	5th	Florida	A	Inf.	Yk. Sq.	2nd	1st Line	13-May-63	---	Ferguson's Factory
Wingler, Isham	26th	North Carolina	D	Inf.	185	2	1	24-Feb-64	Typhoid Fever	Crumpton's Factory
Wise, James W.	38th	North Carolina	D	Inf.	161	4	2	14-Aug-62	Pneumonia	Crumpton's Factory
Wise, Reuben	52nd	Virginia	H	Inf.	160	6	1	19-Jul-62	Febris Typhoides	Knight's Factory
Wiseman, J. F.	60th	Virginia	I	Inf.	198	6	5	11-Oct-64	---	Christian's Factory
Witt, Daniel B., Jr.	58th	Virginia	H	Inf.	160	3	3	07-Jul-62	---	Langhorne's Factory
Womack, Francis S.	3rd	Georgia	G	Inf.	191	4	3	18-Mar-95	Pneumonia	Christian's Factory
Womble, Andrew J.	44th	North Carolina	K	Inf.	193	10	4	27-Jan-63	Febris Typhoides	Ladies Relief Hospt.
Wood, Britton W.	26th	Georgia	D	Inf.	100	3	4	20-May-64	---	Knight's Factory
Wood, G. H.	61st	Alabama	I	Inf.	197	4	1	28-Nov-62	Pneumonia	Crumpton's Factory
Wood, G. S.	33rd	North Carolina	D	Inf.	172	9	1	25-May-64	Small Pox	Claytor's Factory
Wood, James M.	21st	Georgia	C	Inf.	Yk. Sq.	8	2	13-Jun-62	---	Pest House
Wood, Joseph B.	60th	Georgia	F	Inf.	202	24th	4th Line	12-Jan-63	---	Crumpton's Factory
Woodring, John	51st	Virginia	H	Inf.	198	7	5	06-Jul-62	---	Crumpton's Factory
Woods, W. G.	Gilmore's Battn.	Unknown	-	Inf.	194	2	4	31-Dec-64	DOW 5/06/64	Mr. Jones'
Woolf, N. S., Sgt.	20th	Georgia	E	Inf.	190	8	1	30-Jul-64		Reid's Factory
Woolhop, Charles								27-Jun-64		

* See Part III - 110

NAME	REGT. or UNIT	STATE	COMPANY	BRANCH of SERVICE	LOT#	Grave No.	ROW	DATE of BURIAL or DEATH	CAUSE of DEATH	HOSPITAL
Worley, William S.	27th	North Carolina	D	Inf.	185	2	2	25-Apr-64	---	College Hospital
Worthington, John (Wetherington)	60th	Georgia	H	Inf.	180	3	4	26-Sep-62	---	Claytor's Factory
* Wrenn, James W., Sgt.	6th	Virginia	F	Cav.	202	9	4	21-Mar-65	Pneumonia	Christian's Factory
Wright, Alfred Spinks	46th	North Carolina	G	Inf.	193	6	3	19-May-64	---	Knight's Factory
* Wright, Alvin H.	1st	Georgia	E	---	181	4	3	26-Oct-62	---	S. S. Rail Car
Wright, D. N.	13th	Georgia	B	Inf.	Yk. Sq.	19th	3rd Line	31-Dec-62	Small Pox	Pest House
* Wright, Eli	61st	Alabama	E	Inf.	198	5	1	23-Oct-64	---	Camp Davis
Wright, James D.	44th	North Carolina	H	Inf.	200	3	5	22-Oct-63	Phthisis Pulmonaris	Burton's Factory
Wright, John W.	51st	Virginia	E	Inf.	189	5	3	11-May-64	Pneumonia Typhoides	Ferguson's Factory
Wright, W. P.	16th	Mississippi	D	Inf.	171	9	1	31-May-62	---	Crumpton's Factory
* Wyley (also Wylie), Jonathan	17th	South Carolina	A	Inf.	122	1	2	18-Nov-62	Pneumonia	Christian's Factory
Wynn, Robert P.	12th	Alabama	F	Inf.	197	7	4	27-May-64	---	Crumpton's Factory
Yarber, James	16th	Mississippi	F	Inf.	167	6	3	19-May-62	---	Reid's Factory
* Yarber, W. R.	3rd	Georgia	I	Inf.	195	7	4	27-Feb-63	---	Burton's Factory
Yarborough, J. C.	14th	North Carolina	F	Inf.	Yk. Sq.	26th	1st Line	10-Feb-64	Small Pox	Pest House
Yarborough, J. M.	7th	North Carolina	M	Inf.	160	2	2	09-Jul-62	---	Christian's Factory
Yarbrough, Thomas J.	21st	Georgia	F	Inf.	168	6	4	09-May-62	Measles	Christian's Factory
* Yarrington, Andrew B.	26th	Virginia	G	Inf.	198	4	4	30-Oct-64	DOW 6/24/64	Ferguson's Factory
Yawn, Augustus A.	31st	Georgia	I	Inf.	194	7	3	13-Jul-64	---	Camp Davis
Yawn, Ephraim	49th	Georgia	B	Inf.	79	10	4	28-Dec-62	---	Christian's Factory
* York, Alexander B.	24th	Georgia	E	Inf.	172	2	4	11-Jun-62	Gangrene	Ford's Factory
* Young, A. A.	48th	North Carolina	G	Inf.	101	9	4	01-Jan-63	---	Ford's Factory
Young, William	19th	Georgia	Columbus Vol.	Inf.	159	5	3	18-Sep-61	---	Washington Hotel
* Youngblood, Francis M.	8th	Louisiana	E	Inf.	191	5	1	07-Feb-63	Rheumatism Chronic	Claytor's Factory
* Yow, Andrew C.	48th	North Carolina	D	Inf.	187	10	1	12-Feb-63	Diarrhea Chronic	College Hospital
Yow, Moses	5th	North Carolina	B	Inf.	78	5	2	09-Dec-62	---	Reid's Factory
Zimmerman, Samuel R.	21st	North Carolina	K	Inf.	190	10	3	26-Jun-64	DOW 6/18/64	Pratts Hospital

Union Troops

R Ackers, Sidney E. A.	11th	Michigan	M	Cav.	3	5	3	03-Jun-65	Disease	Pratt Hospital
* Adams, A. Q. (NR)	11th	Michigan	M	Cav.	3	3	5th line	03-Jun-65	---	Pratt Hospital
* Allen, Benjamin	10th	New Jersey	G	Inf.	3	1	5th line	22-Dec-64	---	Crumpton's Factory

* See Part III - 111

	NAME	REGT. or UNIT	COMPANY	STATE	BRANCH of SERVICE	LOT#	Grave No.	ROW	DATE of BURIAL or DEATH	CAUSE of DEATH	HOSPITAL
R	Almy, Frank M.	1st	D	Massachusetts	Cav.	3	3	5	01-May-65	Murdered	John Dugans
4719	Andrews, Charles	1st	C	Vermont	Inf.	Yk. Sq.	3	5th line	30-Jul-62	---	Fairgrounds
*	Andrews, Charles E. B. (NR)	1st	H	New York	Cav.				20-Jun-64	KIA BOL?	?
4870	Arnold, William, Corpl.	77th	B	New York	Inf.	3	7	1st line	22-Sep-64	DOW 5/06/64	Crumpton's Factory
4610	Bader, Henry	1st	K	Maryland	Inf.	Yk. Sq.	7	5th line	31-Jul-62	Disease	Fairgrounds
4959	Ballard, Joseph	147th	K	New York	Inf.	2	10	5th line	26-Aug-64	DOW 5/05/64	Crumton's Factory
4714	Barker, John	14th	E	Indiana	Inf.	Yk. Sq.	1	2nd line	30-Jun-64	---	Fairgrounds
4790	Barney, J. P.	1st	A	Deleware	Inf.	2	6	5th line	12-Aug-64	---	Crumpton's Factory
4633	Barnum, Isaac	15th	E	New York	Cav.	2	9	1st line	15-Jul-64	DOW 6/17/64 BOL	Knight's Factory
4737	Beard, James	85th	C	Indiana	Inf.	199	8	2	27-Mar-63	---	Christian's Factory
4791	Beckwith, George	6th	C	Michigan	Inf.	1	4	2nd line	23-Jun-64	DOW 6/12/64	Crumpton's Factory
*	Bell, John (NR)	91st	D	Ohio	Inf.	Yk. Sq.			17-Jun-64	KIA BOL	?
*	Berrick, Merrick C.	1st	H	West Virginia	Inf.		7	5th line	05-Aug-62	---	Fairgrounds
4629	Blacbern, P. (NR)	16th	C	New York	Cav.				?	---	?
*	Blair, George (NR)	116th	E	Ohio	Inf.				18-Jun-64	KIA BOL	Crumpton's Factory
*	Bobson, Allen	27th	E	U.S.C.T.	Inf.	Negro Row			19-Jul-64	---	Crumpton's Factory
4847	Boose, Moses, Sgt.	11th	A	Pennsylvania	Inf.	1	5	1st line	11-Jun-64	---	John Brown's Stable
4582	Bower(?), ******	39th	E	New York	Inf.	169	6	1	17-Jun-62	---	Fairgrounds
4607	Bower, Marquis (also Maroot)	66th	B	Ohio	Inf.	Yk. Sq.	10	2nd line	22-Jul-62	Gun Shot Wound	Massie's Factory
4785	Bowles, Almon E.	1st	L	New Hampshire	Cav.	3	7	2	28-Oct-64	Disease	Crumpton's Factory
*	Boycee, John	1st	B	West Virginia	Art.	2	8	1	11-Jul-64	---	?
4632	Boyd, James A. (NR)	116th	A	Ohio	Inf.				18-Jun-64	KIA BOL	College Hospital
4622	Bradsley, (Beardsly?) John G.	1st	B	West Virginia	Inf.?	1	10	3	13-Jul-64	---	Crumpton's Factory
4665	Brainard, James P.	1st	A	Delaware	Inf.	2	9	4	13-Aug-64	---	Burton's Factory
*	Branson, R. C.	34th	F	Illinois	Inf.	187	6	4	26-Jan-63	---	
*	Breen, Dennis (NR)	34th	H	Massachusetts	Inf.				18-Jun-64	KIA BOL	
4581	Bremer, Andrew	1st	K	Maryland	Inf.	Yk. Sq.	10	6	28-Jul-62	Disease	Fairgrounds
4614	Brommel, H. Fritz	8th	F	New York	Inf.	Yk. Sq.	1	6	24-Jul-62	---	Fairgrounds
4935	Budd, Sebring C.	1st	C	Michigan	Cav.	3	3	3	16-Oct-64	---	Crumpton's Factory
4972	Burdett, C. Henderson F.	11th	G	West Virginia	Inf.	2	6	1	09-Jul-64	DOW 6/18/64 BOL	Camp Davis
4643	Burr, Jewell	4th	C	U.S.	Inf.	3	3	5	06-Sep-64	---	Crumton's Factory
*	Calhoun, George S.	62nd	K	Ohio	Inf.	Yk. Sq.	1	5	28-Jul-62	---	Fairgrounds
4635	Carl, Frank W.	5th	F	New York	Cav.	2	7	4	11-Aug-64	DOW 5/05/64	Crunton's Factory
4781	Carlis, F.	64th	D	New York	Inf.	1	9	1	16-Jun-64	---	Fairgrounds
*	Casterly (Carterwiler?), John	4th	C	Pennsylvania	Cav.	3	3	3	11-Jun-65	---	Pratt Hospital
4586	Choraty, Henry	8th	F	New York	Inf.	Yk. Sq.	3	1	05-Jul-62	---	Fairgrounds
4594	Clearnott, J.	5th	E	New Hampshire	Inf.	2	5	2	29-Jul-64	---	College Hospital
4782	Cocks, John H.	1st	G	Maryland	Inf.	Yk. Sq.	6	1	10-Jul-62	---	Fairgrounds
4782	Coffran, L. F.	3rd	B	Maine	Inf.	1	9	3	11-Jul-64	Wounds?	Crumpton's Factory
4973	Collins, James	10th	G	New Jersey	inf.	3	5	2	16-Oct-64	Chronic Diarrhea	Crumpton's Factory

* See Part III - 112

	NAME	REGT. or UNIT	STATE	COMPANY	BRANCH of SERVICE	LOT#	Grave No.	ROW	DATE of BURIAL or DEATH	CAUSE of DEATH	HOSPITAL
4967	Condin, ****	3rd	Maine	F	Inf.	1	6	1	12-Jun-64	---	Camp Davis
4630	Conley, J.	7th	Maine	C	Inf.	1	3	3	01-Jul-64	Died of Wounds	Dr. Larrndell?
4948	Cooper, E.	7th	Michigan	F	Inf.	2	9	3	31-Jul-64	---	Crumpton's Factory
4720	Coulner/Coultner, Nicholas	4th	New York	H	Inf./Cav.?	Yk. Sq.	3	4	17-Jul-62	---	Fairgrounds
*	Coulter, George M. (NR)	116th	Ohio	E	Inf.				18-Jun-64	KIA BOL	?
*	Counsel, James D. (NR)	12th	Ohio	D	Inf.				17-Jun-64	KIA BOL	?
4944	Coward, Charles A., Corpl.	10th	New Jersey	G	Inf.	3	10	1	01-Oct-64	Gun Shot Wound	Massie's Factory
4640	Crawshaw (Cromshaw), John	128?	Pennsylvania?	I?	Inf.?	3	6	2	26-Oct-64	---	Crumpton's Factory
4956	Dafoe, Edward	1st	Michigan	I	Cav.	2	7	1	12-Jul-64	---	Crumpton's Factory
*	Davis, Charles C.	116th	Ohio	B	Inf.	1	10	-	20-Jun-64	DOW 6/18/64 BOL	Pratt Hospital
4580	Decker, Alonzo (NR)	36th	Maine	B	Inf.	Yk. Sq.	6	2	18-Jun-64	KIA BOL	Fairgrounds
4946	Delano, Leon (Levi?)	1st	Maine	M	Cav.	2	4	4	17-Jul-62	---	Fairgrounds
*	Derr, Samuel A., 2nd Lieut.	34th	Ohio	D	Inf.				30-Jul-64	DOW 6/18/64 BOL	College Hospital
4641	Dickey, William (NR)	91st	Ohio	I	Inf.	2	6	4	17-Jun-64	KIA BOL	?
4587	Dicher, Henry	122nd	Ohio	B	Inf.	Yk. Sq.	4	5	04-Aug-64	---	Fairgrounds
4578	Dockman, George A.	1st	Maine	M	Cav.	Yk. Sq.	4	3	02-Aug-52	---	Fairgrounds
*	Donahue, Peter F.	Knap's Battery	Pennsylvania	-	Art.				08-Jul-62	---	Pratt Hospital
4726	Doting, Henry	3rd Battn. 11th U.S.	U.S.	F	Inf.	172	6	5	04-Aug-66	---	Fairgrounds
*	Dowling, Patrick	1st	West Virginia	B	Art.	172	6	5	19-Jun-62	KIA BOL?	?
*	Downing, Benjamin (NR)	21st	New York	A	Cav.				16-Jun-64	KIA BOL	College Hospital
*	Dunn, Samuel (NR)	123rd	Ohio	F	Inf.				18-Jun-64	DOW 6/18/64 BOL	Fairgrounds
4749	Durbin, John W.	1st	West Virginia	D	Art.	1	3	2	23-Jun-64	Disease	Fairgrounds
4738	Elsworth, Isaac (A.?)	10th	Maine	F	Inf.	Yk. Sq.	8	4	20-Jul-62	KIA BOL	?
*	Emmert, Philip	1st	Maryland	I	Inf.	Yk. Sq.	11	3	28-Jul-62	DOW 6/17/64 BOL	Saunder's Factory
*	Emmons, William J. (NR)	91st	Ohio	K	Inf.				17-Jun-64	DOW 5/05/64	Crumpton's Factory
4646	Esselen, Michaele (NR)	5th	New York	C	Hvy. Art.	?	?	?	02-Jul-64	DOW 6/18/64 BOL	College Hospital
4780	Eustice, William	7th	Wisconsin	C	Inf.	-	3	1	08-Jun-64	---	Fairgrounds
4638	Fairbanks, Forrest G.	6th	Michigan	D	Cav.	2	2	1	04-Jul-64	---	Ferguson's Factory
4745	Parlow, Robert	2nd (PHB)	Maryland	B	Inf.	2	2	4	28-Jul-64	DOW 6/18/64 BOL	?
*	Ferdun, George E.	28th	New York	G	Inf.	Yk. Sq.	12	3	31-Jul-62	---	Fairgrounds
*	Ferguson, John	2nd	North Carolina	?	Inf.	185	1	1	25-Feb-64	KIA BOL	?
4779	Fisher, William (NR)	116th	Ohio	F	Inf.				18-Jun-64	DOW 6/18/64 BOL	Crumpton's Factory
4618	Fisk, Edmund D. (NR)	37th	Massachusetts	A	Inf.				?	DOW 6/18/64 BOL	College Hospital
4962	Forbess, Daniel, Corpl.	5th	West Virginia	B	Inf.	2	3	1	21-Jul-64	---	Fairgrounds
4663	Fowler, Thomas 1st Sgt.	15th	West Virginia	A	Inf.	2	5	1	08-Jul-64	---	Fairgrounds
4604	Freshman, Charles	1st	Maryland	E	Inf.	Yk. Sq.	10	4	25-Jul-62	---	Crumpton's Factory
4772	Frier, Joseph	1st	West Virginia	A	Inf.	Yk. Sq.	6	3	19-Jul-62	DOW 5/12/64	Fairgrounds
4584	Fullmer, Isaiah	148th	Pennsylvania	A	Inf.		4	3	02-Jul-64	---	Fairgrounds
4592	Garfield, Henry Darius	1st	Michigan	B	Cav.	Yk. Sq.	1	3	04-Jul-62	---	Fairgrounds
	Gatton, George W.	1st	West Virginia	?	Cav.	Yk. Sq.	4	1	12-Jul-62	---	Fairgrounds

* See Part III - 113

	NAME	REGT. or UNIT	STATE	COMPANY	BRANCH of SERVICE	LOT#	Grave No.	ROW	DATE of BURIAL or DEATH	CAUSE of DEATH	HOSPITAL
4776	Gatton, Jefferson	116th	Ohio	A	Inf.	1	2	3	30-Jun-64	DOW 6/18/64 BOL	College Hospital
4789	Gibbs, Thomas	14th	New York	D	Inf.	1	8	1	14-Jun-64	---	Crumpton's Factory
R	Gilson, Richard Newton	1st (PHB)	Maryland	C	Inf.	2	5	4	04-Aug-64	DOW 6/18/64 BOL	Crumpton's Factory
4765	Glover, John F.	140th	New York	G	Inf.	2	4	1	05-Jul-64	---	Crumpton's Factory
4654	Gordon, J. W. (NR)	11th	West Virginia	?	Inf.				18-Jun-62	KIA BOL	?
4611	Gosley, Hugh S.	5th	Connecticut	E	Inf.	Yk. Sq.	6	4	18-Jul-62	---	Fairgrounds
*	Goswell, William (NR)	31st	Maine	D	Hvy. Art.				18-Jun-64	KIA BOL	?
4771	Gougins, A. A.	91st	Ohio	D	Inf.	2	8	4	12-Aug-64	---	Crumpton's Factory
*	Graham, Louis (NR)	7th	West Virginia	I	Cav.	1			17-Jun-64	KIA BOL	College Hospital
4774	Green, William A.	12th	Pennsylvania	E	Inf.		6	2	25-Jun-64	DOW? 6/18/64 BOL	?
4648	Haeckey, J. J. (NR)	66th	Ohio	C	Inf.	Yk. Sq.	4	4	?	---	?
4718	Hall, Flemming	3rd	Michigan	K	Inf.	1	4	4	19-Jul-62	---	Fairgrounds
4642	Halsee, J.	116th	Ohio	D	Inf.	2	6	3	10-Jun-64	---	Camp Davis
4957	Hamilton, Evander B.	146th	New York	G	Inf.	2	10	2	24-Jul-64	DOW. 6/18/64 BOL	College Hospital
*	Hammond, Le Roy	1st	Maine	E	Cav.	Yk. Sq.	11	4	04-Aug-64	---	Fairgrounds
4736	Hardison, Hiram P.	29th	Pennsylvania	B	Inf.	Yk. Sq.	2	4	29-Jul-62	---	Fairgrounds
4612	Harps, David S.	8th	New York	C	Inf.	Yk. Sq.	7	1	14-Jul-62	---	Fairgrounds
4754	Hartman, August	3rd	New Jersey	C	Cav.	3	10	2	21-Jul-62	DOW 6/8/62	Fairgrounds
R	Hartman, John B., Capt.	1st	U.S.	A	Cav.	3	4	4	07-Dec-64	---	Crumpton's Factory
4936	Hassacher, G.	15th	New York	B	Cav.				12-Dec-64	KIA BOL	Crumpton's Factory
*	Hawkins, William (NR)	15th	New York	C	Inf.	2	10	1	17-Jun-64	---	Knight's Factory
4763	Hennessey, Michale	39th	Ohio	A	Inf.	1	7	1	15-Jul-64	---	Crumpton'sFactory
4784	Hernandez, J.	55th	Ohio	C	Inf.	Yk. Sq.	10	1	14-Jun-64	---	Fairgrounds
4896	Herring, Daniel	55th	Ohio	?	Inf.	Yk. Sq.	11	4	25-Jul-62	---	Fairgrounds
4744	Hess, Henry H.	?	?	?	?	192	5	3	29-Jul-62	---	Fairgrounds
*	Heter, Gerard	29th	Ohio	G	Inf.	Yk. Sq.	1	6	08-Jul-63	---	Fairgrounds
*	Hueninston, Newton P.	9th	West Virginia	D	Inf.	3	2	4	28-Jul-62	---	Crumpton's Factory
4659	Humphreys, Gabriel, Corpl.	277th	Indiana	D	Cav.	Yk. Sq.	9	5	31-Dec-64	---	Crumpton's Factory
4748	Isert, Peter	5th	West Virginia	H	Inf.	1	1	2	28-Jul-62	DOW 6/18/64 BOL	College Hospital
4943	Johnson, James M.	5th	Ohio	H	Inf.	Yk. Sq.	8	2	25-Jun-64	---	Fairgrounds
4750	Johnte, John G.	5th	New York	A	Hvy. Art.	?	?	2	21-Jul-62	---	?
*	Jolly, James D. (NR)	121st	New York	B	Inf.		?	3	15-May-65	---	Crumpton's Factory
4960	Jones, Jesse	22nd	Wisconsin	F	Inf.	199	8	5	09-Jul-64	Typhoid Fever	V&T Rail Car
4721	Jones, Owen R.	29th	Ohio	D	Inf.	Yk. Sq.	3	5	06-Apr-63	---	Fairgrounds
4606	Jones, William H.	111th	New York	I	Inf.	2	7	3	21-Jul-62	---	Crumpton's Factory
4766	Kelley, T. M.	3rd	West Virginia	K	Cav.	1	2	2	14-Jul-64	---	Crumpton's Factory
4794	Kelly, John	4th	U.S.	Staff	Cav.	3	1	3	23-Jun-64	DOW? 6/18/64 BOL	College Hospital
R	Kerner, H. C., Capt.(AAG)	66th	Ohio	G	Inf.	1	4	1	07-Sep-64	---	Crumpton's Factory
4601	Kettle, John W.	116th	Ohio	B	Inf.	Yk. Sq.	4	2	09-Jul-62	---	Fairgrounds
*	Keys, Edwin, Capt.					2	3	2	19-Jul-64	DOW 6/18/64 BOL	College Hospital

* See Part III - 114

	NAME	REGT. or UNIT	STATE	COMPANY	BRANCH of SERVICE	LOT #	Grave No.	ROW	DATE of BURIAL or DEATH	CAUSE of DEATH	HOSPITAL
*	Kiehl, Cyrus H. (NR)	123rd	Ohio	F	Inf.				18-Jun-64	KIA BOL	?
4739	Killerting, Samuel	3rd	Maryland	F	Inf.	Yk. Sq.	12	5	04-Aug-62		Fairgrounds
*	King, Harry B. (NR)	34th	Massachusetts	E	Inf.				18-Jun-64	KIA BOL	?
4602	King, William C.	46th	Pennsylvania	F	Inf.	Yk. Sq.	3	3	07-Jul-62		Fairgrounds
4769	Kyle, J.	11th	U.S.	D	Inf.	3	8	1	27-Sep-64		Crumpton's Factory
4735	Lambdin, John	1st	Maryland	B	Inf.	171	5	4	23-Jun-52	Starvation(?)	John Brown's Stable
4717	Lannen, Dennis	29th	Pennsylvania	E	Inf.	Yk. Sq.	5	4	12-Jul-62		Fairgrounds
4715	Lapiere, John B.	34th(?)	Massachusetts?	E	Inf.	192	10	4	03-Dec-63		Jail
4752	Leach, William, Sgt.	3rd	Wisconsin	B	Inf.	Yk. Sq.	7	2	18-Jul-62		Fairgrounds
4775	Lenox, S.	8th	New York	A	Inf.	1	1	1	29-May-64	Convulsions	Miller's Factory
4968	Leonard, Frank (H.?)	116th	Pennsylvania	H	Inf.	3	2	1	01-Sep-64		Crumpton's Factory
4951	Lockwood, James E.	10th	Vermont	E	Inf.	2	6	4	08-Aug-64	Disease	Crumpton's Factory
4591	Marson, A. C.	85th	Indiana	C	Inf.	199	7	2	28-Mar-63		Knight'sFactory
*	Martin, Francis (NR)	34th	Massachusetts	K	Inf.				18-Jun-64	KIA BOL	?
*	Matson, James (NR)	12th	Ohio	C	Inf.	2	7	3	17-Jun-64	KIA BOL	Crumpton's Factory
4645	McCluskey, John	140th	New York	A	Inf.		7	3	28-Jul-64		Fairgrounds
4666	McCort, James	110th	Pennsylvania	F	Inf.	Yk. Sq.	9	1	25-Jul-62		?
*	McCowen, Israel T. (NR)	12th	Ohio	F	Inf.				17-Jun-64	KIA BOL	Crumpton's Factory
*	McDonald, Savage (NR)	123rd	Ohio	F	Inf.				18-Jun-64	KIA BOL	?
4623	McGill, S.	6th	New York	F	Inf.	3	5	1	17-Sep-64		Crumpton's Factory
4593	McGinnis, James (John?)	33rd	Indiana	A	Inf.	199	2	2	25-Mar-63	Disease	Knight's Factory
4631	McIntosh, Frank	15th	New York	G	Cav.	2	9	2	26-Jul-64	DOW 6/17/64 BOL	Crumpton's Factory
*	McKee, Samuel (NR)	91st	Ohio	I	Inf.				17-Jun-64	KIA BOL	?
4792	McVey, James	88th	Pennsylvania	D	Inf.	1	5	2	23-Jun-64		Crumpton's Factory
4753	Miller, Samuel (NR)	?	?	?	?				?		?
4595	Monk, Henry	1st	Maryland	I	Inf.	Yk. Sq.	8	1	22-Jul-62		Fairgrounds
4644	Monteith, William	65th	New York	G	Inf.	3	4	2	20-Sep-64		Crumpton's Factory
*	Moore, John Thomas	666th	Ohio	E	Inf.	Yk. Sq.	10	6	31-Jul-62		Fairgrounds
4759	Morse, William W. (NR)	12th	Ohio	D	Inf.				17-Jun-64	KIA BOL	?
4627	Moss, Jacob	5th	New York	A	Hvy. Art.	2	3	4	30-Jul-64	DOW 6/05/64	Crumpton's Factory
4725	Munson, Enos	46th	Pennsylvania	G	Inf.	Yk. Sq.	1	5	24-Jul-62		Fairgrounds
4598	Murphy, Patrick	27th	Indiana	H	Inf.	Yk. Sq.	9	2	22-Jul-62		Fairgrounds
4515	Neal, James L.	11th	New Hampshire	A	Inf.	2	5	3	21-Jul-64	DOW 5/6/64	Crumpton's Factory
4734	Nichols, Langdon H., Corpl.	1st	Vermont	C	Cav.	Yk. Sq.	9	6	27-Jul-62		Fairgrounds
4624	O'Donnell, John	5th	Rhode Island	K	Hvy. Art.	3	6	1	20-Sep-64		Crumpton's Factory
4964	Olf, John	126th	NewYork	E	Inf.	2	10	3	01-Aug-64	DOW 5/6/64	Crumpton's Factory
*	Orton, Martin (NR)	15th	New York	B	Cav.				17-Jun-64	KIA BOL	?
*	Packerman, P.	16th?	New York	C	Cav.?	3	9	1	29-Sep-64		Crumpton's Factory
4762	Parker, Isaac	17th	Maine	F	Inf.	2	6	2	21-Jul-64	DOW 5/6/64	Crumpton's Factory
4778	Parker, James C.	5th	West Virginia	I	Inf.	1	7	3	08-Jul-64	DOW 6/18/64 BOL	Camp Davis

* See Part III - 115

	NAME	REGT. or UNIT	STATE	COMPANY	BRANCH of SERVICE	LOT #	Grave No.	ROW	DATE of BURIAL or DEATH	CAUSE of DEATH	HOSPITAL
4716	Peatt(?), Henry	?	?	?	?	Yk. Sq.	2	5	01-Jul-62	---	Fairgrounds
4768	Phillips, C. Theophilus	140th	Pennsylvania	I	Inf.	2	1	3	15-Jul-64	DOW 5/8/64	Knight's Factory
4583	Phipps, Cyrenius, Corpl.	1st	Michigan	G	Cav.	Yk. Sq.	7	5	11-Aug-62	---	Fairgrounds
4746	Pike, William H.	10th	Maine	I	Inf.	Yk. Sq.	11	2	29-Jul-62	Disease	Fairgrounds
4599	Pitcher, Horace M.	19th	Michigan	D	Inf.	199	9	2	21-Mar-63	Exposure	Knight's Factory
4770	Plattenburgh, Peter	111th	NewYork	F	Inf.	1	2	3	30-Jun-64	DOW 5/5/64	Crumpton's Factory
4730	Preacher, Bruno	1st	Maryland	B	Inf.	Yk. Sq.	4	6	02-Aug-62	---	Fairgrounds
4617	Rand, Joseph	11th	West Virginia	F	Inf.	2	8	3	20-Jul-64	DOW 6/17/64 BOL	Camp Davis
*	Randall, William (NR)	91st	Ohio	F	Inf.	-	-	-	17-Jun-64	KIA BOL	?
4729	Randles, Charles	25th	Pennsylvania	H	Inf.	Yk. Sq.	3	6	30-Jul-62	---	Fairgrounds
4955	Rapp, Levi	149th	Pennsylvania	G	Inf.	2	9	4	13-Aug-64	---	Crumpton's Factory
4647	Redman, John	5th	New York	H	Cav.	2	8	3	29-Jul-64	DOW 5/5/64	Miller's Factory
4760	Reed, Charles E.	12th	Massachusetts	F	Inf.	Yk. Sq.	13	5	09-Aug-62	---	Fairgrounds
4954	Reis, Michael	28th	Ohio	H?	Inf.	2	2	3	16-Jul-64	DOW 6/5/64	Crumpton's Factory
4761	Remington, F. A.	85th	Indiana	G	Inf.	184	3	1	01-May-63	---	Miller's Factory
4616	Rider, John	7th	New York	K	Inf.	2	3	3	19-Jul-64	---	Crumpton's Factory
4741	Roberts, Daniel S.	10th	Maine	B	Inf.	Yk. Sq.	1	4	03-Aug-62	---	Fairgrounds
4577	Robinson (Robison), Charles	27th	Indiana	G	Inf.	Yk. Sq.	4	4	14-Jul-62	---	Fairgrounds
4742	Robinson, Richard	21st	Michigan	K	Inf.	184	2	1	27-Apr-63	---	Burton's Factory
4619	Rogers, Lawson H. (NR)	122nd	Ohio	H	Inf.	-	-	-	18-Dec-64	---	?
4952	Ruck, Cyrus	116th	Pennsylvania	G	Inf.	2	10	4	17-Aug-64	---	College Hospital
4733	Rucker, John W.	25th	Ohio	1	Inf.	172	4	3	24-Jun-62	---	Fairgrounds
4724	Schaum, Rudolph	8th	New York	G	Inf.	Yk. Sq.	4	4	19-Jul-62	---	Fairgrounds
4777	Schwarley, William S. (NR)	163rd	Pennsylvania	H	Inf.	2	-	-	?	---	?
*	Schwartz, William	140th	New York	G	Inf.	2	4	4	05-Jul-64	---	Crumpton's Factory
4783	Sears, William A.	34th	Massachusetts	H	Inf.	1	8	2	29-Jun-64	DOW 6/18/64 BOL	College Hospital
4597	Shannesy, Michale	27th	Indiana	B	Inf.	Yk. Sq.	5	5	15-Jul-64	---	Fairgrounds
4767	Sheehan, Michael	150th	Ohio	A	Inf.	3	3	2	07-Sep-64	DOW 5/6/64	Crumpton's Factory
4764	Sherborne, R.	1st	Michigan	C	Inf.	2	1	1	02-Jul-64	---	Crumpton's Factory
*	Shields, William C. (NR)	12th	Ohio	A	Inf.	-	-	-	17-Jun-64	KIA BOL	?
*	Simpson, Robert J. (NR)	1st	West Virginia	I	Inf.	-	-	-	17-Jun-64	KIA BOL	?
4773	Sink, F.	?	?	B	?	1	2	2	23-Jun-64	---	College Hospital
4731	Sly, Hiram	29th	Ohio	E	Inf.	Yk. Sq.	2	3	06-Jul-62	---	Fairgrounds
4786	Smith, Harrison H.	5th	Vermont	K	Inf.	3	8	2	04-Nov-64	---	Crumpton's Factory
4787	Smith, William	6th	New Hampshire	A	Inf.	1	2	1	02-Jun-64	---	Camp Davis
4722	Sprague, Thomas	4th	Ohio	I	Inf.	Yk. Sq.	5	3	22-Jul-62	---	Fairgrounds
4965	State, William	6th	Ohio	K	Inf.	2	4	2	21-Jul-64	Disease	Camp Davis
4732	Stewart, John	29th	Pennsylvania	I	Inf.	Yk. Sq.	5	2	02-Aug-62	DOW 5/6/64	Fairgrounds
*	Stiles, Colvin, Sgt. (NR)	91st	Ohio	D	Inf.	-	-	-	17-Jun-64	KIA BOL	?
4945	Stout, George H.	6th	Pennsylvania	G	Cav.	2	5	2	21-Jul-64	---	Crumpton's Factory

* See Part III - 116

	NAME	REGT. or UNIT	STATE	COMPANY	BRANCH of SERVICE	LOT#	Grave No.	ROW	DATE of BURIAL or DEATH	CAUSE of DEATH	HOSPITAL
4966	Stowe, Stephen L., Sgt.	6th	Michigan	B	Cav.	2	3	5	30-Jul-64	---	Crumpton's Factory
4968	Stowell, Carlos A.	1st	Vermont	H	Hvy. Art.	?	?	?	22-Aug-64	---	Crumpton's Factory
*	Stratton, Moses C.	6th	Vermont	B	Inf.	3	2	2	03-Sep-64	DOW 5/6/764	Crumpton's Factory
	Strausbaugh, Isaac (NR)	91st	Ohio	D	Inf.				17-Jun-64	KIA BOL	?
4596	Strepler, Jacob	27th	Pennsylvania	D	Inf.	Yk. Sq.	1	1	30-Jun-62	---	Fairgrounds
4961	Strikle, J. M.	?	?	F	?	1	5	3	05-Jul-64	---	Massie's Factory
*	Stroup, George B. 1st Lt. (N?)	91st	Ohio	D	Inf.				17-Jun-64	KIA BOL	?
4628	Strunon, (Sherman?) (NP)	146th	New Jersey	G	Inf.				?	?	?
4661	Sutton, Peter J.	15th	Ohio	F	Inf.	3	2	3	18-Oct-64	---	Massie's Factory
*	Swanger, James J. (NR)	91st	Ohio	D	Inf.				17-Jun-64	KIA BOL	?
4770	Swisher, John H.	66th	Ohio	B	Inf.	Yk. Sq.	10	2	25-Jul-62	---	Fairgrounds
*	Talbot, ****	?	?	?	?	Negro Row			17-May-64	---	Knight's Factory
4609	Taylor, Joseph	1st	Vermont	G	Cav.	Yk. Sq.	2	2	01-Jul-62	---	Fairgrounds
4637	Thompson, David	110th	Pennsylvania	C	Inf.	2	7	2	23-Jul-64	---	Crumpton's Factory
*	Thompson, John, Corpl. (IR)	15th	New York	H	Cav.				17-Jun-64	KIA BOL	?
	Thornburg, W. H.	36th	Ohio	A	Inf.				18-Jun-64	KIA BOL	?
4963	Thornton, David M.	8th	Michigan	C	Inf.	2	3	1	05-Jul-64	DOW 5/6/64	Crumpton's Factory
4949	Thorp, M. Nathan	35th (6th)	Pennsylvania	C	Inf.	2	5	5	11-Aug-64	---	Crumpton's Factory
4639	Tourtellotte, Chester A., Sgt.	18th	Connecticut	H	Inf.				15-Aug-64	DOW 6/05/64	College Hospital
*	Townsend, Calvin W. (NR)	12th	Ohio	B	Inf.				17-Jun-64	KIA BOL	?
	Tripp, Ezra G.	37th	Massachusetts	A	Inf.	1	10	2	01-Jul-64	DOW 5/6/64	Camp Davis
*	Unknown	?	?	?	?	Yk. Sq.			08-Aug-62	---	Fairgrounds?
*	Unknown	?	?	?	?	Yk. Sq.			08-Aug-62	---	Fairgrounds?
*	Unknown	?	?	?	?	Yk. Sq.			08-Aug-62	---	Fairgrounds?
*	Unknown	?	?	?	?	1	10	2	20-Jun-64	DOW 6/18/64 BOL?	Crumpton's Factory
*	Unknown	?	?	?	?				23-Jun-64	DOW 6/18/64 BOL?	College Hospital
4664	Van Horn, Gilbert (NR)	116th	Ohio	I	Inf.				18-Jun-64	KIA BOL	?
*	Vandergraff, Enoch Sgt. (N?)	91st	Ohio	D	Inf.				17-Jun-64	KIA BOL	?
*	VanOrder, Kimble	15th	New York	G	Cav.	1	10	3	24-Jun-64	DOW 6/17/64 BOL	College Hospital
4971	Vinyard, Harvey Corpl.	66th	Ohio	B	Inf.	Yk. Sq.	9	2	25-Jul-62	---	Fairgrounds
4727	Walshe (Welch?), J.	1st	Maine	K	Inf.	3	10	4	09-Nov-64	---	Crumpton's Factory
*	Walton, J. W.	37th	Indiana	?	Inf.	173	2	5	25-Jun-62	---	Fairgrounds
4600	Warwick, Alfred	3rd	New Jersey	A	Inf.	3	12	6	22-Jan-65	---	Crumpton's Factory
4505	Weeks, Joseph W.	10th	Maine	B	Inf.	Yk. Sq.	3	2	02-Aug-62	---	Fairgrounds
4613	Weik, John	54th	New York	K	Inf.	Yk. Sq.			05-Jul-62	---	Fairgrounds
*	Welch, William S. (NR)	67th?	Ohio	D	Inf.				?	?	?
R	Wheeler, George E.	1st	Maryland	A	Inf.	Yk. Sq.	11	1	02-Aug-62	Disease	Fairgrounds
4755	Wheeler, Y. (NR)	?	?	?	?						
R	Whickham, John s., Q.M. Sgt.	135th	Ohio (Nat. Gd.)	B	Inf.	2	2	2	15-Jul-64	---	Crumpton's Factory
*	Wilcox, William S.	67th	Ohio	A	Inf.	Yk. Sq.	8	6	04-Aug-62	---	Fairgrounds

* See Part III - 117

NAME	REGT. or UNIT	STATE	COMPANY	BRANCH of SERVICE	LOT#	Grave No.	ROW	DATE of BURIAL or DEATH	CAUSE of DEATH	HOSPITAL
4636 Willard, James J.	57th	Massachusetts	G	Inf.	2	1	4	26-Jul-64	DOW 5/6/64	Camp Davis
4753 Wilson, W. (NR)	?	?	?	?	-	-	-	?	---	?
* Woodward, Seth A. (NR)	34th	Massachusetts	D	Inf.	-	-	5	18-Jun-64	KIA BOL	?
4626 Wray, Thomas C., Corpl.	72nd	Pennsylvania	E	Inf.	2	1	4	26-Jul-64	---	Camp Davis
4585 York, Calvin B.	33rd	Indiana	A	Inf.	199	4	6	11-Apr-63	---	Miller's Factory
4603 Younger, John	27th	Indiana	D	Inf.	Yk. Sq.	8	4	04-Aug-62	---	Fairgrounds
4747 Ziegler, Franz	45th	New York	B	Inf.	Yk. Sq.	9	5	21-Jul-62	---	Fairgrounds
* Zimmerman, C.	1st	New York	-	Art.	Yk. Sq.	10	5	28-Jul-62	---	Fairgrounds
* Zulker, Benjamin C.	4th	New Jersey	D	Inf.	3	1	5	23-Dec-64	---	Crumpton's Factory

R - Indicates removed & shipped home
4719 - (typ.) Poplar Grove Grave #
(NR) - No Diuguid or No Poplar Grove Record
? - Indicates some question about material or data or is Unknown
* Information on individual in Part III

Yk. Sq. - Yankee Square

KIA - Killed in Action
DOW - Died of Wound(s)
BOL - Battle of Lynchburg

* See Part III - 118

PART II

Listing of Soldiers Interred in Local Lynchburg Cemeteries Other Than The Old City Cemetery

NAME	REGT. or UNIT	STATE	COMPANY	BRANCH of SERVICE	CEMETERY	LOCATION	DATE of BURIAL or DEATH	REMARKS
Anderson, William Edward	Radford's	Virginia	A	Cav.	Methodist	J. Beards Sq., #43	30-Oct-61	-
* Apperson, Robert E.	11th	Virginia	G	Inf.	Presbyterian	Range 10, Lot 14	31-May-62	KIA @ Seven Pines
Armstrong, Samuel	Goochland Batty.	Virginia	-	Art.	Presbyterian	Range 2, Lot 1	29-Mar-65	-
Biggers, A. F., Capt.	-	-	-	-	Presbyterian	Range 11, Lot 10	18-May-63	-
* Boyd, Charles Augustus	Moorman's Batty.	Virginia	-	Art.	Presbyterian	Range 6, Lot 5	26-Nov-63	DOW 10/25/63
Boyd, William Kinckle	-	-	-	-	Presbyterian	Range 6, Lot 5	10-Jul-65	Died of Disease
Crumpton, William	Lynch. City Guard	-	-	Inf.	Methodist	J. Crumpton's Lot	4-May-62	at W. Loyds
Davis, John Willis, Capt.	-	-	-	-	Presbyterian	Range 11, Lot 11	18-May-63	-
Davis, Thomas M.	11th	Virginia	H	Inf.	Methodist	Buried by Sister	4-Nov-61	Curls Row, Virginia
* Didlake, John H., Lt.	34th	Virginia	K	Inf.	Presbyterian	Range 16, Lot 3	9-Jun-62	KIA @ Cross Keys
* Early, Robert Davies, Lt.	Div. Staff	Virginia	F & S	Inf.	Presbyterian	Range 11, Lot 1	5-May-64	KIA @ Wilderness
* Early, William H., Capt.	Braxton's Battn.	Virginia	Lee's	Art.	Presbyterian	Range 11, Lot 1	1-Apr-65	KIA @ Five Forks
Elliott, Edward Howard	11th	Virginia	G	Inf.	Presbyterian	Range 1, Lot 12	31-May-62	KIA @ Seven Pines
Elliott, William Jr	11th	Virginia	I	Inf.	Presbyterian	Range 1, Lot 12	7-Jan-62	-
* Evans, Timothy F.	11th	Virginia	E	Inf.	Presbyterian	Range 1, Lot 1	26-Dec-62	Ferguson's Factory
* Garland, Samuel Jr., Brig. Gen.	Brig. Commd.	Virginia	-	Inf.	Presbyterian	Range 7, Lot 1	14-Sep-62	KIA @ South Mountain
Garrette, John	16th	Virginia	-	Cav.	Presbyterian	Range 2, Lot 2	2-Dec-64	-
* Goggins, William Leftwitch, Jr.	11th	Virginia	H	Inf.	Presbyterian	Range 15, Lot 9	5-Sep-61	At His Fathers
Greene, Daniel S., Dr.	-	-	-	-	Presbyterian	Range 15, Lot 8	7-Mar-64	-
Hewitt, Archer B., Q.M. Sgt.	31st	Virginia	Kirkpatrick's	Art.	Presbyterian	Range 15, Lot 8	30-Jul-64	DOW's 7/20/64
* Hickey, Daniel	Latham's Batty.	Virginia	-	Art.	Methodist	Father's Sq.	14-Nov-62	At Home

* See Part III, 119

NAME	REGT. or UNIT	STATE	COMPANY	BRANCH of SERVICE	CEMETERY	LOCATION	DATE of BURIAL or DEATH	REMARKS
Horner, Edward W., Capt.	-	-	-	-	Presbyterian	Range 9, Lot 6	23-Feb-63	DOW's 12/13/62
Knight, John P.	11th	Virginia	E	Inf.	Presbyterian	Range 15, Lot 7	6-Oct-63	-
* Larrentree, Harry	4th	Alabama	Tracy's	Inf.	Spring Hill	#3, Lot 37	16-Jan-62	College Hospital
Legg, T.	Discharged	-	-	-	Methodist	Refugee Sq., Lot #66	-	-
McKinney, Lineus B.	31st	Virginia	Kirkpatrick's	Art.	Presbyterian	Range 2, Lot 4	31-Mar-65	KIA @ Burgess Mill
* McKinney, Robert M., Col.	15th	North Carolina	-	Inf.	Presbyterian	Range 2, Lot 4	16-Apr-62	KIA @ Lee's Mill
* Meem, Lawrence James Lt.	11th	Virginia	Regt. Adj.	Inf.	Presbyterian	Range 7, Lot 1	31-May-62	KIA @ Seven Pines
* Mitchell, John F., Sgt.	11th	Virginia	A	Inf.	Spring Hill	-	30-Jun-62	At Mr. Purvis's Farm
* Morris, Joshua S.	Portsmouth Batty.	Virginia	C. F. Grimes	Art.	Presbyterian	John Purvis's Lot #13	22-Oct-61	At Mr. Purvis's
* Oliver, Pleasant	11th	Virginia	H	Inf.	Presbyterian	Stanger's Sq.	8-Oct-62	-
Perkins, Benjamin	10th	Virginia	I	Cav.	Presbyterian	Range 13, Lot 8	11-Mar-62	At Home in Amherst
Probst, Jacob	-	Georgia	Dudley's	Inf.	Spring Hill	Lot 37, Sect. W, #2	9-Jul-62	-
Reid, William S., Jr.	Moorman's Batty.	Virginia	-	Art.	Presbyterian	Range 6, Lot 8	19-Sep-62	KIA @ Winchester
* Rodes, Robert E., Maj. Gen.	Div. Commd.	Virginia	-	-	Presbyterian	Range 5, Lot 2	5-Jan-64	-
Rosser, Edward B.	Moorman's Batty.	Virginia	-	Art.	Methodist	#2 from N Cor. Lot #149	25-Jul-64	-
* Stewart, John P.	13th	Virginia	Davidson's	Art.	Presbyterian	Range C, Lot #149	1-Sep-63	KIA @ Petersburg
Stewart, Warren A.	13th	Virginia	Davidson's	Art.	Presbyterian	Range D, Lot 1	21-Jul-61	At A. Pamplin's
* Tarpley, David J.	2nd	Arkansas	B	Inf.	Spring Hill	1 East Cor. Sec. U, Lot 37	2-Aug-62	DOW's @ Seven Pines
Terry, Charles Wentworth, Sgt.	11th	Virginia	G	Inf.	Presbyterian	Range 7, Lot 14	25-Jan-64	KIA @ Beverly 1/25/64
Thomas, James Edward	2nd	Virginia	I	Cav.	Presbyterian	Range 1, Lot 3	18-Jun-64	KIA @ Lynchburg
* Tinsley, Junius Fitz-James	5th	Virginia	Bugler	Inf.	Presbyterian	Range 15, Lot 8	21-Jul-62	DOW's @ Frazier's Farm
Trigg, William King	11th	Virginia	G	Inf.	Presbyterian	Range 3, Lot 3		

* See Part III,120

NAME	REGT. or UNIT	STATE	COMPANY	BRANCH of SERVICE	CEMETERY	LOCATION	DATE of BURIAL or DEATH	REMARKS
* Tyree, Charles Hudson, Lt.	11th	Virginia	E	Inf.	Presbyterian	Range 16, Lot 1	2-Jan-64	MWIA @ Drewry's Bluff
Tyree, Richard J.	2nd	Virginia	B	Cav.	Presbyterian	Range 17, Lot 8	23-Jul-63	Accidentaly Wounded
Tyree, Samuel B.	11th	Virginia	CG	Inf.	Presbyterian	Range 16, Lot 1	1-Jun-62	MWIA Seven Pines
Van Dyke, Richard Smith, Maj.	-	Tennessee	-	-	Presbyterian	Range 3, Lot 13	15-Nov-64	-
Walton, John W.	2nd	Virginia	B	Cav.	Presbyterian	Range 17, Lot 6	20-Nov-63	-
Watts, John H. N.	2nd	Virginia	A	Inf.	Presbyterian	Range 15, Lot 8	6-Jan-64	-
Wheeler, Jerome	11th	Virginia	G	Inf.	Presbyterian	Range 13, Lot 8	7-Feb-64	-
* Wilkerson, P. A.	12th	Mississippi	C. F. Grimes	Inf.	Bedford County	Mrs. Crouch	29-Jun-62	Ladies Relief Hospital
Yancey, Henry D., Lt.	Staff Gen. Rodes	Virginia	F&S	Inf.	Presbyterian	Range 6, Lot 2	8-May-64	KIA Spotsylvania C.H.

* See Part III.121

PART III

Support Information

Additional facts and information on individual Soldiers from Part II

Part III - SUPPORT INFORMATION

The following is a listing of additional, or in some cases support information on the individual Confederate and Union Soldiers who died while in the Lynchburg hospital system. As previously stated these men were handled/prepared for burial by Diuguid's Funeral Home during the four-year period of the War for Southern Independence.

In Part I, the listing of the Confederate Soldiers buried in the Old City (Methodist) Cemetery, several of which were noted by an asterisk (*) with a note referring to Part III. This section will have other information covered in Part I. This information may be a small amount or in some cases lengthy newspaper accounts.

Also within this support data will be a complete listing of the soldiers that either died here in Lynchburg or were shipped here for preparation but were not buried here, their remains were sent home.

The listing of the deceased Confederate and Union soldiers handled by Diuguid's contained in the following pages are in alphabetical order providing specific about the soldiers and has not been previously covered. This additional information may refer to age, home address, wife, parents, or relatives name, birth date, specific cause of death and any other pertinent information available on the individual.

The later section of this listing has been reserved for the Union Soldiers that died while in the Lynchburg Hospital system as Prisoners of War. Only limited information is available for those men. No specific's other than name, unit, and date of approximate death, location and burial site. However, in some cases more specific data was obtained such as age, date of enlistment, rank held, cause of death, spouses name, or other relevant information.

Abbreviations have been used in several cases to conserve space in this roster style listing. The following is a list of some of the abbreviations used:

Inf.	- Infantry	Sgt.	- Sergeant
Cav.	- Cavalry	Corpl.	- Corporal
Art.	- Artillery	Lieut.	- Lieutenant
@	- at	Capt.	- Captain
d.	- died	Maj.	- Major
b.	- born	Col.	- Colonel

#	- number	Lt. Col.	- Lieut. Colonel
col.	- Column	Gen.	- General
Unk.	- Unknown	RR	-Railroad
DOW	- died of wound(s)	Battn.	- Battalion
Brig.	- Brigadier	Batty.	- Battery
POW	- Prisoner of War	St.	- Street
KIA	- Killed in Action	&	- and
WIA	- Wounded in Action	res.	- Residence
DOA	- Dead on Arrival	P.O.	- Post Office
MWIA	- Mortally Wounded in Action		

Roster of Support Information on Soldiers:

* Abbott, Thomas J. - 5th Florida Inf., Company G, d. 3/02/62 of pneumonia @ Burton's Factory. Coffin size was 6 ft. 2 in. in length by 18 in. in width. Enlisted 5/01/62 @ St. Marks as a substitute for N. Strickland. Listed as absent/sick since mid 1862.

* Ackerman, William Lawrence - 6th Louisiana Inf., Company C, the "Orleans Rifles", d. 6/18/61 @ College Hospital, buried in lot #158, grave 7, row 1. Father was shoemaker on Magazine St., located between Clio & Erato Streets in New Orleans. Clio - (myth.) The muse of history. Erato - (Myth.) The muse of love poetry.

Ackerly, John S. - 27th Virginia Inf., Company G, d. 5/20/63 on Packett Boat. Diuguid's entry was, "died on packett boat, & sent to Gilmore's Mill (per order of Quartermaster)". Ackerly was wounded in action (left leg) on 5/3/63 at the Battle of Chancellorsville. Per his military record he was in a Richmond hospital through 5/10/63, transferred to Lexington hospital 5/18/63, died of pneumonia on 5/20/63 while being transported from Lexington to Lynchburg via packett boat. Buried High Bridge Presbyterian Church Cemetery, Rockbridge County. He was born in Rockbridge County, Virginia 11/1/30, 860 census listed his occupation was farmer and newspaperman in the Lexington District. Listed as member of Bolivar Mills Company Militia in June 1861.

Acre, Albert J. - Kirkpatrick's Battery Virginia Light Art., d. 7/10/62 of camp fever @ the residence of James Dinwiddie. Left wife & 4 children. His death notice appeared in the Lynchburg Daily Virginian 7/11/62, page 3, col. 1, and again on 7/24/62 page 3, col. 2. His age at the time of his death was approximately 32. The father of the deceased was Thomas O. Acre.

* **Adams, Andrew Q.** – 15th Alabama Inf., Company F, d. 5/6/62 @ the Warwick House. The brother of the deceased, J. W. Adams, filed a death claim on 12/32/62. The claim was rejected on 1/19/65 based on improper paperwork, "Brother can't make a claim." Per the claim J. W. Adams could be contacted in care of J. H. Hybert in Burndridge, Alabama.

* **Adams, Charles P.** - 58th Virginia Inf., Company B, d. 1/03/64 of diphtheria. Enlisted 5/17/62 @ Jennings Gap, Augusta County born 1845; 1860 census listed age as 15, occupation as a farmhand, res. Davis Mill P.O., Bedford County. Admitted Gordonsville Hospital 11/27/63 with diarrhea.

* **Adams, George B.** - 3rd North Carolina Inf., Company D, d. 5/30/63 of typhoid fever @ Christian's Factory. Coffin size was 5 ft. 11 in. in length by 16 in. in width. Was wounded at Battle of Chancellorsville May 2, 63. Enlisted 7/15/62 in Pitt County at age 18.

Adams, J. H. - 1st South Carolina Inf., Company D, d. 2/15/63 @ Ferguson's Factory. Coffin size was 6 ft. 4 in. in length by 21 in. in width. Originally buried in lot #195, grave #10, row #3. The remains were claimed by the father of the deceased (Mr. Adams). Body was exhumed on 2/18/63. Body was "sent to Chesterville, S.C."

* **Adams, James H., Sgt.** - 11th North Carolina Inf., Company C, d. 1/24/64 of smallpox @ the Pest House. His military records state that his death was from "variola". This is the synonym of smallpox. Adams had been wounded prior to his death, most likely at Gettysburg. He was hospitalized in Richmond with a gunshot wound to the left hand on July 16, 63. Adams rejoined his company prior to 9/01/63. He had been promoted to Sgt. prior to 11/01/63. Adams enlisted 1/23/62 as a Corpl. in Bertie County, North Carolina at age 20.

* **Addy, Simeon Lloyd** - 15th South Carolina Inf., Company C, d. 6/06/64 of wounds & typhoid @ College Hospital. Wounded at Wilderness 5/06/64. Age @ enlistment was 19, 1860 census shows him a resident of the Lexington District.

* **Adkins, John W.** - 38th Virginia Inf., Company B, d. 5/10/62 of Pneumonia @ Ferguson's Factory. His service record states that he was admitted to Gen. Hospital #18 in Richmond on 5/2/62 with measles.

* **Ahrene, Henry William, Sgt. Maj.** - 1st Orr's Rifles South Carolina Inf., Field & Staff, d. 5/18/64 from wounds received during the Battle of the Wilderness 5/6/64. He enlisted 7/20/61 at the age of 18. Appointed Sgt. Maj. 3/1/63. The father of the deceased was D. A. Ahrene.

* **Albritton, Jasper N.** – 8th Florida Inf, Company A, d. 10/15.62 of disease @ Christian's actory. Enlisted 04/01/62 @ Taylor, Fla. Born 1842 Lowndes County, Ga. Son of William & Mariah Albriton. His coffin size was 71 in. in length by 17 in. in width.

* **Aldridge, Francis** - 48th North Carolina Inf. Company K, d. 11/22/62 @ Claytor's Factory of pleuritis. Private Aldridge enlisted 3/18/62 at age 20 in Forsyth County as substitute. Born in Stokes County, resided in Forsyth County, his occupation was listed as a planter. Aldridge was first hospitalized 8/24/62 with typhoid fever. Returned to duty 9/29/62. Re-hospitalized (no date specified) in Lynchburg were he died.

* **Allen, Paul C., 2nd Lieut.** - 1st Orr's Rifles South Carolina Inf., Company A, d. 5/17/64 of wounds received @ Wilderness. Diuguid only listed the last name in his records, no first name. 1860 census showed him as resident of the Barnwell District. His coffin size was 6 ft. 5 in. in length by 18 in. in width.

* **Altman, John Alfred** - 15th South Carolina Inf., Company G, d. 6/19/64 of a gunshot wound @ Knight's Factory. His coffin size was 6 ft. 3 in. in length by 17 in. in width. His military records listed his date of death as 5/06/64 at the Wilderness. Age at enlistment was 19. The 1860 census listed him as a resident of the Williamsburg District.

Andrews, B. B. - 14th Virginia Inf., Company D, d. 1/26/63 @ College Hospital of typhoid fever. Coffin size was 6 ft. 2 in. in length by 18 in. in width. Andrews was originally buried in lot #187, grave #2, row #2. In the Soldiers Book the notions are as follows, "Removed", "R. Atkinson", and "$22.50 Petersburg Va.". Andrews enlisted as a private on 5/4/62 at Camp Randolph, Suffolk, Virginia. Andrews was listed as absent 12/27/62 in Richmond Hospital. He was born in Chesterfield County, Virginia.

Andrews, Charles L. - 30th Virginia Inf., Company H, d. 1/5/63 @ Crumpton's Factory of tubercular consumption. He was originally buried in lot #101, grave #8, row #1. Body was exhumed 01/29/63. H. B. Brooks claimed the remains.

Diuguid's entry was as follows, "Removed & sent to Milford Station". The cost for removal and packing was $25.00. Charles Andrews was born 1840, son of Sarah B. Andrews of Central Point. 1860 Census listed him as Manager @ Moss Point, Caroline County. Andrews enlisted as a private on 3/3/62.

* **Andrews, Daniel** – 47th Alabama Inf., Company I, d. 9/22/62 @ Odd Fellow's Hall. Coffin size was 80 in. in length by 19 in. in width. Andrews enlisted as a private on 4/18/62 at Loachopoka, Alabama. His age at enlistment was listed as 19. He was born in Alabama, he was single, his occupation was listed as a farmer and he was a resident of Tallassee, Alabama. Andrews was listed on the company muster as "Absent Sick" from 8/9/62 (Cedar Run) through 9/17/62 (Sharpsburg). His military records state that his date of death was 9/29/62.

Andrews, Edward R. - 41st Virginia Inf., Company E, d. 5/15/64 of typhoid fever @ Ferguson's Hospital. His coffin size was 6 ft. 1 in. in length and 21 in. in width. He was originally buried in lot #193, grave #9, row #5. Private Andrews was exhumed 1/31/65, "taken up & sent to Sutherland Depot SS (South Side) R Road". Mrs. Andrews, mother of the deceased claimed the remains and paid all expenses associated with removal and packing. Andrews enlisted as a private on 2/17/62 at Petersburg for the war, received $50.00 Bounty. Military records show him on special duty, "Cow Driver", 12/62 to early 64.

* **Apperson, Robert E.** - 11th Virginia Inf., Company G, "Lynchburg Home Guard", **Killed in Action** on 5/31/62 at the Battle of Seven Pines, buried in Lynchburg 06/06/62. He was the son of Washington Apperson - burial from Methodist Protestant Church. Appears in Lynchburg Daily Virginian 06/06/62, page 3, col. 1. "The remains of Robert E. Epperson, of the Home Guard, who was killed in the battle near Richmond, came up on the South Side train last night, and the funeral will take place from the Methodist Protestant Church this morning at 10 o'clock. The Rev. R. B. Thomson will officiate." He is buried in the Presbyterian Cemetery, Range 10, Row 14.

Armstrong, Turner - 46th North Carolina Inf., Company K, d. 1/11/64 of chronic bronchitis and/or chronic diarrhea @ Crumpton's Factory. Coffin size was 6 ft. 2 in. in length by 19 in. in width. Armstrong was originally buried in lot #185, grave #10, row #3. Diuguid's entry, "Removed & sent to

Sherron N.C.". His body was exhumed 01/16/64 at the request of William B. Armstrong, father of the deceased. Private Armstrong was a res. of Catawba County & enlisted @ age 35 on 10/01/62 for the war. Private Armstrong was wounded at Fredericksburg 12/13/62.

Arrowood, Benjamin F. - 37th North Carolina Inf., Company H, d. 04/02/63 of pneumonia @ Ferguson's Factory. The coffin size was listed as 5 ft. 10 in. in length by 18 in. in width. He was originally buried in lot #199, grave #7, row #5. The body was exhumed 04/24/63 at the request of William Arrowood, brother of the deceased. "Was sent to Cherryville N.C.", was the notation made by Diuguid. Born in Gaston County where he resided prior to enlisting in Iredell County 8/12/62 for the war.

Arthur, Armistead Corpl. - 14th Virginia Inf., Company B, d. 12/12/62 @ Christian's Factory of chronic diarrhea. Coffin size was 6 ft. in length by 18 in. in width. Originally buried in lot #180, row #2, grave #2. Body was exhumed 1/1/63 and sent to Bedford County, Virginia. William J. Arthur Paid all expenses, $25.00. Arthur enlisted 04/24/61 @ Fancy Grove, age 20, occupation was listed as carpenter. Elected Corpl. 06/03/61.

* **Athey, John Robert** - 2nd Virginia Inf., Company I, d. 4/22/62 of pneumonia @ Christian's Factory. Athey enlisted as a private on 3/4/62 at Winchester. His age at enlistment was listed as 19. He was born 10/26/1842. Compiled service records state, "was never paid anything", due $44.25.

* **Athey, William A.** - 2nd Virginia Inf., Company I, d. 4/23/62 of typhoid fever @ Warwick House. Athey enlisted as a private on 3/11/62 at Winchester. His age at enlistment was listed as 25. He was born 11/18/1836.

NOTE: John Robert and William Arhey appear to have been brothers, based on age, location at enlistment, date of enlistment and being in the same company.

Atwell, John C. - 42nd North Carolina Inf., Company G, d. 8/17/62 of typhoid fever @ Ladies Relief Hospital of typhoid fever. The body was packed and sent to Salisbury, North Carolina. The coffin size 5 ft. 11 in. in length by 19 in. in width. He enlisted 3/17/62 at age 21, res. of Rowan County, North Carolina.

Austin, Coleman A. - 21st Virginia Inf., Company I, d. 11/23/63 @ Miller's Factory. Coffin size was 6 ft. 3 in. in length by 18 in. in width. Diuguid's entry was, "packed up & sent to Danville Va.". M. R. A. Austin, the brother of the deceased claimed the remains and paid expenses "for packing remains". Austin enlisted as a private on 6/29/61 in Pittsylvania County.

* **Ayers, R. B.** - 7th Tennessee Inf., Company F, d. 9/01/62 @ Burton's Factory. Diuguid made the following notation, "walnut coffin $25.00". Coffin size was 5 ft. 11 in. in length by 18 in. width.

Bagby, Joseph B. - 7th Georgia Inf., Company G, d. 10/25/61 @ College Hospital. His body was prepared and shipped to Atlanta, Georgia. Diuguid did not specify a date. Bagby enlisted as a private on 5/31/61.

* **Baggett, Elisha** – 13th Alabama Inf., Company H, d. 7/27/62 of a fever @ Miller's Factory. Coffin size was 5 ft. 8 in. in length by 18 in. in width. Baggett enlisted as a private on 3/26/62 @ Coosa County, Alabama. His age at enlistment was listed as 20. He was born in Alabama, he was single, his occupation was listed as a farmer, and he was a resident of Rockford, Alabama. He was present for duty during the Siege at Yorktown. Prior to the action at Seven Pines (05/31/62) he was listed as "Absent Sick." Young Baggett had only served 121 days in the service before his death.

* **Bagwell, James** - 13th South Carolina Inf., Company I, d. 12/08/62 of chronic diarrhea @ Claytor's Factory. His coffin size was 6 ft. 1 in. in length by 18 in. in width. Age at enlistment was listed as 23. 1860 census showed him as resident of the Spartanburg District.

Bailey, Henry N., 5t Sgt. - 60th Georgia Inf., Company H, d. 08/13/62 of typhoid fever @ Christian's Factory. Coffin size was 6 ft. 2 in. in length by 20 in. in width. Originally enlisted in Company I, 1st Regiment, 1st Brigade Georgia State Troops on 10/07/61. Was mustered in April of 1862. Bailey enlisted and was appointed 5th Sgt. with 60th Georgia on 4/25/62.

Baker, Richard F. M. - 10th Alabama Inf., Company I, d. 09/13/62 of wounds @ Ladies Relief Hospital. Coffin size was 6 ft. 2 in. in length by 19 in. in width. Baker enlisted as a Private 9/1/61 at Gadsden Alabama. His age at enlistment was listed as 30. He was born in Georgia, occupation was listed as a farmer, his residence was listed as P.O. Duck

Springs, Alabama and he was married. He was present for duty at the following engagements, Dranesville, Yorktown, Williamsburg, Seven Pines, and Gaines' Mill. He was severely wounded at Gaines' Mill. The widow of the deceased, Matilda C. Baker filed a death claim 07/29/63. Mrs. Baker could be contacted in care of C. A. Dunnorby, Atty., Marietta, Georgia.

Ballard, Robert Wesley -   19th Georgia Inf., Company I (Capt. Chamber's Company), d. 10/15/61 @ College Hospital. Body was packed and sent to Palmetto, Georgia. Enlisted 6/22/61.

Ballard, Robert - Capt. Nelson's Company, d. 8/26/62. No other information available.

Ballard, William H. - 37th North Carolina Inf., Company I, d. 3/26/63 of chronic diarrhea @ Ferguson's Factory. Coffin size was 6 ft. 3 in. in length by 18 in. in width. Ballard was originally buried in lot #199, grave #9, row #5. He was exhumed 4/6/63 at the request of Noah Ballard, his father. "Sent to Charlotte N.C.", was the notation made by Diuguid. Resident of Gaston County and was by occupation a farmer. He enlisted in Iredell County at the age of 22 on 08/15/62 for the war.

Bankston, William -   44th Georgia Inf., Company A, d. 3/10/63 @ of chronic diarrhea Langhorne's Factory. Coffin size was 5 ft. 9 in. in length by 18 in. in width. He was originally buried in lot #199, grave #2, row #3. His body was exhumed 3/12/63, wife of the deceased, Mary Bankston (Diuguid spelling was Backston), claimed the remains. The two notations made by Mr. Diuguid were, "Removed" & "Taken up & sent to Jonesborough, (Sic) Claytor Cty, Ga". Diuguid has the name recorded as "Bankstain" in the "Soldier Book". Enlisted 3/17/62.

Banton, Richard H. -   11th Virginia Inf., Company H, d. 7/28/64 @ Charles Mans home. "Buried in family Lot", was the entry made by Diuguid. Banton enlisted as a private on 5/15/61. His age at enlistment was listed as 22. His occupation was listed as a Stone Mason. Banton was detailed as Hospital teamster 7 & 8/61, 9 & 10/62 and 5/8/63. He was arrested as a deserter 09/10/62. He was present for duty then thru 1864.

Barnes, William B. - 4th North Carolina Inf., Company F, d. 6/11/64 of wounds @ Camp Davis. Coffin size was 5 ft. 6 in. in length by 18 in. in width. Barnes was originally buried in lot #201, grave #4, row #2. Body was exhumed 6/16/64, "removed & sent to Wilson N.C.". William Ellis claimed remains. Barnes enlisted as a private on 9/9/61 for the war. His age at enlistment was listed as 19. Place and date of wound(s) not specified. Barnes was a resident of Wilson County.

* **Barnett, Thomas** - 2nd South Carolina Inf., Company H, d. 01/21/63 @ College Hospital. Per his service records, "died of wounds to the head, date unknown". Coffin size was 6 ft. in length by 18 in. in width. Barnett enlisted as a private on 4/15/62 in Pickens, South Carolina.

* **Barry, Howard H., 2nd Sgt.** - 32nd Virginia Inf., Company I, d.11/22/62 @ Miller's Factory. Coffin size was 69 in. in length by 17 in. in wide. Barry enlisted as a private on 5/27/61 at Williamsburg. A personal description; 5' 6", dark complexion, dark hair, blue eyes, occupation farmer. His military records states that his death occurred in Fredericksburg.

* **Barton, David, Jr.** - 28th Virginia Inf., Company D, d. 02/7/63 of diarrhea. Coffin size was 5 ft. 10 in. in length by 20 in. in width. He enlisted as a private on 05/20/61 in Bedford County, Virginia. His age at enlistment was listed as 22.

Barton, N. C. - 50th Virginia Inf., Company D, d. 06/27/63 @ Ferguson's Factory. Coffin size was 76 in. in length by 18 in. in width. He was originally buried in lot #192, grave #9, row #5. Diuguid entry was, "taken up & sent to Marion Smyth Co Va."

Battle, Jesse B. - 21st Georgia Inf., Company D, d. 06/19/62 @ Ferguson's Factory. Battle's coffin size was 73 in. in length by 18 in. in width. Battle was originally buried in lot #172, grave #5, row #4. Battle enlisted 3/01/62. Body was exhumed, packed and shipped to Cedar Town, Polk County, Georgia. Diuguid note the following entries, "(Rome)" and also, "Thomas A. Duke". NOTE: Thomas A. Lipscomb of 13th South Carolina buried in that location.

* **Bear, William Andrew** - 5th Virginia Inf., Company H, d. 03/01/63 of typhoid fever. Coffin size was 69 in. in length by 20 in. in width. Bear originally served in the 14th Virginia Cav., Company I. Bear enlisted as a private in 5th Virginia on 03/23/62. His age at death was 29. The father of the deceased was John H. Bear. Private Bear also was the brother of James H. Bear 14th Va. Cav. (d. 03/14/63 of chronic diarrhea as POW @ Camp Chase, Ill.), " a good young man, and was highly esteemed by all who knew him."

Bedell, Thomas J. - 20th Georgia Inf., Company B, d. 03/16/62 of pneumonia @ College Hospital. Bedell enlisted as a private on 05/23/61. Body was prepared and sent to Auburn, Alabama.

Beckwith, Wiley C., Dr. - 3rd Arkansas Inf., Capt. McGregor's Company, d. 02/10/62 from an accident at the Virginia & Tennessee Railroad Depot. Beckwith was a native of Pine Bluff, Jefferson County, Arkansas. His death notice appears in <u>Lynchburg Daily Virginia</u>, 02/11/62, page 2, col. 5 (the transcribed notice is on the following page). The debtor listed by Diuguid was Lieut. John C. Setson. Was unable to locate a military record for this individual.

Bell, David F. - 5th Virginia Inf., Company C, d. 06/23/63 @ College Hospital of chronic dysentery. Bell was admitted to Lynchburg 04/10/63. Diuguid's entry was, "sent to Staunton Va.". Born Augusta County 8/23/31, son of James Bell of Long Glade, enlisted 6/9/61 @ Shepherdstown. He was buried at Mossy Creek Old Cemetery.

* **Bell, James H.** - 55th North Carolina Inf., Company A, d. 5/24/64 @ Christian's Factory of wounds. Coffin size was 6 ft. 2 in. in length by 18 in. in width. He was wounded 05/05/64 at Battle of the Wilderness. Bell enlisted as a private on 5/08/62. His age at enlistment was listed as 40. He was a substitute for John P. Barden. Bell was born and resided in Wayne County as a farmer.

Berry - Slave of Capt. Barksdale, "In the employ of Quartermaster Department", d. 03/05/65 @ Government Stables. "Was buried in Negro Row".

<u>**Lynchburg Daily Virginian**</u> dated February 11, 1862
Death Notice of Dr. Wiley C. Beckwith
(Transcribed from the original newspaper)

LOCAL AND STATE NEWS

Fatal Accident - As Some Arkansas troops were passing through this city homeward bound on yesterday, Dr. Wiley C. Beckwith of Company ? (Capt. McGregor's) 3rd Arkansas Regiment met his death at the Depot of the Va. & Tenn. Railroad. The deceased attempted to step on the platform when the cars were moving off, when his body came in contact with a post or wall in the building, which threw him down between the cars and the platform running parallel with the track, whereby he was crushed and died a few moments afterwards. Dr.

Beckwith was a native Pine Bluff, Jefferson county Ark.; was a temperate genteel man we are informed, and was the first in his company to reenlist for the war.

? - The Company designation is unreadable

* **Berry, Thomas** - 8th Louisiana Inf., Company G, d. 05/13/64 @ Christian's Factory. Buried in lot #193, row #10, grave #2. Compiled Service Records do not indicate that this soldier was in Lynchburg. The roster states that, "died of wounds received in Battle of Wilderness, May 5, 1864".
* **Best, Thomas J.** - 7th Louisiana Inf., Company H, d. 3/13/62 @ Warwick House. Buried in lot #170, row #3, grave #4. The unit muster roll makes no mention of his death. Roster states, "enlisted June 7, 1861...on rolls from June 1861 to February 1862".
* **Biddle, Benjamin B.** - 3rd Virginia Inf., Company G, d. of pneumonia @ Ford's Factory on 11/13/62. Coffin size was 6 ft. 2 in. in length by 19 in. in width. Enlisted 5/11/61, occupation listed as overseer, age @ enlistment was 27.

Bird, Thomas H. - 42nd Virginia Inf., Company F, d. 1/17/62 of disease @ Warwick House Hospital. Bird was originally buried in lot #170, grave #2, row #2. Body was exhumed 1/24/62, packed and sent to Oak Level, P.O. Henry County, Virginia. His approximate age at death, based on 1860 census would be 19. Bird enlisted as a private on 06/22/61 in Henry County, Virginia. The 1860 census listed him as 18 years of age, occupation laborer, Oak Level P.O. Henry County. He was hospitalized in early January 1862. Father of the deceased was Lewis D. Byrd.
* **Bishop, James M.** – 6th Alabama Inf., Company G, d. 12/09/62 of wounds @ Booker's Factory. The coffin size was 5 ft. 11 in. in length by 18 in. in width. Bishop enlisted 03/1/62 as a private at Autaugaville (sic), Alabama. Private Bishop died of wounds received on 09/17/62 at the Battle of Sharpsburg.
* **Black, Quincy L.** - 48th Georgia Inf., Company F, d. 09/12/62 @ College Hospital. Coffin size was 6 ft. in length by 18 in. in width. Private Black enlisted as a private on 03/04/62. He was born in 1845. His approximate age at time of enlistment would have been 17. This young man served just over 6 months.
* **Blackman, Hiram** – 4th Alabama Inf., Company C, d. 08/02/62 (poss. of wounds) @ Candler's Factory. Coffin Size

was 73 in. in length by 19 inches in width. Blackman enlisted as a private on 3/23/62 in Selma, Alabama. His age at enlistment was listed as 30. His term of enlistment was for 3 years. Per his military records he was listed as "died in Charlottesville Hospital, June 1, 1862." Private Blackman must have been transferred to Lynchburg. He was born in Alabama, listed as single, and his residence was Selma, Alabama.

* **Blair, Anthony, 1st Sgt.** - 14th Louisiana Inf., Company F, buried in lot #173, row #8, grave #1. His unit muster roll indicates that he was 25 years of age and that he died July 1, 1862, no cause stated. However, Diuguid's records indicate that he was buried on June 29, 1862.

* **Blake, Zachariah I.** - 55th Virginia Inf., Company I, d. 8/5/62 of Congestic Cerebri @ Langhorne's Factory. Blake enlisted as a private on 3/14/62. He had previously served in Company B, 109th Virginia Militia. Widow of the deceased was Marry Blake, left one child.

* **Blankenship, King E.** - 41st Virginia Inf., Company D, d. 11/25/62 of secondary hemorrhage as a result of wounds received on 8/30/62 @ 2nd Battle of Manassas. Blankenship enlisted as a private on 6/15/61 in the Clover Hill District of Chesterfield County, Virginia. Occupation was listed as a Carpenter.

* **Blissett, William S.** - 13th Georgia Inf., Company C, d.08/06/62 @ Ladies Relief Hospt. Buried in lot #162, grave #7, row #1, listed as a Baptist Preacher. He enlisted as a private on 03/23/62, mustered into service on same date. He was a resident of Spalding County, Georgia.

Bogue, Z. R. - 15th North Carolina Inf., Company C, d. 11/08/63 of pneumonia @ Burton's Factory. Coffin size was 73 in. in length by 18 in. in width. Diuguid made the following entry, "removed & sent to Goldsboro N.C." Some confusion here, Diuguid also listed in the Soldiers Book that Boague (sic) was a member of 30th North Carolina, Company G. Bogue enlisted as a private in Wake County on 7/15/62, and mustered into service on same date. He was a resident of Wayne County, North Carolina. His age at enlistment was listed as 30.

Boiles, W. L. - Phillip's Legion Georgia Inf., Company B, d. 11/13/62 @ Crumpton's Factory. Diuguid's records state, "(Taken him up & pack him)", no other information.

Bolen, Hayward T. - 12th Virginia Cav., Company I, d. 10/12/64 of pyemia @ Knight's Factory. Originally buried in lot #198, grave #5, row #1. His body was exhumed 10/19/64. The widow of the deceased, Mrs. Rebecca Bolen, claimed the remains. Diuguid's entry was, "For removal & Packing husband $150.00". Diuguid's other entry was, "Removed", "Taken up & sent to Staunton Va."

Boles, Alexander M. - 21st North Carolina Inf., Company G, d. 07/28/62 of wounds and/or febris typhoides @ Claytor's Factory. Coffin size was 71 in. in length by 17 in. in width. Was wounded in the hip at Winchester 5/25/62. Body was prepared and shipped to High Point, North Carolina. Boles enlisted as a private on 5/30/61. His age at enlistment was listed as 18. Born in and a resident of Stokes County.

Bonney, Henry J. - 15th Virginia Cav., Company C, d. 01/14/64 of pneumonia @ Christian's Factory. Coffin size was 75 in. in length by 19 in. in width. He was originally buried in lot #185, grave #10, row #3. "Removed & sent to Princess Ann Cty Va Muddy Creek". Bonney enlisted as a private on 3/27/62 near Ocean View in Company C of the 14th Battn. Va. Cavalry. His age at enlistment was listed as 19. He had previously enlisted 4/20/61 @ Princess Anne Court House in Company A of the 5th Va. Cavalry. The 5th Va. Cav. was reorganized 3/27/62 to the 14th Battn. Va. Cavalry. Te 15th Virginia was formed from the consolidation of the 14th and 15th Battalions on 9/11/62.

* **Booker, S. M.** – 48th Alabama Inf., Company A, d. 10/22/62 of wounds @ Christian's Factory. Coffin size was 70 in. in length by 18 in. in width. Booker enlisted as a private on 4/7/62 at Warrenton, Alabama. His age at enlistment was listed as 19. He was born in Alabama, single, occupation was listed a farmer and was resident of Blountsville, Alabama. Private Booker was wounded on 08/09/62 at the Battle of Cedar Run. His military records state that he died on 11/05/62 at Charlottesville, Va. (sic). Per his records it appears that a death claim was filed on 10/26/63. The certificate #10810 was received 01/18/64. The residence of the claimant could not be "ascertained." At that time the claim was delivered to Col. James Lawrence Sheffield, commanding the 48th Alabama. The amount of the claim was $120.40. Colonel Sheffield was from Huntsville, Alabama. He was appointed Col. Of the 48th in early May 1862. Sheffield spent

$60,000 of his own money to from the regiment. Sheffield resigned his commission in May 1864.

* **Bottoms, Aaron L.** - 53rd Georgia Inf., Company C, d. 2/14/63 @ College Hospital. Coffin size was 6 ft. 1 in. in length by 18 in. in width. Originally enlisted in Company H of 30th Georgia Infantry 9/25/61. He was transferred to 53rd Georgia in exchange for Andrew J. Cox on 05/20/62.

Bost, R. G. - 57th North Carolina Inf., Company F, d. 2/7/63 @ Ferguson's Factory. Private Bost was originally buried in lot #191, grave #5, row #4. His body was exhumed 11/14/63, Rev. Thornton Butler claimed the remains and paid expenses. "Removed & sent to Salisbury N. Carolina", was the notation made by Mr. Diuguid.

Boulware, O. - 17th South Carolina Inf., Company B, d. 09/25/62 @ Burton's Factory. Coffin size was 6 ft. 4 in. in length by 19 in. in width. He was originally buried in lot #180, grave #10, row #4. Exhumed 1/27/63 and sent to Chester Court House, South Carolina. A.R. Jennings claimed remains. NOTE: J. M. Spears of 60th Georgia buried there now.

* **Bowen, B. F.** - 61st Georgia Inf., Company D, d. 10/30/62 @ Miller's Factory. His military record states that, "died Staunton, Virginia hospital 1862". Coffin size was 6 ft. 3 in. in length by 18 in. in width.

* **Bozeman, James S.** - 8th South Carolina Inf., Company F, d. 04/08/62 of pneumonia @ College Hospital. Age at enlisted listed as 27. 1860 census showed him a resident of the Darlington District.

* **Bradford, Hampton** - 8th Florida Inf., Company I, d. 12/26/62 of disease @ Langhorne's Factory. Coffin size was 6 ft. 2 in. in length by 18 in. in width. He enlisted at Orlando on 5/17/62. Sent to Culpepper Hospital 11/18/62. Widow of the deceased was Effie McDougald Bradford. They were married 7/03/55. He was born 1834.

* **Bradshaw, Eaphrum** – 15th Alabama Inf., Company C, d. 01/04/63 of Small Pox @ the Pest House. Coffin size was 6 ft. 2 in. in length by 18 in. in width. Bradshaw enlisted as a Private on 8/15/62 at Dale County, Alabama. His age at enlistment was listed as 34. He was born in South Carolina, occupation was listed as a farmer, he was a resident of Newton, Dale County, Alabama, and was married. Per a "Historical Record Roll, dated near Richmond, Va., Dec. 31, 1864" the following was stated about Private Bradshaw. "This soldier was sent to hospital for treatment in Oct. 1862, having never received any notice of him. Was reported dead and dropped on March and April Rolls, 1864."

* Brady, Francis M. - 28th Georgia Inf., Company B, d. 10/13/62 @ Crumpton's Factory. Coffin size was 6 ft. 1 in. in length by 19 in. in width. An entry in his military record states that he, "Died in Manassas Gap Hospital". Possibly was wounded during the Maryland Campaign admitted at Manassas then moved to Lynchburg.

* Bragg, John W. - 15th North Carolina Inf., Company E, d. 12/24/62 of typhoid fever @ Saunder's Factory. Coffin size was 5 ft. 5 in. in length by 18 in. in width. Bragg had previously served in the 47th North Carolina Inf., Company F. Transferred to Company E, 15th North Carolina 03/10/62. He enlisted 2/24/62 in Franklin County, was a resident of Grandville County.

* Braswell, James C. – 15th Alabama Inf., Company C, d. 05/24/62 of typhoid fever @ Christian's Factory. Coffin size was 6 ft. in length by 18 in. in width. Braswell enlisted as a Private on 3/18/62. He was born in Georgia, occupation was listed as a farmer, he was a resident of P.O. Creek Stand, Alabama, and was married. The widow of the deceased, Eliza Braswell (Macon County, Alabama) filed a death claim 3/16/63. The claim was verified and settled on 5/27/64.

* Brinkley, David - 33rd North Carolina Inf., Company E, d. 01/21/63 of "Febris Typhoides" @ Burton's Factory. Captured at Fredericksburg 12/13/62, paroled and exchanged 12/17/62. Born Gates County where he resided prior to his enlistment on 8/29/61 at age 40. His occupation was listed as a carpenter.

Briscoe, Isaac H., Ord. Sgt. - 17th Virginia Cav., Company F, d. 04/14/65 @ Farmville, Virginia. Briscoe enlisted 9/23/62 @ Sissonville. Listed as sick in Staunton hospital 8/7/64. He was a resident of Parkersburg, Virginia (West Va.) See the information listed below on his brother and the note following that entry.

Briscoe, J. A. - 17th Virginia Cav., Company F, d. 05/02/65 @ Camp Davis. He was originally buried in lot #202, grave #7, row 5. "Removed and buried corner of lot 21 second extension with his brother J. H. Briscoe next to him". In the note section of burial log #6 Mr. Diuguid made the following entry, "J H Briscoe O.S Co F 17th Va Cav Died 14th April at Farmville". He concludes with, "I have to enclose two graves". Diuguid was mistaken the initials J. H. he listed was actually

Isaac H. Private Briscoe enlisted 11/1/64 @ Port Republic. Mr. George Diuguid made another entry in Logbook #7 dated Dec. 16, 1865. The entry was as follows, "Revd. Warwick Briscoe, Parkersburg, Va., for removal of son & burial of another $40.00. Credit by cash in part $20.00. The two brothers buried in West Corner of Lot 21-2nd Extension O G Yard (Old Graveyard). June 29th 1866 by cash in full through express $20.00."

NOTE: The two Briscoe brothers listed above were the sons of Rev. Warwick Briscoe of Parkersburg, West Virginia. On or about December 16, 1865 Rev. Briscoe contacted Mr. Diuguid to remove the one son from the Confederate Cemetery and the burial of the other.

* **Britton, William E.** - 1st Tennessee Inf., Capt. Bennett's Company (Tallahassee Guard), d. 5/27/61 @ College Hospital. The father of the decease was Judge Benjamin Britton of Murphy, Cherokee County, Tennessee.

Brooks, Andrew J. - 10th Virginia Cav., Company K, d. 11/21/63of typhoid fever @ Crumpton's Factory. Brooks was originally buried in lot #200, grave #4, row #1. Body was exhumed 11/28/63 at the request of Robert Lee Brooks, brother of deceased. "Removed" and, "taken up & sent to Big Lick Depot", were the entries made by Mr. Diuguid. Born in Franklin County circa 1846, 1860 census listed him as a student, age 14, Union Hall P.O. Franklin County. Brooks enlisted as a Private on 1/1/63 in Richmond. Personal effects at death were, "...$22.50 and sundries". He was the younger brother of John Meador, David Staples Keen, Peter Henry, Robertson Lee, and William Ebenezer Brooks.

* **Brown, Francis Marion** - 11th Virginia Inf., Company E, d. 6/21/62 of disease @ his fathers residence. His age at death was 29 years 5 months. Enlisted 4/19/61, occupation mechanic (his age at enlistment was listed as 25?). He was the second son of Col. William B. & Sarah Brown. His obituary was published in the Lynchburg Daily Virginian on 7/7/62, page 3, col. 1 (the transcribed obituary is on the following page).

Lynchburg Daily Virginian dated July 7, 1862
Death Notice of Francis Marion Brown
(Transcribed from the original newspaper)

OBITUARY

FRANCIS MARION, second son of Col. William B. and Sarah Brown, died on the 21st of June, at the residence of his father, in Lynchburg, age 29 years and five months. The ligament which bound soul and body has been severed; his spirit has been set free from its prison house, and we trust it winged its way upon the pinions of divine grace to the celestial world there to rest in the house of Abraham and to join in the anthem of praise which is ever chanted around the throne of the Father by the redeemed. Long will be remembered by all who knew him as one of natures bravest son's. He has been cut down the inexorable sickle of death, while his years were yet in the spring time. But dear ones be comforted. We mourn in sympathy with you for your separation from one so fondly loved - so early lost.
    A Friend

Brown, George W. -   14th Virginia Inf., Company H, d. 11/17/62 @ Claytor's Factory of pneumonia. Private Brown's coffin size was 6 ft. 3 in. in length by 18 in. in width. Browns remains were, "sent home by wagon". Home may have been Halifax County, Company H, "The Meadville Greys" were formed in Halifax County April 29, 1861. Brown enlisted 9/1/62 in Richmond, age 20, occupation farmer.

Brown, George W. -   11th Virginia Inf., Company G, "Lynchburg Home Guard", MWIA 8/30/62 at Battle of 2nd Manassas, d. 9/02/62. He was born in Campbell County, his age at the time of his untimely death was 26. He was the son of Col. William B. Brown. Appears in the <u>Lynchburg Daily Virginian</u> on 10/28/62, page 3, col. 1. In Mr. Diuguid's burial records the cost for his services was $33.00. A cost $8.00 was for "sheet, Cotton furnished & gloves". His father paid $24.00 of the cost the remainder was paid by the "Southern Confederacy". NOTE: William B. Brown was in charge of the 131st Virginia Militia formed in Lynchburg in late 1859, he did not serve during the War for Southern Independence. The good Colonel died in 1869 as the result of an accidental gunshot wound at the age of 65.

* **Brown, Lewis T.** - 35th North Carolina Inf., Company A, d. 02/01/63 of typhoid fever @ Burton's Factory. Coffin size was 6 ft. in length by 20 in. in width. Born Onslow County, resided in Duplin County where he was by occupation a farmer. Brown enlisted as a private on 9/6/61 at age 18 in Onslow

County. The last entry in his military records shows him on furlough for January and February of 63.

* **Brown, Patrick** - Madison Light Louisiana Artillery, Capt. Moody's Company, buried in lot #161, row #10, grave #2. He appears on the unit muster roll for December 1863 with the following remarks, "sick in General Hospital in Richmond". This was his last known record.

Brown, Thomas - Possibly Lieut. Thomas Brown of the 7th Georgia Inf., died on or about 02/07/62. Andrew Brown, his brother, paid for packing & shipping of his brothers remains. In addition, Andrew paid for the exhumation, packing and shipment of John B. Furlow, and William Furlow also of the 7th Georgia, Capt. Featherstone's Company. Furlow's remains were shipped to Hogansville, Troup County, Georgia. Brown enlisted 05/31/62 was elected to 2nd Lieut. 09/16/61. His military records listed his cause of death as brain fever and place of death was Camp Sam Jones near Centerville, Va. 01/18/62. NOTE: J. Langston of the 15th Alabama was buried on 02/01/62 in this location.

* **Brown, William N.** - 7th Georgia Inf., Company D, d. 2/24/64 @ Camp Davis. Coffin size was 73 in. in length by 19 in. in width. His military record states, "Accidentally killed at Lynchburg." Diuguid's entry was, "(Stabbed)".

* **Browning, R. A.** - 23rd South Carolina Inf., Company B, d. 09/19/62 @ Langhorne's Factory (Gen. Hospital #2) of febris typhoides. Browning enlisted as a private on 9/25/61. His age at enlistment was listed as 50. Coffin size was 70 in. in length by 18 in. in width.

* **Bruce, John W.** - 1st Orr's Rifles South Carolina Inf., Company C, d. 1/22/63 of fever @ Saunder's Factory. Coffin size was 69 in. in length by 18 in. in width. Bruce enlisted as a private on 8/27/61 in Anderson, South Carolina. His age at enlistment was listed as 39. The widow of the deceased was Mary Bruce. Cost of the funeral was $11.65. Of the $11.65, $1.65 was charged for a shirt, socks, and "drawers".

* **Bryan, Joseph** – 10th Georgia Inf. Battn., Company A, d. 05/10/64 @ Burton's factory. Born 1845, son of John L. & Elisabeth P. Bryan. He was a native of Macon, County, Ga.

Bryant, William H. - Provost Guard, d. 02/11/64 @ College Hospital. Coffin size was 74 in. in length by 19 in. in width. Diuguid's made the following entry, "was buried in Amherst County Mahones G Y (graveyard)". William A. Irvine claimed the remains and paid expenses.

Bryant, William P. - 28th Virginia Inf., Company F, d. 02/13/63 @ home "in Campbell" (County?). The other notation made was, "was buried in family burying (sic) ground". Coffin size was 73 in. in length by 18 in. in width. The father of the deceased, Andrew Bryant, claimed the remains. These additional notations were made by Mr. Diuguid, "(New London)" and "For coffin & box for son $20.00". The "Southern Confederacy" paid $9.00, the balance, $11.00, was paid in cash. There are two "William P. Bryants" listed in the roster of Company F, 28th Virginia. Both enlisted on the same date in Bedford, both are listed in the hospital from Nov. 62 to Feb. 63. For one the record ends the other list him as present in 12/64.

* **Buchanan, Joseph** - 30th North Carolina Inf., Company H, d. 10/15/64 @ Reid's Factory of acute diarrhea. Coffin size was 5 ft. 11 in. in length by 18 in. in width. Buchanan was serving as a substitute for W. T. Yarbrough. Was a resident of Chatham County and enlisted 03/01/62 at Camp Holmes. Possibly Josephs brother, C. B. Buchanan, also a member of the 30th, Company H, died the previous year (08/11/63) in Lynchburg of a fever. Diuguid does not list the later.

* **Buchanan, Robert Edward, Corpl.** - 17th Virginia Inf., Company H, d. 3/23/64 of smallpox @ the Pest House. Coffin size was 6 ft. in length by 18 in. in width. Diuguid made the following notation, "was buried in smallpox lot & board put up". In Diuguid's Burial log the name is spelled "Buckhannon". His occupation was listed as "Gent at large", age 20 when he enlisted on 4/17/61 in Alexandria. Buchanan was captured on 9/17/62 at Sharpsburg, Maryland. He was exchanged and promoted to Color Corpl. June 1863. Wounded in Action at Manassas Gap 7/21/63. Compiled Service Record stated that he died in Lynchburg Hospital 3/23/64 from wounds. Exhumed in November of 1865 and reburied in Methodist Protestant Cemetery Alexandria.

Buckles, Henry - 15th South Carolina Inf., Company G, d. 11/18/62 of pneumonia @ Ford's Factory. His coffin size was 72 in length by 18 in. in width. His military records list his date of death as 6/15/64. Approximately 18 months difference between Mr. Diuguid's records and the Confederate records. His age at enlistment was listed as 28. 1860 census list him as a resident of Williamsburg District.

* **Buckles, John** - 8th Florida Inf., Company I, d. 08/20/64 of disease @ Langhorne's Factory. Coffin size was not listed.

Private Buckles enlisted 02/28/62 at St. John's Bluff. Wife of the deceased was Sarah A. J. Buckles. He was born 1834.

* **Bumgarner, Tobias** - 37th North Carolina Inf., Company G, d. 8/03/62 of typhoid fever @ Saunder's Factory. However, Diuguid's burial records he was not interred until 8/3/62.

Bumpass, Francis Marion - 35th North Carolina Inf., Company E, d. 11/3/62 of chronic diarrhea @ Crumpton's Factory. Coffin size was 6 ft. 6 in. in length by 20 in. in width. He was originally buried in lot #182, grave #10, row #3. His body was exhumed and sent to Roxborough, North Carolina via the South Boston Depot, Virginia. Expenses paid by Mr. J. W. Pearce. Born in Person County where he enlisted 9/25/61. NOTE: W. Gill of 5th South Carolina buried there 12/7/62.

Burch, James B. - 24th Virginia Inf., Company H, d. 6/12/62 @ Ferguson's Factory of disease. Body was prepared and sent to Danville, Virginia. Coffin size was 5 ft. 8 in. in length by 17 in. in width. His approximate age based on existing records indicate he would have been no more than 18. Enlisted 3/17/62 @ age 17; served 2 months 25 days. In Diuguid's notes associated with the death of Pvt. Burch are two names, Lewis E. Burch and Jos. E. Burch (family?).

* **Burdell, Hiram W.** - 14th South Carolina Inf., Company I, d. 7/18/64 @ Ferguson's Factory. His coffin size was 6 ft. in length by 18 in. in width. His military records list his date of death as 5/03/64. This would indicate he was present at the Wilderness, possibly severely wounded, transported to Lynchburg. In addition, Diuguid listed his last name as "Burdett". His age at enlistment was listed as 17. The 1860 census listed him as a resident of Abbeville District.

* **Burks, Rowland** - 5th Texas Inf., Company B, d. 10/2/62 @ Ladies Relief Hospital of disease. Coffin size was 6 ft. in length by 18 in. in width. Private Burks enlisted 3/22/62 @ Columbus, Texas at age 33. He was detailed to CSA Intelligence Office in mid 1862.

* **Burmingham, Benjamin** – 47th Alabama Inf., Company A, d. 1/2/63 of Small Pox @ the Pest House. Coffin size was 75 in. in length by 18 in. in width. The father of the deceased, George W. Burmingham, filed a death claim on 9/18/64. Mr. Burmingham could be contacted in care of Augustis M. McGehee, Dadeville, Alabama.

* **Burns, Henry** - 11th South Carolina Inf., Company H, d. 5/14/64 @ Christian's Factory. Diuguid's and the military date of death differ. The Confederacy shows his death date as

6/15/64. 1860 census list him as resident of the Colleton District.

* **Burton, William John** - 30th Virginia Inf., Company I, was murdered 10/01/63 by a male Negro in Lynchburg. Coffin size was 6 ft. in length by 20 in. in width. Mr. Diuguid's entry in the Soldiers Book was "was killed by a Negro with a spade". Burton enlisted 07/22/61 in Stafford County, listed as 42 years of age, occupation laborer.

* **Butler, Richmond** – 44th Alabama Inf., Company D, d. 06/5/63 @ Claytor's Factory. Coffin size was 76 in. in length by 18 in. in width. Butler enlisted as a private on 03/19/62 at Shelby Springs, Alabama. His age at enlistment was listed as 27. He was born in Virginia, married; occupation was listed as a farmer, and was a resident of Shelby Springs, Alabama. His military records state his date of death to be 06/24/63.

Butter, Isaiah R. - Frazier's Battery Georgia Light Art., d. 1/20/64 @ Ferguson's Factory. Coffin Size was 6 ft. 3 in. in length by 19 in. in width. Private Butter was originally buried in lot #200, grave #6, row #3. Body was exhumed 02/02/64, "Removed & sent to Augusta Ga", was the entry made by Diuguid. D. C. Wellers claimed the remains and paid expenses.

Butterworth, William Whitfield - 11th Virginia Inf., Company E, d. 03/16/62 of disease. Funeral expenses paid in part by Confederacy & father of the deceased, Isaac Butterworth. "...in his 18th year at the residence of his father near Lynchburg, member of Lynchburg Rifles". <u>Lynchburg Daily Virginian</u> dated 03/25/62, page 3, col. 2 (the Transcribed notice is on the following page). Butterworth enlisted 6/5/61 @ age 19 (?). As a sad note his older brother, John W. Butterworth, was **Killed in Action** 09/17/62 at Sharpsburg, Maryland.

<u>**Lynchburg Daily Virginian**</u> dated March 25, 1862
Death Notice of William Whitfield Butterworth
(Transcribed from the original newspaper)

DIED

On the 16th Inst., at the residence of his father, near the city, William Whitfield Butterworth.

This young man was a member of the company known here as Lynchburg Rifles. He was a good soldier; always prompt in the discharge of the duties to which he was called; and ever ready to repair to any post of danger, however imminent the peril to which he exposed himself. His health, from the time he entered the service, until he was attacked by the disease, which terminated his life, was remarkably good. He reached home on Thursday and died the following Sabbath. We are pleased to add that he had no forgotten his responsibility to his Creator. He gave his sorrowing friends the most ample proof that he had made preparation for death. He had not reached his 19th birthday.

* **Buzzard, Presley** - 14th South Carolina Inf., Company B, d. 6/6/62 of typhoid fever @ Odd Fellow's Hall. His coffin size was 6 ft. 1 in. in length by 19 in. in width. Enlisted at age 21 at Camp Butler, South Carolina. Widow of the deceased was Mary Jane Buzzard. The 1860 census list him as resident of the Edgefield District.

* **Bywaters, James Edward** - 6th Virginia Cav., Company B, d. 8/7/62 of typhoid fever @ Reid's Factory. Enlisted 4/1/62 at age 31. Widow of the deceased was Sallie Hill Bywaters (M. 1851)

Cabell, Patrick Henry - 11th Virginia Inf., Company G, d. 09/6/61 at Fairfax Court House of typhoid fever, "in his 22nd year of his age". His death notice was published 9/13/62 in the <u>Lynchburg Daily Virginian</u>, page 2, col. 5. A Tribute form the "Lynchburg Home Guard" was published 9/21/61, page **3**, col. 1. The funeral notice was published 10/11/62, page 3, col., "Funeral discourse on 13th October at Methodist Church". Cabell enlisted as a private on 04/19/61. His age at enlistment was listed as 22. His occupation was listed as a clerk.

Cabell, Samuel Jordan, Dr. - 25th Virginia Inf., Company B ("Upshur Grays", Upshur County, now West Virginia), d. 9/3/61 "...in 26th year of his age at Monteray, Highland County..." Expenses paid by Col. James Langhorne. Notice appeared in <u>Lynchburg Daily Virginian</u> dated 9/13/61, page 2, col. 5. Born 8/23/36. Enlisted Buckhannon, Va. (West Va.) 5/27/61. Requested to be detailed to Monterey General Hospital by Surg. W. A. Carrington, Med. Director, Army of the North West. Cabell was listed as absent 9/1/61 thru 12/31/61. He died at Monterey Hospital, Highland County on 09/03/61 of typhoid fever.

Cagle, Archibald M. - 42nd North Carolina Inf., Company C, d. 08/07/62 of typhoid fever @ Ladies Relief Hospital. Coffin size was 72 in. in length by 18 in. in width. Body was prepared and shipped to Concord, North Carolina. Father, Charles Cagle, paid for the preparation and shipment of his son. He enlisted at age was 18 in Rowan County on 3/24/62. He was a resident of Stanley County, North Carolina.

Cain, William F. - 42nd North Carolina Inf., Company F, d. 7/11/62 @ Reid's Factory. Coffin size was 73 in. in length by 20 in. in width. Body prepared and sent to Davie County, North Carolina. Expenses paid by Capt. Wiley Clements. He enlisted 3/18/62 in Davie County at age 27.

Calhoun, J. Z. - 33rd North Carolina Inf., Company H, d. 1/22/63 of febris typhoides @ Miller's Factory. Coffin size was 73 in. in length by 20 in. in width. He was originally buried in lot #187, grave #9, row #4. "Taken up & sent to High Point N. C.", was the notation made by Mr. Diuguid. Was a resident of Forsyth County where he enlisted 7/15/62 for the war.

* **Cameron, John F.** - 3rd North Carolina Inf., Company C, d. 8/28/62 @ College Hospital, cause not stated. He was originally buried in lot #170, grave #2, Row #2. Mr. Diuguid does not provide any information as to where the remains were shipped, only that the body was "Removed" - we have to assume that he was returned to North Carolina. Cameron enlisted 7/20/62 and was a res. of Cumberland County, North Carolina.

Cameron, John H. - 41st Virginia Inf., Company G, d. 12/1/62 of typhoid fever @ Christian's Factory. Coffin size was 69 in. in length by 18 in. in width. He was originally buried in lot #78, Grave #9, row #3. Body was exhumed and sent to Petersburg, Virginia. Cameron enlisted 03/10/62 @ Petersburg, Virginia for the war, rec. a bounty of $50.00. Per his widows pension application he died 06/11/63 of diphtheria at Fredericksburg. NOTE: T. J. Herren of 15th Alabama buried there 12/15/62.

Campbell, **** - Soldier, d. 07/30/61, paid by father of deceased, Gustavus Campbell. A James W. Campbell, age 21, enlisted in the 11th Virginia inf. 04/23/61, d. 07/28/61 at the Charlottesville Hospital. Could possibly be the individual Diuguid mentions.

* **Campbell, Colin J.** – 6th Alabama Inf., Company l, d. 030/6/63 @ Claytor's Factory. Coffin size was 78 in. in length

by 20 in. in width. The father of the deceased was Colin J. Campbell. Mr. Campbell filed a death claim 07/14/63.

* Campbell, H. H. - 26th North Carolina Inf., Company A, d. 06/05/64 of gunshot wound @ Christian's Factory. Was wounded and captured Gettysburg. He was hospitalized in Gettysburg until transferred to Davis Island, New York that same month. Was paroled at Davis Island and transferred to City Point, Virginia 09/17/63 for exchange. Campbell enlisted as a private on 03/27/62. His age at enlistment was listed as 18. He was a resident of Ashe County.

* Campbell, James - 3rd South Carolina Inf., Company F, d. 02/23/63 of disease @ Langhorne's Factory. His coffin size was 74 in. in length by 18 in. in width. Age at enlistment is shown as 25. 1860 census showed him as a resident of the Richland District. His military records list his date of death as 06/15/63. This is possibly the date of their official notification.

* Campbell, John – 44th Alabama Inf., Company G, d. 03/06/63 @ Crumpton's Factory. Coffin size was 74 in. in length by 18 in. in width. Campbell enlisted as a private on 4/25/62 at Randolph, Alabama. His age at enlistment was listed as 24. He was born in Alabama, single, occupation was listed as a farmer, and he was a resident of Randolph, Alabama. Per his company musters he was listed as "Absent Sick" prior to the Battle on 2nd Manassas (8/31/62) through Sharpsburg (9/17). He was listed as "Present" during the Battle at Fredericksburg on 12/11/62. The following is a final statement made by Lieut. R. H. Croswell on September 20, 1864 at Petersburg, Virginia. "Born in Bibb Co., Ala. Enlisted by B. W. Brown at Bibb Co. Ala. on the 25th of April 62 for 3yrs or the war. Died at Lynchburg, Va. on the 6th of Mch. 63. Last paid by Capt Lapsley, Q. M. to include the 28th of Feb. 63, and is entitled to pay there from to 6th of Mch. 63, at which time he died. He is entitled to commutation for transportation in lieu of furlough from Richmond, Va. to Randolph, Bibb Co., Ala. and back, which is 1900 miles. He is entitled to commutation for clothing from 8th of Oct. 62 to the 6th of Mch. 63 less stoppages for clothing drawn to the amount of $5.10. He is entitled to $100 bounty in compliance with Genl. Order #27, Adjt. Genl. Office."

* Campbell, John W. - 2nd South Carolina Inf., Company F, d. 02/17/63 as a result of a wound to a hand. Coffin size was 72 in. in length by 18 in width. He enlisted at Anderson,

South Carolina 11/23/61. Widow of deceased was Frances Campbell. 1860 census listed him as resident of the Sumter District.

* **Campbell, W. M.** - 13th Georgia Inf., Company D, d. 07/08/64 @ Camp Davis. His coffin size 69 in. in length by 16 in. in width. His military records states that he died of disease in Upson County, Georgia.

* **Canterbury, J. W., 2nd Lieut.** – 8th Alabama Inf., Company B, d. of wounds 12/28/62 @ Burton's Factory. Coffin size was 75 in. in length by 18 in. in width. Canterbury enlisted as 3rd Sgt. 5/13/61 at Watumpka, Alabama. His age at enlistment was listed as 20. His occupation was listed as a carpenter. Born in Georgia circa 1841 and was a resident of Watumpka, Alabama. Saw action at the Siege of Yorktown April 1862, Williamsburg May 5, 62, Seven Pines June 1, 62, Gaines Mill June 26, 62, Frayser's Farm June 30, 62, 2nd Manassas Aug. 29 & 30, 62, and Sharpsburg Sept. 17, 62. Canterbury was promoted to 2nd Lieut. on 06/30/62. He was seriously wounded at Sharpsburg.

* **Cape, William** - 2nd South Carolina Inf., Company C, d. 12/15/62 @ Ferguson's Factory. Coffin Size was 79 in. in length by 19 in. in width. Cape enlisted as a private on 11/23/61 at South Island, South Carolina. Mother of the deceased was Elizabeth Cape.

* **Cardwell, Parker** - 22nd North Carolina Inf., Company K, d. 07/12/64 from wounds @ Knight's Factory. Coffin size 73 in. in length by 20 in. in width. He was wounded in leg and arm at Battle of the Wilderness 5/05/64. Enlisted as a private in Wake County on 3/12/63. Previously wounded at Chancellorsville May, 63.

Cargill, David D., Sgt. - 44th North Carolina Inf., Company K, d. 11/05/63 of chronic diarrhea @ Reid's Factory. Coffin size was 72 in. in length by 17 in. in width. "Packed up & sent to Kitterells (sic) Depot N.C.". The mother of the deceased, "Mrs. Cargill" claimed the remains. Kittrell (correct spelling) is approximately 50 miles north of Raleigh, and just south of Henderson. Cargill was a resident of Franklin County, enlisted in Greenville County at age 24 on 05/18/62 for the war. Promoted to Corpl. 6/15/62. Promoted to Sgt. prior to 03/01/63. "Was a brave & good soldier."

* **Carmical, Robert Y., 4th Corpl.** - 53rd Georgia Inf., Company D, d. 07/03/63 @ Christian's Factory. Coffin size was 6 ft. 2 in. in length by 18 in. in width. Originally enlisted

in Company A, 1st Georgia Infantry 3/18/61. Discharged at Winchester 2/02/62. Enlisted 05/06/62 in Company D, 53rd Georgia and appointed 4th Corpl. Was wounded at Sharpsburg 09/17/62.

* Carney, James - 2nd Tennessee Inf., Company H, murdered 02/26/62. Buried in lot #170, grave #6, row #3. Carney was stabbed to death while on guard duty at the Lawless House at Horses' Ford on the James River, east of Lynchburg, Virginia.

* Carothers, J. R. (James?) - 18th South Carolina Inf., Company H, d. 12/03/62 of disease @ Ferguson's Factory. Coffin size was 76 in. in length by 19 in. in width. James R. Carothers of the 12th South Carolina also Company H is listed as dying @ Winchester 10/29/62. It is possible that these are one in the same. Private Carothers enlisted on 05/15/62 at Charleston, South Carolina. His age at enlistment was listed as 31. The widow of the deceased was Sarah R. Carothers. 1860 census shows him as resident of the York District.

Carpenter, Lawson P. - 23rd North Carolina Inf., Company K, d. 12/22/62 @ Burton's Factory. Coffin size was 74 in. in length by 18 in. in width. Body was prepared and shipped to Lincolnton, North Carolina. Born in Lincoln County where he resided until enlisting 08/20/62 for the war.

Carpenter, Seaborn - 26th North Carolina Inf., Company K, d. 06/27/63 of disease @ Crumpton's Factory. Coffin size was 81 in. in length by 18 in. in width. "Packed up & sent to Concord N.C.". Was a resident of Anson County were he enlisted at age 18 on 02/10/63 for the war.

Carrier, Edward - 7th Louisiana Inf., Company H, d. 07/12/62 @ Burton's Factory, "died from effects of wounds, in June 1862". Originally buried in Spring Hill Cemetery, Section U, South Corner of lot #153, #1. Carrier was exhumed and shipped to New Orleans. Expenses paid by Southern Confederacy & Capt. DeLisle. Carrier enlisted as a private on 06/7/61 at Camp Moore, Louisiana. Born in and resident of New Orleans, occupation clerk, and he was unmarried.

Carroll, Thomas L. - 28th North Carolina Inf., Company B, d. 07/24/62 @ Burton's Factory of diarrhea and from effects of wounds. Carroll enlisted as a private on 08/5/61. His age at enlistment was listed as 21. His coffin size was 69 in. in length by 17 in. in width. Carroll was originally buried in lot #162, grave #2, row #3. Diuguid made the following entry, "taken up & sent (to) Brevard Station, Gaston Cty, N. C.". One source states that he was removed in August of 1862 and returned to North Carolina by a Vincent R. Allen. Thomas Carroll was born in and a resident of Gaston County. NOTE: Leroy Hayes of the 38th Georgia buried in that location 09/07/62.

Carson, James A., 3rd Sgt. - 12th Georgia Inf., Company C, d. 08/27/62 of disease @ Christian's Factory. Coffin size was 72 in. in length by 18 in. width. He was originally buried in lot #178, grave #1, row #2. Body was exhumed and shipped to Reynolds, Taylor County, Georgia. Remains were interred in Carson Cemetery in Macon County. Father of deceased, J. J. Carson, paid all expenses. Enlisted 05/01/62, appointed 3rd Sgt. 06/15/62. NOTE: John J. Huggins 18th North Carolina buried in that location 9/10/62.

Carson, John T., Maj. - 12th Georgia Inf., d. 09/30/64 @ College Hospital from wound received at the Battle of Winchester 9/19/64. Coffin size was 76 in. in length by 20 in. in width. Major Carson, per Diuguid's records, made arrangements prior to his death. A John F. Hobson paid the expenses ($150.00) in cash. Diuguid had noted also the following, "John F. Hobson at College Hos". The only other notation made by Diuguid was, "Was packed up & sent to Reynolds Macon Cty Ga". He enlisted as 1st Lieut. 6/15/61. Elected Capt. 05/08/62. Promoted to Maj. 6/09/63.

* **Carter, Asbury B.** - 15th South Carolina Inf., Company G, d. 06/09/63 of febris typhoides @ College Hospital. His coffin size was 72 in. in length by 18 in. in width. His age at enlistment is shown as 23. 1860 census list his as resident of the Williamsburg District. His military records list his date of death as 06/15/62.

* **Carter, Harvey C., Color Corpl.** - 16th Mississippi Inf., Company E, d. 02/03/62 "Debilitas" @ Ladies Relief Hospital. Diuguid recorded, "was packed in charcoal Feby 4th 1862 and is still in our possession (May 14th)", (prob. in preparation to be shipped home). Private Carter was finally buried 3/30/68 in lot #202, grave #5, row #2. Carter enlisted in Capt. Samuel A. Matthew's Company (Quitman Guards) on 04/23/61 @ Holmesville, Pike County. His age on the muster is listed as 26. This company was mustered into the service of the Confederate States 05/27/61 at Corinth, Mississippi. Records list him as being appointed Color Corpl. on 07/04/61. December, 61 muster listed him as absent. The Jan. 62 muster listed him on a 60-day sick furlough. He was shown as admitted to "Moore Hospital at General Hospital No. 1, Danville, Virginia"

on 01/02/62 with "General Dibility". From Danville it appears that he was sent to Warrenton. His complied Service Record does provide any record when he was transferred to the Lynchburg Hospitals. Personal description, age 28, 5' 11", light complexion, blue eyes, and light hair.

* **Carter, Reuben** -   61st Georgia Inf., Company D, d. 06/14/62 @ Ferguson's Factory. Diuguid listed him as member of Company D 7th Georgia Infantry. In addition, his military records state that he died in Richmond on the above date. His coffin size was 71 in. in length by 18 in. in width.

Carter, William Stinnett - 34th Virginia Inf., Company G, d. 07/21/64 @ Christian's Factory. "Was carried to the country" is the only entry made by Mr. Diuguid. Diuguid recorded the name as W. S. Carter and that he was a member of the 4th Virginia. No W. S. Carter was listed in the ranks of the 4th Virginia Infantry. Carter enlisted as a private on 3/3/62 in Bedford County. He was born in 1826. Based on his muster records Private Carte saw little no action while in the service. He was listed as "Sick" 4/62. Listed in a Richmond hospital 05/14/62. Present for duty 08/62 until sick 06/21/63.

Cates, Henry -   33rd North Carolina Inf., Company F, d. 03/18/63 of chronic diarrhea @ Christian's Factory. Coffin size was 73 in. in length by 18 in. in width. Cates was originally buried in lot #199, grave #10, row #3. Body was exhumed, "taken up & sent to Danville Va", was the notation made by Diuguid. The name recorded by Diuguid in his logbook was "Cutts". Cates was a resident of Orange County were he enlisted as a private on 07/08/62 for the war.

* **Cates, Thomas Jefferson** -   33rd North Carolina Inf., Company F, d. 05/13/64 of wounds @ Christian's Factory. Coffin size was 73 in. in length by 20 in. in width. Cates was wounded in back and hip 05/06/64 at the Battle of Wilderness. Resident of Orange County where he enlisted 07/08/62.

NOTE: Henry & Thomas appear to be family, possibly brothers.

* **Cartwright, James G. W., 2nd Sgt.** -   4th Texas Inf., Company H, d. 06/06/64 @ Christian's Factory from wounds received at Wilderness 05/06/64. Military records state that he was Killed in Action on the above date.

* **Cavanaugh, John R.** -   6th Louisiana Inf., Company B, d. 07/03/62 @ Booker's Factory. Coffin size was 69 in. in length by 18 in. in width. Post war records provide the following

information, "...age 46, born in Ireland, married, died at Culpepper, Va., 1862".

Caviness, Frederick - 29th Virginia Inf., Company F, d. 05/29/63 of smallpox @ Pest House. His widow's pension application stated that he died in "Chickentown, Va in 1863". Caviness was born circa 1827 Randolph County, North Carolina (?). He enlisted as a private on 02/25/63 in Carroll County, Virginia.

* Chaffin, John Robert – 8th Louisiana Inf., Company H, d. 06/23/62 of typhoid pneumonia @ College Hospital.. Born c. 1842 in Cheneyville, Rapides Parrish, Louisiana. He was the son of Anderson Leonard & Sarah Ann Providence Ruthledge Chaffin. Private Chaffin enlisted 05/08/62.

Chalmers, James, Lieut. - 2nd Virginia Cav., Company B, ("Wise Troop"), died October 1, 1861 of wounds received September 29, 1861 at a minor action at Munson's Hill. He was buried on October 2, 1861 in Lynchburg. His service was held in the Episcopal Church, Conducted by Rev. William H. Kunckle. Chalmers left a wife and small child. He was educated at Chapel Hill & The University. His death appears in the <u>Lynchburg Daily Virginian</u> on 10/2/61 page 2, col. 4. A tribute to Lieut. Chalmers by the "Wise Troop" was published 10/08/61 page 2, col. 4. A tribute by the Hastings's Court is published 10/9/61 page 2, col. 4. He was also a member of the Marshall Lodge. His military records list him as Sgt., enlisting in Lynchburg on 05/31/61, occupation listed as a Tobacconist. His wounds were listed as, "left arm broken requiring amputation and in stomach". He was born 09/21/29 at "Woodlawn" in Halifax County. He attended the Univ. of North Carolina & Univ. of Virginia. Practiced law (LLD Lawyer). Interred in Presbyterian Cemetery. The initial death notice published on 10/02/61 is on the following page.

Chamberlain, William - 42nd North Carolina Inf., Company I, d.08/07/62 @ College Hospital of typhoid pneumonia. Coffin size was 71 in. in length by 19 in. in width. Body Prepared and sent to Lexington, North Carolina. Diuguid recorded his name as "Chamblin". He enlisted as a private on 03/04/62. His age at enlistment was listed as 22. He was a resident of Davidson County, North Carolina.

* Chance, V. M. - 1st Texas Inf., Company I, d. 09/25/62 @ Ferguson's Factory. Coffin size was 5 ft. 9 in. in length by 18 in. in width. Chance enlisted as a private on 04/10/62 in

Milam, Texas. His military records state that he was sick most of 1862 & 1863; presumed dead, "Missing 12 months".

* Chandler, Benjamin, Jr. – 5th Battn. Alabama Inf., Company C, d. 05/05/64 of disease @ Crumpton's Factory. Coffin size was 75 in. in length by 19 in. in width. Enlisted as a private on 9/3/61 at White Plains, Alabama. His age at enlistment was listed as 22, and his occupation was a Farmer. He was born in Alabama and was listed as married. His home address was listed as Vernon, Louisiana. Per the company musters Private Chandler spent much of the war absent "Sick". He participated in two engagements during the war. Those were, 06/26/62 at Mechanicsville and at Frayser's (sic) on 06/30/62.

Lynchburg Daily Virginian dated October 2, 1861
Death Notice of Lieut. James Chalmers
(Transcribed from the original newspaper)

LOCAL AND STATE
NEWS

Death of Lieut. Jas. Chalmers - We were deeply pained yesterday, to hear that the wounds received by this gentleman had proven fatal, he having expired about 10 o'clock in the day. Thus has another noble man been taken from the world by this unnatural war. To his poor wife (who seemed to have a presentiment of the fate that awaited him,) and to his little children, the loss will be irreparable. Lieut. Chalmers was an intimate personal friend of ours, and we have often had occasion to admire his high qualities of head and heart. He was a person of most admirable character; a Christian gentlemen, possessed of fine intelligence, discriminating taste, united to very superior scholarship, and was withal a man of unquestioned courage and high resolve. A Union man to the last, he buckled on his armor when the mad course of Abraham Lincoln left us no other alternative consistent with honor, and has sealed with his blood, that devotion which he ever cherished for Virginia. Peace to his ashes; for we trust that he has found a home where the sound of battle never comes, and the tread of armies is never heard.

* Chapman, B. F. (Benj. Franklin?) - 3rd South Carolina Inf., Company H, d. 06/27/64 from wounds received 6/25/64 @

Christian's Factory. Diuguid recorded his initials as B.T. Military records list his date of death as 07/25/64. 1860 census listed him as resident of the Lexington District.

* Chapman, William - 13th South Carolina Inf., Company G, d. 01/14/63 of chronic Diarrhea @ Langhorne's Factory. Coffin size was 73 in. in length by 18 in. in width. Military records list his date of death as 01/19/63. 1860 census listed him as a resident of the Newberry District.

Charles, William F. - 42nd North Carolina Inf., Company F, d. 08/06/62 @ Fairgrounds, cause not stated. Coffin size was 71 in. in length by 18 in. in width. Body was prepared and shipped to Salisbury, North Carolina. He enlisted as a private on 03/18/62. His age at enlistment was listed as 22. He was a resident of Davie County, North Carolina. Expenses paid by Capt. Clements. Diuguid listed "Doct J W Wiseman" as the requestor for the remains of Private Charles.

* Chastain, James E. - 2nd South Carolina Inf., Company E, d. 03/29/63 of pneumonia @ Saunder's Factory. Coffin size was 72 in. in length by 18 in. in width. He enlisted as a private on 04/27/62 at Adams Run, South Carolina. His age at enlistment was listed as 40. Mother of deceased was Elizabeth Chastain. 1860 census listed him as resident of the Anderson District.

* Childers, William - 1st Arkansas Inf., Crawford's Company, d. 06/20/61 @ College Hospital. Diuguid listed "William Workman - Stepfather, Benton P.O. Saline County, Arkansas."

* Chitty, Lafayette - 33rd North Carolina Inf., Company C, d. 06/30/63 @ Miller's Factory. Coffin size was 74 in. in length by 18 in. in width. Wounded during Battle of Chancellorsville May 1-3, 63. Cause of death was reported as "Febris Typhoid".

Citty, Commodore R. - 58th Virginia Inf., Company A, d. 070/8/62 "of disease of the lungs" in Staunton, Virginia. Was hospitalize in Staunton 12/31/61. Per Diuguid's records his body was exhumed, shipped to Lynchburg, prepared and shipped home 01/07/62. Quote, "C. R. Citty box and trip to Bedford". Citty was born in Bedford County circa 1840. His age at death was 22. Per the 1860 census, age 20, Davis Mills P.O. Bedford County, occupation carpenter. Enlisted as a private at Bunker Hill 7/25/61. His age at enlistment was listed as age 22. The father of the deceased was George Whittfield Citty.

Clark, Benjamin F. - 12th Mississippi Inf., Company H, d. 07/23/62 of phithisis pulmonalis @ Ladies Relief Hospital.

Body was prepared and shipped to Vicksburg, Mississippi. He enlisted as a private on 7/06/61 at Union City for 1 year. The February 62 muster had him listed as absent in arrest at Manassas. It appears that he receive a Court Martial on 11/27/61.

* Clark, James J. - 1st Texas Inf., Company H. d. 08/18/62 of chronic diarrhea @ Claytor's Factory. Coffin size was 71 in. in length by 19 in. in width. He enlisted as a private on 03/7/62 at Kickapoo, Texas. His age at enlistment was listed as 19. Private Clark was listed as sick and in hospital in May 1862.

Clark, Stephen A. - 2nd Battn. Georgia Inf., Company C, d. 03/07/63 @ Christian's Factory. Coffin size was 74 in. in length by 18 in. in width. "Packed up & sent to Powersville Ga". He enlisted as a private on 8/18/62.

* Cleland, Robert C. – 14th Alabama Inf., Company A, d. 07/22/62 @ College Hospital. Coffin size was 73 in. by 18 in. in length. Cleland enlisted as a private on 09/20/61 at Chambers County, Alabama. His age at enlistment was listed as 20. The father of the deceased, G. C. Cleland filed a death claim on 3/8/63. The claim was verified and settled on 09/22/64. Mr. Cleland could be contacted in Chambers County, Alabama in care of J. J. Harris, attorney.

* Clemmons, John – 15th Alabama Inf., Company K, d. 05/31/63 @ Knight's Factory. Coffin size was 73 in. in length by 18 in. in width. Clemmons enlisted as a private on 07/03/61 at Eufaula, Alabama. His age at enlistment was listed as 19. He was born in Georgia, occupation was listed as a farmer, was a resident of P.O. Eufaula, Alabama and was single. His military records state that "Died in hospital at Lynchburg, Va., Sept. 20th 62."

* Cleveland, Jackson S., 1st Corpl. – 44th Alabama Inf., Company F, d. 06/08/64 of wounds @ Camp Davis. Coffin size was 75 in. in length by 19 in. in width. Cleveland enlisted as 1st Corpl. on 03/14/62 at Bibb County, Alabama. His age at enlistment was listed as 24. He was born in Alabama, married, occupation was listed as a farmer, and he was a resident of Centerville, Alabama. Cleveland was wounded on 05/06/64 during the Battle of the Wilderness.

* Cobb, W. P. - 2nd South Carolina Inf., Company I, d. 11/26/62 of disease @ Crumpton's Factory. Coffin size was 73 in. in length by 18 in. in width. Military records listed his date of death as 12/26/62. 1860 census listed him as a resident of the Richland District.

Cocke, Lewis T. - 44th Virginia Inf., Company D, d. 05/12/62 @ Ferguson's Factory of pneumonia. He had been discharged 04/24/62 as unfit for duty. At the time of his enlistment he was employed as an Overseer @ Locust Creek, Louisa County, Virginia. His body was prepared and shipped to Richmond, Virginia. Cocke enlisted as a private on 07/12/61 at Isbell's Store. His age at enlistment was listed as 20. 1860 census listed as age 20, occupation Overseer.

* **Cogdell, Lewis D.** - 2nd North Carolina Inf., Company C, d. 02/01/63 of chronic diarrhea @ Crumpton's Factory. Coffin size was 72 in. in length by 20 in. in width. Cogdell previously served in Company E, of 20th North Carolina Infantry. He enlisted as a private on 08/16/61 in Wake County at age 20. His occupation was listed as a student.

* **Colburn, John W.** – 8th Alabama Inf., Company A, d.07/16/62 of disease @ Christian's Factory. Coffin Size was 72 in. in length by 18 in. in width. Colburn enlisted as a Private 05/08/61 at Marion, Alabama. His age at enlistment was listed as 34. He was listed as married, occupation as a farmer. He was born in Alabama circa 1827 and he was a resident of Marion, Alabama. Per his records he had been listed as "Absent Sick" since early April 1862.

* **Cole, J. J.** – 15th Alabama Inf., Company L, d. 05/15/62 of disease @ Saunder's Factory. Coffin size was 74 in. in length by 19 in. in width. Cole enlisted as a private on 03/11/62 at Perote, Alabama. His age at enlistment was listed as 24. He was born in Alabama, occupation was listed as a farmer, he was a resident of Pine Grove, Alabama, and was single. His military records states that he died in Charlottesville, Va. on the date listed above.

* **Cole, S. E.** - 33rd North Carolina Inf., Company K, d. 01/26/63 @ Burton's Factory. Coffin size was 76 in. in length by 20 in. in width. Cole was wounded on 12/13/62 at Fredericksburg. Private Coles died of results of wound and complications. Per his military records his cause of death was stated as "wounds or phthisis pneumonia".

* **Coleman James Jackson (or Jackson James)** – 9th Louisiana Inf., Company H, d. 07/27/62 of Typhoid fever @ Christian's Factory. No date of enlistment found. Born c. 1829 in Alabama. He was the son of William and Sarah Ogden Coleman. Married Margaret Jane Tussell; a resident of Brush Valley, Bienville, Parish, Louisiana.

Coleman, William -   32nd Virginia Inf., Company K, d. 02/04/63 @ Pest House from smallpox. His military records list him as dying at "Hanover Junction" of disease. Initially enlisted in "Lees Guard", Elizabeth County 05/14/61. This company was disbanded, reenlisted in Company "H" 05/27/61. He later enlisted in Company "K" after 08/31/61.

Coleman, William B. -   21st Virginia Inf., Company K, d.0 8/20/62 @ Ladies Relief Hospital. His coffin size was 80 in. in length by 19 in. in width. Body "was packed up & sent to Keysville, Va", was the entry made by Diuguid. Compiled Service Records states that Pvt. Coleman was KIA @ the Battle of Cedar Mountain 08/09/62. It appears that he was critically wounded and sent to Lynchburg. Coleman enlisted as a private on 06/20/61.

* **Colifer, M.** -   33rd North Carolina Inf., Company F, d. 06/02/62 of febris typhoides. He enlisted as a private on 9/9/61. Colifer was a resident of Hyde County, North Carolina.

* **Compton, William H.** -   7th Virginia Inf., Company B, d. 04/26/62 @ the Warwick House. He enlisted as a private on 05/04/61 in Rappahannock County, Virginia. Born circa 1835. Company muster listed him as a deserter 2/14/63. It appears that his unit was never contacted as to his death.

* **Convill, Daniel O.** – 44th Alabama Inf., Company H, d. 06/18/64 of wounds @ Christian's Factory. Diuguid recorded his last name as "Conwill." Convill enlisted as a private on 5/6/62 at Bibb County, Alabama. His age at enlistment was listed as 24. He was born in Alabama, occupation was listed as a framer and was a resident of Randolph, Alabama. On 04/18/63 he as admitted to the hospital with "Extreme Debility." He was granted "30 days leave of absence" on April 19 and again on May 20. He returned to duty on 06/19/63. He was "present for duty" at the Battle of Knoxville 11/29/63 through the skirmish at Dandridge, Tenn. on 01/16/64. He was severely wounded at the Battle of the Wilderness on 05/06/64.

* **Cook, William G., Corpl**. – 11th Georgia Inf., Company I, d. 01/05/62 of disease @ College Hospital. Cook enlisted 07/03/61, he was a resident of Randolph County. The 11th Georgia served in 2nd Corps, Brig. Gen. Samuel Jones Brigade, Dept. of Northern Virginia. See photograph below of postwar tombstone placed in the Old City Cemetery. Per the information on the stone Cook was born 08/19/39 in Quitman

County, Georgia. Also, his age was "22 years 4 months...." Quitman County is located in southwest Georgia on the Alabama line. See photo insert following page of post war headstone.

Cooper, Reuben - 38th Georgia Inf., Company I, d. 07/23/62 of chronic diarrhea @ Ladies Relief Hospital. Coffin size was 71 in. in length by 18 in. in width. Body was packed for his brother, Stephen Cooper, Fort Gains, Alabama. Body was never shipped.

* **Corbett, Jeremiah** - 14th North Carolina Inf., Company K, d. 10/27/63 of "Rheau Extreme" @ College Hospital. The full medical term for cause of death was, "Cardiorhuma Metastasi-sex Rheum Extremitatum". Coffin size was 73 in. in length by 18 in. in width. He enlisted as a private on 07/16/63 in Wake County at age 36. He was a resident of Randolph County.

* **Corbett, Richard William** - 61st Virginia Inf., Company E, d. 11/05/63 of diarrhea. Coffin size was 70 in. in length by 18 in. in width. Enlisted as a private on 03/08/62 at age 40 in the 7th Virginia Battn. Company E, 7th Va. Battalion was transferred as Company E, 61st, Inf. on 08/08/62. Post War he his listed on the Confederate Roll of Honor.

* **Corbin, James** – 48th Alabama Inf., Company D, d. 10/31/62 @ Christian's Factory. Coffin size was 76 in. in length by 19 in. in width. Corbin enlisted as a private on 04/07/62 for 3 years at Warrenton, Alabama. His age at enlistment was listed as 45. He was born in Georgia, he was married, occupation was listed as a farmer and he was a resident of Guntersville, Alabama. His military records state that his date of death was 08/20/62 in Lynchburg.

* **Cordell, Preston J.** - 34th Georgia Inf., Company C, d. @ College Hospital 12/22/62. Coffin size was 74 in. in length by 18 in. in width. Some confusion here, Mr. Diuguid's records shows Private Cordell as member of the 31st Georgia, Company B. The only Cordell listed in either unit is Preston J. Cordell. He enlisted as a private on 10/5/61. The last entry in his military record dated 11/05/64 shows him sick in a hospital in Richmond.

* **Corprew, (also Corfreau) John J.** - 6th Virginia Inf., Company F, d. 11/15/62 of pneumonia Christian's Factory. Coffin size was 70 in. in length by 18 in. in width. He enlisted as a private on 06/28/62 in Norfolk County. The 1860 census listed occupation as farmer, born circa 1838.

Cosar - Slave of Mrs. Ramsey, d. 08/01/64 @ Christian's Factory. Diuguid made the following notation, "Was buried in Negro Row." "Southern Confederacy", $15.00, paid all expenses. Diuguid made another notation in the margin "J. W. Davidson at Randolph".

* **Cotton, Benjamin C.** - 61st Virginia Inf., Company B, died of typhoid/pneumonia 12/27/62 @ Taliaferro's Factory. Coffin size was 73 in. in length by 18 in. in width. He enlisted as a private on 08/08/61 at Oak Grove, Norfolk County, Virginia in Company B, 7th Virginia Battn. Company B was transferred to 61st Virginia on 8/8/62. Cotton was wounded on 12/11/62 at Fredericksburg. Post war listed on the Confederate Roll of Honor.

Counts, W. H. - 13th South Carolina Inf., Company K, d. 10/26/62 @ Ferguson's Factory. Body was prepared and sent to Columbia, South Carolina. Coffin size was 75 in. in length by 19 in. in width.

* **Countz, Charles** - 60th Virginia Inf., Company A, d. 08/14/62. Diuguid has the following notation in the margin, "Died on O&A (Orange & Alexandria) Cars Capt. T. Shers orders". His coffin size was 74 in. in length by 19 in. in width. Countz enlisted as a private on 04/01/62 in Monroe County (now West Virginia). He was listed as present for duty at all musters until his death.

* **Courtney, George W., 4th Corpl.** - 14th Alabama Ins., Company B, d. 05/19/64 of wounds @ Knight's Factory. Coffin size was 74 in. in length by 18 in. in width. The

following is a statement given about Corpl. Courtney the "27th day of Dec. 1864." The statement reads, "Born in Montgomery Co., Ala. Courtney enlisted by Capt. J. J. Williamson at Sandy Ridge Ala. on the 3rd day of July 1861, to serve for the war. Last paid by Capt. J. J. Harris Q.M. to include the...day of..., 1864 and is entitled to pay there from, to the 19th day of May 1864 at which time he died in Linchburg (sic) of wounds. He is entitled to bond of $100 by act of Congress. He is entitled to commutation for transportation in lieu of furlough from Richmond Va. to Montgomery Ala. and back. He is entitled to commutation for clothing from the first day of Nov. 1863 (last paid) to the 19th day of May 1864. He is indebted to the confederate States for stoppage on account of clothing to the amount of $26.00. Genuine, J. K. Elliot, Asst. Agt. for Ala. S. P. Bain 1st Lieut. commanding company." Courtney's age at enlistment was listed as 27. The widow of the deceased, Laura Courtney applied for and received a pension in 1910. The pension was filed from Crenshaw County, Alabama. The pension number was 29820. E. L. Mathis and C. M. Kelly witnessed the pension application.

Cowart, John W. – 5th Alabama Inf., Company, d. 02/03/63 @ Knight's Factory. Coffin size was 77 in. in length by 19 in. in width. His widow, Amelia A. Cowart, filed a death claim that same year. The Claim was honored on 07/26/64. The widow could be contacted in care of B. Fitzpatrick, Troy, Alabama.

Cox, Charles E. - 2nd Virginia Cav., Company B, buried 06/27/62. Died "27th of June in his 19th year", in Campbell County, Virginia. Cause of death as reported by the newspaper was measles. Father of the deceased was Brackenridge Cox. Death notice appears in Lynchburg Daily Virginian, dated 08/30/62, page 3, col. 2 (See next page for Transcribed article). Buried in Mountain View Cemetery, Roanoke County, Virginia.

* **Crabb, Asbury T.** - 28th Georgia Inf., Company H, d. 06/13/62 of erysipelas @ Langhorne's Factory. His military records his date of death as 5/13/62.

Craft, J. M. - 33rd North Carolina Inf., Company H, d. 11/12/62 of chronic dysenteria @ Christian's Factory . Coffin size was 6 ft. 3 in. in length by 17 in. in width. He was originally buried in lot #181, grave #5, row #2. Body was exhumed and shipped to Danville, Virginia. Expenses paid by W. C. Bodenhamer. Resident of Forsyth County were he enlisted on 07/15/62 for the war.

Lynchburg Daily Virginian dated August 30, 1862
Death Notice of Charles E. Cox
(Transcribed from the original newspaper)

DIED

Died, of measles, in Campbell County, June 27th Mr. Charles E. Cox, in his 19th year. He was a member of Company B, 2d regiment Va. Cavalry. Early last spring from a sense of duty he freely left a comfortable home, where he was the center of many affections, to undergo the dangers and privations of a soldier's life. He passed through a short but arduous and glorious campaign and returned home to die in the very morning and the freshness of his youth - another martyr in his country's cause. Amiable, talented and beloved, his unexpected and untimely death has left a gap, which will not be readily filled, in the circle of his acquaintance and in the mourning precincts of his domestic hearth. It is an inexpressible consolation to his friends to believe that their loss is his gain. He consecrated himself to God in the early dawn of his youth. In his fourteenth year Elder Settle baptized him into the fellowship of Flat Creek Church, and when the bridegroom came he found him with the wedding garment on. We cannot reflect upon the ardent expression of his hope. When stretched upon the dying couch, without realizing the power of that scriptural truth. Blessed are the dead, which die in the Lord.

* **Crider, C. W.** - 15th South Carolina Inf., Company C, d. 12/26/62 of disease @ Claytor's Factory. Coffin size was 6 ft. 3 in. in length by 18 in. in width. Diuguid listed his name as "G. Crider". His military records list his date of death as 09/30/62. 1860 census list him as a resident of the Orangeburg District.
* **Crimm, E. E.** – 5th Alabama Inf., Company C, d. 12/08/62 of disease @ Langhorne's Factory. Coffin size was 74 in. in length by 19 in. in width. Crimm enlisted as a Private on 04/20/61 in Pickensville, Alabama. Private Crimm was listed as "On sick furlough" in Dec. of 1861. The muster dated 11/6/62 he was listed as "Sick in Lynchburg, Va." No further record.
* **Crocker, Bethel** – 15th Alabama Inf., Company F, d. 07/2/62 @ Claytor's Factory. Coffin size was 68 in. in length by 17 in.

in width. Crocker enlisted as a Private on 3/1/62 at Brundridge, Alabama. His age at enlistment was listed as 18. He was born in Alabama, occupation was listed as a farmer, and he was married.

*** Croft, Spencer (or Craft)** - 61st Georgia Inf., Company F, d. 08/10/62 @ Saunder's Factory. Coffin size was 69 in. in length by 16 in. in width. Croft enlisted as a private on 02/10/62 as a substitute for W. E. Gray.

Crockett, J. E. - 1st South Carolina Inf., Company D, d. 12/11/62 @ Ferguson's Factory. Was originally buried in lot #146, grave #4, row #2. Coffin size was 74 in. in length by 19 in. in width. Body was exhumed, prepared and shipped to Lancaster Court House, South Carolina. In the margin Mr. Diuguid has entered the following name, "(J. J. Graham)".

Crouch, John T. - 58th Virginia Inf., Company K, d. 05/15/62 @ Booker's Factory of diphteria. Body was prepared and shipped to Bedford County, Thaxton Switch, Virginia for burial. He enlisted as a private on 07/23/61 at Chamblissburg, Bedford County, Virginia. His age at enlistment was listed as 31. His occupation was listed as a farmer. A description of the deceased; 6' 1", fair complexion, gray eyes, and brown hair. The 1860 census listed occupation as farmer, address Davis Mill P.O. Bedford County, age 28, born 1832.

* Crowder, Allen A. - Bedford Light (Virginia) Artillery, Capt. Jordan's Battery, d. 11/22/62 of disease @ Ladies Relief Hospital. He enlisted in service as a private on 07/22/61. Buried in lot #182, grave #1, row #3. Brother, Rev. Joseph A. Allen, paid expenses. Burial cost, including "sheet & cotton" was $33.00 ($8.00 for cotton & sheet). The Southern Confederacy paid $9.00, the balance was paid by cash on Jan. 27, 1863. Coffin size was 77 in. in length by 20 in. in width. His father, Godfrey Crowder, filed death claim to Confederate Government November 17, 1864.

* Crowder, Henderson - 56th Virginia Inf., Company B, d. 01/02/63 @ Ladies Relief Hospital. Coffin size was 73 in. in length by 20 in. in width. Crowder enlisted as a private in Mecklenburg County, Virginia on 06/22/61. He was born in Mecklenburg County. A death claim was filed by executor 02/27/63. Charles W. Thomas, also a member of Company B, wrote that Henderson was in the Hospital 01/10/63 and had not heard from him. Mr. Diuguid's burial records stated that the body was claimed by Levi Tolley of Mecklinburg (sic)

County, "send in care of D. Johnson Petersburg, Va.". In Diuguid's note section of burial log #6 He has the following entry, "Levi Talley Mecklinburg Cty may send for the body of Henderson Crowder Co B 56 Va Reg who died Jany 2nd 1863 send to care of Donnons & Johnson Petersburg". It would appear that two military records exist for this man. The 56th Virginia has a H. C. Crowder and a Henderson Crowder. Based on the information from the Compiled Service Records they appear to be the same person. He was captured at Ft. Donelson, moved from Camp Morton to Vicksburg for exchanged. Admitted to Richmond hospital 08/31/62. Per his service record was discharged from service 01/23/63 at age 27 due to pneumonia. His discharge was a little too late. Born Mecklenburg County, Occupation farmer, light complexion, dark hair, blue eyes, 5 ft. 10 inches in height.

Crowder, Robert - 16th Virginia Cav., Company H, d. 04/30/64 @ home. Diuguid's entry was, "buried in lot 24". The wife of the deceased was Mrs. Martha Crowder. Mrs. Crowder paid $85.00 of the cost, the Southern Confederacy paid $15.00. Compile service record for the 16th Va. Cav. does not list a Robert Crowder.

Colbert, Charles G. - 21st Virginia Inf., Company H, d. 01/09/63 of dropsy @ Ferguson's Factory. Coffin size was 74 in. in length by 19 in. in width. Originally buried in lot #79, grave #5, row #1. Diuguid's only entry was, "Removed". Diuguid listed his name as "C. H. Culbert". He enlisted as a private on 03/10/62 at Chalk Level. Widow of the deceased was Elizabeth Colbert (and 3 small children).

Culverhouse, W. A. - 57th North Carolina Inf., Company B, d. 02/09/63 @ Candler's Factory. Coffin size was 70 in. in length by 18 in. in width. Was originally buried in lot #191, grave #4, row #3. Exhumed 02/16/63, J. F. Moore claimed the remains. "Taken up & sent to Salisbury N.C." was the notation made by Diuguid. The charge "For removal & packing" was $25.00, paid in cash.

Cundiff, James R. - 14th Virginia Inf., Company B, d. 03/25/63 @ Odd Fellow's Hall of pneumonia. Coffin size was 71 in. in length by 17 in. in width. "Was boxed up & sent to Bedford Cty Va". The uncle of the deceased, A. J. Cundiff, claimed remains and paid expenses. Enlisted as a private at Jamestown Island on 027/2/61. Admitted to Chimborazo 02/16/63, transferred to Lynchburg 03/13/63. Six other Cundiffs are shown as members of Company b, 14th Virginia

Infantry. They are; Alfred B., Charles R. d. 11/18/62 of acute diarrhea, Isaac d. 8/9/61 of fever, Jesse, John, and William B., Jr.

Dalton, William F. - 53rd Virginia Inf., Company I (Chatham Grays, Pittsylvania County), d. 06/12/62 of typhoid fever @ Warwick House. Originally buried in lot # 172, grave #8, row #4. Body was exhumed (no other information) probably sent to Pittsylvania County. Enlisted 04/02/62.

Davenport, John - 48th Virginia Inf., Company K, d. 12/31/61 @ Ladies Relief Hospital. Body was shipped to Abingdon, Virginia. He enlisted as a private on 06/25/61 in Russell County, Virginia. His age at enlistment was listed as 28.

* **Davenport William Harvie Andrew, Ord. Sgt** – 35th Georgia Inf., Company C, d. 12/31/62. Born 1836 in Oglethorpe County, Georgia. He was the son of William & Elizabeth Sydnor Andrew Davenport. Sergeant Davenport was not married.

* **Davis, E. Lewis** - 2nd South Carolina Inf., Company K, d. 03/03/63 of disease @ Claytor's Factory. He enlisted as a private at age 36. 1860 census listed as a resident of the Abbeville District.

* **Davis, G. A.** - 14th South Carolina Inf., Company G, d. 01/22/63 of diphtheria @ Reid's Factory. Coffin size was 73 in. in length by 19 in. in width. Davis enlisted as a private on 08/17/61. His age at enlistment was listed as 36. His military records listed his date of death as 06/22/63. Widow of the deceased was Jane A. Davis. 1860 census listed him as a resident of the Abbeville District.

Davis, William M. - 53rd Virginia Inf., Company G, d. 11/22/62 of pneumonia @ Claytor's Factory. Coffin size was 70 in. in length by 18 in. in width. Body was prepared and shipped to Ford's Depot on the Southside Railroad, Dinwiddie County. Davis enlisted as a private on 07/20/61 at Ft. Powhatan in the 5th Virginia Battn. Davis transferred to 53rd Va. on 09/25/62.

Davidson, Joseph W., Lieut. - 1st Tennessee Inf., shot and killed at Fairgrounds 05/19/61. Davidson was the first war related death in Lynchburg. Lieutenant Davidson's body was shipped to Lincoln County, Tennessee on 5/19/61. The following is a portion of what was reported in the <u>Lynchburg Daily Virginian</u>, dated 5/21/61 page 3, col. 1;

"A sad tragedy at the encampment of the 1st Tennessee Regiment, near this city on Sunday morning. It appears that two soldiers were disputing about some articles of clothing, when Lieut. Davidson interposed...The Lieutenant was shot through the heart, and instantly killed by one of the soldiers."

"The body of the murdered officer was dressed out in a new uniform, coffined, and taken charge of by the Masonic fraternity, of which he was member, and sent in charge of a detachment to the home of the deceased in Tennessee". A final note was added, "Whilst recording this sad occurrence, it gives us pleasure to bear testimony to the good deportment of the thousands of troops that have been here in the past few weeks. They have generally deported themselves like gentlemen....this has been the case with Alabama and Mississippi soldiers; a portion of the 1st Tennessee regiment only, constituting an exception to the rule...these men, from a particular section appear to be rough, (they are from Lincoln county) - a bad name - we are told".

The following was recorded in Diuguid's burial log for Lieut. Davidson, "for coffin, box, sheet, & cotton for self - $25.00". The fee was paid in cash.

* **Davis, William H.** - 25th North Carolina Inf., Company D, d. 01/07/63 of wounds @ Ford's Factory. Coffin size was 72 in. in length by 19 in. in width. Davis was wounded in thigh at Battle of Fredericksburg 12/13/62. Leg was amputated at the thigh. He enlisted as a Private in Cherokee County 03/28/62 at age 24. His military records state that death was from wounds and pneumonia.

Day, Thomas J. - Father John Day, Running Water P.O., Marion County, Tennessee. No unit or date of death specified in the Diuguid's records. There is no Thomas J. listed in the Tennessee index. However, there are Thomas's, Pvt. Co. C, 9th (Ward's) Tenn. Cav. and Sgt. Co. E. 6th Tenn. Infantry.

* **Day, Thomas Jefferson** – 6th Alabama Inf., Company I, d. 07/30/61 of disease @ College Hospital. Private Day enlisted 5/20/61. Per the muster roll dated 06/30/61 at Sangsters Cross Roads, Va. stated, "Sick in hospital at Lynchburg, Virginia."

* **Dean, James W.** - 31st Georgia Inf. Company I, d. 10/20/62 @ Miller's Factory. Diuguid made the following entry in the margin, "marked coffin Davis 21st Reg." Coffin size was 70 in. in length by 18 in. in width.

Dearing, James, Brig. General – Died of a gunshot wound on 04/23/65. General Dearing was mortally wounded 04/06/65 during the action at High Bridge, Virginia. His wound was a result of a pistol duel between him and Union General Theodore Read, who was killed. "The desperately wounded officer was taken to Lynchburg and lingered for some time in the Ladies Aid Hospital, dying on April 23, 1865, two weeks after the surrender of the Army of Northern Virginia. Shortly before his death he was visited and paroled by his old West Point classmate, Brigadier General Ranald S. (Slidell) Mackenzie, U.S.A., then commanding in Lynchburg." Dearing was the last general officer to die of wounds received in action. Dearing was born at "Otterburne" in Campbell County, Virginia on April 25, 1840. He was a graduate of Hanover Academy and appointed to West Point in 1858. On April 22, 1861 he resigned from West point to enter service in the Confederacy. He entered as a Lieutenant in the Washington Artillery. He later served in the Lynchburg Artillery (CO. D, 38th Battn., Latham's Battery). He progressively climbed in rank, as a major commanding a Battalion of Artillery at Gettysburg. Following Gettysburg he was transferred to Cavalry and promoted to Colonel. On April 29,64 he was promoted to brigadier general, commanding a brigade of cavalry in W. H. F. Lee's Division. Diuguid's entry in Logbook #7 for Gen. Dearing is short. The following entry was made on 4/23/65, "Est. of Gen. James Dearing, for coffin & box & use of hearse for self $40.00." Diuguid enters one other small notation "Sp Hill Q-13." This is the final resting place of the young general in Spring Hill Cemetery in Lynchburg.

* **DeBoard, Thomas J.** - 37th North Carolina Inf., Company B, d. 06/19/63 of "Pyemia" @ Claytor's Factory. Coffin size was 66 in. in length by 18 in. in width. DeBoard was wounded during the Chancelorsville campaign May 1-4, 63. He was a

resident of Ashe County, enlisted as a Private 8/15/62 in Iredell County at age 18.

* Delaney, Martin - 27th North Carolina Inf., Company G, d. 05/29/64 of wounds @ College Hospital. Coffin size was 75 in. in length by 18 in. in width. Wounded in right arm at Battle of Wilderness 5/05/64. Right arm was amputated 05/15/64. Official cause of death was listed as "Pyaemia". Delaney enlisted as a Private at Fort Macon 5/21/61 at age 22. Occupation was listed as "Hostler" (one in charge of the care of horses at an Inn).

* DeLoach, Andrew – 15th Alabama Inf., Company E, d. 05/21/62 of disease at the Warwick House. Coffin size was 70 in. in length by 18 in. in width. DeLoach enlisted as a Private on 5/3/62 at Westville, Alabama. His age at enlistment was listed as 22. He was born in Alabama, occupation was listed as a farmer, he was a resident of Newton, Alabama and he was married. The widow of the deceased, Nancy J. DeLoach of Newton, Alabama filed a death claim on 9/15/62. The claim was verified and approved on 2/3/65. On the death claim record the name is listed as "Archibald". Possibly the full name was Andrew Archibald DeLoach. His military record states that his place of death was in Richmond, Va. on 05/16/62.

* Derack, C. - 12th South Carolina Inf., Company D, d. 05/26/64 (no cause stated) @ Booker's Factory. Coffin size was 76 in. in length by 19 in. in width. Diuguid listed his name as "G. Delvack". 1860 census listed him as a resident of the Richland District.

* Denham, John T. - 12th Georgia Inf., Company G, d. 06/13/64 of wounds @ Ladies Relief Hospital. His military records state that he was wounded by a "stray shot at Lynchburg" on 5/20/64. Date of death listed by his records indicate 6/19/64.

Dennis, Jasper - 7th Virginia Inf., Company E, d. 04/18/65 @ Crumpton's Factory. Was originally buried in lot #202, grave #7, row #3. Body was exhumed 4/20/65, "Removed", "Packed & sent to Rappahannock". In logbook #7, page 226, on 5/20/65 Diuguid made the following entry, "N. T. Dennis, Woodville Rappahannock, for removal & packing Brother, $35."
 Private Dennis had been paroled in Lynchburg on 04/15/65. Private Jasper Dennis enlisted on 2/20/63 in Rappahannock County.

* **Dennis, T. E.** - 4th Texas Inf., Company D, d. 06/25/62 of meningitis @ Taliferro's Factory. Coffin size was 70 in. in length by 19 in. in width. Denis enlisted as a private on 03/16/62 at Port Sullivan, Texas. His age at enlistment was listed as 28.

* **Denson, Charles** - 13th South Carolina Inf., Company A, d. 10/30/62 of chronic diarrhea @ Crumpton's Factory. Coffin size was 70 in. in length by 17 in. in width. He enlisted as a private on 08/06/61 in the Lauren District, South Carolina. His age at enlistment was listed as 35. Was discharged from service 10/25/62 while in the Lynchburg Hospital system. 1860 census list him as resident of the Laurens District.

* **Diamond, William B.** - 8th Georgia Inf., enlisted 05/14/61, Company E (Miller's Rifles), d. 08/10/61 of disease @ Jed 's. Father of deceased was F. C. Diamond, from Rome, Georgia. Size of his coffin recorded by Mr. Diuguid was (inside dimensions) 6 ft. 10 in. long, 2 ft. 2 in. wide, 16 in. deep.

* **Didlake, John H., Lieut.** - 34th Virginia Inf., Company K, was **Killed in Action** 06/09/62 at the Battle of Cross Key, Virginia. He is buried in Presbyterian Cemetery range 16, lot 3. A very short death notice was published in the <u>Lynchburg Daily Virginian</u> 06/13/62, page 3, col. 1. The short notice is as follows: "We regret to hear that Mr. John Didlake, of this city, was killed in one of Jackson's late battles". Lieutenant Didlake was born in Lynchburg 10/24/34, and had moved to New Orleans in 1859.

* **Dilden, Eli K. R.** – 13th Alabama Inf., Company K, d. 08/17/62 of disease @ Christian's Factory. Coffin size was 5 ft. 11 in. in length by 16 in. in width. Dilden enlisted as a Private on 7/26/61 at Montgomery, Alabama. His age at enlistment was listed as 28. He was born in Georgia, occupation was listed as a mechanic, his residence was listed as P.O. Gold Ridge, Alabama, and he was single. He was listed as present for duty from 04/01/62 the Siege at Yorktown to 5/31/62 Battle of Seven Pines. He was listed as "Absent Sick" prior to the Seven Days Battles around Richmond (6/26/62 – 7/1/62). His records state that his date of death was on 7/20/62 and place was Richmond, Virginia.

* **Dillard, Winberry** - Holcombe's Legion, Company A, d.10/07/62 of chronic diarrhea @ Miller's Factory. Coffin size was 74 in. in length by 18 in. in width. Diuguid listed his first name as "Winsberry". His age at enlistment was listed as 30. 1860 census listed him as resident of the Spartanburg District.

Pvt. Robert W. Dilly
Company B, 12th Mississippi Inf.

* **Dodd, William** - 10th Georgia Inf., Company K, d. around 11/18/62, "an unknown man died at Burton's Hospital, supposed to be Wm. Todd and supposed to belong to Co. K, 10th Georgia. Robert Seabury has some little effects of his". - R. Seabury held $10.00 of his money. - Indications are, the valuables were turned over to Dr. Otaway Owen. Private Dodd's coffin measured 70 in. in length by 18 in. in width.

* **Donaldson, Peter L.** - 3rd Arkansas Inf., Company B, d. 02/08/62 @ Ladies Relief Hospital. Diuguid recorded, "was packed in charcoal Feby 9th 1862". Donaldson was born 01/18/27. Diuguid continues, "was unpacked May 3rd 1864 and buried No 1 1st line lot189", "his uncle Col. W. P. Macklin, Berlin, Ashley Cty, Arkansas".

*** Dorn, William** – 15th Alabama Inf., Company L, d. 05/08/62 of disease @ Saunder's Factory. Dorn enlisted as a Private on 3/11/62 at Perote, Alabama. His age at enlistment was listed as 20. He was born in Alabama, occupation was listed as a farmer, he was a resident of MT. Hilliard, Alabama and he was married. The widow of the deceased, Martha T. Dorn filed a death claim 5/13/63. The claim was verified and settled on 01/21/65. Mrs. Dorn could be contacted in care of B. Fitzpatrick, Troy, Alabama.

*** Dougherty, James** - 14th South Carolina Inf., Company A, d. 01/19/63 of diarrhea @ Langhorne's Factory. Coffin size was 74 in. in length by 18 in. in width. Diuguid listed his name as "Dority". 1860 census listed him as a resident of the Darlington District.

Douglas, Marcellas, Col. - 13th Georgia Inf., **Killed in Action** 09/17/62 @ Battle of Sharpsburg. In Mr. Diuguid's note section of burial log #6 he made the following entry, "Col Marcellas Douglas of Curthbert Ga was Col of 13 Ga Reg killed at Sharpsburg left on storage with us 20th July 1863 by H. W. Morgan Slaughter Decater Cty Ga". Diuguid also notes that, "Delivered to Express Co 14th March 66". Douglas was born Thomaston, Georgia 10/5/20. Douglas was a graduate of the University of Georgia. Wife of the deceased was Menla Davis Douglas. A personal description, "Small, fair-skinned man with light blue eyes and blonde curly hair". "An Alabamian reported seeing Douglas' corpse stripped of clothes the day after the battle" (Lee's Colonels). Enlisted as Capt. 6/19/61 Company E, elected Lieut. Col. 07/18/61 and to Col. 02/01/62.

Douglas, W. A. - Cutt's Battery, Georgia Light Artillery, d. 09/18/62. Originally buried in lot #179, grave #10, row #3. Body was exhumed and shipped to Americus, Sumpter County, Georgia. Coffin size was 73 in. in length by 18 in. in width. NOTE: Franklin Clark of the 33rd North Carolina buried in that location 12/12/62.

Douthatt, Jack - 1st Tennessee Inf., Company F, killed in a street fight 02/23/62, body sent home to Tennessee. Capt. J. S. Butler listed as debtor. Private Douthatt was the only fatality of a street fight that erupted at saloon on Bridge Street. An Irish company of the 16th Mississippi and members of the 1st Tennessee were at a saloon on Bridge Street when a disagreement wound up in a brawl. The melee spread from the saloon up to Main St. in front of

William A. Strother's Drug Store. Lynchburg police with the aid of other soldiers finally restored order. Unfortunately, Douthatt was stabbed and died of the wound. Several others suffered the usual cuts and bruises.

Dove, Thomas - 6th Virginia Cav., Company E (Cabell Edward Flournoy's Company), d. 05/03/62 @ P. Lewis' home from the effects of measles. Body was prepared and sent to Pittsylvania Court House, Virginia. Widow of the deceased was Mary T. Dove. Mary and Thomas were married in 1835. A 1913 roster stated that he died in Camp @ Gordonsville.

* **Dowdey, Benjamin** - 4th Virginia Inf., Company L, d. 09/04/61 @ the Warwick House. Enlisted at age 24, occupation listed as farmer; 5' 4", dark eyes, hair and completion.

* **Doyel, Walter R.** - 2nd South Carolina Inf., Company A, d. 12/31/62 of pneumonia @ Miller's Factory. Coffin size was 74 in. in length by 18 in. in width. He enlisted as a private on 10/22/61 at Abbeville, South Carolina. His age at enlistment was listed as 20. Father of deceased was Richard Doyel. Military records list his initials as "E. W.".

Drewry, Lodewick M. - 53rd Virginia Inf., Company G, d. 11/19/64 of diarrhea @ Chimborazo, Richmond, Virginia. Diuguid has this entry in the note section of burial log #6, "The body of Lodewick Drewry Co G 53rd Va Reg will be here on the 23rd of Nov 1864 and his father Daniel Drewry wishes me to take charge of it he belongs in Pittsylvania Cty Va". Mr. Diuguid concludes with this entry, "Dec 20th 1865 his father carried the remains home". He enlisted as a private on 8/28/61 at Pittsylvania C. H. (now Chatham). Drewry was captured 7/03/63 at Gettysburg, sent Ft. McHenry, Myd., from there to Ft. Delaware on or about 07/12/63. On 10/26/63 he was sent to Point Lookout. He was exchanged 9/30/64 and admitted to Chimborazo #4 on 10/08/64 with diarrhea.

* **Driggers, Christopher Columbus** – 15th Alabama Inf., Company F, d. 07/04/62 of disease @ Christian's Factory. Coffin size was 70 in. in length by 19 in. in width. Driggers enlisted as a Private on 3/1/62 in Brundridge, Alabama. His age at enlistment was listed as 23. He was born in Alabama; occupation was listed as a farmer, and was single. The father of the deceased, Stephen Driggers filed a death claim on 01/13/63. Mr. Driggers could be contacted in care of J. H. Hybert, Burndridge, Alabama.

Drury, J. C. - Capt. Jordan's Battery, Virginia Light Art., d. 05/15/62 @ Taliaferro's Factory. Body was prepared and sent to Liberty, Virginia. Using existing service records, J. C. Drury, is not listed as member of Capt. Jordan's Battery. The spelling could be the problem, or possibly Mr. Diuguid recorded the wrong unit.

* **Duke, W. C. (or W. G.)** - 59th Georgia Inf., Company A, d. 05/29/64 of ascites @ Crumpton's Factory. Coffin size was 69 in. in length by 18 in. in width. Was originally enlisted in Company E, 19th Battn. Georgia Cav. Dule was Transferred to 59th Georgia in exchange for L. B. Faircloth in 1862.

Dulaney, Madison J. - 7th Virginia Inf., Company D, d. 6/26/62 of dysentery @ Crumpton's Factory. Enlisted as a private on 5/13/61 @ Giles Court House. Born in Roanoke County, Virginia. Body was prepared and shipped to Dublin Depot, Virginia for burial. Born Roanoke County, enlisted 5/13/61 @ Giles C.H.

Earnest (Ernest), George W. - 2nd Battn. Georgia Inf., Company C, d. 12/03/62 @ Christian's Factory. Coffin size was 70 in. in length by 18 in. in width. Was originally buried in lot #146, grave #1, row #1. Body was exhumed 12/05/62 (Friday) and shipped to Macon, Georgia. He enlisted as a private on 4/30/62. Military records state that he was discharged in 1862 by furnishing a substitute. NOTE: B. Hardman of 47th Alabama was buried there on or about 12/05/62.

Earnest, S. F. - 4th Georgia Battn. Inf., Company E, d. 08/25/62 @ Reid's Factory. Body was prepared and shipped to Red Clay, Georgia. Coffin size was 73 in. in length by 18 in. in width. Diuguid made the following notation "E T & G RR". This abbreviation was for the East Tennessee & Georgia Rail Road. The town of Red Clay was located on the rail line at the state between Tennessee and Georgia. He enlisted as a private on 09/19/61. Military records state that he was discharged in June 1862

Easley, Luther W. T. - 9th Georgia Inf., Company C, d. 03/14/62 @ College Hospital. Body was prepared and shipped to Social Circle, Georgia. His military state that he died @ College Hospital in Danville, Va. On 3/18/62. Private Easley enlisted on 06/13/61.

Eastment, Robert Albert - from Alabama is listed in Diuguid's records but unfortunately no military record can be located. Private Eastment died 07/16/61 @ the College Hospital. He was born Mobile, Alabama 01/05/1842. His age at death would have been 19. See photograph insert of a post war tombstone erected by family.

Edge, Haywood H. - 33rd North Carolina Inf., Company B, d. 8/21/62 @ Ford's Factory of febris typhoides. Coffin size was 70 in. in length by 18 in. in width. Body was prepared and shipped to Hartsborough, North Carolina. The father of the deceased was James Edge. Private H. H. Edge enlisted at age 19, 05/7/62, he was a res. of Edgecombe County, North Carolina.

Edwards, James B., Jr. - 11th Virginia Inf., Company G, "Lynchburg Home Guard", d. 07/31/62 of disease. He was buried 08/1/62. Father of the deceased was James B. Edwards. Notice appears in <u>Lynchburg Daily Virginian</u> date 08/1/62, page 3, col. 2. He enlisted as a private on 03/10/62. His age at enlistment was listed as 20.

Elder, William W. - 17th Mississippi Inf., Company I (Capt. M. Bell's Company), d. 07/5/61 @ Mrs. Thurmans. His remains were shipped home to his father, Jeremiah Elder, Greenleaf P.O., Desoto County, Mississippi. Burial paid in part by the Confederacy & James Elder of Memphis, Tennessee. Elder enlisted 06/01/61 @ Corinth for 1 year. His age at enlistment was 22 and he was single. Complied Service Records state that his residence was Cockin, Miss., 168 miles from the Corinth (rendezvous point). The June 61 muster states that he was "Left at a private house Lynchburg, Va. June 17th".

* **Eldridge, L. E. W.** - 20th Georgia Inf., Company I, d. 07/1/64 of disease. Compiled Service Records state, "died of disease in Richmond". However, he must have been transferred to Lynchburg sometime prior to his death.

* **Eller, D.** - 51st Virginia Inf., Company H, d.0 6/06/65 @ Camp Davis. Private Eller had surrendered with the Army of Northern Virginia at Appomattox in April.

Ellis, Thomas D. - 58th Virginia Inf., Company I, d. 05/18/62 @ Booker's Factory of Rubeola complicated by diarrhea. He enlisted 03/13/62 @ Huntersville (Bedford County). Private Ellis was originally buried in lot #166, grave #3, row #3. Body was exhumed and shipped home for burial. Ellis was born in Bedford County 1827. 1860 Census listed as age 33, occupation farmer. His brother, James C. Ellis, died of wounds (WIA, fractured thigh) 5/30/63 in Richmond. His wound was received at Fredericksburg 05/03/63. James' description was as follows: age 28, 5' 8", dark complexion, black eyes & black hair. NOTE: T. J. Frazier of the 19th Mississippi Inf. buried in that location 05/20/62.

Ellis, William R. - 42nd North Carolina Inf., Company D, d. 07/01/62 @ Fairgrounds, cause not stated. Body prepared and shipped to Lexington, Davidson County, North Carolina. Coffin size was 70 in. in length by 18 in. in width. Ellis enlisted as a private on 3/24/62 in Rowan County. His age at enlistment was listed as 35. He was resident of Davie County.

* **Ellison, M.** - 1st Texas Inf., Company F, d. 03/07/63 @ Candler's Factory. Coffin size was 75 in. in length by 19 in. in width. He enlisted as a private on 04/10/62 at Milam, Texas.

* **Elliot, John R., 3rd Sgt.** - 21st Georgia Inf., Company E, d. 07/02/64 @ Christian's Factory. Transferred to Company E April 11, 64. His Compiled Service Record, last entry listed on him, "sick in hospital at Lynchburg", dated August 31, 1864.

Epkin, G. A. - 13th South Carolina Inf., Company H, d. @ Christian's Factory 11/26/62. He was originally buried in lot #100, grave #4, row #3. His Coffin size was 72 in. in length by 18 in. in width. Mr. Diuguid made the following entry, "taken up & sent to Hope Station G&C R.R. S.C.". The "G&C" stands for Greenville & Columbia Rail Road, Hope Station and was located about 20 mile northwest of Columbia, South Carolina. NOTE: G. T. Milford of 12th South Carolina buried that location.

* **Etheridge, Lewis M.** - 45th Georgia Inf., Company I, d. 08/27/62 @ Ferguson's Factory. Coffin size was 70 in. in length by 18 in. in width. He enlisted as a private on 03/4/62. His Compiled Service Records states that, "died Orange County Court House May 1863". This is not possible, there must be two Lewis M. Etheridges with the 45th Georgia. Not Likely.

* **Ethridge, Thomas J.** – 5th Alabama Inf., Company G, d. 08/09/62 of disease @ College Hospital. Coffin size was 73 in. in length by 18 in. in width. Listed as "Sick" at Farmville Hospital, no date specified. A death claim was filed in early 1863. Joel Ethridge (poss. Father of the deceased) could be contacted in care of J. Q. Smith Attorney, Selma, Alabama. It appears that the claim was verified and honored on 08/11/64.

Evans, Barnwell - 6th South Carolina Inf., Company K, d. 11/11/62 of pneumonia @ Langhorne's Factory. His coffin size was 75 in. in length by 19 in. in width. His age at enlistment is shown as 24. 1860 census showed him as a resident of the Clarendon District.

Evans, D. E. - 1st South Carolina Inf., Company L, d. 05/16/64 @ Knight's Factory. His coffin size was 73 in. in length by 17 in. in width. Was Originally buried in lot #189, grave #7, row #4. Exhumed 09/06/64, "...sent to Sumpter S.C.". The remains were claimed by W. H. Brunson who paid all expenses associated with removal and packing.

Evans, Timothy F. - 11th Virginia Inf., Company E, d. 12/24/62 of typhoid fever @ Ferguson's Factory. Coffin size was 73 in. in length by 18 in. in width. He was originally buried in lot #123, grave #1, row #2. Body was exhumed 02/10/63 and reburied in Presbyterian Cemetery, Lynchburg, Virginia. Father of the deceased was Timothy Evans. Private Evans was born in Campbell County. He enlisted as a private on 06/10/61. His age at enlistment was listed as 21. His occupation was listed as a farmer. NOTE: J. S. Oxford of the 49th Georgia was buried in that location 05/16/63.

* **Ezell, George Washington -** 21st Georgia Inf., Company G, d. 08/12/62 of chronic diarrhea @ Warwick House. Coffin size was 72 in. in length by 18 in. in width. Ezell enlisted as a Private on 02/18/62 as a substitute for Abraham R. Chandler.

Farmer, James M. - 11th Virginia Inf., Company B, d. 12/02/62 @ Ferguson's Factory. Body was prepared and shipped to Campbell County, Virginia. Coffin size was 68 in. in length by 18 in. in width. He enlisted in service 08/11/62. No Further Record.

Feazle, Frank H. - 11th Virginia Inf., Company A, d. 12/20/64 @ Ladies Relief Hospital. Diuguid's entry was, "Was buried in North Corner of E. Victors lot at Presbyterian grave yard." He enlisted as a private on 04/22/61. His age at enlistment was listed as 21. His occupation was listed as a farmer. His military record list him "absent sick" Jan. - April, 63, and again "absent sick" Mar. - Aug. of 64. No Further Record.

Ferguson, Nimrod - 18th Virginia Inf., Company I (Capt. Luck, "Spring Garden Blues), d. 12/14/61 @ College Hospital. Private Ferguson was prepared and shipped to Pittsylvania County. The compiled service records for the 18th Virginia, a Private Nimrod Ferguson is listed as "died at Manassas 08/24/61". In addition his CSR listed him as a member of Company D (Prince Edward County).

Fesperman, John M. - 42nd North Carolina Inf., Company G, d. 06/28/62 @ Fairgrounds, cause not stated. Body was prepared and shipped to China Grove, Rowan County, North Carolina. He was a resident of Rowan County were he enlisted for the war on 04/24/62 at age 18.

* **Fields, Samuel G. -** 58th Virginia Inf., Company A, d. 05/10/62 of diphtheria @ College Hospital. Enlisted Bunker Hill, Virginia 07/25/61; detailed as nurse in Lynchburg 4/62. Description - age 28, 6' 4", fair complexion, light hair, blue eyes. His occupation was listed as a farmer. Born Bedford County 1834.

Finch, John - 42nd Virginia Inf., Company E, d. 01/21/62 @ the Warwick House. Body shipped home to Lafayette P.O., Montgomery County, Virginia. His approximate age at death based on the 1860 census would have been approximately 20. He enlisted as a private on 06/04/61 at Salem, Virginia. 1860 census listed his age as 19, occupation farmer, Lafayette P.O., Montgomery County, Virginia.

Fink, Nathaniel G. - 33rd North Carolina Inf., Company C, d. 06/05/62 of febris typhoides @ Ferguson's Factory of febris typhoides. His coffin size was 72 in. in length by 19 inches wide. Fink was originally buried in lot #171, grave #4, row #3. On an unspecified date Diuguid recorded the following in his notes, "Doct John Fink may Telegraph us to take up the remains of his brother N. J. Fink Co C 33rd N.C.". Body was exhumed and shipped to Concord, North Carolina. Preparation and shipment of body was paid by his brother Dr. John R. Fink. Private Fink enlisted on 08/31/61 at age 24. He was born in and a resident of Cabarrus County, North Carolina. NOTE: Peter Shepherd of 56th Virginia buried there 06/7/62.

* **Flaniken (or Flanagan) John W., 3rd Lieut.** - 5th Texas Inf., Company I, d. 01/27/63 of
chronic diarrhea @ College Hospital. Coffin size was 77 in. in length by 19 in. in width. Originally joined the company as a private and was promoted to 1st Corpl., then to 5th Sgt. and finally to 3rd Lieut. on Jan. 16, 63.

* **Flemming, J. T.** - 47th Alabama Inf., Company K, d. 01/05/63 of smallpox at the Pest House. Appears to have been a Mason, Mr. Diuguid has drawn the Mason symbol beside his name. Coffin size was 74 in. in length by 18 in. in width.

Fletcher, Lieut. - 57th Virginia Inf. (?), d. 05/10/62. Expenses paid by Alfred Slaughter. Compiled Service Records, list a Allen Fletcher, Lieut., Company B, occupation farmer, which was not re-elected when the regiment reorganized in April 1862.

* **Flippen, Marion Twyman** - 44th Virginia Inf., Company A, found frozen to death 3 miles from Lynchburg near the railroad. Diuguid's exact notation in the Soldiers Book was as follows, "Found dead on Rail Road 3 miles from here frozen." He was buried 01/15/62 in lot #170, grave #1, row #5. Young Flippen had been discharged 7/1/61, reason not specified. He

was carpenter by trade in Appomattox County, Bent Creek, Virginia. Based on the 1860 census his approximate age at his death would be 20. He enlisted as a private on 06/4/61 at Appomattox Court House. 1860 census listed his age 19, apprentice cabinetmaker. Campbell County paid funeral expenses.

Flora, George W. - 24th Virginia Inf. (Early's Regiment), Company B (Capt. Hambrick's Company), d. 07/25/61 @ J. Cundiff's of disease. Body was shipped home to Franklin County, Virginia. Compiled Service Records state, "died of disease in Lynchburg 09/27/61".

* **Flowers, J. C.** – 15th Alabama Inf., Company A, d. 02/19/63 of Small Pox @ the Pest House. Coffin size was 76 in. in length by 19 in. in width. The mother of the deceased, Mary Flowers filed a death claim on 12/24/63. The claim was verified and settled on 02/03/65. Mrs. Flowers could be contacted in care of J. H. Hybert, Burndridge, Alabama.

* **Floyd, Richard** - MacBeth's Battery, South Carolina Light Artillery, (commanded by Capt. R. Boyce), d. 12/17/62 of disease @ Burton's Factory. Coffin size was 75 in. in length by 18 in. in width. He enlisted 03/19/62 in Union, South Carolina. The widow of the deceased was S. A. Floyd. 1860 census showed him as a resident of the Charleston District.

Floyd, Eugenius - 3rd (Stovall's) Battn. Georgia Inf., Company E (Capt. White's Co.), d. 09/25/61 @ Mrs. Collins. Body sent home to Pike County, Georgia. He enlisted 08/08/61. Diuguid had his first name listed as "Yougenius".

* **Forrester, Thomas** - 4th Texas Inf., Company K, d. 07/09/62 of typhoid fever @ Knight's Factory. Coffin size was 68 in. in length by 19 in. in width. Enlisted as a private on 04/15/62 at Athens, Texas.

* **Foster, Baylis B.** – 4th Alabama Inf., Company H, d. 05/29/62 @ College Hospital. Coffin size was 76 in. in length by 19 in. in width. He enlisted as a Private on 04/28/61 in Florence, Alabama for 1 year. His age at enlistment was listed as 24. His occupation was listed as a Farmer. Per his records he was sent to the "Hospital at Lynchburg, Va., Aug. 1862 not heard from since, dropped from roll." Foster was born in Alabama, he was listed as single, and his place of residence was Rogersville, Alabama.

* **Fountain James (also J.A. & A.J.)** - 1st South Carolina Inf., Orr's Rifles, Company G, d. 08/11/63 of pneumonia @ Crumpton's Factory. Coffin size was 74 in. in length by 18 in.

in width. Two military records are found, one for a J.A. and one for a James, both of which died in Lynchburg. Both men were members of the 1st South Carolina. However, one is listed as a member of company E and the other company F. Per the 1860 census, James, was shown as a resident of the Pickens District. This writer considers the men to be one in the same.

* **Fowler, Matthew** - 1st South Carolina Inf., (McCreary's - Gregg's), Company F, d. 12/12/62 at Ferguson's Factory of pneumonia. Coffin size was 74 in. in length by 18 in. in width. He enlisted as a private on 04/25/62 in Conway, South Carolina. His age at enlistment was listed as 33. Widow of the deceased was Nancy Fowler. 1860 census showed him as a resident of the Hoory District.

* **Fowlkes, W. E. (or W. T.)** - 56th Virginia Inf., Company I, d. 02/15/63 of diabetes @ Ferguson's Factory. Coffin size was 77 in. in length by 21 in. in width. Private Fowlkes enlisted as a private on 07/18/61 in Charlotte County. His age at enlistment was listed as 30. He was a substitute for James R. Hill. Fowlkes was one of approximately 80 men of the 56th that were taken prisoner at Fort Donelson, Tenn. on 02/16/62 (Sunday). He was transferred from Camp Morton (Union POW Camp) at Indianapolis, Indiana to Vicksburg where he was exchanged. He was a resident of Lunenburg County, dark complexion, black hair, 6 ft. in height.

* **Fox, James** - 6th Louisiana Inf., d. 12/17/62 from complications of his wound received on 6/9/62 at the Battle of Port Republic. He is buried in lot #123, grave #10, row #1. Burial records state, "one Leg", indicating a leg was amputated prior to his death. Coffin size was 71 in. in length by 18 in. in width.

* **Fox, William** - 7th North Carolina Inf., Company A, d. 11/26/62 of gunshot wound @ Burton's Factory. Coffin size was 73 in. in length by 18 in. in width. Wounded in thigh 8/29/62 at Battle of 2nd Manassas. He enlisted as a private on 07/23/62 in Alexander County. His age at enlistment was listed as 23.

Franklin, Archibald H. - 58th Virginia Inf., Company K, d. 05/14/62 @ Ferguson's Factory of typhoid pneumonia. Body prepared and shipped to Bedford County, Virginia for burial. He enlisted 7/23/61 @ Chamblissburg. Franklin was born in Bedford County circa 1825. His description at death age; 40, light complexion, light hair, light eyes, 6' 4", occupation farmer.

*** Frazier, Brice M., Lieut.** - 24th Virginia Inf., Company I, d. 04/06/63. He enlisted on 05/31/61 at Lynchburg, Virginia. He had resigned his commission 05/10/62.

*** Frazier, James M.** - 1st North Carolina Inf., Company G, d. 07/03/64 of "Diarrhea Chronic" @ Christian's Factory. He was born Washington County, North Carolina. Frazier enlisted as a private on 06/24/61. His age at enlistment was listed as 44. He was transferred to hospital on surgeon's certificate of disability for field duty. Detailed as a nurse on April 11, 63 and remained in that duty until discharged April 20, 1864 "by reason of chronic diarrhea of 18 months standing".

Freeman, Stephen M. - 30th Virginia Cav. (2nd Va.), Radford's Rangers, Capt. Terry's Company (Company A) the "Clay Dragoon's", d. 09/06/61 of typhoid fever @ J. McGehee's. Body was sent home to Bedford County, for burial. <u>Lynchburg Daily Virginian</u> published a tribute to Trooper Freeman from "Clay Troop" on 11/15/61 page 3, col.'s 2 & 3. Enlisted as a private on 5/11/61 at Liberty (Bedford), Virginia. His age at enlistment was listed as 26. His occupation listed as farmer. He was born in Bedford County circa 1835.

* Freestone, Benjamin F. – 4th Texas Inf., Company A, d. 08/04/62 of phthisis pulmonalis (pulmonary tuberculosis – "consumption") @ Langhorne's Factory. Private Freestone enlisted 07/11/62 @ Camp Clark, Guadalupe County, Texas. He was a born c. 1829, possibly in Clinton County, Ohio. He was the son of Jesse & Mary Hunt Freestone.

Frey (Fry), Samuel - 2nd Virginia Inf., Company G, d. 06/06/63 of chronic dysentery @ College Hospital. Coffin size was 71 in. in length by 17 in. in width. Brother of deceased "Mr. Frey" claimed remains and paid expenses. "Was sent to Staunton, Va", was the notation made by Mr. Diuguid. He was interred in Salem Lutheran Church Cemetery at Mt. Sidney. He was born 04/05/35 in Shenandoah County. Frey enlisted as a private on 4/15/62 at Rude's Hill. He was admitted to Lynchburg Gen. Hospital #3 05/8/63.

Fringer, Monroe P. - 34th North Carolina Inf., Company C, d. 06/25/63 @ Ford's Factory. Coffin size was 73 in. in length by 18 in. in width. He was originally buried in lot #192, grave #10, row #4. "Removed & sent to Linconton N.C.".

Fuller, Henry L. C. - 19th Georgia Inf., Company H (Capt. J. B. Bell's Company), d. 03/6/62 of measles @ College Hospital. Body shipped home to Marietta, Georgia.

* Fuller, Joseph L. - 4th Texas Inf., Company I, d. 06/20/64 @ Christian's Factory from wounds receive 5/6/64 at the Battle of the Wilderness. He received wounds to the arm and hip. Coffin size was 73 in. in length by 20 in. in width. Fuller enlisted as a private on 03/24/62 in Navarro County, Texas.

Fullerton, George W. - 11th Virginia Inf. Company G, d. on or about 07/30/61. Funeral was paid by Samuel Andrew Boyd. His funeral notice was published in the Lynchburg Daily Virginian, dated July 30, 1861, page 2, col. 4. The notice read as follows; "**The funeral services of the late Geo. W. Fullerton will take place from the 1st Presbyterian Church at 4 o'clock this evening. His friends and acquaintances, and friends of the families of S. A. Boyd, Andrew Boyd, and Geo. A. Kinner also all members of the Home Guard, or the 11th Regiment Va. Volunteers now in the city, are respectfully invited to attend without further notice.**" His compiled service records states that he was born in Baltimore, Maryland. He enlisted as a Private on 05/28/61 at age 18, occupation clerk. His military record states that he died 07/07/61.

Furlow, John B. - 7th Georgia Inf., Company G (Featherstone's Co.), d. 12/24/61 of disease @ College Hospital. He was originally buried in lot #170, grave #3, row #3. Body was exhumed prior to 2/1/62 and shipped home to Hogansville, Troup County, Georgia. Per the 1860 census he was the son of Lucinda Furlow of Heard County, Georgia. Furlow was born circa 1833. No marked grave located for him in Heard County. Also, Hogansville was the nearest rail station for the Southern section of Heard County. NOTE: Jesse Langston, 15th Alabama was buried in that location 2/1/62.

Furt, William - No Diuguid record on the soldier, only a South Carolina record indicating that Furt died in Lynchburg in 1865. May possibly have been a member of the 1st South Carolina Inf., Company K. 1860 census showed him as a resident of the Charleston District. Another notations makes reference to Brooks, Georgia.

* Furtic, Charles - 1st South Carolina Inf. (Hagood's), Company B, d. 01/17/63 of disease @ Crumpton's Factory. Coffin size was 69 in. in length by 18 in. in width. His military records list his date of death as 12/20/62. 1860 census showed him as a resident of the Charleston District.

* **Gambill, Hugh L.** - 33rd North Carolina Inf., Company D, d. 02/23/63 of smallpox at the Pest House. Coffin size was 79 in. in length by 20 in. in width. Captured at Fredericksburg 12/13/62. Gambill was paroled and exchanged 12/17/62. Military records list cause of death as "Febris Typhoides". Born in Wilkes County where he resided until enlisting 10/04/61 at age 30. Occupation listed farmer.

* **Gardner, S. D.** – 15th Alabama Inf., Company I, d. 07/03/62 @ Ferguson's Factory. Coffin size was 73 in. in length by 18 in. in width. Gardner enlisted as a private on 3/1/62 at Troy, Alabama. His age at enlistment was listed as 24. He was born in Alabama, occupation was listed as a farmer, he was a resident of Olustee, Alabama and he was married. Per his military record his date of death was listed as 06/25/62.

Gardner, William G. (or Wm. E.), Sgt. - 35th Battn. Virginia Cav., Company F, d. 06/08/64 @ Christian's Factory. His coffin size was 73 in. in length by 18 in. in width. "Was packed up & sent to Charlottesville Va". Garner was Wounded In Action 5/6/64 near Shady Grove, Spotsylvania County. Father of the deceased, B. B. Gardner, claimed the remains. Gardner enlisted on 07/15/62 in Albemarle County for the war.

Garland, Samuel Jr., Brig. General - **Killed in Action** September 14, 1862 at South Mountain, Maryland. His North Carolina Brigade was defending Fox's Gap against an overwhelming Union force. During this major action General Garland was struck down by a single Union minnie ball, he died minutes later. He was a native of Lynchburg, graduated from VMI in 1849, and received his law degree from UVa. in 1851. He was the first Captain for the "Lynchburg Home Guard" (Co. G, 11th Va. Vol. Inf. Regt.), Col. of the 11th Virginia Infantry. He was promoted to Brig. Gen. in the spring of 1862. Following a funeral service at St. Paul's Episcopal Church, General Garland was interred in Presbyterian Cemetery, Lynchburg, Virginia. General Garland was interred 9/19/62. Mr. Diuguid made the following entry, "...air tight box & burial service $25.00". See drawing of Gen. Garland on the next page.

* **Garrett, Jesse Newton 1st Sgt.** – 7th Alabama Inf., Company B, d. 01/15/63 of disease @ Talliaferro's Factory. No date of

enlistment found. The 47th Alabama was organized May 1862 in Loachapoka, Alabama. Arrived in Virginia in late June, 62. Garrett was born 1827, Laurens County, South Carolina. Married Sybretta Elizabeth Truss in 1846. His coffin size was 72 in. in length by 18 in. in width.

Garrett, John - 3rd South Carolina Battn. Inf., Company E, d. 10/15/64 of disease @ Crumpton's Factory. Coffin size was 78 in. in length by 18 in. in width. He was originally buried in lot #198, grave #5, row #3. Body was exhumed 11/12/64, "taken up & sent to Lawrence S.C.". In Diuguid's burial Log Book #6 he made this entry, "Doct R. C. Hunter", "For removal & packing John Garrett $180.00". Expenses were paid in full. His age at enlistment is shown as 41. 1860 census showed him as resident of the Laurens District.

Brig. General Samuel Garland Jr.
Killed In Action 09/14/62

Brig. Gen. Samuel Garland, Jr.
CSA

Garrett, J. A. - 14th South Carolina Inf., Company E, d. 12/11/62 of pneumonia @ Ferguson's Factory. Coffin size was 77 in. in length by 19 in. in width. His military records stated that he died of wounds on 09/19/62 (possibly WIA at Sharpsburg on 09/17/62). He was more than likely wounded at Sharpsburg, transported the hospitals in Lynchburg, contracted pneumonia in his weakened state and died. 1860 census showed him as a resident of the Laurens District.

Garrett, Silas - 16th Virginia Inf., Company F, d. 06/15/62 @ Booker's Factory of typhoid fever. Body was prepared and shipped to Henry County, Va. He enlisted as a private on 04/11/62 at Huger's Barracks, Norfolk, Va. He was a resident of Henry County, Virginia.

Garrison, James B. - Jones' Battery Virginia Light Art. (Charlottesville Art.), d. 12/13/63 of pneumonia @ Christian's Factory. Diuguid's entry, "Was sent to North Garden Depot". Garrison enlisted as a Private 04/23/62.

* **Gay, G. M.** – 15th Alabama Inf., Company L, d. 07/31/62 of disease @ Crumpton's Factory. Coffin size was 73 in. in length by 18 in. in width. Gay enlisted as a Private on 03/11/62 at Perote, Alabama. His age at enlistment was listed as 25. He was born in Georgia, occupation was listed as a farmer, he was a resident of Perote, Alabama and he was married. Gay was listed as "Absent" prior to May 25, 1862 (Battle of Winchester).

* **Gay, Henry** - 30th North Carolina Inf., Company F, d. 01/18/63 of typhoid fever @ Claytor's Factory. Coffin size was 68 in. in length by 18 in. in width. His military records state that his place of death was at Guinea Station somewhere between the 1st and 23rd of Feb., 63. His cause of death listed in his records was listed as "typhoid fever or pneumonia".

* **Gayheart, John** - 7th Louisiana Inf., Company B, d. 06/13/62 @ Christian's Factory. Coffin size was 68 in. in length by 17 in. in width. Records state that he was 45 years of age and was born in Germany.

* **Gentry, Allen** - 9th Louisiana Inf., Company B, d. 05/23/62 @ Ferguson's Factory. Coffin size was 77 in. in length by 20 in. in width. The company muster roll for April 1862 stated, "sent to rear sick, in hospital in Lynchburg when last heard from."

Ghean, W. H. - 57th North Carolina Inf., Company K, d. 04/01/63 @ Taliaferro's Factory. Coffin size was 71 in. in length by 18 in. in width. He was originally buried in lot #199, grave #8, row #4. Body was exhumed 04/6/63, prepared and shipped to Salisbury, North Carolina. A. S. Elliott claimed the remains of Ghean.

Gibson, William H. - 18th North Carolina Inf., Company F, d. 12/27/62 of pneumonia @ Burton's Factory. Coffin size was 73 in. in length by 18 in. in width. Originally buried in lot #101, grave #2, row #2. Body was exhumed and shipped to Laurinburg, Richmond County, North Carolina. He was born in Richmond County or in the Marlboro District of South Carolina. His occupation was a farmer in Richmond County where he enlisted at age 22 on 6/01/61. NOTE: W. E. Hurst of 50th Georgia buried in this location on 12/31/62.

Gilbert, John W. - 42nd North Carolina Inf., Company K, d. 08/12/62 @ College Hospital. Coffin size was 72 in. in length by 20 in. in width. Body was prepared and shipped to Hickory Tavern, Catawba, North Carolina. He enlisted 04/24/62 for the war Wilkes County, North Carolina.

Gilliam, William R. - 14th North Carolina Inf., Company G, d. 12/14/62 of chronic bronchitis @ Ferguson's Factory. Coffin size was 71 in. in length by 18 in. in width. Body was prepared and shipped to Danville, Virginia. A resident of Rockingham County and was by occupation a farmer prior to enlisting on 05/10/61. His age at enlistment was listed as 26.

* **Gilligan, John** - Alabama Troops, Capt. Covington's Company, d. 6/30/61 @ College Hospital, buried in lot #158, grave #5, row #2. The widow of deceased was Hannah Gilligan, of Mobile, Alabama.

* **Gillis, Angus 3rd Corpl.** – 15th Alabama Inf., Company I, d. 05/12/62 @ Ferguson's Factory. Gillis enlisted as a Private on 7/3/61 in Troy, Alabama. His age at enlistment was listed as 22. He was born in Alabama, occupation was listed as a farmer, he was a resident of Orion, Alabama and he was single. He was promoted to 3rd Corpl. on 10/3/61. The mother of the deceased, Ann Gillis filed a death claim on 09/2/62. The claim was verified and approved on 2/3/65. Mrs. Gillis could be contacted in care of B. Fitzpatrick, Troy, Alabama.

Gladden, J. D. - 18th Georgia Inf., Company A, d. 07/12/62 @ the Warwick House of chronic Dysentery. Coffin size was 70 in. in length by 18 in. in width. Body was prepared and shipped to Ackworth, Georgia. H. A. Gladden, brother of the deceased paid expenses.

* **Godwin, James** - 5th Florida Inf., Company B, d. 12/02/62 from wound @ Christians Factory. Coffin size was 75 in. in length by 18 in. in width. Godwin enlisted as a private on

03/08/62 at Lake City. He was wounded in the head at Sharpsburg on 9/17/62. A personal description - 6' in height, fair skin, blue eyes, light hair, occupation farmer. Listed as born 1836 in Camden County, Georgia. The widow of the deceased was Amelia Godwin. They were married in 1858. Mr. Diuguid listed his name as "Gardwin".

Goggin, Thomas Stephen - 2nd Virginia Cav., Company F, d. 04/3/63 @ Claytor's Factory of pneumonia (Dr. Minor). Coffin size was 69 in. in length by 18 in. in width. Diuguid also made this entry, "was sent to Liberty Va for burial died at Jno. O. L. Goggin". Goggin enlisted as a private on 05/28/61 at Davis Mills. His age at enlistment was listed as 19, and his occupation listed as farmer. He was buried in Dickerson Cemetery near Moneta, Bedford County, Virginia. Date of birth listed as 8/30/41.

* Goggins, William Leftwich Jr., Lieut. - 11th Virginia Inf., Company H, d. 09/5/61, "...in the 22nd year of his age at the residence of his father in Lynchburg". He was the son of John O. L. Goggins. He was interred in the Presbyterian Cemetery in Lynchburg. An obituary appears in the <u>Lynchburg Daily Virginian</u> on 9/18/61, page 1, col. 4 & 5. A tribute from the "Jeff Davis Guard" was published 9/20/61, page 1, col. 1. Born Liberty, Bedford County 07/21/40. He attended the University of Virginia. Enlisted on 05/15/62, occupation listed as student.

Goin, John - 19th Virginia Inf., Company I, d. 06/10/62 @ Ferguson's Factory. Per Mr. Diuguid's entry, "was packed up and sent to Amherst Cty (Virginia)". Compiled Service Records shows no date of enlistment and no rank.

* Goodman, H. – 5th Alabama Inf., Company K, d. 06/12/63 of wounds @ Knight's Factory. Private Goodman was listed as severely wounded on 05/3/63 at the Battle of Chancellorsville. His records state that he died on 6/10/63. He enlisted as a Private on 3/2/62 at Hayneville, Alabama.

Goodman, Robert L. - 13th Mississippi Inf., Company A (Capt. Samuel J. Randall's Company, Pettus Guards), d. 08/13/61 @ College Hospital. Body was shipped to his home Pemberton Lock, to be buried along side his father in Cumberland County, Virginia. He enlisted on 03/19/61 at Marion for 12 months. His age at enlistment was 27. His occupation was listed as a farmer. Goodman, then a member of Company H was officially mustered into the service of the Confederacy at Corinth, Mississippi on 05/14/61. Distance traveled to the rendezvous (Corinth) was 190 miles. He was transferred to Company "A" on 07/25/61. September/October, 61 musters indicate that he re-enlisted for 9 1/2 months at Camp McIntosh, Stone Bridge, Virginia. His "Death Certificate" provides the following information; Born in the state of Virginia, age 18, 5' 6", dark complexion, blue eyes, light hair and farmer by occupation. This certificate states that he died at Stonebridge, Va. on 8/01/61. His mother was Martha M. Goodman.

* **Grace, Thomas (or Green), Corpl.** - 61st Georgia Inf., Company B, d. 01/03/63 of wounds received during the Battle of Fredericksburg @ Ferguson's Factory. Coffin size was 77 in. in length by 20 in. in width. His military records state that he **Killed in Action** at Fredericksburg 12/13/62. In Diuguid's burial records his name was listed as "T. Green Co B 61st Ga".

* **Graham, Chesley C.** - 23rd Georgia Inf., Company F, d. 08/13/62. He is buried in lot #177, grave #9, row #3. Diuguid made the following notation about the burial of an unidentified infant in the same grave, "A child which was found in Blackwater Creek put in the same grave".

* **Grant, Robert A.** - 14th South Carolina Inf., Company I, d. 10/17/62 of a gunshot wound @ Ford's Factory. Coffin size was 72 in. in length by 19 in. in width. His age at enlistment is shown as 18. 1860 census showed him as a resident of the Abbeville District.

* **Gray, Lorenzo D.** – 44th Alabama Inf., Company C, d. 07/15/64 of chronic diarrhea @ Booker's Factory. Coffin size was 73 in. in length by 18 in. in width. Gray enlisted and mustered into service as a private on 03/8/64 at Greenville, Alabama. His age at enlistment was listed as 18. He was born in Alabama, single, occupation was listed as a farmer, and he was a resident of Monterey, Alabama. Gray was slightly wounded in the arm at the Battle of the Wilderness on 05/06/64. The father of the deceased, J. M. Gray, filed a death claim on 11/30/64. Mr. Gray could be contacted in care of S. J. Bowling, Greenville, Alabama.

* **Gray, Phillip F., 4th Sgt.** - 12th Alabama Inf., Company I, d. 09/13/61 @ Warwick House. The father of the deceased, B. B. Gray on 09/25/63, filed death claim. Mr. Gray could be contacted in care of J. R. Eastborn, Atty., Mobile, Alabama.

Greathouse, Jonas - 31st Virginia Inf., Company C, d. 12/29/62 @ Crumpton's Factory from a gunshot wound. His military records indicate he was at Charlottesville General

Hospital 11/27/62. He received his mortal wound on 11/24/62 during skirmishing around Newtown, Virginia. The Compiled Service Record also states that he died at "C.G.H." (Charlottesville Gen. Hospital). Personal effects turned over to the Q.M. amounted to $2.25. Diuguid listed his coffin size as 70 in. in length by 18 in. in width. He enlisted as a private on 05/21/61 at Clarksburg, Va. (now West Va.). His age at enlistment was listed as 18. His occupation was listed as a Turner, and he was born in Harrison County. Appears to be related to Silas Greathouse (listed below), possibly a younger brother.

* Greathouse, Silas, Sgt. - 31st Virginia Inf., Company C, d. 08/21/62 of smallpox @ Candler's Factory. Greathouse appears to be the first recorded death of smallpox in the Lynchburg Hospital System. He was buried in "Yankee Square", the common grave for smallpox victims. Greathouse was listed as POW of the 115th Penn. Inf. on 06/26/62 (Skirmishing at Woodstock & Mt. Jackson). He was exchanged from Fort Delaware - received at Akiens Landing, Virginia on 8/14/62. Death Cert. #2859 dated 09/16/63. It appears that Sgt. Greathouse contracted smallpox as a prisoner of war @ Fort Delaware. Enlisted on 05/21/61 at age 29, occupation farmer; born in Harrison County.

* Green, Cullen T. - 14th Georgia Inf., Company B, d. 08/19/62 of measles @ Reid's Hospital. However, his military records states, "killed in Virginia, August 1862". Coffin size was 69 in. in length by 19 in. in width.

* Green, Daniel S., Surgeon (M.D.) - Surgeon in the Lynchburg Hospital System, d. 03/05/64. Coffin size was 81 in. in length by 22 1/2 in. width. Interred in Presbyterian Cemetery 03/07/64, "Buried No. 1 in East Corner of lot No. 9 Range Presbyterian". Diuguid's fee for the burial was $225.00. His age at death was listed as "in 53rd year". Served in the C. S. Navy Medical Corps, assigned to Lynchburg early to mid 1862. At one point he was Surgeon-in-Charge of Gen. Hospital #2, 3rd Division. Wilson Cary Nicholas Randolph replaced him on 9/13/62. The **Lynchburg Virginian** carried a tribute from Army Surgeons on March 11th, page 1 col. 5. Also on April 1, page 1 col. 5. He was the son of the late Judge John W. Green, Court of Appeals of Virginia. See photo insert next page of head stone.

Green, Jesse A. - 48th North Carolina Inf., Company K. d. 11/11/62 of febris typhoides @ Miller's Factory. Coffin size was 74 in. in length by 18 in. in width. He was originally buried in lot #182, grave #9, row #5. Body was exhumed and shipped to Thomasville, North Carolina. He was resident of Davidson County where he enlisted for the war on 8/31/62. NOTE: E. E. Crim of the 15th Alabama buried there 12/8/62.

Greenwood, A. H. - 11th Alabama Inf., Company B, d. 8/2/62 @ Ladies Relief Hospital. Body was prepared and shipped to Eutaw, Green County, Alabama for burial.

* **Gregory, William** - 54th North Carolina Inf., Company G, d. 5/23/64 @ Wayside Hospital. "Shot for a deserter" was the entry made by Mr. Diuguid. Appears to have been a for military execution. His military record has the following information, "...deserted near Fredericksburg 19 June, 63. He was apprehended on an unspecified date. Admitted to Richmond Hospital 10/23/63 with a cold. Greggory was transferred to Castle Thunder Prison, Richmond on 10/23/63. Died in Hospital, Lynchburg, 23 May, 64 of gun shot wound received while attempting to desert". Born Wilkes County where he resided until he enlisted 4/24/62 at age 32. Occupation listed as a farmer.

Grey, F. B. - 57th North Carolina Inf., Company A, d. 12/20/62 @ Burton's Factory. He was originally buried in lot #123, grave #10, row #2. Diuguid's records state, "removed", no other information. He was exhumed to be shipped home for burial. Coffin size was 74 in. in length by 18 in. in width. NOTE: G. W. Harriss of 33rd North Carolina buried there 2/9/63.

Grider, G. M. - 15th Alabama Inf., Company L, d. 06/11/62. No other information. This soldier was not interred in the Confederate section, Old City Cemetery.

Groom, John - No Diuguid record, only a military record stating that he died in Lynchburg on 08/29/62 of disease. His service record showed him as member of the 6th South Carolina Infantry. In addition, he was listed also as previously serving in the 2nd South Carolina, Company F.

* **Grounds, John** - 8th Louisiana Inf., Company G, d.07/16/62 @ Claytor's Factory. Coffin size was 76 in. in length by 18 in. in width. The unit muster roll for October 1863 stated, "absent, deserted". However, this young soldier had died on July 16, 1862.

* **Gum, John H.** - 31st Virginia Inf., Company B, d. 08/6/62 @ Booker's Factory of typhoid fever. Coffin size was 71 in. in length by 19 in. in width. Gum enlisted as a private on 4/6/62 at Shenandoah. Compiled Service Records states his death date was 01/12/63. Attorney W. W. Flemming filed Cert. #4118 for $13.75 pay, and 09/06/63 for his effects Cert. #2878. Diuguid's records show him as John H. of Company B.

Hale, Stephen - Not unit stated, died on or about 06/22/61. From Washington City, Mississippi. J. E. Teel listed as debtor.

* **Hall, Edwin M.** - Palmetto Sharp Shooters, Company L, d. 12/06/62 of disease @ Saunder's Factory. Coffin size was 74 in. in length by 18 in. in width. Military records list his date of death as 6/15/63. His age at enlistment is shown as 22. 1860 census listed him as a resident of the Pickens District.

* **Hall, L. J. (James A.?)** - 14th South Carolina, Company L, d. 10/06/62 of hepatitis @ Knight's Factory. Coffin size was 71 in. in length by 17 in. in width. There are two military records listing the death of this man. Both have the same unit/company, and same date of death. Diuguid records "L. J. Hall", the other record list "James A." as dying at Farmville, Virginia. This write considers both to be one in the same.

There appears to be some confusion with the first names. Per the 1860 census both named individuals were residents of the Anderson District.

Hall, James C., 1st Lieut. - 38th Georgia Inf., Company H, d. 08/16/62 @ the Warwick House. Coffin size was 74 in. in length by 18 in. in width. The body was prepared and shipped to Lexington, Georgia. Expenses paid by Mrs. A. H. Hall on 8/30/62. Hall enlisted as 2nd Lieut. 10/15/61. Elected to 1st Lieut. 06/01/62

* **Hall, Richard H.** - 42nd Virginia Inf., Company D, d. 03/12/64 of typhoid fever @ Lynch Adams House. Coffin size was 70 in. in length by 18 in. in width. Had previously served in the 21st Virginia and was transferred to the 42nd Va. Infantry on 09/11/63. Joined Company D of the 42nd on 09/24/63 @ Germanna Ford, Virginia. He was wounded in the nose and hand on 11/27/63 at Payne's Farm. Listed in Richmond Hospital 11/28/63 - 02/02/64.

* **Hall, Richard J.** - 4th North Carolina Inf., Company B, d. 05/26/62 @ Crumpton's Factory of a fever. Coffin size was 75 in. in length by 19 in. in width. Originally hospitalized in Charlottesville 3/22/62 with a fever. Was transferred to Lynchburg 04/23/62. Born Rowan County where he was a resident until he enlisted 06/3/61. Occupation was listed as a farmer.

* **Hamby, Thomas N.** – 47th Alabama Inf., Company B, d. 06/09/64 @ Langhorne's Factory. Coffin size was 74 in. in length by 17 in. in width. Diuguid recorded his name as "T. W. Hamby". Hamby enlisted a private on 04/07/62 at Loachapoka, Alabama. No further record.

* **Hamilton, H.** - 4th Texas Inf., Company B, d. 07/04/62 @ Christian's Factory from typhoid fever. Coffin size was 78 in. in length by 19 in. in width. Hamilton enlisted as a Private on 03/27/62 at Austin, Texas.

Hammond, Benjamin F. - 1st South Carolina (Orr's Rifles) Company D, d. 05/23/64 of wounds @ Knight's Factory. Coffin size was 71 in. in length by 18 in. in width. His age at enlisted is shown as 22. 1860 census listed him as a resident of the Anderson district.

Hamner, N. - Virginia Reserves (no unit stated), Company B, d. 09/23/64 @ Reid's Factory. The brother of the deceased N. G. Hamner claimed the remains and paid all expenses. Diuguid only other entry was, "Was sent to North Garden Depot".

Hamptom - Slave of J. W. Woodson, employed by Seth Halsey, d. 08/01/64 @ Christian's Factory. "Was buried in Negro Row". "Southern Confederacy", $15.00, paid all expenses.

Hancock, Thomas J., Capt. - 21st Virginia Inf., Company A, d. 06/12/62, body shipped to Charlotte, North Carolina. Expenses paid by R. J. Wade. Hancock was a native of Charlotte County Virginia. He was born circa 1838. Enlisted on 6/20/61 at Red House, Charlotte County as a Lieut. Promoted to Capt. 04/22/62. Wife of the deceased was Mary J. Hancock.

Hanirkin, John D. - 18th North Carolina Inf., Company B, d. 06/20/62 @ College Hospital. Coffin size was 74 in. in length by 20 in. in width. He was originally buried in lot #171, grave #6, row #2. Body was exhumed and shipped to Charlotte, North Carolina. NOTE: William A. Sparks of 12th South Carolina buried that location now.

Hardaway, James H. - 18th Virginia Inf., Company G, d. 08/13/62, Diuguid made the following entry, "drowned Soldier...found in canal behind R. Station's Commission House". Diuguid also made notation of two names, "Capt. Rowlett" and "Corner Cross". He was originally buried in lot #177, grave #8, row #5. Body was exhumed and shipped to Prince Edward County, Burkville, Virginia. Compiled Service Record states, enlisted 02/28/62, "struck by shell" at Battle of Gain's Mill 06/27/62. NOTE: Joseph Daniels of Cutt's Battery, Georgia Artillery buried there 08/23/62.

* **Hardee, Isaac** - 1st South Carolina (McCreary's) Inf., Company C, d. 12/17/62 of wounds received during the Battle of Sharpsburg 09/17/62 @ Burton's Factory. Coffin size was 75 in. in length by 20 in. in width. Hardee enlisted as a Private on 08/12/62 at Conway, South Carolina. The widow of the deceased was Mary Hardee. 1860 census listed him as resident of the Hoory District.

* **Hardee, Isaac B., Corpl** - 1st South Carolina (McCreary's) Inf., Company F, d. 07/04/62 of pneumonia @ Burton's Factory. Coffin size was 74 in. in length by 19 in. in width. Hardee enlisted on 08/12/61 in Conway, South Carolina. The widow of the deceased was Susan Hardee. 1860 census listed him as resident of the Hoory District.

NOTE: It would appear that Isaac & Isaac B. were related in some manner, possibly brothers.

* **Hardman, B.** – 47th Alabama Inf., Company G, d.12/11/62 @ Knight's Factory. Coffin size was 74 in. in length by 18 in. in width. Hardman enlisted as a private on 05/14/62 at Loachapoka, Alabama. His age at enlistment was listed as 28. He was born in Alabama, married, occupation was listed as a farmer, and he was a resident of Wedowee, Alabama. He was listed as "Present for Duty" 08/09/62 at the Battle of Cedar Run. He was listed as "Absent Sick" prior to the Battle of 2nd Manassas on 08/30/62. His military records stated that his date of death was 12/14/63. I believe the date stated by the military records was recorded incorrectly.

* **Harper, Benjamin Harrison** – 6th Alabama Inf., Company A, d. 09/16/62 of disease @ Booker's Factory. Coffin size was 70 in. in length by 18 in. in width. Harper enlisted as a Private 03/05/62 at Columbia, Alabama. Muster Roll returns for the month of December 1862 stated "Sick at Richmond Va since Apr 28th, 1862." No further record.

* **Harrell, Benjamin C.** - 48th Georgia Inf., Company E, d. 06/22/63 of pneumonia @ Christian's Factory. He enlisted as a private on 03/04/62. He was wounded at the Battle of Sharpsburg 09/17/62. Born circa 1834.

* **Harris, Alexander H., 3rd Lieut.** - 47th North Carolina Inf. Company C, d. 06/09/64 of wounds @ Booker's Factory. Coffin size was 71 in. in length by 18 in. in width. He had previously served in Company I of this regiment as 1st Sgt. He was promoted to 3rd Lieut. on 04/08/64 and transferred to this company. Harris was wounded 05/08/64 at or near Spotsylvania Court House.

Harris, J. - 28th Georgia Inf., Company C, d. 06/25/62. Not listed in unit roster. No further record.

* **Harris, John** - 25th North Carolina Inf., Company G, d. 12/26/62 of smallpox at the Pest House. Coffin size was 73 in. in length by 18 in. in width. Resident of Georgia, enlisted at Athens, Georgia 4/23/62 at age 19.

* **Harris, John C.** – 11th Alabama Inf., Company K, d. 07/26/62 of disease @ Ladies Relief Hospital. Coffin size was 71 in. in length by 17 in. in width. Harris enlisted as a Private on 03/18/62 at Marion, Alabama. His age at enlistment was listed as 20. He was born in Alabama, occupation was listed as a farmer, he was a resident of Pinetuckey, Alabama and he was single. He was listed as "Absent Sick" prior the Battle of

Seven Pines on 5/31/62. His records also state that "Discharged in consequence of disease June 1862."

Harris, Nehemiah - 61st Alabama Inf., Company B, d. 07/02/64 @ William Crumpton's private home. "Was packed up & sent to Gnereton (sic), Macon County Ala.", "for coffin & packing Nehemiah Harris $225.00". Southern Confederacy paid $15.00, the balance "cash by Mrs. Wm. Crumpton $210.00".

* **Harris, Phillip Andrew Jackson** - 10th Alabama Inf., Company A, d. 06/09/64 @ Camp Davis from severe complications due to wounds received 05/06/64 at the Battle of the Wilderness. The wounds were the loss of three fingers and a minnie ball to the upper arm. He was first treated in Lynchburg at Pratt Hospital were his arm was amputated due to gangrene. His death certificate lists his cause of death as "Vul Sclopt." (gun shot wound), and his age was 25. Coffin size was 71 in. in length by 18 in. in width. Harris enlisted as a private 06/04/61 at Ashville, Alabama at age 22. He was born in Georgia, his occupation was listed as farmer, he was a resident of Bennettsville, Alabama, and he was married. Widow of the deceased was Harriet A. Harris. They were married in 1860. He also left behind one son, Phillip H. Harris that was born the spring of 1861. His widow on 03/20/65 filed a death claim. His widow could be contacted in care of Alfred Turner, Ashville, Alabama.

Harris, Thomas W. - Provost Guard City of Lynchburg, "Silver Greys Home Guard Battalion", d. 12/26/64, "Killed at Provost Office", is the only notation made by Diuguid. No specifics given as to why. Diuguid's other entry was, "Sent to Arrington Depot" (Amherst County). Harris enlisted on 11/01/62. Harris was listed present on 10/31/64 muster. Compiled Service Record states that he died of gunshot wounds. As a member of the Sliver Grays his age would most likely be in and around 40. I have not been able to locate a newspaper account or any other record as the nature of the gunshot wound.

Harris, T. H. - 1st Richmond Howitzer, Virginia Light Art., d.11/08/63 @ of disease Ladies Relief Hospital. The brother of the deceased, "Dr. Harris" claimed the remains and paid expenses. Diuguid's notations were, "was sent to Powhatan Station" and "for coffin & box for brother $50.00"

Harris, W. J – 8th Alabama Inf. Company B, d. 09/14/62 of disease @ College Hospital. Coffin size was 73 in. in length by

18 in. in width. Harris enlisted as a Private 09/30/61 at Wetumpka, Alabama for the duration of the war. His age at enlistment was listed as 30. He was married and his occupation was listed as a farmer. He was born in Georgia circa 1831 and he was a resident of Equality, Alabama. His military records list his date of death as 09/22/62. He was listed as present for duty during the Yorktown Siege, from that point until his death was listed as "Absent on Sick Leave."

Harrison, James B., 2nd Lieut. - 61st Georgia Inf., Company F, d. 06/20/64 of wounds @ Camp Davis. Coffin size was 71 in. in length by 19 in. in width. "Was packed up & sent to Georgia" was the entry made by Mr. Diuguid. The father of the deceased "Mr. Harrison" claimed the remains on 6/22/64. Diuguid's other entry was, "For tight box & packing son". Enlisted on 08/15/61, appointed Ord. Sgt. Dec. 1861; elected 2nd Lieut. 09/23/62. Harrison was wounded 05/12/64 at Spotsylvania.

* **Harrison, John W.** - 17th Georgia Inf., Company G, d. 12/06/61 @ R. A. Lee's. He is buried in lot #170, grave #6, row 1. His Address was listed as Millford P.O., Baker County, Georgia.

* **Hart, Edwin** - 5th Texas Inf., Company F, d. 11/28/62 @ Taliferro's Factory from chronic diarrhea. Coffin size was 74 in. in length by 18 in. in width. Hart enlisted as a private on 03/08/62 in Liberty, Texas.

* **Hart, James H.** – 10th Alabama Inf., Company H, d. 05/13/63 of disease @ Burton's Factory. Coffin size was 79 in. in length by 21 in. in width. Hart enlisted as a Private in early August 1862 at Calhoun County, Alabama. His age at enlistment was listed as 18. He was born in Alabama, occupation was listed as a farmer, his residence was listed as White Plains, Alabama and he was single. Per his records he was listed as "Absent Sick" prior to the battle at 2nd Manassas on 08/30/62. He remained listed as absent until his death.

* **Hartis, John H.** - 30th North Carolina Inf., Company K, d. 01/13/63 of smallpox at the Pest House. Coffin size was 74 in. in length by 18 in. in width. Hartis was captured at or near Boonsboro, Myd. on or about 09/17/62. Was confined to Ft. Delaware, transferred to Aiken's landing (Va.) 10/02/62 for exchange. His military records state that his cause of death was "Diarrhea Chronic".

* **Harvey, Albert G.** - 21st Virginia Inf., Company E, d. 06/19/62 @ Ladies Relief Hospital. Diuguid's records state,

"body sent off". He enlisted as a private on 06/19/61 at Buckingham Court House. Widow of deceased was Martha S. Harvey.

Harvel, Isaac - 42nd North Carolina Inf., Company C, d. 08/05/62 of disease @ College Hospital of disease. Body was prepared and shipped to Concord, North Carolina. Expenses paid by Capt. A. J. Howell. Private Harvel enlisted 03/17/62 at age 29, he was a res. of Stanley County, North Carolina. Diuguid's burial book recorded his last name as "Harville".

* **Hatch, John Robert (or Robert John)** - 44th North Carolina Inf., Company E, d. 10/06/63 of typhoid fever @ Langhorne's Factory. However, his military records state that he was present and accounted for through April of 64 and then listed as a deserter.

Hatton, Robert Hopkins, Brig. General - Of Tennessee was **Killed in Action** on 05/31/62 at the Battle of Seven Pines, "...in the tangled woods around Fair Oaks Station, he was killed instantly at the head of his Brigade (Archer's)." His body was prepared by Diuguid's and shipped home for burial. He was buried in Cedar Grove Cemetery, Lebanon. His death notice appears in the Lynchburg Daily Virginian 06/06/62, page 3, col. 1 (see the Transcribed notice on the next page). Capt. T. H. Bostic paid expenses on 06/05/62.

Lynchburg Daily Virginian
dated June 6, 1862
Death Notice of Gen. Robert H. Hatton
(Transcribed from the original newspaper)

LOCAL AND STATE
AFFAIRS

The remains of Gen. Robert Hatton of Tennessee, were in this city all day yesterday, and were sent to his home this morning.
They were accompanied by his late A. A. General J. Shelby Williams, and Capt. T. H. Bostic Aid-de-Camp.
General Hatton was a gallant man, and his conduct in the last battle won the admiration of President Davis, under whose eye he was. Two horses were killed under the General before he fell pierced through the heart. Gen. Hatton was talented and good as well as a brave man, and represented the Lebanon District in the last Congress of the United States, before the separation.

*   **Hayes, John Harris** – 6th Alabama Inf., Company C, d. 06/25/61 of disease @ College Hospital. Hayes enlisted 05/16/61. The 6th Alabama Inf. Was organized in May 1861. They saw early service at Corinth, Mississippi before being transferred to Virginia in late May or early June 1861. See photographs on next page of postwar tombstone erected by family for Private Hayes.

Hays, E. - 2nd Georgia Inf., Company H, d. 01/10/63 @ Ferguson's Factory. Coffin size was 75 in. in length by 19 in. in width. Hays was originally buried in lot #79, grave #6, row #4. Diuguid only has the entry, "Remove". No one by this name appears on the Georgia index for this unit.

Hayes, John Harris 6th Alabama Inf. Post War Tombstone

Hazelwood, ?, Lieut. - d. 05/30/62, Diuguid's records state "trip with hearse for Lieut. Hazelwood" - expenses paid by Henry Hazelwood. A search of present Virginia records does not list a Hazelwood, Lieut. That died in 1862.

Height, Pasham B. - Pierce's Battery, Virginia Artillery, (Capt. Jacob D. Pierce's Company, Company D, 20th Battn. Virginia Art.), d. 07/2/62 @ Samuel P. Booker's home. He was originally buried in lot #173, grave #7, row #5. Body was exhumed. Born Campbell County, enlisted 3/08/62. NOTE: J. B. Proctor of 22nd Georgia buried there now.

Helms, Solomon - 42nd North Carolina Inf., Company K, d. 07/4/62 @ Fairgrounds. Body was prepared and shipped to Charlotte, North Carolina. Expenses paid by Capt. J. Y. Bryce. Enlisted in Union County on 02/15/62.

* **Hembrey (Hembree?), Robert** - 13th South Carolina Inf., Company I, d. 09/30/62 of disease @ Reid's Factory. Coffin size was 71 in. in length by 18 in. in width. He enlisted in Richland County, South Carolina. The widow of the deceased was Lydia Hembrey. Military date of death listed as 10/11/62. Age at enlistment listed as 23. 1860 census listed him as a resident of the Spartanburg District.

* **Henderson, William H.** – 44th Alabama Inf., Company H, d. 11/04/62 of a fever @ Miller's Factory. Coffin size was 69 in. in length by 18 in. in width. Henderson enlisted as a private on 5/8/62 in Bibb County, Alabama. His age at enlistment was listed as 17. He was born in Alabama, listed as single, occupation was a farmer, and was resident of Randolph, Alabama. The following is a final statement made by Lieut. H. F. Rotenberry at Darbytown, Va. on 01/16/65. "Born in Bibb Co. Ala. Enlisted by Capt F. M. Goode at Randolph, Ala on the 3rd of Apl. 62 for 3 yrs or the war. Died at Lynchburg, Va. on 4th of Nov. 62. Never paid. Entitled to pay to the 4th of Nov. 62, at which time he died. He is entitled to commutation for clothing from the 3rd of Apl. 62 to the 4th of Nov. 62."

Hendricks, Charles T. - 7th Georgia Inf., Company D, d. 06/26/62 of chronic diarrhea @ the Warwick House. The body was prepared and shipped to Marietta, Georgia. A H. M. Whitfield paid the expenses. Private Hendricks enlisted on 05/04/61.

Hendricks, L. (Sgt.?) - 2nd South Carolina Inf., Company E, died @ Christian's Factory 12/28/62. Coffin size was 75 in. in length by 18 in. in width. He was originally buried in lot #101, grave #3, row #1. The body was exhumed 03/10/63, prepared and shipped to Greenville, South Carolina. Father of the deceased, Moses Hendricks, claimed remains and paid expenses. 1860 census listed him as a resident of the Pickens District. NOTE: W. A. Bear of 5th Virginia buried there 03/14/63.

Hendrix, Stephen - 42nd North Carolina Inf., Company E, d. 08/19/62 of typhoid fever @ Ladies Relief Hospital of typhoid fever. The body was prepared and shipped to Lexington, North Carolina. Coffin size was 72 in. in length by 18 in. in width. Henry Hendricks, father of the deceased, paid for the preparation and shipment of his son's body. He enlisted 03/18/62 at age 18 in Davie County, North Carolina.

Henly, C. M. - No Diuguid record - military records indicated that he died in Lynchburg of typhoid 09/15/62. He was a member of the 13th South Carolina Inf., Company I. 1860 census listed him as a resident of the Spartanburg District.

Henry Dablen L. - 3rd South Carolina Inf., Company I, d. 05/21/64 of wounds @ Ferguson's Factory. Coffin size was 72 in. in length by 20 in. in width. He was originally buried in lot #193, grave #1, row #4. Body was exhumed on 06/01/64, "Removed & sent to Lawrence S.C.". The brother of the deceased J. H. Henry claimed the remains and paid all expenses in cash ($100.00). He was interred in the Henry Family Cemetery. Military records list his date of death as 03/20/64. His age at enlistment was 41. 1860 census listed him as a resident of the Laurens District.

Hensley, Mahlon A., 1st Lieut. - 14th Virginia Inf., Company B, "Bedford Rifle Greys", d. 07/26/61 of disease, body was shipped to Bedford County, Virginia for burial. He enlisted as 1st Lieut. on 04/24/61 at Fancy Grove. His age at enlistment was listed as 29 and his occupation teacher.

Herlong, J. A. - 1st South Carolina Inf., Company B, d. 02/04/63 @ Ferguson's Factory. Coffin size was 76 in. in length by 22 in. in width. He was originally buried in lot #191, grave #6, row #3. Body was exhumed and shipped to "St. Matthews P.O. S.C.". Mr. Diuguid made the following notations in the "Soldiers Book", "Jacob W. Redman" and "size of coffin on top 6' 11" x 2' 1".

* **Herrin, J. T.** – 15th Alabama Inf., Company H, d. 12/14/62 @ Ferguson's Factory. Coffin size was 70 in. in length by 18 in. in width. The father of the deceased, William Herrin filed a

death claim on 03/19/63. Mr. Herrin was a resident of Sylvan Grove, Dale County, Alabama.

* Hewitt, Archer B. - Kirkpatrick's Battery, Virginia Light Artillery, d. 07/30/64 from wounds received 7/20/64 during action at Stevenson's Depot. He died at A. G. Hancock's in Lynchburg. According the diary maintained by Henry Robinson Berkeley, Hewitt died in his mother's arms within a few hours after reaching Lynchburg. Was interred in Presbyterian Cemetery, Range 15, Lot #8. Father of the deceased was H. H. Hewitt. Private Hewitt was buried on 07/31/64 at a cost of $80.00.

Hickey, Daniel - Latham's Battery, Company D 38th Battn. Virginia Light Artillery, d. 11/14/62 of disease at his father's home in Lynchburg. Cause of death not stated. Private Hickey was buried in his father's square, public burial grounds of the Old City Cemetery. He enlisted on 04/23/61 in Lynchburg.

* Hicks, James L., 3rd Corpl. – 6th Alabama Inf., Company I, d. 12/19/64 of wounds and disease @ Langhorne's Factory. Hicks enlisted as a Private 05/11/61 in Clifton, Alabama. The Muster dated 6/30/64 stated "absent on wounded furlough in Wilcox Co. Ala." Corporal Hicks in still listed on the Muster dated 02/01/65 at Camp Rodes, Va. No further information.

* Hicks, John M. - 9th Louisiana Inf., Company D, d. 05/23/62 in a Lynchburg Hospital. However, his unit records indicate he died at Stanardsville, Virginia, 1862.

Highsmith, William S. - 44th North Carolina Inf., Company C, d. 09/26/63 of chronic diarrhea @ Ladies Relief Hospital. Coffin size was 75 in. in length by 18 in. in width. J. A. Robertson of Bethel P.O. North Carolina claimed the body of Highsmith. Born and resided in Pitt County were he enlisted on 01/27/62. Age at enlistment was listed as 28 and his occupation Farmer.

* Hight, John C. - 8th Virginia Cav., Company B, d. 01/06/64 at the Norvell House as the result of a gunshot wound. The <u>Lynchburg Daily Virginia</u>, dated 01/06/64, page 2, col. 1, relates the story.

> **"DESERTED SHOT. - John Hite, a deserter from Capt. Paul's Company, of Nelson County, was shot and killed at the Norvell House in the city, yesterday by one of the Provost Guard. He was arrested last week and sent to Charlottesville, but escaped the next day and**

came here. The guard went to the hotel to take him again, when he attempted escape out the back door, and was shot, the ball passing entirely through his body, causing death in a few minutes. He had registered himself as "J. C. Carson". He was detected by Lieuts. Cabell and Boyd of Nelson, who produced the guard and attempted his arrest, resulting as stated."

Hight enlisted on 06/22/61 in Wytheville, Virginia. Compiled Service Records states that he appears on a deceased list, file #3938, amount paid $114.00.

* **Hill, John B.** – 6th Alabama Inf., Company F, d. 04/06/65 @ Camp Davis. Hill enlisted 04/30/61 at Bridgeport, Alabama. He was officially mustered into service on 5/10/61 at Montgomery, Alabama. No further record.

* **Hill, G. G., 2nd Corpl.** – 15th Alabama Inf., Company D, d. 01/02/62 of disease @ College Hospital. Hill enlisted as a Private on 07/03/61 in Ft. Browder, Alabama. His age at enlisted was listed as 45. Born in North Carolina, occupation was listed as a Wagoner, and was married. The widow of the deceased, G. S. Hill filed a death claim on 03/11/62. The claim was verified and settled on 01/20/65. Mrs. Hill was a resident of Browder, Alabama.

* **Hill, Henry G.** - 7th North Carolina Inf., Company F, d. 10/02/62 of typhoid fever @ Burton's Factory. Coffin size was 73 in. in length by 18 in. in width. The Company Muster roll states that he died of wounds on 06/30/62. The Roll of Honor states that he was killed in action at the Battle of Ox Hill on 09/01/62. Born Rowan County where he enlisted on 07/01/61 at age 19. Occupation was listed as a farmer.

* **Hill, Wilson S.** – 6th Alabama Inf., Company G, d. 07/21/62 @ Knight's Factory. Coffin size was 6 ft. 1 in. in length by 18 in. in width. Hill enlisted on 03/01/62 as a Private at Autaugaville, Alabama. A list from Autagua County transmitted to the State Comptroller by G. W. Benson, Judge of Probate, August 18, 1862 Kingston, Ala. showed that Private Hill had 4 dependents. Per Indigent Family Records his family was allowed $175.00 per year.

* **Hillhouse, Samuel Porter, 2nd Sgt.** - 2nd Rifles South Carolina Inf., Company L, d. 11/13/62 of pneumonia @ Ferguson's Factory. He was buried in lot #144, grave #9, row #1. He enlisted in the 2nd South Carolina on 04/27/62 @

Adams Run, South Carolina. However, he originally enlisted on 06/02/61 at Anderson, South Carolina, in the 4th South Carolina Inf., Company K. He was 45 years of age at the time of enlistment. He saw action at Manassas, where he was wounded, receiving a slight wound to the head. According to his Compiled Service Record he was discharged from the 4th South Carolina on 12/19/61, ". . .by reason of disability resulting from the effects of a wound to the head."

In a letter to his wife, dated July 23, 1861, he describes in some detail his head wound.

> "...I am slightly wounded in the left ear. I am mending very pert....You wanted to know how long I lay when hit by the Yankees. They never got me down. When they hit me, the ball knocked me about 2 or 3 steps and turned me around. The ball struck me in the upper part of the fold of my left ear and went through my ear and I supposed about to the skull bone. It ranged or glanced out above my ear and stuck my hat in the lining, carrying the hat about 8 or 10 steps. The bone above my ear is broke in about the width of a bullet."

Following his enlistment (2nd time) in the 2nd South Carolina he saw action in and around Richmond during the "Seven Days" and at 2nd Manassas before succumbing to the hardships associated with hard life and meager rations. On September 30, 1862 Sgt. Hillhouse wrote to his wife his final letter describing his ordeal up to that time. In part the following is that letter.

> "...I went through the fight ruins to our old fighting grounds at the Stone Bridge again, where we had a worse fight than before, two to one, and gained a bigger victory. I got cut (?) of the enemies ball, but was much jarred and jostled. I gave out 10 miles below leesburg, at which place I lay till this day one week ago. I was captured by the Yankees, but they went off and left us and never payrooled (sic) us, so then I Came up to Winchester. I had a hard

scuffle to get there. My main complaint was running off at the bowels and weakness from being broke down hard battles and hard marching and hard fare. I have nearly got over the bowel complaint, but am so weak I cannot get about much yet. Here let me say the ladies of Leesburg nursed me like a child. I don't want to ever forget John Palmer or James Beard for the assistance they gave in getting me to Leesburg and placing me in the hospital. Our army has been in Maryland and whipped the Yankees pretty well and come back to Virginia again. Our regiments are very much worn out and reduced generally very low in ranks and number, though this one has been resting for some days and are recruiting up at this time. The regiments are about 5 or 6 miles from here. I don't know were they will go next. Reports say they may fall back to Richmond. It may be possible. William McChive was killed dead on the Manassas battlefield like a soldier and Christian. George Hammond was wounded.

Now, my dear, I know you want to know how I took sad news of the death of our little girl. I jes (sic) say to you that I took a good cry and gave her up to the lord's will, I hope like a Christian ought to do. Of any of the children we have lost before, I just look at folly and crime of weeping after little children. My dear, I want you to calmly submit to the will of God. Learn the Lord's prayer and say it frequently and the little caterchisms and the ten commandments. If I ever live to come home again. I think I will get you to let us make our daily prayers for this and that if we never meet again on earth, that we with our little family may meet in heaven to enjoy the (several lines not legible) crucified but now atoning Savior. Amen" signed Sam'l. P. Hillhouse

Some time following this last letter he was transferred to Lynchburg were he finally succumb to pneumonia. At the time of his initial enlistment he was described as, 6-foot tall, gray eyes, and had dark hair. In addition, he was the father of 6 children and the widow of the deceased was Mary Hillhouse. Samuel Hillhouse was laid to rest at "9 O'clock Sunday" November the 15th in a pine coffin measuring 74 in. in length, 18 in. in width. Military records list his date of death as 12/15/62. 1860 census listed him as a resident of the Anderson District.

Hines, W. D. - 31st Georgia Inf., Company G, d. 08/15/62 @ Reid's Factory. Body was prepared and sent to Columbus, Georgia. Coffin size was 77 in. in length by 19 in. in width. Expenses paid by W. S. Ward. No one by this name listed in the Georgia index for this unit.

Hobbs, Thomas H., Capt. - 9th Alabama Inf., d. 07/22/62 - "died yesterday at residence of Mother-in-law, Mrs. Benagh". Captain Hobbs was resident of Limestone County Alabama. He was wounded June 27, 1862 at the Battle of Gaines' Mill. His funeral was conducted on 07/23/62 @ Court Street Methodist Church. He was the brother-in-law of James Benagh & A. Rucker. Captain Hobbs was a native of Alabama, however, his parents were originally from Brunswick County, Virginia. The Captain was the son-in-law of Mrs. Elizabeth Benagh of Lynchburg, Virginia. He was interred in Spring Hill Cemetery, Lynchburg, Virginia. His age at death was 35 years. A tribute was published in the <u>Lynchburg Daily Virginian</u>, dated 07/23/62, page 3, col.'s 1 & 2 and his obituary on 09/15/62, page 3, col.'s 2 & 3. On the following page is an insert for the transcribed tribute published on 07/23/62.

Hodge, Joseph P. - Staunton Battery Virginia Light Art., d. 09/05/63 @ Camp Davis of disease(?). In the Soldier Book Diuguid listed him as J. R. Hodges. Compiled Service Record showed him in the hospital at Gordonsville with typhoid fever 05/20/63, transferred to Lynchburg 8/22/63. His service record also states, in hospital through 02/64 and that he died in 1865.

<u>**Lynchburg Daily Virginian**</u> dated July 23, 1862
Death Notice of Capt. Thomas H. Hobbs
(Transcribed from the original newspaper)

Death of A Gallant Officer - We are deeply pained to announce the death of Capt. Thos. H. Hobbs, of the 9th Regiment Alabama Volunteers, which melancholy event occurred at the residence of his mother-in-law, Mrs. Benagh, in this city, yesterday morning. The deceased was a resident of Limestone County, Alabama, where he raised a company at the beginning of hostilities and came to Virginia to meet the invader. Since that time he has been constantly in the service, always at the post of duty, and prompt and faithful in the discharge of all the obligations attaching to his difficult office. During one of the recent bloody battles before Richmond, Capt. Hobbs received a severe wound in the leg which was not supposed to prove fatal - but, as above stated, it terminated his useful life yesterday morning. At home, Capt. Hobbs was a man of great popularity and influence, and as a representative of his county in the Legislature, had taken a high stand among the public men of the State. A Man of high-toned sense of honor, of pleasing manners, amiable disposition, eloquent as a speaker, of excellent information and acquirements, generous, genial, brave, chivalrous and ardent, he was eminently calculated to win the admiration and esteem of all who came within the circle of his acquaintance. No better man has fallen a victim to this war than the deceased - the sacred cause of liberty has no nobler martyr at its shrine than he. As a soldier, as a citizen, as a public man, as a husband, he was irreproachable, and in all those relations performed his duty with a fidelity and promptness rarely if ever surpassed. When the long roll of fallen heroes shall be recorded, brightly on that page will shine the name of the departed; and bright and fragrant will his loved memory be cherished by the long, long list of friends which he leaves behind him. - Peace to the noble spirit which to its final rest.

Holcombe, William Martin, Jr., 1st Corpl. - 35th Georgia Inf., Company A, d. 9/8/62 of wounds @ Burton's Factory. Coffin size was 67 in. in length by 18 in. in width. Originally buried in lot #178, grave #5, row #4. The body was exhumed and shipped to Cartersville, Georgia care of Burton Watson. Enlisted 8/15/61, appointed 1st Corpl. 7/05/62. Wounded at Cedar Mountain 9/07/62. NOTE: G. W. Byrdsong of 1st North Carolina was buried in that location 11/10/62.

* **Holland, B. F.** - 1st Texas Inf., Company B, d. 08/7/64 @ Camp Davis from wounds received 5/6/64 at the Battle of the Wilderness. He enlisted as a private on 1201/63.

Holley, Jacob L., Capt. - 58th Virginia Inf., Company E, d. 03/03/62 @ Huntersville (cause not stated), his body was shipped to Franklin County, Virginia for burial. Holley was born 07/9/39 in Franklin County. The 1860 census listed him as a student with an address Halesford P.O. He enlisted on 07/24/61 at John Pasley's. His Compiled Service Record states his death date as 02/21/62 at Huntersville of disease; his description 5' 7", dark complexion, black eyes, black hair, occupation Tobacconist. Buried in Holley Cemetery Franklin County; age at death 22.

Hollins, James E. - 11th Virginia Inf., Company A, d. 08/12/64 @ private quarters. "Was buried at his fathers in Campbell Cty". Hollins enlisted as a private on 04/22/61. His age at enlistment was listed as 20 and his occupation was listed as a Miller.

Hollomon, Mark - 17th Georgia Inf., Company K, d. 09/27/62 @ Burton's Factory. The body was prepared and shipped to Dawson, Georgia. Coffin size was 75 in. in length by 18 in. in width. No one by this name listed on the Georgia index for this unit.

* **Holloway, John** – 5th Alabama Inf., Company K, d. 08/26/62 @ College Hospital. Coffin size was 71 in. in length by 18 in. in width. Death claim was filed on 06/25/63. The claim was certified (#6384) on 01/18/64. The amount paid was $72.66.

* **Holly, Jesse J.** – 5th Alabama Inf., Company H, d. 09/03/62 @ Crumpton's Factory. Coffin size was 71 in. in length by 18 in. in width. The father of the deceased, D. Holly on 10/23/62, filed a death claim. The claim was verified and honored on 05/02/64. The father D. Holly could be contacted in care of S. Noland, Attorney, Pickensville, Alabama.

Hollycross, Harrison - 23rd Virginia Inf., Company E, d. 04/24/62 @ Booker's Factory of pneumonia. He was originally buried in lot #168, grave #10, row #3. Body was exhumed and shipped to South Boston, Virginia via the Richmond & Danville Railroad. He enlisted as a private on 03/17/62 at Whitlock's. His age at enlistment was listed as 36. Hollycross was born in Halifax County, Virginia. NOTE: J. W. Davis of 12th Georgia was buried in that location 05/07/62.

* **Holmes, James H.** - Chapman's Battery Virginia Light Art., died on or about 11/10/64, drowned to death. "Private James H. Holmes Chapmans Battery detailed on guard duty in Alleghany Cty Va was found drowned in the river above the bridge and was buried...11th Nov 1864".

Holmes, William – 15th Alabama Inf., Company F, d. 05/06/62 @ Warwick House. He enlisted as a Private on

03/01/62 at Brundridge, Alabama. His age at enlistment was listed as 22. He was born in Alabama, occupation was listed as a farmer, and he was single. Per his military records his date of death was listed as 05/15/62.

Holt, Henry A. - 42nd North Carolina Inf., Company C, d. 08/02/62 of febris typhodies @ Ladies Relief Hospital. "Was packed up & sent to Salsbury (sic), N. C.", was the entry made by G. A. Diuguid. Resident of Stanley County, enlisted in Rowan County on 02/01/62 at age 23. Compiled Service Record list his date of death as 09/12/62.

* **Holt, W. S.** - 9th Louisiana Inf., Company F, d. 07/29/62 @ Miller's Factory. Unit records state that, "died May 15, 1862 in hospital", Diuguid's records indicate that he was buried on 07/29/62. The other entry made by Diuguid was, "Tremendous large coffin".

* **Holyfield, Enoch** - 21st North Carolina Inf., Company H, d. 06/18/64, "**Killed in Action**" Battle of Lynchburg. Holyfield was buried on 06/20/64 His military record has the following entries; Enlisted 06/05/61 in Surry County at age 25. Was captured near Chancellorsville around 3rd or 4th of May, 1863. Was confined to Ft. Delaware until paroled and transferred to City Point 23 May, 63 for exchange". His record ends at this point with no additional information. The 21st North Carolina was present and engaged during the Battle of Lynchburg 06/18/64.

* **Honeycutt, William S.** - 4th North Carolina Inf., Company A, d. 09/12/62 @ Langhorne's Factory. Coffin size was 71 in. in length by 18 in. in width. He was wounded, slight wound to head at Battle of Seven Pines on 05/31/62. His military records state that he died in Richmond on the above date and no specific cause of death was stated. Enlisted in Orange County 02/26/62.

* **Hopkins, Charles W** - 32nd Virginia Inf., Company F, d. 11/17/62 @ Christian's Factory. Hopkins enlisted as a Private on 05/20/61 in Williamsburg. His age at enlistment was listed as 21. The 1860 census listed his age as 18 and occupation a sailor. Coffin size was 73 in. in length by 18 in. in width.

Hopkins, John A. - 16th Mississippi Inf., Company F (Capt. James I. Shannon's Company), died on or about 05/31/62. Compiled Service Records state that he died 05/31/62 from phithisis pulmonalis at Gen. Hospital No. 2 in Lynchburg. Hopkins enlisted as a Private on 03/03/61 at Paulding, Mississippi. The term of enlistment was for 3 years or the war.

His age at enlistment was 19. Officially muster into the service of the Confederacy on 05/31/61 at Corinth, Mississippi. Records state that the distance traveled to the rendezvous at Corinth was 247 miles. The Sept., 61 muster states that he was discharged 8/23/61. Surgeons certificate of disability dated 8/23/61 provides the following personal description; born in Jasper County, Miss., age 19, 5' 5", fair complexion, blue eyes, black hair, and occupation farmer. His mother, Nancy L. Hopkins filed an official death claim on 11/14/62. Mrs. Hopkins received $40.60 on 6/05/63

* **Hood, Daniel** – 9th Alabama Inf., Company E, d. 06/24/62 @ Ferguson's Factory. Coffin size was 64 in. in length by 18 in. in width. Hood enlisted as a Private 4/10/62 at Summerville, Alabama. He was born in Alabama, occupation was listed as a farmer, his was a resident of Summerville and he was married. He was listed as present for duty at the beginning of the Siege of Yorktown early April 1862. Per his military records he was listed as Absent Without Leave (AWOL) on 4/10/62. He was listed as AWOL the remainder of the war.

Hood, John J. - 23rd South Carolina Inf., Company G, died of typhoid fever 8/24/62 @ Ferguson's Factory. Hood enlisted as a Private on 10/17/61 in the Marlboro District, South Carolina. His age at enlistment was listed as 17. The father of the deceased was George Hood.

Horn, John J. - 42nd North Carolina Inf., Company F, d. 10/8/62 of scarlatina @ Reid's Factory. The body prepared and shipped to Salisbury, North Carolina. Private Horn's coffin size was 70 in. in length by 18 in. in width. Mr. Diuguid in the margin made the following entry, "D B Tuttorow (father-in-law)". Enlisted in Davie County at age 19 on 3/18/62.

* **Hottle, Joseph** - 5th Virginia Inf., Company K, d. 4/27/62 @ Warwick House. Conscripted on 3/23/62 at Rude's Hill. Listed as sick in Staunton Hospital 4/18/62. Hottle's total time in service 1 month 4 days.

* **Howard, Wiley** - 54th North Carolina Inf., Company G, d. 5/23/63 @ College Hospital. Coffin size was 78 in length by 18 in. in width. His military records state that he had deserted on an unspecified date but was returned to duty 11/05/62. Was listed as sick during the period of Jan. - Apr. of 63. His records state that he died 5/16/63 at Lynchburg, cause of death not specified. Was Born in Wilkes County were he enlisted at age 46 on 4/21/62. Occupation was listed as a farmer.

*** Huckabee, Thomas M.** - 14th Louisiana Inf., Company I, d. 8/6/62 @ Reid's Factory. Buried in lot #177, grave #3, row #3. Company muster roll for June 1862 stated, "absent, wounded". The August muster roll stated, "died August 26, 1862". Based on the information available, he was probably wounded at the Battle of Port Republic fought 6/9/62.

Hughes, James Matthew - 58th Virginia Inf., Company H, (Capt. George Edward Booker's Company), d. 10/4/61 of disease. Originally buried in lot #159, grave #5, row #4. Body was exhumed and shipped to Patrick County, Virginia. Remains were claimed by his brother for burial. Born in Virginia circa 1822. Not listed on muster rolls of unit. NOTE: W. S. Haynes of 19th Georgia buried their 11/11/61.

Humphrey, David Crockett - 21st Georgia Inf., Company K, d. 7/10/62 @ Christian's Factory. The body was prepared and shipped to Dalton, Georgia. Expenses paid by his brother (unnamed). He enlisted as a private on 8/28/61.

Hundley, Thaddeus M., Capt. - 3rd Arkansas Inf., Company C, d. 1/27/62. The body was prepared and shipped to Latonia, Ashley County, Arkansas. Diuguid's records list rank as Capt.; Military Records listed him with the rank of 1st Sgt.

Huneycut, Solman S. - 42nd North Carolina Inf., Company C, d. 6/29/62 @ Fairgrounds of disease. The body was prepared and shipped to China Grove, Rowan County, North Carolina. Honeycutt was a resident of Stanley County. He enlisted on 3/13/62 at age 28 in Rowan County. Expenses paid by Lieut. J. A. Howell.

Hunter, Powhatan B. - 24th Virginia Inf., Company H, d. 5/26/62 of typhoid fever @ Christian's Factory. Originally buried in lot #169, grave #6, row #1. Body exhumed and shipped to Henry County, Virginia. No date provided of removal and shipment. Hunter enlisted as a Private on 3/17/62 at Henry Court House. NOTE: T. B. Cheney of 8th Louisiana buried that location 5/27/62.

Hurlong, J. A. - No Diuguid record - military records list Hurlong as dying in Lynchburg on 2/03/64 of disease. He was a member of 1st South Carolina (Hagood's) Inf., Company B. 1860 census listed him as a resident of the Orangeburg District.

Hurt, Henry Tazewell - 58th Virginia Inf., Company I, d. 05/4/62 typhoid pneumonia @ Christian's Factory. The body was prepared and shipped home to Bedford County, Virginia for burial. Hurt enlisted as a Private 3/13/62 at Huntersville.

Irvine, Alexander - Soldier, no unit stated, d. 07/25/61. No other information listed by Diuguid. A search of military records for Virginia troops revealed a Alexander James Edward Irvine that is more than likely the individual Diuguid listed. Irvine was a member of the 2nd Va. Cav., Company G. Irvine enlisted on 05/28/61 at Forest Depot as a Corporal. He was Killed in Action 07/21/61 (shot in the head) while acting as Color Sergeant of the regiment. Per his enlistment record he was, 6' 3", light complexion, blue eyes, and blonde hair. Irvine was born in 1832. He attended VMI 1854 – 1855. His age at the time of enlistment was 30. He was listed as a resident of Bedford City, Virginia.

Isham, James K. - 23rd Georgia Inf., Company C, d. 8/22/62 @ Taliferro's Factory. The body was prepared and shipped to Calhoun, Georgia. Coffin size was 74 in. in length by 18 in. in width. Expenses paid by his father, W. H. Isham . Isham enlisted as a private on 11/01/61

* **Jackson, Isaac V.** - 19th Mississippi Inf., Company K, d. 7/4/62 of typhoid fever at Claytor's Factory. Jackson enlisted as a private on 2/26/62. The last entry in complied service records stated that he enter Richmond hospital system June 23, 1862. Widow of the deceased was Susan A. Cobb Jackson; married 7/27/56; two daughters.

* **Jackson, Prentiss** - 9th Louisiana Inf., Company C, buried in lot #170, grave #3, row #7. Company records stated that, "died in Richmond hospital 1862". However, Diuguid's records show that Private Jackson died in Lynchburg at the residence of one R. Lee and was buried on 3/1/62.

* **Jackson, William R.** - 38th North Carolina Inf., Company K, d. 6/19/64 @ Knight's Factory. Wounded in right wrist at the Battle of the Wilderness 5/5/64. Right arm was amputated at the elbow. His military record stated that he died of wounds and or "running off of the bowels". Private Jackson enlisted 4/02/64 in Moore County.

* **James, A. J. (Andrew Jackson?)** - 15th North Carolina Inf., Company K, d. 1/16/63 @ Ford's Factory of pneumonia. Coffin size was 67 in. in length by 18 in. in width. Private James was wounded in the shoulder 12/13/62 during the Battle of Fredericksburg. Enlisted as a private on 7/15/62 in

Wake County. His age at enlistment was listed as 18. He was a resident of Davidson County.

* James, Addison - 37th Virginia Inf., Company A, d. 5/1/62 of typhoid & pneumonia @ Christian's Factory. Enlisted as a private on 3/21/62 at Goodson, Virginia. His age at enlistment was listed as 29. A personal description at the time of enlistment; 6' 2", fair complexion, blue eyes, dark hair, occupation laborer. Born in Washington County, Virginia.

Jane - Slave of Col. W. H. Brown, d. 9/25/64 @ Knight's Factory. It appears she was under the employ of Dr. Randolph. "Was buried in Negro Row".

Jenkins, Charles E. - 10th Virginia Inf., Company L, d. 9/02/62 @ Burton's Factory from wounds received @ Battle of Cedar Mountain 8/9/62. Coffin size was 69 in. in length by 18 in. in width. Enlisted as a private on 8/12/61 @ Camp Johnson. The body was prepared and shipped to Orange Court House, Virginia. Compiled Service Records states he died at Gordonsville on 9/2/62. The brother of the deceased, William H. Jenkins, paid expenses.

Jennings, Abner D., 4th Sgt. - 58th Virginia Inf., Company F, d. 4/24/62 of pneumonia @ Bookers Factory. Body was prepared and shipped to Amherst County, Virginia for burial. Enlisted as private on 8/15/61 at Miller's Store. His age at enlistment was listed as 18. Born in Amherst County circa 1844. Physical description - 5' 9", light complexion, blue eyes, light hair, occupation farmer. 1860 census list his address as Buffalo Springs P.O., Amherst County, age 16, occupation farmhand.

* Jennings, John - 45th Virginia Inf., Company C, died on or about 3/25/65 @ Crumpton's Factory. Jennings enlisted as a private on 8/6/62 at Camp Williams. He was listed as a POW at the Battle of Piedmont on 6/5/64. He was a P.O.W. at Camp Morton (Indianapolis, Ind.). Per his records he was exchanged as prisoner of war on 2/26/65.

* Jennings, S. K., 3rd Sgt. – 8th Alabama Inf., Company A, d. 7/16/62 of wounds @ Crumpton's Factory. Coffin size was 71 in. in length by 18 in. in width. Enlisted as 5th Sgt. 9/1/61 at Marion, Alabama (Perry County). Age at enlistment was listed as 33. Sergeant Jennings was listed as married. He was also listed as a Physician at Marion, Alabama. Promoted to 3rd Sgt., date not specified. He was wounded 5/5/62 during the Battle of Williamsburg. The following information came from a "Descriptive list by T. R. Heard, Capt., Plantersville, Ala., Sept.

5th 64 (?)." The information was provided about Sgt. Jennings, "Age 35, dark eyes, dark hair, dark complexion, 5 ft. 8 in. high. Born Baltimore, Md. Occupation Physician. Enlisted May 8th 61 at Marion, Ala. by Capt. Y. L. Royston for period of the war. Last paid by Capt. J. A. Robbins to Feb. 28th 62. Was in the engagement at Williamsburg May 5th, 1862 and received a wound while in the line of his duty. He was 4 mos. & 17 days at $17 per month due him. Bounty $50. Clothing $25."

* **Jeter, Marion J.** – 15th Alabama Inf., Company I, d. 6/12/62 of disease @ Reid's Factory. Coffin size was 67 in. in length by 18 in. in width. Jeter enlisted as a Private on 3/1/62 at Troy, Alabama. His age at enlistment was listed as 21. He was born in Alabama, occupation was listed as a farmer, he was married and was a resident of Troy, Alabama. He was listed as "Absent Sick" prior to the Battle of Winchester on 5/25/62. The widow of the deceased, Lucy P. Jeter, filed a death claim 2/20/63. The claim was verified and approved on 2/3/65. Mrs. Jeter could be contacted in care of B. Fitzpatrick, Troy, Alabama.

* **Johns, James L., 4th Corpl.** – 44th Alabama Inf., Company I, d. 7/6/64 of wounds @ Christians Factory. Johns enlisted as a private on 4/24/62 at Arbacoochee, Alabama. His age at enlisted was listed as 29. Born in Georgia, married, occupation was listed as a farmer, and he was resident of Oakfuskee, Alabama. Johns was elected as 4th Corpl. on 5/1/62, he was reduced to the ranks 10/1/62. This was due to the fact that he was listed as "Absent Sick" between 8/30/62 (2nd Manassas) and 9/17/62 (Sharpsburg). He was listed as "Present for Duty" for the Battle of Fredericksburg (12/13/62) and the actions around Suffolk (5/3/63). He was wounded at Gettysburg on 7/2/63 and again at Chickamauga 9/19/63. He returned to his company and regiment prior to 5/6/64. On that date he was severely wounded during the Battle of the Wilderness. His left leg was amputated above the knee.

* **Johnson, George** – 47th Alabama Inf., Company K, d. 6/13/64 of wounds @ Camp Davis. Coffin size was 71 in. in length by 18 in. in width. Johnson enlisted as a private on 4/29/62 at Loachapoka, Alabama. His age at enlistment was listed as 22. He was born in Alabama, single, occupation was listed as a farmer and a resident of Dudleyville, Alabama. Private Johnson served faithfully. In his two years as a soldier he saw action at Cedar Run, 2nd Manassas, Suffolk, Gettysburg, Chickamauga, Lookout Valley, Knoxville,

Dandridge, and the Battle of the Wilderness. He was listed as "Absent Sick" for Sharpsburg (9/17/62). He was wounded in the right arm at the Wilderness. The arm was amputated in Lynchburg. His military records state that his date of death was on 7/2/64.

* **Johnson, George** - 2nd North Carolina Inf., Company F, d. 12/06/64 of pneumonia @ Knight's Factory. Detailed as a hospital guard in Lynchburg 3/27/64. Resident of Duplin County. He enlisted as a private on 8/15/62 in Wake County. His age at enlistment was listed as 30.

* **Johnson, J. F., Corpl.** - 1st South Carolina (Hagood's) Inf., Company E, d. 7/29/64 of wounds @ Christian's Factory. Coffin size was 76 in. in length by 15 in. in width. Johnson received a wound to left arm at Battle of the Wilderness on 5/6/64. His left arm was amputated.

Johnson, J. H. - 1st Virginia Artillery, d. 1/3/63 @ Capt. McCorkel's Private home. His coffin measured 72 in. in length by 18 in. in width. Diuguid's entries were as follows, "was sent to Salem, Va."..."for coffin & case for self $35.00"..."sheet & cotton $10.00". $9.00 was paid by the Southern Confederacy, the balance ($36.00) was paid by a John B. Logan. No one by the name J. H. Johnson is listed in the units of the 1st Va. Artillery.

* **Johnson, Josiah L.** – 15th Alabama Inf., Company K, d. 5/7/62 @ Ladies Relief Hospital. Johnson enlisted as a Private on 7/3/61 at Eufaula, Alabama. His age at enlistment was listed as 20. He was born in Georgia, occupation was listed as a farmer, he was a resident of Eufaula, Alabama and he was single. His military records state that he died in Haymarket, Virginia on 11/12/61.

* **Johnson, W. A.** - 4th North Carolina Inf., Company I, d. 1/25/65 @ Knight's Factory of pneumonia. His military records state the following, "Resided Randolph County and enlisted in Wake County at age 18, 19 Sept., 63. Deserted 6 Nov, 63 but was apprehended and Court Martialed (sic)19 Jan., 64. Present for duty until he died in hospital, Lynchburg..."

Johnston, William A., 2nd Lieut. - 14th Georgia Inf., Company G, d. 6/24/62 @ Claytor's Factory. Body was prepared and shipped to Isabella, Worth County, Georgia. Expenses paid in part by Dr. William O. Owens and by the deceased. Enlisted as 2nd Lieut. on 7/09/61. Johnston was admitted to Chimborazo #3 (Richmond, Va.) on 5/14/62. He was transferred to Lynchburg on 5/16/62.

Jones, George W. - 3rd Battalion (Stovall's), Georgia Inf., Company E (Captain White's), d. 10/05/61 @ Ladies Relief Hospital. Originally buried in lot #159, grave #8, row #4. Body was exhumed 12/14/61 and shipped to Burnsville, Georgia. He enlisted as a private on 8/08/61. Born in Jones County circa 1838. NOTE: William Hughey of 5th South Carolina buried there 12/15/61.

* **Jones, John H.** – 15th Alabama Inf., Company E, d. 6/17/62 of disease @ Ferguson's Factory. Coffin size was 74 in. in length by 19 in. in width. Jones enlisted as a Private on 3/3/62 at Westville, Alabama. Term of enlistment was for the duration of the war. His age at enlistment was listed as 19. He was born in Georgia, occupation was listed as a farmer, he was a resident of Daleville, Alabama and was single. The following information was taken from "Historical Roll near Richmond, Va., Jan. 3,65." "Enlisted by Capt. W. A. Edwards at Westville, Ala. on 3rd of March 1862, to serve for the War. Died at Lynchburg, Va. on the 3rd of July 1862. He was never paid, and is entitled to pay there from (sic), to 3rd of July 1862, at which time he died. He is entitled to commutation for clothing, from the 3rd of March 1862, to 3rd of July 1862 date of death." "J. R. Edwards, Lieut.", provided all the above information "Camp 15th Alabama Regiment."

* **Jones, John W.** - 1st Texas Inf., Company M, d. 6/6/64 of wounds @ Camp Davis. Jones was wounded at the Battle of the Wilderness 5/6/64. Coffin size was 72 in. in length by 18 in. in width.

* **Jones, Mosias H.** - 56th Virginia Inf., Company H, d. 9/17/62 of chronic diarrhea @ Miller's Factory. First admitted to Chimborazo (Richmond) 7/8/62, transferred to Lynchburg 8/7/62. Widow of the deceased was Susan M. Jones. A death Claim was filed 11/10/62, owed $126.33.

* **Jones, Paul** - 21st Virginia Inf., Company A, d. 12/17/62 of smallpox @ the Pest House. Jones was a resident of Charlotte County, Virginia. Coffin size was 70 in. in length by 18 in. in width. Mr. R. A. Garrett paid a large portion of burial expenses. Cost of burial was $35.00, which included "sheet & cotton.." at a cost of $5.00. The Southern Confederacy paid $9.00 of the cost, the balance was paid in cash.

Jones, Thomas, Maj. - d. 11/27/61, Mt. Zion P.O. Possibly, Thomas P. Jones, Maj., 64th North Carolina Inf. or T. T. Jones Maj./Col. 110th Virginia Militia, Franklin County.

Jones, T. S. - Poague's Battery Virginia Light Art., d. 10/6/63 @ Knight's Factory. Coffin size was 72 in. in length by 18 in. in width. Originally buried in lot #196, grave #3, row #1. Body was exhumed, and per Diuguid, "sent to South Hampton Cty Va". No one by this name listed in the index for this unit.

* **Joyce, Robert** - 56th Virginia Inf., Company E, d. 6/22/63 of chronic diarrhea @ Bookers Factory. Private Joyce left $26.00 in his personal possessions. Born 7/30/27, age at death was 1 month shy of 26 years. Married Caroline F. Thomas of Mecklenburg around 1855. The 1860 census show him residing in Brunswick County with 3 children.

* **Kagle, Henry** – 24th Georgia Inf., Company I, d. 07/31/62 @ Knight's Factory. Buried 08/02/62. Born, 1829, Hall County Ga.; Married Nancy, 10/14/52, in Hall County, father of 3 children. A search of the 24th Ga. Inf. revealed no Henry Kagle (or Cagle) enlisted. No Henry Kagle (or Cagle) was located in the existing Georgia records.

* **Keener, Abraham Lafayette (or Albert Lafayette)** - 24th Georgia Inf., Company E, d. 6/23/62 @ Christian's Factory. Coffin size was 74 in. in length by 22 in. in width by 12 in. in depth. Strange fact, the only Keener listed in the 24th Georgia was captured 8/16/64 at Deep Bottom, Virginia and was released from Elmira, New York June 21, 1865.

* **Kelly, C. H.** – 8th Alabama Inf., Company B, d. 7/16/62 of disease @ Langhorne's Factory. Coffin size was 70 in. in length by 18 in. in width. Kelly enlisted as a Private 5/13/61 at Wetumpka, Alabama. His age at enlistment was listed as 18 and he was single. His occupation was listed as a farmer. He was born in Georgia and a resident of Equality, Alabama. He was listed as "Absent Sick" prior to the Battle of Gains Mill 6/26/62.

Kelly, J. W. - 53rd Virginia Inf., Company H, d. 1/21/63 typhoid & pneumonia @ Saunder's Factory. Coffin size was 70 in. in length by 17 in. in width. Originally buried in lot #183, grave #5, row #2. Body was exhumed 2/18/63 at the request of the brother of the deceased (only listed as Mr. Kelly). Diuguid notation was, "Taken up & sent (to) Wilson's Depot SSR". "SSR" is the Southside Rail Road. Born Brunswick

County, son of Samuel D. Kelly. Enlisted in Richmond 4/06/62, occupation was listed as a student. Age at death was 19.

Kent, James Randal Jr., 2nd Lieut. - 24th Virginia Inf., Company E, d. 9/4/61 from effects of a sever cold, in his 23rd year, at the residence of John Fairfax near Fairfax Station. Native of Pulaski County, Virginia; born there 8/15/38. He was the son of Elizabeth & David F. Kent. He entered VMI in 1856 and graduated 7/4/60. His death notice appears in the Lynchburg Daily Virginian dated 9/16/61, page 2, col. 3. The body was prepared and shipped to Pulaski County, Dublin Depot Virginia for burial. Compiled Service Records state the cause of death as typhoid fever. He enlisted in service 5/27/61 @ Lynchburg, Virginia. His service records state cause of death as typhoid fever.

Key, William J. - 2nd Mississippi Inf., Company A, d. 7/29/62 @ Ferguson's Factory. Body was prepared and shipped to Blountville, Tennessee.

* **Kimbrough, J. H.** - 20th Georgia Inf., Company I, d. 1/5/63 of disease @ Ford's Factory. Coffin size was 70 in. in length by 18 in. in width. Mr. Diuguid's notation in the log was as follows, "Henreatta Kimbrough Columbus Ga." Kimbrough enlisted as a Private on 2/26/62. Was wounded at Malvern Hill 7/01/62.

Kimbrough, William H. - 31st Georgia Inf., Company B, died 8/9/62 of measles @ Maj. J. S. Langhorne's home. Body was prepared and shipped home (address not specified). Coffin size was 74.5 in. in length by 18 in. in width. J. W. Kimbrough paid expenses. Kimbrough enlisted as a Private on 10/05/61.

Kimmey, Augustus A. - No Diuguid Record - military records state that he died in Lynchburg on 5/02/64 of typhoid. No unit provided. 1860 census listed him as a resident of the Charleston District.

* **King, H. B.** – 5th Alabama Battn. Inf., Company C, d. 5/12/64 of disease @ Ladies Relief Hospital. Coffin size was 76 in. in length by 19 in. in width. Enlisted as a Private 3/26/62 at White Planes, Alabama. His age at enlisted was listed as 18 and his occupation was a Farmer. His place of birth was listed as Georgia.

King, William O. - 23rd North Carolina Inf., Company K, d. 4/19/63 @ Camp Davis. Coffin size 76 in. in length by 18 in. in width. Originally buried in lot #184, grave #7, row #1. Body was exhumed 4/30/63, prepared and shipped to Charlotte,

North Carolina. Joseph H. King claimed the remains and paid expenses for removal and packing. King was born in and a resident of Lincoln County. He enlisted in his home county on 8/20/62 for the war. Age at enlistment was 27.

* **Kirby, E. L.** - 9th Louisiana Inf., Company G, d. 5/6/62 @ the Warwick House. Buried in lot #168, grave #2, row #6. Possible brother (or relative) to G. G. Kirby.

* **Kirby, G. G.** - 9th Louisiana Inf., Company G, d. 5/1/62 @ the Warwick House. Buried in lot #168, grave #4, row #9. Possible brother (or relative) to E. L. Kirby.

* **Kirch, Jacob** - A discharged soldier, d. 12/18/62 @ the home of John Merrill. Originally from Franklin County, Virginia. A Jacob Kirch is listed as a member of 24th Virginia Inf., Company B, enlisted on 10/31/61. No further information available in his military record. The "overseer of the poor" paid burial expenses of $7.00 in full. No other information available.

Lackey, Thomas - 2nd Rockbridge Art., Capt. John A. M. Lusk Battery Virginia Artillery, d. 1/19/63 of diphtheria @ Candler's Factory. Coffin size was 76 in. in length by 22 in. in width. Originally buried in lot #183, grave #6, row #2. Diuguid's only notation in the "Soldiers Book" was, "Removed".

In the burial logbook #6 Lackey was exhumed 1/22/63. James Lackey, Father of the deceased claimed the remains. Diuguid's entry was as follows, "For removal & packing son $25.00". Born in Rockbridge County 1838. 1860 census list him living in Saunder's Store District, age 21, occupation as farmhand. Lackey enlisted as a Private on 4/01/62 at Shenandoah Mountain. In Diuguid's records the unit was listed as "Lusts".

Laird, J. W. - 23rd Virginia Inf., Company H, d. 11/11/62 @ Miller's Factory. Coffin size was 74 in. in length by 18 in. in length. Originally buried in lot #182, grave #8, row #3. Body was exhumed and shipped to Jarrett's Depot on P&W Railroad.

Point of information, no "Laird, J. W." listed in the Compiled Service Records for the 23rd Virginia. The destination were the remains were shipped is in Sussex County, due south of Petersburg (approx. 35 miles) the correct spelling of the depot is Jarratt. The P&W rail line would be the Petersburg & Weldon Railroad. Company H (Richmond Sharpshooters) of the 23rd Virginia Inf. was mustered into service in Richmond on 5/16/61.

Lambert, James Taylor - 10th Virginia Cav., a soldier at Lynchburg Depot, killed in accident on Virginia & Tennessee Railroad on 8/14/62. His age according to the obituary was 19. Body was prepared and shipped to Richmond, Virginia for burial. Coffin size was 69 in. in length by 18 in. width. Brother of the deceased was, J. Ben Lambert of Richmond. His death notice appeared in the <u>Lynchburg Daily Virginian</u> dated 8/15/62, page 3, col. 2 and a family thank you notice on 8/22/62, page 3, col. 1. The article printed on the 15th described the accident and the resulting death of Private James Lambert. The following is that article in its entirety.

"Accident On The Va. and Tenn. Railroad - Yesterday morning as the up train from this city was on its way about eleven miles above the city, the engine ran off the track, nearly burying itself in the bank of the narrow cut were the accident occurred. Five persons who were standing or sitting on the platform (three of them soldiers) were badly injured.
We could not learn the names of all the injured men, though one was T. Sprader, of Co. C 42nd Va. Regiment, whose leg was so crushed as to
 require amputation: he was doing well last night. Another was G. A. Nunenger of Bedford, it was thought would die before this morning. Another was a man named Lambeth (Lambert), of Richmond, who died whilst an operation was being performed. George Graybill, of Botetourt, a soldier who was wounded at Seven Pines, was also injured in his wounded arm.
Nobody in the cars was seriously injured. The accident was occasioned by the spreading of the track owing to defective cross ties. Nearly all the coaches were injured.
  Lambert enlisted in Richmond 6/09/61 at age 18. Born Richmond circa 1843. 1860 census listed as a resident of 3rd Ward, age 17, occupation butcher. Two brothers, John H. & William A. Lambert were as members of the 10th Virginia Cavalry.

NOTE: T. Sprader - correct name was Thomas Spradlin, d. 9/8/62 of pneumonia. George Graybill - was Sgt. George W. Graybill, Co. K, 28th Virginia Inf. Regiment (remained in hospital until Jan. 63). G. A. Nunenger, was Giles A. Nininger of the 58th Virginia Inf., Co. K; both legs were amputated at the thigh, d. 8/17/62, age 24, 5' 1" dk. complexion, dk. hair, dk. eyes.

Lanehand, **** - No unit stated, d. 8/3/61. Sarah Lanehand listed as debtor (Big Springs) and listed as wife of soldier.

Langhorne, Edward Alexander, 1st Lieut. - 28th Virginia Inf., Company F, d. 12/26/61 of typhoid fever at his home in Amherst County. Born in Amherst County 12/22/37 (24 years of age). Attended VMI Class of 1857. Death notice published in Lynchburg Daily Virginian 12/27/61, page 3, col. 1 & 2 (see the Transcribed notice, in part, on the following page). A tribute from the 28th was published 1/3/62, page 2, col. 5. Enlisted on 5/25/61 at Good's Crossing, occupation listed as Clerk. Promoted to 1st Lieut. 9/20/61.

Lynchburg Daily Virginian
dated December 27, 1861
Death Notice of Lieut. Edward A. Langhorne
(Transcribed in part from the original newspaper)

LOCAL AND STATE
NEWS

Death of Lieut. Edward A. Langhorne. We are pained to announce the death of our neighbor and friend, Lieut. E. A. Langhorne of Capt. Kent's Company, Col. Robt. Preston's 28th Regiment, Virginia Volunteers. Lieut. L, returned from camp under the influence of the prevailing fever, about two weeks since, and was confined to his bed from that time to the day of his death. All that devoted friendship and unwearied attention could avail to avert the fatal issue were brought to requisition. But the first victim from a family, which has contributed (we say it not invidiously) more, in numbers, than any other that we know of, to the common defense, had to be yielded. Lieut. Langhorne was a brave and true man; a kind neighbor and friend; good citizen; a patriot; a modest and re????? Gentleman, who was justly appreciated by a wide circle of friends who will sincerely mourn his untimely death, and that he did not live to see the ultimate triumph of that cause to which he gave his services and his life. He was in service from the first and passed through the battles of the 18th and 21st of July.

* **Langston, Jesse** – 15th Alabama Inf., Company K, d. 2/1/62 @ College Hospital. Langston enlisted as a Private on 7/3/61 at Eufaula, Alabama. His age at enlistment was listed as 23. He was born in Georgia, occupation was listed as a farmer, he was a resident of Eufaula, Alabama, and was single. His military records state that his date of death was 12/20/61.

* **Lankford, William** – 2nd Virginia Inf., Company E, enlisted @ Mt. Jackson, last entry company muster roll, dated November/December 1863, "sent to hospital March 1863 and never heard from since - supposed dead."

* **Lansford, Benjamin F.** – 47th Alabama Inf., Company H, d. 9/26/62 of disease @ Langhorne's Factory. Coffin size was 78 in. in length by 19 in. in width. Lansford enlisted as a 2nd

Sergeant on 5/5/62 at Cusseta, Alabama. His age at enlistment was listed as 21. He was born in Alabama, married; occupation was listed as a farmer, and was a resident of Milltown, Alabama. It appears that Sgt. Lansford never saw action. He was listed as "Absent Sick" prior to 8/9/62 (Battle of Cedar Run). In addition, he was reduced to the ranks on 7/1/62.

* **Langford, J. M.** – 44th Alabama Inf., Company A, d. 12/29/62 @ Saunder's Factory. Coffin size was 74 in. in length by 18 in. in width. Lanford enlisted as a private on 3/17/62. His age at enlistment was listed as 26. He was born Loundes County, Alabama, married, occupation was listed as a farmer, and was a resident of Loundes County, Alabama. Personal description, light hair, fair complexion, blue eyes and 5 ft. 10 in. in height. Based on the company muster it appears that he was never engaged in any actions. He was listed as "Absent Sick" prior to 2nd Manassas (8/30/62) up to and including the Battle of Fredericksburg (12/13/62). A death claim was filed by the widow of the deceased, May Lanford, 3/20/63. The claim was verified and approved on 7/20/64. Mrs. Lanford could be contacted in care of W. B. Hanes, Selma, Alabama.

Larrentree, Henry (or Harry) - 4th Alabama Inf., Capt. Tracy's Company, Ward Master @ College Hospital, d. 1/16/62 from an accidental gunshot wound. Buried No. 3, lot #37, Section U Spring Hill Cemetery. Larrentree was a native of Philadelphia and a dentist by profession. Death notice was published in <u>Lynchburg Daily Virginian</u> dated 1/18/62, page 3, and col. 1. See full Transcribed article on the following page.

* **Lassiter, Charles** - 2nd North Carolina Inf., Company D, d. 3/18/63 @ Ferguson's Factory of pneumonia. Coffin size was 74 in. in length by 19 in. in width. Lassiter was slightly wounded on 12/13/62 at the Battle of Fredericksburg, returned to duty that same day. He enlisted as a private on 4/12/62 in Wayne County. His age at enlistment was listed as age 22. He was a resident of Wilson County.

Latham, David L. - 14th North Carolina Inf., Company A, d. 1/16/63 of typhoid pneumonia @ Crumpton's Factory. Coffin size was 71 in. in length by 19 in. in width. Was prepared and shipped to Henderson Depot, North Carolina. A Lyman Latham (father of the deceased) paid all expenses. Mr. Diuguid's entry was, "For packing remains of son $15.00".

Born Granville County. Occupation listed as mechanic or blacksmith prior to enlisting in Northampton Count on 6/01/61 at age 26.

Lattimer, J. P. - 18th Mississippi Inf., Company D, 7. 7/10/64 @ Crumpton's Factory. "Was buried in Odd Fellow's Sq. in Spring Hill Cemetery". The cost of the burial was $125.00, the "Southern Confederacy" paid $15.00, the Odd Fellows paid $60.00, and Marshall Lodge No. 39 paid #50.00.

Lawrence, John C. - 2nd Battn. Georgia Inf., Company D, d. 12/16/62 disease @ Christian's Factory. The body was prepared and shipped to Griffin, Georgia. The brother of the deceased, B. O. Lawrence, paid the expenses. Enlisted as a private on 4/20/61.

* **Ledford, John** - 55th North Carolina Inf., Company F, d. 6/1/64 of wounds @ Knight's Factory. Coffin size was 70 in. in length by 20 in. in width. Wounded in hand at Battle of Wilderness 5/05/64. Enlisted at Camp French near Petersburg 10/11/62 at age 33. Resided in Cleveland County, occupation farmer.

Lynchburg Daily Virginian dated January 18, 1862
Death Notice of Henry (Harry) Larrentree
(Transcribed from the original newspaper)

Fatal Accident - Mr. Harry Larrentree a member of Capt. Tracey's Company, 4th Alabama Regiment, who has been acting here for some months past as Ward Master at the College Hospital, accidentally shot himself on Thursday night. The circumstances as detailed by the Surgeon are as follows.

The deceased had a small four barrel revolver in his hand, which he discharged once, in the presence of his companions, into the fire. This drew a remonstrance from the steward, who was somewhat annoyed by the explosion, when the deceased responded playfully, "there are no more loads in it - see;" or words to that effect: at the same time applying the muzzle to his mouth, he pulled the trigger, discharging the contents of the pistol in the top of head, and expired in five minutes afterwards. When the pistol was examined, it was found that every barrel was empty; and it is believed, therefore, that the deceased was under the impression that he had emptied the last barrel into the fire previous to making the rash demonstration, which resulted in his death.

What leads further to the belief that the deceased did not meditate suicide in the foolish act he committed is the fact that he had such demonstration in the presence of his companions on other occasions.

He was lively and in good spirits just previous to the commission of the act, and nothing is known to have existed in his experience or temperament that would have been likely to prompt him to self-destruction. The assistant Surgeon, Steward and one other person was present when the shooting occurred.

Mr. Larrentree was a dentist by profession, and a Philadelphian by birth.

The verdict of the coroner's jury was --------ntal (accidental?) suicide.

* **Lee, James W.** - 42nd Virginia Inf., Company E, d. 7/30/62 @ the Warwick House and was buried 7/31/62. Enlisted as a private on 6/4/61 at Salem, Virginia. His age at enlistment was listed as 17. His occupation was listed as a farmer, 5" 6", bright complexion, blue eyes, and light hair. Diuguid listed his coffin size as 71 in. in length by 19" width.

Lee, John H. - 12th Virginia Inf., Company E, d. 5/16/64 from wounds received 5/5/64 @ the Battle of the Wilderness @ Christian's Hospital. Private Lee's remains were shipped to Petersburg. Captain Samuel McCorkle paid $135.00 of the preparation and the "Southern Confederacy" paid $15.00. Lee enlisted as a private on 3/22/62. Private Lee was born circa 1838, and per the 1860 census his occupation was listed as a bookkeeper for Andrew Kevan. He was the older brother of James W. Lee.

Leftwich, William C., Lieut. - 28th Virginia Inf., Company F, d. 1/6/65 @ Burton's Factory. "Was sent to his fathers in Bedford (at) Goodes. Father of the deceased was Mr. Jack Leftwich. H. Rucker claimed the remains and paid all expenses ($180.00). William is not listed in the roster of the 28th Virginia. Possible a late war entry. At least two other Leftwichs' were members of Company F.

* **Levering, Henry** - 3rd Arkansas Inf., Newman's Company, d. 7/15/61 at a private residence. Buried in lot #158, grave #1, row #3. Father, H. Levering, Midway P.O., Hot Springs County, Arkansas.

Levi - Slave of Dr. Wise, d. 9/16/64 @ Christian's Factory. "Was buried in Negro Row".

Lewis - Slave of Richard Smiley, employed at "Reids Hosp.", d. 11/17/64 @ Reid's Factory. "Was buried in Negro Row". The "Southern Confederacy" paid expenses of $20.00 in full.

* Lewis, James M. - 46th North Carolina Inf., Company I, d. 6/18/64 of wounds @ Camp Nicholls. Purely speculation Private Lewis died from wound or wounds received during the battle for Lynchburg. Private Lewis was more than likely recovering from illness or wound in the Lynchburg Hospital system. He was a member of Cook's Brigade, Hethe's Division, A. P. Hill's Corps. During the Battle for Lynchburg he probably served in the "Convalescents Corps" under the command of Brig. Gen. Francis R. T. Nicholls. Private Lewis was born in Sampson County were here was resident when he enlisted on 3/3/62 at age 26. Occupation was listed as a farmer. His military records only state that he was present for duty until he died in hospital at Lynchburg on the above date. His cause of death was not reported.

* Libscomb Thomas H. - 13th South Carolina Inf., Company I, d. 9/21/62 of typhoid @ College Hospital. Coffin size was 77 in. in length by 19 in. in width. Age at enlistment was 28. 1860 census listed him as a resident of the Spartanburg District.

Liles, E. H. - 37th North Carolina Inf., Company D, d. 06/02/62 of disease. Diuguid did not list the hospital no other entries provided. Liles enlisted in Company D on 09/16/61 at Union County, North Carolina. His age at enlistment was 22 and was listed as a farmer. He was promoted to Sgt. 03/15/62. He was a resident of and born in Union County.

Lilly, **** - (No unit stated Prob. Louisiana), d. 8/12/61, brother of deceased, William Lilly (East Baton Rouge, Louisiana) paid for the packing and shipping of brothers remains.

Linback, J. Allen, Corpl. - 21st North Carolina Inf., Company D, d. 1/21/63 @ Miller's Factory. Coffin size was 73 in. in length by 20 in. in width. Originally buried in lot #187, grave #9, row #4. Remains were exhumed 2/12/63. Diuguid's notation was, "Taken up & sent to High Point North Carolina". George H. Flynt claimed the deceased remains, Diuguid's notation was as follows, "For removal & Packing $25.00". Mr. Flynt also claimed the remains of E. M. H. Vogler. Diuguid recorded the name as "Limback, A. J.". Born in and a resident of Forsyth County. Enlisted in his home county 5/27/62 at age 26. Occupation listed as a farmer.

* Lindsay, Joseph P. – 15th Alabama Inf., Company F, d. 7/7/62 @ Crumpton's Factory. Coffin size was 74 in. in length by 18 in. in width. Enlisted as a Private on 3/1/62 at Brundridge, Alabama. His age at enlistment was listed as 24. Born in Georgia, occupation was listed as a farmer and he was married. The father of the deceased, Dennis Lindsay filed a death claim on 9/16/62. The claim was verified and settled on 10/26/64. Mr. Lindsay could be contacted in care of B. Fitzpatrick, Troy, Alabama. The settlement of the claim was as follows, " Pay for service from March 1, 1862 to July 7, 1862 (four month and seven days at $11.00 per month) $46.56. Six months commutation for clothing $25.00. Total $71.56. Payable to Dennis Linsay, father. %W. L. Fowler, Ag't for Ala., P.O. 1508, Richmond, Va." The above settlement was approved by "T. Calbert, Assistant, Chief Clerk", on or about 11/1/64.

* Lindsey, W. B., Sgt. - 23rd South Carolina Inf., Company H, d. 12/5/62 resulting from wound to the thigh received at the Battle of 2nd Manassas on 8/30/62. Enlisted as a private on 11/10/61 at Marion, South Carolina.

* Lindsey, W. H. – 9th Alabama Inf., Company K, d. 6/9/62 @ Saunder's Factory. Enlisted as a Private 5/19/61 at Guntersville, Alabama. His age at enlistment was listed as 19 and his occupation was a farmer. He was born in Georgia, a resident of Guntersville, and was single. He was listed as "Absent Sick" prior to 4/1/62 at the beginning of the siege of Yorktown.

* Litsey, John W. – 47th Alabama Inf., Company F, d. 9/16/63 of disease @ Knight's Factory. Coffin size was 69 in. in length by 18 in. in width. Litsey enlisted as a private on 4/4/63. His age at enlistment was listed as 18. He was born in Alabama, single, occupation was listed as a farmer and was a resident of Dadeville, Alabama. Per the company musters he was listed as "Present for Duty" and "Unhurt" at Suffolk 5/3/63 thru Gettysburg 7/3/63. He was listed as "Absent Sick" prior to Chickamauga 9/19/63.

Little, Thomas H. - Macbeth's (Capt. R. Boyce) Battery, South Carolina Light Art., d. 12/9/62 @ Christian's Factory. Originally buried in lot #146, grave #3, row #3. Body was exhumed, prepared and shipped to Clinton, South Carolina. Coffin size was 77 in. in length by 18 in. in width. Another source indicates that he is buried at Duncan Creek Baptist Church, Lauren County. 1860 census listed him as resident of the Laurens District. NOTE: Wharton, Bishop, 52nd North Carolina buried in that location.

London, John J. - 19th Georgia Inf., Company D (J. D. Hunter's), d. 9/16/61 of typhoid fever @ the residence of George Lee's. Body was shipped to Morganton, Burk, County, North Carolina. London enlisted as a private on 6/11/61.

* **London, Samuel** - Phillip's Legion, Georgia Inf., Hamilton's Company, d. 10/6/61 @ Ladies Relief Hospital. Buried in lot #159, grave #2, row #5. His home was Dahlonega, Lamkin County, Georgia.

* **Long, Harry** - 33rd North Carolina Inf., Company B, d. 11/18/62 of diarrhea @ Christian's Factory. Long mustered into service 07/01/62 as a substitute (sub. For Mack Jenkins). His age at the time of mustering was 46. He was a resident of Edgecombe County, N. C.

Longcryer, Paul - 23rd North Carolina Inf., Company A, d. 3/2/63 of pneumonia @ Langhorne's Factory. Coffin size was 72 in. in length by 18 in. in width. "Packed up & sent to Younts Store N.C." Longcryer's wife (no first name given) claimed the remains. "For packing husband P. Longcrier $18.00". Diuguid's records listed the name as "Longcrier, P." Resident of Catawba County, enlisted in Iredell County 9/06/62 for the war.

Looper, William F. (M.?) - 37th Battn. Virginia Cav., Company B, d. 10/29/64 @ Ford's Factory from a wound. Coffin size was 73 in. in length by 18 in. in width. "was packed up & sent to Greenville S.C.". The wife of the deceased, Mrs. William F. Looper, claimed the remains, "For packing husbands remains $150.00". Enlisted as a private on 4/1/64 in Pickins South Carolina.

* **Loper, O. H. P.** - 13th Mississippi Inf., Carlton's Company, d. 8/3/61 @ College Hospital. Buried in lot #158, Grave #5, row #3. Uncle, E. Loper, Decator P.O., Newton County, Mississippi.

Love, James D. - 3rd Battn. (Stovall's) Georgia Inf., Company E ("Barncsville Blues"), d. 11/5/61 @ Ladies Relief Hospital. The body was prepared and shipped to Milner, Pike County, Georgia. Brother of the deceased was John Love. No one by this name is listed for this unit or in the Georgia index.

* **Lovell, William C.** - 57th Virginia Inf., Company F, d. 11/27/62 of diarrhea @ Ladies Relief Hospital. His military records indicate date of death as 2/12/63 and the place of death was Winchester, Virginia. Coffin size was 76 in. in length by 18 in. in width. Enlisted in Henry County 3/8/62.

* Lovins, Author B. - 24th Virginia Inf., Company I, d. 8/7/63 of wounds received 7/3/63 at the Battle of Gettysburg. Admitted to Lynchburg Hospital System 7/13/63. Lovins enlisted as a private on 3/10/62 in Patrick Henry County, Virginia. Born 11/33 Rockingham County, North Carolina.

Loyd, **** - Unit not stated, d. 11/01/62, N. S. Loyd paid expenses (brother or son?). Search of Virginia troops under the sir name "Loyd or Lloyd" revealed 8 individuals with that last name that did not survive war, but none under the date specified.

Lyerly, J. R. - 18th North Carolina Inf., Company C, d. 1/14/63 of febris typhoides @ Miller's Factory. Coffin size was 69 in. in length by 18" in width. Originally buried in lot #101, grave #7, row #4. Body was exhumed 2/16/63. "Taken up & sent to Salisbury N.C.", was Diuguid's notation. Moses Lyerly claimed remains, "for removal & packing...", the cost was $25.00. Born Rowan County. Enlisted as a private on 9/06/62 at Camp Hill for the war. His age at enlistment was listed as age 19. Occupation was listed as farmer.

Lyon, J. W. - 10th Alabama Inf., Company K, d. 9/7/62 on rail car of Richmond & Danville Railroad (Southern Railroad). Diuguid made the following entry, "was packed up & sent (to) Wilsonville Depot A & T River RR" (Alabama & Tennessee River Railroad). Wilsonville Depot (on the Coosa River) is approximately 30 miles west of Talladega, Alabama.

Lyon, William - 48th Virginia Inf., Company D, d. 5/16/62 @ Booker's Factory of pneumonia. Body prepared and shipped to Saltville, Virginia. Enlisted as a private on 5/18/61 at Seven Mile Ford, Smyth County, Virginia. His age at enlistment was listed as 19. 1860 census listed as age 19, occupation laborer, resident Smyth County.

Lyons, V. H. - 19th Georgia Inf., Company A, d. 10/25/62 @ College Hospital. Body was prepared and shipped to Social Circle, Georgia. Coffin size was 73.5 in. in length by 18 in. in width. William H. Owens paid the expenses. Social Circle is located approx. 50 miles east of Atlanta, Georgia on the Georgia Railroad. He enlisted 7/15/61.

Madden, John - Lee Battery Virginia Light Art., d.06/14/63 @ Home. Diuguid notation reads, "buried in his fathers Sq.

P.B. (Presbyterian Burial) ground". William Madden, brother of the deceased claimed the body and paid expenses. Madden was born in Mullin, Ireland. Enlisted as a private on 05/20/61. His age at enlistment was listed as 20 and his occupation was listed as a carpenter. Compiled Service Record states he was discharged 10/9/61. The following description is provided; dark complexion, dark hair, blue eyes, 5'8" in height.

Madison, A. N. (also Mattison) - 22nd Georgia Inf., Company E, d. 7/8/62 of pneumonia @ Burton's Factory. Coffin size was 71 in. in length by 19 in. in width. Originally buried in lot #160, grave #8, row #3. Body was exhumed, prepared and shipped to Atlanta, Georgia. Diuguid's entry was, "Removed & left with us to go to Atlanta". William P. Hunnicutt claimed the body and paid expenses. NOTE: William Warwick of Poague's Virginia Artillery is buried that location.

Malone, S. H. - 4th Georgia Inf., Company K, d. 9/23/62 @ Miller's Factory. Originally buried in lot #180, grave #2, row #2. Body was exhumed, prepared and shipped Americus County, Georgia. Coffin size was 77 in. in length by 18 in. in width. Not listed on the roster for this unit, also not on the Georgia Index.

Mandeville, Patrick J. - 19th Georgia Inf., Company F (Capt. Curtis'), d. 10/14/61 of typhoid fever @ the residence of John Brown. Body was prepared and shipped to Carrolton, Georgia (located 45 miles South West of Atlanta on the Tallapoosa River). A. Mandeville listed as the debtor. Mandeville enlisted as a private on 6/24/61.

* **Manning, Robert L.** - 12th South Carolina Inf., Company B, d. 8/7/62 of a fever in Christian's Factory. Coffin size was 71 in. long by 18 in. in width. Private Manning enlisted 8/13/61 at age 28 @ Yorkville, South Carolina. Widow of the deceased was Mary A. Manning. 1860 census listed him a resident of the York District.

Manning, Samuel - 3rd North Carolina Inf., Company D, d. 2/19/63 of phthisis pneumonia @ Candler's Factory. Coffin size was 76 in. in length by 19 in. in width. Originally buried in lot #195, grave #7, row #2. The body was exhumed 3/9/63, the remains were claimed by F. N. Manning. "Removed" and, "Sent to Kingston N.C. (2 O'Clock Friday)" were the notations made by Mr. Diuguid. Resident of Pitt County, he enlisted there 7/15/62 at age 26 for the war.

Maroney, Hacket C. - 21st Georgia Inf., Company B, d. 6/27/62 of disease @ College Hospital. Body was prepared and shipped to Rome, Georgia. Coffin size was 72 in. in length by 18" in width. Maroney enlisted as a private on 6/24/61. The cost of the coffin and preparation was $9.00. Diuguid cost for the packing the remains was $15.00. Total cost came to $24.00 and was paid in full by Mr. Maroney (father or brother?).

* **Marshall, E. M.** - 5th Texas Inf., Company E, d. 1/5/63 of small pox @ the Pest House. Coffin size was 76 in. in length by 18 in. in width. Marshall enlisted as a private on 3/22/62 at Washington, Texas. Sent to hospital 11/14/62, personal effects at death $3.00.

Marshall, Thomas J. - 2nd North Carolina Light Artillery, 1st Company G (Latham's Battery), d. 2/19/63 of typhoid fever @ Wade's Factory. Coffin size was 75 in. in length by 19 in. in width. Originally buried in lot #195, grave #9, row #2. Body was exhumed, Mr. Diuguid's notation was as follows, "Removed & sent to Morehead N.C.". Enlisted as a private in Carteret County on 1/24/62 for 12 months. Transferred to 1st Co. H, 40th N.C. Regiment (3rd N.C. Art.) in April 1862. Age at death was listed as 19.

Marshall, William (Willy) B. - 38th Virginia Inf., Company A, d. 4/2/62 of typhoid fever @ College Hospital. "Was sent home to Ringold Station, Pittsylvania Cty Va", "...Jas Murrell owes for packing". The father of the deceased was Patrick Marshall. Body was prepared (packed) and shipped to Ringgold Station, Pittsylvania County, Virginia on or about 4/9/62. Marshall enlisted as a Private on 5/30/61 in Kentuck, Virginia.

* **Martin, John S.** - 22nd North Carolina Inf., Company B, d. 5/08/63 @ Burton's Factory. Coffin size was 75 in. in length by 18 in. in width. Resident of McDowell County, enlisted 7/08/61 at age 20. Was hospitalized in Lynchburg with pneumonia 4/07/63.

Martin, Thomas F. - 4th Georgia Inf., Company I, d. 5/26/64 of wounds @ Ladies Relief Hospital. Diuguid's entries were as follows, "Packed up & sent to Oglethorp Macon Cty Ga", "Sent off 31st of Oct 1864". Private Martin's remains must have been packed in charcoal and kept on hand; there is no record of him being buried in the city cemetery. The brother of the deceased, Lieutenant Robert Martin paid the expenses for having his brother transported home ($150). He enlisted 5/12/62. Wounded @ Wilderness on 5/05/64.

Buried in Mt. Zion Baptist Cemetery in Macon County, Georgia.

* **Martin, Waitman G., Sgt.** - 55th North Carolina Inf., Company G, d. 5/25/64 @ Knight's Factory of wound. Coffin size was 74 in. in length by 19 in. in width. Wounded in leg at Battle of Wilderness 5/05/64. Born Johnson County and enlisted at age 23 on 5/03/62 in either Johnson or Wayne County. Had been promoted to the rank of Sgt. on the day he was wounded.

* **Mason, Anderson F.** - 22nd South Carolina Inf., Company K, d. 9/18/62 of typhoid fever @ Miller's Factory per the Diuguid records. However, his military records state the death date to be 1/18/63. The mother of the deceased was Jane Mason.

Mason, Jacob - Virginia Reserves, Company B, d. 6/2/64 @ Camp Nichols. Diuguid's entry was, "Was buried in private lot". Also Diuguid made a notation referencing "Col. Burk".

* **Mason, Jeremiah J.** - 110th Virginia Militia, Capt. Joseph LaVenders Company (this Militia unit became Company F "Jeff Davis Guards" 20th Virginia Inf. on 5/29/61, and then was transferred as Company A, 57th Virginia Infantry per Special Order #285 dated 9/23/61). J. M. Mason is listed in Company A of the 57th, age 41, occupation farmer, discharged 5/24/62; height 5' 10", ruddy complexion, sandy hair, & gray eyes. Private Mason is buried in lot #170, grave #6, row #4. His death notice appears in the <u>Lynchburg Daily Virginian</u> on 4/5/62 page 3, col. 1.

Masters, Franklin A. - 37th North Carolina Inf., Company I, d. 2/16/63 of pyemia @ Saunder's Factory. Coffin size was 73 in. in length by 18 in. in width. The father of the deceased A. L. Masters claimed the remains. Diuguid made this entry, "was packed up & sent to Salisbury N.C.". Resident of Mecklenburg County, enlisted in Iredell County on 8/15/62 for the war. His age at enlistment was listed as 24.

* **Matlock, S. S.** - 3rd Tennessee Inf., Company C, d. 8/30/61 @ Ladies Relief Hospital. Father of the deceased was Jason Matlock, "...a Baptist Preacher 3 miles from Benton".

* **Matews, Aaron J., Sr.** - 6th Georgia Inf., Company E, d. 6/27/62 @ Ferguson's Factory. His military records state that he died June 24, 1862 in Danville, Virginia.

* **Matthews, George D.** - 6th South Carolina Inf., Company E, d. 2/15/63 of Small Pox @ the Pest House. Coffin size was 72 in. in length by 18 in. in width. Military records list his date of

death as 6/15/63. His age at enlistment was listed as 35. 1860 census listed him as a resident of the York District.

May, John D. - Soldier transferred to Liberty, Virginia. Not listed on any roster of Bedford County Units.

* **May, Silas M.** - 37th North Carolina Inf., Company A, d. 12/20/62 @ Burton's Factory of typhoid fever. Coffin size was 74 in. in length by 18 in. in width. Was wounded in arm at Battle of Fredericksburg 12/13/63. Was a resident of Ashe County, enlisted 8/15/62 in Iredell County at age 18.

* **Maybin, Thomas M.** - 15th Alabama Inf., Company G, d. 05/11/62 of disease @ Ladies Relief Hospital. Maybin enlisted as a Private on 3/4/62 at Abbeville, Alabama. His age at enlistment was listed as 19. Born in Georgia, occupation was listed as a farmer, he was a resident of Abbeville, Alabama and he was single. Per Diuguid's record the father of the deceased was Henry Maybin of Abbeville, Alabama. Maybin served two months and 7 days in the army and was never involved in any engagements.

Meador, John A. - 58th Virginia Inf., Company E, d. 09/04/62 @ Miller's Factory. Body was prepared and shipped to Franklin County, Virginia. The father of the deceased was Joel Meador. Trip expenses were paid by a Billy Gordon on 9/7/62, as recorded by Mr. Diuguid. Born in Virginia circa 1837. 1860 census list his address as Halesford P.O., Franklin County, age 23, occupation Factory Laborer. Enlisted as a private on 7/24/61 at John Paslet's. Cause of death not listed.

Meador, John J. - 58th Virginia Inf., Company D, d. 5/15/62 @ E. S. Ferguson's from typhoid pneumonia. Body was prepared and shipped to Lick Depot (Roanoke), thence to Franklin County, Virginia. Coffin size was 71 in. in length by 18 in. in width. He entered the Lynchburg Hospital system 4/20/62. Born (circa) 1843. Per the 1860 census his occupation is listed as a farmhand, res. Franklin County, Bandbrook P.O. Enlisted in service 7/23/61. Private Meador was the son of Paschal Meador, and the brother of George W., & James O. Meador. His personal description is as follows; age 18, 5' 8", light complexion, light hair, and blue eyes.

Meeks, Lafayette W. - 2nd Virginia Cav., Company H (Appomattox Rangers), d. 9/04/61 of typhoid fever at Flint Hill of Fairfax Court House at age 19. Father of the deceased F. Meeks, "paid for packing remains of son". Death notice published in the <u>Lynchburg Daily Virginian</u> dated 10/10/61, page 2 col. 3., "...in 19th year of his age near Fairfax Court House". Joel Walker Flood commanded company H. Even through Diuguid does record the location of burial, he was returned to Appomattox Court House for burial and rest within the National Park Grounds at the Surrender Grounds. Meeks enlisted as a Private on 5/24/61 @ Appomattox Court House at age 18, occupation listed as merchant. His death notice published on 10/10/61 can be seen below on this page.

* **Meeks, Thomas J.** – 15th Alabama Inf., Company E, d. 10/11/62 of disease @ Ferguson's Factory. Coffin size was 74 in. in length by 18 in. in width. Meeks enlisted as a Private on 3/3/62 at Westville, Alabama. His age at enlistment was listed as 24. He was born in Georgia, his occupation was listed as a farmer, was a resident of Barnes Cross Roars, Alabama and was single. His military records listed his date of death as 5/12/62 at "Standonsville, Va." The actual name of the town was Standardsville, Va. just North of Charlottesville.

Lynchburg Daily Virginian dated October 10, 1861
Death Notice of LaFayette W. Meeks
(Transcribed from the original newspaper)

DIED

Near Fairfax Court House, on the 4th of October, 1861, after an illness of some four weeks, in the 19th year of his age LA FAYETTE W. MEEKS, in the bloom of youth and in the discharge of the sacred and patriotic duty to defend his country against her ruthless invaders.

The writer knew Fayette (as he was familiarly called) well, and take great pleasure in saying that he was highly esteemed by all who knew him, as an honest, upright young man, against whose fair character no reproach was ever uttered.

He very early, after the breaking out of war, attached himself to Capt. Joel W. Flood's Company of cavalry, and in the month of May last, left his parents and his home, to join the Confederate Army. Never will the citizens of Appomattox who were present forget the parting scene on the occasion of Capt. Floods' company leaving. All of us felt that In all human probability some of our friends in that company would never return to mingle among us and enliven the social circle. Fayette was among the number that on the 31st of May last bid adieu to parents and friends and to home, for the "tented field" never to return. He has gone the way of the earth, and now in his last resting place, he fills a patriot's grave, and the large crowd of persons who were presented to pay the last tribute of respect to his memory attests their sympathy with his bereaved parents. Fayette was an obedient and affectionate son, and the idol of his parents.

The writer has been informed by his comrades that he was a good soldier, ever ready for any duty imposed upon him and beloved by all his officers and comrades in-arms.

May his early death in the Springtime of his life serve as a warning to his comrades and parents, and induce them to be prepared to meet the Judge of all the earth.

A FRIEND

*** Meem, James Lawrence, 1st Lieut.** - 11th Virginia Inf., Company G, **Killed in Action** 5/31/62 @ Battle of Seven Pines. His age at death was 26. His death was listed in a causality list published in the Lynchburg Daily Virginian on 6/2/62 page 3, col. 2 a lengthy obituary was published on 6/17/62 page 3, col. 2. His obituary was in excess of 1,500 words (written by Charles L. Mosby). Meem was the youngest son of John G. and Eliza C. Meem, born 4/02/36 in Lynchburg. He entered VMI in July 1853 and graduated in July of 1856. He later attended the Univ. of Virginia. Following his graduation, in 1858 he spent time in France and England. From Europe he proceeded to Brazil and was employed as an engineer during the construction of the Don Pedro II railroad. In 1859 he returned home and attended the Univ. of Virginia. Meem was a member of the Lynchburg Home Guard prior to 1861. On March 7, 1860 Meem was elected as Company Orderly Sgt., filling the vacancy due to the resignation of Robert M. McKinney (former VMI Class Mate). Enlisted 4/23/61 in Company "G", "Lynchburg Home Guard", with the rank of Orderly Sergeant. Promoted to Lieut. on 5/18/61 and to the Adjutant of the 11th Va. on the same date. Appointed to adjutant-general on or about 5/01/62 of Samuel Garlands Brigade. His promotion coincides with the promotions of Samuel Garland Jr. from Capt. to Colonel and to Brig. General.

Metcalf, S. A., Corpl. - 54th North Carolina Inf., Company I, d. 6/4/63 of fever @ College Hospital. Coffin size 78 in. in length by 19 in. in width. Originally buried in lot #188, grave #6, row #1. Body was exhumed, and "sent to Polk Cty N.C.".

Enlisted in Lenoir County for the war on 7/17/62. Promoted to Corpl. 12/30/62. Discharged from service on the same date as his death.

Milam, William P. - 60th Georgia Inf., Company H, d. 1/8/63 of measles @ Miller's Factory. Coffin size was 70 in. in length by 18 in. in width. Originally buried in lot #79, grave #7, row #5. Body was exhumed 1/11/63 and shipped to Kingston, Georgia. Diuguid's entry was, "For removal & packing son $25.00". The father of the deceased Riley Milam paid expenses in full. Diuguid listed the name as "Millan". He enlisted as a private on 4/25/62. His age at enlistment was listed as 18. Buried in Euharlee Presbyterian Church Cemetery. He was born 2/28/1844.

* **Milford, G. T. (or James T.?)** - 12th South Carolina Inf., Company F., d. 1/16/63 of disease @ Taliaferro's Factory. Coffin size was 72 in. in length by 18 in. in width. A second South Carolinian "James T. Milford" of the 2nd South Carolina, also Company F, and share the same date of death. Both are listed in the 1860 census from the Abbeville District. Possibly both are the same person. Diuguid's recorded the name as "G. T. Milford" in the logbook, it very possible it was a recording error.

* **Miles, John** – 47th Alabama Inf., Company H, d. 8/22/62 of disease @ Ferguson's Factory. Coffin size was 71 in. in length by 19 in. in width. Miles enlisted as a private on 5/5/62 at Cusseta, Alabama. His age at enlistment was listed as 18. He was born in Alabama, single, occupation was listed as a farmer and was a resident of Milltown, Alabama. He was listed as "Absent Sick" prior to 8/9/62 (Battle of Cedar Run).

* **Miller, Atwell** - 33rd Virginia Inf., Company F, d. 8/20/62 of fever @ Crumpton's Factory. Was assigned to Company "F" on 4/8/62. He was admitted to (one of the) Gen. Hospital in Lynchburg 7/1/62. Per Compiled Service Record, Pvt. Atwell Miller was "admitted to Chimborazo (Richmond, Va.) on 5/3/63 with debility; returned to duty 5/21/63". (No further record on Private Miller)

Miller, John R., Jr. - Ringold Battery, 13th Battn. Virginia Light Art., d. 7/25/63 of typhoid fever @ Burton's Factory. Coffin size was 72. in length by 18 in. in width. Originally buried in lot #188, grave #3, row #5. Diuguid's only entry was "Removed" no other information supplied. Born Pittsylvania County 1844. Miller enlisted as a Private at Danville for the war 2/15/62. A death claim was filed the father of the deceased, John Miller on 12/12/63. A total of $88.38 was received for back pay, bounty & clothing. The following was a description of Private Miller, 5' 8", light complexion, light hair, blue eyes, unmarried, occupation farmer.

Miser (Myser), John S. - 5th Virginia Inf., Company K, d. 1/24/63 of typhoid fever @ Saunders Factory. Coffin size was 70 in. in length by 18 in. in width. Originally buried in lot #187, grave #7, row #2. Two notations are adjacent to the deceased name, "Removed" and "Staunton Va". Born Augusta County, occupation farmer. Enlisted as a private on 3/23/62 at Rude's Hill. Age at death listed as 27. Buried at Mt. Tabor Lutheran Church Cemetery, Augusta County. Note: John Jenkins of the 14th North Carolina was buried in that location 7/23/63.

Mitchell, John F. J., Orderly Sgt. - 11th Virginia Inf., Company A, **Killed in Action** at Battle of Frazier's Farm (6/30/62). John was the eldest son of Captain Robert & Mary Ann Mitchell. Sergeant Mitchell was buried in Spring Hill Cemetery 7/3/62. Appears in Lynchburg Daily Virginian on 7/3/62, page 2, col. 3 and his obituary on 7/9/62, page 3, col. 1 (the Transcribed notice is on the following page). Funeral services were conducted from his father's residence (corner of 5th and Madison Street) on 7/03/62 at 9 o'clock. He enlisted as a private on 4/22/61 at Lynchburg. His age at enlistment was listed as 22. His occupation was listed as an Architect. Promoted to Sgt. 5/24/61. He was born in Lynchburg 10/26/38. (His age at death was 23).

* **Mitchell, Pryon M.** - 12th Alabama Inf., Company B, d. 4/4/62, as the results of a fall @ Ladies Relief Hospital. Mr. Diuguid made the following notation, "killed by falling from window". Death notice was published in the Lynchburg Daily Virginian on 4/5/62, page 3, col. 1. The notice read as follows; *"Distressing Causality - Mr. P. M. Mitchell, a member of Co. B 12th Alabama Regiment, who was confined by indisposition, at the Ladies Relief Hospital*
in this city, while delirious with fever, threw himself from the sixth story of the building, yesterday morning, about seven o'clock, and was instantly crushed to death." The father of the deceased, John Mitchell on 7/24/63, filed a death claim. Mr. Mitchell was listed as the administrator and his address was Socopotoy, Alabama. The claim was verified and approved 1/28/65.

Lynchburg Daily Virginian dated August 9, 1862
Obituary of John F. Mitchell
(Transcribed in part from the original newspaper)

OBITUARY

John F. Mitchell fell mortally wounded in the battle before Richmond, on Monday evening, June 30th, 1862, whilst leading a charge the company he had temporary in command. After the fighting subsided on that night, a comrade of the deceased shouldered his precious remains and carried them nine miles to the city of Richmond. His remains were then brought to Lynchburg where his funeral services were numerously attended, after which all that was mortal of him was laid besides loved members of his family who sleep in Spring Hill Cemetery.

John F. was the eldest son of Robert and Mary Ann Mitchell, born in the city of Lynchburg, on 26th Oct'r, 1838, and at his death not quite 24 years of age. As a youth he was good, kind and affectionate boy, deeply attached to parents and home. He made rapid progress in his studies when young, particularly in mathematics, drafting and architectural...   When the war broke out he was one of the first that rallied under the flag of the Confederacy, and left here as a member of the Rifle Greys, Co. A, 11th Virginia Regiment, on the 23d of April, 1861. A few weeks thereafter he was elected to the post of Orderly Sergeant in his Company,...He served through the campaigns of the Army of the Potomac and of the Peninsula, and participated in the terrible battles of Williamsburg and Seven Pines, fighting bravely through both engagements. He was always at his post, in rain or sunshine, in winter or summer.

But a few weeks ago being detailed to attend to some Government business here, he seized the opportunity and united himself in holly wedlock to one whose troth he had long since plighted....   ...His memory will be cherished as a chivalrous volunteer, whose history will be written in letters of gold upon the hearts of those liberties he sacrificed himself to defend.

Lynchburg, July 8th, 1862

* **Montgomery, R. B.** – 9th Alabama Inf., Company A, d. 10/4/62 of wounds @ Reid's Factory. Coffin size was 71 in. in length by 20 in. in width. Montgomery enlisted as a Private on

5/18/61 at Mobile, Alabama. His age at enlistment was listed as 30. He was born in Alabama, occupation was listed as a laborer. Montgomery was a resident of Mobile and was listed as single. He was listed as present for duty at Yorktown, Williamsburg and at Seven Pines. He was listed as severely wounded on 6/27/62 at the Battle of Gains Mill. A second entry in his records states that, "Died of wounds received June 30th 1862, at Gordonsville, Va. Nov. 15th 1862."

* **Moody, Joel** - 1st South Carolina (Orr's Rifles) Inf., Company E, d. 11/01/62 of disease @ College Hospital. Coffin size was 74 in. in length by 18 in. in width. Military records list his date of death as 9/01/62. His age at enlistment was 35. 1860 census listed him as a resident of the Pickens District.

Moon, Dilmus J., Corpl. - 9th Georgia Inf., Company C, d. 5/28/64 of wounds @ Miller's Factory. His coffin size was 74 in. in length by 18 in. in width. Originally buried in lot #197, grave #5, row #5. Exhumed in January 1866, "Removed & sent to Atlanta Ga". Diuguid's Log #7, page 256. He enlisted 9/22/61. Wounded at Cedar Mountain 8/9/62. He was appointed Corpl. prior to May 1864. Wounded @ Wilderness 5/06/64. Died from complications after the amputation of a limb (not specified).

* **Moon, John S., 5t Sgt.** - 38th Georgia Inf., Company H, d. 10/01/64 @ Christian's Factory. His coffin size was 71 in. in length by 18 in. in width. Was originally a member of the 15th Georgia Inf., Company I. Was discharged in Richmond 10/25/61 due to disability. Enlisted in 38th Georgia 3/01/62. Appointed 5th Sgt. in December, 1863.

* **Moore, J. F.** – 15th Alabama Inf., Company L, d. 5/17/62 of disease @ Ladies Relief Hospital. Coffin size was 74 in. in length by 20 in. in width. Moore enlisted as a Private on 3/11/62 at Perote, Alabama. His age at enlistment was listed as 26. He was born in Georgia, occupation was listed as a farmer, he was a resident of MT. Hilliard, Alabama, and he was single. Moore served 3 months 6 days in the army and was never involved in any engagement.

* **Moorman, George Washington** - 15th Alabama Inf., Company D, d. 4/29/62 @ Ladies Relief Hospital. Death notice published in the <u>Lynchburg Daily Virginian</u> on 5/1/62, page 3, col. 1.

* **Morgan, John L.** - 9th Louisiana Inf., Company C, d. 7/22/62 @ College Hospital. Was originally buried in lot #161,

grave #1, row #4. Body was claimed by brother James Morgan, exhumed, prepared and shipped to Bienville Parrish, Mount Lebanon, Louisiana. Coffin size was 6' in length by 19" in width. The Company Muster states, "died Lynchburg, Va. July 20, 1862 of disease".

Morgan, William C. - 28th Virginia Inf., Company G, Capt. Minter's Company d. 12/25/61 of Measles @ College Hospital. Original buried in lot #170, grave 4, row 2. "Taken up 17th Jany 62 & sent to Bedford Cty Va.". Private Morgan was from the Chestnut Fork area of Bedford County. His approximate age based on the 1860 census would be 24. Enlisted as a private on 4/27/61 at Chestnut Fork, Virginia. His age at enlistment was listed as 23. Occupation was listed as a farmer. The deceased was the son of Thomas Morgan of Bedford County, Virginia. An Unknown Soldier now buried in this location on 1/27/62.

* **Moore, Green W.** - 9th Virginia Inf., Company H, d. 8/4/62 of typhoid fever @ Taliaferro's Factory. Enlisted as a private on 6/19/61 at Fletcher's Chapel, Lunenburg County, Virginia. Private Moore's entire company was transferred to the 28th Virginia Inf. Battalion 5/8/62. No further record.

* **Moore, James A.** - 2nd South Carolina Inf., Company C, d. 1/3/63 of fever and pneumonia @ Ladies Relief Hospital. Coffin size was 72 in. in length by 19 in. in width. Widow of the deceased was Mary Moore.

* **Moore, John Charles** - 6th Louisiana Inf., Company K, d. 3/2663 in jail. Mr. Diuguid's entry was as follows, "John Charles alias King alias Moore died in jail". His name is not included among the soldiers listed in the main burial book, only in the "Soldiers Book".

Moore, Owen - 31st Georgia Inf., Company I, d. 9/22/62 from wounds @ Christian's Factory. Body was prepared and shipped home to Mr. Green Moore, Brainbridge, Decatur, Georgia. Coffin size was 74 in. in length by 18 in. in width. He enlisted 11/11/61. Wounded at Cold Harbor 6/27/62. Diuguid listed his first name as "Oren".

* **Moose, William A.** - 4th North Carolina Inf., Musician, d. 6/26/64 from gunshot wound @ Knight's Factory. Was detailed as a musician and transferred from Company K of this regiment between Sept & Oct. of 1861. He was prem. Transferred to the regimental band 2/11/63. His military records do not indicate were he received his wound. It is very possible that he could have been mortally wounded at the Battle for

Lynchburg 6/17-18/64. Soldiers in the Lynchburg Hospital system that were in the "convalescents" stage of recuperation were mustered together and used in the defense of the city.

* **Morris, Joshua S.** - Portsmouth Battery, (Carey F. Grimes' Batty.) Virginia Light Art., d. 10/22/61 at Mr. Parrish's home. Interred in Presbyterian Cemetery, John Purvis's Lot #13.

Morris, S. J. - 16th Mississippi Inf., Company F, d. 5/23/62 @ Sauer's Factory. Body was prepared and shipped to DeSoto, Clark County, Mississippi.

Morrow, George Washington - 44th Alabama Inf., Company D, d. 11/18/62 Christian's Factory. Originally buried in lot #144, grave #6, row #1. Coffin size was 6 ft. in length by 20 in. in width. Body was exhumed 2/11/63, prepared and shipped to Monticello, Alabama. Thomas L. Morrow, brother of the deceased, claimed remains. Note: A. S. Sons of the 15th South Carolina buried in that location on May 11, 1863.

* **Moynehan, Cornelius** - 7th Louisiana Inf., Company D, buried in lot #172, grave #5, row #4, compiled service records state, "Killed June 9, 1862". Diuguid's records indicate that he died on or about 6/26/62 at Reid's (Factory) Hospital. It would appear that he was severely wounded in the Battle of Port Republic on June 9, 1862, transported to Lynchburg, and dying later that same month in the hospital of his wounds.

Munday, Jesse Y. - 45th North Carolina Inf., Company I, d. 1/21/64 of pneumonia @ Langhorne's Factory. Coffin size was 75 in. in length by 18 in. in width. Originally buried in lot #200, grave #7, row #3. "Removed & sent to South Boston Depot R & D RR (Richmond & Danville Railroad)". Resident of Person County where he enlisted at age 34 on 5/03/62.

Munnerlyn, Robert N. - 23rd North Carolina Inf., Company A, d. 11/25/62 of enteritis @ Ford's Factory. Originally buried in lot #100, grave #6, row #2. There are no specific records of exhuming this soldier by Diuguid's, however, the body must have been exhumed and buried elsewhere. Born in Anson County, resided in and enlisted in Montgomery County on 9/23/62. NOTE: George W. Stanley of the 57th Virginia Inf. was buried there 11/30/62.

* **Murphy, Thomas J.** - 13th Georgia Inf., Company I, d. 1/26/63 of Pneumonia @ Knight's Factory. Coffin size was 77 in. in length by 18 in. in width. Private Murphy had been wounded at Sharpsburg on 9/17/63. His death was more than likely connected to his wound.

* Murray, James Hilliard – 7th North Carolina Inf., Company E, d. 02/08/64 of smallpox @ the Pest House. Diuguid listed the name as "Murry" with no first or middle name. Private Murray enlisted 08/03/61 at Alamance County at age 45. He was wounded at Gains Mill 06/26/62 and returned to duty 03/31/63. He was wounded a second time at Gettysburg on 07/03/63. The 7th was a part of Lane's Brigade, Pender's Division, 3rd Corps. On the 3rd the 7th was a part of Pickett's Charge. They suffered 11 KIA, 61 WIA, and 67 POW's. Private Murray returned to duty 09/30/63 and was placed on light duty 12/04/63. Private Murray was a resident of Nash County, North Carolina.

Murrell, John H. - 11th Virginia Inf., Company G "Lynchburg Home Guard", was **Killed in Action** 05/31/62 @ Battle of Seven Pines. Buried in Lynchburg 06/05/62. Death Notice Appeared in the <u>Lynchburg Daily Virginian</u> dated 6/6/62 page 3, col. 1. The notice read as follows, *"The remains of the late John Murrell, of the Home Guard, who was killed in the battle before Richmond, were brought to this city, and interred yesterday. He was a most worthy young gentleman."* He enlisted in Company G of the 11th Virginia on 3/10/62.

Myers, Fredrick W. - 6th Virginia Cav., Company E, d. 5/12/62 @ Ferguson's Factory of rubeola. Body was prepared and sent to Pittsylvania County, Virginia. He enlisted as a private on 4/01/62.

* Myers, Henry L. - 21st Georgia Inf., Company C, d. 5/30/62 @ Ferguson's Factory. Coffin size was 70 in. in length by 18 in. in width. Private Myers' name last appears on the Company Muster Roll dated 8/17/64 in the remarks col., "Dropped from rolls - was ordered from hospital". No further military records

McAlphin (or McCalpin), Joseph M. - 1st Rockbridge (Virginia) Light Artillery, d. 2/28/63 of pneumonia @ Christian's Factory. Coffin size was 76 in. in length by 18 in. in width. "Was sent to mouth of North River", was the entry made by Diuguid in the Soldiers Book. **Wounded in Action** at Fredericksburg, amputation of foot. Buried in Falling Springs Church Cemetery, Rockbridge County. Enlisted in Lexington 3/3/62. "A fine soldier", "Brave, generous, frank; truthful and noble in nature, he won the hearts of everyone associated with him". Born Rockbridge County 7/21/35. Diuguid's entry in the main burial log was, "For coffin & box for self $15.00".

* McAulay, Hugh E. - 37th North Carolina Inf., Company C, d. 5/23/62 of "Febris Typhoides" @ the Warwick House. Coffin size was 77 in. in length by 21 in. in width. Diuguid had his name recorded as McCauley. Born Mecklenburg County, were he resided until his enlistment 9/16/61 at age 21. His occupation was listed as a farmer.

McCallay (or McCauley), William P. - 60th Georgia Inf., Company B, d. 8/9/62 @ Burton's Factory. Originally buried in lot #161, grave #4, row #2. Body was exhumed and shipped to LaGrange, Georgia. Diuguid made the following notation, "Taken up 15th Aug & sent to Le Grange (sic) Geo". In addition, Mr. Diuguid has the name "John Scott" in parenthesis. William was the son of William & Susan Fish McCalley (William Sr. died in 1848). Private McCallay's coffin size was 70 in. in length by 18 in. in width. The inscription on his head stone reads, "In Memory of William McCalley, Jr. Born Nov. 27, 1842 Died Aug. 8, 1862 In Lynchburg, Va." (McCalley Cemetery Land Lot #217, 4th Land District, Troup County, Georgia). Note: J. W. Wise of 38th North Carolina buried in that location on 8/15/62.

McChristian, Sam - Virginia Conscript, d. 10/15/63 @ Knight's Factory. Coffin size was 76 in. in length by 18 in. in width. Originally buried in lot #200, grave #2, row #5. Diuguid's entry was, "Removed & sent Amherst C. House Va". No other information.

* McClendon, Burwell – 10th Alabama Inf., Company A, d. 6/11/62 of disease @ Booker's Factory. Coffin size was 74 in. in length by 19 in. in width. McClendon enlisted as a Private 3/1/62 at Ashville, Alabama. His age at enlistment was listed as 21. He was born in Alabama, occupation was listed a farmer, he was a resident of Ashville, Alabama, and was married. He was listed as present for duty at the outset of the siege of Yorktown 4/1/62. He was listed as "Absent Sick" at the Battle of Williamsburg on 5/5/62.

* McClendon, H. - 31st Georgia Inf., Company K, d. 8/1/64 @ Christian's Factory. Coffin size was 73 in. in length by 17 in. in width. Enlisted as a private on 8/12/61. His Compiled Service Record states, "Absent with leave", dated August 31, 1861. No further information.

McClung, Charles Bell, Jr. - 11th Virginia Cav., Company I, d. 9/27/64 of typhoid fever @ Christian's Factory. Coffin size was 70 in. in length by 17 in. in width. Diuguid's entry was, "was packed up and sent to Rockbridge". Diuguid's burial logbook had the following entry, "Est. of Charles H. McClung, for coffin & packing remains of self $300.00, For cotton furnished $3.50", total amount $303.50. The "Southern Confederacy paid $15.00 and Capt. Samuel S. McCorkle paid $288.50 in cash. Born in Rockbridge County circa 1824. Had prior service in Company A of 11th Va. Cavalry. Listed as wounded at Gettysburg 7/?/63. No record of a discharge in records. Enrolled as conscript on 4/02/64 in Richmond. Was assigned to 11th Va. Cav. on 4/04/64. Was listed as present 4/01-30/64. He owned his own horse appraised at $850.00. Compiled Service Records states that was absent sick with dysentery 7/09/64 thru 7/18/64. His records indicate that the cause of death was from a wound but does not specify any date. He left a widow, no name available.

* **McCloud, Elisa, Sr.** - 31st Virginia Inf., Company E, d. 6/15/64 @ College Hospital of disease. Enlisted 3/31/62 in Allegheny County, Virginia. Listed as AWOL 4/62 on march from Shenandoah to Valley Mills; apparently served with the 62nd Virginia, Imboden's Command, before returning to the 31st Virginia.

McClure, Noah B. - 37th Virginia Inf., Company H, d. 5/2/62 of diarrhea @ Christian's Factory. Originally buried in lot #168, grave #5, row #2. Body was taken up, prepared and shipped to Glade Springs, Virginia. Enlisted as a private on 7/24/61 at Abingdon, Virginia. His age at enlistment was listed as 18. Note: A. Q. Adams of the 15th Alabama buried there 5/6/62.

* **McCool, William** - 2nd South Carolina "Rifles" Inf., Company A, d. 11/1/64 of chronic diarrhea. Coffin size was 70 in. in length by 18 in. in width. Enlisted as a private at Balls Gap, Tennessee on 2/19/64.

* **McCord, John Thomas** - 2nd Battn. Georgia Inf., Company D, d. 6/26/63 of smallpox at the Pest House. Coffin size was 68 in. in length by 18 in. in width. His military records state only that he died in Lynchburg, no dates or other information.

McCormick, Rollin S. - 38th Virginia Inf., Company C, d. 3/16/62 @ College Hospital of pneumonia. He was admitted in Lynchburg 3/4/62. Private McCormick's body was prepared and shipped to Pittsylvania County, Virginia. He enlisted as a private on 5/30/61 at Laurel Grove, Virginia.

McCoy, Henry - d. 2/5/64 of smallpox, "Negro Hospital Nurse". Burial expenses paid by Southern Confederacy, $25.00. Buried in Negro's Row.

McCready, Edwin H. - Soldier, unit not stated, d. 7/29/61. Diuguid records listed John H. Oury as debtor and also stated that the coffin was returned.

* **McCullough, Nathaniel** - 60th Georgia Inf., Company I, d. 8/06/62 @ Burton's Factory. Coffin size was 75 in. in length by 18 in. in. width. He enlisted on 5/06/62 as a substitute for J. B. Wheeler.

* **McDade, Benjamin Franklin** - 21st Georgia Inf., Company C, d. 4/29/62 of congestion @ Saunder's Factory. He enlisted as a private on 6/26/61. McDade was born 1811, age at death was approximately 51.

McDaniel, William H. - 48th Virginia Inf., Company F, d. 4/26/62 of pneumonia @ Warwick House Hospital. Originally buried in Lot #168, grave #2, row #5. Body was exhumed, prepared and shipped to Bristol, Tennessee. He was born 2/27/1839 in Washington County, Virginia. McDaniel enlisted as a Private on 6/15/61 at age 22. Detailed as teamster 2/28/62. He was 23 years of age at the time of his death. Note: John E. Gizer, 8th Louisiana, Company B, now buried in that location.

* **McDermott, Addison** - 22nd Virginia Inf., Company G, d. 7/6/64 of disease @ Langhorne's Factory. Enlisted as a private on 3/5/64 at New Castle, Virginia. His personal effects were turned over to the regimental Quarter Master.

* **McDonald, (also McDonold) Charles** - 12th Virginia Cav., Company I, d. 10/3/63 of febris continua communis @ Christian's Factory. Coffin size was 79 in. in length by 20 in. in width. Death possibly was the result of a wound received 6/21/63 at Upperville, Virginia.

* **McDonald, Harvey** - 12th Virginia Cav., Company I, d. 11/6/64 of chronic bronchitis @ Knight's Factory. Coffin size was 75 in. in length by 20 in. in width. Enlisted as a private on 1/22/64 at New Market, Virginia. His Military records state that he died in Gen. Hospital #2.

McDonald, G. W., Sgt. - 3rd South Carolina Inf., Company F, d. 8/15/62, @ Langhorne's Factory. Originally buried in lot #165, grave #8, row #3. Body was exhumed, prepared and shipped to Clinton, Lauren District, South Carolina. Coffin size was 73 in. in length by 18 in. in width. Note: G. B. Adams of 3rd North Carolina was buried in that location 5/30/63.

McKinney, Bartlett M. - Wise Legion, Company H, d. 12/31/61 @ Ladies Relief Hospital. Body was prepared and sent to Halifax County, Virginia. Expense, paid in part by

George W. McKinney, Mt. Laurel P.O., Halifax County, Virginia. As best can be determined this young man was more than likely a member of the 2nd Regiment Inf., Wise Legion. Company H of the 2nd Regiment was transferred and became part of the 59th Va. Infantry that was organized 11/1/62. In the muster of the 59th is a B. W. McKinney that enlisted as a private on 7/11/61 in Halifax County, Virginia. That date coincides with the date the 2nd Regt., Company H "The Bruce Rifles" were organized. B. W. McKinney was listed as age 18 at his enlistment. No further record.

* **McKinney, Robert M., Col.** - 15th North Carolina Inf., d. 4/16/62 (Wednesday), **Killed in Action** @ Lee's Mill, Virginia (Yorktown Defenses). By one source Col. McKinney received a bullet to the head during the initial action against a Vermont Regiment. Buried in the Presbyterian Cemetery, Range 2, Lot #4. Colonel McKinney's obituary appears in the Lynchburg Daily Virginian dated 5/10/62, page 3, col. 2 and also in the Petersburg Express on 4/18/62. Son of Thomas M. McKinney, Esq., was born in Lynchburg 2/15/35. Entered VMI in 1852, graduated on 7/04/56. Following his graduation Mr. McKinney opened a male school in Lynchburg, which he continued until March 1860. At that time he accepted the position as professor of French at North Carolina Military Inst. in Charlotte, North Carolina. Prior to moving to North Carolina he was a pre-war member of the "Lynchburg Home Guard" serving as the company Orderly Sergeant. He resigned that position on 3/07/60. Captain of Company A 6th North Carolina Inf., 5/16/61; Colonel 15th North Carolina 6/24/61.
  NOTE: When the 6th North Carolina arrived in Lynchburg in the spring of 1861 for training, McKinney's arrival was announced in the local newspaper.

  McLaurin, D. McQ. - 23rd South Carolina Inf., Company G, d. 8/25/62 @ Ferguson's Factory. Originally buried in lot #178, grave #9, row #3. Coffin size was 77 in. in length by 18 in. in width. Body was exhumed, "packed up & sent to Laurenburg, Richmond Cty, N. C.". Diuguid also has a notation, "to move Monday". Without a doubt that Monday would have been Dec. 8, 1862. W. H. Clark of the 18th North Carolina buried in that location 12/6/62, a Saturday.

* **McMillian, Warren J.** - 6th Virginia Cav., Company G, d. 5/14/62 of Icterus @ Warwick House Hospital. Coffin size was 71 in. in length by 18 in. in width. McMillian enlisted as a

Private on 8/19/61 at age 27. Name was also listed as McMillen.

McNew, John - Abingdon Provost Guard, d. 8/8/64. "Found dead on V&T Rail Road (car)". Pronounced dead @ Wayside Hospital. Coffin size was 75 in. in length by 20 in. in width. Originally buried in lot #198, grave #9, row #2. Body was exhumed on 8/14/64. Bother of the deceased Daniel McNew claimed the remains. Diuguid made this entry, "sent to Garden Springs Depot". Was unable to locate any military (Virginia) record on this soldier. The "Provost Gurad" was a Home Guard unit from Abingdon (Washington County). The unit was formed in the fall of 1862 and commanded by Capt. J. G. Martin.

* **McPherson, Jesse A.** - 61st Virginia Inf., Company B, d. 8/18/64 of febris interimittens quotidiana. Wounded in right thigh 7/3/63 @ Gettysburg. Returned to duty early 1864. Hospitalized 5/6/64 "intermitten fever" @ Charlottesville, transferred to Lynchburg 6/6/64.

* **McSwain, John** – 15th Alabama Inf., Company E, d. 8/29/62 of disease @ Crumpton's Factory. Coffin size was 68 in. in length by 18 in. in width. Diuguid listed his last as "McSween." McSwain enlisted as a Private on 3/3/62. His age at enlistment was listed as 18. He was born in Alabama, occupation was listed as farmer, he was a resident of Newton, Alabama and he was single. His military records state his date of death as 5/28/62 and place of death as "Standonsville, Va." The actual town name would have been Standardsville, Va. just North of Charlottesville, Va.

* **NeSmith, Robert P.** – 5th Alabama Inf., Company K, d. 5/25/62 @ Ferguson's Factory. Coffin size was 68 in. in length by 18 in. in width. His widow on 12/10/62 filed a death claim. The claim was not verified and honored until 1/26/65. Martha J. NeSmith widow of the deceased could be contacted in care of N. B. Clark, Attorney, General Hospital, Petersburg, Virginia.

Neuffer, **** - Unit not stated, d. 8/14/61. Per Diuguid's records he was from South Carolina. The father of the deceased, Harman F. Neuffer, paid the expenses "for packing corpse of son".

Neville, Brandon P. - 11th Virginia Inf., Company H, Musician, d. 10/3/62 as a result of wounds received 8/30/62 at Battle of Manassas. Enlisted as a private on 5/15/61 in

Lynchburg. His death notice appears in <u>Lynchburg Daily Virginian</u> on 10/14/62 page 3 col. 2. Capt. Pleasant Labey & the Southern Confederacy paid funeral expenses. The Obituary printed on Oct. 14th read as follows; "**Died in this city on the 3rd inst., BRANDON P. NEVILLE, from effects received at the second battle of Manassas. The deceased was a member of the 11th regiment Va. Volunteers, and participated in the battles with his regiment up to the time of his death and was a brave and efficient soldier.**"

* **Newman, William G.** - 58th Virginia Inf., Company A, **Wounded in Action** on 8/9/62 at Battle of Cedar Run (also Cedar Mountain), d. 9/13/63 @ Burton's Factory from result of wound(s). Newman enlisted as a Private on 7/25/61 at Bunker Hill, Virginia. Born Bedford County, Virginia 1839. The 1860 census listed his occupation as Farmhand, res. Davis Mill P.O. Bedford County. Description - 5' 5", fair complexion, light hair, blue eyes, age 23. Private Newman's coffin measured (externally) 69 in. in length by 18 in, in width. Brother of James H. Newman - James was captured 1864, P.O.W. at Elmira New York, d. 12/21/64 of pneumonia.

Newsom, Edmond T. - 37th North Carolina Inf., Company D, d. 9/5/62 of typhoid fever @ Claytor's Factory. Body was prepared and shipped to Charlotte, North Carolina. Coffin size was 70 in. in length by 18" in width. Born and resided in Union County were he enlisted on 9/16/61 at age 20. Listed as a POW between 5/27-28/62 at Hanover Court House. Confined at Ft. Columbus in New York Harbor. Paroled and transferred to Aiken's Landing on the James River and received there 7/12/62 for exchange. Officially exchanged on 8/05/62.

* **Newsom, John R.** - 1st Texas Inf., Company G, d. 7/7/62 of typhoid fever @ Christian's Factory. Coffin size was 70 in. in length by 19 in. in width. Enlisted as a private on 3/17/62 at Palestine, Texas, age 19.

Nichols, Jesse Griffin, 1st Lieut. - 58th Virginia Inf., Company I, d. 11/7/61 @ Staunton (Hospital). Diuguid only made the following entry, "Nov. 10, 61 trip to Bedford with Lieut. Nichols". Expenses were paid J. C. Adams.

Lieutenant Nichols was more than likely railed to Lynchburg, prepared by Diuguid, and taken to Bedford County for burial. Born circa 1835, per the 1860 census, age 25, Davis Mills P.O., Bedford County. Enlisted in Liberty City (Bedford) 7/24/61.

* **Nicholson, Sylvester** - 8th Florida Inf., Company D, d. 12/27/62 of fever @ Claytor's Factory. Buried in lot #101, grave #2, row #5. Coffin size was 73 in. in length by 18 in. in width. Diuguid made the following notation, "by mistake his coffin is labeled J. Otom". Enlisted with his brother Robert 4/12/62 @ Columbus. Born circa 1843. His widowed mother, Ann, & 3 children appear on a list of needy families seeking assistance during the war.

Nixon, Thomas R. - 27th North Carolina Inf., Company F, d. 1/3/63 of chronic diarrhea @ Burton's Factory. Originally buried in lot #162, grave #7, row #5. Diuguid's only entry was, "Removed & sent to Boykin Depot". Nixon enlisted as a Private on 7/01/61 in Perquimans County.

Noel, James H. - 11th Virginia Inf., Company E, d. 4/4/65 @ Crumpton's Factory. "Was buried in his fathers lot" (location not specified, no other information supplied by Mr. Diuguid). Private Noel enlisted 6/6/61 at age 21, occupation carpenter. Compiled Service Record end stated that private Noel was sick 11/64 and was given a furlough for 60 days.

* **Norris, J. R.** - 14th South Carolina Inf., Company A, d. 1/02/63 of pneumonia @ Taliaferro's Factory. Coffin size was 75 in. in length by 19 in. in width. Norris enlisted as a Private 8/10/61 at age 35. Widow of deceased was Susasanna E. Norris. Another enlistment record shows his age as 23. 1860 census listed him as a resident of the Darlington District.

* **Norwood, J. C.** – 48th Alabama Inf., Company I, d. 10/15/62 @ Knight's Factory. Coffin size was 66 in. in length by 16 in. in width. Based on Diuguid's coffin dimensions Private Norwood was very small, approximately 5' 3" in height by approximately 13" in width and his weight was no more than 90 to 100 pounds. Norwood enlisted as a private on 4/26/62 at Abernathy, Alabama. His age at enlistment was listed as 19. He was born in Georgia, single, occupation was listed as a farmer and he was a resident of Kemps Creek, Alabama. It appears that a death claim was filed 10/27/63. Certificate #10599 was received on 1/18/64. However, the residence of the claimant could not be "ascertained." The claim in the amount of $87.33 was delivered to Col. James Lawrence Sheffield, commanding the 48th Alabama.

Nunn, Crockett - 4th Virginia Inf., Company C, d. 4/27/62 of pneumonia @ Christian's Factory. Body was prepared and shipped to Dublin Depot, Virginia. The compiled Service Records states he enlisted 3/17/62 and died 5/8/62 in Lynchburg of pneumonia. Company C was from Pulaski County, Company A was formed in Wythe County.

Nutt, R. R. - 57th North Carolina Inf., Company I, d. 4/13/63 @ Candler's Factory. Coffin size was 69 in. in length by 16 1/2 in. in width. R. T. Nutt claimed body and paid expenses. "Was packed up & sent to Haw (?) River N.C.".

* **Obarr, J. Hezekiah (or O'Barr)** - 15th Georgia Inf., Company H, d. 7/03/63 of chronic diarrhoea @ Miller's Factory. Coffin size was 71 in. in length by 18 in. in width. Captured at Carrsville, Va. May, 1863. Paroled at Ft. Monroe May 13, 1863. Exchanged at City Point May 23, 1863.

Ochiltree, David Leech - 52nd Virginia Inf., Company E, d. 4/27/62 of pneumonia @ Christian's Factory. Originally buried in lot #168, grave #10, row #3. His body was exhumed, prepared and shipped to Rockbridge County, Virginia. David A. Ochiltree (the father) paid for the removal, packing and shipment of his son's body. He was buried at the High Bridge Presbyterian Church Cemetery near Natural Bridge. His age at death was 21. David was the brother to Thomas Alexander Ochiltree. Born Rockbridge County 9/13/40. He enlisted in Staunton on 8/01/61. NOTE: J. W. Davis of the 12th Georgia buried in that location 5/7/62.

Ochiltree, Thomas Alexander - 52nd Virginia Inf., Company E, d. 7/24/62 of typhoid fever @ Christian's Factory. His coffin size was 69 in. in length by 17 in. in width. Originally buried in lot #162, grave #1, row #3. His body was exhumed, prepared and shipped to Rockbridge County, Virginia for burial at High Bridge Presbyterian Church near Natural Bridge. Thomas was born in Rockbridge County 3/1/-29. Personal description, age 20, 5' 5" in height, fair complexion, gray eyes, light red hair, occupation farmer. Enlisted @ Camp Alleghany 3/20/62. NOTE: Sgt. John M. Danielly of the 6th Georgia Inf. was buried in that location 8/8/62.

* **O'Donnell, Peter** - 24th Virginia Battn. Cav., Company B, d. 7/22/62 of a gunshot wound at Ladies Relief Hospital. Diuguid recorded the following, "Shot in a fray 21st July 62". Coffin size was 73 in. in length by 20" in width.

* **Oliver, Pleasant** - 11th Virginia Inf., Company H, d. 4/22/62 @ his home in Amherst County. Was buried in Strangers Square in the Presbyterian Cemetery. Occupation Blacksmith, age 45.

* **O'Neal, W. R.** – 14th Alabama Inf., Company F, d. 1/12/64 of Small Pox @ the Pest House. O'Neal enlisted as a Private on

2/27/63 at LaGrange, Georgia. His occupation was listed as a farmer. The following was taken from his military records, "Descriptive List deceased member's dated near Orange County Court House Virginia March 23 1864." "Due government $55.60 for clothing." "Bounty paid $50.00."

Organ, John H., Sgt. - 11th Virginia Inf., Company C, d. 8/13/61 of disease. Company muster reported him as absent and sick in June of 61. Age 29, occupation farmer, address was Pigeon Run, Campbell County, Virginia. Father of deceased was James Organ. Enlisted as a Sergeant on 5/16/61. His occupation was listed as a farmer.

* **Osborne, Thomas J.** - 1st South Carolina (Orr's Rifles) Inf., Company D, d. 5/19/64 from wounds received 5/5/64 during Battle of the Wilderness. He was wounded in the head, bone on right side fractured by piece of exploding shell. Enlisted as a private on 3/17/62 at Anderson, South Carolina.

Otis, James - 23rd South Carolina Inf., Company F, d. 11/13/62 @ Ferguson's Factory from wounds received at the Battle of 2nd Manassas 8/29/62. Enlisted as a private on 10/17/61 at Chester, South Carolina.

Orenburn, William H. - 2nd Rockbridge Battery, Virginia Light Artillery, d. 7/29/62 of typhoid fever @ Ford's Factory. Coffin size was 74 in. in length by 18 in. width. Originally buried in lot #162, grave #9, row #5. His remains were exhumed, prepared and shipped to Rockbridge County, Virginia. Enlisted as a private on 7/16/61 @ Fairfield, Virginia. Born Rockbridge County circa 1831. 1860 census lists as age 29, occupation farmer, res. South River District of Rockbridge County. Note: G. D. Howell of 31st Georgia was buried in that grave 7/30/62.

Otey, George Gaston, Capt. - Captain in command of Otey's Battery, Virginia Light Artillery, d. 10/ 21/62 at the residence of his mother in Lynchburg. Funeral was conducted at 4th Street Methodist Church. His death notice appears in the <u>Lynchburg Daily Virginian</u> dated 10/22/62 page 3, col. 1. A tribute to Capt. Otey was published in the <u>Lynchburg Daily Virginian</u> dated 11/14/62. The following excerpt is taken from that tribute.

> "He reached this city a few days since, suffering from disease induced by hardships of the campaigns and which has terminated his valuable life."

Otey entered VMI in 1851 as a part of the Class of 55 (did not graduate). Resigned to become a merchant in Richmond. Personal wealth listed at $1,700.00 in 1860. He was 29 years of age at his death, born 5/25/34, the son of John and Lucy W. Otey. He was the grandson of Maj. Isaac Otey, member of the Virginia Senate. Otey was listed as Orderly Sgt. in Company H (Richmond Howitzers) 1st Virginia 1859-60. Adjutant of 1st Va. Inf. in Feb. 1861. Muster into State service with 1st Va., Provisional Army of Va. on 5/25/61. Formed Otey's Battery 3/22/62 and elected Captain. His Battery served under Gen. Loring in the Western Theater at the time of his death. Captain Otey was wounded 5/24/62 @ Lewisburg. Returned to duty by early July of 62. One account indicates that a carbuncle at the base of his spine was the initial cause of his illness a subsequent death. On 11/23/63 a death claim was filed by Daniel B. Lucas, Atty. for his wife Mary E. "Morgan". He had 2 daughters. He had six brothers that served in the Confederacy, Col. Kirkwood Otey (Class of 1849) 11th Va. Inf., 2nd Lieut. Samuel Dexter 2nd Va. Cav. (d. 8/20/63), Capt. Van Renselar Commander Lynchburg Public Guard (d. 09/13/64), Capt. Walter Hays (Class 1859) Light Art. Company, John Marshall & Maj. Peter Johnston Otey (both Class of 1860) 30th Va. Sharpshooters Battn.

Otey, Van Renselar, Capt. - Provost Marshall of Lynchburg, d. 09/13/64 of disease. He was buried in Spring Hill Cemetery. At the outbreak of war he enlisted 05/13/61 in Company B, 2nd Va. Cav., as 3rd Sergeant. His age at enlistment was 34, occupation listed as farmer. Appointed to 2nd Lieut. 8/27/61. Listed as absent on detail with Gen. J. E. B. Stuart 10/01/61 through 01/06/62. Appointed as Captain & Commander of the Lynchburg Public Guard 3/22/62. Remained as Commander through 12/62. Otey was born 4/25/27.

Overton, J. R. - 23rd North Carolina Inf., Company G, d. 12/05/62 of typhoid fever @ Reid's Factory. Coffin size was 71 in. in length by 19 in. in width. Originally buried in lot #122, grave #6, row #2. His body was exhumed 12/12/62, prepared and shipped to Kittrell, Grandville County, North Carolina. He enlisted in Wake County 7/08/62 for the war. Resident of Granville County. Note: S. Bexley of the 22nd North Carolina was buried in this location on 12/12/62.

Overton, J. W. - 12th North Carolina Inf., Company K, d. 1/2/63 of pneumonia @ Candler's Factory. Coffin size was 72 in. in length by 18 in. in width. Originally buried in lot #79, grave # 10, row #3. Body was exhumed 2/2/63 at the request of John Overton, Father of the deceased ("taken up & sent to Franklinton's, Franklin Cty N.C."). Diuguid's entry was "For removal & packing of sons remains $25.00". The location/address supplied was Lewisburg, Franklin County, North Carolina. Resident of Franklin County where he enlisted at age 24 on 5/24/62 for the war.

* **Overtrout, Preston** - Died 9/10/62 @ Christian's Factory, buried in lot #178, grave #5, row #2. Diuguid's records state that he was from Rockingham County, Virginia, and was a member of a Company J, no other information was available. Research indicated that he was possibly a member of Company I, "The Rockingham Confederates", 33rd Virginia Infantry. The letters I & J were often confused when transcribed.

* **Owens, Adolphus, Sgt.** – 9th Alabama Inf., Company D, d. 5/16/64 of wounds @ Knight's Factory. Coffin size was 73 in. in length by 17 in. in width. Owens enlisted as a Private 5/27/61 at Oakland, Alabama. His age at enlistment was listed as 20. He was born in Kentucky, occupation was student and was a resident of Paducka, Kentucky and was listed as single. His military records show his only rank as Private, Diuguid listed him as a Sergeant. This young warrior was present during 12 major engagements from 1862 to 1864. He saw service at Yorktown, Williamsburg, Seven Pines, Gaines' Mill, Frayser's Farm, 2nd Manassas, Sharpsburg, Fredericksburg, Salem Church, Gettysburg, Mine Run, and Wilderness. He was severely wounded at Gettysburg 7/3/63 and returned to duty prior to Mine Run on 12/1/63. His was mortally wounded 5/6/64 at the Battle of Wilderness.

* **Owens, Ezra S., Sgt. (?)** - 26th Georgia Inf., Company M, d. 8/24/62 @ Miller's Factory. Owens enlisted as a private on 8/13/61. Diuguid's records and the military records differ. Owens compiled service records states, "wounded and disabled at Gettysburg 7/3/63, and wounded again 8/31/64, no other records. It is very possible that there were two Ezra Owens in Company N of the 26th Georgia (father and son).

* **Pace, William H.** - Captain Garden's Company, South Carolina Light Artillery, d. 12/12/62 of pneumonia @ Langhorne's Factory. He enlisted as a private on 6/1/62 in Sumter, South Carolina. His age at enlistment was listed as

34. The widow of the deceased was Elizabeth S. Pace. 1860 census listed him as a resident of the Sumter District.

Paden, William J. - 7th Georgia Inf., Company H, d. 8/1/62 @ Ferguson's Factory. Enlisted 5/21/61, per his Complied Service Records he was discharged for disability in August 1862.

Padgett, Arenton R. - 19th South Carolina Inf., Company A, d. 5/23/63 of smallpox at the Pest House Hospital. He was captured after the Battle of Stone River, Tennessee on 1/5/63. Exchanged by the Union on 1/9/63. The widow of the deceased was Lucinda Padgett. His age at enlistment was listed as 26. 1860 census listed him as a resident of the Edgefield District.

Padgett, William M. - Amherst Battery, Capt. Thomas J. Kirkpatrick's Battery Virginia Light Artillery, d. 5/29/62 @ Mr. Coffee's Home. Body was prepared and shipped to Bedford County, Virginia for burial. Padgett enlisted as a private on 4/01/62 at Orange Court House. 1860 census shows him a resident of Amherst County, age 14, and a student.

Painter, Arthur R. - 48th Virginia Inf., Company C, d. 4/25/62 @ Ladies Relief Hospital of pneumonia. Body was prepared and shipped to Abingdon, Virginia. Enlisted in Washington County on 6/18/61 at age 18. 1860 census list his occupation as apprentice bricklayer, res. Washington County, Virginia, and his age was list as 19.

Palmer, F. M. - 1st Georgia Inf., Company H, d. 4/5/62 @ Ladies Relief Hospital. Compiled Service Records show that he enlisted 3/18/61. Private Palmer was mustered out & Discharged of service at Augusta, Georgia on 3/18/62. No further information available.

Pamplin, **** - No unit stated by Diuguid, the remains were handled by Diuguid on 12/27/61. Father of the deceased was Nicholas Pamplin of Pamplin's Depot, "coffin and box for son". This is possibly Corpl. Peter R. Pamplin of the 18th Virginia Inf., Company H. Corporal Pamplin died of typhoid fever at his home, per his service record, on 12/25/61. Born 07/17/38, occupation tanner. Enlisted in Company H on 05/07/61. He was buried in the Pamplin family cemetery, Pamplin, Virginia.

Parker, Jaby - 6th South Carolina Inf., Company K, d. 7/25/64 of wounds @ Camp Davis. Coffin size was 74 in. in length by 19 in. in width. Age at enlistment was listed as 28. 1860 census listed him as a resident of the Williamsburg District.

* Parker, M. Turner - 14th South Carolina Inf., Company B, d. 2/17/63 of ascities @ Christian's Factory. Coffin size was 67 in. in length by 17 in. in width. Age at enlistment was 22. 1860 census listed him as a resident of the Edgefield District.

Parks, J. M. - 17th South Carolina Inf., Company K, d. 11/20/62 @ Claytor's Factory. Originally buried in lot #122, grave #10, row #2. Body was exhumed, prepared and shipped to Chesterville, South Carolina. Coffin size was 73 in. in length by 18 in. in width. In the margin Mr. Diuguid has written this name, "(W. C. Gwinn). Note: E. M. Hall of the Palmetto Sharpshooters, South Carolina was buried in that Location 12/06/62.

* Parson, George W., Sgt. - 17th Virginia Cav., Company H, d. 6/19/64 from wounds @ Ladies Relief Hospital. His coffin size was 73 in. in length by 17 in. in width. His wound was received 6/18/64 during the Battle for Lynchburg from a bursting shell. His age at death was around 42. The widow of the deceased was Marry Asbury Parson. They were married 11/26/46.

Parsons, William A., 3rd Corpl. - 52nd Virginia Inf., Company E, d. 5/29/64 of pyemia @ Christian's Factory. His coffin size was 72 in. in length by 18 in. in width. Originally buried in lot #197, grave #5, row #1. Exhumed 5/31/64, "removed & sent to Gilmore's Mill". Richard Parson, brother of the deceased, claimed the remains and paid expenses for removal and packing ($100.00). 1860 census listed Parsons occupation as farmhand, age 18, residing in Natural Bridge District of Rockbridge County. Enlisted as a private on 8/01/61 at Staunton, Virginia. Promoted to 3rd Corpl. in early 1864. Wounded in hip at Spotsylvania Court House 5/19/64. His age at death was 21. In his service record was entered "an excellent Soldier".

Parramore, Henry C., Corpl. - 31st Georgia Inf., Company E, d. 9/12/62 of typhoid fever @ Claytor's Factory. Coffin size was 71 in. in length by 18 in. in width. Body was prepared and shipped to Columbus, Georgia. In addition, Diuguid entered, "Florence Stewart Cty Ga". The father of the deceased, W. E. Parramore, paid all expenses. Parramore enlisted as a Private on 11/13/61. Corporal Parramore was wounded at Cold Harbor 6/27/62.

Patterson, David R., Sgt. - 56th Virginia Inf., Company D (Buckingham Yancey Guard), d. 10/17/61 of typhoid fever "in 20th year of his age at Sycamore Island, residence of his father

Dr. David Patterson of Buckingham". Death notice was published in the <u>Lynchburg Daily Virginian</u> on 10/24/61, page 3, col. 1. (See insert next page of transcribe article). Death claim was filed 10/28/61, owed $26.63. He enlisted as Sgt. on 7/08/61 in Buckingham County.

Patterson, J. W. B., Corpl. - 2nd Georgia Inf., Company C, d. 10/6/62 @ Christian's Factory. Patterson was wounded (finger) on June 27, 1862 (Gaines Mill). Admitted to Charlottesville Gen. Hospital for wounds on Sept. 3, 1862. His coffin size was 72 in. in length by 18 in. in width. Originally buried in lot #181, grave #2, row #1. Body was exhumed 10/22/62, prepared and shipped to Columbus, Georgia. His father Robert C. Patterson paid all expenses.

Patterson, S. J. - 10th Georgia Battn., Company C, d. 2/8/63 @ Claytor's Factory. Coffin size was 75 in. in length by 19 in. in width. Originally buried in lot #191, grave #1, row #3. Diuguid has two notations, "Removed" and "Sent to Forsyth Ga".

Paulett, Henry L. - 35th Georgia Inf., Company E, d. 8/17/62 @ Langhorne's Factory. Coffin size was 78 in. in length by 19 in. in width. Originally buried in lot #162, grave #2, row #3. Body was exhumed on or about 9/7/62, prepared and shipped to Atlanta, Georgia. Dr. John W. Suber paid all expenses. Private Paulett enlisted on 8/12/61.

Lynchburg Daily Virginian dated October 24, 1861
Death Notice of Sgt. David R. Patterson
(Transcribed from the original newspaper)

DIED,

Of typhoid fever, on Thursday, the 17th October, at Sycamore Island, the residence of his father, Dr. David Patterson of the county of Buckingham. David R. Patterson, in the 20th year of his age, Sergeant in Buckingham Yancey Guard, Capt. Camin Patterson, 56th Regiment Virginia Volunteers; and on the following day, his little sister, Jesie M. Patterson, aged 2 years, 1 month and 22 days. Both were buried in the same grave.

This is a simple record of what has carried mourning and anguish to many hearts. The youth of manly (sic) promise, about whom many high hopes of future usefulness and distinction were thickly clustered, and the dear child, sweet bud of innocence and beauty, both cut down within a few hours of each other by the ruthless hand of death, and consigned to the cold and darksome grave.

May the God of love and mercy comfort and support the hearts of the bereaved parents and other mourning relatives, and enable them to find sweet consolation in the thought that their loved ones "are not lost, but gone before" to a land of everlasting bliss.

Paxton, Cyrus H., 2nd Lieut. - 18th Virginia Inf., Company A, d. 6/12/64 @ Burton's Factory. "Was packed up to go to Amherst C.H.". Wounded In Action 5/16/64 at Battle of Drewry's Bluff, left arm was amputated, died of hemorrhage. Paxton enlisted on 4/23/61 at age 27. His occupation was listed as a mechanic. Promoted to Corpl. on 10/15/61, to 2nd Sgt. on 3/01/62, and to 3rd Lieut. on 4/23/62. Paxton was promoted to 2nd Lieut. on 8/12/63. Diuguid's notation in the logbook was, "For oak coffin, tight box & packing self $250.00." Southern Confederacy paid $15.00, balance of $235.00 paid in cash.

* **Payne, Joseph M.** - 47th Virginia Inf., Company H, d. 7/1/62 of typhoid fever @ Knight's Factory. Diuguid listed the initials of the deceased as J. E. Father of the deceased was

Thomas A. Payne. The widow of the deceased, Nicey A. Payne, applied for a pension on 5/14/88 and received $35.00 per year.

* Pearcy, John A., 1st Sgt. - 48th Virginia Inf., Company A, d. 9/20/62 of carditis @ Langhorne's Factory. Coffin size was 78 in. in length by 19 in. in width. Enlisted as a Private on 3/13/62 at Stone Creek, Virginia. Personal description, 6' 2", dark complexion, gray eyes and brown hair. 1860 census list him as age 33, occupation farmer, and a resident of Scott County, Virginia.

Peebles, Arron G. - 10th Virginia Cav., Company B, d. 1/19/63 @ Ferguson's Factory of Pneumonia. Coffin size was 74 in. in length by 18 in. in width. Originally buried in lot #183, grave #4, row #2. The body was exhumed and shipped to Lexington, North Carolina. The Compile Service Records states that Peebles died in Richmond. The 1860 census lists him as, Student, age 20, Shady Grove District, Davie County, North Carolina. He enlisted as a private on 1/6/62 in Davie County. His age at enlistment was listed as 22.

Peek, **** - No unit stated, d. 8/21/61. Brother of the deceased, Julius Peek, paid expenses "for packing brothers remains".

Pelfrey, Joseph - No Diuguid record - 12th South Carolina Inf., Company K, d. 1/22/63 in Lynchburg per his records. Age at reenlistment was 25. 1860 census listed him as a resident of the Pickens District.

* Pendergrass, Phillip H. – 48th Alabama Inf., Company E, d. 8/12/62 @ Knight's Factory. The widow of the deceased, Hanna O. Pendergrass, filed a pension application n on 6/17/87 in Marshall County, Alabama.

Perkins, E. A. - 50th Virginia Inf., Company D, d. 1/18/64 @ Odd Fellows Hall. Diuguid's only entry was "Sent to Grayson Cty Va".

* Perry, James Calvin- 44th Alabama Inf., Company B, d. 11/5/62 @ Odd Fellow's Hall. Coffin size was 74 in. in length by 18 in. in width. The only information available on Private Perry is a date of admission to the hospital (Gen. Hospital, Selma, Ala.) on 4/17/62. He was treated for Rheumatism and returned to duty on 4/24/62. Private Perry enlisted at age 24, most likely from Bibb County as Company B was from Bibb County, Alabama. The 44th was mustered into service 05/16/62 at Selma Alabama. The unit reached Richmond 07/01/62. No other military records on the soldier located. It is believed the he was born in North Carolina, married Francis Holder and was a resident of Scottsville, Alabama.

Peters, Asa C. – 6th Alabama Inf., Company F, d. 5/11/64 of wounds @ Christian's Factory. Coffin size was 70 in. in length by 18 in. in width. Peters enlisted as a private on 5/2/61 at Crawford, Alabama. He was officially mustered into service 5/15/61 at Montgomery, Alabama. The Company Muster dated 7/1/64 at Bunker Hill, Virginia only states "Wounded at Hospital". Based on Private Peters date of death and the fact that he was reported wounded he date of wounding was more than likely 5/6/64 at the Wilderness. The 6th Alabama was part of Battles Brigade, Rodes Division, Ewell's Corps (2nd Corps ANV). Ewell's Corps suffered 1250 killed and wounded.

Peters, James C. – 15th Alabama Inf., Company E, d. 5/21/62 of disease @ Reid's Factory. Coffin size was 70 in. in length by 20 in. in width. Peters enlisted as a Private on 3/3/62 at Westville, Alabama. His age at enlistment was listed as 23. He was born in Georgia, occupation was listed as a farmer, he was a resident of High Bluff, Alabama, and he was single. His military records stated his date of death as 1/8/62. A death claim was file by the widow of the deceased(?), Rachel A. Peters on 2/5/63. Mrs. Peter's address was listed as High Bluff, Dale County, Alabama.

Peters, John R. – 15th Alabama Inf., Company E, d. 6/12/62 of disease @ Ferguson's Factory. Coffin size was listed as 68 in. in length by 18 in. in width. Peters enlisted as a Private on 3/3/62 at Westville, Alabama. His age at enlistment was listed as 27. He was born in Georgia, occupation was listed as a farmer, he was a resident of High Bluff, Alabama, and he was married. His military records listed his place of death as Farmville, Virginia. The widow of the deceased, Mintie Peters applied for pension on 5/9/87. Her place of residence was listed as Geneva County, Alabama.

Peters, William, Sgt. - 58th Virginia Inf., Company I, d. 6/01/62 of disease @ Mr. Bowyer's residence. Diuguid recorded, "was sent to Bedford Cty". William Peters was born 1818. Was listed as age 44 when he enlisted on 7/24/61. 1860 census listed him as age 42, occupation farmer, and residing in Davis Mills P.O., Bedford County, Virginia.

Pharr, W. R. - 57th North Carolina Inf., Company B, d. 11/28/63 @ Reid's Factory. Coffin size was 74 in. in length by 19 in. in width. Elam King claimed the remains and paid expenses. "Packed up & sent to Harrisburg Depot N.C. Cabanas Cty".

* **Phillips, John** -   1st Arkansas Inf., Capt. McGregor's Company, d. 6/23/61 @ College Hospital. From Pine Bluff P.O., Jefferson County, Arkansas.

Phillips, Franklin -   No Diuguid Record   - 12th South Carolina Inf., Company K, d. 12/05/62 of disease. His age at enlistment was listed as 20.   1860 census listed him as a resident of the Pickens District.   Another record lists him as buried in the Oakwood Cemetery #145, Row L, Div. A.

* **Phillips, Robert** – 15th Alabama Inf., Company B, d. 5/10/62 of disease @ Saunder's Factory.   Phillips enlisted as a Private on 3/14/62 at Midway, Alabama.   His age at enlistment was listed as 20.   He was born in Alabama, occupation was listed as a farmer, he was a resident of Spring Hill, Alabama and he was single.   Phillips served 57 days in the army and was never involved in any engagement.   No birth date other than year, 1842.   Her was the son of Hester Phillips and was a resident of Spring Hill, Barbour County, Alabama.

* **Pickett, P. Willey** -   2nd North Carolina Inf., Company H, d. 7/14/64 of pneumonia @ Knight's Factory.   Coffin size was 73 in. in length by 18 in. in width.   His military indicate that he was place on a furlough in August after receiving a wound. Date and place of wounding not stated.   The father of the deceased filed a claim for "pay due" for his son on 9/13/64. The father stated that his son died in Richmond.

Pierce, **** - No unit stated, d. 8/17/61. Father of deceased John Pierce, listed as debtor, Diuguid only stated "son of soldier".

* **Pilgrim, T. F.** -   Hampton's Legion South Carolina Inf., Company K, d. /1/20/63 of pneumonia @ Langhorne's Factory.   Coffin size was 73 in. in length by 19 in. in width. Enlisted as a private on 4/14/61 at Pendelton, South Carolina. Brother of deceased was William H. Pilgrim.

Pittard, William G. -   14th North Carolina Inf., Company A, d. 3/2/63 of erysipelas @ Crumpton's Factory. Coffin size was 75 in. in length by 19 in. in width.   Originally buried in lot #195, grave #4, row #2.   Body was exhumed 3/19/63 and "..sent to Gaston N.C.".   The father of the deceased, Jesse Pittard, claimed the remains and paid expenses. Diuguid has the name recorded as "Pittence" in the "Soldier Book".   Enlisted in Warren County 3/30/61 at age 29.   Occupation listed as farmer.

Pleasant, William T. - 15th North Carolina Inf., Company G, d. 5/19/64 @ Ladies Relief Hospital. His coffin size was 71 in. in length by 18 in. in width. His military record is very brief, only provides his date of enlistment, 11/25/62 at Fredericksburg, Virginia. He was a resident of Franklin County; and that he was present for duty through April 1864.

Plemons (Plemiens), W. E. - 60th Georgia Inf., Company G, d. ? (late 1865). The only entry on the soldier is in Diuguid's note section of burial log #6. The entry was as follows, "W E Plemiens Co G 60th Ga was buried in a rifle pit at the South Corner of lot 183 buried from Ladies Hospital". Company roll dated 4/29/65 showed him as present. Plemons enlisted enlisted as a private on 5/14/62.

* **Pope, Elijah T.** - 45th North Carolina Inf., Company K, d. 8/02/64 @ Camp Davis. Coffin size was 72 in. in length by 17 in. in width. Enlisted at Camp Mancum near Raleigh 3/27/62 at age 43. Occupation was listed as a farmer. His military record states that he deserted the army at Kinston on or about 5/02/63. The next report listed him as sick and in hospital between May & Dec. of 64. The last entry stated that he was dropped from the company rolls between Jan. & Feb., 65. No other information available.

* **Potts, James H.** - 9th Virginia Inf., Company H, d. 7/5/62 of a fever @ Burton's Factory. Coffin Size was 73 in. in length by 18 inches in width. Enlisted as a private on 6/19/61 at Fletcher's Chapel, Lunenburg County, Virginia. Company H was transferred to the 28th Battn. Inf. on 5/8/62.

* **Powe, J. W.** – 13th Mississippi Inf., Company B, d. 08/16/62 @ Christian's Factory. His coffin size was 70 in. in length by 16 in. in width. A search of military records list a John W. Powe as a member of Company B 13th Mississippi Inf. with no other details. Diuguid's records only provided initials in his records for this soldier. There were Powes' listed in the records of the 13th Mississippi, Company B.

* **Powell, John B.** - 3rd Arkansas Inf. d. 7/15/61 @ J. W. Murrell's Home. The sister of the deceased was Mrs. Marry Berry, Jon P.O., Drew County, Arkansas.

Powell, James M. - 6th Georgia Inf., Company A, d. 8/19/62 @ Burkville, Virginia. Body was prepared by Mr. Diuguid and shipped to Warrenton, Georgia. Coffin size was 6 ft. 2 in. in length by 18 in. in width. Powell enlisted as a private on 8/03/61.

* **Powell, Willey** – 38th Georgia Inf., Company F, d.01/25/64 of Tuberculosis @ Ferguson's factory. Enlisted 07/29/62; a resident of Elbert County, Georgia. Was wounded in action at 2nd Manassas 08/26/62.

* **Prater, Thomas L.** - 16th North Carolina Inf., Company F, d. 11/28/63 of meningitis @ Ladies Relief Hospital. His coffin size was 74 in length by 19 in. in width. His military stated that he deserted in January 1863. Rejoined his company prior to March 26, 1863 when he was court martialed. After that date he was carried on the company muster as absent-sick from May 1863 until his death.

Preston, L. Perry - 11th Virginia Inf., Company G, d. 1/24/62 of typhoid fever @ Centerville, Virginia. Preston enlisted as a Private on 4/23/61 at age 20, occupation clerk. Tribute from Home Guard published in Lynchburg Daily Virginian on 2/04/62, page 2, col. 4 (see the following page for the Transcribed tribute).

* **Presnell, John** - 54th North Carolina Inf., Company K, d. 1/07/63 of typhoid fever @ Burton's Factory. Coffin size was 77 in. in length by 18 in. in width. Wounded at Battle of Fredericksburg 12/13/62. Born Randolph County where he resided until he enlisted 5/07/62. Occupation was listed as a farmer.

* **Prevatt, Thomas K.** - 8th Florida Inf., Company B, d. 5/03/63 of diarrhea @ Burton's Factory (Gen. Hospt. #1). Coffin size was 71 in. in length by 18 in. in width. Prevatt enlisted as a Private on 5/10/62 in Quincy, Florida. Listed as slightly wounded on 12/11/62 at Fredericksburg. Description, 5' 7" in height, sallow skin, blue eyes, light hair, occupation farmer. Born 1832 in Roberson, North Carolina. Wife of the deceased was Sarah Prevatt. Diuguid had listed his name as "Privatt".

* **Price, William** – 11th Alabama Inf., Company K, d. 5/3/63 of disease @ Reid's Factory. Coffin size was 70 in. in length by 19 in. in width. Price enlisted as a Private 6/11/61 at Marion, Alabama. His age at enlistment was listed as 45. He was born in Alabama, occupation was listed as a farmer, he was a resident of Pinetuckey, Alabama, and was single. Price was never actively engaged with the 11th. He was listed as "Absent Sick" at Seven Pines 5/31/62, Gaines' Mill 6/27/62, and Frayser's Farm 6/30/62. He was listed as "Absent on Furlough" for 2nd Manassas 8/30/62, Sharpsburg 9/17/62,

and Fredericksburg 12/13/62. He was also listed as absent for Salem Church on his date of death 5/3/63.

Lynchburg Daily Virginian dated February 4, 1862
Tribute to Pvt. L. Perry Preston
(Transcribed from the original newspaper)

Tribute of Respect - At A meeting of the "Lynchburg Home Guard," held at their camp near Centerville, on the 29th day of January, 1862, the following resolutions were unanimously adopted:

Whereas, it has pleased Almighty God in his wise Providence, to take from this world our honored and respected friend - fellow soldier, L. Perry Preston, in the bloom of early manhood - therefore be it

Resolved, That we express our hearty sorrow at this early loss of our friend, grieving to think that one whose youth was so promising should have been so soon called away from this world.

Resolved, That we take this opportunity of expressing also high appreciation of the merits of the deceased, as a soldier and a gentleman, and our sincere regret that our intercourse with him has thus early been brought to a close.

Resolved, That a copy of these resolutions be sent to the Lynchburg papers for publication, and also to the family of the deceased.

W. J. H. Hawkins Lieut. Commanding.

Ro. C. Berkeley, Sec'y.

See note below

NOTE: Lieut. William James Holcomb Hawkins – Mentioned above survived the war, died just prior to his 38th birthday in 1875.

Robert C. Berkeley – Mentioned above survived the war, wounded at Seven Pines 5/31/62, transferred to 7th Virginia, paroled at Appomattox, listing as still living in 1891.

* Price, William B. - 4th Texas Inf., Company K, d. 2/4/63 of pleuritis @ College Hospital. Coffin size was 74 in. in length by 18 in. in width. Enlisted as a private on 4/1/62 at Athens, Texas.

* **Pruden, Kinch T.** – 44th Alabama Inf., Company F, d. 12/17/62 of Small Pox @ the Pest House. Coffin size was 71 in. in length by 18 in. in width. Diuguid had recorded his name as "T. R. Prudem." Pruden enlisted as a private on 3/28/62 in Bibb County, Alabama. His age at enlistment was listed as 38. He was born in Alabama, married; occupation was listed as a farmer and was a resident of Centerville, Alabama. His military records state that he died in Richmond, Va. on 12/19/62. A Col Fowler filed a death claim on 9/7/63 for the widow of the deceased, Nancy Pruden. It appears that a second claim was filed on 8/29/64 by Mrs. Purden. Mrs. Purden could be contacted in care of J. Gardner, Centerville, Alabama. Nancy Pruden applied for a pension, no date was specified. She was a resident of Tuscaloosa County. Two witnesses listed on the application were J. M. Krout and L. L. Wyatt.

Pugh, L. J. - Georgia Regiment, Governor's Horse Guard, d. 10/8/61 @ Ladies Relief Hospital. Originally buried in lot #159, grave #9, row #4. "Was packed up and sent to Millidgeville, Georgia". Private Pugh was exhume by the request of his brother N. J. Pugh and shipped home. No one by this name is listed on the Georgia index. Note: L. B. Williams, 20th Mississippi now buried in that location.

Pulman, W. - No Diuguid record - 14th South Carolina Inf., Company H, no date of death. 1860 census listed him as a resident of the Barnwell District.

* **Purvis, Robert L.** - 46th North Carolina Inf., Company D, d. 2/08/64 of smallpox at the Pest Hose. Born in Richmond County where he resided until enlisting 2/20/62 at age 23. Occupation was listed as a farmer. Reported as AWOL 5/1/63. He was apprehended 6/13/63 and returned to duty to 11/1/63. His military records state his cause of death as "variola".

* **Quiett, James H.** - 2nd Florida Inf., Company L, d. 7/17/63 @ Knight's Factory. Coffin size was 78 in. in length by 18 in. in width. Enlisted as a private on 7/03/61 in Madison. Was wounded during the Seven Day's Campaign in June 62 and again at Sharpsburg on 9/17/62. Following Sharpsburg he was absent on all subsequent company musters. The final entry in his military record only states that he died in 7/17/63 at General Hospital #2 in Lynchburg. Records indicated that

Quiett was born in Tennessee in 1840. Diuguid listed his name as "Quiatt, J. H.".

Quillian James R., Sgt. - 37th Virginia Inf., Company D, d. 4/30/62 @ Ladies Relief Hospital from the results of a gun shot wound (vulnus sclopeticum) received at The Battle of Kernstown on 3/23/62. Body was prepared and shipped to Bristol Depot, Virginia. He enlisted as a private on 5/20/61 at Estillville. His death notice was published in the Lynchburg Daily Virginian on 5/1/62 page 3, col. 1 (see the following page for the transcribe notice).

Lynchburg Daily Virginian dated May 1, 1862
Death Notice of Sgt. James R. Quillian
(Transcribed from the original newspaper)

LOCAL AND STATE
NEWS

J. R. Quillian, of Company D, 37th Va. Regiment, died at Ladies Relief Hospital, in this city, on the morning of 30th April, of a wound received at the battle of Kernstown. He was a brave and gallant soldier, and displayed his coolness in the heroic manner he bore the amputation of his arm, and the quiet manner he endured all his sufferings. Few men have produced such a favorable impression upon those who privilege it was to administer to his wants. Peace to his ashes.

G. W. Momon, Company G, 15th Alabama, died at the same hospital on the evening of April 29th.

*NOTE: the G. W. Momon listed in the obituary above was George Washington Moorman.

Radford, Edmund Winston, Capt. - 30th Virginia Cav. (2nd Va. Cav.), Company G, **Killed in Action** at the Battle of Manassas 7/21/61 (shot in abdomen). Funeral services conducted at St. Stephens Esp. Church, Forest, Virginia (Bedford County) on 7/25/61. Captain Radford was a member of the vestry of St. Stephens. His death notice was published in the Lynchburg Daily Virginian on 7/29/61 (a Monday). Born 7/9/20 in Bedford County. Attended Washington College (now Washington & Lee) & V.M.I. 1837-38. Enlisted 5/28/61 @ Forest Depot, Age 40, occupation Farmer, and a resident of Bedford city.

Ramage, Isaac, W. T. - 13th South Carolina Inf., Company A, d.11/18/62 @ College Hospital.
Private Ramage's Coffin size was 79 in. in length by 19 in. in width. Originally Buried in lot #122, grave #2, row #2. Body was exhumed 5/13/63, prepared and shipped to Martin's Depot, on the Lawrence Railroad, South Carolina. In the margin of the log book Mr. Diuguid has written the name, "Isaac Adair". Diuguid had recorded his name as "J. W. Rammage". Another source indicates that he was buried in the Duncan Creek Baptist Church Cemetery, Laurens County. 1860 census listed him as a resident of the Lauren District.

Ratliff, Isaac P. - 4th Virginia Inf., Company L, d. 5/2/62 of typhoid fever @ Christian's Factory. Body was prepared and shipped to Christiansburg, Virginia. Ratliff enlisted as a private on 7/16/61.

Reid, G. H. - 48th Alabama Inf., Company G, d. 8/15/62 @ Ladies Relief Hospital. Originally buried in lot #172, grave #5, row #4. His remains were exhumed, prepared and shipped to Casetta, Alabama. Coffin size was 74 in. in length by 19 in. in width. Note: Thomas H. Lipscomb of the 13th South Carolina was buried in that location on 9/21/62.

Render, Thomas C. - 8th Georgia Inf., Company D, d. 8/19/61 of fever @ Orange Court House. On 8/23/61 Diuguid noted that James A. Render, brother of the deceased, was listed as debtor "packing brothers remains". J. H. Houseworth paid the expenses. In the notes section of burial log #4 Mr. Diuguid list the name, "James A. Render" and address, "Greenville Meriweather Cty Geo." This may possibly be the father of the deceased or it may be the deceased.

* **Reynolds, Samuel** - 24th Georgia Inf., Company B, d. 6/24/64 of wounds @ Ferguson's Factory. Coffin size was 78 in. in length by 25 in. in width. Enlisted as a Pvt. in Company C, 16th Georgia Inf. on 7/17/61. Transferred to Company B, 24th Georgia Inf. 9/30/62. His military record only states that he was wounded in 1864 and died of those wounds in Lynchburg.

Reynolds, M. A. - No unit stated, d. 8/23/61 @ Mrs. Hare's residence. Expenses paid by W. R. Reynolds "for coffin and packing".

* **Rich, Hiram N.** - 48th Virginia Inf., Company D, d. 10/21/62 of tuberculosis @ Miller's Factory. Buried in lot #181, grave #3, row #3, was interred under the name of "Rich, R. H., 48th Va. Inf., Company C". Coffin size was 73 in. in

length by 18 in. in width. Enlisted as a private on 5/18/61 at Seven Mile Ford, Symth County, Virginia. His age at enlistment was listed as 24. Listed AWOL 7/1/61, the company muster stated, "a great annoyance to the community at large". 1860 census listed his occupation as a laborer, age 21 (?).

Ricketts, James A. – 6th Alabama Inf., "Lynch's Company", d. 6/24/61 @ College Hospital. He was buried in lot #158, grave #4, row #2. Diuguid noted the following "Brother-in-law John B. Kane, Bethel P.O., Wilcox County, Alabama".

Riddle, Ariel - 2nd Mississippi Inf., Bramley's Company (Town Creek Company), d. 5/24/61 @ College Hospital. Buried in lot #158, grave #4, row #1. See photograph of tombstone (following page) erected after the war by family. Address: A. D. Martin, Woodlawn P.O., Attawamba County, Mississippi.

Riddle, George M. A. C. - 6th South Carolina Inf., Company D, d. 2/2/63 @ Claytor's Factory. Coffin size was 72 in. in length by 21 in. in width. Originally buried in lot #191, grave #6, row #2. "Taken up & sent to Charlotte N.C.", is the only notation made by Mr. Diuguid in the "Soldiers Book". George L. Riddle, cousin of the deceased, made the request for the removal of Riddle. The body was exhumed on 2/24/63. In the main burial log Mr. Diuguid has this entry, "York District S.C. Zeno P.O.". His age at enlistment was 30. 1860 census listed him as a resident of the York District. Note: James D. Amos of the 26th Georgia was buried in that location 3/14/63.

Riley, George – 15th Alabama Inf., Company G, d. 6/16/63 of disease @ Camp Davis. Coffin size was 76 in. in length by 20 in. in width. Riley enlisted as a private on 8/15/62 at Dale County, Alabama. His age at enlistment was listed as 20. He was born in Alabama. His occupation was listed as a farmer, he was a resident of Echo, Alabama, and was married. He was listed as "Absent on Furlough" 12/13/62. He was listed as "Present" 5/3/63 during the operations in and around Suffolk, Virginia. The widow of the deceased, Nancy A. Riley filed a death claim on 9/18/63. The claim was verified and settled on 6/2/64. Mrs. Riley was listed as a resident of Echo, Dale County, Alabama.

Rinehart, Caleb M. - 1st North Carolina Cav., Company F, d. 3/7/62 of gastritis @ College Hospital. Body was prepared and shipped to Concord, Cabarras County, North Carolina.

Born in Cabarrus County where he enlisted on 6/15/61 for the war. Age at enlistment was listed as 18.

Ringo, D. W., Capt. - No unit specified, buried 01/26/65. Expenses paid by Samuel Tyree.

Riddle, Ariel
Post War Tombstone

Ritchie, R. Lieut. - No unit specified, d. 10/30/64. Father-in-law of the deceased, William Simpson claimed remains. Diuguid's entry was "For carrying out son in laws remains Lieut R Ritchie". Expenses for Mr. Diuguid's services were paid in full on 12/3/64, in the sum of $50.00 cash.

* **Roberts, John R.** - 6th North Carolina Inf., Company E, d. 8/29/62 of peritonitis @ College Hospital. Coffin size was 70 in. in length by 18 in. in width. His military record states that he was discharged 7/20/62 due to phthisis Pulmonalis. Roberts was born in Yancey or Mitchell County. Enlisted as a private on 7/15/61 in Alamance County. His age at

enlistment was listed as 20. Occupation was listed as a farmer.

* **Roberts, W. M., 4th Corpl.** – 9th Alabama Inf., Company H, d. 12/24/62 of wounds @ Knight's Factory. Coffin size was 70 in. in length by 18 in. in length. Roberts enlisted as a private on 6/10/61 at Athens, Alabama. His age at enlistment was listed as 25. He was born in Alabama, occupations was list as a farmer, he was a resident of Athens, and was single. He was present for duty at the following engagements, Yorktown, Williamsburg, Seven Pines, Gaines' Mill and Frayser's Farm. He was severely wounded at Frayser's Farm on 6/30/62

Robertson, Eldridge P. - Latham's Battery Virginia Light Art., d. 8/30/61 @ Mrs. Adams. Body was prepared and shipped to his father in Bent Creek, Virginia. Robertson enlisted as a private on 4/23/61. Cost of the funeral was $23.00, which included the cost "cotton & sheet". The Southern Confederacy paid $10.00 of the cost. Diuguid noted that the remaining balance was paid by "Thos H. Robertson" possibly the father of the deceased.

Robinson, A. Samuel E. - 53rd Georgia Inf., Company F, d. 6/11/63 of wounds @ Christian's Factory. Coffin size was 74 in. in length by 18 in. in width. Originally buried lot #188, grave #1, row #5. The body was exhumed 2/12/64, W. A. Stewart claimed the remains. Diuguid's entry was, "removed sent to Jonesboro Ga". Private Robinson enlisted 5/02/62. Robinson was wounded 9/17/62 at Sharpsburg. However, the specific cause of death was not stated.

* **Robinson, James A.** - 11th Mississippi Inf., "Chickasaw" Company, d. 5/23/61 @ College Hospital. The uncle of the deceased was listed as, Major Robinson, Red Hand P.O., Ponito County, Mississippi. A Lieut. Galbreath appears to have made the arrangements. Diuguid made the following entry, "Sheet, gloves & cotton - $3.00". Total fee was $23.00. Thirteen of which was paid in cash the balance was paid by the "Southern Confederacy".

Rodes, Robert Emmet, Maj. General - Killed **in Action** 9/19/64 @ Winchester (Opequon Creek). Born 3/29/29 in Lynchburg, Virginia. He was the son of General David Rodes and Martha Yancey. Young Robert entered VMI in July 1845. Cadet Rodes graduated from VMI in July 1848. He ranked 10th out of 24 graduates. Young Rodes remained on at VMI as an Assistant Professor from 1848 to 1850. Rodes worked in Alabama on several railroad projects. On September 10th

1857 he married Virginia Hortense Woodruff of Tuscaloosa, Alabama. He returned to VMI in 1860 as a Professor of Applied Mechanics. However, due to the outbreak of the war he never served in his capacity. In January 1861 he raised a volunteer company "The Warrior Guard." In May 1861 these volunteers became part of the 5th Alabama Infantry. Rodes was elected as Colonel of the 5th. In October of 1861 he was promoted to Brig. General. His brigade saw action at Fair Oaks, Gaines's Mill, Sharpsburg, Fredericksburg and Chancellorsville. Rodes was promoted to the rank of Maj. General in May 1863. His division served gallantly at Gettysburg, The Wilderness and Spotsylvania. Served under Jubal Early in the 1864 Valley Campaign from June until his death in September. General Rodes was interred in Presbyterian Cemetery on 9/23/64 (Friday) in Range #5, Lot #2. The Lynchburg Daily Virginian carried five announcement and stories on Gen. Rodes's death. The first appeared on the 21st and the last on the 30th. See following page for a sketch of General Rodes.

Roebuck, J. - 3rd South Carolina Inf., Company G, d. 9/28/61 @ Warwick House Hospital. Originally buried in lot #158, grave #3, row #4. Body was exhumed 10/6/61, prepared and shipped Lauren Court House, South Carolina. John P. Roebuck paid for the "removal and packing brothers remains" on 10/7/61. Note: B. M. Burress of the 8th Tennessee now buried in that location.

Rogers, Albert, Lieut. - 54th North Carolina Inf., Company D, d. 10/9/64 of febris typhoides @ Burton's Factory. Coffin size was 72 in. in length by 18 in. in width. "Was packed up & sent to Margarettville N.C.". On 10/11/64 J. M. S. Rogers, father of the deceased, claimed the remains and paid all expenses ($150.00). Rogers previously served in Company A of the 15th Reg. N.C. Troops (5th N.C. Vols). He was transferred to the 54th on7/28/62. Was mustered in as 1st Sergeant. Rogers was promoted to 2nd Lieut. on 4/09/63 and to 1st Lt. 5/08/63. Severely wounded in both thighs on 9/19/64 at the Battle of Winchester.

Maj. Gen. Robert E. Rodes
Killed in Action 9/19/64 @ Winchester

Maj. Gen. Robert E. Rodes
CSA

* **Roland, S. David** - 12th Georgia Inf., Company K, d. 9/04/64 @ Camp Davis. His coffin size was 71 in. in length by 15 in. in width. The Compiled Service records state that he died on 5/30/64 at Staunton or Lynchburg.
* **Rooks, Noah** - 1st Texas Inf., Company L, d. 7/9/62 of disease @ Ladies Relief Hospital. Coffin size was 71 in. in length by 18 in. in width. Rooks enlisted as a Private on

4/11/62 at Galveston, Texas. His age at enlistment was listed as 29.

* Rosser, Edward B. - Moorman's (also Shoemaker's) Battery Virginia Light Art., d. 1/05/64 of chronic diarrhea @ a Private home. Coffin size was 68 in. in length by 18 in. in width. "Was buried No. 2 from north corner of lot 149". William & Mrs. S. A. Rosser paid expenses. Diuguid listed his first name as "Edwin". He enlisted as a private on 5/11/61 at age 18.

Rousey, Mitchell G. - 38th Georgia Inf., Company H, d. 10/23/63 of typhoid fever @ College Hospital. Coffin size was 73 in. in length by 18 in. in width. Diuguid's entry was, "Sent to Lexington Ga".

* Rowland, Waddy T. - 1st Tennessee Inf., Capt. Bennett's Company the "Tallahoma Guards", d. on or about 5/31/61 @ College Hospital. Buried in lot #158, grave #6, row #1. Diuguid had made the following entry in the "Soldiers Book", "Emma E. Wagstaff - his love, William Rowland his father formerly of Pendelton Anderson District, South Carolina, T. S. Reed his cousin." No other information available.

Rucker, Paulus G. - 11th Virginia Inf., Company H, d. 5/23/65 in Lynchburg (cause not known). Enlisted as a private on 5/15/61 in Lynchburg. His age at enlistment was listed as 18 and his occupation was listed as a farmer. Private Rucker was listed as "Absent Sick" for the musters from 10/61 to 5/62. He was discharged from service 11/8/62. The father of the deceased was G. W. Rucker. Paulus Rucker was buried in Rucker Square (Block 1 Section 9) of the Old City Cemetery. His age at death was listed as 21.

Ruddle, Michael - 28th Virginia Inf., Company I, d. 7/19/63 from wounds and tetanus @ Ladies Relief Hospital. Ruddle was wounded 7/03/63 at Gettysburg. "Was sent to Gishes Mill Roanoke Cty". Expenses paid by E. McDermed.

Rudisail, H. A. - 57th North Carolina Inf., Company E, d. 3/3/63 @ Knight's Factory. Coffin size was 78 in. in length by 20 in. in width. Originally buried in lot #195, grave #4, row #4. Body was exhumed 3/10/63 and per Mr. Diuguid's notes shipped to "Charlotte N.C.". Also in burial log #6 made this notation, "Soloman Rudisail Lincoln Cty N C Iron P.O. Should D R Rudisail & J R Stroup Die write as above Directed". Soloman Rudisial was notified by Mr. Diuguid and claimed his son's remains and paid the associated expenses. Based on Diuguid's records Private Stroup did not die in Lynchburg and live to serve the Confederacy.

* **Runnells, Richard** - 10th Virginia Inf., Company C, d. 5/27/64 (approx. date of death) @ Camp Davis. He was conscripted 2/22/64 Camp Lee near Richmond. Was discharged 4/23/64 with "acute rheumatism of knees, feeble constitution and want of muscular development". Born circa 1824 in Caroline County, Virginia. Dark Complexion, dark hair, 5' 6", occupation farmer.

* **Russell, J. Larkin** - 22nd North Carolina Inf., Company A, d. 6/2/62 of febris remittent @ College Hospital. He enlisted as a private on 3/19/62. His age at enlistment was listed as 19. Russell was a resident of Caldwell County, North Carolina. In one Diuguid record Private Russell was exhumed and shipped home 8/2/62, with all expenses paid by his father Captain James Russell. In "The Soldier Book" Private Russell in still listed as buried in lot #171, grave #2, row #3, and not removed. Normally Mr. Diuguid would make the notation "Removed".

* **Rutledge, Marion** - Listed as a member of the 63rd Tennessee Inf., Company G, buried in lot #189, grave #10, row #3. Private Rutledge died 4/30/64 @ College Hospital. Coffin size was 69 in. in length by 17 in. in width. Based on existing sources the only "Marion Rutledge" can be found under Company A of the 36th Tennessee Infantry. However, the 63rd was present at Appomattox with the Army of Northern Virginia on April 9, 1865.

Rutledge, William - 60th Georgia Inf., Company B, died on or about 8/24/62 @ Candler's Factory. Body was prepared and shipped to LaGrange, Troup County, Georgia. Coffin size was 75 in. in length by 18 in. in width. His remains were delivered via the West Point & LaGrange Rail Road. W. G. Marcus claimed the remains. The fee charged by Diuguid was $35.00, of which $26.00 was paid in cash and $9.00 paid by the "Southern Confederacy". William was the son of John & Martha Marcus Rutledge. He was born (circa) 1838. In 1860 he was living in the household with his mother and stepfather, Dr. John Baugh. There is no marked grave located for him in Troup County, Georgia.

Sanford, William John - 9th Louisiana Inf., Company B, d. 5/4/62 @ Saunder's Factory. Buried in lot #166, row #3, grave #1. The Company muster roll for March 1 - June 30, 1862 stated, "died at Standardsville, Va.". Diuguid's records show that the death and burial took place on or about 5/4/62. Also

Diuguid made the following notation, "W. J. Saunders was transported to Liberty Jno Sanford Co B 9 La died." Initially the name "John Saunders" had been entered in the logbook. It is possible that he did die at Standardsville and was transported to Lynchburg for burial or was transferred from a hospital there to Lynchburg where he died.

Saunders, R. W. - Courtney's (also Henrico) Battery Virginia Light Art., d. 9/7/62 @ Ferguson's Factory. Body was prepared and shipped to Richmond, Virginia. Coffin size was 76 in. in length by 19 in. in width. Diuguid has this entry above the name, "Quartermasters Orders".

Seabury, John Kirk, Sgt. Major - 11th Virginia Inf. Company G (Lynchburg Home Guard), was **Killed In Action** @ Battle of Frazier's Farm on 6/30/62. Death notice appeared in the Lynchburg Daily Virginian dated 7/2/62, page 3, col. 1, funeral notice on 7/3/62 page 2, col. 3, "Funeral today from 2nd Presbyterian Church, this afternoon at 3 o'clock. The Rev. R. B. Thomson, D. D. will officiate...", and a tribute (obituary) from the 11th Virginia dated 7/24/62, page 3, col. 2 (the Transcribed notice is on the following page). Seabury was born 7/26/38. He enlisted as a Corpl. on 4/23/61. His age at enlistment was listed as 23. Promoted to Sgt. on 5/18/61. See photo insert next page of head stone.

Lynchburg Daily Virginian dated July 24, 1862
Death Notice of Sgt. Major John Kirkpatrick Seabury
(Transcribed in part from the original newspaper)

OBITUARY

The Late John Kirkpatrick Seabury, Sergeant Major of the 11th Regiment Va. Vols.

The announcement in the Virginian a few weeks since of the fall of our gallant young townsman above in the battle of 30th June, 1862, before Richmond, awakes emotions of sadness in many a heart in this community.

Gifted with a vigorous and cultivated mind, endowed with those social qualities, which bind man to his fellow, and possessing a moral character without reproach, the death of this estimable young man would have been, under any circumstances, painful in the extreme to his friends. But falling as he did, in one of the bloodiest conflicts of this malignant war, and almost in the moment of victory, this dispensation of Providence is rendered much more distressing. 'Tis true, he fell in the discharge of his duty; he "died at his post," nobly vindicating our right to be free, and in defending his land and home, and all he held dearest on earth, against the approach of our ruthless invaders!

...for the subdued sorrow of friends, compassion-in-arms, and superior officers, testify their love and recognize the worth of his character.

Sears, Thomas A. - 11th Virginia Inf. Company G (Lynchburg Home Guard), d. 7/30/61 of disease. Father of the deceased was John A. Sears, "son - soldier". Sears enlisted as a Private on 4/23/61. His age at enlistment was listed as 22. His occupation was listed as a merchant.

Seay, William G. - 2nd Regiment Wise Legion Inf., Company H (Capt. John Willis Lewis' Company), d. 12/28/61 @ Ladies

Relief Hospital. Originally buried in lot #170, grave #5, row #2. Body was exhumed 1/3/62, prepared and shipped to Clover Depot, Halifax County, Virginia. Private Seay at the time of his death was a member of the 59th Virginia Inf. Company E (3rd) as of August, 1861. He enlisted 7/20/61 in Richmond, Virginia at age 18. Per the Compiled Service Records Private Seay was, "Detailed to extra duty as a carpenter on 10/31/61 at White Sulphur Springs Hospital". NOTE: Private G. W. Cook of the 11th Georgia was buried in that location 1/5/62.

* **Scott, George P.** - 20th Georgia Inf., buried in lot #170, grave #9, row #2. Father of deceased was Perry R. Scott, Catawba P.O., Harris County, Georgia.

* **Scroggins, John** – 6th Alabama Inf., Company F, d. 1/31/63 @ College Hospital. Coffin size was 76 in. in length by 20 in. in width. The widow of the deceased, Patience Scroggins, filed a pension application 7/21/97 in Coffee County, Alabama.

* **Segreest, Charles T.** – 61st Alabama Inf., Company H, d. 6/11/64 of wounds @ Crumpton's Factory. Coffin size was 68 in. in length by 18 in. in width. Segreest was wounded during the Battle of the Wilderness 5/6/64. Diuguid had recorded his name as "Segrest." Eliza J. Segreest, widow of the deceased, filed a death claim on 11/30/64. Mrs. Segreest could be contacted care of D. Clopton, Tuskegee, Alabama

* **Self, M. M.** - 4th Texas Inf., Company F, d. 6/20/62 of pneumonia @ Claytor's Factory. Coffin size was 77 in. in length by 20 in. in width. Enlisted as a private on 3/22/62 at Hallettsville, Texas.

Sellers, D. T. - 57th North Carolina Inf., Company I, d. 8/23/63 @ Camp Davis. Coffin size was 73 in. in length by 18 in. in width. Originally buried in lot #196, grave #8, row #2. Body was exhumed 8/26/63. Father of deceased, L. Sellers claimed remains. "Removed & sent to Company Shop N.C.".

* **Sellers, E. D.** – 15th Alabama Inf., Company L, d. 5/27/62 of disease at Ferguson's Factory. Coffin size was 73 in. in length by 19 in. in width. Sellers enlisted as a Private on 3/11/62 at Perote, Alabama. His age at enlistment was listed as 20. He was born in Alabama, occupation was listed as a farmer, was resident of Perote, Alabama and was single. The father of the deceased, Elisha H. Sellers filed a death claim on 1/5/63. The claim was verified and settled on 1/21/65. Mr. Sellers could be contacted in care of B. Fitzpatrick, Troy, Alabama.

* **Senn, John D.** - 13th South Carolina Inf., Company D, d. 3/23/63 of disease @ College Hospital. Coffin Size was 74 in.

in length by 18 in. in width. Military records list his date of death as 5/15/64 from wounds. His age at enlistment was 24. 1860 census listed him as a resident of the Newberry District.

Severence, E. J. - No Diuguid Record - Member of the 14th South Carolina Inf., Company A, d. 2/09/63 of disease. Age at enlistment was listed as 30. 1860 census listed him as a resident of the Darlington District.

* **Shadrock, John D.** – 6th Alabama Inf., Company A, d. 5/26/62 @ Langhorne's Factory. Coffin size was 73 in. in length by 20 in. in width. Private Shadrocks Widow filed a death claim on 8/29/62 and again 2/16/63. The widow of the deceased was Margaret Shadrock, she could be contacted in care of J. L. Pugh at Eufaula, Alabama. The claim was verified and approved 1/26/65.

* **Sheehe, Christopher** - 27th Virginia Inf., Company E, d. 8/2/61 of wounds @ College Hospital. His death resulted from a wound to the head received 7/21/61 at the Battle of Manassas.

Shelly, J. H. - Provost Guard in Lynchburg, d. 12/26/62 @ Christian's Factory. Shelly was interred in the City Cemetery. Diuguid entry was as follows, "Was buried beside of mother in the Old part of the yard". Coffin size was 74 in. by 18 in. in width.

* **Shelor, George T.** - Stuart's Virginia Horse Art., d. 7/22/62 @ Saunder's Factory. Coffin size was 76 in. in length by 19 in. in width. He is listed as buried in lot #173, grave #3, row #2. However, James J. Clark is also listed as being buried in that location. It is unclear, but it is quite possible that Shelor was exhumed and shipped home. On two occasions Diuguid has made notations to this man. First in the Soldiers Book under his name, "(unreadable) & Pack". In Log Book #5 in the notes section he made this entry, "Jesse W. Alltizer after the remains of Geo T Shelor", then adds "Christiansburg V&TRR". Also he has entered the date "28th". Clark was interred on 8/18/62.

Shelton, A. J. - 2nd Virginia Cav., Company I, d. 1/12/63 of pneumonia @ College Hospital. Coffin size was 72 in. in length by 18 in. in width. "Was carried home (unreadable) Wards Bridge", was the notation made by Mr. Diuguid. A Littleberry Hughs claimed the body. The main entry made by Mr. Diuguid was, "For coffin & box for A. J. Shelton & Trip $50.00". The Southern Confederacy paid $9.00, the balance of $41.00 was paid in cash. Shelton enlisted at Campbell Court House 8/07/62. Death claim was filed 11/9/63.

Shelton, Martin V., Corpl. - 28th Virginia Inf., Company F, d. 8/29/62 from wounds received 6/27/62 @ Battle of Gain's Mill. Coffin size was 70 in. in length by 18 in. in width. Receive a bullet wound in right side. Enlisted as a private on 4/26/61 at Good's Crossing. His age at enlistment was listed as 22 and his occupation was listed as a farmer. Born in Bedford County, Virginia, unmarried. He was the son of James and Citty J. Shelton.

Sheppard, Lewis H. - 28th Virginia Inf., Company G, d. 1/16/62 from typhoid fever at the home of A. J. Cundiff. Body sent to Bedford County, Virginia. Sheppard enlisted as a Private on 8/1/61. His age was 22 at the time of his death. He was born in Bedford County, Virginia, and was the son of Thomas and Elizabeth Sheppard.

Shepherd, Robert F. - 2nd Virginia Inf., Company H, d. 5/4/62 @ Ferguson's Factory from pneumonia. Originally buried in lot #166, grave #9, row #1. Body was exhumed in the spring of 1866 and shipped to Kerneysville on B&O Railroad. Diuguid's entry in the note section read as follows, "R F Shepherd Co H 2nd Va Reg Kerneysville B&O R R Care of Jas H Shepherd". Private Sheppard enlisted 2/15/62 at Winchester, Virginia.

Sherer, G. H. - 44th Georgia Inf., Company B, d. 5/14/64 @ Ladies Relief Hospital. His coffin size was 74 in. in length by 19 in. in width. Originally buried in lot #193, grave #9, row #4. Sherer was exhumed on 8/28/64, "taken up & sent to Yorkville S.C.". The brother of Private Sherer (no name supplied) claimed the remains and paid the expenses of removal and packing. Unable to locate anyone by this name is listed in the Georgia Index.

Shields, Joseph M. - 48th Georgia Inf., Company K, d. 3/24/63 of pneumonia @ Claytor's Factory. Coffin size was 74 in. in length by 18 in. in length. Originally buried in lot #199, grave #6, row #1. "Removed & sent to Thompson Ga". Private Shields enlisted 4/24/62.

* Shierling, John Andrew, Sr. - 59th Georgia Inf., Company H, d. 6/15/64 of typhoid fever & wounds. Originally enlisted in Company G, 10th Georgia State Troops. Was mustered out in May 1862. Enlisted in Company H of 59th Georgia 5/06/62. His military record only states that he was wounded in 1864, does not specify where.

* Shropshire, Henry Clay - Brumsby's Regt., 14th Georgia Inf., enlisted 07/09/61 as a member of Capt. Wallace Jordan's

Company (Co. C), d. 9/1/61 @ H. Bocock's. His coffin size was recorded as 82 in. in length by 25 1/2 in. in width. He was buried in lot #159, grave #2, row #2. Death notice published <u>Lynchburg Daily Virginian</u> 9/5/61, page 3, col. 1. His home was listed as Hillsborough, Jasper County, Georgia.

* **Shuford, Phillip S.** - 23rd North Carolina Inf. Company F, d. 5/30/64 of wounds @ Knight's
Factory. Coffin size was 70 in. in length by 19 in. in width. Wounded at Battle of Wilderness 5/05/64. Enlisted as a private on 3/01/62 in Catawba County. Reported as deserted 8/02/63. Returned to duty 9/25/63 and Court Martialed. Was in confinement thru April 64.

* **Simmons, William** – 5th Alabama Inf., Company C, d. 1/21/63 @ Crumpton's Factory. Coffin size was 73 in. in length by 18 in. in width. The widow of the deceased was Abcillie, Simmons. Mrs. Simmons applied for a pension on 5/31/94.

Simpson, J. W., Lieut. - From Alabama, d. 7/28/61. Paid for by Hon. Judge R. W. Walker of Florence, Alabama.

Simpson, Robert M. - 38th Georgia Inf., Company A. Company Records state that he died in Lynchburg from wounds received near Winchester, Va. on 8/11/64. Nothing recorded in the Diuguid burial records for this man. He enlisted as a private on 9/26/61.

* **Simpson, Sampson C., Corpl.** – 48th Alabama Inf. Company E, d. 9/3/62 @ Christian's Factory. Coffin size was 77 in. in length by 19 in. in width. Based on Diuguid's records of coffins Corpl. Simpson was very tall fellow for the 1860's. His height would have been approximately 6' 2" by approximately 16" in width. His weight was probably less than 170 pounds. The widow of the deceased, Keziah Simpson, filed a death claim on 11/18/62. Her claim was verified and approved on 9/12/64. Widow Simpson residence was listed as Lebanon, Alabama.

* **Sims, Patrick Henry** - 23rd Virginia Inf.. Company A, d. 6/06/62 of diphtheria @ Booker's Factory. Enlisted as a private on 5/15/62 at Thompson's Cross Roads for 1 year. Born Louisa County, Virginia. Age at enlistment listed as 22. His occupation was listed as a farmer. Personal description 5'11" light complexion, light hair and blue eyes.

* **Singletary, B.** – 6th Alabama Inf., Company I, d. 2/1/63 @ Christian's Factory. Coffin size was 72 in. in length by 20 in.

in width. Singletary enlisted as a Private 9/24/62 in Clarke County, Alabama. The only entry in his military records after enlistment was "Missing since battle of Chancellorsville, May 3rd, 1863." No further record.

Sink, Jacob - 33rd North Carolina Inf., Company C, d. 1/29/63 of chronic diarrhea @ Langhorne's Factory. Coffin size was 69 in. in length by 18 in. in width. "Packed & sent to Lexington N.C." was the notation made by Diuguid. Joseph H. Miller claimed the remains, "For packing remains $20.00", paid in full. Resident of Forsyth County also were he enlisted on 7/01/62 at age 23.

Sink, Valentine - 48th North Carolina Inf., Company H, d. 3/21/64 of chronic diarrhea @ Camp Davis. Coffin size was 72 in. in length by 18 in. in width. Originally buried in lot #185, grave #6, row #2. Diuguid made the following entries, "Removed & sent to Danville Va" and "(Readsville N. C.)". Enlisted in Wake County for the war on 10/18/63.

Skipper, H. - 13th Georgia Inf., Company B, d. 8/24/62 @ Crumpton's Factory. Body prepared and sent to Grantsville, Georgia. Coffin size was 80 in. in length by 21 in. in width.

Slave - "Doct. Carmichales servant an employee at Pratt Hospital", d. 4/6/65 @ Camp Davis.

* **Sligh, David J. -** 12th Georgia Inf., Company C, d. 5/27/64 @ Burton's Factory from wound to arm received during Battle of the Wilderness 5/5/64. Arm amputated, died from complications. Coffin size was 78 in. in length by 19 in. in width. Enlisted as a private on 6/15/61. Wounded at Battle of McDowell 5/8/62.

Smith, Andrew J. - 47th Alabama Inf., Capt. Russell's Company, d. 3/16/63 @ Knight's Factory. Coffin size was 74 in. in length by 19 in. in width. Originally buried in lot #195, grave #5, row #3. Body was exhumed on request. Diuguid's entry, "was taken up & sent to Loachapoka Alabama". In the note section of burial log #6 Mr. Diuguid has made the following entry, "Mrs Adaline E. Smith Widow of Andrew J. Smith Direct to John J. Smith care of J. N. Brown Montgomery Ala."

* **Smith, B. T.** - 2nd South Carolina Inf., Company D, d. 8/24/63 @ Crumpton's Factory. Coffin size was 73 in. in length by 18 in. in width. Smith enlisted 10/20/61. Last report, based on military records, listed him in hospital in

Lynchburg on 12/31/61. 1860 census listed him as a resident of the Anderson District. No other information.

* Smith, Bennett - 37th North Carolina Inf., Company B, d. 6/30/63 of dropsy @ Camp Davis. Coffin size was 72 in. in length by 20 in. in width. Resident of Watuga County were he enlisted 9/08/61 at age 25. He was captured at Hanover Court House 5/27/62. Confined at Fort Monroe until he was paroled and transferred to Aiken's Landing on 7/12/62. Was listed as AWOL Oct. through Dec. of 62. Returned to duty by Feb. 63.

* Smith, Charles W. - 35th Virginia Battn. Cav., Company B, d. 10/16/64 @ Camp Davis. His military records state that he was discharged from service 10/15/64 with pleuritis.

* Smith, Conrad - 6th Louisiana Inf., Company H, d. 9/17/62 Ferguson's Factory. Company Muster Roll for May - August, 1862 Stated, "absent sick in general hospital". The Company Muster for Sept. - Oct. 1862 stated, "discharged from hospital". Coffin size was 69 in. in length by 18 in. in width.

Smith, John L. - 48th North Carolina Inf., Company K, died on or about 9/18/62 from wounds @ Camp Davis. Military records do not give a date or place but it would appear to have been Sharpsburg 9/17/62. Coffin size was 73 in. in length by 19 in. in width. Originally buried in lot #179, grave #4, row #2. Body was exhumed, and shipped to Max Meadows, Virginia. Diuguid's records indicate this grave was not filled. Smith was a resident of Forsyth County were he also enlisted on 7/24/62 for the war. His age at enlistment was listed as 30.

* Smith, John - 28th North Carolina Inf., Company I, d. 2/05/64 @ Booker's Factory. Coffin size was 69 in. in length by 18 in. in width. Death resulted from a self-administered overdose of morphine. Enlisted as a private on 1/06/62 in Yadkin County at age 18.

Smith, R. R. - 61st Georgia Inf., Company F, d. 8/12/62 @ Candler's Factory. His military records state that he died in Richmond. Coffin size was 71 in. in length by 18 in. in width. Body was prepared and shipped to Georgetown, Georgia. Recorded in Diuguid's main burial log, "For packing remains of R. R. Smith Aug 12th/62 $20.00", and also included the name Joel E. Smith. Private Smith enlisted on 8/15/61.

* Smith, Thomas - 12th North Carolina Inf., Company I, d. 6/04/62 of typhoid fever @ Reid's Factory. Coffin size 73 in. in length by 19 in. in width. Private Smith had served a total of

99 days in the military. Smith enlisted as a Private on 2/25/62 at age 43 for the war.

*** Smith, W. T.** - 14th South Carolina Inf., Company G, d. 2/22/63 of chronic diarrhea @ Ferguson's Factory. Coffin size was 75 in. in length by 18 in. in width. His age at enlistment was 40. 1860 census listed him as a resident of the Abbeville District.

*** Smith, William** - 16th North Carolina Inf., Company M, d. 1/14/63 @ Ford's Factory. His coffin size was 74 in. in length by 18 in. in width. Based on his military records it appears that he died of complications from wounds received 8/30/62 at the Battle of 2nd Manassas. Using the regimental history the following is listed as cause of death, "Bronchitis Chronic" and/or "Hepatitis" and/or "Wounds". Enlisted as a private on 5/01/61 in Gaston County, North Carolina. His age at enlistment was listed as 19. He was also a resident of Gaston County.

Snead, Micajah - No unit stated, d. 1/24/65 @ his home. Diuguid made the following entry, "Was buried in private square", "lot 44". Diuguid does not specify which cemetery. Very possibly in Spring Hill. Zachariah Woodall claimed remains and paid expenses. Diuguid also entered, "For burial service for Micajah Snead $400.00". Of this amount the "Southern Confederacy" paid $25.00.

*** Snipes, Asa** - 2nd South Carolina Inf., Company H, d. 12/17/62 of disease @ Knight's Factory. Coffin size was 75 in. in length by 18 in. in width. His age at enlistment was 31. 1860 census listed him as resident of the Lancaster District.

*** Sparks, William** – 47th Alabama Inf., Company K, d. 10/23/62 @ Knight's Factory. Coffin size was 71 in. in length by 18 in. in width. Sparks enlisted as a private on 4/29/62 at Loachapoka, Alabama. His age at enlistment was listed as 42. Private Sparks was a substitute for Isaac Williamson. Sparks was born in Alabama, married, occupation was listed as a farmer and was a resident of Dadeville, Alabama. The widow of the deceased filed a death claim, Mary Sparks, on 12/15/62. The claim was verified and approved on 1/21/65. Mrs. Sparks could be contacted in care of James M. Phillips, Attorney, Dadeville, Alabama. On 3/13/94 Mrs. Sparks applied for a pension. Her address was listed as Dadeville, Tallapoosa County, Alabama. The two witnesses listed on her application were W. B. Roberts and W. J. Mann.

Sparks, William M. - 12th South Carolina Inf., Company H, d. 3/6/63 of pneumonia @ Langhorne's Factory. Enlisted as a private on 8/13/61 at Rock Hill, South Carolina. His age at enlistment was listed as 22. Mother of deceased was Catherine Sparks. 1860 census listed him as a resident of the York District.

Spaugh, Benjamin A. - 35th North Carolina Inf., Company I, d. 2/15/63 of febris typhoides @ Burton's Factory. Coffin size was 71 in. in length by 18 in. in width. Body was exhumed 5/15/63 and "sent to Lexington N.C.". Ordan Rominger claimed the remains and paid expenses. Resident of Forsyth County where he also enlisted on 7/08/62 for the war. His age at enlistment was listed as 36.

* **Spiller, Hubbard (also Herbert?) M., Corpl.** - 1st (Hagood's) South Carolina Inf., Company J, d. 4/3/64 of chronic diarrhea @ Ferguson's Factory. Spiller enlisted as a Private on 3/29/62 at Union South Carolina. He was wounded at the 2nd Battle of Manassas 8/30/62. Deserted near Blackwater, Virginia, and returned to duty. Widow of deceased was Mary Spiller. Military records state his date of death as 5/15/64 as a result of wounds. 1860 census listed him as a resident of the Union District.

Spradlin, James Hardy - 58th Virginia Inf., Company I, d. 8/7/62 of typhoid fever @ Crumpton's Factory. Coffin size was 73 in. in length by 18 in. in width. His age at death was approximately 25. He was listed absent sick with typhoid fever in Lynchburg hospital 4/30/62. Personal description, 5' 8", fair complexion, bright hair, blue eyes, occupation farmer. He was the son of John and Sarah Spradlin. Originally buried in lot #162, grave #5, row #4, body was exhumed, prepared and shipped to Liberty (Bedford) Depot, Virginia. Note: J. J. Mathews of the 49th Georgia was buried there 8/31/62.

Spradlin, Paschal T., 2nd Corpl. - 58th Virginia Inf., Company I, d. 8/27/62 of Typhoid fever @ Langhorne's Factory. Coffin size was 77 in. in length by 19 in. in width. Body was prepared and shipped to Liberty (Bedford), Virginia. Born Bedford County circa 1841, his approximate age at death was 21. Personal description, 5' 10", fair complexion, auburn hair, blue eyes, occupation farmer. He was the son of James & Lucinda Spradlin. He was unmarried.

Spradlin, Thomas, Color Corpl. - 42nd Virginia Inf., Company C, d. 9/8/62 of pneumonia @ Burton's Factory. His coffin size was 74 in. in length by 18 in. in width. Corporal

Spradlin was severely injured in August, both legs were crushed and amputated. Body was prepared and shipped to Burford's Depot (Montvale), Virginia. For additional details related to the accident, see the entry under "Lambert, James Taylor", in this section. Spradlin enlisted as a private on 5/18/61 at Lisbon, Bedford County, Virginia. His age at enlistment was listed as 28. Promoted to Color Corpl. on or about 10/01/61. Was reduced to Pvt. by 12/31/61, reason no specified. Admitted to Lynchburg Hospital on 6/25/62 with debility. Had probably been released to return to duty when his legs were crushed.

Springer, Israel - 42nd North Carolina Inf., Company C, d. 8/18/62 of febris typhodies @ College Hospital. Coffin size was 68 in. in length by 20 in. in width. Body was prepared and shipped to Concord, North Carolina. Expenses paid by Captain J. A. Howell. Private Springer enlisted 3/13/62 in Rowan County at age 22. He was a resident of Stanley County, North Carolina.

* **Spurlock, Green W.** – 15th Alabama Inf., Company H, d. 5/28/62 of disease @ Crumpton's Factory. Coffin size was 69 in. in length by 18 in. in width. Spurlock enlisted as a Private on 3/10/62 at County Line, Alabama. His age at enlistment was listed as 25. He was born in
Alabama; occupation was listed as a farmer, was a resident of Kings, Alabama and was married. His military records list his date of death as 5/1/62.

* **Staggs, John** - 16th North Carolina Inf., Company I, d. 8/25/62 @ Claytor's Factory. His coffin size was 71 in. in length by 18 in. in width. He was wounded 6/26/62 at the Battle of Mechanicville. Military records state the cause of death as "Gastro Enteritis". Enlisted as a private on 3/8/62 in Henderson County. His age at enlistment was listed as 18. He was a resident of Transylvania County.

* **Starkey, John Jr.** - 58th Virginia Inf., Company E, d. 7/1/62 of congestion of brain @ Knight's Factory. Enlisted as a private on 7/24/61. Born Franklin County, Virginia circa 1822. 1860 census listed as age 38, occupation overseer, and a resident of Halesford P.O. Franklin County. Description, 5' 7", fair complexion, black hair, blue eyes, occupation farmer.

Starling, T. S. - 16th Mississippi Inf., Company F, d. 8/2/62 @ Christian's Factory. Body was prepared and shipped to Paulding, Jasper County, Mississippi. Diuguid also has made this notation, "Shubota Station Clark Cty Miss".

* **Steuart, John C.** - 31st Virginia Inf., Company E, d. 5/12/62 of erysipelas @ Booker's Factory. Enlisted in Bath County, Virginia as a private on 8/31/61. Death Cert. #853, "left $205.40 in charge of Capt. Hutter", turned over to G.M. cert #1084, Q.M. #585.

Stewart, Hezekiah - 42nd North Carolina Inf., Company F, d. 8/01/62 of febris typhoidies @ College Hospital. Coffin size 70 in. long by 20 in. wide. Body was prepared and shipped to Salisbury, North Carolina. He enlisted as a private on 3/18/62 in Davie County, North Carolina. His age at enlistment was listed as 30.

Stewart, Robert A., Asst. Surgeon - 9th Louisiana Inf., Company C, d. 9/03/61 of typhoid fever @ Camp Beauregard (Manassas). Mr. Diuguid made the following entry in the notes of burial log #4, "...remains sent to Bossier Parrish Louisiana accompanied by his friend & relative Wm W Carloss of New Orleans Oct 1st 1861". Stewart was appointed surgeon 07/19/61. Bossier Parrish is located in upper northwest corner of Louisiana with Caddo Parrish to the west, Webster Parrish to the east and Arkansas to the north. Stewart enlisted 7/19/61 @ Camp Moore, Louisiana. He was a resident of Mt. LeBanon, age at enlistment was 26 and listed as single.

* **Stewart (also Stuart?), R. M.** - MacBeth's Battery, South Carolina Light Art., (formerly Capt. R. Boyce's Battery), d. 12/14/62 of pneumonia @ Miller's Factory. Coffin size was 77 in. in length by 18 in. in length. Compiled Service Records state the he was, "listed as missing at Gordonsville, Virginia 8/1/63". He enlisted at age 39, on 11/15/61 at Unionville, South Carolina.

* **Stewart, William** - 6th South Carolina Inf., Company C, d. 12/14/62 of pneumonia @ Miller's Factory. Coffin size was 71 in. in length by 18 in. in width. Enlisted as a private on 3/14/62 at Camden, South Carolina. Captured at the Battle of Seven Pines (Fair Oaks). At the time of his capture he was listed as 32 years of age. He was exchanged 8/5/62 at Aiken's Landing, Virginia and returned to duty 9/29/62. Description - 5' 5", black hair, black eyes, and a light complexion. The widow of the deceased was Rebecca Stewart.

* **Stewart, William G., Corpl.** – 48th Alabama Inf., Company A, d. 6/24/64 @ Christian's Factory. Coffin size was 74 in. in length by 18 in. in width. Stewart enlisted as a private 4/7/62 at Warrenton, Alabama. His age at enlistment was listed as

31. He was born in Georgia, Married, occupation was listed as a farmer and his residence was Blountsville, Alabama. Diuguid in his records listed Stewart as a Corporal. Corporal Stewart was in 8 major battles and 6 other engagements from Aug. 1862 until Dec. 1863. He saw or participated in the following battles; Cedar Run, 2nd Manassas, Sharpsburg, Fredericksburg, Gettysburg, Chickamauga, Knoxville, and Beams Station. He was listed as "Absent Sick" prior to an engagement at Dandridge, Tenn. on 1/1/64.

Stidham, L. D. - No Diuguid Record - member of the 14th South Carolina Inf., Company A, d. 8/11/62 of disease. Was a resident of the Darlington District. However, Diuguid does list a Thomas L. Steudham, also a member of the 14th South Carolina, but part of Company K, same death date, cause of death typhoid fever @ Christian's Factory. Coffin size 74 in. in length by 18 in. in width. Very possibly these are one in the same.

Still, Thomas - 11th Virginia Inf., Company H, **Killed in Action** 5/31/62 at the Battle of Seven Pines. Enlisted as a private on 5/15/61. His age at enlistment was listed as 22 and occupation was listed as a Laborer. He was buried 7/21/62 in Lynchburg. Casualty notice published in the Lynchburg Daily Virginian dated 6/4/62, page 3, col. 2. This notice only listed the members of Company H that were killed or wounded.

* **Stinson, Samuel** – Phillips Legion, Battalion, Georgia Inf., Company B, d. 01/05/63 of pneumonia@ Ford's Factory. Not confirmed but believed to have been wounded at or near Fredericksburg, December 1862. Born 1835, resident of Whitfield County, Georgia.

* **Stogdale, Elias P.** - 52nd Virginia Inf., Company G, d. 6/7/64 of wounds @ College Hospital. Stogdale was wounded in his side at the Battle of Spotsylvania Court House on 5/19-/64. Enlisted as a private on 8/2/61. 1860 census listed him as 21 years of age, occupation farmhand, residing in Augusta County, Virginia. He was the brother of Henry T. Stogdale also a member of the 52nd Virginia, Company G, d. 8/18/64 at Elmira, New York (Union Prisoner of War Camp).

* **Stokes, T. A.** - 18th North Carolina Inf., Company C, d. 12/20/62 @ Claytor's Factory. His coffin size was 74 in. in length by 19 in. in width. He was wounded on 12/13/62 during the Battle of Fredericksburg. His military records list cause of death as "Diarrhoea Chronic". He enlisted as a

private on 8/20/62 at Camp Hill. His age at enlistment was listed as 23.

*** Stone, H. A.** - 8th Georgia Inf., Company H, d. 4/01/63 @ Claytor's Factory. His coffin size was 6 ft. 3 in. in length by 18 in. in width. Last entry in his service record stated that he was assigned to the ambulance corps 12/31/62.

Stone, John H. - 2nd North Carolina Inf., Company A, d. 2/25/63 of phthisis pneumonia @ Burton's Factory. Coffin size was 77 in. in length by 18 in. in width. Originally buried in lot #195, grave #7, row #2. Body was exhumed and "sent to Max Meadow Va". No date on removal, remains claimed by E. F. Lovill. He was a resident of Surry County. Enlisted as a private on 9/05/62 for the war in Wake County at age 28.

* Storie, Jesse P., Sgt. - 37th North Carolina Inf., Company B, d. 8/01/63 @ Candler's Factory of wound & disease. Born Davidson County, resident of Watauga County were he enlisted 9/14/61 at age 28. His occupation was listed as farmer. Mustered in at the rank of Corpl. Was reduced to rank of private by April 1862. Was reported as AWOL 11/01/62. Returned to duty by February 63. He was promoted to Sgt. sometime prior to 8/01/63. Was wounded at Gettysburg July 1-3, 63.

* Strickland, Leburn - 15th Alabama Inf., Company I, d. 8/16/62. "Died on O & A RR cars & buried from Warwick House", was the entry made by Diuguid. Diuguid also made the following entry, "John Strickland same Co is his brother". Coffin size was 73 in. in length by 18 in. in width.

Strum, Joseph - 15th Alabama Inf., Company C, d. 9/4/62 @ College Hospital. Originally buried in lot #178, grave #4, row #5. Body was exhumed, prepared and shipped to Union Springs, Alabama. Coffin size was 70 in. in length by 18 in. in width. Note: P. G. Long of the 37th North Carolina was interred that location 9/30/62.

Stuart, Nora - Daughter of General J. E. B. Stuart, d. 11/3/62, buried in #1, in south corner of Capt. Whiteheads Sq, Springhill Cemetery, paid by Maj. J. S. Langhorne. Funeral was conducted from the residence of Maj. John S. Langhorne, death notice was published the <u>Lynchburg Daily Virginian</u> dated 11/4/62, page 3, col. 1. (Note from 1863-64 logbook) "removed General Stuarts child buried in #1, South corner of lot 36, Section V, Springhill Cemetery - Capt. Whitehead's Sq."

* **Stubbs, Marcellus** – 47th Alabama Inf., Company A, d. 11/30/62 @ Langhorne's Factory. Coffin size was 76 in. in length by 18 in. in width. Stubbs enlisted as a private on 3/20/62 in Tallapoosa County, Alabama. Alcy Stubbs, the mother of the deceased, filed a death claim on 5/29/63. The claim was verified and approved on 2/3/65. The claim stated that Private Stubbs had no wife, child or father. Mrs. Stubbs could be contacted in care of M. J. Bulger, Chaneyhatchie, Alabama.

* **Sturdivant, William R.** – 41st Alabama Inf., Company A, d 5/6/64 @ Knight's Factory. Coffin size was 76 in. in length by 18 in. in width. Enlisted as a private on 3/13/62 at Tuscaloosa County, Alabama. His age at enlistment was listed as 28. The following information comes from the "Roll Book" of Orderly Sgt. H. H. Sartain. "Furloughed for thirty days from 17th April, 1863, by D. P. Davice, M.D. of Tuscaloosa Co., Ala." The next entry by Sgt. Sartain was "Deserted at Jackson, Miss. July 1, 1863." Sartain's next three entries are as follows; "W. R. Sturdivant is at Liberty until the 20th inst. At 11 o'clock A.M. – by order of Major S. G. Spann, Comdg. Rendezvous, Tuscaloosa Nov 12, 1863." "Headquarters, Tuscaloosa, Nov. 20, 1863. Extended until Nov. 25, 1863 – S. G. Spann, Maj. Comdg. Rendv." Nov. 25, 1863; extended until 30th inst. – W. C. Dunham, Lieut. Commanding Rendz., Tuscaloosa." Sergeant Sertain next entry was "Deserted – Returned to Company at Morries (sic) Town (Tenn.), Jan. 23, 1864." The final entry was "Sent to hospital at Lynchburg, Va., April 28 (1864)."

* **Styers, N. R.** - 21st North Carolina Inf., Company D, d. 6/18/64 "**Killed in Action**" at Battle of Lynchburg. His military record provides the following information. Enlisted as a private on 7/08/62. His age at enlistment was listed as age 23. He was a resident of Forsyth County. He was present for duty thru 8/03/63. At that point his records end with no additional information.

* **Suber, Enoch** - 1st South Carolina (McCreary's/Greg's) Inf., Company B, d. 2/28/63 of pneumonia @ Candler's Factory. Coffin size was 74 in. in length by 20 in. in width. Age at enlistment was 45. 1860 census listed him as a resident of the Newberry District.

Suiter, Arthur T., Sgt. - 12th North Carolina Inf., Company G, d. 3/13/63 of pneumonia @ Claytor's Factory. Coffin size was 69 in. in length by 18 in. in width. "Packed up & sent to

Petersburg Va." Brother of the deceased, J. W. Suiter, claimed remains. Mr. Diuguid in his note section of burial log #6 made this entry, "Mr. J. W. Suiter Petersburg Va will send for Remains his Bro who is packed up & ready to ship". At the top of this note in smaller letters is entered, "Conductor on Petersburg & Weldon R. R.". Was a resident of Halifax County and a merchant. He also enlisted in his home county on 4/25/61 at age 24. Was promoted to Sgt. between March & October of 1862.

* **Sullins, Nathan Ashbury** – 61st Alabama Inf., Co. H, d. 4/01/65 @ Ladies Relief Hospital. His coffin size was 73 in. in length by 18 in. in width. Diuguid had recorded his name as "Saulins". Sullins enlisted (no date specified) as Quarter Master Sergeant. Per his postwar tombstone he was born 03/27/23. He would have celebrated his 42nd birthday in March 1865. This soldier is one of the few in the cemetery that has had postwar tombstone erected by family. See the photograph this page. Diuguid identified him as N. S. Sullins, his marker has N. A. Sullins. His place of birth was McMinn County, Tennessee. He was married to Mary Keitt in 1855.

Sultan, Joseph R. - No Diuguid Record - Member of 15th South Carolina Inf., Company I, d. 5/15/64 from wounds per his military records. His age at enlistment was listed as 47. 1860 census listed him as a resident of the Lexington District.

Sutherlin, B. J. - 23rd Virginia Inf., Company E, d. 4/25/62 @ Booker's Factory. Body was packed and shipped to Barksdale Station, Halifax County, Virginia. No soldier with the above name listed as a member of the 23rd Virginia. Compiled Service Records list a "Christopher T. Sutherlin, 1st Sgt." also Co. E, listed as on leave 5/62 and discharged for being over the age of 35.

* **Swink, James William** - 5th Virginia Inf., Company F, d. 12/19/62 of smallpox @ the Pest House. Coffin size was 69 in. in length by 18 in. in width. Compiled Service Records for Private Swank states, "died of smallpox at Lovingston Hospital, Winchester (Va.). Swink enlisted as a Private on 3/15/62 in Augusta County, Virginia. Served approx. 8 months 26 days.

Swink, John H., 2nd Corpl. - 52nd Virginia Inf. Company C, d. 6/18/63 of typhoid fever @ Crumpton's Factory. Coffin size was 64 in. in length by 18 in. in width. Mr. Swink, father of the deceased claimed body. "Sent to Staunton Va" was the entry made by Diuguid. 1860 census listed as 21 years of age, a residing in the Northern District of Augusta Co., and occupation farmhand. Enlisted as a private on 7/16/61 at Staunton, Virginia. His age at enlistment was listed as 21. Wounded in action at Port Republic 6/09/62. Returned to duty 8/31/62. Brother of George Washington and Martin Van Buren Swink. Born Augusta County circa 1839. "A brave soldier and a true Christian."

* **Swinson, B. Frank** - 20th North Carolina Inf., Company E, d. 9/07/63 of fever @ Miller's Factory. Coffin size was 70 in. in length by 19 in. in width. Wounded at Battle of Gaines Mill 6/27/62. He was a resident of Duplin County, North Carolina. His occupation was listed as a carpenter. Enlisted as a private on 4/27/61 in Duplin County. His age at enlistment was listed as 28.

Tabour, Phillip - 4th Virginia Inf., Company L (Capt. Robert G. Newlee's Company) d. 9/10/61 @ Ladies Relief Hospital. Body was prepared and shipped to Christiansburg, Virginia, Montgomery County. He enlisted 7/16/61. Served 55 days in the military.

* **Talbert, Calvin R.** - 34th North Carolina Inf., Company K, d. 9/24/62 @ College Hospital of "Febris Typhoides".

* **Talbot, C. R.** - 34th North Carolina Inf., Company K, d. 9/24/62 of typhoid fever @ College Hospital. Coffin size was 77 in. in length by 18 in. in width. Father of deceased was Wesley Talbot of Windhill, Montgomery County, North Carolina.

* **Tankersley, J. M.** - 38th Georgia Inf., Company A, d. 7/19/62 @ Ford's Factory. Company muster roll dated 2/21/64 states, "sent to hospital", no other information. Enlisted 5/10/62.

Tarpley, David J. - 2nd Arkansas Inf., Company B, d. 7/11/61 @ A. Pamphlin's. A funeral notice was published in the Lynchburg Daily Virginian on 7/12/61, page 2, col. 5. The notice read as follows; "The funeral services of private David J. Tarpley, of Capt. J. H. Carpers, Company B, 2nd Arkansas Regiment, will take place at the residence of A. Pamphlin, on Lynch Street, at 4 o'clock this evening.

* **Tarpley, S. S., Dr.** - 11th Mississippi Inf., buried 8/4/61. Diuguid recorded, "died north of us, brought here for burial". Sterling O. Tarpley on New Orleans was the father of the deceased.

* **Tart, Vernon H.** – 6th Alabama Inf. Company C, d. 5/13/62 @ College Hospital. Enlisted as a Private 4/20/61 in Wilcox County, Alabama. The mother of the deceased, Eliza Harper, filed a death claim on 7/6/63. Her residence was listed as Clifton, Alabama. It appears that the claim was verified and approved on 8/12/64.

Tate, Charles C. - 22nd Virginia Cav., Company K, d. 10/7/64 of typhoid fever @ Camp Davis. Coffin size was 72 in. in length by 18 in. in width. "Was packed up & sent to 7 Mile Ford Smyth Cty Va". The father of the deceased claimed the remains and paid all expenses, "For coffin & tight box & packing sons remains $300.00". Was originally a member of the 51st Virginia Inf., transferred to the Cav. in 1863. Enlisted in 51st Va. 9/01/62 in Wythe County. 1850 census listed as a resident of Smyth County and age 5.

Taylor - Slave of Col. Withers (or Capt. Getty) d. 8/12/64 @ Christian's Factory. Coffin size was 71 in. in length by 20 in. in width. "Was buried in Negro Row". "Southern Confederacy" paid $15.00, balance paid in cash ($25.00).

* **Taylor, Joab** - 24th Virginia Inf., Company C, d. 12/20/62 of pneumonia @ Ferguson's Factory. Coffin size was 78 in. in

length by 19 in. in width. Enlisted as a private on 5/24/61 at Lynchburg, Virginia. He was born in Pittsylvania County, Virginia.

Taylor, Josiah F. - 2nd Virginia Cav., Company D, d. 8/07/62 of typhoid fever at the home of T. C. S. Ferguson. Body was prepared and shipped to Franklin County, Virginia. Diuguid had his name listed as "Joseph S". Admitted to Charlottesville Hospital with typhoid fever 7/22/62. Transferred to Lynchburg 7/23/62. Description, 5' 6", fair complexion, blue eyes, dark hair, occupation farmer. Buried in Price-Taylor Cemetery in Franklin County.

Taylor, Thomas Skelton, Capt. - 24th Virginia Inf., Company D, d. 10/4/61 of typhoid fever. Captain Taylor was in his 24th year of age when his untimely death occurred while stationed near the Potomac. Born 8/19/37 in Franklin County, he was the son of Christopher C. & Julia Taylor. He entered VMI on 8/02/54 and graduated 7/04/58 (one of 19 graduates). After study under Judge Brokenbrough he opened his law practice in Franklin County, Virginia prior to the war. His body was returned to Franklin County for burial. Taylor enlisted as a Private on 6/11/61 in Lynchburg, Virginia. The <u>Lynchburg Daily Virginian</u> published his obituary on 10/22/61 page 3, col. 1 & 2; and a tribute from the Franklin County Circuit Court was published on 10/30/61 page 2, col. 4.

Teaford, Joseph H. - 14th Virginia Cav., Company I, d. 3/14/65. Mr. Diuguid made the following entry, "Killed in camp near Fairgrounds". His military record list his death as accidental, "Accidentally wounded near Lynchburg 3/1/65 d. 5/15/65". However, Diuguid's entry in Burial Log Book #7 was made 3/15/65, "Was sent to Lone Mills Rockbridge Cty". Major Thomas J. Jenkins made the arrangements. The father of the deceased Henry Teaford paid all expenses ($350.00). Private Teaford enlisted as a private on 2/12/63 in Salem. 1860 census listed him as age 19, occupation clerk, and residing in Lexington, born Augusta County. Detailed as Brigade Ordinance Clerk 12/31/63 through 12/31/64. Age at death was listed as 22.

Team, John W. - 2nd South Carolina Inf., Company E (Capt. Kennedy's Company), d. 9/1/61. Father of the deceased was James Team. Although Diuguid does not specify his remains were sent home. His age at enlistment was listed as 18. 1860 census listed him as a resident of the Kershaw District.

Tearn, John - Died 7/15/61, his body was prepared and shipped to Kershaw District, South Carolina. No other information.

* **Thomas, John E.** – 8th Alabama Inf., Company D, d. 11/18/62 @ Crumpton's Factory. Coffin size was 71 in. in length by 18 in. in width. A death claim was filed April 27, 1864. William B. Thomas filed the death claim. William B. was listed as guardian and could be contacted in care of James M. Landrum, Attorney, Encheranna, Florida.

* **Thomas, William H.** – 14th Alabama Inf., Company G, d. 11/4/62 @ Ferguson's Factory. Coffin size was 72 in. in length by 18 in. in width. The widow of the deceased was Sarah J. Thomas. She applied for a pension 5/22/91 in Etowah County, Alabama.

* **Thomason, Arnold P.** – Holcombe Legion, Regiment, South Carolina Inf., Company G, d. 08/31/62 @ College Hospital. Born 02/06/31; married Harriet Suber of Newberry, South Carolina c. 1855. He was the father of 4 children.

* **Thompson, Allen** - 26th Georgia Inf., Company E, d. 8/6/62 @ Miller's Factory. Unit muster dated 2/28/62 listed him as present, no other information. Coffin size 76 in. in length by 18 in. in width.

* **Thompson, Blount James** - 2nd North Carolina Inf., Company F, d. 2/18/64 of smallpox at the Pest House. Coffin size was 72. in length by 19 in. in width. Private Thompson's military records state that he was discharged at Lynchburg 2/05/64 with "Valvular Heart Disease". Per his records his cause of death is listed as variola. Was Born in Bertie County and resided there until he enlisted 6/10/61 in Wilson County at age 33. His occupation was listed as a farmer.

* **Thompson, J. N.** - 1st North Carolina Cav. Company C, d. 3/15/62 of pneumonia @ the Warwick House. Enlisted as a private on 6/3/61. His age at enlistment was listed as 35 He was born in Mecklenburg County, North Carolina.

Thompson, James Sidney - 28th North Carolina Inf., Company G, d. 5/31/64 wounds @ Crumpton's Factory. His coffin size was 76 in. in length by 20 in. in width. Original buried in lot #193, grave #2, row #4. Exhumed 6/3/64, "removed & sent to Manbanville, N.C." was the entry made by Mr. Diuguid. The brother of the deceased, A. G. Thompson, claimed the remains and paid all associated expenses. He was a resident of Alamance County. Enlisted as a private on 9/02/61 in Orange County. His age at enlistment was listed as 21. Wounded in the arm and thigh during the Battle of the Wilderness 5/05-07/64.

* **Thompson, P. N.** – 44th Alabama Inf., Company K, d. 6/3/63 @ Langhorne's Factory. Coffin size was 74 in. in length by 18 in. in width. The widow of the deceased, Ruth E. Thompson, field a death claim on 10/3/63. The claim was verified and approved on 1/21/65. Mrs. Thompson could be contacted in care of A. Woods, Jacksonville, Alabama.

* **Thompson, Samuel R., Sgt.** - 1st South Carolina Cav., Company D, d. 8/13/63 of typhoid fever @ Crumpton's Factory. Military records list his date of death as 9/15/63. His age at enlistment was listed as 23. 1860 census listed him as a resident of the Chester District.

* **Thornberg, Andrew M.** – 48th Alabama Inf., Company E, d. 10/2/62 @ Miller's Factory. Coffin size was 72 in. in length by 18 in. in width. Diuguid had recorded his name as "Thornburg, A." Thornberg enlisted as a private on 3/31/62 at Guntersville, Alabama. His age at enlistment was listed as 19. He was born in Alabama, single, occupation was listed as a farmer, and he was a resident of Guntersville, Alabama. Per his company muster he was listed as "Absent Sick" prior to the Battle of Cedar Run on 8/9/62. His records state that his date of death was 8/11/62 at Gordonsville, Virginia.

* **Tinsley, Junius Fitz-James** - Stonewall Brigade Bugler, 5th Virginia Inf., Company G, **Mortally Wounded in Action** 6/17/64, d. of wounds 6/18/64. Originally buried on the battlefield. Exhumed on 6/20/64 and interred in Presbyterian Cemetery, Range 15, Lot 8. Diuguid's only entry was made in logbook No. 6 which stated, "For Removal & Burial of Mr. Tinsley". The charge was $75.00, which was paid in cash by Mr. Chas. L. Mosby. Tinsley enlisted 3/17/62 at Staunton, Va., his age was listed as 20. Birthplace listed as Richmond. (See photo of headstone on next page.)

* **Todd, James Erskine** - 1st Orr's Rifles, South Carolina Inf., Company C, d. 8/28/63 of typhoid fever @ Crumpton's Factory. Coffin size was 76 in. in length by 19 in. in width. Private Todd enlisted on 7/20/61 in Pickens, South Carolina. His age at enlistment was listed as 37. The widow of the deceased was Catharine Todd. Todd was born 07/14/25 in Pickens, South Carolina. He was married to Catherine Wilson in 1845. He was the father of 7 children.

* **Todd, Houston James E.** - 12th Georgia Inf., Company D, d. 5/8/62 @ Ferguson's Factory. Military record states cause

of death as "measles", and place of death as "Stribling Springs, Virginia".

Todd, Levia A. – 14th Alabama Inf., Company E, d. 7/3/62 @ Crumpton's Factory. Coffin size was 76 in. in length by 19 in. in width. Todd enlisted as a Private on 9/2/61 at Chambers County, Alabama. His age at enlistment was listed as 18. The father of the deceased, Levi Todd filed a death claim on 2/23/63. The claim was verified and approved on 2/4/65. Mr. Todd could be contacted in Chambers County, in care of Henry M. Cox, Attorney.

Junius Fitz-James Tinsely Tombstone in the Presbyterian Cemetery

Todd, John R. - "Niter Worker" (no unit stated), d. 8/4/63.
* **Todd, S. D.** - Palmetto Sharp Shooters, Company H (M?) d. 1/28/64 of disease @ Ladies Relief Hospital. Coffin size was 67 in. in length by 16 in. in width. His age at enlistment was

18. 1860 census listed him as a resident of the Pickens District.

* **Todd, Thomas L.** - 14th South Carolina Inf., Company F, d. 10/17/62 of typhoid fever @ Miller's Factory. Coffin size was 6 ft. in length by 18 in. in width. Todd enlisted as a private on 8/18/61 in Lawrence County, South Carolina. His age at enlistment was listed as 24. The widow of the deceased was Ruthet E. Todd.

* **Tormey, John** - 10th Louisiana Inf., Company D, d. on or about 9/25/64 @ College Hospital. He was buried (per Diuguid) on 9/28/64 in lot #198, grave #6, row #2. A post war record stated, "Sent to hospital in Richmond, never heard from again".

Traver, R. B. (or L. B.) - 3rd Georgia Inf., Company B, d. 9/2/61 @ Warwick House. Originally buried in lot #159, grave #5, row #1. Body was exhumed 9/15/61, prepared and shipped to Augusta, Georgia. Only one "Traver" listed in the Georgia Rosters, a "E. L.", of Company E, 60th Georgia Inf. that enlisted 9/19/61. NOTE: W. C. Peak of the 9th Georgia was buried in that location 9/15/61.

Trent, Timothy - Capt. William N. Patterson's Campbell Battery (possible), d. 5/21/62 @ Christian's Factory. Coffin size was 75 in. in length by 20 in. in length. Body was prepared and shipped to Campbell County, Virginia. Diuguid had recorded in the Soldiers Book the unit name As "Pierson's Art." There was no Pierson's Art. listed among the Virginia Units. However there was a Capt. Jacob D. Pierce, which commanded Co. D of the 20th Battn. Hvy. Artillery. To make things more confusing Patterson's Battery of Hvy. Art. was disbanded in June of 1862. 84 men of this unit were reassigned to the 18th Battn. Co. D. In addition 27 men were re-assigned to the 20th Battn. Virginia Heavy Art., Company D. Two Trents are listed in the 18th Battn. Co. D, both from Campbell County. No Trents are listed on the roster for the 20th Battalion. It's very possible he could a member of either unit but his name was never transferred in the muster due to his date of death.

* **Tribett, J. E.** - 37th North Carolina Inf., Company E, d. 1/15/63 of Phley Erysipelas @ Fords Factory. His coffin size was 74 in. in length by 18 in. in width. In the Soldier Book Diuguid made the Notation "one arm". Tribett most have been wounded and had an arm amputated.

* **Trigg, William King** - 11th Virginia Inf., Company G, d. 7/2/62, MWIA on 6/30/62 at the Battle of Frazier's Farm. Trigg was born 2/26/41. Enlisted as a private on 4/23/61. His occupation was listed as a clerk. He was interred in the Presbyterian Cemetery in Rang #3, Lot #3 on 7/21/62.

Trimble, Toby - Soldier's Negro Man, d. 10/13/62, no other Information. Possibly buried in Negro Row.

* **Trivett, John E.** - 37th North Carolina Inf., Company E, d. 1/15/63 of "Phley Erysipelas" @ Ford's Factory. Coffin size was 74 in. in length by 18 in. in width. Wounded at Battle of Fredericksburg 12/13/62, "thumb shot off".

* **Trotter, William L.** - 2nd South Carolina Inf., Company K, d. 5/20/64 @ Christian's Factory. Enlisted as a private on 1/13/62 at Pickens, South Carolina. The widow of the deceased was A. Trotter.

Truman, W. R. - 2nd Virginia Reserves, Company B, d. 3/15/65 @ Christian's Factory. Coffin size was 68 in. in length by 18 in. in width. Originally buried in lot #202, grave #10, row #2. Body was exhumed 3/27/64, "sent to Depot Monday the 27th", "Removed", "Packed up & sent to Big Lick Depot", were the entries made by Mr. Diuguid.

* **Tucker, Charles B., Corpl.** - 5th Florida Inf., Company I, d. 4/19/63 of pneumonia @ College Hospital (Gen. Hospt. #2). Coffin size was 68 in. in length by 18 in. in width. Enlisted at Camp Anderson as a private on 3/14/62. Promoted to Corpl. on 3/15/63. Tucker was born in 1843. He listed as unmarried. Father of the decease was Rufus Tucker.

* **Tucker, Levi T.** - 33rd North Carolina Inf., Company A, d. 6/01/64 of wounds @ Camp Davis. Coffin size was 73 in. in length by 18 in. in width. Enlisted in Wake County 5/26/63 at age 24. He was a resident of Lincoln County. Wounded at the Battle of the Wilderness 5/5-7/64 in thumb, left arm, & right shoulder. Compiled service records also state that he was captured.

Tucker, M. W. - 27th North Carolina Inf., Company H, d. 1/19/63 of hepatitis @ Crumpton's Factory. Coffin size was 73 in. in length by 18 in. in width. Originally buried in lot #189, grave #10, row #2. Exhumed on 1/24/63 at the request of William D. Tucker, brother of the deceased. "Taken up & sent to Lexington N.C.", was Mr. Diuguid's notation. Diuguid's entry was, "For removal & packing brother $25.00". There appears to be some confusion in the Diuguid records, in the "Soldiers Book" he is listed as a member of the 27th, in Log

Book #6 he is listed as member of the 22nd North Carolina. Private Tucker enlisted in the 27th N.C. in Pitt County on 4/20/61.

Turner, William W. - 2nd South Carolina Inf., Capt. Kennedy's Company, d. 9/2/61 at J. Cundiff's. Originally buried in lot #159, grave #3, row #2. His body was exhumed 12/30/61. The body was prepared and shipped to Camden, South Carolina per the instructions of Capt. McKagen. Diuguid made the following notation "removal and packing". His age at enlistment was listed as 18. 1860 census listed him as a resident of the Kershaw District. NOTE: J. J. Jenlins of the 20th Georgia was buried in that location on 12/31/61.

* **Tyree, Samuel Branford** - 11th Virginia Vol. Inf., Company G, **Killed in Action** 5/31/62 at Battle of Seven Pines. Tyree enlisted as a Private on 3/10/62. His age at enlistment was listed as 21. In Diuguid's Log Book #5 the following entry was made on 8/02/62 "John H. Tyree, Removal of Sons Remains". The cost for removal and reburial was $80.00. Private Tyree was reinterred in Presbyterian Cemetery Range 16, Lot 1. (See photo of headstone on next page.)

Ulmer, Adam A. - 1st South Carolina Inf., Company B, d. 11/12/62 of disease @ Ferguson's Factory. Coffin size was 73 in. in length by 19 in. in width. He was originally buried in grave no. 8 row no. 2 of lot no. 182. He was exhumed and shipped to South Carolina. His age at enlistment was 24. 1860 census listed him as a resident of the Orangeburg District. The only notation that Diuguid made in his logbook was, "St. Matthews P.O. S.C.". Diuguid listed his name as "A. A. Ullmer".

* **UNKNOWN** - This unknown soldier was buried 1/27/62 in lot #170, grave #4, row #2. Diuguid provided the following description; approximately 18 to 20 years of age, 5' 8" in height, light hair, sharp nose, upper teeth projecting and slightly decayed, mark of blister on his breast, grey kersey pants, white shirt much worn, hickory shirt, grey overcoat & white blanket in coffin, bare footed - taken on cars (railroad) at Gordonsville, Virginia. The blister on the chest probably came from the medical practice of "Cupping" a treatment for pneumonia

* **UNKNOWN** - An Unknown man was found dead on South Side Railroad - died on rail car - Diuguid made this entry, "supposed to be a Fort Donaldson prisoner". Unsure of the

date of death, he was interred on 10/12/62, buried in lot #180, grave #5, row #1. Coffin size was (external) 74 in. in length by 20 in. in width. Based on these dimensions his approximate height would have been 5 ft. 10 in. in height and 16 in. in width.

Note – The stone identifies his middle initial as "E." and the date of death is June 1, 1862. These do not coincide with the military records. This stone was erected in the late 1990's and certain material were not available.

* **Unknown** - "An unknown man brought to the Wayside Hospital a corpse supposed to be a North Carolinian". Died 6/26/64, buried in lot #190, grave #10, row #1.

Urquehart, B. W. E. - No unit stated, d. 10/12/61 @ Arnold Town, Campbell County. Approximately 24 years of age.

Death notice published in the Lynchburg Daily Virginian on 10/14/61, page 3, col. 1.

Utz, (poss. Calvin) - No unit recorded by Mr. Diuguid, d. 7/25/61, recorded as "son - soldier". Morgan Utz listed as debtor, expenses paid by McCorkle and Company. George Baxter McCorkle "Rockbridge Grays" commanded company H of the 4th Virginia Inf. A Private Calvin Utz from Botetourt County, served in Company I, enlisted 6/2/61, age 19 (student), died 7/25/61 from wounds received 7/21/61 at the Battle of Manassas.

* **Vail, J. (H.?) W.** – 5th Alabama Inf., Company E, d. 6/9/62 @ Langhorne's Factory. Coffin size was 76 in. in length by 19 in. in width. Enlisted as a Private 3/24/61 at Antiock, Alabama for a term of 3 years. Per Private Vail's military record it does not state that he died during the course of the war. Diuguid recorded the name as J. H. Vail, the only Vail that served in the 5th Alabama was J. W. Vail. Per his records he was listed as "Sick" at Richmond on the 11/6/62 muster roll. The next muster is dated 3/31/64 at Orange CH, Va. and he is listed as "Prisoner of War." Then the muster for 6/30/64 near Bunker Hill, Va. states, "Prisoner – Due commutation for clothing for year commencing Oct. 1861. Has drawn clothing in kind to the amount of $20.30." The muster dated from 7/1/64 to 9/1/64, stationed at New Market, Va., states "Corps Provost Guard. $7.00 additional pay per month from 9th June 1864." Also for that period on the same muster it stated "last paid May 1863" and in addition he was still listed as a POW. To make matters more confusing the muster dated 10/31/64 stationed at New Market, Va. states, "Prisoner of War. Exp 1 clothing 8 Oct. 63", "Last Paid 1/1/63." On the same dated muster it states, "Corps Prvt Guard", "Last paid 9/1/64."

Vandyke, Richard Smith, Maj. - 1st Tennessee Cav. (Carter's), d. 11/14/64. Diuguid does not specify his place of death. It appears that he may have died at the residence of John William Murrill. Mr. Murrill paid the burial expenses on Dec. 1, $275.00. Major Vandyke final resting place was Lynchburg, "was buried in west corner of Jno Wm Murrills lot No 13 Range 3 PGY (Presbyterian Grave Yard)".

Vaughn, Lewis M. - 2nd South Carolina Inf., Captain Kennedy's Company, d. 9/3/61 @ Mr. Farris's. Body was prepared and shipped to Kershaw District, South Carolina.

Cost of Mr. Diuguid's services was $25.00. The Name "J. H. Vaughn" is also listed in this entry.

Venable, Hugh - No Diuguid Record - 5th South Carolina Inf. Company K, no date of death supplied. His age at enlistment was listed as 25. 1860 census listed him as a resident of the York District.

* **Venters, Washington Harmon** - 7th South Carolina Inf., Company E, d. 6/21/64 from wounds @ Booker's Factory. His age at enlistment was 24. 1860 census listed him as a resident of the Williamsburg District. He was born c. 1837; son of David Blunt & Annie Flowers Venters. He was married to Eleanor Carter c. 1858.

Vest, David H. - 63rd Virginia Inf., Company A, d. 8/28/63 @ Ferguson's Factory. Coffin size was 76 in. in length by 18 in. in width. Originally buried in lot #196, grave #6, row #5. "Removed & sent to Botetourt Cty Va". No one by the name "Vest" served in the 63rd Virginia.

Via, James W. - 19th Virginia Inf., Company B, d. 6/29/62 of diphtheria @ Knight's Factory. His body was prepared and shipped to Charlottesville, Virginia. Via enlisted as a Private on 5/25/61 at Manassas. His age at enlistment was listed as 20. His occupation was listed as a farmer.

* **Vinson, John** - 26th North Carolina Inf., Company G, d. 8/05/64 of wounds @ Ladies Relief Hospital. Coffin size was 76 in. in length by 18 in. in width. The following is summary of Private Vinson's military record. "Enlisted Chatham County at age 26, 6 March, 62 as substitute. Present for duty until wounded at Malvern's Hill 1 July, 62. Returned to duty by December of 62. Listed as a deserter 29 March 63. Court Martialed & sentenced to be shot. His sentence was revoked on an unspecified date. He had returned to duty prior to 1 July, 63 when he was wounded at Gettysburg while carrying colors. Returned to duty prior to 1 Sept., 63. Present for duty until wounded in right leg at Wilderness 5 May, 64. Right leg was amputated. Died Hospital at Lynchburg on or about 5 August, 64 of wounds".

Vogler, Elisha M. H. - 33rd North Carolina Inf., Company H, d. 2/04/63 of chronic diarrhea @ Saunder's Factory. Coffin size was 74 in. in length by 18" in width. Mr. Diuguid's entry was, "Packed up & sent to High Point N.C.". George H. Flynt claimed the remains. Resident of Forsyth County where he also enlisted on 7/15/62. The body was exhumed 2/12/63. The fee for removal and packing was #20.00. See A. J.

Limback, Mr. Flynt claimed both bodies for return to North Carolina. Mr. Diuguid made interesting entry in the notes of burial log #6 in reference to Private Vogler, "Elisha Vogler Co H 33 N. C. at Saunders Factory is to be packed up if he dies & we are to write to Jas E Vogler Winston P.O. Forsythe Cty N.C.". Also in the same notation but in parenthesis is, "Saml Vest also of 33rd N.C. Reg.". Based on Diuguid's records Mr. Vest did not die and live to serve the Confederacy.

Vogler, J. L. - 24th North Carolina Inf., Company K, d. 12/25/62 @ Claytor's Factory. Coffin size was 75 in. in length by 19 in. in width. Originally buried in lot #123, grave #6, row #2. Body was exhumed 1/26/63, prepared and shipped to Danville, Virginia. Mr. Diuguid listed the name James E. Vogler as claiming the remains. Private Vogler was a resident of Forsyth County were he also enlisted on 7/08/62 for the war. His age at enlistment was listed as 30. NOTE: James D. Amos of the 26th Georgia was buried in that location 3/14/63.

* **Walden, Francis M.** - 44th Georgia Inf., Company D, d. 2/27/63 of typhoid fever, found in rail car, Southside Railroad. Diuguid's entry states, "Died on S. S. Car's, buried by Waldrop's order".

Waldon, J. A. - 15th Alabama Inf., Company E , d. 6/6/62 @ Christian's Factory. Body was
prepared and shipped to Fort Gains, Georgia.

Walker, R. W. - 22nd Virginia Battn. Inf., Company D, d. 8/13/63 @ Ladies Relief Hospital.
"Was sent to Mcherrin (sic) Depot R & D RRoad".

Wallace, Frederick J. - No Diuguid Record. 1st South Carolina Inf., Company D, d. 12/15/62. 1860 census listed him as a resident of the Lancaster District.

Waller, Richard H. - 21st Virginia Inf., Company H, d. 8/11/62 of bronchitis @ the home of Wilson O. Harvey. The attending doctor was a Dr. Patterson. Diuguid made the following entry, "was packed up & sent to Pittsylvania Cty" (Virginia). The widow of the deceased was Louisa B. Waller. Private Waller enlisted 3/10/62.

* **Ward, Peter D.** - 48th North Carolina Inf., Company B, d. 1/01/63 of wounds @ Burton's Factory. Coffin size was 74 in. in length by 19 in. in width. Wounded in hand 12/13/62 at Battle of Fredericksburg. Was a resident of Davidson County were he enlisted 8/08/62.

Ward, Patrick H. - 48th Georgia Inf., Company G, d. 12/20/62 of erysipelas @ Claytor's Factory. Coffin size was 73 in. in length by 18 in. in width. Originally buried in lot #101, grave #1, row #1. Body was exhumed, prepared and shipped to Macon, Georgia. Private Ward enlisted 3/04/62. NOTE: J. M. Trout of the 18th North Carolina was buried in that location 5/18/63.

Warner, Tefonius - 21st North Carolina Inf., Company K, d. 10/02/62 of phthisis pulmonalis @ College Hospital. Coffin size was 72 in. length by 18 in. in width. Body was prepared and shipped to High Point, North Carolina. His brother, Jacob, paid all expenses. Was a resident of Forsyth County were he enlisted on 7/08/62 for the war. His age was listed as 25 when he enlisted.

* **Warren, Micajah** - 13th North Carolina Inf., Company I, d. 7/04/63 @ Camp Davis of "Febris Remittens". Coffin size was 78 in. in length by 21 in. in width. His regimental history indicates that he "fell at Gaines Mill on 27 June, 62". This would indicate that he was more than likely wounded and transported to Lynchburg were he succumbs to his wound. Enlisted in Rockingham County 5/03/61 at the age of 26. His occupation was listed as a Ditcher.

* **Watson, John T.** – 15th Alabama Inf., Company G, d. 12/16/61 of disease @ College Hospital. Watson enlisted as a Private on 7/3/61 at Abbeville, Alabama. His age at enlistment was listed as 29. He was born in Georgia, occupation was listed as a farmer, he was a resident of Lawrenceville, Alabama, and he was single. His military records state that he died on 10/25/61 at "Hay Market" (sic).

* **Watson, John William, Sgt.** – 47th Virginia Inf., Company I, d. 05/03/64 of pneumonia @ Knight's Factory. Enlisted 03/08/62 as a Corpl. WIA @ Gettysburg 07/01/63 in right thigh; @ Chimborazo Hospital (Richmond) 07/29/63. He was born 1831 Brooke Station, Stafford County, Virginia. Married Margaret Watson.

* **Watts, Benjamin F.** - 1st Texas Inf., Company G, d. 6/12/62 of rubeola @ Langhorne's Factory. Coffin size was 68 in. in length by 18 in. in width. Enlisted as a private on 4/8/62 at Palestine, Texas. His age at enlistment was listed as 25.

* **Watts, William Archibald** - 3rd Georgia Inf., Company C, d. 11/25/63 of disease @ Miller's Factory. Enlisted as a private on 11/5/62 as a substitute for William R. Wilson.

* **Weatherly, Samuel S.** - 5th Texas Inf., Company I, d. 1/27/63 of typhoid fever @ Burton's Factory. Coffin size was 72 in. in. in length by 18 in. in width. Enlisted as a private on 3/28/62 at Independence, Texas.

* **Weaver, John** - 60th Georgia Inf., Company I, d. 11/13/63 of acute liver inflammation @ College Hospital. Coffin size was 72 in. in length by 18 in. in width. Captured at Fredericksburg 12/13/62. Sent to Old Capitol Prison, Washington, D. C. Exchanged at City Point Virginia 3/29/63. Private Weavers' name was listed as " Wever" in Mr. Diuguid's records.

Weaver, William H. - 37th North Carolina Inf., Company K, d. 6/02/63 of diphtheria @ Christian's Factory. Coffin size was 73 in. in length by 18 in. in width. Originally buried in lot #188, grave #10, row #3. "Removed & sent to Marion Depot". He was a resident of Alleghany County. Enlisted as a private on 8/15/62 in Iredell County for the war. His age at enlistment was listed as 21.

* **Webb, Peter D.** - 45th Virginia Inf., Company I, d. on or about 3/25/65 @ Knight's Factory. Enlisted as a private on 5/29/61 at Wytheville, Virginia. 1860 census listed age as 19. Was captured at Battle of Piedmont 6/5/64. Webb was confined as a P.O.W. at Camp Morton, Indianapolis, Indiana. He was exchanged in February of 1865, listed in the hospital system of Richmond 2/26/65.

* **Webb, Thomas** - 11th Virginia Cav., Company B, d. 7/1/63 of febris contina @ Reid's Factory. Buried in lot #192, grave #7, row #3, left $14.40 at the time of his death. Enlisted as a private on 3/10/62 at Winchester, Virginia.

* **Weddington, William A. G.** - 20th North Carolina Inf., Company B, d. 12/23/62 of diarrhea @ Reid's Factory. Coffin size was 74 in. in length by 18 in. in width. Enlisted as a private on 4/18/61 in Cabarrus County. His age at enlistment was listed as 37. He was a resident on Cabarrus County, and his occupation was listed as a teacher.

* **Weeks, Cornelius** - 22nd Virginia Inf., Company K, d. 5/21/64 @ Wayside Hospital. Diuguid's entry was, "Shot for deserter". Appears to have been a formal Military execution.

West, Jesse D. - 41st Virginia Inf., Company A, d. 9/08/62 of disease @ Ford's Factory. Coffin size was 74 in. in length by 18 in. in width. Diuguid made the following entry, "Was packed up and sent to Waverly Station Va.". He also references "P & N RR", (Petersburg & Norfolk Railroad, connecting Petersburg and Suffolk). Diuguid also references the name "Burton Watson".

* Whately, Cicero Columbus - 21st Georgia Inf., Company F, d. 6/26/62 @ Crumpton's
Factory. The father of the deceased was Rev. V. D. Whately, Antiach P.O., Troup County, Georgia. Whately was born 12/4/35, His age at death was 26.

Wheeler, George W. - 12th Alabama Inf., Capt. Brown's Company, d. 10/9/61 @ the Warwick House. Diuguid recorded the following, "packed up 10 October to be sent home, staid in our possession until 4 November without becoming offensive". "Cousin A. D. Lowry owes $15 on Him". Father of the deceased was Samuel Wheeler, Coffee County, Alabama.

* Whitacker, Hugh H. – 48th Alabama Inf., Company F, d. 1/18/63 @ Langhorne's Factory. Coffin size was 74 in. in length by 18 in. in width. Per Diuguid's burial logbook his name was recorded as "Whittaker, H. H." Whitacker enlisted as a private on 4/10/62 at Blountsville, Alabama. His age at enlistment was listed as 19. He was born in Alabama, single, occupation was listed as a farmer, and he was a resident of Blountsville, Alabama. Per the company muster he was listed as "Absent Sick" prior the Battle of Cedar Run on 8/9/62. In addition, his records state his date of death as 11/17/62.

* White, Harmon - 46th North Carolina Inf., Company I, d. 6/03/64 of wounds @Burton's Factory. Coffin size was 73 in. in length by 20 in. in width. Wounded 5/5/64 at Battle of the Wilderness. Born and resided in Sampson County where he enlisted on 3/12/62 at age 32. His occupation was listed as a farmer.

Whitehead, A. - No Diuguid Record - 5th South Carolina Inf., Company E, d. 1/01/63. 1860 census listed him as a resident of the York District.

Whitehurst, Cornelius - 11th Georgia Inf., Company K (Capt. Wimberly's Company), d. 12/26/61 of disease @ College Hospital. Body was prepared and shipped to his home in Fort Valley, Georgia. He enlisted 7/03/61.

Whitehurst, William A. - 44th North Carolina Inf., Company C, d. 11/5/63 of dysenteria chronic @ Burton's Factory. Coffin size was 72 in. in length by 18 in. in width. Dr. J. R. Jenkins claimed remains and paid expenses. "Was packed up & sent to Tarborough (sic) N.C.". Resident of Pitt County where he enlisted for the on 1/25/63. His age was listed as 43 when he enlisted.

Whitten, John W. - 52nd Virginia Inf., Company E, d. 5/8/62 of typhoid fever @Warwick House. Body was prepared and shipped to Lexington, Virginia. Born in Rockbridge County, Virginia 12/07/45. Enlisted as a private on 8/1/61 in Staunton. 1860 census lists his age as 16, occupation farmhand, and residing in the Lexington District of Rockbridge County.

Whitlock, J. S - 60th Tennessee Inf., Company C, d. 10/26/64 @ Crumpton's Factory. Coffin size 72 in. in length by 18 in. in width. "Was buried No 3 in 3rd line 3rd lot yankee lot". Very unusual, may have been a Union Soldier Diuguid does not specify.

* **Whitlock, Thomas A.** - 4th Texas Inf., Company G, d. 5/18/64 of dropsy @ Ferguson's Factory. Coffin size was 75 in. in length by 19 in. in width. Assigned as Brigade teamster Jan. 1862 through March 1864. Admitted to hospital April 1864.

* **Wiggins, William E.** - 59th Georgia Inf., Company B, d. 6/30/63 of typhoid pneumonia @ Ferguson's Factory. Coffin size was 73 in. in length by 18 in. in width. Wiggins was formerly a member of Capt. Horatio's N. Hollifield's Battery Light Art. Georgia State Troops. Was mustered out in Savannah 5/30/62. Enlisted in the 59th Georgia later that same year.

Wilkes, Benjamin T. - 14th Virginia Inf., Company B, d. 4/4/65 @ Christian's Factory. "Was sent to Liberty Depot Bedford Cty". Wilkes enlisted as a Private on 4/24/61 at Fancy Grove, Virginia. His age at enlistment was listed as 28 and his occupation was listed as a farmer. Admitted to Farmville Hospital 5/08/63 with rheumatism. He was listed as AWOL several times; the last was in October 1864. No further record.

Wilkerson, P. A. - 12th Mississippi Inf., Company C, d. 6/29/62 @ Ladies Relief Hospital. Body was taken to Mrs. Couche's for burial. Private Wilkerson was possibly taken to Bedford County for burial, the Couches and Wilkerson's were related by marriage.

* **Wilkes, James H.** - 4th Georgia Inf., Company I, d. 12/09/62 of Pneumonia @ Taliaferro's Factory. Coffin size was 74 in. in length by 18 in. in width. Per his military records Private Wilke's was wounded at the Battle of Malvern Hill 7/02/62. His death may or may not have been connected to his wound.

Willett, John - 3rd Georgia Battn. (Stovall's Battn.) Georgia Inf., Company E (Capt. White's Company), d. 11/04/61 @ Ladies Relief Hospital. Body was prepared and shipped to Thomason, Upson County, Georgia. Born in Chatham County, North Carolina in 1826. He enlisted as a private on 9/08/61.

Willhoit, A. S. - 10th Virginia Inf., Company L, d. 10/14/63. Diuguid made this entry, "A man supposed to be a soldier found in the river above the S. Side island on the 14th of Oct 1863 & was buried No 1 in 1st line of lot 200". A second entry by Diuguid was as follows, "found today Abram S. Wilhite Co L 10th Va who left the Way Side Hos whilst delerious". "Removed", "taken up & sent to Gordonsville Va". Based on Diuguid's records Willhoit appears to have been buried and exhumed in the same day. His service record states he died on 10/4/63.

* **Williams, D. R.** - 5th Texas Inf., Company H, d. 9/5/62 of tuberculosis @ Claytor's Factory. Coffin size was 72 in. in length by 18 in. in width. Enlisted as a private on 3/15/62 at Cold Spring, Polk County, Texas.

* **Williams, Hartwell Spain, Sgt.** - 34th North Carolina Inf., Company E, d. 8/23/62 of "Febris Typhoides" @ Christian's Factory. Diuguid also recorded "lay dead 3 or 4 days". Coffin size was 78 in. in length by 20 in. in width. His regimental records state that he died 8/27/62.

* **Williams, J. W.** – 5th Alabama Inf. Company G., d. 9/16/62 @ Langhorne's Factory. Coffin size was 71 in. in length by 18 in. in width. A death claim was filed on 10/15/62. The claim was verified and honored on 9/29/64. Alexander Williams was listed as the administrator, Henrico County, Virginia. The specific relation between J. W. and Alex was not specified. Sumpter County, Alabama was listed, possibly his residence.

Williams, Thomas. H. - 1st North Carolina Inf., Company C, d. 6/08/63 of gastritis @ Ferguson's Factory. Coffin size was 69 in. in length by 18 in. in width. Originally buried in lot #188, grave #8, row #5. "Removed & sent to Marlboro Depot N.C.". Resident of New Hanover County where he enlisted at age 18 on 6/11/61.

Williams, Jacob W., Corpl. - 42nd North Carolina Inf., Company E, d. 7/20/62 of typhoid fever @ Ladies Relief Hospital. Body was prepared and shipped to Lexington, North Carolina. Expenses paid by Capt. T. J. Brown. Enlisted in Davie County at age 32 on 3/18/62.

* **Williams, James W.** - 1st North Carolina Art., Company E, d. 12/26/62 @ Christian's Factory. Coffin size was 71 in. in length by 19 in. in width. His military record states, "Transferred from 1st Company G, 40th Regiment North Carolina Troops (3rd N.C. Art.) 8 Oct. 62. Absent sick after 12 Nov., 62. Reported dead 7 March, 63".

Williams, W. C. - 42nd Virginia Inf., Company H, d. 5/03/62 of pneumonia @ Christian's Factory. Body was prepared and shipped to Patrick County, Virginia. Enlisted 3/17/62 @ Tatum's Store, Patrick Henry County, Virginia. Mustered in 4/14/62 @ New Market.

Williams, William T. - 6th Virginia Cav., "Cabell Edward Flournoy's Company" (Company E), d. 5/7/62 of rubeola @ the home of P. Lewis. Body was prepared and shipped to Ringold's Station (Pittsylvania County) via the Richmond & Danville Railroad. Expenses paid by the father of the deceased, Charles B. Williams. He enlisted 4/01/62.

* **Willingham, John H.** – 47th Alabama Inf., Company D, d. 10/2/62 @ Langhorne's Factory. Coffin size was 73 in. in length by 18 in. in width. Willingham enlisted as a private on 4/26/62 at Loachapoka, Alabama. Per his records his was paid in camp near Loachapoka on 5/23/62. No further record.

Willis, Charles A. - 1st Rifles South Carolina Inf., Company A, d. 6/3/64 of wounds @ Crumpton's Factory. His coffin size was 74 in. in length by 18 in. in width. "Was packed up & sent to White Pond Depot S.C.". Diuguid did not provide a first name or the relation only that "Mrs. Willis" claimed the remains. 1860 census listed him as a resident of the Barnwell District.

Wilner, A. A. - 1st South Carolina Inf., Company B, d. 11/12/62 @ Ferguson's Factory. Originally buried in lot# 1-82,grave #8, row #2. Coffin size was 73 in. in length by 19 in. in width. Body was exhumed, prepared exhumed, prepared and shipped to St. Matthews P.O., South Carolina. NOTE: William J Beckham of the 9th Louisiana was interred in that location on or about 6/8/63.

* **Wilson, J. B.** - 5th Texas Inf., Company K, d. 9/25/62 of wounds @ Booker's Factory. Wilson was wounded 8/22/62 at Freeman's Ford. Freeman's Ford is located on the Rappahannock River. Skirmishing took place at this and two other river fords on the 21st and 22nd. Coffin size was 74 in. in length by 18 in. in width. Wilson enlisted as a Private on 2/26/62 at Monroe, Louisiana.

* **Wilson, John W.** – 48th Alabama Inf., Company D, d. 10/13/62 @ Knight's Factory. Coffin size was 74 in. in length by 18 in. in width. Wilson enlisted as a private on 4/7/62 for 3 years at Warrenton, Alabama. His age at enlistment was listed as 18. He was born in Alabama, single, occupation was listed as a farmer and he was a resident of Warrenton, Alabama. Wilson was officially mustered into service on 5/31/62 at Auburn, Alabama. His military record stated his date of death was 9/5/62 at Liberty Mills, Virginia. Joseph M. Wilson, father of the deceased, filed a death claim on 2/17/63. The claim was verified and approved on 1/21/65. Mr. Wilson could be contacted in Marshal County, Alabama.

* **Wilson, Marion** - 2nd South Carolina Inf., Capt. Manning's Company, d. 6/21/61 @ College Hospital. The father of the deceased was Henderson Wilson, Hamburg P.O., Ashley County, Arkansas.

Wilson, Peter P. - 5th North Carolina Inf., Company K, d. 3/06/62 of pneumonia @College Hospital. Body was prepared and shipped to Danville, Virginia. Enlisted as a private on 6/13/61 in Caswell County. His age at enlistment was listed as 19. Wilson was also born in Caswell County.

* **Wimberly, George E.** - 6th Georgia Inf., Company I, d. 12/27/62 @ Ferguson's Factory. Coffin size was 72 in. in length by 18 in. in width. Wimberly enlisted as a private on 5/27/61. Per his military record he died at "Guinea Station", on Dec. 25 or 27, 1862.

Windes, F. M., Lt. Col. - 4th Alabama Cav. (Roddey's), was interred in the City Cemetery 9/19/68. He was buried in lot #250, grave #4, row #5. This was the last Confederate soldier listed by Mr. Diuguid in the "Soldiers Book".

Windham, Allen - No Unit Specified, d. 12/26/62 @ Knight's Factory. Body was prepare and shipped to Quitman, Georgia. Coffin size was 72 in. in length by 19 in. in width. The father of the deceased, E. C. Windham, paid for preparation, coffin & shipment.

Withers, Sawney, Dr. - 2nd Virginia Inf., Asst. Surgeon, d. 6/21/61 @ Bellevue Hospital in Richmond, Virginia. He was about 25 years old and a native of Lynchburg. His death notice appears in the Lynchburg Daily Virginian 6/22/61, page 3, col. 1 (see following page for Transcribed notice). Doctor Withers is not listed in the compiled service records of the 2nd Virginia Inf. or Cav., or any of the other units from Lynchburg.

This it not to say that he did serve in the military, only that there is no current listing.

Lynchburg Daily Virginian dated June 22, 1861
Death Notice of Dr. Sawney Withers
(Transcribed from the original newspaper)

SUDDEN DEATH - Dr. Withers, Assistant Surgeon of the 2nd Regiment of Virginia Volunteers, a native of Lynchburg, we regret to learn, died very suddenly yesterday evening at Bellevue Hospital. He was carried thither about 10 1/2 o'clock on Wednesday night, by a stranger, as we were informed. The deceased was apparently about 25 years of age, and is said to have been a gentleman of great social wealth, and beloved by a large circle of friends, who can but grieve at hearing of his sudden and untimely demise. Of the nature of his malady, we know nothing. His body will, as we understand, will be committed to its last resting place, with military honors, this evening, but at what hour we are unable to state. D. Patch

* **Witt, Daniel B., Jr.** - 58th Virginia Inf., Company A, d. 7/7/62 of typhoid fever @ Christian's Factory. Born Bedford County; 1860 census listed him as age 17, occupation farmhand, res. Davis Mills P.O., Bedford County.
  Wolfe, **** - No unit stated, d. 8/24/61, Martin R. Wolfe listed as debtor, "packing corpse of brother".
  Wood, E. B. - Phillips Legion, Georgia Inf., d. 10/31/61 @ H. R. Sumpter's. Body was prepared and shipped to the father of the deceased, John Wood, Greensboro, Georgia.
  Wood, John William - Capt. Winston Radford's Company, 30th Virginia Cav. (2nd Va. Cav., Company G "Radford Rangers", Bedford County), d. 9/11/61 of "Febris Remittens" (Diuguid does not state location of death, his military records indicated a Lynchburg Hospital). John B. Wood listed as debtor. Born circa 1839. Enlisted at Forest Depot 5/28/61 at age 23, occupation listed as farmer.
  Woods, William H. - 11th Virginia Inf., Company G, **Killed in Action** 9/17/62 @ Sharpsburg, Maryland. Mr. Diuguid in Log Book #5 about Private Woods supplies a brief notation. The following was enter by Diuguid, "Thos D. Woods (of) Christiansburg Va has a son Wm H. Woods Co G 11 Va buried at Shepperdstown and wants him removed" Diuguid continues, "Dabney Percival buried Robt T. Calhoun of same Co is at same

place. Diuguid provides no other information as to whiter one or both of the young men were exhumed and returned to Virginia. Private Woods enlisted 4/23/61 in company G at age 20 his occupation was listed as a Merchant. Robert T. Colhoun enlisted 4/23/61 in company G at age 23 his occupation was listed as Merchant. C. Dabney Percival enlisted 4/23/61 in company G at age 25 and his occupation was listed as a Carpenter. I have not been able to locate any record of Woods or Colhoun being buried in Lynchburg. It is very possible that that they may have been buried in family plots outside of Lynchburg. It would also appear these three young men were very close friends.

* Woodring, J. - 60th Georgia Inf., Company F, d. 7/6/62 @ Crumpton's Factory. Coffin size was 71 in. in length by 19 in. in width. Diuguid's records state, "To be packed and sent to Mountain Town P.O., Gilmore County". Woodring was buried 68 months later, Diuguid's recorded the following, "Buried No. 7 in 5th line Lot 202 March 30, 1868".

Woodruff, William D. - 1st North Carolina Cav., Company H, d. 9/13/62 of febris typhoides@ College Hospital. Coffin size was 71 in. in length by 18 in. in width. Diuguid's only notation was "Packed up and sent home". Conscripted in Wake County 7/15/62 for the war.

Woods, Joshua Brandon - 46th North Carolina Inf., Company B, d. 5/20/64 of diarrhea chronic @ Camp Davis. His coffin size was 74 in. in length by 18 in. in width. Originally buried in lot #193, grave #5, row #1. Exhumed on 12/5/64, "Removed & sent to China Grove Depot Rowan Cty N.C.". Thomas S. Atwell claimed the remains and paid all associated expenses for the removal and preparation for shipment home ($175.00). Woods was a resident of Rowan County where he enlisted on 4/13/63 for the war. Age at enlistment was 40.

Word, Alexander - 11th Mississippi Inf., Van Dorms Reserve, d. 5/29/61 @ Norvell House. Diuguid recorded the following, "was sent in Metallic to Thomas Word Okolona Chickasaw Cty Miss". The reference "Metallic" was the type of coffin used.

* Wrenn, James W., Sgt. - 6th Virginia Cav., Company F, d. 3/21/65 of pneumonia @ Christian's Factory. Enlisted as a private on 10/1/61.

Wright, Abraham B., 1st Sgt. - 51st Georgia Inf., Company E, d. 11/01/62 @ Odd Fellow's Hall. Coffin size was 75 in. in length by 18 in. in width. Originally buried in lot #182, grave

#1, row #3. Body was exhumed 11/22/62, prepared and shipped to Grantville, Georgia. The brother of the deceased, Young F. Wright paid, "for removal & packing brothers remains". The cost was $20.00, paid in full by cash. Enlisted as 1st Sgt. 3/04/62 (born in 1833). NOTE: Allen Crowder of Jordan's Battery, Virginia Light Art., was buried in that location 11/22/62.

* **Wright, A. H.** - 1st Georgia Inf., Company E, "died Monday (10/27/62)". The following was recorded in Diuguid's burial book, "A. H. Wright a soldier found dead on the South Side Cars having in possession transportation to Calhoun Ga and $112.60 in money he was buried in No 4 in 3rd Line of Lot 181", he continues, "Coroner A W Cross has his effects". His death notice appeared in the <u>Lynchburg Daily Virginian</u> dated 10/30/62, page 3, col. 1, which stated that he was discharged from a Richmond Hospital and had died in the rail car on Monday just as the train was arriving in Lynchburg. A second article was published on 11/3/62 identified him and stating he was on furlough to Calhoun, Georgia and had $112.60 in his possession. Deducting the cost of his funeral, $102.60 was deposited in a local bank for his relatives to claim.

* **Wright, Alfred Spinks** - 46th North Carolina Inf., Company G, d. 5/19/64 of pneumonia@ Knight's Factory. Was a resident of Randolph County. Enlisted as a private on 6/21/62 as a substitute, @ Drewry's Bluff, Virginia. His age at enlistment was listed as 16 Wright was wounded at Bristoe Station 10/14/63. Returned to duty by Nov. 1, 63.

Wright, James C., 2nd Corpl. - 4th Virginia Inf., Company F, d. 7/4/62 of wounds @ College Hospital. Wright was wounded @ Battle of Kernstown on 3/23/62. He enlisted on 4/24/61. His age at enlistment was listed as 21 and his occupation was listed as a farmer. Originally buried in lot #171, grave #4, row #2. Body was exhumed, prepared and shipped to Wytheville, Virginia. Arrangements for removal and packing the remains were done by John J. Cannoy. NOTE: Henry Taylor of the 26th Georgia was buried in that location on 8/8/62.

Wright, John Quincy Adams, 1st Sgt. - 58th Virginia Inf., Company E, d. 7/19/62 @ Hancock's Private Hospital of typhoid fever. Coffin size was 69 in. in length by 19 in. in width. Body was prepared and shipped to Gish's Mill, Bedford County, Virginia. Born Bedford County 1826. Enlisted in Co. K @ Chamblissburg on 7/23/61. His age at enlistment was listed as 35. Elected 1st Sgt. and transferred to Co. E on 5/28/62.

Wright, Louis - 11th North Carolina Inf., Company A, d. 8/24/61 @ the Warwick House. Originally buried in lot #158, grave #5, row #4. Body was exhumed on 8/29/61, prepared and shipped to Salem, North Carolina. Father of the deceased was James R. Wright.

Wright, Theodore F. - 4th Virginia Inf., Capt. (Edmondson's) Company B, d. 7/25/61 in Charlottesville Hospital from complications of wounds received 7/21/61 at Manassas. Enlisted as a private on 4/18/61. His age at enlistment was listed as 22 and his occupation was listed as a merchant. Born Franklin County, Virginia. His body was prepared and shipped to Shawsville, Montgomery County, Virginia.

Wyley, J. Ross - No Diuguid Record - 17th South Carolina Inf., Company D, d. 10/22/62 of disease in Lynchburg. His age at enlistment was 24. 1860 census records listed him as a resident of the Chester District. Possibly Jonathan Ross Wyley, or related to, see below.

* **Wyley, Jonathan** - 17th South Carolina Inf., Company A, d. 11/18/62 of pneumonia @ Christian's Factory. Enlisted at College Green, South Carolina, date not specified. The father of the deceased was listed as Samuel Wylie (sic). Coffin size for Private Wyley was 73 in. in length by 18 in. in width. His age at enlistment was 19. 1860 census listed him as a resident of the Chester District.

* **Yarborough, J. C.** - 14th North Carolina Inf., Company F, d. 2/10/64 of smallpox at the Pest House. Coffin size was 76 in. in length by 19 in. in width. His military records state that he died in Lynchburg prior to January 1, 1864 and that the exact cause of death was unknown. Also, Mr. Diuguid recorded his name as "Yarber". He was a resident of Montgomery County, enlisted in Wake County 6/16/62 at age 26.

* **Yarrington, Andrew B.** - 26th Virginia Inf., Company G, d. on wounds 10/30/64 @ Ferguson's Factory. Yarrington was wounded on 6/24/64. Was wounded accidentally in left arm. Enlisted as a private on 12/4/63 at Little Plymouth. His age at enlistment was listed as 18.

* **York, Alexander B.** - 24th Georgia Inf., Company E, d. 6/11/62 @ Ford's Factory. The last company muster, dated 10/31/61, listed him as, "present for duty", no other information.

* **Young, A. A.** - 48th North Carolina Inf., Company H, d. 1/01/63 of gangrene @ Ford's Factory. Coffin size was 75 in. in length by 18 in. in width. Wounded in foot 12/13/62 at Battle of Fredericksburg. Resident of Davidson County where he enlisted 8/14/62.

* **Youngblood, Francis M.** - 8th Louisiana Inf., Company E, d. on or about 2/10/63 @ Claytor's Factory. Coffin size was 76 in. in length by 18 in. in width. The company muster for April to August of 1864 stated, "absent, not heard from since November 20, 1862, supposed to be dead".

* **Yow, Andrew C.** - 48th North Carolina Inf., Company D, d. 2/12/63 of rheumatism chronic @ College Hospital. Coffin size was 76 in. in length by 20 in. in width. Resident of Moore County where he enlisted 3/10/62 at age 28. Occupation was listed as a farmer. Listed as deserter 9/7/62. Was arrested and sent to camp 10/4/62.

Zimmerman, Thomas - 10th Virginia Inf. Cav., Company B, d. 2/26/63 of typhoid fever @ Christian's Factory. Coffin size was 70 in. in length by 18 in. in width. "Sent to Lexington N.C.". Matthew Mackland claimed remains. Diuguid's entry was, "For coffin & packing T. Zimmerman $40.00". Diuguid also entered, "Effects $110.00 and sundries." Zimmerman was born circa 1840, enlisted 10/29/61 in Davie County, North Carolina, at age 21.

Union Soldiers:

Ackers, Sidney E. A. - 11th Michigan Cav., Company M, d. 6/03/65 of disease @ Pratt Hospital. Coffin size was 68 in. in length by 18 in. in width. "Was buried No 3 in 5th line of 3rd lot". Enlisted 8/27/64 at Reading for one year. Age at enlistment listed as 20. Mustered in on 9/13/64. Joined his regiment at Lexington, Ky. on 10/17/64. Listed as prisoner at Lynchburg, Va. (no date stated). Died of disease while a P.O.W. Pension information indicates that his mother (Jane Acker) applied for a pension on 6/7/88, application #394,030. This soldier's remains were exhumed from the Old City Cemetery in Oct. 1866 and reinterred in a National Cemetery. All Union soldiers remove from Lynchburg were to be reinterred at Poplar Grove National Cemetery, Petersburg, Virginia.

Allen, Benjamin - 10th New Jersey Inf., Company G, P.O.W., d. 12/22/64 @ Crumpton's Factory. Coffin size was 74 in. in length by 17 in. in width. "Was buried No 1 in 5th line 3rd lot". Allen enlisted and mustered in to service on 4/05/64. Caused of death or place of capture not stated. He was a resident of Harrisonville, Glouster County, New Jersey. No birth date or age provided. He was unmarried. This soldier's remains were exhumed from the Old City Cemetery in Oct. 1866 and reinterred in a National Cemetery. All Union soldiers that were removed from Lynchburg were supposed to be reinterred at Poplar Grove National Cemetery, Petersburg, Virginia.

Almy, Frank M., Corpl. - 1st Massachusetts Cav., was killed in a street fight 5/1/65. Diuguid made the following entries in the "Soldier's Book", "Killed in street fight by Stockton Terry", "Killed on Bridge Street near John Duggans". Diuguid's burial book entry listed his name as ***"Alma"*** Originally buried Lot #3, Grave #3, row #5. Body was exhumed, "Packed up & marked Newbury Port, Rhode Island (delivered to Express Co. on the 5th day of Sept. 1865)". Diuguid made the following concerning the removal of Corpl. Almy, *"8/18/65 Capt. Geo. C. Almy, for removal & packing brother F M Almy $45.00 - delivered to the Express Co. 5th Sept. 1865"*. Almy enlisted as a Pvt. 8/4/62 at age 21. His occupation was listed as a tinsmith. He mustered into the 1st Mass. Cav. on 8/4/62. Almy was promoted to Corpl. 3/17/64. His residence was listed as Newport, Rhode Island.

Andrews, Charles E. - 1st Vermont Inf., Company H, P.O.W., d. 7/30/62 @ the Fairgrounds. Was buried in Yankee Square, #3, in 5th line. Enlisted as a private on 12/01/61. He was mustered in on 12/10/61. His age at enlistment was listed as 26 and his occupation was listed as a shoemaker. He was resident of Essex Massachusetts. His military records state that he was **Killed in Action** at Glendale, Va. on 6/30/62 (Seven Days around Richmond). His widow (Amelia A. C. Andrews) applied for a pension on Jan. 2, 1863, Application #9,492. His son (John E. Lee) applied for pension on Sept. 24, 1866 application #134,170. This soldier's remains were exhumed from the Old City Cemetery in Oct. 1866 and reinterred in Poplar Grove National Cemetery, Petersburg, Virginia. Grave #4719.

Arnold, William, Corpl. - 77th New York Inf., Company B, P.O.W., d. 9/22/64 of disease @ Crumpton's Factory. "Was buried No 7 in 1st line of 3rd lot". Arnold enlisted as a Private 9/17/61 at Ballston, N.Y. at age 19. He was promoted to

Corpl. 3/30/63. He was wounded & captured on 5/3/63 at Fredericksburg then paroled. Returned to duty 10/12/63. He was wounded and captured on 5/6/64 during the battle of the Wilderness. This soldier's remains were exhumed from the Old City Cemetery in Oct. 1866 and reinterred in Poplar Grove National Cemetery, Petersburg, Virginia. Grave #4870.

Bader, Henry - 1st Maryland Inf., Company K, P.O.W., d. 7/31/62 @ the Fairgrounds of "disease contracted while in military". Was buried in Yankee Square, #7, in 5th line. He was captured 5/23/62 at the Battle of Front Royal, Virginia. He enlisted as a private and was mustered into service 5/28/61 at Relay House, Maryland. His age was listed as 42 went he enlisted. This soldier's remains were exhumed from the Old City Cemetery in Oct. 1866 and reinterred in Poplar Grove National Cemetery, Petersburg, Virginia. Grave #4610.

Ballard, Joseph - 147th New York Inf., Company K, P.O.W., d. 8/26/64 @ Crumpton's Factory. "Was buried No 10 in 5th line of 2nd lot". Enlisted and was mustered in as a private at Hanover, N.Y. on 8/8/63. His military records list him as **Killed in Action** at the Wilderness 5/5/64. This soldier's remains were exhumed from the Old City Cemetery in Oct. 1866 and reinterred in Poplar Grove National Cemetery, Petersburg, Virginia. Grave #4959.

Barker, John - 14th Indiana Inf., Company E, P.O.W., d. 6/30/62 @ the Fairgrounds. Was buried in Yankee Square, #1, in 2nd line. A search of the records for the 14th Indiana could not locate a John Barker. However, this soldier's remains were exhumed from the Old City Cemetery in Oct. 1866 and reinterred in Poplar Grove National Cemetery, Petersburg, Virginia. Grave #4714.

Barney, J. P. - 1st Delaware Inf., Company A, P.O.W., d. 8/12/64 @ Crumpton's Factory. His coffin Size was 72 in. in length by 15 in. in width. "Was buried No 6 in 5th line of 2nd lot". This soldier's remains were exhumed from the Old City Cemetery in Oct. 1866 and reinterred in Poplar Grove National Cemetery, Petersburg, Virginia. Grave #4790.

Barnum, Isaac - 15th New York Cav., Company E, P.O.W., d. 7/15/64 of wounds @ Knight's Factory. Barnum was wounded and taken prisoner 6/18/64 at the Battle for Lynchburg. The causality records for Hunter's Army June 10 thru 23 listed the 15th New York with 15 wounded and 23 captured. Barnum "Was buried No 9 in 1st line 2nd lot". He enlisted and was mustered into service as a private at Liberty (NY?) on 1/26/64 at age 23. This soldier's remains were exhumed from the Old City Cemetery in Oct. 1866 and reinterred in Poplar Grove National Cemetery, Petersburg, Virginia. Grave #4633.

Beard, James - 85th Indiana Inf., Company C, d. 3/27/63 @ Christian's Factory. Coffin size was 72 in. in length by 18 in. in width. Was buried in lot #199, grave #8, row #2. An initial search of the records for the 85th Indiana could not locate a James Beard. The entire 85th Indiana, per its unit history, was capture on 3/5/63 at Thompson's Station Tennessee. They were sent to Libby prison in Richmond, Virginia. The members of this regiment were exchanged on 3/31/63. However, this soldier's remains were exhumed from the Old City Cemetery in Oct. 1866 and reinterred in Poplar Grove National Cemetery Poplar Grove at Petersburg, Virginia. Grave #4737.

Beckwith, George - 6th Michigan Cav., Company C, P.O.W., d. 6/23/64 from wound(s) @ Crumpton's Factory. "Was buried No 4 in 2nd line 1st lot". Beckwith enlisted as a private at Flint, Mich. on 1/4/64. He was mustered into service 1/5/64. His age at enlistment was listed as 17. He was wounded and captured at the battle of Trevilian Station, Virginia on 6/12/64. This soldier's remains were exhumed from the Old City Cemetery in Oct. 1866 and reinterred in Poplar Grove National Cemetery, Petersburg, Virginia. Grave #4791.

Berrick, Merrick C. - 1st Virginia Inf. (West Virginia), Company H, P.O.W., d. 8/5/62 @ Fairgrounds. Coffin size was 72 in. in length by 20 in. in width. Was buried in Yankee Square, #7, in 5th line. This soldier's remains were exhumed from the Old City Cemetery in Oct. 1866. All Union soldiers that were removed from Lynchburg were supposed to be reinterred at Poplar Grove National Cemetery, Petersburg, Virginia.

Bobson, Allen - 27th U. S. Colored Troops Inf., Company E, P.O.W., d. 7/19/64 @ Crumpton's Factory. Coffin size was 70 in. in length by 20 in. in width. Diuguid's entry in the "Soldiers Book" stated that Bobson was a member of the 27th Ohio and "Was buried in Negro Row". Private Bobson enlisted as a private on 3/5/64 at age 18. The 27th was organized at Camp Delaware, Ohio between Jan. 6th and Aug. 6th, 1864. As a part of the 9th Corps (1st Brigade, 4th Division) the unit saw limited service until Petersburg on Saturday July 30, 1864 (The Mine Explosion and assault). The 27th suffered 14 killed,

11 wounded, 1 POW & 8 MIA Very sketchy information on Bobson, no record of his death, capture and or any type of discharge. This soldier's remains were exhumed from the Old City Cemetery in Oct. 1866. All Union soldiers removed from Lynchburg were supposed to be reinterred at Poplar Grove National Cemetery, Petersburg, Virginia.

Boose, Moses, Sgt. - 11th Pennsylvania Inf., Company A, P.O.W., d. 6/11/64 of wounds @ Crumpton's Factory. His coffin size was 69 in. in length by 20 in. in width. "Was buried No 5 in 1st line 1st lot", "...in far corner". Mr. Diuguid's burial log had the last recorded as "Booze". Poplar Grove records listed the last name as "Broose". Boose enlisted as a private 9/30/61. He was promoted to the rank of Sgt. On 4/1/64. He was wounded and captured 5/6/64 during the battle of the Wilderness. This soldier's remains were exhumed from the Old City Cemetery in Oct. 1866 and reinterred in Poplar Grove National Cemetery, Petersburg, Virginia. Grave #4847.

Bower, ** -** 39th New York Inf., Company E, P.O.W., d. 6/17/62 @ John Brown's Stable, under the care of a Dr. Maguire (sic). This Union Soldier was the first to die in Lynchburg as a P.O.W. Coffin size (external) was 71 in. in length by 19 in. in width. He was interred in lot #169, grave #6, row #1. A search of the 39th New York did not reveal any soldier by the name "Bower". There were Bauers and Browers but their death records indicated a later date. This was very unusual, since all other Union P.O.W. dead were buried in Yankee Square. There is nothing to indicate he was exhumed and reinterred in Yankee Square. To further complicate matters, on 5/27/62 Private T. B. Cheney of the 8th Louisiana was listed as buried in that same location (coffin size 6' 1" by 20"). There is nothing to indicate that Private Cheney was exhumed or moved to another location. North and South seem to have been buried in the same plot. However, this soldier's remains were exhumed from the Old City Cemetery in Oct. 1866 and reinterred in Poplar Grove National Cemetery, Petersburg, Virginia. Grave #4582

Bower, Maroot (also Marquis) - 66th Ohio Inf., Company E, P.O.W., d. 7/22/62 from a gunshot wound(s) @ the Fairgrounds. A note by Diuguid states that he was shot by (sic) "Sentinell" (the guard). Was buried in Yankee Square, #10, in 2nd line. His death notice was published on 8/28/62 in **The Delaware Gazette**, Delaware, Ohio. An abstract states, *"We learn from Lt. Watkins that Maroot Bower, one of our*

German Citizens and a member of Capt. Buxton's Company was killed by a rebel soldier at Lynchburg, VA. He was among the prisoners captured at Port Republic, and having stepped a few feet beyond the limits prescribed to the prisoners to procure a bucket of water was shot dead by the guard." Bower enlisted as a private on 11/19/61, mustered into service 12/26/61. His age at enlistment was listed as 36. The 66th first major engagement was in Shenandoah Valley at Port Republic on 6/9/62. The 66th lost 109 men Killed, wounded and captured of the approx. 400 engaged. This soldier's remains were exhumed from the Old City Cemetery in Oct. 1866 and reinterred in Poplar Grove National Cemetery at Petersburg, Virginia. Grave #4607.

Bowles, Almon E. - 1st New Hampshire Cav., Company L, P.O.W., d. 10/28/64 of disease @ Massie's Factory (Prison). "Was buried No 7 in 2nd line 3rd lot". Enlisted as private on 2/16/64, officially muster into service on the same date. Was born in and a resident of Francoinia, New Hampshire. Age at enlistment was 18. He was captured 8/17/64 @ Winchester, Virginia. This soldier's remains were exhumed from the Old City Cemetery in Oct. 1866. All Union soldiers that were removed from Lynchburg were supposed to be reinterred at Poplar Grove National Cemetery, Petersburg, Virginia.

Boycee, John - 1st Virginia (West Va.) Art., Battery B, P.O.W., d. 7/11/64 @ Crumpton's Factory. Boycee was captured 6/18/64 during the Battle for Lynchburg. "Was buried No 8 in 1st line 2nd lot". Enlisted 9/08/63 @ Mt. Pleasant, W. Va. at age 20. Mustered into service @ Wheeling West Virginia. Military records listed him as captured at Lynchburg but no record of his death. His records state that he was mustered out in 1865 and still listed as a P.O.W. This soldier's remains were exhumed from the Old City Cemetery in Oct. 1866 and reinterred in Poplar Grove National Cemetery, Petersburg, Virginia. Grave #4785

Bradsley (or Beardsly), John G. - 1st Virginia (West Va.) Inf., Company B, P.O.W., d. 7/13/64 @ College Hospital. Possibly captured during the Battle for Lynchburg. The causality report for the 1st West Va. Inf. June 10-23, 1864 listed 29 men wounded or captured. "Was buried No 10 in 3rd line 1st lot". This soldier's remains were exhumed from the Old City Cemetery in Oct. 1866 and reinterred in Poplar Grove National Cemetery at Petersburg, Virginia. Grave #4632.

Brainard, James P. - 1st Delaware Inf., Company A, P.O.W., d. 8/13/64 @ Crumpton's Factory. "Was buried No 9 in 4th line of 2nd lot". This soldier's remains were exhumed from the Old City Cemetery in Oct. 1866 and reinterred at Poplar Grove National Cemetery, Petersburg, Virginia. Grave #4622.

Branson, R. C. - 34th Illinois Inf., Company F, d. 1/26/63 @ Burton's Factory. Coffin size was 72 in. in length by 18 in. in width. He was buried in lot #187, grave #6, row #4. Based on a research of the 34th Ill. Company "F", no one by the name "R. C. Branson" served. There were two individuals by the name Bronson that did serve in this unit. These men were Corpl. William L. and Pvt. Lewis C. Bronson. William enlisted 9/07/61 for 3 years. Personal description, 5' 8" in height, brown hair, blue eyes, light complexion, single, occupation farmer, age listed as 19. He was a native Oswego, New York. He was resident of Ogel County, Illinois. However, he died of typhoid fever 12/06/61 in Kentucky. Lewis also enlisted 9/07/61 for 3 years. Personal description, 5' 9" in height, black hair, black eyes, dark complexion, single, occupation farmer, age listed as 21. He was a native Lake, Pennsylvania. He was resident of Lafayette, Ogel County, Illinois. His record ends here with no additional information. His remains were removed from the Old City Cemetery in Oct. 1866 and reinterred in Poplar Grove National Cemetery at Petersburg, Virginia. Grave #4665.

Bremer, Andrew - 1st Maryland Inf., Company K, P.O.W., d. 7/28/62 @ the Fairgrounds of "disease contracted while in military service". Enlisted as a private on 5/28/61. It is not stated in his military records, but was probably captured on 5/23/62 at Front Royal, Virginia. Was buried in Yankee Square, #10, in 6th line. Coffin size was 78 in. in length by 20 in. in width. Poplar Grove's burial records listed the last name as "Bummer". Bremer enlisted as a private on 5/28/61. He was mustered into service on the same date. This soldier's remains were exhumed from the Old City Cemetery in Oct. 1866 and reinterred in Poplar Grove National Cemetery, Petersburg, Virginia. Grave #4581.

Broemmel, H. Fritz - 8th New York (1st German Rifles) Inf., Company B, P.O.W., d. 7/24/62 @ the Fairgrounds. Was buried in Yankee Square, #1, in 6th line. Coffin size was 72 in. in length by 20 in. in width. In Diuguid's burial log book the last name was recorded as "Brohnmel". It" quite possible he was captured at Cross Keys on 6/8/62. This was the first major engagement the 8th participated in. The 8th lost 220 men out of 550 engaged at the battle of Cross Keys. His military records stated that he was mustered out of service at Lynchburg, Va. (no date given). This soldier's remains were exhumed from the Old City Cemetery in Oct. 1866 and reinterred in Poplar Grove National Cemetery, Petersburg, Virginia. Grave #4614.

Budd, Sebring C. - 1st Michigan Cav., Company C, P.O.W., d. 10/16/64 @ Crumpton's Factory. "Was buried No 1 in 3rd line of 3rd lot". The name recorded in Diuguid's burial Log was, "S. Budd". Poplar Grove's records listed the name as "J. Bud". Budd enlisted as a private 10/7/63 at Detroit, Michigan. He was mustered into service 10/13/63. His age at enlistment was listed as 18. He was a resident of Detroit, Michigan. He was captured 8/16/64 at Front Royal, Virginia. This soldier's remains were exhumed from the Old City Cemetery in Oct. 1866 and reinterred in Poplar Grove National Cemetery, Petersburg, Virginia. Grave #4935.

Burdett, C. Henderson F. - 11th Virginia (West Va.) Inf., Company G, d. 7/9/64 of wounds @ Camp Davis. Wounded and captured during the Battle for Lynchburg on 6/18/64. "Was buried No 6 in 1st line, 2nd lot". Enlisted as a private at Mt. Pleasants, W. Va. (no date). His age at enlistment was listed as 19. "Wounded, left leg shot off June 18, 1864 at Lynchburg, Va., died July 9, 1864 of the wound received in action at Lynchburg, Va.". This soldier's remains were exhumed from the Old City Cemetery in Oct. 1866 and reinterred in Poplar Grove National Cemetery, Petersburg, Virginia. Grave #4972.

Burr, Jewell - 4th U.S. Inf., Company C, P.O.W., d. 9/6/64 @ Crumpton's Factory. Coffin size was 75 in. in length by 17 in. in width. "Was buried No 3 in 1st line of 3rd lot". In Mr. Diuguid's burial log the first name was recorded as "Joel". This soldier's remains were exhumed from the Old City Cemetery in Oct. 1866 and reinterred in Poplar Grove National Cemetery, Petersburg, Virginia. Grave #4643.

Calhoun, George S. - 62nd Ohio Inf., Company K, P.O.W., d. 7/28/62 @ the Fairgrounds. Coffin size was 72 in. in length by 18 in. in width. Buried in Yankee Square, #1, in 5th line. Cause of death and place of capture not specified. Enlisted as a private on 10/31/61 for three years. Age at enlistment listed as 22. His record only states that he was captured in action.

The only action the 62nd participate in was at Port Republic, Va. on 6/9/62. This soldier's remains were exhumed from the Old City Cemetery in Oct. 1866. All Union soldiers that were removed from Lynchburg were to be reinterred at Poplar Grove National Cemetery, Petersburg, Virginia.

Carl, Frank W. - 5th New York Cav., Company F, P.O.W., d. 8/11/64 @ Crumpton's Factory. Coffin size 72 in. in length by 18 in. in width. "Was buried No 7 in 4th line of 2nd lot". Enlisted as a private 2/6/64 at Nichols, New York. Mustered into service on same date. Age at enlistment was 19. His military records state that he was ***"Killed in Action"*** on 5/5/64 at Parker's Store, Virginia. This soldier's remains were exhumed from the Old City Cemetery in Oct. 1866 and reinterred in Poplar Grove National Cemetery, Petersburg, Virginia. Grave #4635.

Carlis, F. - 64th New York Inf., Company D, P.O.W., d. 6/16/64 @ Crumpton's Factory. "Was buried No 9 in 1st line 1st lot". Was unable to locate anyone by this name in the 64th New York. This soldier's remains were exhumed from the Old City Cemetery in Oct. 1866 and reinterred in Poplar Grove National Cemetery, Petersburg, Virginia. Grave #4781.

Casterly, John - 4th Pennsylvania Cav., Company C, d. 6/11/65 @ Pratt Hospital. Coffin size 70 in. in length by 17 in. in width. "Was buried No 3 in 4th line of 3rd lot". No John Casterly served in Company "C" of the 4th Penn. Cav. The 4th was permanently station at Lynchburg until early July, 1865 when the unit was mustered out of service. I was able to locate a "John Carterwiler" of Company "C" that died in Lynchburg on 6/12/65. Carterwiler enlisted on 1/1/64 as a private. This soldier's remains were exhumed from the Old City Cemetery in Oct. 1866. All Union soldiers that were removed from Lynchburg were supposed to be reinterred at Poplar Grove National Cemetery, Petersburg, Virginia.

Chorarty, Henry - 8th New York Inf., Company F, P.O.W., d. 7/5/62 @ the Fairgrounds. Was buried in Yankee Square, #3, in 1st line. This soldier's remains were exhumed from the Old City Cemetery in Oct. 1866 and reinterred in Poplar Grove National Cemetery at Petersburg, Virginia. Grave #4586.

Clearnott, Joseph - 5th New Hampshire Inf., Company E, P.O.W., d. 7/29/64 @ College Hospital. "Was buried No 2 in 5th line 2nd lot". Diuguid listed his name as "Clearmont, J.". Poplar Grove records also listed him as "Clearmont, but a member of Company "B", 5th New York Infantry. A search of the 5th New Hampshire does not list anyone by the name "Clearmont". A Private Joseph Clearnott, Company E was wounded 6/17/64 at Petersburg. His military records state that he died of these wounds on 6/22/64 near Petersburg. Joseph Clearnott enlisted as a substitute on 10/03/63 and mustered in on the same date. He was born in and a resident of Canada. His age at enlistment was 19. The 5th was heavy engaged from early June into July. They were active on both the 16th and 17th Of June but do not list any soldiers captured. Only one individual by the name "Clearnott" served in any New Hampshire units, and that was Joseph Clearnott. This soldier's remains were exhumed from the Old City Cemetery in Oct. 1866. All Union soldiers that were removed from Lynchburg were supposed to be reinterred at Poplar Grove National Cemetery, Petersburg, Virginia.

Cocks, John H. - 1st Maryland Inf., Company G, P.O.W., d. 7/10/62 @ the Fairgrounds. Enlisted as a private on 5/27/61. Mustered into service on the same date. His age at enlistment was listed as 23. His coffin size was 72 in. in length by 20 in. in width. He was buried in Yankee Square, #6, in 1st line. Poplar Grove burial records listed his last name as "Cox". He was captured at Front Royal, Va. on 5/23/62. This soldier's remains were exhumed from the Old City Cemetery in Oct. 1866 and reinterred in Poplar Grove National Cemetery, Petersburg, Virginia. Grave #4594.

Coffran, L. F. - 3rd Maine Inf., Company B, d. 7/11/64 @ Crumpton's Factory. "Was buried No 9 in 3rd line 1st lot". A search of the roster for the 3rd provides only one individual with the above last name. Seba F. Coffran (also Coffrin), initially enlisted in the 11th Maine but was discharged in Oct. 1862 for disability. This same man enlisted in the 3rd Maine 9/28/63. He was transferred to the 17th Maine 6/04/64 an again on 6/04/65 to the 1st Maine Heavy Artillery. Whoever this soldier was he was exhume from the Old City Cemetery in Oct. 1866 and reinterred in Poplar Grove National Cemetery, Petersburg, Virginia. Grave #4782. Burial ,records at Poplar Grove listed his last name as "Coffin".

Collins, James - 10th New Jersey Inf., Company G, d. 10/16/64 of chronic diarrhea @ Crumpton's Factory. "Was buried No 5 in 2nd line of 3rd lot". Enlisted 4/09/62 mustered into service 6/12/62. Re-enlisted 1/03/64. Listed as P.O.W., place of capture not stated (possibly Winchester 8/17/64, Charlestown, Wva. 8/21/64 or Openquan 9/19/64). The 10th

New Jersey was a part of the Army of Shenandoah from 8/64 – 12/64. Collins was a resident of Newark, New Jersey. The wife of the deceased was Mary J. Collins. Collins had one son, William D. Collins born circa 1861 (listed as age 4 in 1865). This soldier's remains were exhumed from the Old City Cemetery in Oct. 1866 and reinterred in Poplar Grove National Cemetery, Petersburg, Virginia. Grave #4973.

Condin, ***** - 3rd Maine Inf., Company F, P.O.W., d. 6/12/64 @ Camp Davis. Coffin size was 73 in. in length by 18 in. in width. "Was buried No 6 in 1st line 1st Lot", "in far corner". A search of the 3rd Maine indicates no one by the above last name served in that unit. There was an Elijah Cowden. However, he was transferred to the 17th Maine 6/17/64 and later transferred to the 1st Maine Heavy Artillery on 6/03/65. Whoever this soldier's remains were exhume in Oct. 1866 and reinterred in Poplar Grove National Cemetery at Petersburg, Virginia. Grave #4967.

Conley, J. - 7th Maine Inf., Company C, P.O.W., d. 7/01/64 wounds @ Dr. Larrndell(?) Factory. Coffin size 72 in. in length by 17 in. in width. "Was buried No 3 in 3rd line in far corner (lot #1)". Possibly John Conley. Listed as wounded, no discharge furnished. Also listed as assigned to the 1st Veterans Inf. on 9/20/64. Enlisted as a private on 12/29/63 for 3 years. Age 37, married, light complexion, blue eyes, dark hair, 5' 6 1/2" in height, occupation laborer. Born Galway, Ireland. He was a resident of Portland. This soldier was exhumed and reinterred in Poplar Grove National Cemetery at Petersburg, Virginia. Grave #4630.

Cooper, E. - 7th Michigan Inf., Company F, P.O.W., d. 7/31/64 @ Crumpton's Factory. Coffin size was 72 in. in length by 17 in. in width. "Was buried No 9 in 3rd line 2nd lot". A search of the 7th Michigan no one is listed as E. Cooper. A Henry Cooper was listed member of Co. I WIA 5/6/ 64 and discharged 4/15/65. A total of 8 Coopers served in Michigan units that did not survive the war. None of these men share the same death date as the Cooper listed above. This soldier's remains were exhumed from the Old City Cemetery in Oct. 1866 and reinterred in Poplar Grove National Cemetery, Petersburg, Virginia. Grave #4948.

Coulner or Coultner, Nicholas - 4th New York Inf. (Cav.?), Company H, P.O.W., d. 7/17/62 @ the Fairgrounds. Was buried in Yankee Square, #3, in 4th line. Coffin size was 78 in. in length by 20 in. in width. This soldier's remains were exhumed from the Old City Cemetery in Oct. 1866 and reinterred in Poplar Grove National Cemetery at Petersburg, Virginia. Grave #4720. Military burial records at Poplar Grove list his name as "Coulther, Mike". In addition Poplar Grove list him as a member of 4th New York Inf., Diuguid listed him as 4th New York Cavalry. In either unit there is no one by the above name that served.

Coward, Charles A., Corpl. - 10th New Jersey Inf., Company G, P.O.W., d. 10/1/64 from a gunshot wound @ Massie's Factory. Diuguid's entry was, "Yankee Prisoner shot at prison Massie's Factory". Originally buried in lot #3, grave #10, row #1. Enlisted on 5/31/62, mustered into service 6/12/62. Re-enlisted 1/03/64, listed as Corpl. 8/03/64. Diuguid noted that his remains were exhumed in January of 1866, "sent to Highstown, New Jersey". His military records states, "Shot by guard at rebel prison, Lynchburg, Va. Oct. 1, 64 while a Pris. of War". No specific date or place of capture stated in his records. The 10th New Jersey served in the Shenandoah Valley 8/64 – 12/64. A fellow member of the 10th (see James Collins), and same company was captured at about the same time. Coward was a resident of Mercer County, Hightown, New Jersey. 20 years old at death. Place of birth East Windsor, New Jersey. Parents of the deceased were Clayton & Lydia Coward.

Crawshaw (also Cromshaw), John (Pvt.?) - Listed as Federal citizen, d. 10/26/64 @ Crumpton's Factory. "Was buried No 6 in 2nd line of 3rd lot". Diuguid's burial logbook listed his last name as "Crawshaw", Poplar Grove lists his name as "Cromshaw". A search of records for an individual with either name (that did not survive the war) listed a John Crawshaw. Private Crawshaw enlisted 8/15/62 and was mustered into Co. "I" of the 128th Pennsylvania. He was listed as deserted on 9/8/62 with no further record. This individual, soldier or not, remains were exhumed from the Old City Cemetery in Oct. 1866 and reinterred in Poplar Grove National Cemetery at Petersburg, Virginia. Grave #4944. In addition, military records for interment at Poplar Grove list him with the rank of Private.

Dafoe, Edward - 1st Michigan Cav., Company I., P.O.W., d. 7/12/64 @ Crumpton's Factory. "Was buried No 7 in 1st line 2nd lot". Poplar Grove listed the name as "Edry De Foe". Dafoe enlisted as a private 10/29/63 at Clinton, Mich. at the age of 18. He was mustered into Co. "I" 1st Mich. Cav. on 11/13/63. His records do not specify a place of capture. This soldier's remains were exhumed from the Old City Cemetery in Oct. 1866 and reinterred in Poplar Grove National Cemetery at Petersburg, Virginia. Grave #4640.

Davis, Charles C. - 116th Ohio Inf., Company B, P.O.W., d. 6/20/64 of wounds @ Pratt Hospital. Coffin size was 76 in. in length by 20 in. in width. Capture during the Battle for Lynchburg, and died of wound(s) received on the afternoon of 6/18/64. "Was buried No 10 in 1st line 1st lot", "in far corner". Enlisted as a private on 8/13/62 for three years. Age at enlistment was listed as 19. This soldiers remains were exhume from the Old City Cemetery in Oct. 1866 and reinterred in Poplar Grove National Cemetery at Petersburg, Virginia. Grave #4956. Poplar Grove lists list the middle initial as "E."

Delano, Leon (Levi?) - 1st Maine Cav., Company M, P.O.W., d. 7/17/62 @ the Fairgrounds. Was buried in Yankee Square, #6, in 2nd line. Coffin size was 72 in. in length by 20 in. in width. A search of the 1st Maine Cav. provides one individual that may be the above soldier. A Levi Delano of Company "M" is listed as "died of exposure". His muster out date is June 1862. Enlisted 10/07/61 for 3 years at Augusta at age 20. He was listed as single, light complexion, blue eyes, 5' 9 1/4" in height, occupation farmer. He was born in Guilford, and was resident of Abbot. This soldier's remains were exhumed from the Old City Cemetery in Oct. 1866 and reinterred in Poplar Grove National Cemetery, Petersburg, Virginia. Grave #4580. Burial records at Poplar Grove listed the last name as "Deleno".

Derr, Samuel A., 2nd Lieut. - 34th Ohio Vol. Inf., Company D, P.O.W., d. 7/30/64 of wounds @ College Hospital. Coffin size 71 in. in length by 17 in. in width. Captured during Battle for Lynchburg. "Was buried No 4 in 4th line 2nd lot". Enlisted on 7/22/61 as a Corpl. for three years. Mustered into service, Co. "G" 34th Ohio on 8/20/61. Age at enlistment was listed as 24. Promoted from Corpl. to 2nd Lieut. of Company "D" 3/15/64. This soldier's remains were exhumed from the Old City Cemetery in Oct. 1866 and reinterred in Poplar Grove National Cemetery at Petersburg, Virginia. Grave #4946. Poplar Grove's burial log recorded the last name as "Dun". Also his military records state that he died in Richmond, Virginia on 9/13/64.

Dilcher, Henry - 122nd Ohio Inf., Company B, P.O.W., d. 8/4/64 @ Crumpton's Factory. Coffin size was 70 in. in length by 16 in. in width. "Was buried No 6 in 4th line 2nd lot". Both Diuguid's and Poplar Grove burial logs listed the last name as "Dilchner". Cause of death and place of capture not specified. Drafted with an enlistment date of 6/02/64 for three years. Age at enlisting was listed as 32. This soldier's remains were exhumed from the Old City Cemetery in Oct. 1866 and reinterred in Poplar Grove National Cemetery, Petersburg, Virginia. Grave #4641.

Dockhman, George A. - 1st Maine Cav., Company M, P.O.W., d. 8/2/62 of "exposure" @ the Fairgrounds. Was buried in Yankee Square, #4, in 5th line. Possibly capture during Jackson's 1862 Valley Campaign. He enlisted 10/09/61 for 3 years at age 18. He was listed as single, dark complexion, black eyes, black hair, 5' 10" in height, and occupation farmer. Born in Dover, was a resident of Sebec. His remains were exhumed in Oct. 1866 and reinterred in Poplar Grove National Cemetery, Petersburg, Virginia. Grave #4587. Burial records at Poplar Grove list his last name as "Dockam".

Donahue, Peter F. - Knap's Battery, Pennsylvania Light Art. (Independent Battery "E"), P.O.W., d. 7/8/62 @ the Fairgrounds. Buried in Yankee Square, #4, in 3rd line. Poplar Grove burial log listed his name as "Peter Donohue". Donahue enlisted on 2/15/62 as a private. He was mustered into service on the same date into Penn. Battery E light Artillery. It's very possible that Donahue was capture during Jackson's Valley Campaign of 62. This soldier's remains were exhumed from the Old City Cemetery in Oct. 1866 and reinterred in Poplar Grove National Cemetery, Petersburg, Virginia. Grave #4578.

Dotting, Henry - 3rd Battn. 11th U.S. Inf., Company F, d. 8/4/66 @ Pratt Hospital. Coffin length was listed as 69 inches. No burial location was specified. Private Dotting was the last Union Solider listed in Diuguid's "Soldier Book". This soldier's remains were exhumed from the Old City Cemetery in Oct. 1866. All Union soldiers that were removed from Lynchburg were supposed to be reinterred at Poplar Grove National Cemetery, Petersburg, Virginia.

Dowling, Patrick C. - 1st Virginia (West Virginia) Art., Company B, P.O.W., d. 6/19/62 @ the Fairgrounds. Was buried in lot #172, grave #6, row #5. There are no records to indicate that Dowling was exhumed and moved to Yankee

Square. Initially Albert Harvey of the 21st Virginia was slated for burial in that location. However, Harvey was shipped home for burial. Enlisted as a private on 10/01/61 at Coredo, W. Va. at age 20. Mustered into service in same location. Rank was listed as "Artificer". Captured June 1862 near Strasburg, Virginia. He was still listed as a P.O.W. at the date of the units Muster Out. This soldier's remains were exhumed from the Old City Cemetery in Oct. 1866 and reinterred in Poplar Grove National Cemetery at Petersburg, Virginia. Grave #4726.

Durbin, John W. - 1st Virginia (West Va.) Art., Battery D, P.O.W., d. 6/23/64 of wounds @ College Hospital. Wounded and captured during the Battle for Lynchburg 6/18/64. Enlisted as a private and mustered in at Wheeling W. Va. at age 18 on 08/30/62. His unit listed him as **Killed in Action** on 6/18/64. "Was buried No 3 in 2nd line 1st lot". His remains were exhumed from the Old City Cemetery in Oct. 1866. All Union soldiers that were removed from Lynchburg were supposed to be reinterred at Poplar Grove National Cemetery, Petersburg, Virginia. Poplar Grove does have a J. Y. Derlin in Grave #4953. He was a member of an artillery unit listed as 1st Co. D. This writer considers these to be one in the same.

Elsworth, Isaac (A.?) - 10th Maine Inf., Company F, P.O.W., d. 7/20/62 of disease @ the Fairgrounds. Was buried Yankee Square, #8, in 4th line. His coffin size was 6 ft. in length by 20 in. in width. Enlisted as a private on 9/10/61 for 2 years at age 36. Mustered into service on 10/04/61. Listed as married, light complexion, blue eyes, light hair, 5' 6" in height, occupation farmer. Elsworth was born in and a resident of Salem, Maine. His remains exhumed in Oct. 1866 and reinterred in Poplar Grove National Cemetery at Petersburg, Virginia. Grave #4749.

Emmert, Philip - 1st Maryland Inf., Company I, P.O.W., d. 7/28/62 @ the Fairgrounds. Coffin size was 71 in. in length by 20 in. in width. Enlisted as a private on 5/27/61 at age 40. He was mustered into service on the same date. Was buried in Yankee Square, #11, in the 3rd line. He was captured on 5/23/62 at Front Royal, Virginia. His company records state that he died in Richmond. This soldier's remains were exhumed from the Old City Cemetery in Oct. 1866 and reinterred in Poplar Grove National Cemetery, Petersburg, Virginia. Grave #4738.

Eustice, William - 7th Wisconsin Inf., Company C, d. 6/8/64 of wounds @ Saunder's Factory. Coffin size was 71 in. in length by 18 in. in width. "Was buried No 3 in 1st line lot", "...in far Corner". Private Eustice was a resident of Mifflin, Iowa County, Wisconsin. Sgt. John Enloe enlisted him on 1/18/64 at Mifflin. His term of enlistment was for 3 years. Officially mustered in on 2/12/64 by Lt. J. H. Purcell at Camp Randall, Madison Wisconsin. Description at enlistment, age 22, gray eyes, dark hair, fair complexion, height 5' 6", occupation was listed as farmer. He was wounded and captured on 5/05/64 during the Battle of the Wilderness. Diuguid had his name spelled "Eustace". The remains of Private Eustice were exhumed in Oct. 1866 for reinterrment in Poplar Grove National Cemetery, Petersburg, Virginia. Grave #4646. The Burial Log at Poplar Grove has Pvt. Eustice listed as a member of the 7th Michigan.

Fairbanks, Forrest G. - 6th Michigan Cav., Company D, P.O.W., d. 7/4/64 @ Crumpton's Factory. "Was buried No 2 in 1st line 2nd lot". Fairbanks enlisted as a private on 2/20/64 at Cohoctah, Michigan. He was mustered into service on 2/29/64. His age at enlistment was 41. He was wounded and captured 6/12/64 at Trevilian Station, Virginia. This soldier's remains were exhumed from the Old City Cemetery in Oct. 1866 and reinterred in Poplar Grove National Cemetery, Petersburg, Virginia. Grave #4780.

Farlow, Robert - 2nd Maryland Inf. (Potomac Home Brigade), Company B, P.O.W., d. 7/28/64 @ College Hospital. "Was buried No 2 in 4th line 2nd lot". Farlow enlisted as a private 3/3/63. He was mustered into service on the same date. He was wounded and captured on 6/18/64 at Lynchburg, Virginia. His military records state no date of death. Only that he was wounded and left in Confederate hands. This soldier's remains were exhumed from the Old City Cemetery in Oct. 1866 and reinterred in Poplar Grove National Cemetery, Petersburg, Virginia. Grave #4638.

Ferdun, George E. - 28th New York Inf., Company G, P.O.W., d. 7/31/62 @ the Fairgrounds. Coffin size was 72 in. in length by 18 in. in width. Buried in Yankee Square, #12, in 3rd line. Ferdun enlisted as a private on 5/3/61 at Albion, New York. He was mustered into service on 5/22/61. Hi age at enlistment was 20. He was captured at Winchester, Va. on 5/25/62. This soldier's remains were exhumed from the Old

City Cemetery in Oct. 1866 and reinterred in Poplar Grove National Cemetery, Petersburg, Virginia. Grave #4745.

Ferguson, John - 2nd North Carolina Inf., P.O.W., d. 2/25/64 @ Ferguson's Factory. Coffin size was 73.5 in. in length by 19 in. in width. Was buried in lot #185, grave #1, row #1. This soldier's remains were exhumed from the Old City Cemetery in Oct. 1866. All Union soldiers that were removed from Lynchburg were supposed to be reinterred at Poplar Grove National Cemetery, Petersburg, Virginia.

Forbess, Daniel, Corpl. - 5th Virginia (West Va.) Inf., Company B, P.O.W., d. 7/21/64 of wounds @ Crumpton's Factory. Wounded and captured during the Battle for Lynchburg on 6/18/64. Coffin size was 74 in. in length by 19 in. in width. "Was buried No 4 in 3rd line 2nd lot". Enlisted on 8/10/61 at age 26 at Ceredo, West Virginia. Mustered into service on same date and location. Poplar Grove burial record listed his name as "Forbs, B.". His military records listed as **Killed in Action** on 6/18/64 at Lynchburg, Virginia. His remains were exhumed from the Old City Cemetery in Oct. 1866 and reinterred in Poplar Grove National Cemetery, Petersburg, Virginia. Grave #4618.

Fowler, Thomas, 1st Sgt. - 15th Virginia (West Va.) Inf., Company A, P.O.W., d. 7/8/64 of wounds @ College Hospital. Wounded & captured during the Battle for Lynchburg on 6/18/64. "Was buried No 5 in 1st line 2nd lot". Enlisted 8/30/62 @ Claysville, W. Va. at age 31. Mustered into service at Wheeling, West Virginia. Military records listed him as **Killed in Action** on 6/18/64. This soldier's remains were exhumed from the Old City Cemetery in Oct. 1866 and reinterred in Poplar Grove National Cemetery, Petersburg, Virginia. Grave #4962.

Freshman, Charles - 1st Maryland Inf., Company E, P.O.W., d. 7/25/62 @ the Fairgrounds. Was buried in Yankee Square, #10, in 4th Line. Coffin size was 72 in. in length by 20 in. in length. This soldier's remains were exhumed from the Old City Cemetery in Oct. 1866 and reinterred in Poplar Grove National Cemetery at Petersburg, Virginia. Grave #4663.

Frier, Joseph - 1st Virginia (West Virginia) Inf., Company A, P.O.W., d. 7/19/62 @ Fairgrounds. Coffin size was 72 in. in length by 20 in. in width. Was buried Yankee Square, #6, in 3rd line. This soldier's remains were exhumed from the Old City Cemetery in Oct. 1866 and reinterred in Poplar Grove National Cemetery at Petersburg, Virginia. Grave #4604.

Fullmer, Isaiah - 148th Pennsylvania Inf., Company A, P.O.W., d. 7/2/64 @ Crumpton's Factory. "Was buried No 4 in 3rd line in far corner". Diuguid's burial logbook recorded his name as "Fulner, J.". Fullmer enlisted as private on 8/21/61 at Rebersburg, Pennsylvania. He was mustered into service 8/25/62. His age at enlistment was listed as 18. He was wounded and captured on 5/12/64 at Po River, Virginia. His records "estimated" his date of death as "soon" after capture at Petersburg, Virginia. Point of interest, William Fullmer was Killed in Action at Po River on 5/10/64. William was also a member of Co. A 148th Pennsylvania. His age at enlistment was 20. A Levi H. Fullmer (age 25 at enlistment), Co. A, 148th was discharged 2/11/63 for disability. All three were from Rebersburg, Pennsylvania. This soldier's remains were exhumed from the Old City Cemetery in Oct. 1866 and reinterred in Poplar Grove National Cemetery at Petersburg, Virginia. Grave #4772.

Garfield, Henry Darius (or Darius Henry?) - 1st Michigan Cav., Company B, P.O.W., d. 7/4/62 @ the Fairgrounds. Was buried in Yankee Square, #1, in 3rd line. Enlisted as a private on 3/15/62 at Detroit, Michigan. He was mustered into service on the same date. He was a resident of Pontiac, Michigan. His age at enlistment was listed as 22. This soldier's remains were exhumed from the Old City Cemetery in Oct. 1866 and reinterred at Poplar Grove National Cemetery, Petersburg, Virginia. Grave #4584.

Gatton, George W. - 1st Virginia (West Virginia) Cav., P.O.W., d. 7/12/62 @ the Fairgrounds. Coffin size was 78 in. in length by 20 in. in width. Was buried in Yankee Square, #4, in 1st line. Enlisted East Richland, Ohio on 10/01/61 at age 20. Mustered into service at Wheeling, West Virginia. His military record stated that he was captured, no date specified. In addition, his record states that he died in Richmond, Virginia. Polar Grove's burial log recorded the last name as "Getton". This soldier's remains were exhumed from the Old City Cemetery in Oct. 1866 and reinterred in Poplar Grove National Cemetery at Petersburg, Virginia. Grave #4592.

Gatton, Jefferson - 116th Ohio Inf., Company A, P.O.W., d. 6/30/64 of wounds @ College Hospital. Wounded and captured on the afternoon of 6/18/64 during the Battle for Lynchburg. "Was buried No 2 in 3rd line in far corner (lot #1)". Diuguid's burial log recorded his last name as "Gatten". Poplar

Grove records listed the name as "Getton" and "Galtin." The Ohio State Archives has no listing for J. Getton or Gatten in the 116th Ohio. Jefferson Gatton enlisted as a private on 8/22/62. He was mustered into service on 9/18/62. His age was listed as 21 when he enlisted. This soldier's remains were exhumed from the Old City Cemetery in Oct. 1866 and reinterred in Poplar Grove National Cemetery, Petersburg, Virginia. Grave #4776.

Gibbs, Thomas - 14th New York Inf., Company D, d. 6/14/64 @ Crumpton's Factory. Coffin size was 66 in. in length by 16 in. in width. "Was buried No 8 in 1st line 1st lot". A search for "Thomas Gibbs" from New York that did not survive the war revealed only two. Thomas S. died 4/29/63. The second Thomas O. Gibbs, 2nd Lieut. Was listed as Killed in Action on 5/12/64. Neither of these men served in the 14th New York Infantry. The 14th New York was a two year regiment and was discharged the later part of July, 1863. This soldier's remains were exhumed from the Old City Cemetery in Oct. 1866 and reinterred in Poplar Grove National Cemetery, Petersburg, Virginia. Grave #4789.

Gilson, Richard Newton - 1st Maryland (Potomac Home Brigade) Cav., Company C, P.O.W., d. 8/4/64 of wounds @ Crumpton's Factory. His military record does not specify that he was captured only "died of wounds". Gilson was probably wounded and captured on 6/18/64 during the Battle for Lynchburg. Gilson enlisted as a private 8/27/62 (location not specified). He was mustered into service on the same date. Originally buried in lot #2, grave #5, row #4. Body was exhumed 11/16/65, "Packed up & sent to Emmetsburg (sic) Md." Brother of deceased C. A. Gilson claimed remains and paid all expenses for removal and packing of his brother. Gilson is buried at Gettysburg National Cemetery, A-7 Maryland Plot.

Glover, John F. - 140th New York Inf., Company G, P.O.W., d. 7/5/64 @ Crumpton's Factory. "Was buried No 4 in 1st line 2nd lot". Glover enlisted as a private 8/11/63 at New York City. He was mustered into service on the same date. The only other item in his records state that he was transferred to the Veterans Reserve Corps on 6/3/65. No date or place of discharged specified. This soldier's remains were exhumed from the Old City Cemetery in Oct. 1866 and reinterred in Poplar Grove National Cemetery, Petersburg, Virginia. Grave #4765.

Gosley, Hugh S. - 5th Connecticut Inf., P.O.W., d. 7/18/62 @ the Fairgrounds. Was buried in Yankee Square, #6, in 4th line. Gosley enlisted as a private on 6/22/61 at Litchfield, Connecticut. Was mustered into service by Col. James Loomis at Hartford, Conn. on 7/22/61. He was captured at Front Royal, Virginia on 5/23/62. His records state that he died as a POW at Belle's Isle (Island) Richmond, Virginia. This soldier's remains were exhumed from the Old City Cemetery in Oct. 1866 and reinterred in Poplar Grove National Cemetery at Petersburg, Virginia. Grave #4611. Diuguid recorded his name as "Gozze" and Poplar Grove recorded it as "Gooze".

Gougins, A. A. - 31st (11th?) Maine Inf., Company D, P.O.W., d. 8/12/64 @ Crumpton's Factory. Coffin size was 75 in. in length by 15 in. in width. "Was buried No 8 in 4th line of 2nd lot". This soldiers remains were exhume in Oct. 1866 and reinterred in Poplar Grove National Cemetery at Petersburg, Virginia. Grave #4771.

Green, William A. - 7th Virginia (West Va.) Cav., Company I, P.O.W., d. 6/25/64 @ College Hospital (cause of death not stated). Coffin size was 74 in. in length by 18 in. in width. Possibly wounded and captured at the Battle for Lynchburg 6/18/64. "Was buried No 6 in 2nd line first lot in far corner". Enlisted 3/20/64 at Brownstown, W. Va. at age 20. Mustered into service at Charleston, West Virginia. Personal description, 5 ft. 9 in. in height, fair complexion, gray eyes, light hair. Born circa 1844 in Kanawha County. His military records only state that he died in Lynchburg as a Prisoner of War. This soldier's remains were exhumed from the Old City Cemetery in Oct. 1866 and reinterred in Poplar Grove National Cemetery, Petersburg, Virginia. Grave #4774.

Hall, Flemming - 66th Ohio Inf., Company C, P.O.W., d. 7/19/62 @ the Fairgrounds. Was buried in Yankee Square, #7, in 4th line. Coffin size was 72 in. in length by 20 in. width. Possibly captured at Port Republic on 6/9/62. The 66th lost 109 men out of 400 engaged. Enlisted as a private on 10/09/61 for 3 years. Mustered into service on the same date at Camp McArthur at Urbana. Age at enlistment was listed as 43. Widow of the deceased was Elizabeth Jane Dagger Flemming. They were married 9/22/53. He was a resident of Concord, Ohio, Champaign County. This soldier's remains were exhumed from the Old City Cemetery in Oct. 1866 and reinterred in Poplar Grove National Cemetery, Petersburg, Virginia. Grave #4718.

Halsee, J. - 3rd Michigan Inf. Company K, P.O.W., d. 6/10/64 @ Camp Davis. Coffin size was 68 in. in length by 20 in. in width. "Was buried No 4 in 1st line 1st lot", "...in far corner". Unable to locate anyone by this name (or Halsey) in the 3rd Michigan Cav. or Infantry that did not survive the war. This soldier's remains were exhumed from the Old City Cemetery in Oct. 1866 and reinterred in Poplar Grove National Cemetery possibly Poplar Grove at Petersburg, Virginia. Grave #4642.

Hamilton, Evander B. - 116th Ohio Inf., Company D, P.O.W., d. 7/24/64 of wounds @ College Hospital. Wounded and captured on the afternoon of 6/18/64 during the Battle for Lynchburg. "Was buried No 6 in 3rd line of 2nd lot". Enlisted as a private on 8/14/62 for three years. Mustered into service 9/18/62. His age at enlistment was listed as 32. This soldier's remains were exhumed from the Old City Cemetery in Oct. 1866 and reinterred in Poplar Grove National Cemetery at Petersburg, Virginia. Grave #4957.

Hammond, Le Roy - 146th New York Inf., Company G, P.O.W., d. 8/4/64 @ Crumpton's Factory. Coffin size was 71 in. in length by 18 in. in width. Hammond enlisted as a private on 9/4/62 at Bridgewater, New York. Mustered into service on 10/10/62 at Rome, New York. Hammond's age at enlistment was listed as 22. "Was buried No 10 in 2nd line 2nd lot". This soldier's remains were exhumed from the Old City Cemetery in Oct. 1866. All Union Soldiers removed from Lynchburg were supposed to be reinterred at Poplar Grove National Cemetery. Petersburg, Virginia.

Hardison, Hiram P. - 1st Maine Cav., Company E, P.O.W., d. 7/29/62 of disease @ the Fairgrounds. Was buried in Yankee Square, #11, the 4th line. Coffin size was 71 in. in length by 20 in. in width. Enlisted as a private on 10/08/61 for 3 years. His age at enlistment was listed as 25. Officially mustered in 10/19/61 in Augusta. Listed as married, light complexion, blue eyes, light hair, 5' 10" in height, occupation farmer. Born in Sangerville. He was a resident of Fremont Place. His remains were exhume in Oct. 1866 and reinterred in Poplar Grove National Cemetery, Petersburg, Virginia. Grave #4736.

Harps, David - 29th Pennsylvania Inf., Company B, P.O.W., d. 7/14/62 @ the Fairgrounds. Was buried in Yankee Square, #2, in 4th line. Coffin size was 72 in. in length by 20 in. in width. Harps enlisted as a private on 7/5/61. He was mustered into service on the same date in Philadelphia. His records do no indicate where he was captured but most likely at Winchester on 5/25/62. This soldier's remains were exhumed from the Old City Cemetery in Oct. 1866 and reinterred in Poplar Grove National Cemetery at Petersburg, Virginia. Grave #4612.

Hartmann, August - 8th New York Inf., Company C, P.O.W., d. 7/21/62 of wounds @ the Fairgrounds. Coffin size was 72 in. in length by 20 in. in width. Was buried in Yankee Square, #7, in 1st line. Poplar Grove records list the last name as "Hartinar". Enlisted 4/23/61 at New York City as a private. Mustered into service on the same date. Wounded and captured at Cross Keys, Virginia on 6/8/62. This soldier's remains were exhumed from the Old City Cemetery in Oct. 1866 and reinterred in Poplar Grove National Cemetery, Petersburg, Virginia. Grave #4754.

Hartman, John B., Capt. - 3rd New Jersey Cav., Company C, d. 12/7/64 @ Crumpton's Factory. Originally buried in lot #3, grave #10, row #2. Caused of death and place of capture not stated (captured prior to 11/01/64). Enlisted 1/21/64 as Captain, mustered into service on 1/22/64 for three years. Age at enlistment was 45. Body was exhumed (no date provided by Diuguid), "Taken up & sent to Philadelphia".

Hassacher, G. - 1st U.S. Cav., Company A, P.O.W., d. 12/12/64 @ Crumpton's Factory. "Was buried No 4 in 4th line 3rd lot". Diuguid burial log recorded his last name as "Hansaker". This soldier's remains were exhumed from the Old City Cemetery in Oct. 1866 and reinterred in Poplar Grove National Cemetery, Petersburg, Virginia. Grave #4936.

Hennessey, Michael (Philip?) - 15th New York Cav., Company B, P.O.W., d. 7/15/64 @ Knight's Factory. Was buried No. 10 in 1st line 2nd lot". Diuguid's burial log recorded his last name as "Henesey". Poplar Groves listed the name as "P. Henisey" and "Philip Hennessee." Hennessey enlisted as a private on 8/6/63 at Syracuse, New York. He was mustered into service on 8/12/63. His age at enlistment was listed as 18. Captured at Lynchburg, Virginia on 6/17/64. His records state that he was transferred to Co. "B" NY 2nd Prov'l. Cavalry. A final entry stated, thought to be dead no further records. This soldier's remains were exhumed from the Old City Cemetery in Oct. 1866 and reinterred in Poplar Grove National Cemetery at Petersburg, Virginia. Grave #4763.

Hernandez, J. - 39th New York Inf., Company C, P.O.W., d. 6/14/64 @ Crumpton's Factory. Coffin size was 68 in. in length by 18 in. in width. "Was buried in No 7 in 1st line 1st lot", "in far corner". Diuguid's burial log recorded the last name as "Hernandas". His remains were exhumed from the Old City Cemetery in Oct. 1866 and reinterred in Poplar Grove National Cemetery at Petersburg, Virginia. Grave #4784.

Herring, Daniel - 55th Ohio Inf., Company A, P.O.W., d. 7/25/62 @ the Fairgrounds. Was buried in Yankee Square, #10, in 1st line. Coffin size was 72 in. in length by 20 in. in width. Herring was captured on 5/27/62 at Franklin, Virginia. Enlisted as a musician on 9/30/61 for three years. He was mustered into service on the same day at Norwalk, Ohio. Age at enlistment was listed as 23. This soldier's remains were exhumed from the Old City Cemetery in Oct. 1866 and reinterred in Poplar Grove National Cemetery, Petersburg, Virginia. Grave #4589.

Hess, Henry H. - 55th Ohio Inf., Company C, P.O.W., d. 7/29/62 @ the Fairgrounds Was buried in Yankee Square, #11, in 4th line. Coffin size was 70 in. in length by 18 in. in width. Cause of death not stated. Hess was captured on 5/08/62 at the Battle of McDowell, Virginia. Enlisted as a private on 12/14/61 for three years. Mustered into service on the same date at Norwalk, Ohio. Age at enlistment was listed as 45. The 55th was not engaged during the Battle of McDowell but was held in reserve protecting an artillery unit that did not enter the battle due to the nature of the ground. The only men lost by the 55th were 3 POW's. This soldier's remains were exhumed from the Old City Cemetery in Oct. 1866 and reinterred in Poplar Grove National Cemetery, Petersburg, Virginia. Grave #4744.

Heter, Gerard - "A German who cut his throat was buried No 5 in 3rd line of lot 192", died 7/8/63. Diuguid did not specify which hospital he died in, he did state, "Buried...with soldiers". This writer has not been able to locate this individual (Heter, Hetzer, Hezer) via a search existing records. This individual, soldier or not, remains were exhumed from the Old City Cemetery in Oct. 1866. All Union soldiers that were removed from Lynchburg were scheduled to be reinterred at Poplar Grove National Cemetery, Petersburg, Virginia.

Hueninston, Newton P. - 29th Ohio Inf., Company G, P.O.W., d. 7/28/62 @ the Fairgrounds. Was buried in Yankee Square, #1, in 6th line. Coffin size was 72 in. in length by 20 in. in width. Enlisted as a private on 9/30/61, term of service 3 years. Mustered into service on the same date at Jefferson, Ohio. His age at enlistment was listed as 23. The only major engagement the 29th was involved in was Port Republic, Virginia on 6/9/62. This was the last major battle of the Valley Campaign. The 29th suffered less than fifty casualties at Port Republic, approximately 20 of which were POW's. Diuguid's burial records listed the last name as "Hummuston". This soldier's remains were exhumed from the Old City Cemetery in Oct. 1866. All Union soldiers removed from Lynchburg were supposed to be reinterred at Poplar Grove National Cemetery, Petersburg, Virginia.

Humphreys, Gabriel, Corpl. - 9th Virginia (West Va.) Inf., Company D, d. 12/31/64 @ Crumpton's Factory. Wounded & captured during the action at Lynchburg on the afternoon of 6/18/64. Enlisted as a private on 2/26/62 at Guyandotte, W. Va. at age 40. Mustered into service in same location. Occupation listed as a carpenter. Born in Lawrence County, Ohio. His military records state that he was transferred to Company D, 1st West Va. Inf. by consolidation of 5th and 9th regiments Infantry (no date given). "Was buried No 2 in 4th line 3rd lot". This soldier's remains were exhumed from the Old City Cemetery in Oct. 1866 and reinterred in Poplar Grove National Cemetery, Petersburg, Virginia. Grave #4659.

Isert, Peter - 27th Indiana Cav (?)., Company D, P.O.W., d. 7/28/62 @ the Fairgrounds. Was buried in Yankee Square, #9, in 5th line. Coffin size was 78 in. in length by 20 in. in width. There was not a 27th Ind. Cav. regiment. The highest was the 13th Ind. Cav. It is very possible he was a member of the 27th Ind. Infantry. They saw service in the Valley Campaign of 62 under Banks. This soldier's remains were exhumed from the Old City Cemetery in Oct. 1866 and reinterred in Poplar Grove National Cemetery at Petersburg, Virginia. Grave #4748.

Johnson, James M. - 5th Virginia (West Va.) Inf., Company H, P.O.W., d. 6/25/64 of wounds @ College Hospital. Wounded and captured during the Battle for Lynchburg. "Was buried No 1 in 2nd line far corner (lot #1)". Enlisted (originally) as a private on 11/21/61 at Ceredo, W. Va. at age 21. Mustered into service at Gauley Bridge, West Virginia. Reenlisted as a veteran vol. 1/04/64. His military record stated he as wounded and left on the field on 6/18/64 at Lynchburg. Occupation listed as gentleman, born in Kanawha County, West Virginia. This soldier's remains were exhumed from the Old City Cemetery in Oct. 1866 and reinterred in Poplar Grove National Cemetery, Petersburg, Virginia. Grave #4943.

Johnte, John G., Corpl. - 5th Ohio Inf., Company H, P.O.W., d. 7/21/62 @ the Fairgrounds. Was buried in Yankee Square, #8, in 2nd line. Coffin size was 72 in. in length by 20 in. in width. Johnte's records are very confusing. He is shown enlisting on 4/20/61 for three years at age 30. Also listed as muster out of service on 6/19/61. Another record for this soldier dated 8/25/62 states he was rejected by examining surgeon and discharged. The State of Ohio Official Roster listed his enlistment date as 6/19/61. He enlisted as a private and was mustered into service on 6/19/61 at Camp Dennision. Johnte's age at enlistment was listed as 26. His military records do not specify were he was captured. The 5th Ohio was actively engaged in the Valley Campaign of 62 from Kernstown (3/24/62) to Port Republic (6/9/62). This soldier's remains were exhumed from the Old City Cemetery in Oct. 1866 and reinterred in Poplar Grove National Cemetery, Petersburg, Virginia. Grave #4750. Poplar Grove's burial log recorded the last name as "Jones".

Jones, Jesse - 121st New York Inf., Company B, P.O.W., d. 7/08/64 of wounds @ Crumpton's Factory. "Was buried No 8 in 3rd line far corner". Originally enlisted as a private on 8/22/61 at Amsterdam, New York. Age at enlistment was 26. He was mustered into service 5/31/61 at New Dorp, Staten Island in Co. "D", 32nd New York Infantry. As a 3-year veteran he was transferred into the 121st New York on 5/24/63. Jones was wounded and captured on 5/10/64 at Spotsylvania Court House, Virginia. This soldier's remains were exhumed from the Old City Cemetery in Oct. 1866 and reinterred in Poplar Grove National Cemetery, Petersburg, Virginia. Grave #4960.

Jones, Owen R. - 22nd Wisconsin Inf., Company F, P.O.W., d. 4/06/63 of typhoid pneumonia on "V&T Rail Car". Buried in lot #199, grave #3, row #5. Enlisted by Capt. Owen Griffith on 8/15/62 at Racine, Wisconsin. Term of enlistment was for 3 years. Officially muster into service 9/01/62 by Capt. Trowbridge. Description, age 26, blue eyes, brown hair, dark complexion, height 5' 8", occupation teamster, marital status, single. His military records indicated he was a prisoner of war but does not indicate where he was captured. The 22nd served in the Western theater in the Army of Kentucky. On 3/25/63 a force totaling about 300, which included members of the 22nd, were guarding the railroad at Brentwood, Tenn. were surprised and captured. These men were transported eastbound for Richmond, Virginia. His remains were exhumed from the City Cemetery in Oct. 1866 and reinterred in Poplar Grove National Cemetery at Petersburg, Virginia. Grave #4721.

Jones, William H. - 29th Ohio Inf., Company D, d. P.O.W., 7/21/62 @ the Fairgrounds. Was buried in Yankee Square, #7, in 3rd line. Coffin size was 72 in. in length by 20 in. in width. Cause of death and place of capture not stated. Enlisted as a private on 9/10/61 for three years. Mustered into service on same date as enlistment at Jefferson, Ohio. Age at enlistment was listed as 18. The 29th participated in the battles of Winchester and Port Republic in the spring of 1862. Jones was probably captured during this time frame. This soldier's remains were exhumed from the Old City Cemetery in Oct. 1866 and reinterred in Poplar Grove National Cemetery at Petersburg, Virginia. Grave #4606.

Kelley, T. M. - 111th New York Inf., Company I, P.O.W., d. 7/14/64 @ Crumpton's Factory. "Was buried No 1 in 2nd line 2nd lot". Diuguid's burial log recorded the last name as "Keller". This soldier's remains were exhumed from the Old City Cemetery in Oct. 1866 reinterred at Poplar Grove National Cemetery, Petersburg, Virginia. Grave #4766.

Kelly, John - 3rd Virginia (West Va.) Cav., Company K, P.O.W., d. 6/23/64 @ College Hospital. Coffin size was 72 in. in length by 18 in. in width. Possibly captured during the Battle for Lynchburg. It is assumed that he was wounded in Action. "Was buried No 1 in 3rd line 1st lot". This soldier's remains were exhumed from the Old City Cemetery in Oct. 1866 and reinterred in Poplar Grove National Cemetery at Petersburg, Virginia. Grave #4794. The burial records at Poplar Grove listed only a first name "John".

Kemer, H. C., Capt. - A.A.G. 4th Federal Cav., P.O.W., d. 9/7/64 @ Crumpton's Factory. Coffin size was 74 in. in length by 20 in. in width. Originally buried in Lot #3, grave #4, row

#1. Body was exhumed January 1866, "sent to Chattanooga Tenn.".

Kettle, John W. - 66th Ohio Inf., Company G, P.O.W., d. 7/09/62 @ the Fairgrounds. Was buried Yankee Square, #4, in 2nd line. Coffin size 78 in. in length by 20 in. in width. Cause of death and place of capture not specified. Enlisted as a private on 10/06/61 for three years. Mustered into service 12/26/61 at Camp McArthur, Urbana, Ohio. Age at enlistment was listed as 40. The only action the 66th participated in prior to his death date would have been Port Republic (6/9/62). This regiment lost 109 men of 400 engaged. This soldier's remains were exhumed from the Old City Cemetery in Oct. 1866 and reinterred in Poplar Grove National Cemetery, Petersburg, Virginia. Grave #4601.

Keys, Edwin, Capt. - 116th Ohio Inf., Company B, P.O.W., d. 7/19/64 from wounds and complications @ College Hospital. Captains Keys coffin size was 77 in. in length by 18 in. in width. "Was buried No 3 in 2nd line 2nd lot". A second entry by Diuguid read, "Capt. Keys by Government count in removal is No 43". His age at death was 35 years, 11 months and 28 days. Widow of the deceased was Sibyl D. Sergeant Keys. They were married 4/13/54. He was a resident of Troy, Ohio, Athens County. Keys enlisted as a Captain on 8/12/62. He was commissioned on 9/19/62. Captain Keys was wounded during the battle of Lynchburg. By one account he was wounded in the left knee and left elbow. His wounds were received during the actions on Saturday afternoon of June 18th when the 116th for a brief instant breached the Confederate lines. Captain Keys and Color Sgt. Fred Humphrey, both severely wounded, were carried back to Union lines. They were taken to the Union field hospital located in a barn on the Hutter farm. Captain Keys arm and leg were amputated. Several of the Union soldiers, were seriously wounded, and left behind by Gen. Hunter when he retreated. The records of Diuguid make no mention of Color Sgt. Humphrey. (1st Sgt. Frederick E. Humphrey was Killed in Action 4/02/65 during the assault on Fort Gregg, Petersburg, Virginia. No record of being wounded at Lynchburg, June 1864.) Keys remains were exhumed from the Old City Cemetery in Oct. 1866 and reinterred in Poplar Grove National Cemetery at Petersburg, Virginia. Grave #4950. Captains Keys is also listed as interred in the Old Hockingport Cemetery in Troy, Ohio were his wife is also interred. She died 5/16/79 at age 51 years, 6 months, and 7 days.

Killering, Samuel - 3rd Maryland Inf., Company F, d. 8/4/62 @ the Fairgrounds. Coffin size was 78 in. in length by 20 in. in width. Was buried Yankee Square, #12, in 5th line. Diuguid's burial log recorded the last name as "Kittering". Have been unable to locate anyone by the name **"Killering"** or **"Kittering"** in either the 3rd Maryland Inf. or the 3rd Inf. Maryland Potomac Home Brigade. An additional search through Maryland service records revealed no such names. This soldier's remains were exhumed from the Old City Cemetery in Oct. 1866 and reinterred in Poplar Grove National Cemetery at Petersburg, Virginia. Grave #4739.

King, William C. - 46th Pennsylvania Inf., Company F, P.O.W., d. 7/7/62 @ the Fairgrounds. Was buried Yankee Square, #3, in 3rd line. Enlisted as a private and mustered into service on 9/16/61. The 46th was officially mustered into service on 10/31/61 at Harrisburg, Pennsylvania. Private King was possibly captured at Winchester on 5/25/62. This was the only major engagement the 46th participated in prior to Cedar Mountain on 8/9/62. This soldier's remains were exhumed from the Old City Cemetery in Oct. 1866 and reinterred in Poplar Grove National Cemetery, Petersburg, Virginia. Grave #4602.

Kyle J. - 11th U.S. Inf., Company D, P.O.W., d. 9/27/64 @ Crumpton's Factory. "Was buried No 8 in 1st line of 3rd lot". This soldier's remains were exhumed from the Old City Cemetery in Oct. 1866 and reinterred in Poplar Grove National Cemetery at Petersburg, Virginia. Grave #4769.

Lambdin, John - 1st Maryland Inf., Company B, P.O.W., d. 6/23/62 @ John Brown's Stable. It states in his record that he died of starvation. Enlisted as a private on 5/11/61 at Baltimore, Maryland. He was mustered into service on the same date as enlistment. His age at enlistment was recorded as 32. He was captured 5/23/62 at Front Royal, Virginia. One record states that he died of starvation. Was buried in lot #171, grave #5, row #4. His remains were exhumed from the Old City Cemetery in Oct. 1866 and reinterred in Poplar Grove National Cemetery, Petersburg, Virginia. Grave #4735.

Lannen, Dennis - 29th Pennsylvania Inf., Company E, P.O.W., d. 7/14/62 @ the Fairgrounds. Coffin size was 72 in. in length by 20 in. in width. Was buried Yankee Square, #5, in

4th line. Lannen enlisted as a private on 7/8/61. He was mustered into service on the same date at Philadelphia, Penn. His military records only state that he was a POW not where. The 29th served with Bank's in the Shenandoah Valley in 1862. The 29th was lightly engaged at both Front Royal and Winchester in late May 1862. This soldier's remains were exhumed from the Old City Cemetery in Oct. 1866 and reinterred in Poplar Grove National Cemetery at Petersburg, Virginia. Grave #4717.

Lapiere, John - Diuguid's only entry in the burial log was, "A Yankee who died in jail was buried No 10 in 4th line lot 192". His date of death was 12/3/63. The "jail" Diuguid refers to would have been Massie's Factory. It was being used as a holding area for Federal POW's. A search of available records with this spelling located a John Lapiere, a member of the 34th Massachusetts Inf., Company E. However, his records indicate that he was discharged at Fort Lyon, Va. on 11/24/62. He had enlisted on 7/19/62 at age 21. He was resident of Shirley, Mass., occupation listed as a bootmaker. This soldier's remains were exhumed from the Old City Cemetery in Oct. 1866 and reinterred in Poplar Grove National Cemetery, Petersburg, Virginia. Grave #4715.

Leach, William, Sgt. - 3rd Wisconsin Inf., Company B, P.O.W., d. 7/18/62 of convulsions @ the Fairgrounds. Was buried Yankee Square, #7, in 2nd line. Coffin size was 72 in. in length by 20 in. in width. Enlisted as a private on 4/21/61 in Oshkosh, Wisconsin. Term of enlistment was for 3 years. Officially muster into service by Capt. McIntyer at Fond du Lac on 6/29/61. Enlisted with Company as Sgt., his recorded also indicate that he was promoted to Sgt. 7/09/61. The causality report for May, 62 list him as missing in action at Winchester on 5/25/62. On the company muster for 7/62 to 9/62 he was listed as a prisoner of war from 5/25/62. Description, age 29, gray eyes, brown hair, sandy complexion, height 5' 7", occupation farmer. Marital status, single. Resident of Marion, Waupaca County, Wisconsin. Place of birth listed as Ruthland, New York. His remains were exhumed from the City Cemetery in Oct. 1866 and reinterred in Poplar Grove National Cemetery at Petersburg, Virginia. Grave #4752.

Lenox, S. - 8th New York Inf., Company A, d. 5/29/64 @ Miller's Factory. Coffin size was 74 in. in length by 18 in. in width. "Was buried No. 1 in 1st line in the far corner lot no. 1". This soldier's remains were exhumed from the Old City

Cemetery in Oct. 1866 and reinterred in Poplar Grove National Cemetery, Petersburg, Virginia. Grave #4775.

Leonard, Frank (H.?) - 116th Pennsylvania Inf., Company H, P.O.W., d. 9/1/64 @ Crumpton's Factory. Coffin size was 75 in. in length by 15 in. in width. "Was buried No 2 in 1st line of 3rd lot". Enlisted as a private on 2/16/64. Mustered into service on same date. Captured on 6/22/64 at Williams' Farm, Virginia (Petersburg?). His military records list his date of death as 9/10/64. This soldier's remains were exhumed from the Old City Cemetery in Oct. 1866 and reinterred in Poplar Grove National Cemetery, Petersburg, Virginia. Grave #4958.

Lockwood, James E. - 10th Vermont Inf., Company E, P.O.W., d. 8/08/64 of disease @ Crumpton's Factory. "Was buried No 6 in 4th line 2nd lot". Enlisted as a private on 12/24/63, officially mustered in 12/30/64. He was a resident of Pownal, Vermont. Lockwood was captured 5/09/64 at Battle of the Wilderness. His remains were exhumed in Oct. 1866 from Lynchburg and reinterred in Poplar Grove National Cemetery, Petersburg, Virginia. Grave #4951.

Marson, A. C. - 85th Indiana Inf., Company C, P.O.W., d. 3/28/63 @ Knights Factory. Coffin size was 70 in. in length by 18 in. in width. Was buried in lot #199, grave #7, grave #2. A search of the records for the 85th Indiana could not locate an A. C. Maren. The 85th was engaged at Thompson's Station, Tenn. on 3/3/63 were a large portion of the regiment was captured. Those captured were exchanged at Richmond on 3/31/63. However, this soldier's remains were exhumed from the Old City Cemetery in Oct. 1866 and reinterred in Poplar Grove National Cemetery, Petersburg, Virginia. Grave #4591.

McCluskey, John - 140th New York Inf., Company A., P.O.W., d. 7/28/64 of wounds(?) @ Crumpton's Factory. "Was buried No 7 in 3rd line 2nd lot". Enlisted as a private on 3/4/64. He was mustered into service on the same date. His age at enlistment was listed as 42. His military records list him as **Killed in Action** at the Battle of the Wilderness on 5/5/64. This soldier's remains were exhumed from the Old City Cemetery in Oct. 1866 and reinterred in Poplar Grove National Cemetery, Petersburg, Virginia. Grave #4645.

McCort, James - 110th Pennsylvania Inf., Company F, P.O.W., d. 7/25/62 @ the Fairgrounds. Was buried Yankee Square, #9, in 1st line. Coffin size was 72 in. in length by 20 in. in width. Enlisted as a private on 8/30/61. He was mustered into service on the same date at Huntington, Pennsylvania. His available records do not state were he was captured. The 110 served under both Bank's and Shield's Divisions in the Shenandoah Valley in the spring of 1862. They saw action at Winchester and were lightly engaged at Port Republic. It's quite like he was capture during this time frame. This soldier's remains were exhumed from the Old City Cemetery in Oct. 1866 and reinterred in Poplar Grove National Cemetery, Petersburg, Virginia. Grave #4666.

McGill, S. - 6th New York Inf., Company F, P.O.W., d. 9/17/64 @ Crumpton's Factory. "Was buried No. 5 in 1st line of 3rd lot". The 6th New York was a two-year unit, which was discharged in June 1863. Also the 6th only saw service in Florida and Louisiana. To date have not been able to locate this individual. This soldier's remains were exhumed from the Old City Cemetery in Oct. 1866 and reinterred in Poplar Grove National Cemetery, Petersburg, Virginia. Grave #4623.

McGinnis, James (John?) - 33rd Indiana Inf., Company A, P.O.W., d. 3/25/63 of disease @ Knights Factory. Coffin size was 80 in. in length by 21 in. in width. Was buried in lot #199, grave #2, row #2. Enlisted as a private on 8/30/61 at Indianapolis, was mustered in 9/16/61 also at Indianapolis. He was a native of Owen County, Indiana. His age at enlisted was 23 and his occupation was listed as a farmer. Physical description, 6 ft. 2 in. in height, blue eyes and light hair. The 33rd Indiana was in the Western Theater as a member of the Army of Kentucky. On March 3, 1863 they were engaged at Thompson's Station, Tenn. where approximately 400 of the regiment were captured. They were sent to Richmond, Virginia and paroled by the end of March. McGinnis' remains were exhumed from the Old City Cemetery in Oct. 1866 and reinterred in Poplar Grove National Cemetery at Petersburg, Virginia. Grave #4593.

McIntosh, Frank - 15th New York Cav., Company G, P.O.W., d. 7/26/64 @ Crumpton's Factory. Coffin size was 70 in. in length by 17 in. in width. "Was buried No 9 in 2nd line 2nd lot". McIntosh enlisted as a private on 1/20/64 at Mina, New York. He was mustered into service on the same date. His age at enlistment was listed as 18. He was wounded and captured on 6/17/64 at Lynchburg, Virginia. Diuguid's burial log recorded the last name as "McItosh." Poplar Grove recorded the name as "Mac Kentosh." This soldier's remains were exhumed from the Old City Cemetery in Oct. 1866 and reinterred in Poplar Grove National Cemetery, Petersburg, Virginia. Grave #4631.

McVey, James - 88th Pennsylvania Inf., Company D, P.O.W., d. 6/23/64 @ Crumpton's Factory. "Was buried No 5 in 2nd line 1st lot". Enlisted as a private on 3/12/64. He was mustered into service on the same date. The available records do no state where he was captured. The 88th was active the entire spring of 64 from Wilderness to Petersburg. This soldier's remains were exhumed from the Old City Cemetery in Oct. 1866 and reinterred in Poplar Grove National Cemetery, Petersburg, Virginia. Grave #4792.

Monk, Henry - 1st Maryland Inf., Company I, P.O.W., d. 7/22/62 @ the Fairgrounds. Coffin size was 78 in. in length by 20 in. in width. Enlisted as a private on 5/27/61 at Relay House, Maryland. His age at enlistment was recorded as 30. His occupation was listed as "Morocco Dresser"(?). He was captured 5/23/62 at Front, Royal, Virginia. Was buried Yankee Square, #8, in 1st line. Personal description was as follows, 5 ft. 11 in. in height, dark complexion, dark eyes and black hair. This soldier's remains were exhumed from the Old City Cemetery in Oct. 1866 and reinterred in Poplar Grove National Cemetery, Petersburg, Virginia. Grave #4595.

Monteith William - 65th New York Inf., Company G, P.O.W., d. 9/20/64 @ Crumpton's Factory. "Was buried No 4 in 2nd line of 3rd lot". Poplar Grove burial log recorded the last name as "Monteal". He enlisted as private on 8/26/61 at New York City. He was mustered into service on the same date. His age at enlistment was listed as 29. He was wounded and captured 5/6/64, Battle of the Wilderness. His records also state that he was paroled on 5/10/64. This soldier's remains were exhumed from the Old City Cemetery in Oct. 1866 and reinterred in Poplar Grove National Cemetery, Petersburg, Virginia. Grave #4644.

Moore, John Thomas - 66th Ohio Inf., Company E, P.O.W., d. 7/31/62 @ the Fairgrounds. Was buried Yankee Square, #10, in 6th line. Enlisted as a private on 11/8/61. Was officially mustered into service on 12/26/61. His age at enlistment was listed as 19. He was listed as a POW, place of capture not specified. It's quite likely he was captured at Port Republic, 6/9/62. the 66th lost 109 men (killed, wounded & captured) of the 400 engaged. This soldier's remains were exhumed from the Old City Cemetery in Oct. 1866. All Union soldiers removed from Lynchburg were scheduled to be reinterred at Poplar Grove National Cemetery, Petersburg, Virginia.

Moss, Jacob - 5th New York Heavy Art., Company A, P.O.W., d. 7/30/64 of wounds @ Crumpton's Factory. Coffin size was 69 in. in length by 16 in. in width. Enlisted as a private on 12/28/63 at Greig, New York. Officially muster into service on 1/08/64. His age at enlistment was listed as 42. Wounded and captured at Piedmont, Va. on 6/5/64. His records state that he died of wounds as a POW on 11/02/64. Was buried No 3 in 4th line 2nd lot". Four companies, A, B, C, & D of this unit participated in Hunter's expedition and the Battle for Lynchburg June 17-18, 1864. This soldier's remains were exhumed from the Old City Cemetery in Oct. 1866 and reinterred in Poplar Grove National Cemetery, Petersburg, Virginia. Grave #4627.

Munson, Enos - 46th Pennsylvania Inf., Company G, P.O.W., d. 7/24/62 @ the Fairgrounds. Coffin size was 73 in. in length by 20 in. in width. Was buried Yankee Square, #1, in 5th line. Diuguid's burial log recorded the first name as "Aenas". Enlisted as a private on 9/13/61. Mustered into service on the same date. Captured at Winchester, Va. on 5/25/62. This soldier's remains were exhumed from the Old City Cemetery in Oct. 1866 and reinterred in Poplar Grove National Cemetery, Petersburg, Virginia. Grave #4725.

Murphy, Patrick - 27th Indiana Inf., Company H, P.O.W., d. 7/22/62 @ the Fairgrounds. Was buried Yankee Square, #9, in 2nd line. Coffin size was 72 in. in length by 22 in. in width. Enlisted as a private on 9/01/61 at Indianapolis, was mustered in 9/16/61. No age or date of birth provided. No physical description supplied in his records. The 26th served in 1862 Valley (Shenandoah) Campaign under Banks. In May of 1862 it participated in the battles at Front Royal and Winchester. It's quite likely he was capture at one of these battles. His military records only stated that he died in Lynchburg as a prisoner of war in July 1862. His remains were exhumed from the Old City Cemetery in Oct. 1866 and reinterred in Poplar Grove National Cemetery, Petersburg, Virginia. Grave #4598.

Neal, James L. - 11th New Hampshire Inf., d. of wounds or complications 7/21/64 @ Crumpton's Factory. Coffin size was 71 in. in length by 16 in. in width. "Was buried No 5 in 3rd line 2nd lot". Enlisted as a private for three-year term on 8/13/62. Officially mustered into service 8/28/62. Born in and a resident of South Newmarket, New Hampshire. Age at enlistment was listed as 22. Occupation was listed as a farmer. Neal was wounded and captured 5/06/64 during the Battle of the Wilderness. A personal description, 5 ft. 9 1/2 in. in height, blue eyes, light hair, and light complexion. This soldier's remains were exhumed from the Old City Cemetery in Oct. 1866 and reinterred in Poplar Grove National Cemetery, Petersburg, Virginia. Grave #4615.

Nichols, Langdon H., Corpl. - 1st Vermont Cav., Company C, P.O.W., d. 7/27/62 @ the Fairgrounds. Coffin size was 78 in. in length by 20 in. in width. Was buried Yankee Square, #9, in 6th line. Enlisted as a Corpl. on 10/03/61. Officially mustered into service on 11/19/61. He was a resident of Roxbury, Vermont. He was captured 5/24/62 at Middletown, Virginia in an action associated with the Battle of Front Royal. Nichols was one of approximately 80 men captured of the 1st Vermont. Erastus W. Nichols, possibly a brother, died 3/31/63 of disease. Both were from Washington County, members of company C and muster in at the same time. This soldier was exhumed from City Cemetery in Oct. 1866 and reinterred in Poplar Grove National Cemetery, Petersburg, Virginia. Grave #4734.

O'Donnel, John - 5th Rhode Island Heavy Artillery, Company K, P.O.W., d. 9/20/64 @ Crumpton's Factory. "Was buried No 6 in 1st line of 3rd lot". Enlisted as private 12/18/-62. Officially mustered into service on 2/23/63 at Smithfield, Rhode Island. Occupation listed as Seaman, age 27, 5' 7" in height, hazel eyes, brown hair, and florid complexion. He was listed as resident of New York, New York. Listed as M.I.A. or deserted 4/29/64 at New Bern, North Carolina. Possibly captured during the actions in and around New Bern. Diuguid's burial log listed the name as "Dounold, J. O." His remains were exhumed from the Old City Cemetery in Oct. 1866 and reinterred in Poplar Grove National Cemetery at Petersburg, Virginia. Grave #4624.

Olf, John - 126th New York Inf., Company E, P.O.W., d. 8/1/64 @ Crumpton's Factory. Coffin 68 in. in length by 16 in. in width. "Was buried No 10 in 3rd line 2nd lot". Enlisted as a private on 7/28/62 at Potter, New York. Mustered into service on 8/22/62. Age at enlistment was listed as 31. He was captured on 5/06/64 at the Battle of the Wilderness. Poplar Grove's burial records the last name as "Oulf". This soldier's remains were exhumed from the Old City Cemetery in Oct. 1866 and reinterred in Poplar Grove National Cemetery, Petersburg, Virginia. Grave #4964.

Packerman, P. - 16th New York Cav., Company C, P.O.W., d. 9/29/64 @ Crumpton's Factory. "Was buried No 9 in 1st line of 3rd lot". I was unable (to date) to locate this individual by the above spelling. This soldier's remains were exhumed from the Old City Cemetery in Oct. 1866. All Union soldiers removed from Lynchburg were scheduled to be reinterred at Poplar Grove National Cemetery, Petersburg, Virginia.

Parker, Isaac - 17th Maine Inf., Company F, P.O.W., d. 7/21/64 of wounds @ Crumpton's Factory. Coffin Size was 78 in. in length by 19 in. in width. "Was buried No 6 in 2nd line 2nd lot". Enlisted as a private 7/25/62 for 3 years at age 26. Officially mustered in at Portland, Maine on 8/06/62. Listed as married, dark complexion, black eyes, black hair, 6' 1" in height, occupation trader. Born in and a resident of Hiram, Maine. His military record states that he was "Killed in Battle" on May 6, 64 at the Wilderness. His remains were exhumed in Oct. 1866 and reinterred in Poplar Grove National Cemetery, Petersburg, Virginia. Grave #4762.

Parker, James C. - 5th Virginia (West Va.) Inf., Company I, P.O.W. d. 7/8/64 of wounds @ Camp Davis. Parker was wounded and captured during Battle for Lynchburg on 6/18/64. Enlisted as a private on 9/14/61 @ Ceredo, W. Va. at age 18. Mustered into service in same location. Re-enlisted as a veteran vol. on 12/24/63. His military record states he was **Killed in Action** on 6/18/64. "Was buried No 7 in 3rd line far corner". This soldier's remains were exhumed from the Old City Cemetery in Oct. 1866 and reinterred in Poplar Grove National Cemetery at Petersburg, Virginia. Grave #4778.

Peaft(?), Henry - Unit not stated, P.O.W., d. 7/1/62 @ the Fairgrounds. Was buried Yankee Square, #2, in 5th line. Have been unable to locate this individual by the above spelling. This soldier's remains were exhumed from the Old City Cemetery in Oct. 1866 and reinterred in Poplar Grove National Cemetery, Petersburg, Virginia. Grave #4716.

Phillips, C. Theophilus - 140th Pennsylvania Inf., Company I, P.O.W., d. 7/15/64 @ Knight's Factory. He was buried, "No 1 in 3rd line 2nd lot". Enlisted as a private on 8/25/62.

Mustered into service on the same date. Wounded and captured at Todd's Tavern, Virginia on 5/08/64 (a part of the Wilderness Campaign). This soldier's remains were exhumed from the Old City Cemetery in Oct. 1866 and reinterred in Poplar Grove National Cemetery, Petersburg, Virginia. Grave #4768.

Phipps, Cyrenius, Corpl. - 1st Michigan Cav., P.O.W., d. 8/11/62 @ the Fairgrounds. Coffin size was 72 in. in length by 18 in. in width. Was buried Yankee Square, #7, in 5th line. Diuguid listed his first name as "Serenas". A record of this soldier was found in the regimental records for the 1st Mich. Cav., Company G. He enlisted as a Corpl. on 8/19/61 at Pontiac for three years at age 19. Listed as a P.O.W at Middletown, Va. on 5/25/62. Then his records list him as promoted to Sgt. 5/01/63, re-enlisting at Stevensville, Va. on 12/21/63. A final entry in his records state that he died in Michigan of disease on 9/09/65. This soldier's remains were exhumed from the Old City Cemetery in Oct. 1866 and reinterred in Poplar Grove National Cemetery at Petersburg, Virginia. Grave #4583.

Pike, William H. - 10th Maine Inf., Company G, P.O.W., d. 7/29/62 of disease(?) @ the Fairgrounds. Coffin size was 76 in. in length by 20 in. in width. Was buried Yankee Square, #11, in 2nd line. Enlisted as a private on 9/09/61 at age 20 for 2 years. Officially mustered in 10/04/61 (his military records state, "for a term of 2 yrs from May 3, 61"). Listed as single, dark complexion, hazel eyes, brown hair, 5' 10" in height, occupation farmer. He was born in Wells, and was a resident of Harrison, Maine. The 10th had the duty of being the rear guard on 5/25/62 covering Bank's retreat from Winchester. As rear guard they lost an estimated 90 men, private Pike was most likely one of this number. His military records state, "Died at Lynchburg, Va. July 15,'62, Prisoner of war". His remains were exhumed in Oct. 1866 and reinterred in Poplar Grove National Cemetery, Petersburg, Virginia. Grave #4746.

Pitcher, Horace M. - 19th Michigan Inf., Company I, P.O.W., d. 3/20/63 @ Crumpton's Factory. Coffin size was 68 in. in length by 18 in. in width. Pitcher was buried in lot #187, grave #2, row #2. Both Diuguid and Poplar Grove records listed his name as **"Beacher, John"**. Poplar Grove also had a listing of his name as "H. M. Ritcher." Pitcher enlisted as a private at St. Josephs, Michigan on 8/9/62. He was officially mustered into service on 9/05/62. His age at enlistment was listed as 18. Pitcher was a resident of Hager, Michigan. The 19th Michigan served in the Western theater. Based on his date of death and the engagements the 19th participated in, it's highly likely he was captured at Thompson's Station, Tenn. on 3/5/63. The 19th suffered 20 killed, 20 wounded and listed 15 men captured. His records state that he died from exposure, hunger and cold. This soldier's remains were exhumed from the Old City Cemetery in Oct. 1866 and reinterred in Poplar Grove National Cemetery at Petersburg, Virginia. Grave #4599.

Plattenburg, Peter - 111th New York Inf., Company D, P.O.W., d. of wounds on 6/30/64 @ Crumpton's Factory. "Was buried No 2 in 3rd line in far corner (lot #1)". He enlisted as a private on 12/30/63 at Sodus, New York. He was mustered into service on 1/02/64. His age at enlistment was listed as 27. He was wounded and captured on 5/5/64 during the Battle of the Wilderness. This soldier's remains were exhumed from the Old City Cemetery in Oct. 1866 and reinterred in Poplar Grove National Cemetery, Petersburg, Virginia. Grave #4770.

Preacher, Bruno - 1st Maryland Inf., Company F, P.O.W., d. 8/2/62 @ the Fairgrounds. Coffin size was 72 in. in length by 20 in. in width. Enlisted as a private on 5/27/61. Mustered into service on the same date. He was captured 5/23/62 at Front Royal, Virginia. Was buried Yankee Square, #4, in 6th line. This soldier's remains were exhumed from the Old City Cemetery in Oct. 1866 and reinterred in Poplar Grove National Cemetery, Petersburg, Virginia. Grave #4730.

Rand, Joseph - 11th Virginia (West Va.) Inf., Company B, P.O.W., d. 7/20/64 of wounds @ Camp Davis. Wounded and captured during the Battle for Lynchburg 6/17/64. Enlisted 3/26/64 at Ravenwood, W. Va. at age 18. Mustered into service in same location. Occupation listed as a farmer, born Jackson County, W. Virginia. "Was buried No 8 in 3rd line of 2nd lot". This soldier's remains were exhumed from the Old City Cemetery in Oct. 1866 and reinterred in Poplar Grove National Cemetery, Petersburg, Virginia. Grave #4617.

Randles, Charles - 25th Pennsylvania Inf., Company H, P.O.W., d. 7/30/62 @ the Fairgrounds. Was buried Yankee Square, #3, in 6th line. The only record on this individual is a post war. This soldier's remains were exhumed from the Old

City Cemetery in Oct. 1866 and reinterred in Poplar Grove National Cemetery at Petersburg, Virginia. Grave #4729.

Rapp, Levi - 149th Pennsylvania Inf., Company G, P.O.W., d. 8/13/64 @ Crumpton's Factory. "Was buried No 9 in 4th line of 2nd lot". Rapp enlisted as a private 8/15/63. He was mustered into service on the same date. He was captured on 5/5/64 during the Battle of the Wilderness. This soldier's remains were exhumed from the Old City Cemetery in Oct. 1866 and reinterred in Poplar Grove National Cemetery, Petersburg, Virginia. Grave #4955.

Redman, John - 5th New York Cav., Company H. P.O.W., d. 7/29/64 @ Crumpton's Factory. Coffin size was 77 in. in length by 16 in. in width. "Was buried No 8 in 3rd line 2nd lot". Enlisted as a private on 12/30/63 at Crown Point, New York. He was mustered into service on 12/30/63. His age at enlistment was listed as 39. Wounded and captured at Parker's Store, Va. on 5/5/64. His records list him as "died in Richmond, Va." This soldier's remains were exhumed from the Old City Cemetery in Oct. 1866 and reinterred in Poplar Grove National Cemetery, Petersburg, Virginia. Grave #4647.

Reed, Charles E. - 12th Massachusetts Inf., Company F, P.O.W., d. 8/9/62 @ the Fairgrounds. Coffin size was 72 in. in length by 20 in. in width. Was buried Yankee Square, #13, in 5th line. Enlisted as a private on 7/02/61. Mustered into service on the same date. His age at enlistment was listed as 20. He was a resident of North Bridgewater, Massachusetts. His records do not specify his place of capture or cause of death. The 12th was in the Shenandoah Valley in 1862 but not actively engaged. This soldier's remains were exhumed from the Old City Cemetery in Oct. 1866 and reinterred in Poplar Grove National Cemetery at Petersburg, Virginia. Grave #4760.

Remington, F. A. - 85th Indiana Inf., Company G, P.O.W., d. 5/1/63 @ Miller's Factory. Was buried in lot #184, grave #3, row #1. Enlisted 8/14/62 and mustered into service on 9/02/62 at Terre Haute, Indiana. He was 34 years old at enlistment, occupation listed as a farmer. Physical description, gray eyes, sandy hair, 6 ft. 1 in. in height. He was a native of Putnam County, Indiana. The 85th had heavy losses at Thompson's Station, Tenn. on 3/3/63. This was their first engagement. His military records stated that he died in Libby Prison in Richmond, Virginia as a prisoner of war in March, 1863. His remains were exhumed from the Old City Cemetery in Oct. 1866 and reinterred in Poplar Grove National Cemetery,

Petersburg, Virginia. Grave #4761. Poplar Grove burial records listed his initials as "T. M.".

Reis, Michael - 28th Ohio Inf., Company H, P.O.W., d. 7/16/64 of disease @ Crumpton's Factory. "Was buried No 2 in 3rd line 2nd lot". Enlisted as private on 6/13/61. Mustered into service 7/6/61. His age at enlistment was listed as 35. His was listed as wounded at Piedmont, Va. on 6/5/64. Both Diuguid and Poplar Grove recorded the last name as "Rice." This soldier's remains were exhumed from the Old City Cemetery in Oct. 1866 and reinterred in Poplar Grove National Cemetery, Petersburg, Virginia. Grave #4954.

Rider, John, Sgt. - 7th New York Heavy Art., Company K, P.O.W., d. 7/19/64 @ Crumpton's Factory. Coffin size was 75 in. in length by 19 in. in width. Poplar Grove burial log recorded the last name as "Ryder". Both Diuguid and Poplar Grove listed his branch of service as Infantry. "Was buried No 3 in 3rd line 2nd lot". Enlisted as a private 8/4/62 at Westerlo, New York. He was mustered into service on 8/12/62. Rider was promoted to Sgt. on 8/18/62. He was captured 6/16/64 at Petersburg, Virginia. The 7th NY Hvy. Art. This unit at Petersburg (on 6/16/64) suffered over 400 men killed, wounded and captured. A total 252 men were take prisoners. Diuguid listed the name as "Rider" Poplar Grove recorded the name as "Ryder." This soldier's remains were exhumed from the Old City Cemetery in Oct. 1866 and reinterred in Poplar Grove National Cemetery, Petersburg, Virginia. Grave #4616.

Roberts, Daniel S. - 10th Maine Inf., Company B, P.O.W., d. 8/03/62, of unspecified cause @ the Fairgrounds. Coffin size was 78 in. in length by 20 in. in width. Was buried Yankee Square, #1, in 4th line. Enlisted as a private on 9/17/61 at age 43 for 2 years. Officially mustered into service 10/04/61. His military records state, "for a term of 2 yrs from May 3, '61". Listed as married, dark complexion, gray eyes, black hair, 6' in height, occupation cordweimer(?). Born in Brunswick and was resident of Portland. His remains were exhumed in Oct. 1866 and reinterred in Poplar Grove National Cemetery, Petersburg, Virginia. Grave #4741.

Robinson (also Robison), Charles - 27th Indiana Inf., Company G, P.O.W., d. 7/14/62 @ the Fairgrounds. Coffin size was 72 in. in length by 20 in. in width. Was buried in Yankee Square, #1 in 4th line. Enlisted as a private on 9/01/61 at Indianapolis. Officially mustered into service on

9/12/61 at age 44. Occupation listed as a farmer. No physical description, no place or date of birth supplied. His military records stated that he died in Richmond, Virginia and that he was taken prisoner at Winchester, Virginia 5/25/62. His remains were exhumed from the Old City Cemetery in Oct. 1866 and reinterred in Poplar Grove National Cemetery, Petersburg, Virginia. Grave #4577.

Robinson, Richard - 21st Michigan Inf., Company K, P.O.W., d. 4/27/63 @ Burton's Factory. Was buried in lot #184, grave #2, row #1. Enlisted as a private on 8/11/62 at Grand Haven, Michigan in Company G for three years. Was mustered into service on 9/03/63. He was a resident of Allendale, Michigan. His age at enlistment was listed as 18. The 21st was in the Western theater in the Army of Cumberland. This regiment suffered 130 men lost at Stone River, Tenn. on 12/31/62 & 1/1/63. It's highly likely Robinson was captured during this battle. His military record list his date of death as 2/23/63. This soldier's remains were exhumed from the Old City Cemetery in Oct. 1866 and reinterred in Poplar Grove National Cemetery, Petersburg, Virginia. Grave #4742.

Ruck, Cyrus - 116th Pennsylvania Inf., Company G, P.O.W., d. 8/17/64 @ College Hospital. "Was buried No 10 in 4th line of 2nd lot". Diuguid and Poplar Grove listed the name as "Silas Ruck". Ruck enlisted as a private on 3/25/64. He was mustered into service on the same date. He was captured on 6/22/64 at William's Farm, Virginia (Petersburg). This soldier's remains were exhumed from the Old City Cemetery in Oct. 1866 and reinterred in Poplar Grove National Cemetery possibly Poplar Grove, Petersburg, Virginia. Grave #4952.

Rucker, John W. - 25th Ohio Inf., Company I, P.O.W., d. 6/24/62 @ the Fairgrounds. Was buried in lot #172, grave #4, row #3. Enlisted as a private on 6/26/61 for three years. Was mustered into service on the same date. His age at enlistment was stated as 20. Cause of death and place of capture not specified. The 25th was engaged in the Shenandoah Valley in the spring of 1862. The 25th participated at McDowell on 5/08/62 and again at Cross Keys on 6/8/62. Military records listed 2 men missing at Cross Keys. Diuguid's burial log recorded his first name as "James". This soldier's remains were exhumed from the Old City Cemetery in Oct. 1866 and reinterred in Poplar Grove National Cemetery, Petersburg, Virginia. Grave #4733.

Sears, William A. - 34th Massachusetts Inf., Company H, P.O.W., d. 6/29/64 of wounds @ College Hospital. Coffin size was 71 in. in length by 18 in. in width. "Was buried No 8 in 2nd line far corner (lot #1)". Sears enlisted as a private on 7/11/62. He was mustered into service on 7/31/62. His age at enlistment was listed as 33. His occupation was listed as a "Carder". He was resident of Southbridge, Massachusetts. Sears was wounded and captured at Lynchburg, Virginia on 6/18/64. This soldier's remains were exhumed from the Old City Cemetery in Oct. 1866 and reinterred in Poplar Grove National Cemetery, Petersburg, Virginia. Grave #4783.

Schaum, Randolph - 8th New York Inf., Company G, P.O.W., d. 7/19/62 @ the Fairgrounds. Coffin size was 72 in. in length by 20 in. in width. Was buried Yankee Square, #4, in 4th line. Enlisted as private On 4/23/61 at New York City. He was mustered into service on the same date. He was captured at Cross Keys, Va. on 6/08/62. Diuguid's burial log recorded only the last name "Shanm" no first name or initial. Poplar Grove recorded his last name as "Shuan". This soldier's remains were exhumed from the Old City Cemetery in Oct. 1866 and reinterred in Poplar Grove National Cemetery at Petersburg, Virginia. Grave #4724.

Schwartz, William - 140th New York Inf., Company G, P.O.W., d. 7/5/64 @ Crumpton's Factory. "Was buried No 4 in 1st line 2nd lot". No one by the above name "Schwartz" served in this unit. This soldier's remains were exhumed from the Old City Cemetery in Oct. 1866. All Union soldiers that were removed from Lynchburg were scheduled to be reinterred at Poplar Grove National Cemetery, Petersburg, Virginia.

Shannesy, Michael - 27th Indiana Inf., Company B, P.O.W., d. 7/15/62 @ the Fairgrounds. Coffin size was 78 in. in length by 20 in. in width. Was buried Yankee Square, #5, in 1st line. To date a search of the 27th Indiana has not located a Michael Shannessy. The 27th participated in the Battles of Front Royal on 5/23/62 and Winchester on 5/25/62. Quite likely this soldier was captured at one of these battles. This soldier's remains were exhumed from the Old City Cemetery in Oct. 1866 and reinterred in Poplar Grove National Cemetery, Petersburg, Virginia. Grave #4597.

Sheehan, Michale - 150th Pennsylvania Inf., Company A, P.O.W., d. 9/7/64 of wounds @ Crumpton's Factory. Coffin size was 75 in. in length by 16 in. in width. "Was buried No 3 in 2nd line of 3rd lot". Diuguid listed his name as "Shuan". Enlisted as a private on 9/19/62. He was mustered into service on the same date. This soldier's remains were exhumed from the Old City Cemetery in Oct. 1866 and reinterred in Poplar Grove National Cemetery, Petersburg, Virginia. Grave #4767.

Sherborne, R. - 1st Michigan Inf., Company C, P.O.W., d. 7/2/64 @ Crumpton's Factory. Coffin size was 69 in. in length by 16 in. in width. "Was buried No 1 in 1st line 2nd lot". Diuguid's burial log recorded only a last name, "Sherburon", no first name or initial. Have not been able to locate this individual to date. This soldier's remains were exhumed from the Old City Cemetery in Oct. 1866 and reinterred at Poplar Grove National Cemetery, Petersburg, Virginia. Grave #4764.

Sink, F. - Co. B, Union P.O.W., d. 6/23/64 at College Hospital. "Was buried No 2 in 2nd line 1st lot". Diuguid's burial log had his last name listed as "Cink". A search of available records has not identified this individual. This soldier's remains were exhumed from the Old City Cemetery in Oct. 1866 and reinterred in Poplar Grove National Cemetery, Petersburg, Virginia. Grave #4773.

Sly, Hiram - 29th Ohio Inf., Company E, P.O.W., d. 7/6/62 @ the Fairgrounds. Was buried Yankee Square, #2, in 3rd line. Enlisted as a private 9/16/61 for three years. Mustered into service on 99/27/61. Age at enlistment was listed as 18. His records do no specify where he was captured. The 29th was engaged at Winchester on 5/25/62 and again at Port Republic on 6/9/62. Sly was mostly captured at one of these engagements. Diuguid recorded the name as Henry Sly. Poplar Grove listed the name as Henry Sky. This soldier's remains were exhumed from the Old City Cemetery in Oct. 1866 and reinterred in Poplar Grove National Cemetery at Petersburg, Virginia. Grave #4731.

Smith, Harrison H. - 5th Vermont Inf., Company K, P.O.W., d. 11/4/64 of disease @ Crumpton's Factory. "Was buried No 8 in 2nd line of 3rd lot". Enlisted as a private 12/30/63, officially mustered into service 1/07/64. No listing of his place of capture. The 5th participated in several battles in the Shenandoah Valley in the fall of 1864, which included Fisher's Hill (9/22/64) and Cedar Creek (10/19/64). His remains were exhumed from City Cemetery in Oct 1866 and reinterred in Poplar Grove National Cemetery, Petersburg, Virginia. Grave #4786.

Smith, William - 6th New Hampshire Inf., Company A, d. 6/2/64 @ Camp Davis. "Was buried No. 2 in 1st Line Lot No. 1 in far Corner". Diuguid specifically recorded "Wm Smith Co A 6 NH YP (Yankee Prisoner)." Poplar Grove listed the state of service as New York. A search of the 6th New Hampshire reveals a total of 7 William Smiths. Five of which were listed as deserters in January 1864 from Camp Nelson in Kentucky. The 6th New Hampshire was a part of the 9th Corps that was sent to the Western theater after Fredericksburg 12/62. The 9th Corps returned to the Easter Theater by the spring 1864. Of the five deserters 2 were members of Company A. The 1st William Smith enlisted 1/01/64, officially mustered in 1/04/64. Age 35 at enlistment, born in Pennsylvania, resident of Winchester, New Hampshire. Listed as deserted 1/18/64. The 2nd William Smith enlisted 12/30/63 and officially mustered in on the same date. Age at enlistment 22, born in New York, resident of Wakefield, New Hampshire. Listed as a deserter 1/25/64. Sources indicate that this was a common alias of the time. The other three men were members of Companies G, H & I respectively. There desertions were around the same time frame. It would appear that one of these men was captured some time after their desertion and wound up in the hospital in Lynchburg. This soldier's remains were exhumed from the Old City Cemetery in Oct. 1866 and reinterred in Poplar Grove National Cemetery, Petersburg, Virginia. Grave #4787. Point of interest, William State also a member of the 6th New Hampshire was wounded and capture at the Wilderness on 5/6/64 and died at Lynchburg on 7/21/64.

Sprague, Thomas - 4th Ohio Inf., Company I, P.O.W., d. 7/22/62 disease @ the Fairgrounds. Coffin size was 72 in. in length by 20 in. in width. Was buried Yankee Square, #5, in 3rd line. Enlisted as a private 10/12/61 for three years. Mustered into service on same date. Age at enlistment was listed as 38. Captured at Strausburg, Va. (no date given) while sick in hospital. This soldier's remains were exhumed from the Old City Cemetery in Oct. 1866 and reinterred in Poplar Grove National Cemetery at Petersburg, Virginia. Grave #4722.

State, William - 6th New Hampshire Inf., Company K, P.O.W., d. 7/21/64 of wounds @ Camp Davis. "Was buried No 4 in 2nd line 2nd lot". Enlisted as a private on 12/30/63 and mustered into service on the same date. His age at enlistment was listed as 22. State was born in Ireland and a resident of

Plymouth, New Hampshire. Listed as wounded 5/06/64 at Wilderness. Military records state that he was on the mustered out roll 7/17/65 as absent sick since 5/06/64. No further record on the soldier. Poplar Grove burial records listed the last name as "Slate". This soldier's remains were exhumed from the Old City Cemetery in Oct. 1866 and reinterred in Poplar Grove National Cemetery, Petersburg, Virginia. Grave #4965.

Stewart, John - 29th Pennsylvania Inf., Company I, P.O.W., d. 8/2/62 @ the Fairgrounds. Coffin size was 72 in. in length by 20 in. in width. Was buried Yankee Square, #5, in 2nd line. Enlisted as a private on 7/9/61, mustered into service on the same date. No date given to his capture. The 29th fought at both Front Royal (5/23/62) and at Winchester (5/25/62). Stewart was more than likely captured at one of these engagements. This soldier's remains were exhumed from the Old City Cemetery in Oct. 1866 and reinterred in Poplar Grove National Cemetery at Petersburg, Virginia. Grave #4732.

Stout, George N. - 6th Pennsylvania Cav., Company G, d. 7/21/64 @ Crumpton's Factory. Coffin size was 70 in. in length by 16 in. in width. "Was buried No 5 in 2nd line 2nd lot". Enlisted as a private on 3/21/64, mustered into service on same date. The 6th was heavy engaged from the Wilderness (5/6/64) through to Trevilian Station (6/11/64). During that time frame the 6th listed 82 killed, wounded and captured or missing. This soldier's remains were exhumed from the Old City Cemetery in Oct. 1866 and reinterred in Poplar Grove National Cemetery, Petersburg, Virginia. Grave #4945.

Stowe, Stephen L., Sgt. - 6th Michigan Inf., Company B, P.O.W., d. 7/30/64 @ Crumpton's Factory. Coffin size was 74 in. in length by 20 in. in width. "Was buried No 3 in 5th line 2nd lot". Diuguid recorded his name as "S L Stow." Poplar Grove's burial log listed the last name as "Stone". Stowe enlisted as private on 9/1/62 at Grand Rapids, Michigan. Officially mustered into service on 10/11/62. His age at enlistment was listed as 32. He was promoted to Corpl.11/01/63 and to Sgt. 3/16/64. He was captured 6/11/64 at Trevilian Station, Virginia. This soldier's remains were exhumed from the Old City Cemetery in Oct. 1866 and reinterred in Poplar Grove National Cemetery at Petersburg, Virginia. Grave #4966.

Stowell, Carlos A. - 1st Vermont Heavy Art., Company H, P.O.W., d. 8/22/64 @ Crumpton's Factory. Coffin size was 69 in. in length by 16 in. in width. Diuguid listed his name as "C A Stovill". His unit was listed as Co. H, 11th Vermont Infantry. Research of the Vermont troops revealed he was a member of the 1st Vt. Heavy Artillery. Enlisted as a private on 7/19/62, officially mustered into service on 9/01/62. Was a resident of Chelsea, Vermont? He was captured 6/23/64 at Weldon, Railroad South of Petersburg. Military records state that he died 8/08/64 at Danville, Virginia. This soldier's remains were exhumed from the Old City Cemetery in Oct. 1866 and reinterred in Poplar Grove National Cemetery, Petersburg, Virginia. Grave #4968.

Stratton, Moses C. - 6th Vermont Inf., Company B, P.O.W., d. 9/03/64 of wounds @ Crumpton's Factory. "Was buried No 2 in 2nd line of 3rd lot". Diuguid recorded the name as "M C Strattin 6th VT YP (Yankee Prisoner)." The Poplar Grove records recorded the name as "M C Stratam." Stratton enlisted as a private and was mustered into service on 11/30/63. He was a resident of Bradford, Vermont. Wounded and taken prisoner 5/06/64 at the Wilderness. His remains were exhumed from Old City Cemetery in Oct. 1866 and reinterred in Poplar Grove National Cemetery, Petersburg, Virginia. Grave #4969.

Strepler, Jacob - 27th Pennsylvania Inf., Company D, P.O.W., d. 6/30/62 @ the Fairgrounds. Was buried Yankee Square, #1, in 1st line. Diuguid recorded his last name as "Shippler". Poplar Grove has the name recorded as "Jacob Shippler." A search of the roster for the 27th did not list anyone with the name "Shippler". Jacob Strepler, very similar sounding did enlisted on 6/1/61 as a private. He was mustered into service on the same date. His records do not specify were he was captured. His records state that he died in Richmond, Va. on 7/14/62. The first major actions the 27th was engaged would have been at Cross Keys, Va. on 6/08/62. The losses listed for the 27th was less than a 100. This soldier's remains were exhumed from the Old City Cemetery in Oct. 1866 and reinterred in Poplar Grove National Cemetery, Petersburg, Virginia. Grave #4596.

Strikle, J. M. - New York "Dragoons", Company F, P.O.W., d. 7/05/64 @ Massie's Factory. "Was buried No 5 in 3rd line far corner". Diuguid recorded the name as listed above. Poplar Grove burial records indicate the soldier was a member of the 148th Pennsylvania Inf., Company A. However, a search of the 148th did not locate this individual by the above spelling. This soldier's remains were exhumed from the Old City Cemetery in Oct. 1866 and reinterred in Poplar Grove National Cemetery, Petersburg, Virginia. Grave #4961.

Sutton, Peter J. - 15th New Jersey Inf., Company F, P.O.W., d. 10/18/64 @ Massie's Factory (Prison). "Was buried No 2 in 3rd line of 3rd lot". Enlisted as a private on 8/11/62 for 3 years. Officially mustered into service on 8/25/62. Occupation was listed as a Laborer. Listed as "Missing In Action" at Winchester, Virginia on 8/17/64. His age at death is listed as 30. He was a resident of Washington, New Jersey, Morris County. The widow of the deceased was Julia Ann. A daughter Lydia Ann, born circa 1860, survived Sutton. He was the son of John and Ann Sutton. This soldier's remains were exhumed from the Old City Cemetery in Oct. 1866 and reinterred in Poplar Grove National Cemetery, Petersburg, Virginia. Grave #4661.

Swisher, John H. - 66th Ohio Inf., Company B, P.O.W., d. 7/25/62 @ the Fairgrounds. Coffin size was 72 in. in length by 20 in. in width. Was buried Yankee Square, #10, in 2nd line. Enlisted as a private on 10/08/61 for three years. Mustered into service on 12/26/61. Age at date of enlistment was listed as 42. The place and date of captured not stated. However the 66th participated in the Battle of Port Republic on 6/09/62. The widow of the deceased was Anna W. Demsey Swisher. Anna and John were married 5/29/50. Swisher was a resident of Champaign County, Ohio. This soldier's remains were exhumed from the Old City Cemetery in Oct. 1866 and reinterred in Poplar Grove National Cemetery, Petersburg, Virginia. Grave #4740.

Talbot, *** - Union P.O.W., d. 5/17/64 @ Knight's Factory. Diuguid's entry was, "Yankee Negro named Talbot was buried". Diuguid supplied no other information. This man was buried in Negro Row in the City Cemetery. A search of available records has not located the above individual. Several Talbots served in the 39th & 43 U.S. Colored Troops regiments but none fit the date of death. This soldier's remains were exhumed from the Old City Cemetery in Oct. 1866. All Union soldiers that were removed from Lynchburg were scheduled to be reinterred at Poplar Grove National Cemetery, Petersburg, Virginia.

Taylor, Joseph - 1st Vermont Cav. Company G, P.O.W., d. 7/01/62 @ the Fairgrounds. Coffin size was 68 in. in length by 18 in. in width. Was buried Yankee Square, #2, in 2nd line. He enlisted as private on 10/7/61. He was mustered into service on 11/19/61. He was a resident of Bennington, Vermont. He was captured on 5/24/62 at Middletown, Virginia. His remains were exhumed in Oct. 1866 and reinterred in Poplar Grove National Cemetery, Petersburg, Virginia. Grave #4609.

Thompson, David - 110th Pennsylvania Inf., Company C, P.O.W., d. 7/23/64 @ Crumpton's Factory. Coffin size was 78 in. in length by 17 in. in width. "Was buried No 7 in 2nd line 2nd lot". Enlisted as a private on 10/24/61. Mustered into service on same date. As a part of the 2nd Corps the 110th was active from May 64 (Wilderness) to the end of June, 64 (Petersburg). Thompson could have been capture at any of several engagements in that time frame. This soldier's remains were exhumed from the Old City Cemetery in Oct. 1866 and reinterred in Poplar Grove National Cemetery at Petersburg, Virginia. Grave #4637.

Thornton, David M. - 8th Michigan Inf., Company C, P.O.W., d. 7/5/64 of wounds @ Crumpton's Factory. "Was buried No 3 in 1st line 2nd lot". Enlisted as a private on 1/01/62 in Ingham County, Michigan. Mustered into service on 1/10/62. Thornton was wounded and captured on 5/06/64 at the Battle of the Wilderness. This soldier's remains were exhumed from the Old City Cemetery in Oct. 1866 and reinterred in Poplar Grove National Cemetery, Petersburg, Virginia. Grave #4963.

Thorp, M. Nathan - 35th Pennsylvania Inf. (also known as 6th Penn. Reserves), Company C, P.O.W., d. 8/11/64 @ Crumpton's Factory. "Was buried No 5 in 5th line of 2nd lot". Enlisted as a Corpl. on 5/13/61. He was mustered into service on the same date. No date specified when he was capture. As a part of the 5th Corps the 35th was engaged Wilderness and Spotsylvania Court House. Thorp was mostly likely captured during that time frame. The 35th was mustered out of service on 6/11/64 as a three-year unit. Also, per his records Thorp was transferred to the 191st Penn. On 5/31/64. Several Thorps listed none of which were Nathan Thorp. This soldier's remains were exhumed from the Old City Cemetery in Oct. 1866 and reinterred in Poplar Grove National Cemetery, Petersburg, Virginia. Grave #4949.

Tourtellotte, Chester A., Color Sgt. - 18th Connecticut Inf., Company H, P.O.W., d. 8/15/64 of wounds @ College

Hospital. "Was buried No 1 in 1st line of 3rd lot". Diuguid's burial log listed the last name as "Fourtelotte". Poplar Grove records listed his name as "Fourtalot" with the 10th Connecticut. He enlisted as a Sgt. on 7/21/62 at Tolland, Connecticut. He was mustered into service on 8/18/62 At Camp Aiken, Norwich, Connecticut. One record has him listed as the Color Barer for the 18th. At the Battle of Piedmont, Va. on 6/5/64 the 18th all but one of the Color Guard was wounded. Among the wounded was Sgt. Tourtellotte, captured and transported to Lynchburg. The town of Tolland, Conn. supplied 120 men to the war effort out a population of 1,310. The good Sgt. was the only one to die as a POW. This soldier's remains were exhumed from the Old City Cemetery in Oct. 1866 and reinterred in Polar Grove National Cemetery, Petersburg, Virginia. Grave #4639.

Tripp, Ezra G. - 37th Massachusetts Inf., Company A, P.O.W., d. 7/01/64 @ Camp Davis. Coffin size was 71 in. in length by 15 in. in width. "Was buried No 10 in 2nd line in far corner (lot #1)". Enlisted as a private 7/11/62 at Chicopee, Mass. at age 32. Officially mustered into service 9/02/62. His occupation was listed as a farmer. Tripp was wounded and take prisoner on 5/06/64 during the Wilderness battle. This soldier's remains were exhumed from the Old City Cemetery in Oct. 1866 and reinterred in a National Cemetery. All Union Soldiers removed from Lynchburg were scheduled to be reinterred at Poplar Grove National Cemetery, Petersburg, Virginia.

Unknown - 3 unknown Union soldier's, d. 8/8/62, location not specified. Diuguid does not specify but they were probably buried Yankee Square. These soldier's remains were exhumed from the Old City Cemetery in Oct. 1866. All Union Soldiers removed from Lynchburg were scheduled to be reinterred at Poplar Grove National Cemetery, Petersburg, Virginia.

Unknown - Union P.O.W., "Yankee Prisoner" d. 6/20/64 @ Crumpton's Factory. Possibly this individual was wounded and captured during the Battle for Lynchburg. "Was buried No 10 in 2nd line 1st lot", "in far corner". This soldier's remains were exhumed from the Old City Cemetery in Oct. 1866. All Union Soldiers removed from Lynchburg were scheduled to be reinterred at Poplar Grove National Cemetery, Petersburg, Virginia.

Unknown - Union P.O.W., "Yankee Prisoner", d. 6/23/64 @ College Hospital. Possibly this individual was wounded and captured during the Battle for Lynchburg. "Was buried in far corner bottom". This soldier's remains were exhumed from the Old City Cemetery in Oct. 1866. All Union soldiers that were removed from Lynchburg were scheduled to be reinterred at Poplar Grove National Cemetery, Petersburg, Virginia.

VanOrder, Kimble - 15th New York Inf., Company G, P.O.W., d 6/24/64 @ College Hospital. "Was buried in far corner". Enlisted as a private on 8/27/63. Mustered into service on 10/03/63. His age at enlistment was listed as 23. Diuguid recorded his last name as "Vanerder". His military record state that he was wounded and captured at Lynchburg, Virginia on 6/15/64. The Battle at Lynchburg was fought on 6/17-18/64. It is possible that this individual was capture prior to the battle. This soldier's remains were exhumed from the Old City Cemetery in Oct. 1866. All Union Soldiers removed from Lynchburg were scheduled to be reinterred at Poplar Grove National Cemetery, Petersburg, Virginia.

Vineyard, Harvey, Corpl. - 66th Ohio Inf., Company B, P.O.W., d. 7/25/62 @ the Fairgrounds. Coffin size was 78 in. in length by 20 in. in width. Was buried Yankee Square, #10, in 3rd line. Cause of death not specified. Enlisted as a private on 9/24/61, mustered into service on same date. He was a resident of Champaign County, Ohio. Date and place of captured not stated. The 66th lost 109 men out 400 engaged at Port Republic on 6/09/62. This soldier's remains were exhumed from the Old City Cemetery in Oct. 1866 and reinterred in Poplar Grove National Cemetery, Petersburg, Virginia. Grave #4664.

Walshe, J. - 1st Maine Inf., Company K, P.O.W., d. 11/9/64 @ Crumpton's Factory. "Was buried No 9 in 2nd line 3rd lot". To date have not been able to locate this individual. This soldier's remains were exhumed from the Old City Cemetery in Oct. 1866 and reinterred in Poplar Grove National Cemetery at Petersburg, Virginia. Grave #4971.

Walton, J. W. - 37th Indiana Inf., P.O.W., d. 6/25/62 @ the Fairgrounds. Was buried in lot #173, grave #10, row #4. With a search of the 27th Indiana I have not been able to locate the above named J. W. Walton. As a part of the Army of Ohio the 37th served in Tenn. & Kentucky from early 62 through the winter on 62. It was engaged at Murfreesboro in December of 62. This soldier's remains were exhumed from the Old City Cemetery in Oct. 1866 and reinterred in Poplar Grove National Cemetery, Petersburg, Virginia. Grave #4727.

Warwick, Alfred - 3rd New Jersey Cav., Company A, d. 1/22/65 @ Crumpton's Factory. "Was buried No 2 in 5th line of 3rd lot". Enlisted as a private on 1/04/64 as was mustered into service on 1/26/64. His age at death was listed as 21. Born in Dennisville, New Jersey, unmarried and a resident of Cape May County. The 3rd served in the Shenandoah Valley from 8/64 to 3/65. Very possible Warwick was captured at one of the several engagements in that time frame. This soldiers remains were exhumed from the Old City Cemetery in Oct. 1866. All Union soldiers removed from Lynchburg were scheduled to be reinterred at Poplar Grove National Cemetery, Petersburg, Virginia. His military records state that he was reinterred at Poplar Grove. However, Poplar Grove does not list him.

Weeks, Joseph W. - 10th Maine Inf., Company B, P.O.W., d. 8/2/62 of unspecified cause @ the Fairgrounds. Was buried Yankee Square, #12, in 6th line. Enlisted as a private on 9/19/61 at age 45 for 2 years. Officially mustered into service on 10/04/61. His military records state, "for a term of 2 yrs from May 3, '61". Listed as single, light complexion, blue eyes, brown hair, 5' 6 1/2" in height, occupation tanner. Born in and was a resident of Portland, Maine. His remains were exhumed in Oct. 1866 and reinterred in Poplar Grove National Cemetery, Petersburg, Virginia. Grave #4600.

Weik, John - 54th New York Inf. (Barney Black Rifles), Company K, P.O.W., d. 7/5/62 @ the Fairgrounds. Coffin size was 78 in. in length by 20 in. in width. Was buried Yankee Square, #3, in 2nd line. Enlisted as a private on 9/17/61 at Hudson City, New Jersey. Mustered into service on the same date. His age at enlistment was listed as 28. His records do not specify his date or place of capture. The 54th was in Blenker's Division of Fremont's Command and saw service at the Battle of Cross Keys on 6/08/62. Causality figures for this unit were less than 50. This soldier's remains were exhumed from the Old City Cemetery in Oct. 1866 and reinterred in Poplar Grove National Cemetery, Petersburg, Virginia. Grave #4605.

Wheeler, George E. - 1st Maryland Inf., Company A, P.O.W., d. 8/2/62 @ the Fairgrounds of disease. Was originally buried Yankee Square, #11, in 1st line. To date I have been unable to locate this individual. His body was exhumed on 9/14/65, prepared and shipped to Baltimore, Maryland. Henry A. Wheeler, the father of the deceased made arrangements for the removal and shipment of his sons remains to Baltimore. Diuguid's fee was $30.00.

Wickham, John S., Q. M. Sgt. - 135th Ohio (National Guard) Inf., Company B, P.O.W., d. 7/15/64 @ Crumpton's Factory. Originally buried lot #2, grave #2, row #2. Captured at North Mountain, W. Va. 7/03/64. His age at death was listed as 23 years and 4 months. His remains were exhumed January 5, 1866, "Removed & sent to Clay Rick, Licking Cty Ohio, Newark Ohio". The father of the Deceased "Mr. Wickham" made and paid for all arrangements. Diuguid also entered, ""for removal and packing of sons remains $40.00...by cash in full." He was interred in Newark Cedar Hill Cemetery, Newark, Ohio, Licking County. He was the son of Gideon & Sarah Wickham. Note of interest, the 135th Ohio Vol. Regiments was 100 day regiment formed and mustered into service May 11, 1864. It was used to guard the Baltimore & Ohio Railroad. The Companies stationed at North Mountain were surrounded and after a three-hour fight were compelled to surrender. The regiment was mustered out of service on Sept 1, 1864 at Champ Chase, Ohio. Sergeant Wickham only served 64 days in the Federal army.

Wilcox, William S. - 67th Ohio Inf., Company A, P.O.W., d. 8/4/62 @ the Fairgrounds. Cause of death specified. Was buried Yankee Square, #8, in 6th line. Enlisted as a private on 11/05/61 for three years. Mustered into service on the same date. Age at enlistment was listed as 27. His records do not specify where he was captured. The 67th was in the Shenandoah Valley briefly in 1862. They served between March and May seeing only limited action, primarily at Winchester on 03/23/62. In that engagement the 67th lost approximately 50 men. This soldier's remains were exhumed from the Old City Cemetery in Oct. 1866. All Union soldiers removed from Lynchburg were scheduled to be reinterred at Polar Grove National Cemetery, Petersburg, Virginia.

Willard, James J. - 57th Massachusetts Inf., Company G, P.O.W., d. 7/26/64 of wounds @ Camp Davis. Coffin size was 75 in. in length by 18 in. in width. "Was buried No 1 in 4th line of 2nd lot". Enlisted as a private on 2/27/64 at Worcester, Massachusetts. Mustered into service on 3/10/64.

His age at enlistment was listed as 21. He was a resident of Worcester. He was wounded a captured 5/06/64 during the Battle of the Wilderness. His physical description was 5' 7", light complexion, dark hair and gray eyes. This soldier's remains were exhumed from the Old City Cemetery in Oct. 1866 and reinterred in Poplar Grove National Cemetery, Petersburg, Virginia. Grave #4636.

Wray, Thomas C., Corpl. - 72nd Pennsylvania Inf., Company E, P.O.W., d. 7/26/64 @ Camp Davis. "Was buried No 1 in 5th line 2nd lot". Diuguid recorded the name as "T C Wray." Poplar Grove records listed his name as "T. C. W. Ray". Enlisted as Corpl. on 8/10/61, mustered into service on the same date. Captured on 5/06/64 during the Battle of the Wilderness. This soldier's remains were exhumed from the Old City Cemetery in Oct. 1866 and reinterred at Poplar Grove National Cemetery, Petersburg, Virginia. Grave #4626.

York, Calvin B. - 33rd Indiana Inf., Company A, P.O.W., d. 4/11/63 @ Miller's Factory. Coffin size was 74 in. in length by 18 in. in width. Was buried in lot #199, grave #4, row #4. Enlisted as a private 8/30/61 at Indianapolis and muster into service on 9/16/61. His age at enlistment was listed as 23. York was a native of Randolph County, North Carolina. Physical description, gray eyes, light hair, 5 ft. 9 in. in height, and occupation listed as farmer. The first engagement for the 33rd was on 3/4/63 at Thompson's Station, Tenn. (Spring Hill, Tenn.). The following day the 33rd along with the remainder of the brigade were compelled to surrender. The 33rd lost 100 in killed and wounded and 400 captured. This soldier's remains were exhumed from the Old City Cemetery in Oct. 1866 and reinterred in Poplar Grove National Cemetery, Petersburg, Virginia. Grave #4585.

Younger, John - 27th Indiana Inf., Company D, P.O.W., d. 8/4/62 @ the Fairgrounds. Was buried Yankee Square, #8, in 6th line. Enlisted as a private at Indianapolis, no date given. The 27th was mustered into service on 9/12/61 at Indianapolis. His age at enlistment was listed as 22. The 27th participated in the Shenandoah Valley campaigns of 1862. It saw action at Winchester on 3/23/62, Front Royal on 5/23/62 and Winchester on 5/25/62. Younger was most likely captured at one of the latter battles. This soldier's remains were exhumed from the Old City Cemetery in Oct. 1866 and reinterred in Poplar Grove National Cemetery, Petersburg, Virginia. Grave #4603.

Ziegler, Franz - 45th New York Inf., Company B, P.O.W., d. 7/21/62 @ the Fairgrounds. Coffin size was 72 in. in length by 20 in. in width. Was buried Yankee Square, #9, in 4th line. Diuguid's burial log recorded the name as "Frank Zigler". Poplar Grove recorded the last name "Frank Zergler." Enlisted as a private on 9/16/61 at New York City, NY. Was mustered into service on 9/17/61. His record does not specify his place of capture. However, the 45th was engaged at Cross Keys, Virginia on 6/08/62. This soldier's remains were exhumed from the Old City Cemetery in Oct. 1866 and reinterred in Poplar Grove National Cemetery, Petersburg, Virginia. Grave #4747.

Zimmerman, Charles - 1st New York Light Art., Battery I, P.O.W., d. 7/28/62 @ the Fairgrounds. Was buried Yankee Square, #10, in 5th line. Coffin size was 72 in. in length by 20 in. in width. Enlisted as a private 9/05/61 at Lancaster, New York. Mustered into service 9/12/61. His age at enlistment was listed as 34. Available records do not specify his place of Capture. This unit was a part of the famed 6th Corps, Army of the Potomac during 1862. This soldier's remains were exhumed from the Old City Cemetery in Oct. 1866 and reinterred in a National Cemetery. All Union soldiers removed from Lynchburg were scheduled to be reinterred at Polar Grove National Cemetery, Petersburg, Virginia.

Zulker, Benjamin C. - 4th New Jersey Inf., Company D, P.O.W., d. 12/23/64 @ Crumpton's Factory. "Was buried No 1 in 5th line 3rd lot". Enlisted as a private on mustered into service on 8/13/61. Officially mustered into service on 8/17/61. Listed as missing in action at Opequan (Winchester), Virginia on 9/19/64. Cause of death not specified. His was married, and a resident of Kensington, Pennsylvania (Kensington is Northeast of Philadelphia and my now be part of the city). This soldier's remains were exhumed from the Old City Cemetery in Oct. 1866. All Union soldiers removed from Lynchburg were scheduled to be reinterred at Poplar Grove National Cemetery, Petersburg, Virginia. All Union soldiers removed from Lynchburg were scheduled to be reinterred at Polar Grove National Cemetery, Petersburg, Virginia. His military records list him as buried at Poplar Grove. However, Poplar Grove does not have a listing for him.

The following is a listing of soldiers that by their military records died in Lynchburg but Diuguid has no record of the burial. Thirteen of these men were reportedly exhumed from Lynchburg after the war and reinterred in Poplar Grove. The remaining individuals were reported as **Killed In Action** during the Battle for Lynchburg in June of 1864. The correct spelling with the names of those reinterred at Poplar Grove for this group has been a problem. Several of the others I have not been able, with available records, find any military service.

Andrews, Charles E. B. - 1st New York Veteran Cav., Company H, **Killed in Action** 6/20/64. His records list his place of death as Lynchburg. However, on the 20 of June, 1864 Hutter had retreated from Lynchburg and fought a small action at Burfordville, Va. (between Bedford & Salem, Va.). It's uncertain if he was actually killed at Lynchburg or during Hutter's retreat. Enlisted as a private on 9/17/63 at Masonville, New York. Mustered into service on 10/10/63. His age at enlistment was listed as 17. Diuguid and Poplar Grove have no record. However, Diuguid made an entry in his logbook on 1/31/65, "Mrs. Andrews, for removal & packing son E. R. Andrews...$200.00".

Bell, John, Corpl. - 91st Ohio Vol. Inf., Company D, **Killed in Action** 6/17/64, Battle for Lynchburg. Enlisted as a private on 8/02/62. Mustered into service on 9/07/62. His age at enlistment was listed as 30. Promoted to Corpl. 3/01/64. No Diuguid or Poplar Grove Record.

Blacbern, P. - 16th New York Cav., Company C, no date of death. Exhumed from Lynchburg and reinterred at Poplar Grove in grave #4629. No Diuguid Record.

Blair, George - 116th Ohio Inf., Company E, **Killed in Action** 6/18/64, Battle for Lynchburg. Enlisted as a private on 8/17/62. Mustered into service on 9/18/62. His age at enlistment was listed as 26. No Diuguid or Poplar Grove record.

Boyd, James A. - 116th Ohio Inf., Company F, **Killed in Action** 6/18/64, Battle for Lynchburg. Enlisted as a private on 8/14/62. Mustered into service on 9/18/62. Age at enlistment listed as 25. No Diuguid or Poplar Grove record.

Breen, Dennis - 34th Massachusetts Inf., Company H, **Killed in Action** 6/18/64, Battle for Lynchburg. Enlisted as a

Corpl. on 7/16/62. Mustered into service on 7/31/62. His age at enlistment was listed as 21. His occupation was listed as "Operative". He was a resident of Weber, Massachusetts. No Diuguid or Poplar Grove record.

Coulter, George M. - 116th Ohio Inf., Company E, **Killed in Action** 6/18/64, Battle for Lynchburg. Enlisted on 8/22/62 as a private. Mustered into service on 9/18/62. Age at enlistment was listed as 23. No Diuguid or Poplar Grove Record.

Counsel, James D. - 12th Ohio Vol. Inf., Company D, **Killed in Action** 6/17/64, Battle for Lynchburg. Enlisted as a private on 6/20/61, mustered into service on same date. Age at enlistment was listed as 18. No Diuguid or Poplar Grove Record.

Decker, Alonzo - 23rd Ohio Inf., Company B, **Killed in Action** 6/18/64, Battle for Lynchburg. Enlisted as a private on 6/05/64(?) mustered into service on same date. His age at enlistment was listed as 18. No Diuguid or Poplar Grove record.

Dickey, William - 91st Ohio Vol. Inf., Company I, **Killed in Action** 6/17/64, Battle of Lynchburg. Enlisted as a private on 8/13/62. Mustered into service on 9/07/62. His age at enlistment was listed as 19. Records indicated that he was exhumed from Lynchburg and reinterred at Poplar Grove National Cemetery, Petersburg, Virginia. Neither Diuguid nor Poplar Grove shows any record of Pvt. Dickey.

Downing, Benjamin, 1st Sgt. - 21st New York Cav., Company A, **Killed in Action** 6/16/64. Place of death is listed as Tinker's Gap, Virginia. This is a questionable record. The date of 6/16/64 placed Hunter's Army (which the 21st was part of) in Liberty (Bedford), Virginia advancing towards Lynchburg. Tinker's Gap is approx. 45 miles west of Lynchburg. Hunter's army retreated in this direction arriving at Tinker's gap on or about 21st of June. It's all most impossible to determine if Downing was killed at Lynchburg or during the retreat. Enlisted as private on 7/20/63 at Troy, New York. Mustered into service on 8/28/63. His age at enlistment was listed as 20. Promoted to 1st Sgt. 9/20/63. Total causalities for the 21st during the Lynchburg Campaign were low. A total of 2 killed, 5 wounded, 11 POW's, and 1 MIA between 6/5/64 Battle of

Piedmont, Va. and Salem, Va. on 6/22/64. No Diuguid or Poplar Grove record.

Dunn, Samuel, Sgt. - 123rd Ohio Inf., Company F, **Killed in Action** 6/18/64, Battle for Lynchburg. Enlisted as Sgt. on 8/21/62. Mustered into service on 9/24/62. His age at enlistment was listed as 28. He was previously captured at Winchester, Va. on 6/15/63. Paroled 7/19/63. No Diuguid or Poplar Grove record.

Emmons, William J. - 91st Ohio Vol. Inf., Company K, listed as **Killed in Action** 6/17/64 at Battle of Lynchburg. Enlisted as a private on 8/12/62 for three years. Age at enlistment was listed as 24. His military records state that he was mustered out of Company K on 6/24/65. In addition, he is listed as buried in Byers Cemetery, Washington Township, Jackson County, Ohio with a death date of July 1, 1914. His birth date is listed as 8/12/37. No Diuguid or Poplar Grove record.

Esselen, Michael - 5th New York Heavy Art., d. 7/02/64 of wounds, Battle of Lynchburg. Enlisted as a private on 12/10/63 at Lansing, New York. Mustered into service on 3/10/64. His age at enlistment was listed as 34. Wounded on the afternoon of 6/17/64. His available records only state that he died on 7/02/64. His records do not specify if he was taken prisoner after Hunter's withdrawal from Lynchburg or if he died still with Hunter's Army. No Diuguid or Poplar Grove record.

Fisher, William – 116th Ohio Inf., Company F, **Killed in Action** 6/18/64, Battle for Lynchburg. Enlisted as a private on 8/21/62. Mustered into service on 10/27/62. His age at enlistment was listed as 43. No Diuguid or Poplar Grove Record.

Fisk, Edmund D. - 37th Massachusetts Inf., Company A, no date of death. Buried in Poplar Grove National Cemetery, Petersburg, Virginia, grave #4779. Fisk enlisted as a private on 9/02/62 for three years. Age at enlistment listed as 24, his occupation was listed as a farmer. Residence or place of enlistment was Chicopee, Massachusetts. Very strange, his military records state that he was mustered out of service on 6/21/65. No Diuguid record.

Gordon, J. W., Lt. - 11th West Virginia Inf. Company ?, no date of death. Listed as **KIA**, possibly **Killed in Action** at Lynchburg 6/17-18/64. Grave #4654. No Diuguid record.

Goswell, William - 5th New York Heavy Art., Company D, **Killed in Action** 6/18/64, Battle for Lynchburg. Enlisted as a private on 2/05/62 at Brooklyn, New York. Mustered into service on 2/06/62. His age at enlistment was listed as 30. He reenlisted on 2/06/64. No Diuguid or Poplar Grove record.

Graham, Louis (Lewis) - 91st Ohio Vol. Inf., Company C, **Killed in Action** 6/17/64 at Battle of Lynchburg. Enlisted as a private on 8/04/62 for three years. Age at enlistment was listed as 31. No Diuguid or Poplar Grove record.

Haexley, J. J. - 12th Pennsylvania Inf., Company E, no date of death. Exhumed from Lynchburg and reinterred at Poplar Grove in grave #4648. No Diuguid record.

Hawkins, William - 15th New York Cav., Company B, **Killed in Action** 6/17/64, Battle for Lynchburg. Enlisted as a Sgt. on 6/08/63 at Batavia, New York. Mustered into service on 8/13/62. Age at enlistment was listed as 30. Reduce in rank back to a private on 2/20/64. No Diuguid or Poplar Grove record.

Jolly, James D. - 5th New York Heavy Art., d. 5/15/65 in Lynchburg. Enlisted as a private on 12/09/63 at Fremont, New York. Mustered into service on 1/05/64. His age at enlistment was listed as 18. He was captured 6/18/64 at Lynchburg, Virginia. His records state that he died as a POW in Lynchburg. Lynchburg was occupied by Union troops on April 12th 1865. Jolly died a month later after the Union occupation. He would not have been a POW. No Diuguid or Poplar Grove record.

Keihl, Cyrus H. - 123rd Ohio Inf., Company F, **Killed in Action** 6/18/64, Battle for Lynchburg. Enlisted as a private on 8/18/62. Mustered into service on 9/24/62. His age at enlistment was listed as 20. Was previously captured. He was listed as a POW at Winchester on 6/15/63. Paroled 7/19/63. No Diuguid or Poplar Grove record.

King, Harry B. - 34th Massachusetts Inf., Company E, **Killed in Action**, 6/18/64 Battle for Lynchburg. Enlisted as Sgt. on 7/04/62. Mustered into service on 7/13/62. Age at enlistment listed as 22. He was a resident of Barre,

Massachusetts. Promoted to 1st Sgt. date no specified. No Diuguid or Poplar Grove record.

Martin, Francis - 34th Massachusetts Inf., Company K, **Killed in Action** 6/18/64, Battle for Lynchburg. Martin enlisted as a private on 1/12/64. He was mustered into service on same date. His age at enlistment was listed as 18. Occupation listed as a mechanic. He was a resident of New York City, NY. No Diuguid or Poplar Grove record.

Matson, James - 12th Ohio Vol. Inf., Company C, **Killed in Action** 6/17/64, Battle for Lynchburg. Enlisted as a private on 6/03/61, mustered into service on same date. His age at enlistment was listed as 23. No Diuguid or Poplar Grove Record.

Miller, Samuel - No unit or date of death. Exhumed from Lynchburg and reinterred at Poplar Grove in grave #4753. No Diuguid record.

Morse, William W. - 12th Ohio Inf., Company D, **Killed in Action** 6/17/64 at Battle for Lynchburg. Exhumed from Lynchburg and reinterred at Poplar Grove in grave #4759. He was exhumed from Lynchburg. Possibly was buried on the battlefield where he fell. Poplar Grove Cemetery records only listed him as W. W. Morse, no unit stated and no place of death. Enlisted as a private on 6/25/62 for three years. Mustered into service on same date. His age at enlistment was listed as 24. Diuguid has no record of this soldier.

McCowen, Israel T., Sgt. - 12th Ohio Vol. Inf., Company F, **Killed in Action** 6/17/64, Battle for Lynchburg. Enlisted as a private on 6/19/61, mustered into service on same date. His age at enlistment was listed as 22. Promoted to Sgt. 3/31/63. No Diuguid or Poplar Grove record.

McDonald, Savage - 123rd Ohio Inf., Company F, **Killed in Action** 6/18/64, Battle for Lynchburg. Enlisted as a private on 12/04/63, mustered into service on same date. His age at enlistment was listed as 18. No Diuguid or Poplar Grove record.

McKee, Samuel L. - 91st Ohio Vol. Inf., Company I, **Killed in Action** 6/17/64 at Battle of Lynchburg. Enlisted as a private on 8/11/62 for three years. Age at enlistment was listed as 18. State of Ohio records indicate that he was buried in the National Cemetery, Poplar Grove, Petersburg, Virginia. However, Poplar Grove Records does not include his name as being exhumed in Lynchburg. No Diuguid record.

Orton, Martin - 15th New York Cav., Company B, listed as **Killed in Action** at Lynchburg, Va. on 6/25/64. This must be incorrect, by 6/25 the Lynchburg campaign is over and Hunter has retreated into West Virginia. If he was killed at Lynchburg it would have been either the 17th or 18th of June, 1864. Enlisted on 7/24/63 as a trumpeter at Syracuse, New York. Mustered into service on 8/08/63. His age at enlistment was listed as 18. No Diuguid or Poplar Grove Record.

Randall, William - 91st Ohio Vol. Inf., Company F, **Killed in Action** 6/17/64 at Battle of Lynchburg. Enlisted as a private on 8/02/62 for three years. Age at enlistment was listed as 18. No Diuguid or Poplar Grove record.

Rogers, Lawson H. - 122nd Ohio Inf., Company H, d. 12/18/64 in Lynchburg. Exhumed from Lynchburg and interred in Poplar Grove Cemetery in Grave #4619. Poplar Grove lists his unit as the 128th Ohio. Enlisted as a private on 9/15/62 for three years. Mustered into service on 9/30/62. His age enlistment was listed as 21. His military records state that his place of death was Charlottesville, Virginia (same date as recorded above). No Diuguid record.

Schwarley, William S. - 163rd Pennsylvania Inf., Company H, (Poplar Grove listed the unit as the 18th Penn.) no date of death. Exhumed from Lynchburg and reinterred in Poplar Grove in grave #4777. No Diuguid record.

Shields, William C., Corpl. - 12th Ohio Vol. Inf., Company A, **Killed in Action** 6/17/64, Battle for Lynchburg. Enlisted as a private on 4/20/61. Officially mustered into service on 5/30/61. His age at enlistment was listed as 21. Promoted to Corpl. the date was not specified. No Diuguid or Poplar Grove Record.

Simpson, Robert J. - 1st Va. (West Va.) Light Inf., Company I **Killed in Action** 6/18/64 at Battle of Lynchburg. Enlisted as a private on 11/17/61, age at enlistment was 38. No Diuguid or Poplar Grove record.

Stiles, Colvin, Sgt. - 91st Ohio Vol. Inf., Company D, **Killed in Action** 6/17/64, Battle for Lynchburg. Enlisted as a private on 8/05/62 for three years. Mustered into service on 9/07/62. Age at enlistment was listed as 32. Promoted to Corpl. 8/22/62, promoted to Sgt. 2/03/63. Ohio State records indicate that he was buried in the National Cemetery,

Poplar Grove, Petersburg, Virginia. However, Poplar Grove Records do not include his name as being exhumed in Lynchburg. No Diuguid record.

Strausbaugh, Isaac - 91st Ohio Vol. Inf., Company A, **Killed in Action** 6/17/64, Battle for Lynchburg. Enlisted as a private on 8/11/62. Mustered into service on 9/07/62. His age at enlistment was listed as 18. Ohio state records indicate that he was buried in the National Cemetery, Poplar Grove, Petersburg, Virginia. However, Poplar Grove Records do not include his name as being exhumed in Lynchburg. No Diuguid record.

Stroup, George B. 1st Lieut. - 91st Ohio Vol. Inf., Company D, **Killed in Action** 6/17/64 at Battle of Lynchburg. Enlisted as a 2nd Lieut. on 8/11/62 for three years. Officially mustered into service on 9/07/62. Age at enlistment was listed as 31. Promoted to 1st Lieut. on 2/17/64. Stroup was a resident of Adams County, Scott Township, 1860 census. Ohio state records indicate that he was buried in the National Cemetery, Poplar Grove, Petersburg, Virginia. However, Poplar Grove Records do not include his name as being exhumed in Lynchburg. No Diuguid record. There are 58 Union soldiers that were buried at Poplar Grove that were listed as "Unknown." Two of these "Unknown" were officers. One is in grave #4931 and the other is in Grave #4658. One of these graves is where Lieut. Stroup was interred.

Sturnmon, (Sherman?) - 146th New York Inf., Company G, no date of death. Exhumed from Lynchburg and reinterred in Poplar Grove in grave #4628. No Diuguid record.

Swanger, James J. - 91st Ohio Vol. Inf., Company D, **Killed in Action** 6/17/64, Battle for Lynchburg. Enlisted as a private on 8/11/62. Mustered into service on 9/07/62. His age at enlisted was listed as 23. Ohio state records indicate that he was buried in the National Cemetery, Poplar Grove, Petersburg, Virginia. However, Poplar Grove Records do not include his name as being exhumed in Lynchburg. No Diuguid record.

Thompson, John, Corpl. - 15th New York Cav., Company H, **Killed in Action** 6/17/64, Battle for Lynchburg. Enlisted as private on 1/04/64 at Otisco, New York. Mustered into service on same date. Promoted to Corpl. date not specified. No Diuguid or Poplar Grove record.

Thornburg, W. H., Corpl. - 36th Ohio Inf., Company A, **Killed in Action** 6/18/64, Battle for Lynchburg. Enlisted as a Corpl. on 7/29/61. Mustered into service 8/27/61. His age at enlistment was listed as 29. No Diuguid or Poplar Grove record.

Townsend, Calvin W. - 12th Ohio Inf., Company B, **Killed in Action** 6/17/64, Battle for Lynchburg. Enlisted as a private on 2/09/64, mustered into service on same date. His age at enlistment was listed as 19. No Diuguid or Poplar Grove Record.

Van Horn, Gilbert - 116th Ohio Inf., Company I, **Killed in Action** 6/18/64, Battle for Lynchburg. Enlisted as a private on 1/01/64. Mustered into service on same date. Age at enlistment was listed as 38. No Diuguid or Poplar Grove record.

Vandergraff, Enoch - 91st Ohio Inf., Company D, died as a POW, date not specified. Place of death was specified as Andersonville, Georgia. Enlisted as a private on 8/06/62. Mustered into service on 9/07/62. His age at enlistment was listed as 27. He was promoted to Corpl. on 9/1/62 and to Sgt. on 10/01/63. Diuguid in his logbook on 3/01/66 made to following entry, "H. W. Vandergrift (sic) for removal of sons remains...$40.00."

Welch, William S. - 67th Ohio Inf., Company D, no date of death. Welch was exhumed from Lynchburg and reinterred at Poplar Grove in grave #4613. A review of the Ohio Civil War Roster revealed no listing for such a person in the 67th Ohio Infantry. A Search for a similar spelling (i.e. Walsh, Welsh) also yielded no match. No Diuguid record.

Wheeler, Y. - No unit or date of death. Exhumed from Lynchburg and reinterred at Poplar Grove in grave #4755. No Diuguid record.

Wilson, W. - No unit or date of death. Exhumed from Lynchburg and reinterred at Poplar Grove in grave #4753. No Diuguid record.

Woodward, Seth A. - 34th Massachusetts Inf., Company D, **Killed in Action** 6/18/64, Battle for Lynchburg. Woodward enlisted as a private on 10/30/63, mustered into service on same date. His age at enlistment was listed as 28. His occupation was a "Miller". He was a resident of Warwick, Massachusetts. No Diuguid or Poplar Grove record.

On 6/21/64 <u>The Lynchburg Virginia</u> had an article on the battle listing some of the Union soldiers that were killed at Lynchburg on the afternoon of June 17, 1864. The names listed were **Emmons** 91st Ohio, **Graham** 91st Ohio, **McKee** 91st Ohio, **Randall** 91st Ohio, **Stroup** 91st Ohio and **Simpson** 1st Va. (West Va.). The 5 men of the 91st Ohio were in shallow graves with wooden headboards. The West Virginia soldier was laid out on a blanket with his name on a white piece of paper pinned to the breast of his uniform. Diuguid makes no mention of these men in his records.

PART IV

Disease & Definitions

A listing of the primary illnesses, diseases, and wounds of the day – with a general description and definition (present and from the mid 1800's)

Part IV – Disease & Definitions

During their four arduous years of war both the Confederate and Union soldier suffered more from disease behind the lines than from **"Shot and Shell"** on the field of battle. The death toll for the **"War Between the States"** (1861 - 1865) is estimated that an estimated 620,000 to 850,000 Americans serving in both armies died. Depending on the figures provided, roughly two-thirds died from disease and illnesses and not combat. The more conservative estimates list the death toll at 620,000 of which 414,000 died of disease and illness. The Union losses for the war are listed at 110,070 battlefield deaths (including deaths from wounds) and 224,586 deaths from disease and 24,872 deaths from accidents, suicides, etc. The Union death total comes to 359,528. This would leave the Confederate death toll at approximately 260,472. An estimated 94,000 Confederate deaths resulted in battlefield and another 164,000 died of disease. It is almost impossible to accurately determine Confederate total losses with the loss and destruction of records. The Confederate deaths due to disease and illness would be equal to, if not slightly greater than, the Union losses. In this case this author estimates, as a minimum, the death toll for the Confederates would be another 85,458 under the category of death due to illness. This would bring the Confederate death toll to 345,930. The total death toll for the war, based of the above figures, would be 705,458.

Based on existing information, the Confederate soldier, during his enlistment, was treated in a hospital (including field hospitals) or required some type of medical attention on the average four times. Using the records of one North Carolina regiment, we have the following data for an eighteen-month period. Beginning April 1862 and ending September 30, 1863, this unit reported 2,180 men suffering from various illnesses. The numerical strength of a Confederate infantry regiment during this time frame probably did not exceed 600 to 800 men. So, based on the preceding information for this one unit, each soldier was treated at least twice, possibly three times during this eighteen-month period. However, a factor for deaths and medical discharges must be considered for the above numbers.

The primary ailment suffered by all Southern fighting men, enlisted and officers alike, were intestinal disorders such as diarrhea and dysentery. Confederate field reports from east of the Mississippi during the first two years of the war reported 848,555 cases of disease. Out of this figure, 226,828 were for diarrhea and dysentery, with a conservative death total of 12,000. Confederate Surgeon Paul F. Eve stated these aliments as, "**the disease**" of the Confederate forces. In addition, Eve stated, "**Chronic diarrhoea was very prevalent and quite difficult of management. Indeed, so common was looseness of the bowels of the army, that few soldiers ever had natural or moulded evacuation. The camping grounds, privies everywhere and too often the depots, streets, etc., of villages and towns presented disgusting evidence of this fact**". Another Confederate medical officer, Bedford Brown, pointed out that diarrhea struck early, indicating that 9 out of every 10 new recruits were stricken with this condition. Once stricken with diarrhea the individual would fall into a weakened physical condition becoming an easy victim for other diseases. "**No matter what else a patient had,**" wrote a Confederate surgeon, "**he had diarrhoea**". An estimated thirty to forty percent of the deaths suffered by the Southern soldier were attributable to Acute/Chronic Diarrhea or Dysentery. Following the war, Confederate Surgeon Joseph Jones made the following eye opening statement, "**Chronic diarrhoea and dysentery were most abundant and most difficult to cure amongst army diseases; and whilst the more fatal diseases, as typhoid fever, diminished, chronic diarrhoea and dysentery progressively increased, and not only destroyed more soldiers than gunshot wounds, but more were permanently disabled and lost from service from these diseases than from the total disability from the accidents of battle**".

Two other illnesses suffered by the common soldier and resulted in a high mortality was "**pneumonia**" and "**typhoid fever**". Both shared equally in the mortality among the soldiers, approaching one-forth of all deaths reported. As an example, a period from January 1862 to March 1863, 4,864 cases of pneumonia were reported in Virginia (excluding Richmond) with 1,261 deaths (25.9%). Chimborazo Hospital in Richmond, for the war, reported 1,568 cases of pneumonia and pleurisy, with 583 deaths (37.1%). Statistics on typhoid fever were much the same. For a period from January 1, 1862 to April 1, 1863, 4,749 cases of typhoid fever were reported in the general hospitals in Virginia (excluding Richmond) with 1,619 deaths (34.1%).

The Lynchburg Hospital system was no different than her sister hospitals in the South and shared a representative mortality rate with the same illnesses reported above. By far, diarrhea, dysentery, pneumonia and typhoid fever were the primary messengers of death.

Other diseases such as tuberculoses, heart attacks, blood disorders, gangrene, scarlet fever, catarrh, measles, venereal diseases, bronchitis, rheumatism, scurvy, camp itch and many more were common during the war. However, one deadly and dreaded disease to the Confederate soldier was **"Smallpox"**. This disease was devastating to the Army of Northern Virginia with two epidemics. The first, a major outbreak, during the winter of 1862-63 and second, of less magnitude, the winter of 1863-64. This powerful disease left its mark on the Army of Northern Virginia and on the Lynchburg Hospital system.

The first recorded death in the Lynchburg Hospital system related to smallpox was on August 21, 1862. Its first victim was Sgt. Jonas Greathouse of the 31st Virginia Infantry. Greathouse had been hospitalized in the Candler Tobacco Factory. The second reported death was on September 25, 1862. The victim was David Cofield of the 35th Georgia Infantry. Cofield had been hospitalized in Reid's Factory. It appears that Greathouse contracted this disease as Prisoner of War. He was captured on June 26, 1862, exchanged from Fort Delaware and received at Akeins Landing, Virginia on August 14, 1862.

To combat the oncoming smallpox epidemic, the Surgeon General issued directives, the first on September 22, 1862. This directive stated, "**...to have each patient as he enters the hospital thoroughly examined...have each patient vaccinated**". His second directive was issued on October 13, 1862 stating, "**...cases of smallpox should be placed in the building set apart for these patients and other suspicious cases occurring in any of these hospitals should be at once removed**". In Lynchburg the "Pest House" was designated site for the smallpox hospital. A third directive was issued November 3, 1862, **"In order to prevent the spreading of smallpox you will without delay establish a receiving hospital for all patients that will be sent to the rear from Genl Lee's Army..."** The Wayside Hospital was established in Lynchburg to serve this purpose. The forth and final directive was issued on December 3, 1862 stating, **"In order to prevent the extension of smallpox...furloughs shall not be granted to officers of enlisted men who have recently been exposed to the contagion."**

The majority of the small pox deaths in Lynchburg occurred between October 1862, to April 1863. The death toll progressively increased over time. During the early weeks of January, it was not uncommon to have 5 to 10 deaths per day at the "Pest House" hospital in Lynchburg. During the same time frame Richmond and others were dealing with smallpox. At a smallpox hospital in Richmond between December 12, 1862 and December 19, 1862 (one week), out of 250 admissions there were 110 deaths. George Diuguid's burial records reported 99 deaths by smallpox of Confederated Soldiers whose burials were paid by family or friends. In addition, there was an additional 375 smallpox victims that were not given "formal burials". They were placed in a common grave (a pit) measuring approximately 60 feet by 80 feet. The bodies were placed in layers, limed, covered with a thin layer of dirt and another layer of bodies placed over them. This section was designated as "Yankee Square" and was adjacent to the other burial lots in the cemetery.

The last recorded death by smallpox in Lynchburg was reported on February 19, 1865 at Crumptom's Factory.

A total of 145 diseases were listed in the Confederate Medical regulations published during the early part of the war. These diseases fell under the following headings: **"Fevers" (9 listed), "Eruptive Fevers" (5 listed), "Diseases of the organs connected with the digestive system" (19 listed), "Diseases of the respiratory system" (10 listed), "Diseases of the circulatory system" (9 listed), "Diseases of the brain and nervous system" (14 listed), "Diseases of the urinary and genital organs and venereal afflictions" (14 listed), "Diseases of the serous exhalent vessels" (5 listed), "Abscesses and ulcers" (6 listed), "Diseases of the eye" (7 listed), "Diseases of the ear" (4 listed), "Diseases of the fibrous and muscular** structures (4 listed)", **"Wounds and injuries"** (15 listed), and **"all other diseases"**. Under the last heading, twenty-four ailments were listed, including, **"Dibilitas", "Nostalgia"** and **"Scorbutus"**.

The following is a listing of illnesses, number of cases and the number of deaths by each, reported by Union Army. The time period is not specified. The total number of admissions per sick reports for the Union Army was 5,825,480 during the war.

# of Cases	Disease	Deaths	%
76,368	typhoid	27,050	35.4
2,501	typhus	850	33.98
11,898	continued fever	147	1.23
49,871	malaria Fever	4,059	8.13
1,155,266	acute diarrhea	2,923	.25
170,488	chronic diarrhea	27,588	16.16
233,812	acute dysentery	4,084	1.75
25,670	chronic dysentery	3,229	12.58
73,382	syphilis	123	.17
95,833	gonorrhea	6	>.001
30,714	scurvy	383	1.25
3,744	delirium tremens	450	12.02
2,410	insanity	80	3.32
2,837	paralysis	231	8.14
1,933.794	Total	71,173	3.68

The following are the diseases, illnesses and wounds of the period. The majority of which are spelled out in the Confederate manual plus Diuguid mentions a few others in his burial logs or notes. The physicians that treated the men in the Lynchburg hospitals mentioned or listed others.

These diseases are arranged by the Greek name followed by the current or present day definition. This will be followed by a period definition taken from a Medical Dictionary published in 1858. This period entry will be made in italics. This a first attempt, to my knowledge of person to list and define the illnesses and disease of that age. I take full responsibility for this listing. I'm sure there will be misspelling and some incorrect definitions. I'm not a physician. Some physicians were contacted to look over the material for correctness and content but did not except to offer. If you the reader find errors please inform and correction can and will be made. Thank you.

DISEASE/TITLE   **DEFINITION**

Abscessus: (Abscesses and Ulcers) A localized collection of pus in the tissue of the body often accompanied by swelling and inflammation and often caused by bacteria. (abscessus - Latin; "a going away".) **(Potentially Fatal)**

Acute: Also "Acuta" or "Actus"; extremely severe, intense.

Amaurosis: (am"aw-rosis) **(Disease of the Eye)** Partial or total loss of sight. Dimming or darkening. *Diminution, or complete loss of sight, without any perceptible alteration in the organization of the eye; generally, perhaps, owing to loss of power of the optic nerve or retina. Counter-irritants are the most successful remedial agents, although the disease is always very difficult of removal, and generally totally incurable.* **(Disabling)**

Ambustio: (Wounds or Injuries) To burn or scald.

Anaemia: (ah-ne'meah) **(Circulatory System)** Anemia/anemic. Reduction below normal of the number of erythrocytes, quantity of hemoglobin, or volume of packed red cells in the blood; a symptom of various diseases and disorders. *Privation of blood - the opposite of plethora. It is characterized by every sign of debility. Also, diminished quality of fluids in the capillary vessels: - the opposite to* **Hyperaemia**. *– The essential character of the blood in anaemia in diminution in the ratio of red corpuscles.* (Potentially Disabling**)**

Anasarca: (Serous Exhalent Vessels) *A pronounced (also Anasaica) general dropsy. An abnormal collection, accumulation* *of fluids in the body - generalize edema.* Commonly, it begins to manifest itself by swelling around the ankles; and it characterized by tumefaction of the limbs and of the soft parts covering the abdomen, thorax, and even face, with paleness and dryness of the skin, and pitting when any of these (especially the ankles) are pressed upon. Like dropsy in general, Anasarca may be active or passive; and its treatment must be regulated by the rules that are applicable to general dropsy. At times, the symptoms are of an acute character, and the effusion sudden, constituting Dermatochysis, Hydrops Anasarca acutus. See Hydrops *(Potentially Fatal)*

Anchylosis: (General) (ang"ki-lo'sis) Stiffening of joints. To unite or grow together, as bones of a joint or the root of a tooth and its surrounding bone. Also anchylose & ankylosis. *Anchylosis is said to be complete or true, when there is an intimate adhesion between the synovial surfaces, with union of the articular extremities of the bones. In the incomplete or false anchylosis, there is obscure motion, but the fibrous parts around the joint are more or less stiff and thickened. In the treatment of this last state, the joint must be gently and gradually exercised; and oily, relaxing applications be assiduously employed.* **(Disabling)**

Aneurisma: (Circulatory System) A permanent ardiac or arterial dilatation usually caused by weakening of the vessel wall by disease such as syphilis or arteriosclerosis. Also aneurism or aneurysm (an'u-rizm). *Properly, Aneurism signifies a tumor, produced by dilatation of an artery; but it has been extended to various lesions of arteries, as well as to dilatations of the heart.* **(Potentially Fatal)**

Angina Pectoris: (Circulatory System) A syndrome characterized by constricting paroxysmal pain below the sternum, most easily precipitated by exertion or excitement and caused by ischemia of the heart muscle, usually due to a coronary artery disease. such as arteriosclerosis. *The principal symptoms are violent pain about the sternum, extending towards the arms, anxiety, dyspnoea, and sense of suffocation. It is an affection of great danger, and is often connected with ossification, or other morbid condition of the heart.* **(Disabling & Potentially Fatal)**

Anthrax: (an'thraks) (Abscesses or Ulcers) An often fatal, infectious disease of ruminants due to ingestion of spores of *Bacillus anthracis* in soil; acquired by man through contact with contaminated wool or other animal products or by inhalation of airborne spores. A malignant carbuncle that is a diagnostic lesion of anthrax in man. *An inflammation, essentially gangrenous, of the cellular membrane and skin, which may arise from an internal or external cause. Anthrax is a malignant boil, and its treatment is similar to that which is required in case of gangrene attacking part.* **(Potentially Fatal)**

Aphonia: (a-fo'ne-ah) **(Respiratory System)** A loss of voice due to organic or functional disturbance of the vocal organs. Greek - "speechlessness". *Privation of voice, or of the sound that ought to be produced in the glottis.*

Apoplexia: (ap'o-plek"se) **(Brain or Nervous System)** A sudden, (Apoplexy) unusually marked loss of bodily functions due to the rupture of or the occlusion of a blood vessel. A hemorrhage into the tissue of any organ, especially the brain. *Hemmorrhage from the meninges of the brain or spinal marrow, generally into the great cavity of the arachnoid.* **(Potentially Fatal)**

Asoites: (Serous Exhalent Vessels) An accumulation of serous fluids in the peritoneal cavity; dropsy of the peritoneum. **(Disabling)**

Asthma: (az'mah) **(Respiratory System)** A paroxysmal disorder of respiration, with labored breathing, a feeling of constriction in the chest, and coughing. *Difficulty of breathing, recurring intervals, accompanied with a wheezing sound and sense of constriction in the chest; cough and expectoration. Asthma is a chronic disease, and not curable with facility. Excitant and narcotic antispasmodics are required.* **(Disabling)**

Atrophia: (General) Also "Atrophy" (at'ro-fe); a wasting or failure in development of body or any of its parts. **(Disabling)**

Bilious: also **Biliousness** (bil'yus-nes). Pertaining to bile or to an excess secretion of bile. Suffering from, caused by or attended by trouble with the bile or liver. A symptom complex comprising nausea, abdominal discomfort, headache, and constipation, formerly attributed to excessive bile secretion. *That which relates to bile, contains bile, or is produced by bile. An epithet given to certain constitutions and disease, which are believed to be the effect of superabundance of biliary secretion;* **(Disabling)**

Bronchitis: (Respiratory System) (brong-kit'is) A chronic or acute inflammation of the mucous membrane of the bronchial

tubes. Inflammation of one or more bronchi. Acute infection marked by fever, pain in the chest (especially during coughing). Chronic, a long-continued, recurrent inflammation due to repeated attacks or acute bronchitis or to chronic general disease and marked by coughing, expectoration, and secondary changes in the lung tissue. Other forms of bronchitis are; catarrhal, croupous, fibrinous, infectious avain, and obliterans. *Inflammation of the lining membrane of the bronchial tubes. This is always more or less present in cases of pulmonary catarrh; and is accompanied by cough, mucous expectoration, dyspnoea, and more or less uneasiness in breathing.* **(Disabling)**
Bronchitis Acuta: See bronchitis - acute.
Bronchitis Chronica: See bronchitis - chronic.
Bubo Syphilitcum: (bu'bo) **(Urinary, genital organs, and venereal affections)** An inflammatory swelling of a lymphatic gland, especially in the groin of armpit. Pertaining to, noting, or affected with syphilis. *The moderns apply the term to an inflammatory tumor seated in the groin or axilla, and the generally distinguish – 1. Simple or Sympathetic Bubo, which is independent of any virus in the economy. 2. Venereal Bubo, which is occasioned by the venereal virus. Primay Bubo, shows itself with the first symptoms of syphilis: the consecutive not till afterwards.* **Syphilitcum** *(Syphilitic), belonging, or related to syphilis – as a syphilitic ulcer.* **(Disabling Potentially Fatal)**
Bubo Simplex: (bu'bo) **(Inflammation)** An inflammatory swelling of a lymphatic gland, especially in the groin or armpit. Simple, single action, Latin - one-fold. **(Disabling)**
Calculus (Calculi): (kal'ku-lus) **(Urinary, Genital Organs, & Venerial Affections)** A stone, or concentration, found in the gall bladder, kidneys, or other parts of the body. (i.e.) Biliary Calculi stones of the gallbladder (cholelithiasis & cysthepatolithiasis), urinary calculi one in any part of the urinary tract, renal culculi one in the kidney **(Disabling)**
Carditis: (kahr-di'tis) **(Circulatory System)** An inflammation of the pericardium, myocardium or endocardium, separately or in combination. *Inflammation of the fleshy substance of the heart. Carditis, indeed, with many, includes both the inflammation of the external investing members and that of the interior of the heart.* See Pericarditis, and Endocarditis. **(Potentially Fatal)**
<u>Pericardium</u> (-kahr'de-um) the fibrous sac enclosing the heart

and the roots of the great vessels.
Pericarditis: Membranous sac enclosing the heart and the Inflammation of.
Myocardium: The muscle tissue of the heart.
Endocardium (-kahr'de-um) the endothelial (interior) lining membrane of the cavities of the heart and connective tissue bed on which it lies.
Endocarditis Inflammation of the endocardium.
Cataracta (Cataract): (Disease of the Eye) Opacity of the lens of the eye, causing partial or total blindness. *A deprivation of sight, which comes on as if a veil fell before the eyes. Cat6aract consists in opacity of the crystalline lens or its capsule, which prevents the passage of the rays of light, and precludes vision. The causes are obscure.* **(Disabling)**
Catarrh: (kah-tahr') **(Respiratory System)** (also Catarrhus) An inflammation of the mucous membrane, especially of the respiratory tract (particularly of the head and throat), accompanied by excessive secretions (free discharge). Greek - "a flowing down". *A discharge of fluid from a mucous membrane. It is characterized by cough, thirst, lassitude, fever, watery eyes, with increased secretions of mucous from the air-passages. The antiphlogistic regimen and time usually remove it. Sometimes, the inflammation of the bronchial tubes is so great as to prove fatal.* **(Disabling)**
Catarrhus: See "Catarrah".
Cephalalgia: (sef'al-al'jah) **(Brain or Nervous System)** Sever headache. *Every kind of headach (sic), whether symptomatic or idiopathic, is a cephalalgia. It is ordinarily symptomatic, and has to be treated accordingly.* **(Disabling)**
Cerebrospinal Meningitis: An acute inflammation of the meninges of the brain and spinal cord, accompanied by fever. Also called brain fever, or cerebrospinal fever. **(Potentially Fatal)**
Cholera: (kol'er-ah) **(Organs connected with digestive system)** An acute infectious, often fatal disease endemic and epidemic in Asia, caused by Vibrio cholerae - characterized or marked by sever or profuse diarrhea, extreme fluid and electrolyte depletion (dehydration), vomiting, muscle cramps, and prostration. *A disease charterized by anxiety, gripings, spasms in the legs and arms, and by vomiting and purging (generally bilious) vomiting and purging are, indeed, the essential symptoms.* **(Usually Fatal if untreated)**

Cholera Asiatica: **(Organs connected with digestive system)** of or pertaining to Asia.
Cholera Morbus: (mor-bus, Latin) **(Organs connected with digestive system)** Sickness, sickly, disease, unhealthy, etc. **(Disabling, Potentially Fatal)**
Chorea: (kor-e' ah, Latin) **(Brain or Nervous System)** Any of (Chorea Sancti Viti) several disease of the nervous system characterized by ceaseless occurrence of rapid, jerky, involuntary movements, chiefly in the face and extremities. Also called St. Vitus's Dance. A disease of the central nervous system caused by bacterial or organic degeneration. *The charteristics are: irregulare and involuntary motions of one or, more limbs, and of the face and truck. It is a disease which usually occurs before puberty; and is generally connected with torpor of the system, and of the digestive organs in particular. Its duration is long, but is devoid of danger; although frequently but little under the control of medicine. The spasms do not continue during sleeping. The indications of treatment are: to strengthen the general system, and stimulate the intestinal canal. Purgatives, once or twice a week, and chalybeates (impregnated with the salts of iron), with appropriate regimen, will fill these.* **(Disabling)**
Chronic: Constant - habitual - continuing a long time or recurring frequently.
Colica (Colic): (kol'ik) **(Organs connected with digestive system)** Paroxysmal (sever/acute) pain in the abdomen or bowels, usually caused by abnormal conditions in the bowels. Also called "colic" **(Disabling)**
Compressio Cerebri: (Wounds & Injuries) A violent shock to some organ, especially the brain by a fall, sudden blow or blast; concussion to the cerebrum. See Concussion Cerebri **(Disabling)**
Concussion Cerebri: (kon-kush'in) **(Wounds & Injuries)** Compression of a portion or all of the brain. A violent shock or jar, or the condition resulting from such an injury. Loss of consciousness, transient or prolonged, due to a blow to the head; there may be transient amnesia, vertigo, nausea, weak pulse and slow respiration. *Concussion of the brain, sometimes gives rise to alarming symptoms, even to abolition of the function of the brain, yet without any sensible organic disease...After sever concussion, a patient, although apparently well, is not safe till some time after the accident.* **(Disabling - Possibly Fatal)**

Congestic Cerebri: (con-jes'chin) **(Brain or Nervous System)** Congestic or congestion is to surcharge (an organ or part) with an abnormal or excessive amount of blood. Cerebri or cerebrum is the upper anterior part of the cranial cavity; its two hemispheres united by the corpus callosum, from the largest part of the central nervous system in man. Link these two words together and you have a large accumulation of blood on the brain. **(Potentially Fatal if untreated)**

Conjunctivitis: (kon-junk"ti-vit'is) **(Disease of the Eye)** Inflammation of the eye or eyelid. "Conjunctiva" the mucous membrane that lines the inner surface of the eyelid. Acute epidemic conjunctivitis, pinkeye; a highly contagious form of conjunctivitis caused by Haemophilus aegyptius **(Disabling)**

Consecutiva: (General) Probably Latin, more modern it would be "consecutive". Medically, during the War it was an unrelated illness followed by another illness. *Consecutivus, from "con", 'with', and "sequor, secutus", 'to follow.'*

Constipatio (Constipation): (kon sti-pa'shun) **(Organs connected with digestive system)** A condition of the bowels in which the feces are dry and hardened and evacuation is difficult and or infrequent. *A state of the bowels, in which the evacuations do not take place as frequently usual; or are inordinately hard, and expelled with difficulty. Cathartics will usually remove it; after which its exciting and predisponent (predispose) cause must be inquired into obviated, to render the cure permanent.* **(Disabling)**

Consumption: (kon-sup'shun) **(Respiratory System)** A wasting of tissue, Tuberculosis; a communicable disease, caused by microorganism, manifesting itself in lesions of the lung, bone, and other parts of the body. *Progressive emaciation or wasting away. This condition precedes death in the greater part of chronic diseases, and particularly in* **phthisis pulmonalis**: *on this account it is, that phthisis has received the name* **consumption**. **(Disabling - Potentially Fatal)**

Contusio: (Wound & Injuries) To bruise by a blow, the skin is not broken. **(Disabling)**

Cystitis: (Urinary, Genital Organs, & Venerial Affections) An inflammation of the urinary bladder. *Inflammation characterized by pain and swelling in the hypogastric* (mid abdominal) *region; discharge of urine painful or obstructed, and tenesmus* (painful straining)*...It must be treated upon the same* *energetic principals as required in other cases of internal inflammation; venesection, general and local, the warm bath, warm fomentations, warm, soothing enemata, diluents &c.* **(Disabling)**

Debilitus (Debility): (de-bil'i-te) **(General)** A condition of the body in (Debilitas) which there is a weakening of the vital functions. The lack or loss of strength; weakness. In today's military this would be classified as "battle fatigue". **(Disabling - Potentially Fatal)**

Delirium Tremens: (de-ler'e-um) **(Brain or Nervous System)** a violent restlessness due to excessive and prolonged use of alcohol, characterized by trembling, terrifying visual hallucinations. A acute mental disturbance marked by delirium with trembling and excitement, attended by anxiety, mental distress, sweating, gastro-intestinal symptoms, and precordial pain; a form of alcohol psychosis seen after withdrawal from heavy alcohol intake. *It is caused by the habitual and intemperate use of ardent spirits or of opium or tobacco; or rather abandoning them after prolonged use.* **(Disabling)**

Diabetes: (Urinary, Genital Organs, & Venerial Affection) Also called "diabetes mellitus"; a disease that impairs the ability of the body to use sugar and causes sugar to appear abnormally in the urine. *A disease, characterized by great augmentation and often manifest alteration in the secretion of urine; with excessive thirst, and progressive emaciation.* **(Disabling)**

Diarrhea: (-re'ah) **(Organs connected with Digestive System)** (Diarrhoea) An intestinal disorder characterized by frequency and fluidity of fecal evacuations. Greek "diarrhoia" - "a flowing through". Abnormally frequent evacuation of watery stools. *A disease characterized by frequent liquid alvine evacuations, and generally owing to inflammation or irritation of the mucous membrane of the intestines. It is commonly caused by errors in regimen, the use of food noxious by its quality or quantity, &c. It may be acute or chronic...If caused, as it often is, by improper matters in the intestinal canal, these must be evacuated; and the astringent plan of treatment must not be adopted, unless the discharges seem kept up by irritability of the intestines, or unless they are colliquative. The indiscriminate use of astringents is to be deprecated.* **(Disabling/Potentially Fatal)**

Diarrhoea Acuta: See Diarrhea - Acute.
Diarrhoea Chronica: See Diarrhea – Constant or Chronic.
Diphtheria (Diphtheritis): (dif-ther'e-ah) **(General)** An acute febrile, infectious (highly contagious) disease caused by bacillus "Corynebacterium diphtheriae" and its toxins, affecting the membranes of the nose, throat, or larynx, and marked by formation of a gray-white pseudomembrane (false), with white fever, pain, and, in the laryngeal form, aphonia and respiratory obstruction. The toxin may also cause myocarditis and neuritis. air passages, especially the throat. *A name given by M. Bretonneau to a class of disease, which are characterized by a tendency to formation of false membranes; and affect the dermoid tissue. As the mucous membranes, and even the skin.* **(Disabling/Potentially Fatal)**
Dropsy: (drop'se) Edema. An excessive accumulation of serious fluid in the serous cavity or in the subcutaneous cellular tissue (especially the heart).
Dysentery (Dysenteria): (dis'in-te"re) **(Organs connected with digestive system)** An infectious disease marked by inflammation and ulceration of the lower part of the bowels, with diarrhea that becomes mucous and hemorrhagic. Any of a number of disorders marked by inflammation of the intestine, especially of the colon, with abdominal pain, tenesmus, and frequent stools containing blood and mucus. *Inflammation of the mucous membrane of the large intestine; the chief symptom of which are; fever, more or less inflammatory, with frequent mucous or bloody evacuations; violent tormina and tenesmus. When the evacuations do not contain blood, it has been called simple dysentery. It occurs...frequently, also, in camps and prisons, in consequence of impure air, and imperfect nourishment: and is often epidemic...At times, the inflammations runs so speedily to ulceration, that, unless a new action be rapidly excited, death will be the consequence. In such cases, mercury must be rapidly introduced into the system, and narcotics may be combined with it.* **(Disabling/Potentially Fatal)**
Dysenteria Acuta: See Dysentery - Acute.
Dysenteria Chronica: See Dysentery - Chronic.
Dyspepsia: (dis-pep'se-ah) **(Organs connected with digestive system)** Impairment of the power or function of digestion; usually applied to epigastric discomfort after meals. Deranged or impaired digestion; indigestion. *A state of the stomach, in*

which its functions are disturbed, without the presence of other diseases, or when, if other diseases be present, they are of but minor importance. It is usually dependent on irregularity of living; either in the quantity or quality of the food taken: and the most successful treatment is, to put the patient on a diet easy of digestion; to combat the cause, where such are apparent; and, by proper remedies and regimen, to strengthen the system in every practical manner. **(Disabling)**

Ebrietas (Temulentia/Temulence): (General) *Plater gave this name to delirium*; Ettmuller, to an apoplectic condition, depending drunkenness; the Apoplexia Temulenta or dead drunkenness. Commonly, Temulentia is used synonymously with drunkenness. **(Disabling)**

Enuresis: (en ur-e'sis) **(Urinary, Genital Organs, & Venerial Affections)** Involuntary discharge of urine; usually referring to involuntary discharge of urine during sleep at night (incontinence). (enuretic). *This affection is most common in advanced life. It may depend on too great irritability of the bladder, or on distension, or injury of the fiber about its neck...rupture of the bladder and urethra; renal disease; or on pressure exerted on the bladder by the distended womb or by a tumor.* **(Disabling)**

Epidemicus (also Epidemy or Epidemic): (ep I-dem'ik) **(Respiratory System)** Attacking many people in a region at the same time; widely diffused and rapidly spreading. A disease of high morbidity which is only occasionally present in the human community. *A disease which attacks at the same time a number of individuals, and which is referred to some particular* **constitutio aeris**, *or condition of the atmosphere, with which we are utterly ignorant.*

Epilepsy (Also Epilepsis): (Brain or Nervous System) A Disorder of nervous system, characterized by fits of convulsions that end with loss of consciousness. Any of a group of syndromes characterized by paroxysmal transient disturbances of brain function that may be manifested as an episodic impairment or loss of consciousness, abnormal motor phenomena, psychic or sensory disturbances, or perturbation of the autonomic nervous system; symptoms are due to disturbance of the electrical activity of the brain. *It is a disease of the brain, which may either be idiopathic or symptomatic, spontaneous or accidental and which occurs in paroxysms, with* uncertain intervals between...At times, before the loss of consciousness occurs, a sensation of a cold vapour is felt. This appears to rise in some part of the body, proceeds towards the head; and as soon as it reaches the brain the patient falls down...After the fit, the patient retains not the least recollection of what has passed, but remains, for sometime, affected with headach, stupor, and lassitude. **(Disabling)**

Epistaxis: (-stak'sis) **(General)** a nosebleed; hemorrhage from the nose, usually due to rupture of small vessels overlying the anterior part of the cartilaginous nasal septum. *This is one of the most common varieties of hemorrhage;...A common case of epistaxis requires but little treatment.... Light diet and a dose or two of sulphate of magnesia will be sufficient. In more severe attacks, cold and astringent washes of alum, sulphate of zinc, weak sulphuric acid, or creosote, may be used, and the nostrils plugged anteriorly.* **(Disabling)**

Erysipelas: (er i-sip i-lis) **(Eruptive Fever)** An acute febrile infectious disease, caused by specific streptococcus, characterized by diffusely spreading deep red inflammation on the skin or mucous membranes. A contagious disease of the skin and subcutaneous tissues due to infection with *Streptococcus pyogenes*, with redness and swelling of affected areas, constitutional symptoms, and sometimes vesicular and bullous lesions. *A disease, so called because it generally extends gradually to the neighboring parts. Superficial inflammation of the skin, with general fever, tension and swelling of part; pain and heat more or less acrid; redness diffused, but more or less circumscribed, and disappearing when pressed upon by finger, but returning, but returning as soon as the pressure is removed. Frequently, small vesicles appear upon the inflamed part, which dry up and fall off, under the form of branny scales. Erysipelas is, generally, an acute affection: its medium duration being from 10 to 14 days. It yields, commonly, to general refrigerant remedies. Topical applications are rarely serviceable. At times, when the disease approaches the phlegmonous character, copious bleeding and other evacuants may be required, as in many cases of erysipelas of the face; but this is not commonly necessary. When erysipelas is of a highly inflammatory character, and invades the parts beneath, it is termed Erysipelas phlegmonodes. When accompanied with phlyetenae, and the inflammation terminates in gangrene.* **(Fatal)**

Exostosis: (ek sos-to sis) **(General)** The abnormal formation of bony growth or a bone or a tooth. A benign bony growth projecting outward from a bone surface. *An osseous tumour, which forms at the surface of bones, on in their cavities. Exostoses are sometimes distinguished into the true, which seem to be a projection of the osseous substance, which have the same organization and hardness as that substance; and the false or osteo-sarcoma. Exostosis may depend on syphilis, scrofula, rickets, gout, &c. In such cases, it is important to get rid of the primary disease.* **(Disabling)**

Exposure: (General) The body exposed to extremes of weather, cold wet, heat, privations, lack of proper food, clothing, warmth, rest, etc. resulting in the weakening or physical deterioration of a soldier in the field. **(Disabling/Potentially Fatal)**

Febrile: (Fever) Pertaining to or marked by fever. Related to fever. (Latin - ***Febris***)

Febris Congestiva: (Fever) A fever and congestion of the lungs. *Belonging or related to, or affected with, congestion – as congestive fever.* **(Disabling/Potentially Fatal)**

Febris Continua: (Fever) A constant or continuous fever; Communis (common) unremitting, unceasing. **(Disabling/Potentially Fatal)**

Febris Interimittens Tertiana: (Fever) Characterized by paroxysms, which recur every other day. *An intermitten, whose paroxysms recur every third day, or every 48 hours. The mildest, sand the most pernicious, intermittens belong to the head. As a general rule, it is the most manageable form of ague.* **(Disabling/Potentially Fatal)**

Febris Interimittens Quartana: (Fever) Characterized by paroxysms, which recur every fourth day, both days of connective occurrence being counted. **(Disabling/Potentially Fatal)**

Febris Interimittens Quotidiana: (Fever) Daily, everyday, a fever characterized by a paroxysms which recur daily. *...is an intermitten, the paroxysms of which recur every day. A simple, double, or triple quotidian, ia a quotidian, which has one, two or three paroxysms in 24 hours* **(Disabling/Potentially Fatal)**

Febris Remittens: (Fever) A fever that may abate for a time or return at intervals; the symptoms diminish considerably at intervals without disappearing entirely. **(Disabling/**

Potentially Fatal)
Febris Typhoides: (Fever) See typhoid.
Febris Typhus: (Fever) See typhus.
Febris Typhus Icterodes (Ictericus): (Fever) See Typhus - also type of jaundice. *A disease, principle symptoms of which is yellowness of the skin and eyes, with white feces and high coloured-urine. It admits of various causes; in fact, anything which can directly or indirectly obstruct the course of the bile, so that it is taken into the mass of blood and produces the yellowness of surface; the bile being separated by the kidney, causes yellowness of urine, and its being prevented from reaching the intestine occasions the pale-coloured feces. The prognosis, in ordinary cases, is favorable. When complicated with hepatic disease, unfavorable. The treatment is simple. An emetic or purgative, give occasionally so as to elicit the return of the bile to its ordinary channels; light tonics; unirritating diet; cheerful company, &c.*
Fistula: (fis tu-lah) **(Abscesses & Ulcers)** A narrow passage or duct formed by disease or injury, as one leading from an abscess to a free surface, or from one cavity to another. Any of various suppurative inflammations. Characterized by the formation of passages or sinuses through the tissue and the surface of the skin. **(Disabling)**
Fractura: (Wounds & Injuries) A fracture of a bone, the breaking or cracking of a bone; also sometimes the tearing of cartilage. **(Disabling)**

Gangrene: (General) The dying or death of soft tissue on part of the body; as from the interruption of circulation. Death of tissue, usually in considerable mass, generally with loss of vascular (nutritive) supply and followed by bacterial invasion and putrefacation. *When the gangrene has become developed, the separation of the eschars* (hard crust or scab) *must be encouraged by emollient applications, if there be considerable reaction: or by tonics and stimulants, if the reactions be insufficient.* **(Potential Fatal)**
Gastritis: (Organs connected with digestive system) Inflammation of the stomach, especially of its mucous membrane. *A disease, characterized by pyrexia; great anxiety; heat and pain in the epigastrium, increased by taking anything into the stomach; vomiting or hiccup. Gastritis may either be seated in the peritoneal or mucous coat. It is most frequently in*

the latter, being excited directly by acrid ingesta. It requires the most active treatment; bleeding, blistering, fomentation, diluents, &c. Some degree of inflammation of the mucous coat of the stomach was considered by the followers of Broussais to be present in almost all fevers; and various forms of dyspepsia have been supposed by some to be nothing more than chronic endogastritis. **(Disabling)**
Gelatic: (Wound & Injuries) Freezing – frostbite; solidification by cold. **(Disabling)**
Gonorrhoea: (Urinary, Genital Organs, & Venereal Affections) See Venereal Disease. **(Disabling)**

Haematemesis: (Organs connected with digestive system) Comes from the Greek, meaning "I vomit." *Haematemesis is generally preceded by a felling of oppression, weight, and dull or pungent pain in the epigastric and in the hypochondriac region; by anxiety, and, occasionally, by syncope. Blood is then passed by vomiting, and sometimes, also, by stool – the blood being generally of a aspect. Haematenesis may be active or passive, acute or chronic. The blood effused proceeds from rupture of vessel, or from a sanguineous exhalation at the surface of the mucous membrane of the stomach. Complete abstinence from food; rest; the horizontal posture; bleeding, if the hemorrhage be active; cold, acidulous drinks, &c., constitute the usual treatment.* **(Disabling)**
Hematocele: (he mah-to-sel) **(General)** Also see Hydrocele. An effusion of blood into a cavity, especially into the tunica vaginalis testis (male gonad). **(Disabling)**
Hemoptysis: (he-mop ti-sis) **(Respiratory System)** Also "Hemophthis", excessive spitting up of blood from the lungs. **(Disabling/Potentially Fatal)**
Haemorrhois: (General) Also hemorrhoid; a tumor or dilation of a vein in the anal region, usually painful. **(Disabling)**
Hemorrhia: (General) Very heavy bleeding - a discharge of blood from a ruptured blood vessel. **(Potentially Fatal)**
Hepatitis: (Organs connected with digestive system) Inflammation of the liver. *The treatment must be bold. Bleeding, general and local, fomentation, blisters, purgatives, and the antiphlogistic regimen. In hot climates especially, a new action must be excited by mercury as early as possible.* **(Disabling/Potentially Fatal)**
Hepatitis Acuta: See Hepatitis - Acute.

Hepatitis Chornica: See Hepatitis - Chronic.
Hernia: (Wounds & Injuries) The protrusion of an organ or part of an organ, as of the intestine, through an opening in the wall surrounding it; rupture. **(Disabling)**
Hydrarthus: (Disease of the Serous Exhalent Vessels) Also known as hydrarthosis, an accumulation of effused watery fluid in a joint cavity. *It may attack any one of the joints; but is most commonly met with in the knee, the haunch, the foot, the elbow, and generally occurs in scrofulous children. The treatment consist in the employment of counter-irritants; the use of iodine internally and externally &c.* **(Disabling)**
Hydrocele: (Disease of the Serous Exhalent Vessels) An accumulation of serous fluids, usually about the testis. *A term generally applied to a collection of serious fluid in the areolar texture of the scrotum or in some of the coverings, either of the testicle or spermatic cord.* **(Disabling)**
Hydrothorax: (Disease of the Serous Exhalent Vessels) The presence of serous fluid in one or both pleural cavities (lungs). *Is a rare disease, and difficult to diagnosis. It generally exists only on one side, which, if the fluid effusedbe considerable, projects more than the other. Dyspnoea, and fluctuation perceptible to the ear, are characteristic symptoms. When the chest is examined with the stethoscope, respiration is found to be wanting every where, except at the root of the lung. The sound is also dull on percussion. Effusion into the chest, as a result of inflammation of some thoriacic viscus, is as common as the other is rare. It is usually a fatal symptom. It has been called symptomatic hydrothorax. In hydrothorax, the course of treatment proper in dropsies in general must be adopted. Diuretics seem, here, to be especially useful; probally on account of the great activity of pulmonary absorption. Paracentesis can rarely be serviceable.* **(Disabling/Potentially Fatal) Incipt** - Beginning; initial
Hypertrophy: (Circulatory System) Enlargement or overgrowth of a part or organ due to increase in size of its constituent cells, especially the heart; excessive growth. **(Disabling/Potentially Fatal)**

Icterus: (Organs connected with digestive system) Jaundice. *A disease, the principle symptoms of which is yellowness of the skin and eyes, with white feces and high-coloured urine. It admits of various causes; in fact, anything which can directly or*

indirectly obstruct the course of the bile, so that it is taken into the mass of blood and produce the yellowness of surface; - the bile being separated by the kidneys, causes yellowness of urine, and its being prevented from reaching the intestine occasions the pale-coloured feces. The prognosis, in ordinary cases, is favorable; - when complicated with hepatic disease, unfavorable. The treatment is simple: - an emetic or purgative, given occasionally so as to elicit the return of the bile to its ordinary channels; light tonics; unirritating diet; cheerful company, &c. **(Disabling)**
Ictus Solis: (Brain or Nervous System) a fit; a stroke, as sunstroke. **(Potentially Fatal)**
Iritis: (Disease of the Eye) Inflammation of the iris. *The chief symptoms are; - change in colour of the iris; fibres less movable; tooth-like processes shooting into the pupil; pupil irregularly contracted, with the ordinary signs of inflammation of the eye. If the inflammation does not yield, suppuration takes place; and although the matter may be absorbed, the iris remains immovable. It is often caused by syphilis. The general principles of treatment are, to deplete largely and exhibit mercury freely; along with attention to other means advisable in ophthalmia. Free use of quinia is sometimes serviceable.* **(Disabling)**
Irritatic Spinalis: (Brain or Nervous System) The bringing of a body part or organ to an abnormally excited or sensitive condition. Of or pertaining to the spine. **(Disabling)**
Ischuria et Dysuria: (Urinary, Genital Organs, & Venerial Affections) Difficult or painful urination. *Ischuria (Ishu'ria) – stoppage of urine; Retention of, or impossibility of discharge, the urine. Dysuria (Dysr'ria) – Difficulty of passing urine. In this affection the urine is voided with pain, and a sensation of heat in some parts of the urethra. Dysuria is the first degree of retention of urine. It differs from strangury, in which the urine can only be passed in drops and with great straining.* **(Disabling)**

Laryngitis: (Respiratory System) Also Laryngitis - inflammation of the larynx. **(Disabling)**
Lumbago: (Fibrous & Muscular Structures) Pain in the lumbar region of the back, especially in the small of the back. **(Disabling)**
Luxatio: (luk-sa'shun) **(Wounds or Injuries)** Dislocation, to put out of joint. Luxation is divided into simple, compound,

primary, consecutive, complete, incomplete, and subluxation. A displacement of a part from its proper situation. A pulling out of joint. A displacement or two or mor bones, whose articular surface have lost, wholly, or in part, their natural connexion; either owing to external violence, (accidental luxation,) or to disease of some of the parts about the joint (spontaneous luxation), Luxation is complete when the bones have entirely lost their natural connexion; incomplete, when they partly preserve it; and compound, when a wound communicates with the luxated joint. The general indications of treatment are; - 1. To reduce the protruded bone to its original place. 2. To retain it in situ. 3. To obviate any attendant or consequent symptoms. **(Disabling)**

Mania: (Brain or Nervous System) A form of insanity characterized by great excitement, with or without delusion, and in its acute state by great violence. **(Disabling)**
Measles: (Eruptive Fever) An acute infectious disease occurring mostly in children, characterized by catarrhal and febrile symptoms and an eruptions of small red spots. **(Disabling/Potentially Fatal)**
Melancholia: (Brain or Nervous System) Mental disease characterized by great depression of spirits and gloomy foreboding. Rubelola, see Rubeola **(Disabling)**
Meningitis: (Brain or nervous System) Inflammation of the meninges (brain). *From meningina, and it is, denoting inflammation. Inflammation of the meningina.* **(Potentially Fatal)**
Morbi Cutis: (General) Disease of the skin; CUTIS - the corium or true skin. **(Disabling)**
Morbi - Related to disease. Cutis - layer of skin below the epidermis.
Morbi Varii: (General) Various diseases or illnesses. **(Disabling)**
Morsus Serpentis: (mor'sus) (Wound & Injuries) Morsus means bite. The term "Serpentis" is most likely Latin for serpent or snake – the term would most like be interpreted as "snake bite."

Necrosis: (ne-kro-'sis) **(General)** Also "Necrocytosis". Death of a circumscribed piece of tissue of an organ. Death of tissue in a living animal, resulting from infection or burns; gangrene. **(Potentially Fatal)**

Nephritis: (ne-fri-tis) **(Urinary, Genital Organs, & Venerial Affections)** An inflammation of the kidneys, especially in Bright's disease. *Inflammation of the kidney . . . is characterized by acute pain; burning heat, and sensation of weight in the region of one or both kidneys; suppression or diminution of urine; fever; dysuria; ischuria; constipation, more or less obstinate; retraction of the testicle, and numbness of the thigh of the same side. It may be distinguished into simple and calculous nephritis – Lithonephritis. In the later, the urine often contains small particles of uric acid or of urate of ammonia. The most common causes of nephritis are; - excess in irritating and alcoholic drinks; abuse to diuretics; blows or falls on the region of the kidneys; the presence renal calculi, &c.* **(Disabling)**

Neuralgia: (Brain or Nervous System) Sharp and paroxysmal (sever attack) pain along the course of a nerve. *A generic name for a certain number of diseases, the chief symptoms of which is a very acute pain, exacerbating or intermitting, which follows the course of a nerve branch, extends to its ramifications, and seems, therefore, to be seated in the nerve.* **(Disabling)**

Nostalgia: (General) A longing for familiar or beloved circumstances that are now remote or irrecoverable. **(Disabling)**

Nyctalopia: (nik-tah-lo'pe-ah) **(Disease of the Eye)** Also "Night Blindness"; A condition of the eyes in which sight is abnormally poor or wholly absent at night or in dim light. NYCTO - Night; OPIA - Eye. From the Greek words meaning "night" and "I see." *The faculty of seeing during in the night, with privation of the faculty during the day. It affects both eyes at once, when idiopathic. Its duration is uncertain, and treatment very obscure. It is, however, a disease of nervous irritability, and one of excitement of the visual nerve in particular. The indications of cure will consequently be – to allay direct irritation in every way; to excite counter-irritation by blisters; and to gradually accustom the eyes to the impression light.* **(Disabling)**

Odontalgia: (o'don-tal'jah) **(General)** A pain in a tooth - toothache. From the Greek words meaning "a tooth" and "pain." *A disease dependent on upon a variety of causes affecting the cavity of the tooth; but generally owing to caries, which exposes the cavity to the action of the air, and to extraneous matters in general. Hence, the treatment consist in plugging the tooth, or destroying the sensibility of the nerve by* *powerful stimulants; and, if these means fail, in extracting the tooth.* **(Disabling)**

Ophthalmia: (of-thal'me-ah) **(Disease of the Eye)** Inflammation of the eye, especially of its membrane or external surface. **(Disabling)**

Orchitis: (or-kit'is) **(Urinary, Genital Organs, & Venerial Affections)** The word Orchea refers to the Scrotum; and "it is" generally refers to inflammation. **(Disabling)**

Otalgia: (o-tal'jah) **(Disease of the Ear)** An earache. **(Disabling)**

Otitis: (Disease of the Ear) An inflammation of the ear. **(Disabling)**

Otorrhoea: (-ra'jah) **(Disease of the Ear)** Bleeding from the ear or ears.

Paralysis: (Brain or Nervous System) A loss or **(Palsy)** impairment of sensation or especially of muscle function, caused by injury or disease of the nerves, brain, or spinal cord. **(Disabling)**

Paronychia: (par'o-nik'e-ah) **(Abscesses & Ulcers)** Also "Whitlow". Inflammation of the folds of skin bordering a nail or a finger or toe, usually characterized by infection & pus formation. **(Disabling)**

Parotitis: (par'o-tit'is) **(Organs connected with digestive system)** Inflammation of a parotid - mumps. "Parotid - a salivary gland situated at the base of each ear." **(Disabling)**

Peritonitis: (Organs connected with digestive system) Inflammation of the peritoneum. A serous membrane that lines the abdominal cavity and is more or less complete covering for the viscera. Greek - **peri** "around" + **teinein** "to stretch". *The characteristic signs of acute inflammation of the peritoneum are, - violent pain in the abdomen, increased by the slightest pressure, often by the simple weight of the bed clothes. It generally occurs in the parturient state; Lochoperitoni'tis, and begins on the second or third day after delivery.* **(Disabling/Potentially Fatal)**

Phlebitis: (fle-bit'is) **(Circulatory System)** Inflammation of a vein. **(Disabling)**

Phlegmon: (fleg'mon) **(General)** An inflammation, especially of the connective tissue, leading to ulceration or abscess. **(Disabling/Potentially Fatal)**

Phthisis: (thi'sis) **(Respiratory System)** Tuberculosis of the

lungs - lung disease - a wasting away. **(Disabling/Potentially Fatal)**
Pleuritis: (Respiratory System) Inflammation of the pleura, with or without liquid effusion. **(Disabling)**
Phthisic Pulmonalis: (Respiratory System) Tuberculosis of the lungs - lung disease - a wasting away. **(Disabling/Potentially Fatal)**
Pneumonia: (Respiratory System) Inflammation of the lungs and being acute affection of the lungs regarded as caused by the pneumococcus. **(Disabling/Potentially Fatal)**
Podagra: (pah-dag'rah) **(Fibrous & Muscular Structures)** Gout of the foot. **(Disabling)**
Prolapsus Ani: (General) To fall out of place, to become detached from its normal position or place, as an organ or part, such as the bladder. **(Disabling/Potentially Fatal)**
Pulmonaris: (Respiratory System) Pertaining to the lungs.
Punitio: (Wounds & Injuries)
Pyemia: (-em'e-ah) **(General)** A disease condition in which pyogenic bacteria are circulating in the blood, characterized by the development of abscess in various organs. **(Usually Fatal)**
Retinitis: (Disease of the Eye) Inflammation of the retina. **(Disabling)**
Rheuma: (roo'mah) **(Respiratory System)** A thin, or serous catarrhal discharge. Catarrh; cold. Also Rheuma Extreme. *Also, inflammation of a fibrous tissue, as in rheumatism and gout.* **(Disabling)**
Rubeola: (roo-be'o-lah) **(Eruptive Fever)** See "Measles". *One of the major exanthemata; generally affecting individuals but once, and produced by specific contagion. The rash usually appears on the fourth, but sometimes on the third, fifth, or sixth day of a febrile disorder; and, after a continuance of four days, gradually declines with the fever. The disease generally commences from ten to fourteen days after the contagion has been received. The eruption first shows itself in distinct, red, and nearly circular spots, somewhat less than the ordinary areola of flea-bites. As these increase in umber, they coalesce; forming small patches of an irregular figure, but approaching nearest to that of semicircles or crescents. These patches are intermixed with single, circular dots and with interstices of the natural colour of the skin. On the face they are slightly raised, so as to give the sensation of inequality of surface to the finger passed over the cuticle. The disappearance of the eruption is followed by*

desquamation of the cuticle. Measles is not dangerous of itself; but it is liable to induce pneumonia in winter, and dysentery in the summer, which are, at times, very fatal. These are apt to come on come on at the time of, or soon after, the disappearance of the eruption. When they supervene, they must be treated as idiopathic affections. It demands a general antiphlogistic treatment.
Rheumatism: (Fibrous & Muscular Structures) A **(Rheumtismos)** disease commonly affecting the joints and accompanied by constitutional disturbances, now usually thought to be a micro organism; rheumatic fever. **(Disabling)**
Rheumatism Actus: See Rheumatism - Acute.
Rheumatism Chronicus: See Rheumatism - Chronic.

Sarcocele: (-sel) **(Urinary, Genital Organs, & Venerial Affections)** A fleshy tumor. "Sarco" from Greek meaning "Flesh". "Cele" from greek meaning tumor. Both "Sarco" and "Cele" are used in compound word. *This disease affects adults particularly; and appears most commonly after an inflammatory swelling of the testicle. Sometimes it is dependent upon a blow; at others, it makes its appearance without any appreciable cause. It is well known by a hard, heavy, ovoid or spherical swelling of the testicle, which is at first, slightly, or not at all painful, which is, at first, slightly, and merely causes an unpleasant traction on the spermatic cord. There is no heat or change of colour of the skin; the spermatic cord is swollen, and participates in the affection; very painful shootings occur; the lymphatic glands of the abdomen become swollen, and form a tumor, which may, at times, be felt through the abdomen; and the patient, at length, dies with every sign of the cancerous diathesis. The prognosis is very unfavorable. The only means, indeed, that can save life, is the extirpation of the testicle.* **(Disabling)**
Scarlatina: (skahr'lah-te'nah) **(Eruptive Fever)** See Scarlet Fever. *The characteristic symptoms of Scarlatina are: - a scarlet flush, appearing about the second day of fever on the face, neck, and fauces; and progressively spreading over the body; terminating about the 7th day. . . . Scarlatina belongs to the Major exanthemata, and is a disease, chiefly, of children. The eruption differs from that of measles, in being an efflorescence not raised above the cuticle. Measles, too, is attended with catarrhal symptoms, whilst the complication, in Scarlatina, is cynanche. (Any inflammatory disease of the throat). The treatment of*

simple Scarlatina need not be much. It must be antiphlogistic. If the throat be very much ulcerated, acid gargles and counter-irritants must be employed; and if the affection becomes manifestly typhoid, and the sore throat of a malignant character, the case must be treated like typhus gravior; with antiseptic gargles of bark, acid, &c. Anasarca sometimes supervenes on Scarlatina, and requires attention. Purgatives are here demanded as well as the use of sorbefacients, such as mercury and squill, &c. (Squill was an expectorant from dried sea onion; sorbefacients is a compound word – "facient" from the Latin "that makes or cause (something)." Sorbefacients – Herbs which cause absorption. Antiphlogistic – An herb which reduces inflammation.

Scarlet Fever: (Eruptive Fever) A congestive febrile disease, caused by streptococci and characterized by a scarlet eruption. **(Usually Fatal)**

Scirrhus: (skir'us) **(General)** A hard, indolent tumor; a hard cancer. See under carcinoma. **(Disabling/Potentially Fatal)**

Scorbutus: (skor-bu'tus) **(General)** Pertaining to, of the nature of, or affected with scurvy. *That which belongs to scurvy. One affected with scurvy.* **(Disabling)**

Scrofula: (skrof''ya-la) **(General)** A constitutional disorder of a tuberculosis nature, characterized chiefly by swelling and degeneration of the lymphatic glands, especially of the neck, and by inflammation of the joints, etc. *A state of the system characterized by indolent, glandular tumors, chiefly in the neck; suppurating slowly and imperfectly, and healing with difficulty; the disease ordinarily occurring in those of a sanguine temperament, with thick upper lip, &c. . . . The best treatment is; - to strengthen the system by animal diet; pure air, and exercise, cold bathing, or salt-water bathing, &c.* **(Disabling)**

Sequela: (General) An abnormal condition resulting from a previous disease; example, "measles sequela", measles alone was not a killer, however, once weakened, fevers, pneumonia, diarrhea, typhoid fever, and phthisis followed out breaks measles. Also see "Consecutiva" **(Disabling/Potentially Fatal)**

Smallpox: (Eruptive Fever) An acute, highly contagious, febrile disease characterized by a pustule eruption, which often leaves permanent scars or pits. Also see Variola. **(Potentially Fatal)**

Splenitis: (Organs connected with digestive system) Inflammation of the spleen. **(Disabling)**

Strictura Urethrae: (Urinary, Genital Organs, & Venerial Affections) An abnormal contraction of the urethra tube extending from the bladder to the exterior. **(Disabling)**
Sub-laxatio: (Wounds & Injuries) An incomplete dislocation. **(Disabling)**
Suicidium: (General) The intentional taking of ones own life. **(Fatal)**
Surditas: (Disease of the Ear) Deafness. **(Disabling)**
Syphilis Primitiva: (Urinary, Genital Organs, & Venerial Affections) Early signs of the primary venereal disease; See "Venereal Disease". **(Disabling/Potentially Fatal)**
Syphilis Consecutiva: (Urinary, Genital Organs, & Venerial Affections) The primary venereal disease in or and its peak having completed the full or uninterrupted sequence. See "Venereal Disease". **(Disabling/Potentially Fatal)**

Tetanus: (Brain or Nervous System) An infectious, often fatal disease, caused by bacterium that enters the body through wounds, and characterized by tonic spasms and rigidity of voluntary muscles, especially of the neck and lower jaw (Lockjaw). Also called Tetanus Bacillus. **(Potentially Fatal)**
Tonsillitis: (Organs connected with digestive system) Inflammation of a tonsil or the tonsils. **(Disabling)**
Toxicum: (General) Poisoning. **(Disabling/Potentially Fatal)**
Tuberculosis: (Respiratory System) An infectious disease affecting any of various tissues of the body, due to the tubercle bacillus, and characterized by the production of tubercles. **(Disabling/Potentially Fatal)**
Tumores: (General) An abnormal or diseased swelling in any part of the body, especially a more or less circumscribed overgrowth of new tissue that is autonomous, differs in structure from the part in which it grows, and serves no useful purpose. **(Disabling/Potentially Fatal)**
Typhoid: (Fever) Also called typhoid fever, or "febris typhoides", an infectious, often fatal, febrile disease, characterized by intestinal inflammation and ulceration, caused by the typhoid bacillus. **(Usually Fatal)**
Typhus: (Fever) An acute, infectious disease **(Typhus Fever)** characterized by great prostration, sever nervous symptoms, and a peculiar eruption of reddish spots on the body; now regarded as due to a specific microorganism transmitted by lice and fleas. **(Potentially Fatal)**

Ulcus: (Abscesses & Ulcers) An open sore on an external or internal surface of the body usually accompanied by degeneration of tissue with formation of pus. **(Disabling)**

Ulcus Penis Non Syphiliticum: (Urinary, Genital Organs, & Venereal Affections) Non syphilitic ulcers of the penis. Sores open either to the surface or the urethra lining accompanied by degeneration of tissue, the formation of pus, etc. **(Disabling)**

Varicocele: (Circulatory System) A varicose condition of the spermatic veins of the scrotum. **(Disabling)**

Variola: (Eruptive Fever) The medical synonym for smallpox; Latin "varius", various, spotted. A disease, now of somewhat less interest than before the discovery of vaccination. It is of a very contagious nature, and is supposed to have been introduced into Europe from Asia, at an early period of the middle ages. It is characterized by fever, with pustules appearing from the third to the fifth day, and it possesses all the distinctive properties of the major exanthemata (Exanthemata are diseases associated with a rash and a fever.) **(Fatal)**

Varioloides: (Eruptive Fever) Resembling variola or smallpox. A mild smallpox, especially as occurring in persons who have been vaccinated or have previously had smallpox. **(Disabling)**

Varix: (Circulatory System) (Also Varicosity) A permanent abnormal dilation and lengthening of a vein, usually accompanied by some tortuosity; a varicose vein. **(Disabling)**

Venereal Disease: (Urinary, Genital Organs, & Venereal Affections)
GONORRHEA - A contagious, purulent inflammation of the urethra due to the gonococcus.
SYPHILIS - A chronic, infectious venereal disease caused by microorganism spirocheta pallida or treponema pallidum, also see Spirochete.

Vermes: (General) Worms. **(Disabling)**

Vulnus: (vul'nus) **(Wounds & Injuries)** of or pertaining to a wound or injury.

Vulnus Incisum: (Wounds & Injuries) Incise or cut with a sharp instrument; (vulnerae - to wound). **(Disabling/ Potentially Fatal)**

Vulnus Contusum vel Laceratum: (Wounds & Injuries) To wound the flesh by tearing - severely bruised; jagged wound.

(Disabling/Potentially Fatal)
Vulnus Punctum: (Wounds & Injuries) A puncture wound.
(Disabling/Potentially Fatal)
Vulnus Sclopeticum: (Wounds & Injuries) A gunshot wound.
(Disabling/Potentially Fatal)

Whitlow: An inflammatory tumor, esp. on the terminal phalanx (bone forming the joint) of a finger or toe, seated between the epidermis and true skin.
Wounds: Wounds are classed into incised, lacerated, contused, punctured, and gunshot

Bibliography

Primary & Printed Sources:

The Diuguid Records – Burial Log Books; Log Book #6 June 1861 – Dec. 1862; Log Book #6 Jan. 1863 – Dec. 1864; Log Book #7 Jan. 1865 –
The Soldiers Book 1861 - 1865

Compiled by Lucy Baber, research and writing by Evelyn Moore; Behind the Old Brick Wall – A Cemetery Story, published by The Lynchburg Committee of The National Society of the Colonial Dames of America in The Commonwealth of Virginia 1968

H. E. Howard, Inc. The Virginia Regimental History Series

Hartman, David W. & Coles, David, compilers. Biographical Rosters of Florida's Confederate and Union Soldiers, 1861 - 1865. 6 vols. Wilmington, NC: Broadfoot Publishing Company, 1995

Henderson, Lillian, compiler. Roster of Confederate Soldiers of Georgia 1861 - 1865. 6 vols. + index. Atlanta: State of Georgia, Longino & Porter, Inc., printers, 1955-1964.

Booth, Andrew B., compiler. Records of Louisiana Confederate Soldiers and Louisiana Confederate Commands. 3 vols. Spartanburg, SC: The Reprint Co. 1984 reprint of the 1920 edition.

Jordan, Weymouth T. and Manarin, Louis H., compilers. North Carolina Troops, 1861 - 1865, A Roster. 15 vols. Raleigh, NC: Division of Archives and History, 1966-2003.

Robley Dunglison, M.D. LL.D, professor of the institute of medicine, etc., in the Jefferson Medical College of Philadelphia. A Dictionary of Medical Science, published by Blanchard and Lea 1858, Philadelphia, Pa.

Dorland's Pocket Medical Dictionary 25th Edition, 1995, published by W. B. Saunders Company, Philadelphia, Pa.

Peter W. Houck, A Prototype of a Confederate Hospital Center in Lynchburg, Virginia, published by Warwick House Publishing 1986

H. H. Cunningham, Doctors in Gray, The Confederate Medical Service, published by Louisiana State University Press 1958, reprinted, 1970, by permission of Louisiana State University Press

United States Department of Interior, National Park Service, Petersburg National Battlefield, Petersburg, Virginia. Listing of Union soldiers exhumed from Lynchburg and re-interred at Poplar Grove Cemetery, Petersburg, Virginia.

Robert E. Denney, Civil War Prisons & Escapes, A Day-by-Day Chronicle, Sterling Publishing Co., Inc. New York 1995

Secondary Printed Sources:

Robert K. Krick, Lee's Colonel's A Biographical Register of the Field Officers of the Army of Northern Virginia, Morningside Bookshop, Dayton, Ohio, 1984

Regulations for the Army of the Confederate States, 1863 – J.W. Randolph, Richmond, Va. 1863. Republished by The National Historical Society, Harrisburg, PA 1980.

Charles D. Walker, late assistant professor V.M.I., Memorial, Virginia Military Institute, Biographical Sketches of the Graduate And Eleves of the Virginia Military Institute, who fell during the War Between the States, published 1875 by J. B. Lippincott & Co.

Ezra J. Warner, Generals in Gray, Lives of the Confederate Commanders, published by Louisiana State University Press 1983

Ann Chilton, <u>Remnants of War 1861 – 1865, Civil War Records Bedford County, Va.</u>, 1986

Edited by William B. Styple, <u>Writing & Fighting from the Army of Northern Virginia, A Collection of Confederate Correspondence</u>, published by Belle Grove Publishing Co., Kearny, N. J. 2003

Ida C. Brown, <u>Michigan Men in the Civil War</u>, The University of Michigan, Michigan Historical Collections Bulletin No. 9, January 1959

<u>State & Local Archives;</u>

State of Alabama, Department of Archives and History, Montgomery, Alabama, Confederate Military Records 1861 – 1865.

Illinois State Archives, Springfield, Illinois – Muster and Descriptive Rolls of Illinois Civil War Units

State of Indiana, Indiana State Archives, Indianapolis, Indiana, Indiana Commission on Public Records

Jones Memorial Library, Lynchburg Virginia

Maine State Archives, Augusta, Maine, Adjutant General's Report, muster roll listing 1861 - 1865

The Commonwealth of Massachusetts, State Archives, Military Records 1861 – 1865; information from Massachusetts Soldiers, Sailors and Marines in the Civil War.

Mississippi Department of Archives and History, Archives and Library Division, Jackson, Mississippi - Muster roll records 1861 - 1865

The State of New Hampshire, Division of Records Management and Archives, Concord, New Hampshire, military records 1861 – 1865.

State of New Jersey, New Jersey State Archives, Trenton New Jersey, Officers and Men of New Jersey in the Civil War, 1865, Vol. I & II Complied in the Office of the Adjutant General – Published by authority of the Legislature, William S. Stryker Adjutant General, 1876

The State Library of Ohio, Columbus, Ohio, Military Service Records 1861 - 1865

Rhode Island State Archives and Public Records Administration, Providence Rhode Island, Military Records 1861 – 1865

Troup County Archives, LaGrange, Georgia

Vermont State Archives, <u>Revised Roster of Vermont Volunteers and list of Vermonters Who Served in the Arm and Navy of the United States During the War of the Rebellion 1861-1865</u>, Compiled by authority of the Gen. Assembly under direction of Theodore S. Peck, Adj. Gen., Montpelier, VT, Watchman Publishing Co., 1892

West Virginia Division of Culture and History, Charleston, West Virginia, Military Service Records 1861 - 1865

The State Historical Society of Wisconsin, Madison, Wisconsin Adjutant General's Records. Records of Regiments, 1861 – 1865, Regimental Muster Rolls, series #1142 & 1144.

Newspapers:

Lynchburg Daily Virginian, 1861 - 1865

ABOUT THE AUTHOR

JERALD (JERRY) MARKHAM is a native of Botetourt County, Virginia. He graduated from James River High School and attended the University of North Dakota while serving in the U. S. Air Force. His interest in the War Between the States began in his early youth. He has been actively engaged in Civil War historical research for several years. Several of his Virginia ancestors served in the Confederate Army, including his great-grandfather John Owen Markham that served in the Botetourt Artillery. Jerry has been an active member of the Civil War reenacting unit, 11th Virginia Infantry, Company G since 1986. He currently serves as the unit's Captain.

This book is the third publication by Mr. Markham. All three have been a labor of love. The first was a listing, *Confederate Veterans Buried in Hollywood Cemetery from Camp Lee Soldiers Home 1894–1946*. His second book was *The Botetourt Artillery* – a part of the *Virginia Regiment History Series*, published by H. E. Howard.

Jerry and his wife, Mary Jo, live in Salem, Virginia. He is an employee of Accellent Cardiology in Salem and works in the Research & Development Department.

www.ingramcontent.com/pod-product-compliance
Lightning Source LLC
Chambersburg PA
CBHW070057020526
44112CB00034B/1429